Lecture Notes in Computer Science

Lecture Notes in Artificial Intelligence 15201

Founding Editor

Jörg Siekmann

The series Lecture Notes in Artificial Intelligence (LNAI) was established in 1988 as a topical subseries of LNCS devoted to artificial intelligence.

The series publishes state-of-the-art research results at a high level. As with the LNCS mother series, the mission of the series is to serve the international R & D community by providing an invaluable service, mainly focused on the publication of conference and workshop proceedings and postproceedings.

Xuguang Lan · Xuesong Mei · Caigui Jiang ·
Fei Zhao · Zhiqiang Tian
Editors

Intelligent Robotics and Applications

17th International Conference, ICIRA 2024
Xi'an, China, July 31 – August 2, 2024
Proceedings, Part I

Springer

Editors
Xuguang Lan
Xi'an Jiaotong University
Xi'an, China

Xuesong Mei
Xi'an Jiaotong University
Xi'an, China

Caigui Jiang
Xi'an Jiaotong University
Xi'an, China

Fei Zhao
Xi'an Jiaotong University
Xi'an, China

Zhiqiang Tian
Xi'an Jiaotong University
Xi'an, China

ISSN 0302-9743 ISSN 1611-3349 (electronic)
Lecture Notes in Artificial Intelligence
ISBN 978-981-96-0770-9 ISBN 978-981-96-0771-6 (eBook)
https://doi.org/10.1007/978-981-96-0771-6

LNCS Sublibrary: SL7 – Artificial Intelligence

This Springer imprint is published by the registered company Springer Nature Singapore Pte Ltd.
The registered company address is: 152 Beach Road, #21-01/04 Gateway East, Singapore 189721, Singapore

Preface

With the theme "AI & Robotics for Smart Society", the 17th International Conference on Intelligent Robotics and Applications (ICIRA 2024) was held in Xi'an, China, July 31 – August 2, 2024, and designed to encourage advancement in the field of robotics, automation, mechatronics, and applications. It aimed to promote top-level research and globalize quality research in general, making discussions and presentations more internationally competitive and focusing on the latest outstanding achievements, future trends, and demands.

ICIRA 2024 was organized and hosted by Xi'an Jiaotong University, co-hosted by Zhejiang University, Harbin Institute of Technology, Shenyang Institute of Automation Chinese Academy of Sciences, and Huazhong University of Science and Technology. Also, ICIRA 2024 was technically co-sponsored by Springer. ICIRA 2024 was a successful event. It attracted more than 490 submissions, of which 489 were sent for peer review, and the Program Committee undertook a rigorous review process to select the most deserving research for publication. The Advisory Committee gave advice for the conference program. Also, they helped to organize special sections for ICIRA 2024. Finally, a total of 321 papers were selected for publication in 10 volumes of Springer's Lecture Note in Computer Science. For the review process, single-blind peer review was used. Each review took around 2–3 weeks, and each submission received at least 2 reviews and 1 meta-review.

In ICIRA 2024, 12 distinguished plenary speakers delivered their outstanding research works in various fields of robotics. Participants gave a total of 180 oral presentations and 142 poster presentations, enjoying this excellent opportunity to share their latest research findings. Here, we would like to express our sincere appreciation to all the authors, participants, and distinguished plenary and keynote speakers. Special thanks are also extended to all members of the Organizing Committee, all reviewers for peer review, all staff of the conference affairs group, and all volunteers for their diligent work.

August 2024

Xuguang Lan
Xuesong Mei
Caigui Jiang
Fei Zhao
Zhiqiang Tian

Organization

Conference Chair

Xuguang Lan	Xi'an Jiaotong University, China

Program Chairs

Xuesong Mei	Xi'an Jiaotong University, China
Xinjun Liu	Tsinghua University, China
Heping Chen	Texas State University, USA
Bo Tao	Huazhong University of Science and Technology, China
Lianqing Liu	Chinese Academy of Sciences, China
Geng Yang	Zhejiang University, China

Organizing Chairs

Honghai Liu	Harbin Institute of Technology, China
Jun Zou	Zhejiang University, China

Award Committee Chairs

Fei Zhao	Xi'an Jiaotong University, China
Xuetao Zhang	Xi'an Jiaotong University, China

Publication Chairs

Caigui Jiang	Xi'an Jiaotong University, China
Zhiyong Wang	Harbin Institute of Technology, China

Local Arrangement Chairs

Zhiqiang Tian	Xi'an Jiaotong University, China
Jianyi Liu	Xi'an Jiaotong University, China

Registration Chair

Liangjun Chen	Xi'an Jiaotong University, China

Regional Chairs

Zhiyong Chen	University of Newcastle, Australia
Naoyuki Kubota	Tokyo Metropolitan University, Japan
Zhaojie Ju	University of Portsmouth, UK
Eric Perreault	Northeastern University, USA
Peter Xu	University of Auckland, New Zealand
Simon Yang	University of Guelph, Canada
Houxiang Zhang	Norwegian University of Science and Technology, Norway
Imad Elhajj	American University of Beirut, Lebanon
Yaguo Lei	Xi'an Jiaotong University, China

Program Committee Members

Yuwen Sun	Dalian University of Technology, China
Zeyang Xia	Shanghai Jiao Tong University, China
Guimin Chen	Xi'an Jiaotong University, China
Weijun Tian	Jilin University, China
Lei Jiang	Shanghai Humanoid Robot Manufacturing Innovation Center, China
Xiaofeng Liu	Hohai University, China
Daqi Zhu	University of Shanghai for Science and Technology, China
Duanling Li	Beijing University of Posts and Telecommunications, China
Baiquan Su	Beijing University of Posts and Telecommunications, China
Jihua Zhu	Xi'an Jiaotong University, China
Ning Sun	Nankai University, China

Yang Gao	Chang'an University, China
Xing Liu	Northwestern Polytechnical University, China
Jiyu Cheng	Shandong University, China
Yanfeng Lv	Chinese Academy of Sciences, China
Liang Zhao	Henan University of Technology, China
Anzhu Gao	Shanghai Jiao Tong University, China
Yixing Gao	Jilin University, China
Laihao Yang	Xi'an Jiaotong University, China
Yuquan Leng	South University of Science and Technology, China
Honghao Lv	Zhejiang University, China
Weiliang Zuo	Xi'an Jiaotong University, China

Contents – Part I

Innovative Design and Performance Evaluation of Robot Mechanisms

Online Performance Assessment of UAV Formations via the Belief Rule Base with Asynchronous Sequential Inputs

Jiayue Fang[1], Haoran Zhang[2(✉)], Ruohan Yang[3], Yan Lv[1], Shuo Miao[1], and Zhichao Feng[4]

[1] Key Laboratory of Information System and Technology, Beijing Institute of Control and Electronic Technology, Beijing, China
[2] School of Electronic Engineering, Xidian University, Xi'an, China
zhr20000720@163.com
[3] School of Electronics and Information, Northwestern Polytechnical University, Xi'an, China
[4] School of Missile Engineering, Rocket Force Engineering University, Xi'an, China

Abstract. Recently, UAV formations, as a typical instance of aerospace multi-robot systems, have played an increasingly crucial role in military confrontation due to their extraordinary synergy. As the basis of performance optimization for UAV formations, performance assessment not only provides credible reference for the offline design of their parameters and structure, but also offers strong decision support for the online update of their configuration, thus becoming the key to maintaining their high-performance operation. In most cases, the program for iteratively assessing the performance of UAV formations is deployed and operated in ground stations. During periodic information transmission between the UAV formation and the ground station, delay is inevitable, leading to the asynchrony of temporal information received from different UAVs. Moreover, for each assessment, it is the observation information of UAV formations over a time period, rather than that at a time instant, that should be utilized to reduce the risk of poor decision-making. Therefore, the belief rule base with asynchronous sequential inputs is constructed with the help of cross correlation and discrete wavelet transformation, on which a strategy is further designed for the online performance assessment of UAV formations. Pertinent simulation is performed, showing the feasibility and validity of the proposal.

Keywords: UAV formation · Performance assessment · Belief rule base · Transmission delay

1 Introduction

As an instance of aerospace multi-robot systems, the UAV formation plays an increasingly significant role in the military field [27,28], such as intelligent air

J. Fang and H. Zhang—Contribute equally to this work.

X. Lan et al. (Eds.): ICIRA 2024, LNAI 15201, pp. 3–16, 2025.
https://doi.org/10.1007/978-981-96-0771-6_1

combat [11,16] and vicinagearth security [12,23]. The synergy achieved by the interaction among each member inside renders the formation more intelligent, dramatically boosting its comprehensive combat effectiveness.

For UAV formations, maintaining prolonged high-performance running is the key to completing the task or winning the battle. Performance assessment serves as an effective safeguard for the UAV formation in the environment with strong uncertainty and fast changeability, which can not only provide useful reference basis for offline tactic planning, but also offer faithful decision support for online configuration switching [25].

The belief rule base (BRB), a powerful decision-making tool developed with the joint research on fuzzy theory, D-S evidence theory and optimization theory [21,22], has been widely adopted in the offline performance assessment of single complex systems [8] and further expanded to the online performance assessment of multiagent systems in our previous work [24]. The superior comprehensibility in model representation and model inference makes the BRB highly favored by military departments. As a result, it is appropriate to select the BRB for researching the online performance assessment of UAV formations.

Generally, the performance assessment software is installed and operated in the ground station, an essential digital infrastructure in the scene of multi-UAV flight control. After receiving the information sent by each UAV in the swarm, the ground station will synthesize it and further capture discriminative characteristics that correspond to the entire swarm. Then, the ground station will invoke the program to assess the performance status of the UAV formation, and the result will be sent back to the UAV formation after postprocessing automatically or artificially. However, in real-world applications, the delay during information transmission between the UAV formation and the ground station is inevitable and cannot be ignored, which leads to the asynchrony of the information sent by different members of the UAV formation and further hinders the execution of the performance assessment program mounted on the ground station.

On the other hand, as aforementioned, one of the functions that performance assessment possesses is to provide decision support for the online reconfiguration of UAV formations. In our previous work [26], the observation information collected from the UAV formation at a single time instant was utilized for one execution of the performance assessment program, which poses the risk of poor decision-making and may further affect flight safety and mission achievement for the UAV formation. By contrast, using the observation information collected from the UAV formation over a time period for one invocation of the performance assessment program appears to be more reasonable.

Motivated by the above, we propose a solution based on the belief rule base with asynchronous sequential inputs (BRB-ASI) to assess the synergistic performance of UAV formations online, taking into account the transmission delay between the UAV formation and the ground station. The main contributions of this work are as follows.

Contribution 1. A new belief rule representation is proposed for the BRB-ASI, making it an end-to-end model capable of mapping multiple asynchronous characteristic sequences to one element of the discernment frame as well as enhancing its comprehensibility to assist specialists to provide more accurate knowledge for model initialization.

Contribution 2. Two links, i.e., asynchronous input alignment and sequential input conversion, are devised and integrated into the inference of the BRB-ASI, with the help of cross-correlation and discrete wavelet transformation (DWT), thereby synchronized time-frequency characteristics can be captured.

Contribution 3. By virtue of the BRB-ASI, an online performance assessment strategy for UAV formations is constructed, taking the transmission delay between the UAV formation and the ground station into consideration. To the best of our knowledge, there is no relevant work regarding the online performance assessment of multi-robot systems that pays attention to delay.

The rest is organized as follows. Section 2 models the motion of UAV formations and clarifies the target issues. Section 3 elaborates on the corresponding solutions, including the BRB-ASI and the performance assessment approach based on it, whose validation is revealed in Sect. 4. Section 5 concludes this work and looks to future work.

2 Problem Formulation

2.1 Motion Modeling of UAV Formations

Take a UAV formation with N members into account, which maneuvers horizontally. The motion of the n-th member ($n \in \{1, \ldots, N\}$) is modeled as follows [17]:

$$\begin{cases} \dot{x}_n(t) = v_n(t) \cdot \cos\theta_n(t), \\ \dot{y}_n(t) = v_n(t) \cdot \sin\theta_n(t), \\ \dot{v}_n(t) = -\frac{1}{\tau} \cdot v_n(t) + \frac{1}{\tau} \cdot r_n(t), \\ \dot{\theta}_n(t) = \omega_n(t). \end{cases} \tag{1}$$

Therein, $\dot{(\cdot)}$ is the derivative operator. $(x_n(t), y_n(t))$ is the real-time position in the Cartesian coordinate system. $v_n(t)$ is the real-time cruise speed. τ is the time constant. $r_n(t)$ is the control command of $v_n(t)$. $\theta_n(t)$ is the real-time course angle and $\omega_n(t)$ is its rate of change.

By virtue of the dynamic feedback linearization [5], the state space representation of the n-th UAV inside the formation is obtained as follows:

$$\begin{cases} \dot{\mathbf{s}}_n(t) = \mathbf{A}_n \cdot \mathbf{s}_n(t) + \mathbf{B}_n \cdot \mathbf{i}_n(t), \\ \mathbf{o}_n(t) = \mathbf{C}_n \cdot \mathbf{s}_n(t). \end{cases} \tag{2}$$

Therein, $\mathbf{s}_n(t)$ is the state vector satisfying $\mathbf{s}_n(t) = \left[x_n(t)\ y_n(t)\ v_n(t)\ \theta_n(t)\right]^\top$, where $(\cdot)^\top$ is the transpose operation. $\mathbf{i}_n(t)$ is the input vector satisfying

$$\mathbf{i}_n(t) = \begin{bmatrix} \frac{1}{\tau} \cdot \cos\theta_n(t) & -v_n(t) \cdot \sin\theta_n(t) \\ \frac{1}{\tau} \cdot \sin\theta_n(t) & v_n(t) \cdot \cos\theta_n(t) \end{bmatrix} \cdot \begin{bmatrix} r_n(t) \\ \omega_n(t) \end{bmatrix}, \tag{3}$$

where $v_n(t) \neq 0$. $\mathbf{o}_n(t)$ is the output vector. $\mathbf{A}_n$, $\mathbf{B}_n$ and $\mathbf{C}_n$ are all constant matrices.

Further introducing component malfunction and ambient interference yields the following:

$$\begin{cases} \dot{\mathbf{s}}_n(t) = \mathbf{A}_n \cdot \mathbf{s}_n(t) + \mathbf{B}_n \cdot \mathbf{i}_n(t) \cdot \varrho_n^a(t) + \mathbf{E}_n \cdot \varrho_n^d(t), \\ \mathbf{o}_n(t) = \mathbf{C}_n \cdot \mathbf{s}_n(t) \cdot \varrho_n^s(t). \end{cases} \tag{4}$$

Therein, $\varrho_n^a(t)$ is the time-varying actuator failure vector. $\varrho_n^s(t)$ is the time-varying sensor failure vector. $\varrho_n^d(t)$ is the time-varying environmental disturbance vector. $\mathbf{E}_n$ is a constant matrix.

The following control protocol is adopted for the assembly and maintenance of the UAV formation [18]:

$$\mathbf{i}_n(t) = \mathbf{K}_1 \cdot \sum_{n'=1, n' \neq n}^{N} (\mathbf{o}_n(t) - \delta_n - \mathbf{o}_{n'}(t) + \delta_{n'}) + \mathbf{K}_2 \cdot (\mathbf{o}_n(t) - \delta^*). \tag{5}$$

Therein, δ_n is the time-invariant geometric pattern vector corresponding to the n-th UAV inside the formation. δ^* is the time-invariant reference vector shared by all UAVs inside the formation. $\mathbf{K}_1$ and $\mathbf{K}_2$ are both constant matrices.

2.2 Target Problem Clarification

The target problems of this work are twofold. One is the asynchrony of the information sent by different UAVs resulting from transmission delay, the other is the risk of decision-making error due to utilizing the observation information of UAV formations at a single time instant. To address these problems, the BRB-ASI is built, on which an online performance assessment strategy for UAV formations is devised, as introduced in Sect. 3.

3 Main Results

3.1 Construction of the BRB-ASI

As a rule-based fuzzy expert system, construction of the BRB-ASI involves three aspects: representation, inference and optimization, which will be expounded successively.

Model Representation. Denote the number of belief rules in the BRB-ASI as K. Denote the k-th belief rule as R_k, which has the following structure ($k \in \{1, \ldots, K\}$):

$$\begin{aligned}&\text{If } \zeta_1(\xi_1(C_1(T^*))) \text{ is } A_{k,1} \wedge \cdots \wedge \zeta_M(\xi_M(C_M(T^*))) \text{ is } A_{k,M},\\ &\text{Then } \{(D_l, \beta_{k,l}) \mid l = 1, \ldots, L\},\\ &\text{With } \omega_k^r \text{ and } \{\omega_{k,m}^c \mid m = 1, \ldots, M\}.\end{aligned} \tag{6}$$

Therein, T^* is the nominal moment sequence. M is the number of characteristics extracted from the observation information of the multiagent system. N is the scale of the multiagent system. $C_m(T^*)$ ($m \in \{1, \ldots, M\}$) is the set satisfying $C_m(T^*) = \{C_m^n(T_n) \mid n = 1, \ldots, N\}$, where T_n is the real moment sequence corresponding to the n-th agent and $C_m^n(\cdot)$ is the corresponding characteristic value sequence of the n-th agent. Subject to the delay existing in the communication between the multiagent system and the master control entity, the characteristic sequences corresponding to each agent are asynchronous, meaning $T^* \neq T_1 \neq \cdots \neq T_N$. Yet, $|T^*| = |T_1| = \cdots = |T_N|$, where $|\cdot|$ is the length. $\xi_m(\cdot)$ ($m \in \{1, \ldots, M\}$) is the map to be devised for aligning the characteristic sequences corresponding to each member inside the multiagent system. $\zeta_m(\cdot)$ ($m \in \{1, \ldots, M\}$) is the map to be designed for extracting the distinguishable characteristic corresponding to the multiagent system from the synchronized characteristic sequences corresponding to each agent. $A_{k,m}$ ($k \in \{1, \ldots, K\}$, $m \in \{1, \ldots, M\}$) is the reference value of the m-th characteristic corresponding to the multiagent system in R_k. $\{D_l \mid l = 1, \ldots, L\}$ is the frame of discernment, where L is its potential, and $\{\beta_{k,l} \mid l = 1, \ldots, L\}$ is the corresponding confidence distribution in R_k. ω_k^r is the weight of R_k and $\omega_{k,m}^c$ is the weight of the m-th characteristic corresponding to the multiagent system in R_k.

Then, the BRB-ASI can be described as follows:

$$\{(D_l, \beta_l(\bar{T})) \mid l = 1, \ldots, L\} = \textbf{BRB-ASI}(\{\zeta_m(\bar{T}) \mid m = 1, \ldots, M\}). \tag{7}$$

Therein, $\bar{T}$ is the moment sequence after alignment. $\{\beta_l(\bar{T}) \mid l = 1, \ldots, L\}$ is the real-time confidence distribution of the discernment frame. **BRB-ASI** is the model.

Model Inference. The natural advantage of the BRB in interpretability makes it highly valued in the military field. The intuitive IF-THEN representation facilitates specialists in leveraging their rich experience to determine the initial structure and parameters of the BRB. At the same time, the transparent and traceable inference mechanism centered on the D-S evidence theory makes the output of the BRB trustworthy enough and the man-in-the-loop idea achievable.

For better understanding, we divide the inference of the BRB-ASI into the following steps, where **Step 1** and **Step 2** are first introduced in this work.

Step 1. Asynchronous input alignment

Analyze the correlation or similarity between the m-th characteristic value sequence ($m \in \{1, \ldots, M\}$) sent by the n-th agent and that sent by the $(n+1)$-th agent ($n \in \{1, \ldots, N-1\}$) using the following formula [20,30]:

$$\mathcal{R}^m_{n,n+1}(\phi^m_{n,n+1}) = \sum_{t \in T^*} C^n_m(t) \cdot C^{n+1^*}_m(t + \phi^m_{n,n+1}). \tag{8}$$

Therein, $(\cdot)^*$ is the complex conjugate operation. $\phi^m_{n,n+1} \in \Phi^m_{n,n+1}$ is the time lag of the second sequence relative to the first one, where $\Phi^m_{n,n+1}$ is the corresponding set. $\{\mathcal{R}^m_{n,n+1}(\phi^m_{n,n+1}) \mid \phi^m_{n,n+1} \in \Phi^m_{n,n+1}\}$ is the cross-correlation sequence between $C^n_m(T_n)$ and $C^{n+1}_m(T_{n+1})$.

Seek the maximum point of $\{\mathcal{R}^m_{n,n+1}(\phi^m_{n,n+1}) \mid \phi^m_{n,n+1} \in \Phi^m_{n,n+1}\}$ and denote it as $\hat{\phi}^m_{n,n+1}$ ($n \in \{1, \ldots, N-1\}$, $m \in \{1, \ldots, M\}$). The process can be formulated as follows:

$$\hat{\phi}^m_{n,n+1} = \underset{\phi^m_{n,n+1} \in \Phi^m_{n,n+1}}{\operatorname{argmax}} \mathcal{R}^m_{n,n+1}(\phi^m_{n,n+1}). \tag{9}$$

Shift $C^{n+1}_m(T_{n+1})$ to the left by $\hat{\phi}^m_{n,n+1}$ units provided $\hat{\phi}^m_{n,n+1} > 0$, otherwise shift $C^{n+1}_m(T_{n+1})$ to the right by $\hat{\phi}^m_{n,n+1}$ units ($n \in \{1, \ldots, N-1\}$, $m \in \{1, \ldots, M\}$).

Denote the shifted moment sequence corresponding to the n-th agent as T'_n ($n \in \{1, \ldots, N\}$). Then, the following formula related to $\bar{T}$ in (7) holds:

$$T'_1 \cap \cdots \cap T'_N = \bar{T}. \tag{10}$$

By retaining the subsequence of $C^n_m(T_n)$ over $\bar{T}$ and discarding the rest ($m \in \{1, \ldots, M\}$, $n \in \{1, \ldots, N\}$), the alignment of the asynchronous M characteristic value sequences sent by N agents within the multiagent system is achieved. Here, denote the synchronized sequence of the m-th characteristic value corresponding to the n-th agent as $C^n_m(\bar{T})$ ($m \in \{1, \ldots, M\}$, $n \in \{1, \ldots, N\}$).

Thereupon, the m-th characteristic value sequence corresponding to the multiagent system, denoted as $\tilde{C}_m(\bar{T})$, can be obtained with specific signal synthesis strategies and $\xi_m(\cdot)$ in (6) is devised ($m \in \{1, \ldots, M\}$).

Step 2. Sequential input conversion

For the sake of computation reduction, the DWT is adopted to extract discriminative time-frequency characteristics from M characteristic value sequences corresponding to the multiagent system. In the context of this work, the formula of the DWT can be formulated as follows [14,19]:

$$\Gamma_m(\lambda; \mu, \rho) = \sum_{t'=1}^{|\bar{T}|} \tilde{C}_m(t') \cdot \psi(t'; \mu, \rho). \tag{11}$$

Therein, μ is the scale. ρ is the translation. $\psi(\cdot)$ is the discretized mother wavelet. $t' \in \{1, \ldots, |\bar{T}|\}$ is an intermediate variable. $\Gamma_m(\cdot)$ is the DWT sequence corresponding to the m-th characteristic value sequence of the multiagent system and λ is its independent variable.

Further, the time-frequency characteristic of $\tilde{C}_m(\bar{T})$ can be obtained by the following formula:

$$\hat{C}_m(\bar{T}) = \sum_{\lambda \in \Lambda} |\Gamma_m(\lambda; \mu, \rho)|^2. \tag{12}$$

Therein, $|\cdot|$ is the modulo operation. Λ is the set corresponding to λ. $\hat{C}_m(\bar{T})$ is the m-th energy feature corresponding to the multiagent system over T^*.

As a result, the design of $\zeta_m(\cdot)$ in (6) is completed ($m \in \{1, \ldots, M\}$).

To yield $\{(D_l, \beta_l(\bar{T})) \mid l = 1, \ldots, L\}$ in (7), four routine links of the BRB inference remain to be performed, including: **Step 3.** Reference value membership calculation, **Step 4.** Belief rule membership calculation, **Step 5.** Belief rule activation calculation and **Step 6.** Discernment frame confidence distribution calculation. Limited by space, they are omitted here, which can be found in our previous work [9,25].

Model Optimization. As a learning expert system, the BRB-ASI is initialized by empirical knowledge and optimized by historical data. In this work, we only take into account the parameter tuning of the BRB-ASI and formulate it as the following constrained continuous static single optimization problem:

$$\begin{aligned} &\min\ f_1(\mathbf{h}) \\ &\text{s.t. } \{\Xi_k^1 \mid k = 1, \ldots, K\}, \{\Xi_k^2 \mid k = 1, \ldots, K\}, \{\Xi_k^3 \mid k = 1, \ldots, K\}. \end{aligned} \tag{13}$$

Therein, $\mathbf{h}$ is the decision vector satisfying

$$\mathbf{h} = \left[\beta_{1,1} \cdots \beta_{K,L}\ \omega_1^r \cdots \omega_K^r\ \omega_{1,1}^c \cdots \omega_{K,M}^c\right]. \tag{14}$$

$f_1(\cdot)$ is the accuracy of assessment. Ξ_k^1 is the interpretability constraint imposed on R_k, which can be formulated as follows [29]:

$$\beta_{k,l} \geq \frac{\beta_{k,l-1} + \beta_{k,l+1}}{2}, l \in \{2, \ldots, L\}. \tag{15}$$

Ξ_k^2 is the integrity constraint imposed on R_k, requiring $\sum_{l=1}^{L} \beta_{k,l} = 1$. Ξ_k^3 is the boundary constraint imposed on R_k to ensure

$$\begin{cases} \beta_{k,l} \in [0, 1], l \in \{1, \ldots, L\}, \\ \omega_k^r \in [0, 1], \\ \omega_{k,m}^c \in [0, 1], m \in \{1, \ldots, M\}. \end{cases} \tag{16}$$

Then, both deterministic optimization algorithms like the gradient descent [10] and metaheuristic algorithms like the gray wolf optimizer [25] can be used to seek the optimal hyperparameter combination of the BRB-ASI.

3.2 Design of the Online Performance Assessment Strategy via the BRB-ASI

It should be noted that the BRB-ASI presented in the last subsection is a general model based on the BRB. In this subsection, we will utilize the BRB-ASI to further devise the online performance assessment strategy for the UAV formation, taking into account the transmission delay between it and the ground station, a factor overlooked by most of the existing literature for the sake of facilitating research.

The strategy can be applied according to the following steps.

Step 1. System construction

In order to utilize the BRB-ASI for constructing the corresponding system that can online assess the performance status of the UAV formation in the presence of the transmission delay between it and the ground station, several elements are required to be determined in advance, including the antecedent of the belief rule in (6), the maps that the belief rule in (6) involves and the consequent of the belief rule in (6).

First, select M characteristics corresponding to N UAVs within the formation according to their respective dynamics. Then, in turn determine an appropriate observation period for one assessment, a pertinent strategy for fusing the synchronized characteristic value sequences corresponding to each UAV inside the formation over the observation period and a suitable mother wavelet for further extracting time-frequency characteristics from the synthesized characteristic value sequences corresponding to the entire formation over the observation period. Last, empirically assign the reference values for each captured time-frequency characteristic corresponding to the UAV formation, the discernment frame, which is referred to as the performance status set in this sense, and the confidence distributions for it.

Step 2. System optimization

For the sake of reducing the impact of expert cognitive biases on the accuracy of the performance assessment system, it is imperative to leverage the accumulated historical operation data of UAV formations for optimizing the initial performance assessment system in both offline and online manners.

First, a metaheuristic algorithm or a combination of multiple metaheuristic algorithms is to be chosen as the solver for the optimization problem in (13), which will be integrated into the performance assessment system as an auxiliary module, aimed at obtaining the optimal hyperparameter combination of the BRB-ASI prior to the formal operation of UAV formations. Moreover, another auxiliary module for tuning the hyperparameters within the BRB-ASI during the flight of UAV formations can be introduced selectively, depending on the actual situation. In this module, the deterministic algorithm is preferable for the search of the optimal hyperparameter combination due to the expensiveness of computation time in the online context, and additional consideration needs to be given to the conditions triggering the online adjustment and the amount of data used in a single adjustment.

Step 3. System deployment

In the practical application of the performance assessment system based on the BRB-ASI, two objects are involved: the ground station and the UAV formation. The core program for performance assessment is to be deployed in the ground station, and both the ground station and each member within the formation are required to be equipped with a signal transmitter and a signal receiver. The online performance assessment strategy for UAV formations using the BRB-ASI is illustrated in Fig. 1.

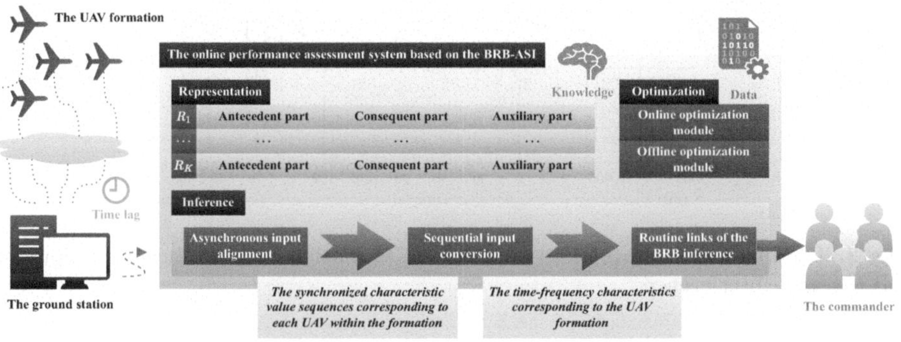

Fig. 1. The schematic of the BRB-ASI-based online performance assessment system for UAV formations

4 Simulation

For the validation of our proposal, corresponding simulation has been conducted, with the core results revealed in this section.

4.1 Preparation

A multi-UAV simulation platform conforming to the dynamics in (4) and applying the control law in (5) is implemented with $N = 5$. On this platform, 6 rounds of experiments are conducted successively and the characteristic value sequences corresponding to each UAV with varying performance statuses are acquired by observing with a frequency of 5 Hz. The performance statuses involved include 'Nominal', 'Good', 'Above average', 'Average', 'Below average' and 'Poor'. Note that the UAVs with 'Nominal' follow the dynamics in (2), which are free of equipment failure and environmental disturbance. Here, the kinematic information of the UAV formation with 'Nominal' is used solely for blank control, as shown in Fig. 2.

Apply the sliding window approach [4] to segment the characteristic sequences corresponding to each UAV with different performance statuses, where the window size is set to 10 s and the step size is set to 5 s, followed by shifting each subsequence by random units to simulate the delay.

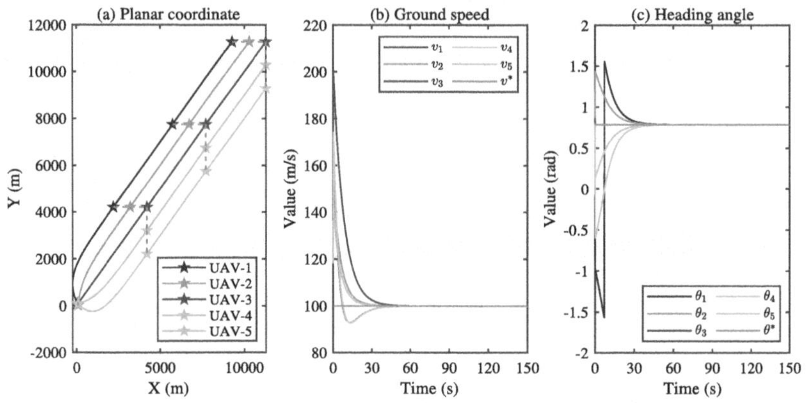

Fig. 2. The kinematic information of the UAV formation free of internal malfunction and external interference

4.2 System Implementation

We select the Haar wavelet [7] as the mother wavelet in (11). Through the two links of asynchronous input alignment and sequential input conversion, 28 pairs of time-frequency characteristics for each performance status are captured, as exhibited in Fig. 3. Accordingly, the sample library for the training and testing of the BRB-ASI-based performance assessment system is built. Based on the analysis of it, as well as the guidance of empirical knowledge, the initialization of the system is accomplished. Additionally, the improved gray wolf optimizer [15] corresponding to the problem in (13) is chosen to implement the optimization module, where the population size is set to 100 and the iteration number is set to 50.

4.3 System Validation

To observe the performance of the implemented system, 10 rounds of experiments are conducted. In each round, 75% samples from the library are used for the training, while the rest are used for testing. Figure 4 shows the fitness curves of the system in the 10 rounds of experiments, all of which can converge to zero within 100 iterations at varying rates. The corresponding assessment results are displayed in Fig. 5, where the maximum, minimum and mean of the accuracy in the 10 rounds of experiments are 100%, 88.57% and 96%, respectively.

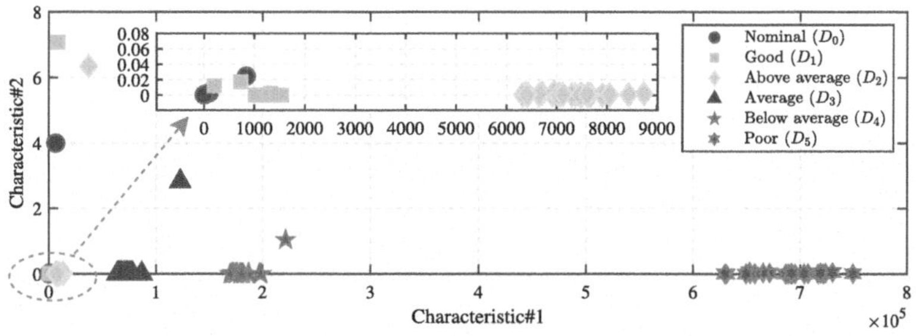

Fig. 3. The time-frequency characteristics corresponding to the UAV formation

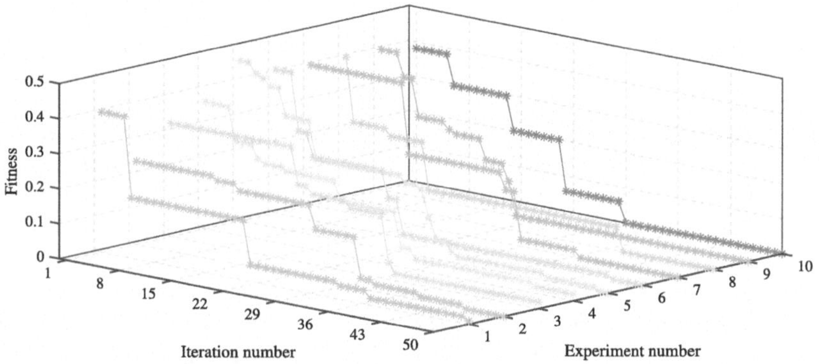

Fig. 4. The fitness curves in the 10 rounds of experiments

4.4 Summary

Based on the established simulation platform, the delayed characteristic value sequences corresponding to the UAV formation with different performance statuses are obtained in turn. Then, the performance assessment system for the UAV formation is implemented using the BRB-ASI, which is initialized by the ambiguous empirical knowledge and optimized by the lagging observational data from different UAVs. Multiple rounds of experiments are performed on the system and the results preliminarily manifest its feasibility and validity, while the superiority will be further verified by designing relevant comparison and ablation studies in our future work.

5 Conclusion

In response to the asynchrony of the information sent by different UAVs caused by transmission delay and the risk of bad decision-making caused by observation information at a single time instant, a BRB-ASI-based solution for the online performance assessment of UAV formations is proposed with the help of cross-correlation and DWT, and the corresponding simulation is conducted,

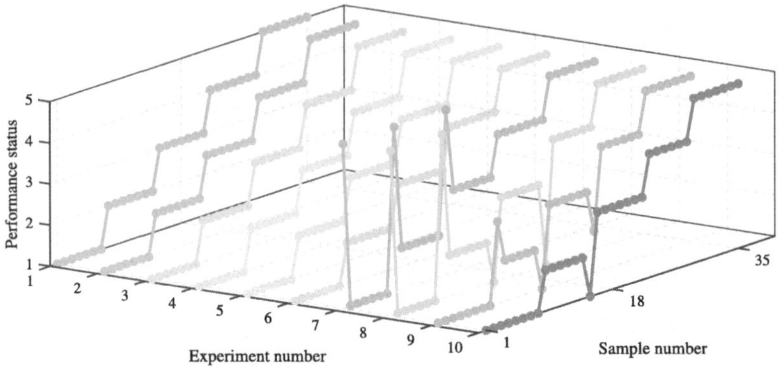

Fig. 5. The assessment results in the 10 rounds of experiments

validating its engineering practicability. In the future, we will further delve into the scalability [2], interpretability [1] and robustness [3] of the BRB-ASI at the quantification level, thus providing more valuable insights for the improvement of the performance assessment strategy based on it. Additionally, delay also exists in the communication among UAVs [6], posing a great threat to the safety of the formation. Given that the model predictive control or receding horizon control serves as an effective measure for the stable operation of multi-robot systems subject to delay [13], we plan to establish a BRB-based predictive control scheme for UAV formations to maintain their stability in the presence of communication delay.

Acknowledgments. This work is supported partly by National Natural Science Foundation of China under Grant No. 62203365 and No. 62203461, partly by China Postdoctoral Science Foundation under Grant No. 2023M742843, partly by Young Talent Promotion Program of Shaanxi Association for Science and Technology under Grant No. 20220121 and No. 20230125, partly by Aeronautical Science Foundation under Grant No. 2023Z034053.

References

1. Cao, Y., Zhou, Z., Hu, C., He, W., Tang, S.: On the interpretability of belief rule-based expert systems. IEEE Trans. Fuzzy Syst. **29**(11), 3489–3503 (2021). https://doi.org/10.1109/tfuzz.2020.3024024
2. Cao, Y., Zhou, Z., Hu, C., Tang, S., Wang, J.: A new approximate belief rule base expert system for complex system modelling. Decis. Support Syst. **150**, 113558 (2021). https://doi.org/10.1016/j.dss.2021.113558
3. Cao, Y., Zhou, Z., Tang, S., Ning, P., Chen, M.: On the robustness of belief-rule-based expert systems. IEEE Trans. Syst. Man Cybern. Syst. **53**(10), 6043–6055 (2023). https://doi.org/10.1109/tsmc.2023.3279286
4. Dai, Q., Liu, J., Yang, J.: SWSEL: sliding window-based selective ensemble learning for class-imbalance problems. Eng. Appl. Artif. Intell. **121**, 105959 (2023). https://doi.org/10.1016/j.engappai.2023.105959

5. D'Souza, R., Louwers, R., Nielsen, C.: Piecewise linear path following for a unicycle using transverse feedback linearization. IEEE Trans. Control Syst. Technol. **29**(6), 2575–2585 (2021). https://doi.org/10.1109/tcst.2021.3049715
6. Du, Z., Qu, X., Shi, J., Lu, J.: Formation control of fixed-wing UAVs with communication delay. ISA Trans. **146**, 154–164 (2024). https://doi.org/10.1016/j.isatra.2023.12.036
7. Eliasof, M., Bodner, B., Treister, E.: Haar wavelet feature compression for quantized graph convolutional networks. IEEE Trans. Neural Netw. Learn. Syst. **35**(4), 4542–4553 (2024). https://doi.org/10.1109/tnnls.2023.3285874
8. Feng, Z., He, W., Zhou, Z., Ban, X., Hu, C., Han, X.: A new safety assessment method based on belief rule base with attribute reliability. IEEE/CAA J. Automatica Sinica **8**(11), 1774–1785 (2021). https://doi.org/10.1109/jas.2020.1003399
9. Feng, Z., Yang, R., Zhou, Z., Hu, C.: Trustworthy fault diagnosis method based on belief rule base with multi-source uncertain information for vehicle. IEEE Trans. Ind. Electron. 1–10 (2023). https://doi.org/10.1109/tie.2023.3277095
10. Feng, Z., Zhou, Z., Hu, C., Ban, X., Hu, G.: A safety assessment model based on belief rule base with new optimization method. Reliab. Eng. Syst. Safety **203**, 107055 (2020). https://doi.org/10.1016/j.ress.2020.107055
11. Li, S., Chen, M., Wang, Y., Wu, Q.: Air combat decision-making of multiple UCAVs based on constraint strategy games. Defence Technol. **18**(3), 368–383 (2022). https://doi.org/10.1016/j.dt.2021.01.005
12. Li, X.: Positive-incentive noise. IEEE Trans. Neural Netw. Learn. Syst. 1–7 (2022). https://doi.org/10.1109/tnnls.2022.3224577
13. Luo, Z., Zhu, B., Zheng, J., Zheng, Z.: Robust distributed model predictive control for formation tracking of nonholonomic vehicles. IEEE/CAA J. Automatica Sinica **11**(2), 560–562 (2024). https://doi.org/10.1109/jas.2023.123732
14. Mallat, S.: A theory for multiresolution signal decomposition: the wavelet representation. IEEE Trans. Pattern Anal. Mach. Intell. **11**(7), 674–693 (1989). https://doi.org/10.1109/34.192463
15. Nadimi-Shahraki, M., Taghian, S., Mirjalili, S.: An improved grey wolf optimizer for solving engineering problems. Expert Syst. Appl. **166**, 113917 (2021). https://doi.org/10.1016/j.eswa.2020.113917
16. Pope, A., et al.: Hierarchical reinforcement learning for air combat at darpa's alphadogfight trials. IEEE Trans. Artif. Intell. **4**(6), 1371–1385 (2023). https://doi.org/10.1109/tai.2022.3222143
17. Qiu, H., Duan, H.: Pigeon interaction mode switch-based UAV distributed flocking control under obstacle environments. ISA Trans. **71**, 93–102 (2017). https://doi.org/10.1016/j.isatra.2017.06.016
18. Ren, W.: Consensus strategies for cooperative control of vehicle formations. IET Control Theory Appl. **1**(2), 505–512 (2007). https://doi.org/10.1049/iet-cta:20050401
19. Shensa, M.: The discrete wavelet transform: wedding the a trous and mallat algorithms. IEEE Trans. Signal Process. **40**(10), 2464–2482 (1992). https://doi.org/10.1109/78.157290
20. Tugnait, J.: Time delay estimation with unknown spatially correlated Gaussian noise. IEEE Trans. Signal Process. **41**(2), 549–558 (1993). https://doi.org/10.1109/78.193197
21. Yang, J., Liu, J., Wang, J., Sii, H., Wang, H.: Belief rule-base inference methodology using the evidential reasoning approach-rimer. IEEE Trans. Syst. Man Cybern. Part A Syst. Hum. **36**(2), 266–285 (2006). https://doi.org/10.1109/tsmca.2005.851270

22. Yang, J., Liu, J., Xu, D., Wang, J., Wang, H.: Optimization models for training belief-rule-based systems. IEEE Trans. Syst. Man Cybern. Part A Syst. Hum. **37**(4), 569–585 (2007). https://doi.org/10.1109/tsmca.2007.897606
23. Yu, D., Li, J., Wang, Z., Li, X.: An overview of swarm coordinated control. IEEE Trans. Artif. Intell. 1–22 (2023). https://doi.org/10.1109/tai.2023.3314581
24. Zhang, H., He, W., Yang, R., Feng, Z.: Performance assessment for leader-following multi-agent systems with unpredictable disturbances and switching topologies via belief rule base. J. Intell. Robot. Syst. **109**, 62 (2023). https://doi.org/10.1007/s10846-023-01990-4
25. Zhang, H., Yang, R., He, W.: Efficacy assessment for multi-vehicle formations based on data augmentation considering reliability. Adv. Eng. Inform. **61**, 102504 (2024). https://doi.org/10.1016/j.aei.2024.102504
26. Zhang, H., Zhang, G., Yang, R., Feng, Z., He, W.: Resilient formation reconfiguration for leader-follower multi-UAVs. Appl. Sci. **13**(13) (2023). https://doi.org/10.3390/app13137385
27. Zhang, J., Cui, Y., Ren, J.: Dynamic mission planning algorithm for UAV formation in battlefield environment. IEEE Trans. Aerosp. Electron. Syst. **59**(4), 3750–3765 (2023). https://doi.org/10.1109/taes.2022.3231244
28. Zhang, J., Yan, J., Zhang, P.: Multi-UAV formation control based on a novel backstepping approach. IEEE Trans. Veh. Technol. **69**(3), 2437–2448 (2020). https://doi.org/10.1109/tvt.2020.2964847
29. Zhou, Z., Cao, Y., Hu, G., Zhang, Y., Tang, S., Chen, Y.: New health-state assessment model based on belief rule base with interpretability. Sci. China Inf. Sci. **64**(7), 1–15 (2021). https://doi.org/10.1007/s11432-020-3001-7
30. Zhou, Z., Zhang, D., Helleseth, T., Wen, J.: A construction of multiple optimal ZCZ sequence sets with good cross correlation. IEEE Trans. Inf. Theory **64**(2), 1340–1346 (2018). https://doi.org/10.1109/tit.2017.2756845

Design and Kinematics Characteristic Analysis of a 3-PURU/S Photoelectric Stabilized Platform

Bo Han[1,2], Zizhao Jia[1], Yuan Jiang[1], Jiayao Liu[1], Meng Han[3], and Jiantao Yao[1,2,3](✉)

[1] School of Mechanical Engineering, Yanshan University, Qinhuangdao 066004, China
{bohan,jtyao}@ysu.edu.cn
[2] Hebei Provincial Key Laboratory of Parallel Robot and Mechatronic System, Yanshan University, Qinhuangdao 066004, China
[3] School of Control Engineering, Northeastern University at Qinhuangdao, Qinhuangdao 066004, China

Abstract. This paper introduced a three-degree-of-freedom (3-DOF) photoelectric stabilized platform (PSP), and the Finite-Step-Integration (FSI) method was applied to analyze the kinematics characteristics. The motion process of the mechanism is segmented linearly, and the mathematical model of forward kinematics (FK) with iterative parameters is created and solved. The kinematic simulation is verified in ADAMS software, and the calculated results are compared with the simulation. The workspace of the PSP is analyzed to describe the working dimensionality characteristics. The results show that: the FK algorithm based on the FSI method has enough computational precision and can be efficient for the workspace analysis. This paper's research provides a good reference for the design and kinematics characteristic analysis of PSP.

Keywords: Photoelectric Stabilized Platform · Finite-Step-Integration Method · Kinematic Characteristics · Workspace

1 Introduction

The photoelectric stabilized platform (PSP) is a kind of electromechanical equipment with integrated multidisciplinary technology. Its function is to compensate the disturbance of the carrier by external factors in real time to make the optical axis of the photoelectric detector stable and quickly implement the acquisition, tracking, hit, aiming and positioning of the target. It is widely used in aerospace, navigation, and other fields [1–3]. The parallel mechanism (PM) has the characteristics of high precision, high stiffness, high bearing capacity, symmetrical structure and simple, which has been widely used in the field of stabilized platform [4–6].

Analysis of the forward kinematics (FK) of PMs is the basis for dynamic control and trajectory planning. However, the problem of modeling forward kinematics involves a group of strongly coupled nonlinear equations that are very difficult to solve, so that the analysis of the FK of a PM becomes a difficult problem [7, 8]. Huang et al. [9] proposed an efficient graphical representation of geometric algebra approaches for the

X. Lan et al. (Eds.): ICIRA 2024, LNAI 15201, pp. 17–27, 2025.
https://doi.org/10.1007/978-981-96-0771-6_2

FK of PMs with 3-PPS; Yang et al. [10] used the unit dual quaternion method to solve the FK model of a mechanism with 6-UPS; Patel et al. [11] used the iterative method to solve the FK model of an overloaded 6-DOF mechanism and verified it with the Monte Carlo method. The results show that this method has good convergence; Wang et al. [12] solved a parallel mechanisms based on the kinematic mapping of constrained planar motions and planar quaternions.

Workspace of PM is an important index for measuring its performance. Zaccaria et al. [13] presented an exploratory algorithm based on the iterative solution of the inverse geometric-static problem; Hao et al. [14] used the coordinate transformation method to solve the workspace of the 3-PCR mechanism.

This paper introduces a PSP and the Finite-Step-Integration (FSI) method [15]. The FK analysis of the PSP is carried out, and the error analysis is given by ADAMS. Finally, the FK model based on the FSI method is established to solve the workspace of the mechanism.

2 Photoelectric Stabilized Platform and the FSI Method

2.1 Photoelectric Stabilized Platform

The PSP researched in this paper is shown in Fig. 1, where it is designed based on a three-degrees-of-freedom (3-DOF) PM and its moving platform can rotate about any direction in space.

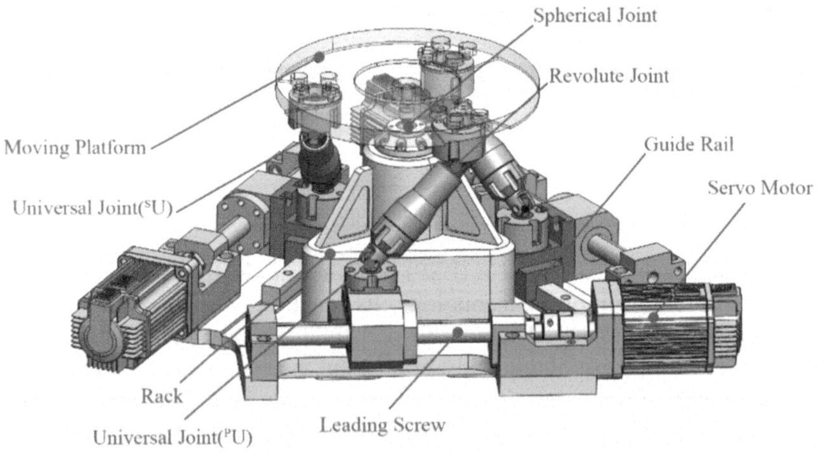

Fig. 1. The components of the PSP, where the universal joint closed to the prismatic joint (denoted as P) is represented as ^{P}U, and the universal joint closed to the moving platform is represented as ^{S}U.

The prismatic joint consists of a servo motor, a leading screw, a sliding block, and a guide rail (the guide rail is fixed to the rack). The universal joint fixed to the prismatic joint can only move in a straight line along the guide rail. The universal joint fixed to the moving platform can follow the moving platform to perform three-dimensional rotation in space. The motion of the branch is driven via the servo motor and the leading screw. The motion is transmitted to the moving platform and restrained by the spherical joint. As a result, the moving platform can provide 3-DOF rotation motion.

2.2 The FSI Method

The motion process of the PM is shown in Fig. 2. It is known that the position and pose of the moving platform in three-dimensional space can be uniquely confirmed by three non-collinear points on the moving platform. The basic principle of the FSI method is to convert the static solution of the FK of the PM into a dynamic linear superposition process solution.

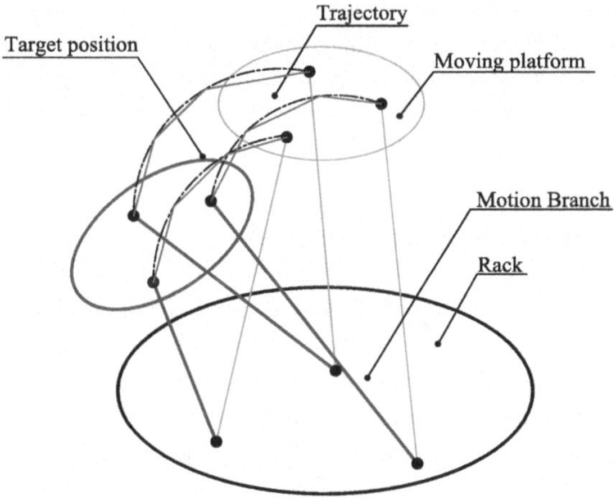

Fig. 2. Geometric concept of the FSI method, where the continuous motion process can be transformed into a superposition of a series of continuous linear motion.

The FK analysis process is shown in Fig. 3 by applying the FSI method. The information of the driving joint is known, and the entire motion stroke of the driving joint is divided into finite and small intervals. By solving the linear equations, the coordinate information of the moving platform of the mechanism at the end of the first tiny interval can be obtained, and then the obtained coordinate information is taken as the known quantity of the next iteration to perform a finite number of iterations. The result obtained at the end of the last iteration is the target posture of the moving platform under the given driving conditions.

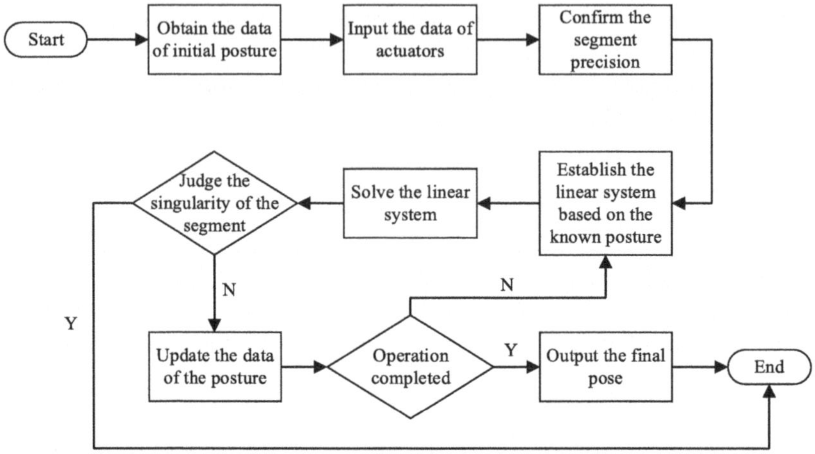

Fig. 3. Flow chart of the FSI method. The linear system is also a linear equations system, where there is a coefficient matrix used for judging the singularity of the configuration. When the determinant of the matrix is small enough, the system will identify that the mechanism is closing to the singularity and give out the singular result.

3 Kinematics Characteristics Analysis

The schematic diagram of 3-PURU/S PM is shown in Fig. 4. The three control-type motion branch chains are uniformly distributed on the circumference, and the constraint-type motion branch chain is the driven branch. The center of the spherical joint on the constraint-type motion branch chain is taken as the origin of the coordinate system, and the fixed frame $\boldsymbol{P} : \{O, x, y, z\}$ coincides with the dynamic frame $\boldsymbol{P'} : \left\{O, x', y', z'\right\}$ at their initial posture.

Since the revolute joint on the control-type motion branch chains is perpendicular to the secondary-type universal joint, the revolute joint on the control-type motion branch chains and the secondary-type universal joint are regarded as a spherical joint in the following analysis. To facilitate analysis, the reference point on the moving joint is taken as the center point of the moving joint.

The initial posture information of the PSP is known. When the driving joint moves a certain distance l_i during the movement of the mechanism, and the moving platform reaches the target pose. The FSI method divides the process into a set of finite small intervals.

The known information of the initial conductions of the PSP is ${}^{P}U_i^{\langle 0\rangle}$ and ${}^{S}U_i^{\langle 0\rangle}$. As the input data, the value of the actuator is denoted as Δp_i, and the variation of actuators P_i in every interval is $\Delta p_i \big/ n$, where the number of steps is n.

The establishment process of the first-type equations is shown in Fig. 5, Since the position of the upper level universal joint relative to the prismatic joint is always unchanged during the movement of the mechanism, the motion process of the control-type motion branch chains can be described as follows: in the first stage, the ${}^{P}U_i$ and the ${}^{S}U_i$ driven by the prismatic joint move a certain distance along with the driving joint. In the secondary stage, the ${}^{S}U_i$ rotates around the first-type universal joint at an angle

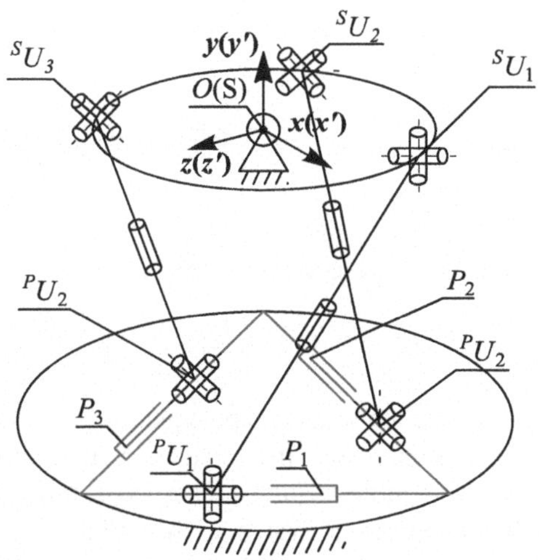

Fig. 4. Simplified mechanism model of 3-PURU/S PM. The prismatic joint (actuator) is denoted as the unit vector $\mathbf{p}_i$ $(i = 1, 2, 3)$, the unit vector the centers of two types of universal joint is denoted as points ^PU_i and ^SU_i, and the spherical joint is denoted as the point S coincided with the point O.

$\alpha_i^{\langle k\rangle}$ to reach the target posture. Since the whole motion process is divided into a finite number of tiny stages, the value of $\alpha_i^{\langle k\rangle}$ is very small, which is linearized according to the differential principle.

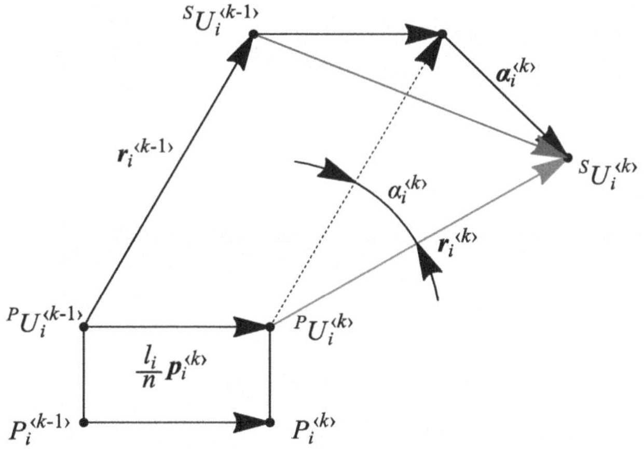

Fig. 5. Geometric principle of the first-type equations, where the vector $\overrightarrow{^SU_i^{\langle k-1\rangle}\,^SU_i^{\langle k\rangle}}$ is equivalent to the superposition of $\overrightarrow{^PU_i^{\langle k-1\rangle}\,^PU_i^{\langle k\rangle}}$ and $\boldsymbol{\alpha}_i^{\langle k\rangle}$.

According to the differential geometric and the Maclaurin series, the first-type equations are established as follows:

$$\boldsymbol{r}_i^{\langle k-1\rangle}\cdot\boldsymbol{\alpha}_i^{\langle k-1\rangle}=\boldsymbol{r}_i^{\langle k-1\rangle}\cdot\left(\overline{{}^{S}U_i^{\langle k-1\rangle}{}^{S}U_i^{\langle k\rangle}}-\frac{l_i}{n}\boldsymbol{p}_i^{\langle k\rangle}\right)=0 \tag{1}$$

where $\boldsymbol{r}_i^{\langle k-1\rangle}=\overline{{}^{P}U_i^{\langle k-1\rangle}{}^{S}U_i^{\langle k-1\rangle}}$.

After simplification, the first-type equations are as follows:

$$\boldsymbol{r}_i^{\langle k-1\rangle}\cdot\overline{{}^{S}U_i^{\langle k-1\rangle}{}^{S}U_i^{\langle k\rangle}}=\frac{l_i}{n}\left(\boldsymbol{r}_i^{\langle k-1\rangle}\cdot\boldsymbol{p}_i^{\langle k\rangle}\right) \tag{2}$$

The establishment process of the second-type equations is shown in Fig. 6. Since the mechanism has only three rotational DOF, in a fixed coordinate system, the movement of the moving platform in each tiny interval can be regarded as turning from the initial pose around the origin of the fixed coordinate system to the end posture of the stage. With the same operation as the first-type equations, the second-type equations are established as follows:

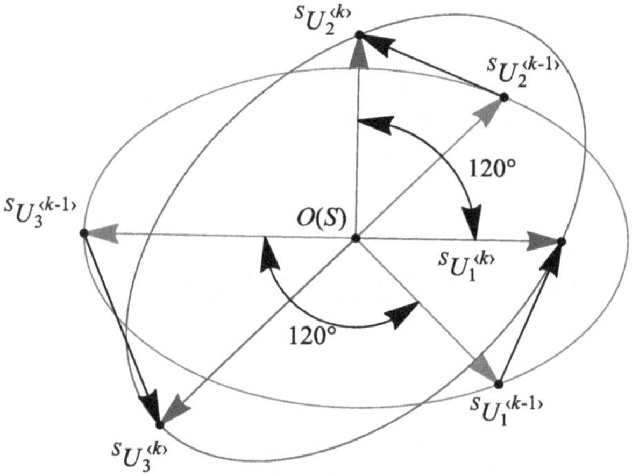

Fig. 6. Geometric principle of the second-type equations and third-type equations.

$$\overline{O^{S}U_i^{\langle k-1\rangle}}\cdot\overline{{}^{S}U_i^{\langle k-1\rangle}{}^{S}U_i^{\langle k\rangle}}=0 \tag{3}$$

The establishment process of the third-type equations is shown in Fig. 6. Analyzed in a fixed coordinate system, it is known from the configuration characteristics of the PSP that the four joints' center are always on a plane in the process of movement, and the spherical joints on the three control-type motion branch chains are all distributed on the circular arc with the spherical joint of the constraint-type motion branch chain as the center of the circle.

$$\overline{O^{S}U_1^{\langle k\rangle}}+\overline{O^{S}U_2^{\langle k\rangle}}+\overline{O^{S}U_3^{\langle k\rangle}}=\sum_{i=1}^{3}\left(\overline{O^{S}U_i^{\langle k-1\rangle}}\right)+\sum_{i=1}^{3}\left(\overline{{}^{S}U_i^{\langle k-1\rangle}{}^{S}U_i^{\langle k\rangle}}\right)=\boldsymbol{0} \tag{4}$$

Simultaneous Eq. (2)–Eq. (4) nine systems of linear equations with nine unknowns can be constructed, the coefficient matrix of the linear system is $\mathbf{M}_{9\times9}$. The unknown quantity of the constraint system is $\mathbf{d}_{9\times1}$ which comes from coordinates of vector $\overline{{}^{S}U_i^{\langle k-1\rangle}{}^{S}U_i^{\langle k\rangle}}$ The constant vector of the system is denoted as $c_{9\times1}$.

As a result, the linear arithmetic system is described as follows:

$$\mathbf{M}_{9\times9}\cdot \boldsymbol{d}_{9\times1} = \boldsymbol{c}_{9\times1} \tag{5}$$

The nine unknowns in the vector $\boldsymbol{d}_{9\times1}$ can be obtained with n times iteration calculations. The FK program is coded by MATLAB, and the posture of the end of the moving platform of the PSP can be obtained by solving it for n times.

In order to verify the reliability of the FK solution obtained by FSI method, the 3-PURU/S mechanism model was established in ADAMS (as shown in Fig. 7) and simulation analysis was carried out, the input functions of three actuators are given as:

$$\begin{cases} \Delta p_1(t) = \left|\overline{{}^{P}U_1^{\langle 0\rangle}{}^{P}U_1^{\langle 0\rangle}}\right| = 20\sin(t) \\ \Delta p_2(t) = \left|\overline{{}^{P}U_2^{\langle 0\rangle}{}^{P}U_2^{\langle 0\rangle}}\right| = -30\cos(t) \\ \Delta p_3(t) = \left|\overline{{}^{P}U_3^{\langle 0\rangle}{}^{P}U_3^{\langle 0\rangle}}\right| = 50\sin(t) \end{cases} \tag{6}$$

Fig. 7. The simulation model in ADAMS, where it has been simplified to facilitate the software operation.

The simulation time is set as $t_{\max} = 10$ s, and the interval is divided into $n = 3000$. To obtain the posture of the fixed platform of the PSP in space, the center point of the universal joint connected to the moving platform on the three driving branches is taken as the observation point. The curve of reference point coordinates x, y and z over time is compared with the result obtained by FSI method (simulation value and calculated value), as shown in **Fig. 8**.

On this basis, the error between the calculated value and the simulation value is obtained as shown in Fig. 9.

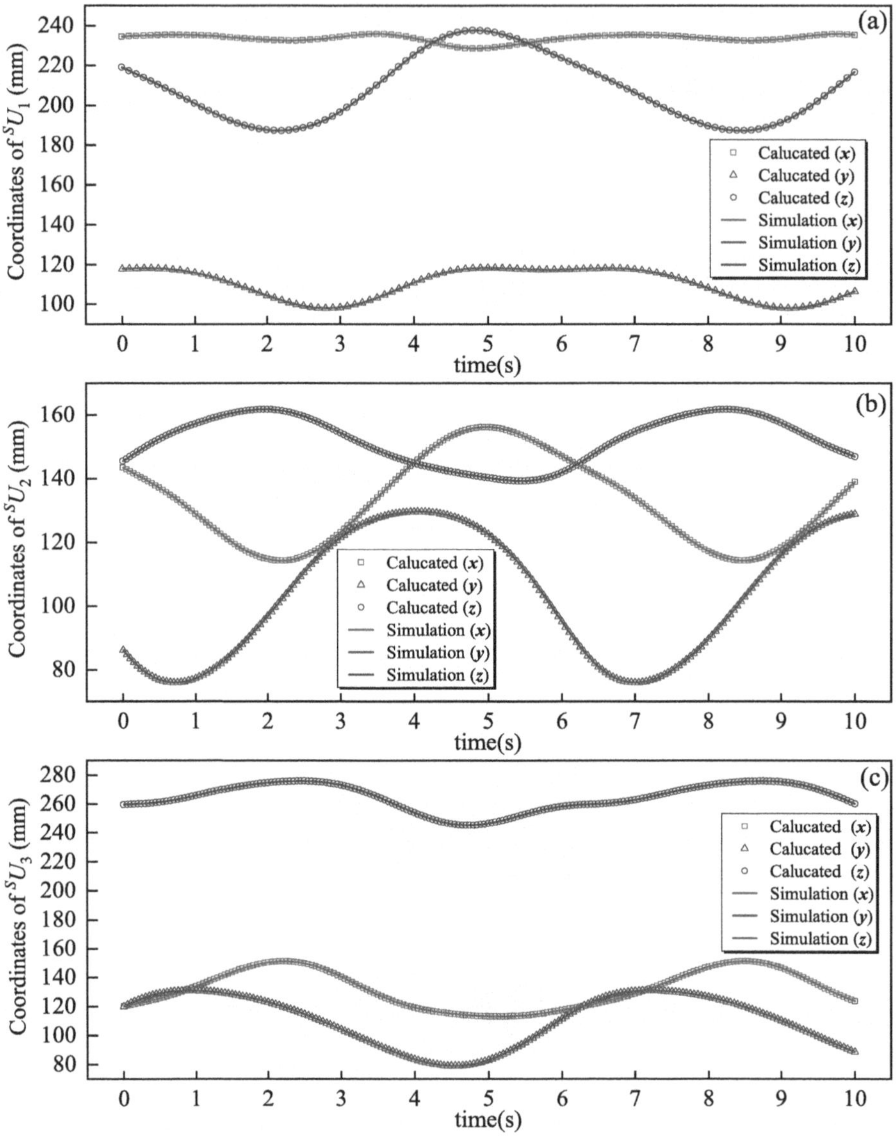

Fig. 8. The motion trajectory of point $^{S}U_i$, where (a), (b), and (c) respectively represent in each case the change of the coordinate values of the reference points on three branches with the time under the influence of the driving joint.

The analysis of the above figures shows the temporal changes of the driving joint. The error between the results of the FSI method and the true value is limited to about 10 μm. This indicates that the results of the FSI method for the FK analysis of the PSP have a high degree of agreement with the real situation and the error value is very minute. The reliability of the FK analysis with the FSI method is proved.

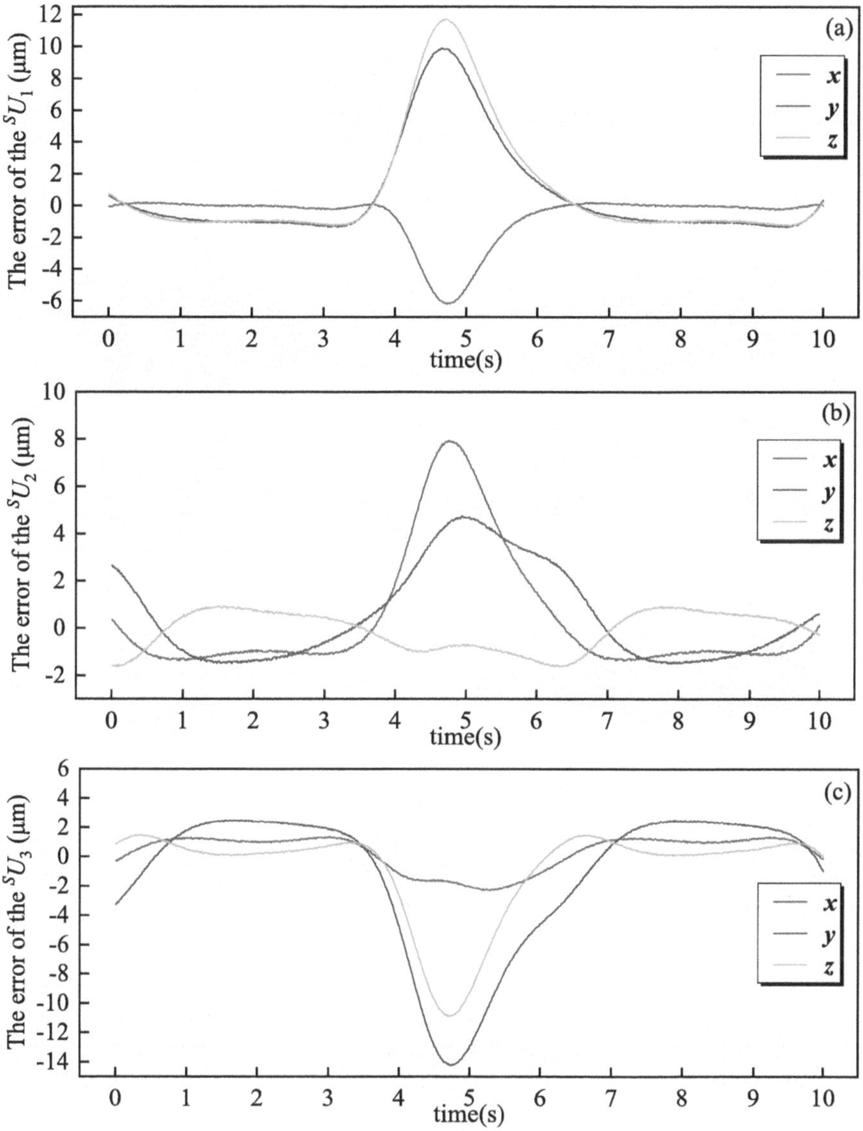

Fig. 9. The position error of point ^SU_i, where (a), (b), and (c) represent the error between the calculated value and the true value of the reference point on the three driving branches respectively. The error value can be used to quantify the reliability of the FK of the PSP using the FSI method.

4 Workspace Analysis

The application of the FSI method to solve the workspace flow of the PSP is as follows: based on the established model of the FK, three continuous Euler angles are derived by solving the posture matrix of the moving platform, which are the reachable points in the workspace of the PSP. According to the requirements workspace: the rotating range of the moving platform should be $[-10°, 10°]$ in three directions respectively. Due to the limitation of the size of the PSP, the moving range of the driving joint should be $[-40\ \text{mm}, 40\ \text{mm}]$. Based on the above known conditions, the workspace of the PSP is solved, and the workspace is obtained as shown in Fig. 10.

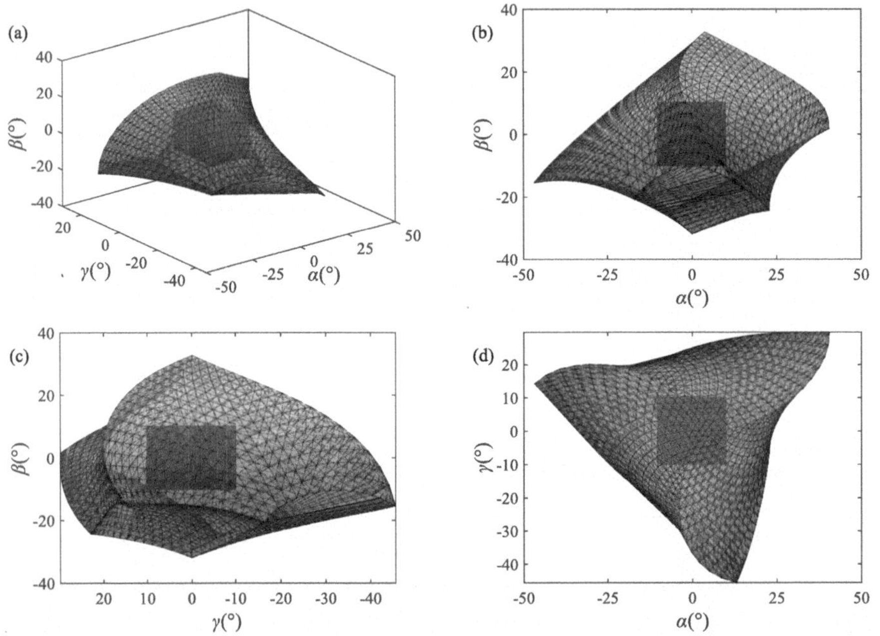

Fig. 10. The accessible and the required workspace of the PSP, where the number of steps is $n = 3000$. The red patterning is the required workspace, and the colorful patterning is the accessible one: (a) The axonometric. (b) The front view. (c) The left view. (d) The top view.

It shows that the workspace of the PSP meets the basic workspace requirements. From the perspective of the FK of the PSP, the FSI method is used to solve the workspace, which overcomes the disadvantage of the traditional ergodic search method based on inverse kinematics and has the advantage of accurate workspace boundary calculation.

5 Conclusion

In this paper, a PSP was proposed and its kinematics characteristics were studied. The FSI method for solving the FK of the parallel mechanisms was introduced. Given the input function of the driving joint, the FK position solution of the PSP was solved by using the FSI method, and the simulation was verified in ADAMS. Finally, the workspace of the PSP was solved. The results show that the FSI method can establish and solve the FK analysis model of PMs accurately, and it can also provide an effective solution for the search problem of accessible workspace.

Acknowledgement. This work was supported by the National Natural Science Foundation of China [Nos. 52105035 & 62203094], the Special Central Funds for Guiding Local Scientific and Technological Development [No. 236Z1801G], the Higher Education Youth Top Talent Project of Hebei Province of China [No. BJK2024042], the Natural Science Foundation of Hebei Province of China [Nos. E2021203109 &F2023501021] and the Graduate Student Innovation Capability Training and Support Project of Hebei Province [No. CXZZBS2024053].

References

1. Qiang, H.B., Jin, S., Feng, X.Y., et al.: Model predictive control of a shipborne hydraulic parallel stabilized platform based on ship motion prediction. IEEE Access **8**, 181880–181892 (2020)
2. Han, B., Yuan, Z.T., Zhang, J.C., et al.: Design and analysis of modular deployable antenna mechanism based on a class of self-limiting position units. Mech. Mach. Theory **191**, 105509 (2024)
3. Song, X.R., Chen, H., Xue, Y.G.: Stabilization precision control methods of photoelectric aim-stabilized system. Optics Commun. **351**, 115–120 (2015)
4. Meng, X.D., Gao, F., Wu, S.F., et al.: Type synthesis of parallel robotic mechanisms: framework and brief review. Mech. Mach. Theory **78**, 177–186 (2014)
5. Li, L.Q., Fang, Y.F., Yao, J.Q., et al.: Type synthesis of a family of novel parallel leg mechanisms driven by a 3-DOF drive system. Mech. Mach. Theory **167**, 104572 (2022)
6. Chen, Z.M., Li, M., Kong, X.W., et al.: Kinematics analysis of a novel 2R1T 3-PUU parallel mechanism with multiple rotation centers. Mech. Mach. Theory **152**, 103938 (2020)
7. Wang, L.P., Xu, H.Y., Guan, L.W., et al.: A novel 3-PUU parallel mechanism and its kinematic issues. Robot. Comput.-Integrated Manuf. **42**, 86–102 (2016)
8. Ye, H., Wang, D., Wu, J., et al.: Forward and inverse kinematics of a 5-DOF hybrid robot for composite material machining. Robot. Comput.-Integrated Manuf. **65**, 101961 (2020)
9. Huang, X., Ma, C., Su, H.: A geometric algebra algorithm for the closed-form forward displacement analysis of 3-PPS parallel mechanisms. Mech. Mach. Theory **137**, 280–296 (2019)
10. Yang, X., Wu, H., Li, Y., et al.: A dual quaternion solution to the forward kinematics of a class of six-DOF parallel robots with full or reductant actuation. Mech. Mach. Theory **107**, 27–36 (2017)
11. Patel, S., Nguyen, V.L., Caverly, R.J.: Forward kinematics of a cable-driven parallel robot with pose estimation error covariance bounds. Mech. Mach. Theory **183**, 105231 (2023)
12. Wang, L.K., Song, Z.C., You, J.J., et al.: A fast forward kinematics algorithm based on planar quaternion solution for a class of 3-DoF planar parallel mechanisms. Meccanica **59**(3), 461–473 (2024)
13. Zaccaria, F., Ida, E., Briot, S., et al.: Workspace computation of planar continuum parallel robots. IEEE Robot. Automation Lett. **7**(2), 2700–2707 (2022)
14. Han, B., Yuan, Z.T., Hu, X.Y., et al.: Design and analysis of a hoop truss deployable antenna mechanism based on convex pentagon polyhedron unit. Mechanism Mach. Theory **186**, 105365 (2023)
15. Han, B., Jiang, Y., Yang, W., et al.: Kinematics characteristics analysis of a 3-UPS/S parallel airborne stabilized platform. Aerosp. Sci. Technol.. Sci. Technol. **134**, 108163 (2023)

Vibration Analysis and Test of Working Arm of the Anchor Drilling Robot

Xu Zhou[1], Qihang You[3], Xin Wang[3](✉), Licai Zhang[2], Siyuan An[2], and Aibin Zhu[4]

[1] School of Mechanical Engineering, Northwestern Polytechnical University, Xi'an, Shaanxi, China
[2] Shanxi Tiandi Coal Mining Machinery Co., Ltd., Taiyuan, Shanxi, China
[3] School of Construction Machinery, Chang'an University, Xi'an, Shaanxi, China
wangxin@chd.edu.cn
[4] School of Mechanical Engineering, Xi'an Jiaotong University, Xi'an, Shaanxi, China

Abstract. Aiming at the problems of complex and harsh working environments and low reliability of the working arm of the anchor drilling robot, the dynamic characteristics of the working arm are studied based on the dynamic simulation analysis and vibration test analysis. In view of the influence of working load and deformation on the rigidity of the working arm, the static finite element analysis is implemented by simulating the actual working conditions. The stress and strain distribution of the working arm under the roof anchor drilling condition is derived, and on this basis, the modal analysis of the working arm with pre-stress is carried out. The six orders of vibration mode and the corresponding inherent frequencies are obtained. A vibration test system of the working arm is set up to achieve the three-dimensional vibration accelerations of the working arm under the roof anchor drilling condition. The fast Fourier transform of the vibration acceleration signals is conducted to obtain the vibration spectrum. The dynamic characteristics of the working arm are analyzed through the vibration frequency and the inherent frequency, which is of great reference value for improving the reliability of the working arm.

Keywords: Working arm · Anchor drilling robot · Vibration analysis

1 Introduction

With the in-depth advancement of intelligent construction of coal mines, support technique and equipment are becoming increasingly widely used to improve the safety of the coal mine tunnel. As a new mine support machine, the anchor drilling robot is developed to conduct the whole working process of walking, positioning, drilling, anchor rod placing and fastening automatically and efficiently, without the human involvement [1].

The working arm is the key component of the anchor drilling robot, and it overtakes the most tasks of the drilling work with the heavy drilling device mounted on it. As a long cantilever component with complex and harsh working environments, the working arm bears a random and violently fluctuating load and exhibits complex coupled vibration

X. Lan et al. (Eds.): icira 2024, LNAI 15201, pp. 28–40, 2025.
https://doi.org/10.1007/978-981-96-0771-6_3

characteristics, which leads to lower positioning accuracy of the working arm and shorter MTBF (Mean Time Between Failures), thus affecting the automatic execution capability and the reliability of the robot [2]. Therefore, in this paper, with the purpose of improving the reliability of the working arm, the pre-stress modal analysis and the vibration test analysis are combined to analyze the dynamic characteristics of the working arm.

In most previous research, the analysis of dynamic characteristics mainly focuses on the dynamic simulation of the working arm and the study of the wear mechanism. Yang *et al.* [3] take the 9t loader as the research object and established a rigid-flexible coupling dynamic model that can reflect the dynamic characteristics of the working device based on the modal superposition method. As a result, the dynamic stress changes of the boom, the rocker, and the connecting rod are derived. In [4], Chaphalkar *et al.* describe an experimental apparatus and the associated theory which allows to obtain the natural frequencies and modes of vibration of a cantilever beam and analyze the low, medium and high frequency values by using ANSYS finite element package. Mekalke *et al.* in [5] determine the natural frequencies and mode shapes of a free cantilever beam of different material and geometries by ANSYS simulation and experimentation. In [6], Liu *et al.* use finite element analysis software and dynamics simulation software to establish the rigid-flexible coupling model of an excavator, and used the displacement curves of the hydraulic cylinders as the driving force to obtain the stresses at each point on the movable arm and the bucket rod. Chen *et al.* [7] analyze the dynamic load data at the joints of the movable arm under two typical working conditions by using finite element numerical simulation technology.

In this paper, an anchor drilling robot is taken as the research object, and the dynamic characteristics analysis of its working arm is carried out based on the combination of modal analysis and vibration test analysis. Through the pre-press modal analysis and the vibration spectrum analysis, the vibration characteristics of the working arm is revealed and thus the optimization and improvement measures are proposed.

2 Problem Description

The outside view and the structure of the anchor drilling robot are shown in Fig. 1 and Fig. 2, respectively. The robot consists of for main components, i.e. the driving chassis, the working arm and two drilling devices. In general, the working arm of the anchor drilling robot is a typical long and heavy-loaded cantilever and always has a relatively large weight. In order to ensure its efficiency, the movement speeds of all the actuators are relatively high. Moreover, the size of the working arm is also designed to meet the operation requirements of the narrow working space, the maintenance of the roadway roof, and the tip nest.

The environment of the underground coal mine is commonly complex and harsh. Differences in the coal seam hosting conditions, gangue, faults, trapped columns, and changes in the hardness of the rock layer bring random and violently fluctuating loads upon the working arm. The heavy, alternating, and complex working loads coupled with multiple sources of excitation and the inertia of the actuators cause the working arm to exhibit a complex vibration characteristic, resulting in low positioning accuracy of the working arm, increased fatigue damage of the structural parts, wear of shafts, decreased accuracy of sensors, early failure of electrical control components and other reliability problems.

The working arm studied in this paper is assumed to be a linear elastomer. It obeys Hooke's law in the elastic range, the material is uniformly continuous and isotropic, and the vibrations satisfy the micro-vibration prerequisites. Firstly, the force analysis of the working arm is conducted, and the load boundary conditions are obtained. Next, the actual working conditions are simulated to establish the working arm finite element analysis model, and the static analysis is carried out to obtain the stress distribution. Then, the static load of the working arm is taken as the pre-stress, with which the modal analysis is implemented to obtain the inherent frequency and the vibration mode. After that, a vibration test system is set up to achieve the vibration acceleration signals under the roof anchor drilling condition, and the fast Fourier transform of the vibration signal is done to obtain the vibration spectrum. Finally, the dynamic characteristics analysis of the working arm is completed by combining the inherent frequency and the vibration spectrum.

Fig. 1. Outside view of the anchor drilling robot.

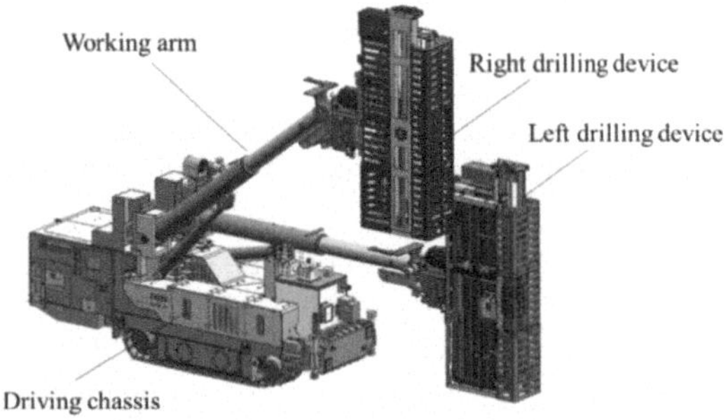

Fig. 2. Structure of the anchor drilling robot.

3 Research Procedure

3.1 Force Analysis

Force analysis of the working arm of the anchor drilling robot can be shown in Fig. 3. The working arm of the robot is hinged to the frame through the pin shaft. The swing hydraulic cylinder is regarded as a two-force rod and is subjected to the frame force F at the hinged point O_1.

According to Newton's third law, F and the hydraulic cylinder force are acting force and reaction force to each other, so F is along the direction of the cylinder axis. The outer sleeve of the working arm is hinged to the frame through the pin shaft, and it is acted upon by the frame force F_x, F_y, and F_z at the hinge point O. The gravity force G acts vertically downward upon the working arm at its centroid. For the roof anchor drilling condition, the drill frame is acted by the feeding resistance P and the rotary resistance moment T. The acting points of P and T are both the head of the drill pipe.

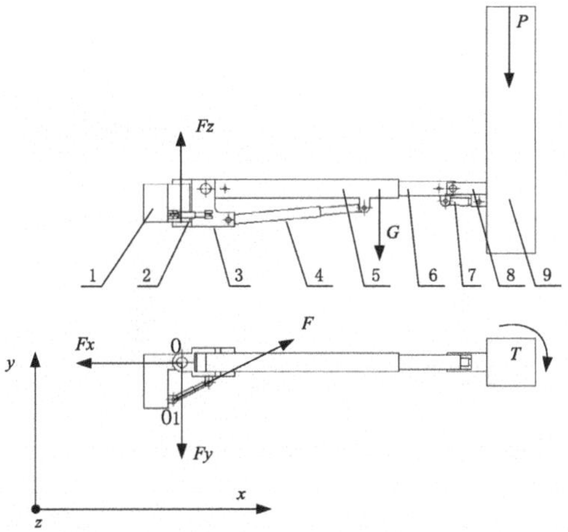

1.Robot frame 2. Swinging hydraulic cylinder 3. Base 4. Lifting hydraulic cylinder 5. Outer sleeve 6. Inner sleeve 7. Swinging hydraulic cylinder of the drilling frame 8. Drilling frame connecting seat 9. Drilling frame

Fig. 3. Force analysis of the working arm.

3.2 Static Finite Element Analysis

The drilling frame and the robot frame can be simplified into two equivalent mass blocks. The 3D model of the working arm is established and imported into the finite element analysis software ANSYS, and the contact of the articulation points is established between the working arm and the robot frame, as while as the articulation points of each joint with the friction contact type. It should be noted that the working arm contact belongs to the metal articulated pair with lubrication conditions, and the friction coefficient can be consulted from the design manual [8]. The working arm contact setting stated above is shown in Fig. 4.

The finite element model of the working arm is shown in Fig. 5. Since the body of the anchor drilling robot is fixed when drilling, fixed constraints are applied to the robot frame to simulate drilling conditions. Gravity is applied at the mass centroid of the working arm, and the feed resistance and rotational resistance are applied to the drilling frame simultaneously.

The length of the working arm is 2600 mm, the sleeve cross-section is 200 mm by 200 mm, and the working arm mass is 2.5t. To create the finite element mesh model of the working arm, the physical field type needs to be determined first. Considering that the working arm belongs to structural parts, containing multiple articulated pairs, the problem is nonlinear [9]. To do this, the physical field type is set to nonlinear mechanical. Furthermore, the global mesh size is set to 10 mm according to the actual size. Finally, the local mesh size of the articulated pin shafts is set to 5 mm after a local mesh refinement. Thus, the generated finite element analysis mesh model of the working arm can be shown in Fig. 6. The number of working arm grid cells is 151629 and the number of nodes is 295917.

By solving the finite element analysis model of the working arm, the stress distribution of the working arm under the roof anchor drilling condition is derived as shown

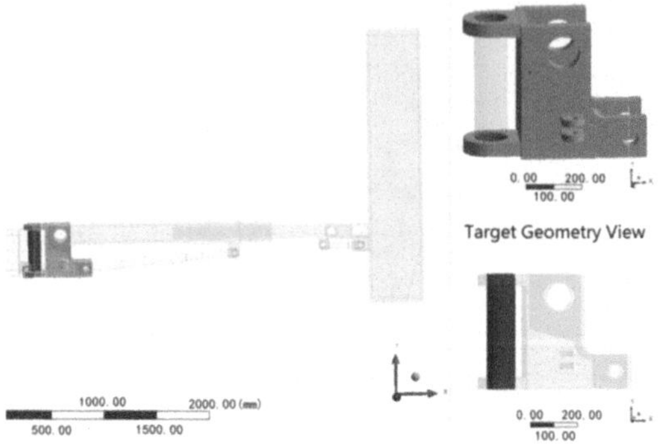

Fig. 4. Contact setting of the working arm.

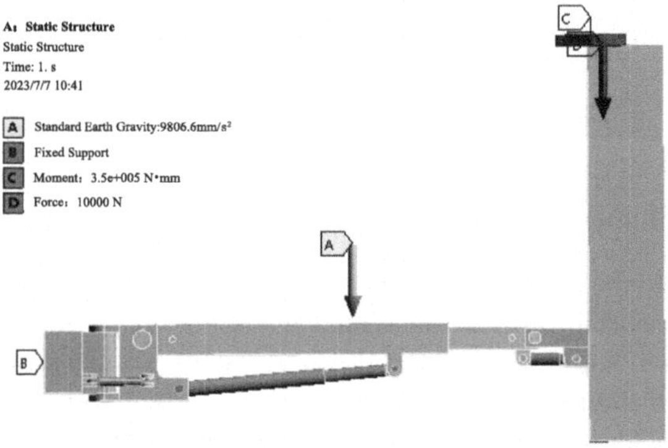

Fig. 5. Finite element model of the working arm.

in Fig. 7. From Fig. 7, it can be seen that for the roof anchor drilling condition, the maximum stress of the working arm is 279.44 MPa, which appears at the lower corner point of the drilling frame connecting seat.

Fig. 6. Finite element mesh model of the working arm.

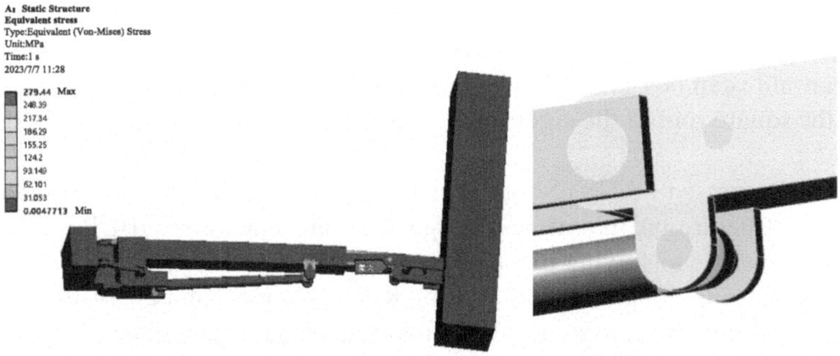

Fig. 7. Stress distribution of the working arm and local amplification diagram.

3.3 Pre-stress Modal Analysis

An important procedure in the structural dynamics analysis is the inherent vibration characteristics analysis. Since the inherent vibration characteristics are only related to the mass and stiffness distribution of the structure itself, it is also known as the self-oscillation characteristics which determine the response behavior of the structure under dynamic loading.

Each component or part has its own inherent frequency and corresponding modal vibration mode shape, which are inherent properties of the structure itself. The essence of modal analysis is to calculate the eigenvalues of the structural vibration. For a typical undamped structure, the free vibration equation is denoted by

$$M\ddot{X} + KX = 0 \tag{1}$$

where M is the mass matrix, K is the stiffness matrix,X is the displacement vector, and $\ddot{X}$ is the acceleration vector. If the structure vibrates at a certain fixed frequency and mode in the form of

$$x = \varphi \sin(\omega t + \varphi) \tag{2}$$

where φ is the amplitude, ω is the angular frequency, and φ is the initial phase, then we have

$$\ddot{X} = -\omega^2 \varphi \sin(\omega t + \varphi) \tag{3}$$

Substituting Eq. (3) into Eq. (1), the free vibration equation of the structure can be obtained as

$$\left(K - \omega^2 M\right)\varphi = 0 \tag{4}$$

Obviously, $\varphi = 0$ is one of the solutions of Eq. (4), but this solution implies that all the mass points of the structure are in a stationary state. To obtain a non-zero solution, the following conditions must be satisfied:

$$\det\left(K - \omega^2 M\right) = 0 \tag{5}$$

Equation (5) is called the eigenvalue equation of structural vibration, and its eigenvalues are $\omega_i{}^2$. By substituting the eigenvalue into Eq. (5), the eigenvector φ_i corresponding to the eigenvalue can be obtained, which is also the vibration mode vector of the structure, and the square root of the eigenvalue ω_i is the self-oscillation angular frequency of the structure.

The basic purpose of ANSYS modal analysis is to calculate the self-oscillation frequency of the structure and its corresponding vibration mode shape [10]. Pre-stress modal analysis is applicable to solving the inherent vibration characteristics of structures with pre-stress. Regarding the gravity, the drilling feed resistance, and the drilling rotational resistance as pre-stresses, the six orders of inherent frequencies of the working arm can be picked up through pre-stress modal analysis, as shown in Table 1.

Table 1. Inherent Frequency of the Working Arm.

Order	Inherent frequency/Hz
1	4.8952
2	6.1454
3	9.9625
4	13.465
5	34.849
6	65.883

The pre-stress modal analysis of the working arm drilling is carried out, and the vibration modes corresponding to the nth-order of the inherent frequency are shown in (a) ~ (f) of Fig. 8, respectively.

From Fig. 8(a), we can see that the first-order inherent frequency of the working arm is 4.8952 Hz, which corresponds to the vibration mode of the left-to-right swing of the drilling frame, and the maximum deformation appears at the left front corner of the top of the drilling frame, with a maximum deformation of 1.6176 mm. From Fig. 8(b), it can be seen that the second-order inherent frequency is 6.1454 Hz, which corresponds to the vibration mode of the back-to-forth swing of the drilling frame, and the maximum deformation appears at the right front corner of the top of the drilling frame, with a maximum deformation of 1.7099 mm.

From Fig. 8(c), we can see that the third-order inherent frequency is 9.9625 Hz, which corresponds to a combined vibration mode of the left-to-right oscillation of both the drilling frame and the front end of the working arm, and the maximum deformation appears at the right front corner of the bottom of the drilling frame, with a maximum deformation of 1.9362 mm. From Fig. 8(d), it can be seen that the fourth-order inherent frequency is 13.465 Hz, which corresponds to the vibration mode of a superposition of the back-and-forth swing of the drilling frame and the up-and-down swing of the front end of the working arm, and the maximum deformation appears at the right back corner of the top of the drilling frame, with a maximum deformation of 1.6213 mm.

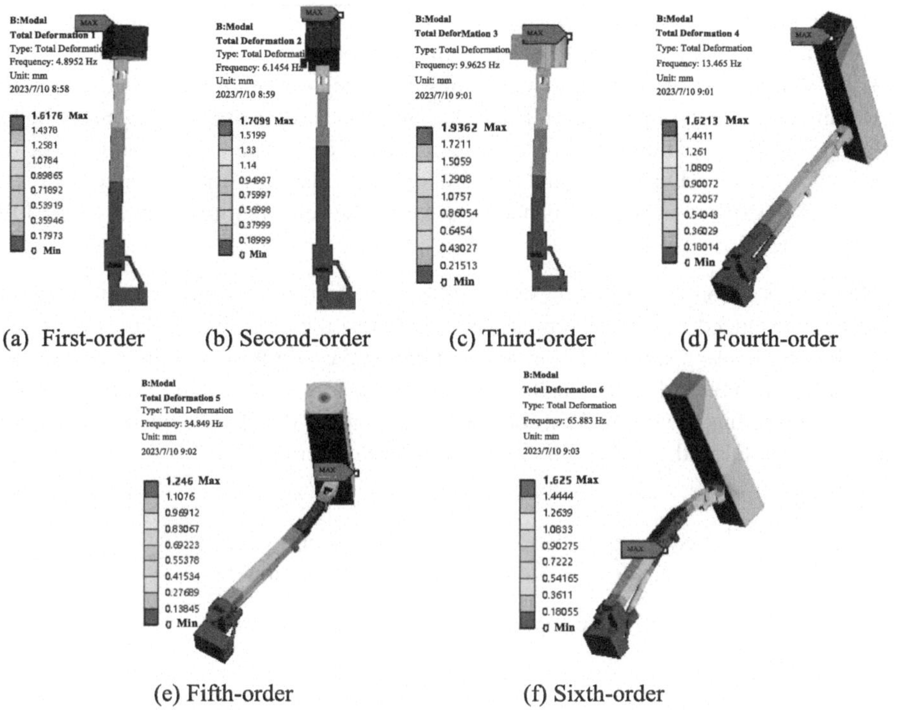

Fig. 8. The nth-order inherent frequency vibration modes.

From Fig. 8(e), we can see that the fifth-order inherent frequency is 34.849 Hz, which corresponds to the vibration mode of a superposition of the left-to-right swing and the lateral quadratic curve swing of the working arm, with a maximum deformation of 1.246 mm. From Fig. 8(f), it can be seen that the sixth-order inherent frequency is 65.883 Hz, which corresponds to the vibration mode of a superposition of the back-and-forth swing and the up-and-down quadratic curve swing of the working arm, and the maximum deformation appears near the hinge point of the elevating hydraulic cylinder in the middle of the working arm, with a maximum deformation of 1.625 mm.

4 Vibration Test Analysis of the Working Arm

To study the actual vibration characteristics of the working arm, the vibration of the working arm is tested under the roof anchor drilling condition. A vibration testing platform is built to simulate the practical working environment, with the granite testing block mounted overhead at a same height of the coal mine roadway roof. The practical machine is used to drill the testing block, and during the drilling period the typical working parameters are set and controlled. Thus the load boundary conditions including the gravity of the earth, the feed resistance and the rotational resistance are all the same as those in the practical working condition. In the vibration test analysis, the Fourier transform will be adopted to process the vibration acceleration time-domain signal of the testing point, and the vibration spectrum is analyzed based on the modal theory of the vibration mechanics. From the results of the modal analysis of the working arm, we know that among the inherent frequencies of the six orders of the working arm, the maximum deformations corresponding to the first four orders are all located at the top of the drilling frame. Therefore, we arrange the vibration measurement points at the top of the drilling frame. Due to the fact that the top of the drilling frame is in contact with the roof when drilling upward, it is hard to arrange the sensors directly at the top of the drilling frame.

The composition of the test system is shown in Fig. 9. A sound vibration testing instrument produced by LMS Company is used to test the vibration of the working arm [11]. The acceleration sensor [12] is selected to test the vibration and the measurement point is placed on the side of the drilling frame near its top, as shown in Fig. 10. The measurement directions are defined as: the vertical upward is the X-axis-positive direction, and the horizontal to the right is the Z-axis-positive direction.

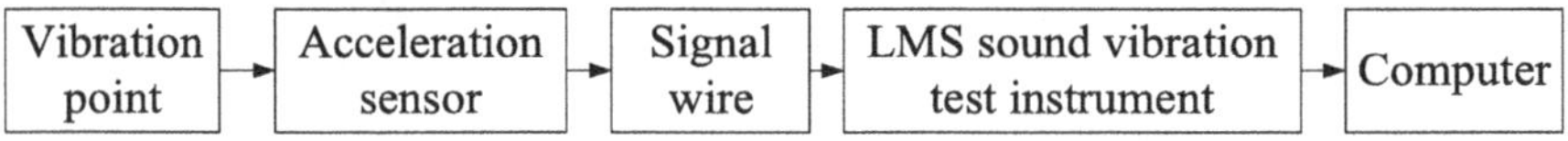

Fig. 9. The composition of the vibration test system.

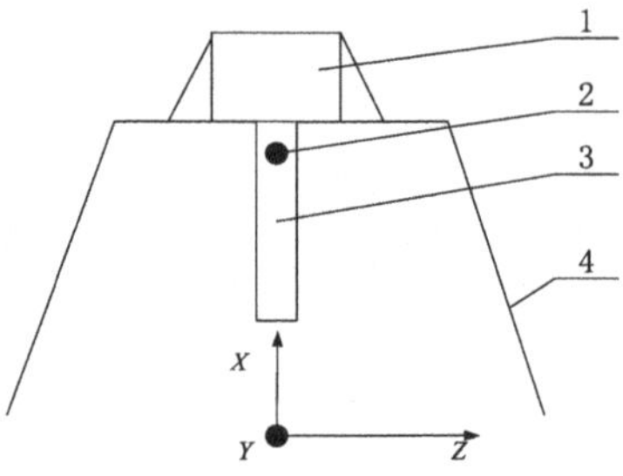

1. Rock specimen 2. Three-directional acceleration sensor 3. Drilling frame 4. Test bench

Fig. 10. Arrangement of the measurement points.

First, the three-directional acceleration sensor is fixed at the drilling frame measuring point by means of a magnetic holder and protected as necessary, and then the acceleration sensor is connected with the test instrument and the computer through the data cable. Next, the channel setup and sensor configuration are completed in the computer software and the test instrument, and the system is debugged to ensure that the test system works normally. Then the drilling robot is started and the roof anchor drilling test is carried out. The vibration acceleration signals of the working arm are collected during the test.

Spectrum analysis calculation is based on Fourier integration, which decomposes the complex signal into simple harmonic components of a finite or infinite number of frequencies [13]. The fast Fourier transform is done on the acquired vibration signal to obtain the vibration signal spectrum, as shown in Figs. 11, 12 and 13. From Figs. 11, 12 and 13, it can be seen that the vibration spectrum of the measurement point is symmetrical at about 1024 Hz which is the signal sampling frequency. Thus we only need to analyze the vibration spectrum during the 0-1024 Hz frequency band.

Table 2. Inherent Frequency and Spectrum.

Order	Inherent frequency/Hz	Vibration spectrum/Hz
1	4.8952	18, 55.5, 73.5, 109
2	6.1454	127, 129, 182, 212
3	9.9625	250.5, 251.5, 389.5
4	13.465	395.5, 484, 486
5	34.849	492.5, 670, 882, 934
6	65.883	1002, 1020

5 Dynamic Characteristics Analysis of the Working Arm

All six orders of inherent frequencies and the vibration spectrums of the working arm are shown in Table 2, from which we can see that 18 Hz is the 3 times frequency of the second-order inherent frequencies 6.1454 Hz, 250.5, 129, 670, and 1002 Hz are the times frequency of the third-order inherent frequency 9.9625 Hz, and 395.5 Hz is the 3 times frequency of the sixth-order inherent frequency 65.883 Hz.

From the above analysis, we know that the vibration of the working arm of the anchor drill robot is intense under the roof anchor drilling working condition, which is due to the fact that the second-order, the third-order, and the sixth-order inherent frequencies and even the multiplication frequency resonate with the main frequency components of the vibration spectrum. It should be noted that components with frequencies higher than 100 Hz in practical applications are usually of low energy efficient and have negligible effects on the system. Optimizing the mass distribution of the working arm and adjusting its low-order inherent frequency will be effective technical measures to solve this vibration problem [14].

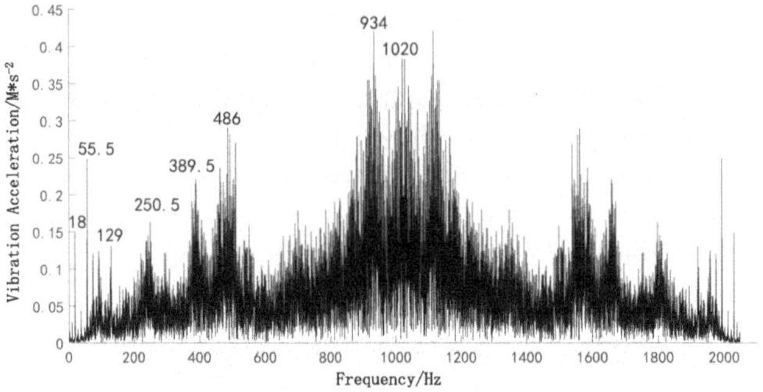

Fig. 11. X-direction vibration spectrum of the measuring point.

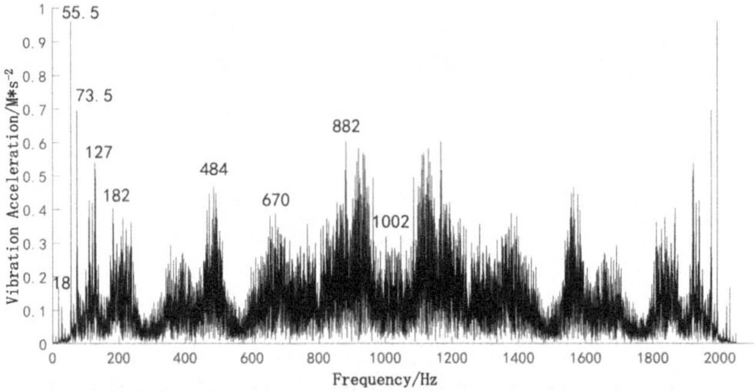

Fig. 12. Y-direction vibration spectrum of the measuring point.

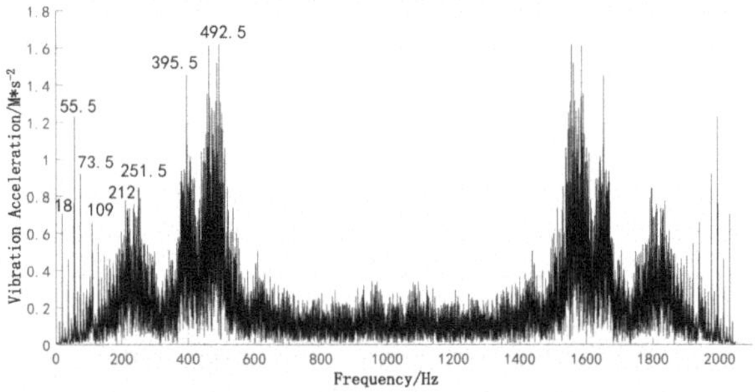

Fig. 13. Z-direction vibration spectrum of the measuring point.

6 Conclusions

In this paper, the working arm of the anchor drilling robot is taken as the research object, and the pre-stress modal analysis and the vibration test analysis are comprehensively applied to study the dynamic characteristics of the working arm. The following conclusions are drawn:

(1) The working arm of the anchor drilling robot belongs to the long-cantilever heavy-load device, which is a structure with pre-stress, and the pre-stress modal analysis can accurately reflect its inherent vibration characteristics.
(2) The combination of modal analysis and vibration test analysis overcomes the limitations of the theoretical analysis and the blindness of experimental analysis and can be used to analyze the dynamic characteristics of the structure in a more efficient way.
(3) The inherent frequency of the working arm of the anchor drilling robot and its multiplication frequency coincide with the main frequency components of the vibration spectrum, which excites the structural resonance, and it is recommended to optimize the mass distribution of the working arm.

Acknowledgments. This paper is supported by the National Key Research and Development Program of China (2020YFB1314003), Shanxi Provincial Major Science and Technology Special Project (2020XXX001), and the Self-support Project of Shanxi Tiandi Coal Mining Machinery Co., Ltd. (M2023-MS01).

References

1. Sun, X.Y., Wang, H.S., Guo, X.P., He, X.: Kinematics study on redundant manipulator with serial-parallel hybrid mechanism of Bolter-drilling rig. Mech. Sci. Technol. Aerospace Eng. **42**, 493–503 (2023)
2. Jiao, H.Z.: Configuration design and kinematic characteristics analysis of operation manipulator on coal mine roadway slotting machine. Coal Mine Machinery **44**, 71–73 (2023)
3. Yang, S.Y., Song, X.D., Wan, Y.P.: Fatigue life assessment of loader working device based on rigid-flexible coupling dynamics analysis. J. Mach. Des. **39**, 6–12 (2022)
4. Chaphalkar, S.P., Khetre, S.N., Meshram, A.M.: Modal analysis of cantilever beam structure using finite element analysis and experimental analysis. Am. J. Eng. Res. **4**(10), 178–185 (2015)
5. Mekalke, G.C., Sutar, A.V.: Modal analysis of cantilever beam for various cases and its analytical and fea analysis. Int. J. Eng. Technol. Manage. Appl. Sci. **4**(2), 60–66 (2016)
6. Liu, K., Sun, B.: Multibody dynamic analysis and simulation of backhoe hy-draulic excavator working device based on rigid-flexible coupling. J. Tongji Univ. (Natural Sci.) **49**(7), 1053–1060 (2021)
7. Chen, X.H., et al.: Excavator working device based on dynamic characteristics analysis of clearance wear mechanise of end face friction pair. J. Mech. Eng. **58**, 191–205 (2022)
8. Lv, J.S.: Vibration model analysis of rotary drill pipe of bolt drilling rig. Coal Mine Mach. **43**, 88–91 (2022)
9. Zhang, L.C.: Prestress modal analysis on test bench for Mine-used cutting reducer. Mining Mach. **50**, 11–14 (2022)
10. Li, B., et al.: Pre stress modal analysis and optimization of parallel frame of seven rocket engines. J. Astronautics **44**(2), 178 (2023)
11. Liang, L.J., Ma, M.Y., Wang, Y., Li, J.: Analysis on the lateral vibration of drill string in horizontal wells. Chinese J. Appl. Mech. **40**, 690–701 (2023)
12. Zheng, G.Q., Li, Y.M., Ji, K.Z., Liang, Z.W., Ma, X., Cheng, J.H.: Vibration analysis and structural optimization of header frame of millet combine harvest. Agric. Mechanization Res. **46**, 41–45 (2024)

13. Tu, J.H., Hu, G., Tan, X.L., Liang, J.Q., Zhang, P.: Study on spectrum characteristics of vortex-induced vibration of three tandem circular cylinders. Chinese J. Theoretical Appl. Mech. **53**, 1552–1568 (2021)
14. Zhang, J., Wang, T.Y., Yao, X.X.: Modal analysis and physical test verification of a certain type of automobile exhaust system. J. Guangxi Univ. Sci. Technol. **34**, 1–6 (2023)

Design and Optimization of Vibration Sieve for Specific Sandy Soil and Its Screening Motion Parameters

Zhenxing Liu, Chengzhou Fan(✉), Yanxia Li, Shiguo Li, Yongdong Bi, and Jinshuai Yang

Northwest Institute of Nuclear Technology, Xi'an, China
fanchengzhou@126.com

Abstract. As an efficient and continuous screening equipment, vibrating screens are widely used in the screening process of various raw materials. However, aim at the screening of specific sandy soil, traditional vibrating screens often suffer from issues such as low screening efficiency and unstable motion performance. Therefore, this paper designs a vibrating screen specifically for sandy soil, which mainly includes a screen body, an automatically replaceable screen mesh mechanism, and a screen mesh cleaning mechanism. The vibrating screen can automatically change the screen mesh during the screening process, greatly improving the screening efficiency, and adopts a screen mesh cleaning method combining extrusion and high-pressure air knives to reduce dust volatilization. Subsequently, a screening model of the vibrating screen is established, and a sandy soil particle model is constructed using the weighted roundness method based on the discrete element overlapping particle family ODEC method. The impact of various model parameters on screening efficiency is analyzed. Based on multi-parameter orthogonal experimental analysis, the key parameters of the screening motion are optimized using the ant colony algorithm based on four-dimensional path planning, thereby improving the screening efficiency and stability of the vibrating screen.

Keywords: linear vibrating screen · discrete element method · multi-parameter orthogonal experiment · ant colony optimization algorithm

1 Introduction

Vibrating screen, as a key equipment for screening bulk granular materials, is widely used in agriculture, chemical industry, mining and other fields. According to the different vibration trajectories of vibrating screens, they can be divided into linear vibrating screens, circular vibrating screens and elliptical vibrating screens [1–3]. Among them, the ZKB series of linear vibrating screens [4] are relatively common. They use the vibration motor excitation principle to achieve the purpose of screening through reasonable matching of the screen mesh. It is suitable for impurity removal, classification and screening work in coal preparation, mineral processing and other industries, and can ensure stable operation in harsh environments.

X. Lan et al. (Eds.): ICIRA 2024, LNAI 15201, pp. 41–53, 2025.
https://doi.org/10.1007/978-981-96-0771-6_4

The screening efficiency [5], as a key performance indicator to measure the effect of vibrating screen, directly affects the effective utilization and quality performance of the screening results. In the research of screening technology, virtual simulation can shorten the design cycle of vibrating screen. However, the movement of granular materials such as sand and soil is complex during the screening process, and it is difficult to directly measure or observe their microscopic movement through experimental methods [6]. The application of continuous medium mechanics methods, such as the finite element method [7], to study granular materials often ignores the interactive relationship between the movements of individual particles in the material.

However, the Discrete Element Method (DEM) [8–10], as a highly nonlinear numerical method for solving and analyzing the motion laws and mechanical properties of complex discrete systems, can demonstrate the interactive relationships among the motions of individual particles. Therefore, through the analysis and research of screening equipment parameters using the DEM, the relationship between various screening parameters and screening efficiency can be obtained, providing a reference for the design of the parameters and structural body of the vibrating screen. In related research, Ma Xuedong et al. [11] analyzed the effects of the vibration direction angle, excitation frequency, and amplitude of the KZX936 vibrating screen on the screening efficiency of coal particles using EDEM software. The results showed that when the screen size is fixed, the various parameters have a greater impact on the screening efficiency during the initial stage of screening, and have less impact during the steady state. Yang Longfei [12] studied the screening process of asphalt mixtures on multi-layer linear vibrating screens based on DEM, and compared and analyzed the effects of various screening parameters on the screening efficiency of the vibrating screen. Li Yongxiang et al. [13] conducted numerical simulations of the screening process of reciprocating vibrating screens using EDEM, analyzing the effects of amplitude, vibration frequency, vibration direction angle, and screen inclination angle on screening efficiency. In summary, the analysis of key parameters in the screening motion of vibrating screens is particularly important, as it directly affects the screening efficiency of the vibrating screen [14].

However, the parameters obtained through the virtual simulation analysis mentioned above are only approximate ranges and cannot be used as the final design parameters. Therefore, parameter optimization is necessary. To further obtain reliable results, this paper proposes to design relevant orthogonal experiments based on considering the interactions among various parameters. Additionally, an ant colony optimization algorithm [15–17] is proposed to determine the key parameter values for the screening motion, with the maximum screening efficiency as the indicator.

2 Key Structural Design of Vibrating Screens

As shown in Fig. 1, the vibrating screen mainly includes a spiral discharge mechanism 1, a support box 2, a vibrating screen frame 3, a screen cleaning mechanism 4, and an automatically replaceable screen cylinder mechanism 5. Each part of the vibrating screen adopts a modular design, allowing for the disassembly and installation of independent modules. The feeding and discharging mechanisms are designed in a split-body configuration, facilitating the transportation of fine sand and waste materials. The vibrating screen frame is placed inside the support box, ensuring the sealing of the sand screening process. The built-in dust cleaning mechanism can recover dust and fine sand from the front screen, ensuring thorough cleaning of the screen and avoiding dust emissions.

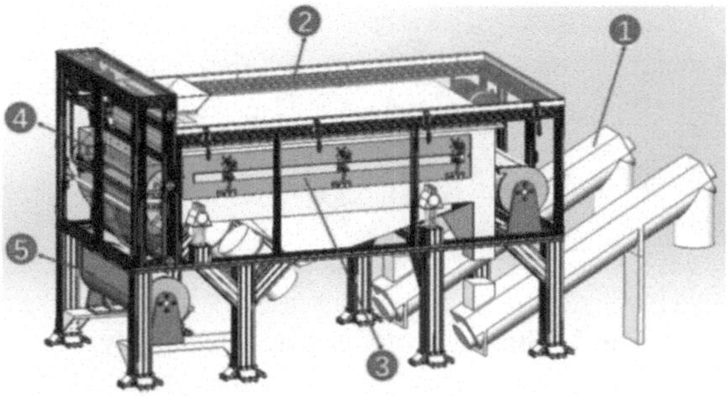

Fig. 1. Structural model of a specific sand vibrating screen

2.1 Vibrating Screen Body

As shown in Fig. 2, the invention relates to a linear vibrating screen principle prototype which can automatically change the screen surface, realizing the functions of automatically unlocking, replacing, pressing and cleaning the screen surface, so as to realize the automatic, rapid and efficient control of the particle size under the screen in the process of sand screening. The traditional design concept of linear vibrating screens is adopted to effectively screen various granular materials. As the main working part of the vibrating screen, the vibrating screen body mainly completes the function of vibrating and screening sand. Since the screen body needs to bear high-frequency vibration during sand screening, the structure of the vibrating screen body is particularly important. To facilitate the automatic replacement of screens, adjustment of vibration frequency and amplitude, and factors such as reliability, the vibrating screen body structure mainly consists of screens, screen frames, screen supports, tensioning mechanisms, support springs, and frequency-adjustable exciters. The screen body is connected to the support box through four support springs, and the frequency-adjustable exciters are installed at the bottom of the box. Two exciters are used to provide vibration output through symmetrical excitation, which can achieve amplitude adjustment of the screen body.

The screen is fixed to the screen frame through a tensioning mechanism. Since the screen is made of steel wire mesh, which has a certain flexibility, the tensioning mechanism is required to perform two actions of tensioning and pressing to secure the screen on the screen holder and better improve the screening efficiency. Considering the reliability of tensioning and the positioning requirements of the screen, the drive of the tensioning mechanism adopts the trapezoidal structure principle, as shown in Fig. 3(a). The front end of the tensioning mechanism is the screen clamping mechanism, which adopts a claw design structure. Through the limiting block, the movement is converted into clamping movement, thereby realizing the clamping and pulling actions on the screen, making the screen smoother and with greater tensioning force, and achieving the

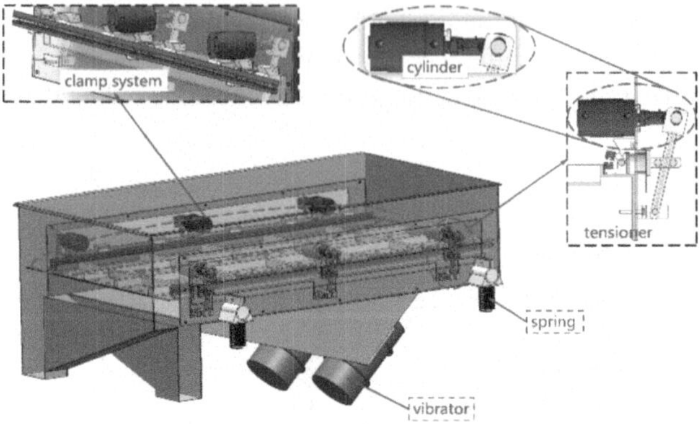

Fig. 2. Structural of vibrating screen body

purpose of improving the overall screening efficiency. The simplified motion diagram of the screen clamping mechanism is shown in Fig. 3(b). The pressing plate of the tensioning mechanism is made of Q235 steel through integral processing, improving the structural strength and flatness of the pressing strip, and making the pressing force and tensioning force more uniform. Fig. 3(c) is a simplified diagram of the screen clamping mechanism movement. In addition to the active pressing force provided by the position of the cylinder, there is an additional passive pressing device in the middle position to enhance the pressing force of the screen.

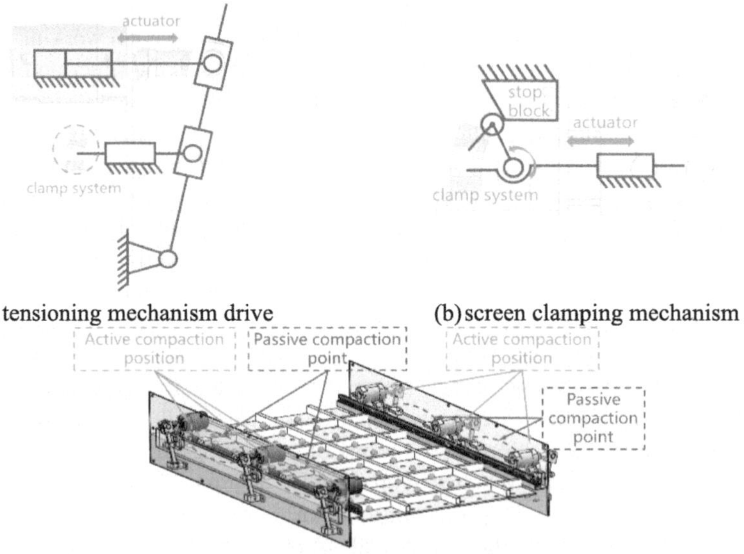

(c) Schematic diagram of screen clamping mechanism motion

Fig. 3. Screen clamping mechanism

2.2 Automatic Replacement of Screen Drum Mechanism

To achieve an integrated design of the screen-changing mechanism and the screen body of the vibrating screen, it is proposed to use a roller to perform the screen-changing task of the vibrating screen. As shown in Fig. 4, the roller mechanism can achieve automatic screen replacement, storage, and retrieval, thereby completing the automatic replacement and tensioning of the screen. The assembly modules outside the roller include the upper shell of the roller, the lower shell of the roller, and the roller shaft. The roller shaft module comprises a roller shaft and a serially woven metal screen. There are two guiding fronts (guiding grooves and screen guide columns) on the upper and lower shells of the roller, which facilitate the smooth movement of the screen during operation. To meet different fine sand requirements, the replacement of screens with different aperture sizes can be achieved by using a pair of automatically replaceable screen roller mechanisms. The screens have aperture sizes of 20mm, 10mm, 5mm, 2mm, and 1mm, respectively, with a thickness of 4mm. Each metal woven screen is connected with a rope.

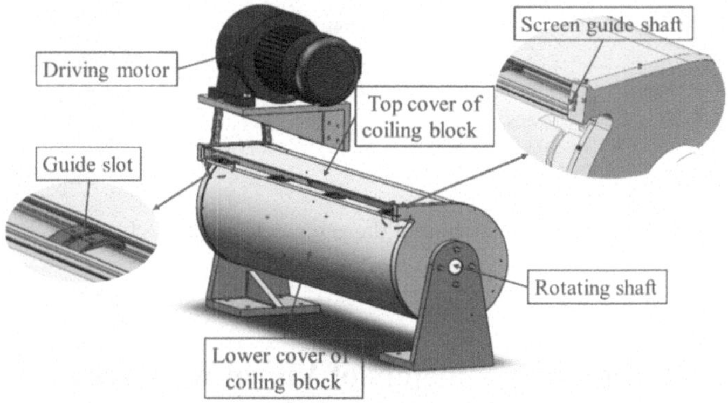

Fig. 4. Automatic replacement of screen drum mechanism

2.3 Screen Cleaning Mechanism

In this article, the method of extrusion and high-pressure air knife blowing is adopted to clean the screen before recycling, ensuring thorough cleaning of the screen. As shown in Fig. 5, the screen extrusion and cleaning mechanism mainly consists of four parts: the driving mechanism, the screen extrusion mechanism, the screen conveyor belt, and the high-pressure blowing mechanism. The driving mechanism mainly provides power output for the entire module. The motor transmits power to the screen extrusion roller through the chain wheel and chain. The extrusion rollers are driven by a pair of intermeshing gears to achieve the extrusion action. The spacing between the rollers is 4mm, which allows for rolling when larger sand particles pass through. Afterward, the high-pressure air knife blows the screen to clean it. At the same time, the ends of the rollers are wrapped with rubber to increase the friction between the screen and the rollers, facilitating the conveyance of the screen. The screen conveyor belt consists of passive rollers, and three groups of rollers have screen-limiting channels designed at both ends. The three groups of passive rollers also serve the function of supporting the screen during the conveyance process, preventing the screen from detaching from the limiting channel due to the action of high-pressure air, thereby providing a certain supporting effect. The high-pressure air knife is installed directly above the screen conveyor belt, and the airflow blows downward in the form of an air curtain to clean the dust on the screen. The entire mechanism (excluding the drive motor and transmission device) is sealed within a dust collection chamber. It serves the purpose of overall sealing.

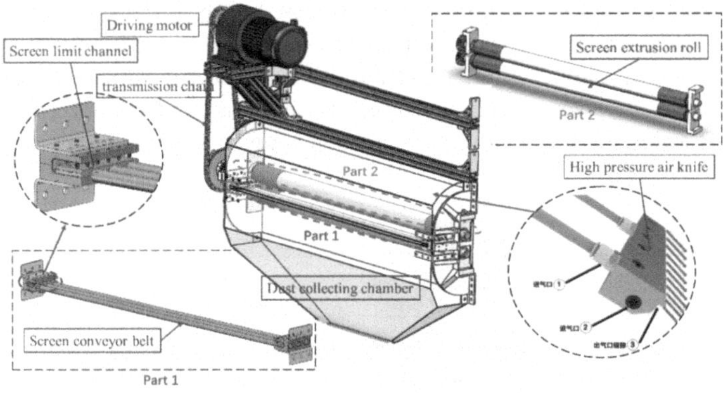

Fig. 5. The composition of the screen cleaning mechanism

3 Analysis of Motion Parameters of Vibrating Screen

The screening performance of vibrating screens for sieving specific sand and soil particles is influenced by numerous factors, such as the inherent properties of the sand and soil particles themselves and the process parameters of the screening equipment. Additionally, it is also affected by other factors, including amplitude, vibration frequency, and the inclination angle of the screen surface. Based on the practical application requirements of the vibrating screen's sieving motion, In this chapter, the proportion of the total mass per unit time is used as the evaluation index of screening efficiency, according to the practical application requirements of the screening movement of the vibrating screen, laying the foundation for the optimization of relevant motion parameters.

3.1 Screening Modeling and Model Parameters

The model imported into EDEM retains the four main screening components: the screen frame, screen mesh, inlet, and outlet. The screen frame measures 2100mm × 1084mm, and the screen mesh material is made of 304 stainless steel with square mesh holes measuring 5mm × 5mm and a gap of 5mm between each mesh hole. After the material is screened, it is separated into two outlets, A and B. Outlet A collects the undersized

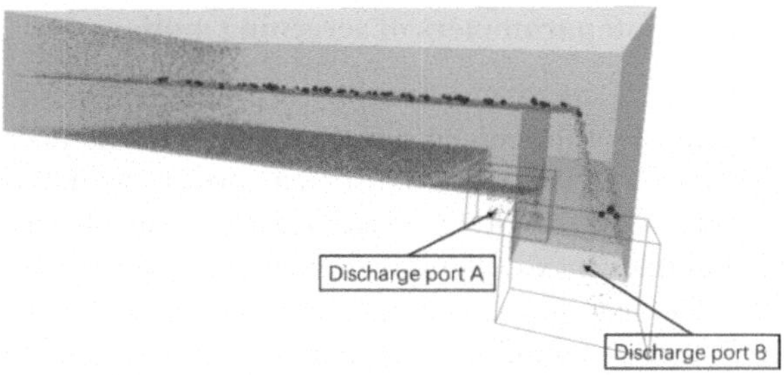

Fig. 6. Sieve motion model

particles that pass through the mesh holes, while Outlet B collects the oversized particles that do not pass through the mesh holes, as shown in Fig. 6.

Commonly used discrete element methods typically employ single spherical or multi-sphere combined models to simulate bulk granular materials [18]. However, sand soil has a complex contour shape, and using such methods can easily lead to significant errors. Therefore, based on the discrete element method of overlapping discrete element clusters (ODEC), a weighted circularity method is adopted to establish a sand particle model according to the size, shape, density, and other characteristics of sand soil sample particles. The modeling process is shown in Fig. 7, and some of the established particle models are depicted in Fig. 8. Additionally, three graded particle libraries have been established.

Fig. 7. Sand samples and modeling processes

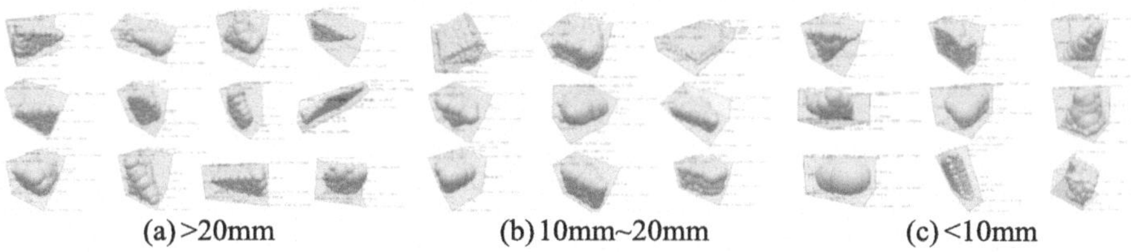

Fig. 8. Sand particle model

3.2 Analysis of key motion parameters of screening motion

A. Screen frequency

The vibration frequency of the screen surface refers to the number of vibrations of the screen mesh per unit time. With a fixed screen surface inclination angle of 3°, a vibration direction angle of 45°, and a screen surface amplitude of 5mm, equally spaced changes in the vibration frequency of the screen surface are applied to the cross-section of the screen mesh to simulate the screening conditions of the linear vibrating screen under different screen surface vibration frequencies, as shown in Table 1.

Table 1. Screening efficiency of different vibration frequencies

Frequency	Amplitude	Dip angle	Efficiency
20	5	3	0.93661
25	5	3	0.868746
30	5	3	0.694844

It can be seen from Table 1 that the screening efficiency decreases with the increase of vibration frequency, and the maximum efficiency is 93.66% when the vibration frequency is 20 Hz.

B. Screen amplitude

The amplitude of the screen surface refers to the maximum distance that the screen mesh can move in the vibration direction relative to its initial position. In this section, with a fixed screen surface inclination angle of 3°, a vibration direction angle of 45°, and a screen surface vibration frequency of 25 Hz, the screening conditions of the vibrating screen under different amplitudes are simulated, as shown in Table 2.

Table 2. Screening efficiency of different amplitude

Frequency	Amplitude	Dip Angle	Efficiency
25	8	3	0.750363
25	5	3	0.868746
25	2	3	0.924160

As can be seen from Table 2, the screening efficiency decreases as the amplitude increases. The maximum efficiency of 92.4% is achieved when the amplitude is 2mm, but at the same time, with the increase of amplitude, the time of the material running in the air during the screening process increases, and it cannot fall back to the screen surface quickly, resulting in the material not being screened in time, and the residence time of the material on the screen surface becomes longer.

C. Screen Angle

The screen surface inclination angle refers to the angle between the screen mesh and the horizontal plane. When the vibration direction angle is set to 45°, the screen surface amplitude is 5mm, and the screen surface vibration frequency is 25Hz, the screening conditions of the linear vibrating screen under different screen surface inclination angles are simulated by varying the angle between the cross-section of the screen surface and the horizontal plane.

Table 3. Screening efficiency of different angles

Frequency	Amplitude	Dip angle	Efficiency
25	5	3	0.868746
25	5	5	0.823674
25	5	7	0.731262

As can be seen from Table 3, the screening efficiency decreases as the inclination angle increases, with the maximum efficiency of 86.87% occurring at an inclination angle of 3°.

The overall motion speed of particles in the vibrating screen is shown in Figure 9. Before contacting the screen mesh, the particles undergo accelerated motion, reaching their maximum velocity upon contact with the screen mesh. After contact, the velocity decreases, and the particles bounce up and down on the screen mesh at a certain frequency for screening. The velocity decreases when the particles jump up and increases when they jump down. After traversing the length of the screen mesh, the particles accelerate and exit the vibrating screen through the feed inlet and discharge outlet, respectively.

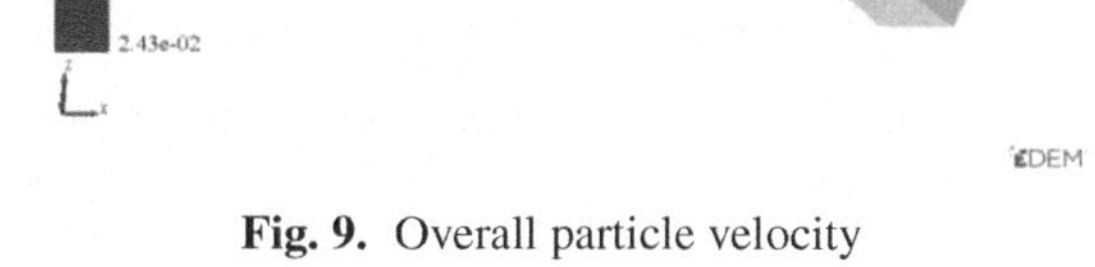

Fig. 9. Overall particle velocity

4 Optimization Design of Ant Colony Algorithm

4.1 Multi-parameter Orthogonal Experimental Analysis

Using the discrete element analysis software EDEM, a simulation analysis was conducted for the three parameters of vibration frequency, vibration amplitude, and vibration direction angle of the vibrating screen. To obtain reliable results, orthogonal experiments were designed to consider the interactions among these three factors. Seven levels were designed for each factor: vibration frequencies of 18, 20, 22, 24, 26, 28, and 30 Hz, vibration amplitudes of 2, 3, 4, 5, 6, 7, and 8 mm, and vibration directions of 30°, 35°, 40°, 45°, 50°, 55°, and 60°. After EDEM simulation, the screening efficiency corresponding to each factor level was obtained. The relationship between the screening efficiency of the vibrating screen and the three parameters of vibration frequency, amplitude, and direction angle is shown in Fig. 10.

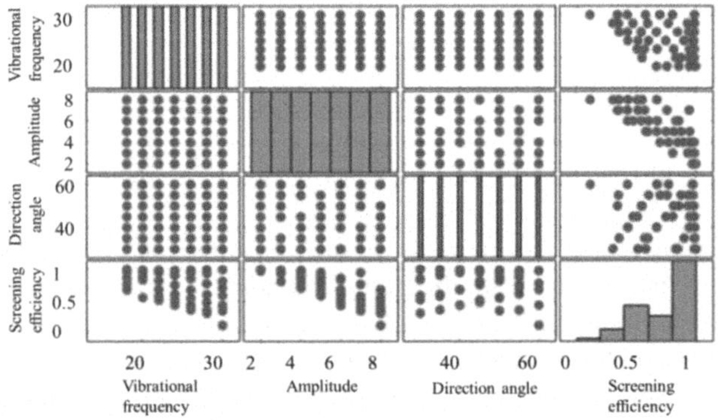

Fig. 10. The influence of three parameters on the sieving efficiency

The screening efficiency of the vibrating screen exhibits a significant nonlinear functional relationship with the vibration parameters. To obtain the optimal parameters, a relationship equation between the screening efficiency of the vibrating screen and the vibration frequency, amplitude, and direction angle is established. A multivariate nonlinear fitting is performed on the results obtained from the orthogonal experiments. Let x represent the screening efficiency, and a, b, and c represent the vibration frequency, amplitude, and direction angle, respectively. The assumed fitting equation is:

$$y = a_1 + a_2x_1 + a_3x_2 + a_4x_3 + a_5x_1^2 + a_6x_2^2 + a_7x_3^2 \tag{1}$$

The function fitting vibration frequency and screening efficiency are shown in Fig. 11.

The fitting functions of vibration parameters such as vibration frequency, amplitude, direction Angle and screening efficiency are shown in formula 2. Among them, the effect of vibration frequency on screening efficiency is weaker than that of amplitude and direction Angle.

$$\begin{aligned} y = {} & 1.28498 - 0.01578x_1 - 0.04537x_2 + 0.01737x_3 \\ & -0.00025x_1^2 - 0.00510x_2^2 - 0.00020x_3^2 \end{aligned} \tag{2}$$

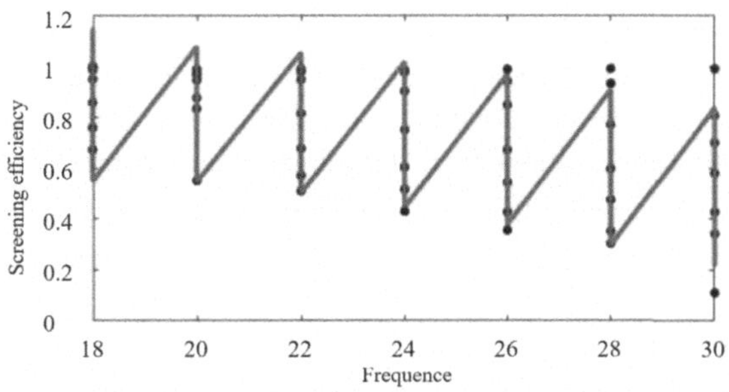

Fig. 11. Frequence and sieving efficiency fit plot

4.2 Multi-parameter Optimization Based on Ant Colony Algorithm

The optimization problem of vibration screen parameters is to find the parameter values that maximize the screening efficiency of the vibration screen. The ant colony algorithm is a heuristic probabilistic algorithm used to find optimized paths, and it has extensive applications in path planning, task allocation, and combinatorial optimization [19, 20]. Ant colony optimization algorithm has strong global searching ability in parameter optimization of vibrating screen. It has the advantages of strong robustness and easy combination with other methods, and the positive feedback mechanism makes the algorithm gradually converge to the optimal solution during the search process. This mechanism not only speeds up the convergence of the algorithm, but also helps to find better solutions. In this paper, the ant colony algorithm is applied to a four-dimensional space composed of vibration frequency, amplitude, direction angle, and screening efficiency. The feasible solutions to the optimization problem represent the walking paths of individual ants, and the walking paths of the entire ant colony constitute the solution space for the optimization problem.

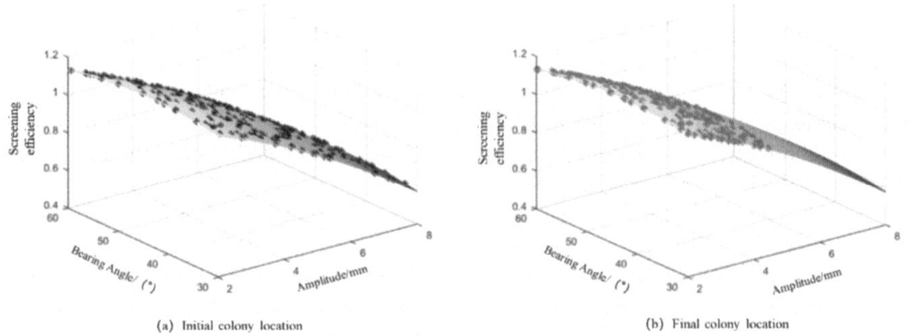

Fig. 12. Map of ant colony walking process

The optimization walking path of the ant colony on the three-dimensional surface composed of direction angle, amplitude, and screening efficiency is shown in Fig. 12 [21]. The ant colony moves towards the position with the smallest amplitude and the highest screening efficiency, which is consistent with the results of the compound orthogonal experiment. After optimization using the ant colony algorithm, the optimal parameters for maximizing the screening efficiency of the vibration screen are finally obtained: an amplitude of 2mm, a vibration frequency of 18 Hz, and a vibration direction angle of 44°. Comparison with the results of the orthogonal experiment shows that the calculated results are reliable, demonstrating the effectiveness of the ant colony algorithm for optimization.

5 Conclusion

In this paper, a modularized vibrating screen specifically designed for sand soil is introduced, which mainly consists of a vibrating screen body, an automatically replaceable screen mesh cylinder mechanism, and a screen mesh cleaning mechanism. The screen body employs a tensioning mechanism to achieve real-time tensioning of the screen mesh. Additionally, the designed automatic screen mesh replacement mechanism enables the replacement of the screen mesh during the operation of the vibrating screen, thereby enhancing its adaptability and screening efficiency. The screen mesh cleaning mechanism at the end effectively reduces the emission of harmful dust and purifies the working environment. To obtain reliable screening motion parameters, a sand soil particle model is established based on the discrete element overlapping particle cluster (ODEC) method and the weighted circularity method. Orthogonal experiments are designed to analyze the influence of various parameters on screening efficiency. Finally, the ant colony optimization algorithm is used to optimize and obtain the design parameters of the vibrating screen that correspond to the maximum screening efficiency.The plan is to actively seek cooperation with industry in future studies so that data can be collected for practical applications and in-depth case studies can be conducted.

References

1. Yang, W., et al.: Spatial motion trajectory calculation and simulation of linear screen. Coal Eng. (2018)
2. Djoković, J.M., et al.: Screening efficiency analysis of vibrosieves with the circular vibrations. Civil Environ. Eng. **13**(1), 77–83 (2017)
3. Chen, Z.: Numerical Simulation of elliptical vibrating screen and optimization of screening performance. Huaqiao University (2020)
4. Shi, P.: Structural Dynamic Analysis and Optimal Design of ZKB Linear vibrating screen. Hebei University of Technology (2018)
5. Meng, Q.: Research on Screening Performance of Double-layer Linear Vibrating Screen Based on Discrete Element Method. University of Science and Technology Liaoning (2023)
6. Wang, B.: Simulation analysis of corn linear vibrating screen based on DEM discrete element technology. Food & Machinery (2021)
7. Yu, J., Fu, H., et al.: Discrete element method and its application in research and design of working parts of agricultural machinery. Chinese J. Agric. Eng. (2005)
8. Cundall, P.A., Strack, O.D.L.: A discrete numerical model for granular assemblies. Géotechnique **29**, 47–65 (1979)
9. Thornton, C.: Coefficient of restitution for collinear collisions of elastic-plastic spheres. J. Appl. Mech. **55**(1), 118–122 (1988)

10. Cleary, P.W.: Industrial applications of the discrete element method. Int. J. Rock Mech. Mining Sci. Geomechanics Abstracts **32**(7), 627–644 (1995)
11. Ma, X., Zhang, Y., et al.: Research on screening efficiency based on three-dimensional discrete element method. J. Henan Univ. Technol. (Natural Science Edition), pp. 841–844 (2015)
12. Yang, L.: Estimation and experimental study of vibration screening efficiency of asphalt mixture based on DEM. Chang 'an University (2015)
13. X Li Yongxiang, Li Yang et al.: Analysis of screening effect of Large yield raw grain vibration cleaning screen based on EDEM. China Oils and Fats, (2018).
14. Chen, G.: Research on Screening Efficiency of Cantilever Vibrating Screen based on EDEM. University of Science and Technology Liaoning (2021)
15. Dorigo, M., Maniezzo, V., Colorni, A.: Ant system: optimization by a colony of cooperating agents. IEEE Trans. Syst. Man Cybern. Part B (Cybern.) **26**(1), 29–41 (1996)
16. Stützle, T., Dorigo.: Ant colony optimization: overview of meta-heuristics. In Metaheuristics, pp. 241–272 (2002)
17. Gambardella, L.M., Dorigo, M.: Ant colonies for the traveling salesman problem. Biosystems **53**(1–3), 167–17 (1999)
18. Jian, Z.: Research on simulation and test of screening of vibrating screen of crank linkage mechanism based on discrete element method. Northwest A & F University (2018)
19. Merkle, D., Middendorf, M., Schmeck, H.: Ant colony optimization for resource-constrained project scheduling. IEEE Trans. Evol. Comput. **6**(4), 333–34 (2002)
20. Bilchev, G., Parmee, I.C.: The ant colony metaphor for searching continuous design spaces. In: Evolutionary Computing: AISB Workshop Sheffield (1995)
21. Li, Y., Zhang, Z., Wang, Z.: Optimization design of vibrating screen parameters based on ant colony algorithm. J. Chongqing Technol. Bus. Univ. Natural Sci. Edition **41**(2), 34–41 (2024)

Design of a Trajectory-Tracking Controller for OMRs Based on Minimizing Tire Wear

Zhaoyun Luo[1], Jieling Wang[2](✉), Bingchen Ju[1], Chuanyang Li[3], and Changhua Hu[2]

[1] Combat Support Academy, Rocket Force University of Engineering, Xi'an 710025, China
[2] Department of Basics, Rocket Force University of Engineering, Xi'an 710025, China
2602973060@qq.com
[3] Laboratory of Intelligent Control, Rocket Force University of Engineering, Xi'an 710025, China
li_chuanyang@yeah.net

Abstract. Omnidirectional mobile robots (OMRs), which have full mobility on a plane, have been widely used in various applications, such as warehousing and logistics. However, the high tire wear and power consumption of the OMRs have become to difficulties needed to be solved urgently. In this paper, to address the issues of interest, a novel trajectory-tracking algorithm for OMRs with Mecanum wheels is proposed. A controller is then designed in light of the model-prediction control algorithm. A joint simulation is conducted by using the V-rep and MATLAB for verification. It turns out that the algorithm presented effectively reduce the tire wear and power consumption. This study is expected to lay a foundation for the further popularization and application of OMRs.

Keywords: OMRs · Trajectory-tracking algorithm · Controller design · Joint simulation

1 Introduction

The omnidirectional mobile robots (OMRs) are robots capable of motions with three degrees of freedom (DOFs) in a plane, possessing excellent navigation performance in narrow and complex spaces. As a typical form of OMRs, the Mecanum wheel OMR has been widely used in various application scenarios such as warehousing and logistics, industrial production, and more. Due to its multiple DOFs, its control becomes more challengeable to control OMRs than traditional wheeled mobile robots. To achieve precise trajectory tracking, therefore, the interactions among various motion modes and more optimized control algorithms should be considered.

Energy consumption is an important indicator in trajectory tracking algorithms, as well as a key factor for omnidirectional mobile technology passenger vehicles with

Supported by the National Natural Science Foundation of China (52205040, 62227814) and Young Talent Fund of Xi'an Association for Science and Technology (959202313096). Chuanyang Li gratefully acknowledges the support of the Three Qin Talents" program.

X. Lan et al. (Eds.): ICIRA 2024, LNAI 15201, pp. 54–67, 2025.
https://doi.org/10.1007/978-981-96-0771-6_5

Mecanum wheel. The Mecanum wheels have special structures, leading to the increased friction in operation, thereby increasing the energy consumption. Therefore, it is meaningful to reducing the friction loss during the robot's movement for larger endurance, while ensuring precise trajectory tracking. Zhou et al. [1] analyzes the impact of vertical load, inflation pressure, and road conditions on tire wear. Das et al. [2] establishes a model to calculate fuel consumption rate based on the influence of toe-in angle and tire pressure on vehicle fuel efficiency. Meena et al. [3] develops an on-board real-time tread wear monitoring system. Chen et al. [4] estimates the lateral tire wear using a nonlinear dynamic model of a multi-axle steering vehicle, which demonstrates that the nonlinear model outperforms the linear model in tire wear calculations.

Besides, many researchers focus the studies on the design of accurate trajectory-tracking algorithms based on OMRs platforms. Shojaei et al. [5] designs a nonlinear adaptive controller for wheeled robots. Lu et al. [6] proposes an adaptive sliding mode control method based on neural networks. Che [7] proposes an OMRs trajectory tracking algorithm based on dual-loop sliding mode control. Shui et al. [8] proposes a generalized predictive control algorithm based on an extended state observer. Huang et al. [9] proposes a dual-loop control strategy combining Model Predictive Control (MPC) with differential-first proportional-integral-derivative (PID). Mohammad et al. [10] proposes a MPC scheme based on different model prediction errors and solution times, allowing flexible adjustments based on various vehicle models. Du et al. [11] proposes a MPC method based on online recognition of vehicle lateral stability status and fuzzy algorithms. Considering both tracking accuracy and controller response speed, the MPC algorithm is an excellent choice for controlling OMRs in trajectory tracking. The Literature [5–11] do achieve good trajectory tracking performance, however, these studies fail to discover energy optimization for OMRs. Wang et al. [12] constructs a novel robot energy consumption model. Gao et al. [13] proposes a new method for optimal energy consumption motion trajectory planning based on frequency domain analysis. Du et al. [14] presents a longitudinal control strategy based on MPC that takes energy consumption into account. However, none of the controllers designed above take into account the energy loss caused by friction during trajectory tracking.

In this paper, a tire wear model for the OMRs with Mecanum wheel based on tire wear theory is proposed to address the optimization of tire wear during trajectory tracking. Subsequently, a novel trajectory-tracking algorithm, as well as a hierarchical controller based on MPC is proposed to address the trajectory tracking problem for the Mecanum wheel OMRs. Finally, through collaborative simulation experiments utilizing V-rep and MATLAB, we empirically validated the effectiveness of our control scheme in accurately accomplishing trajectory tracking tasks across diverse operational scenarios. Additionally, our findings demonstrate the system's ability to mitigate tire wear and reduce power consumption during motion, highlighting its efficiency and durability.

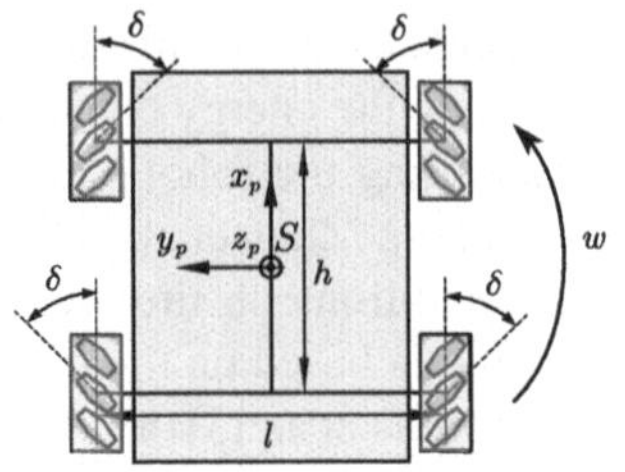

Fig. 1. Schematic diagram of omnidirectional mobile

2 System Modeling and Analysis

2.1 Kinematic Description of the OMR with Mecanum Wheel

The model of the OMR with Mecanum wheel is shown in Fig. 1. Where S denotes the centroid of the mobile robot. ω denotes the rotational speed of the robot around S. The four Mecanum wheels have the same angle δ with the x_p axis. As well, l indicates the left-right wheelbase distance of the robot, h being the front-rear wheelbase distance.

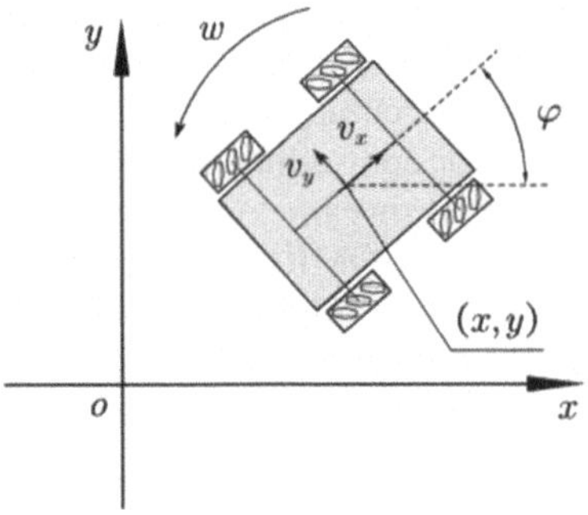

Fig. 2. Overall framework for path tracking

The kinematics model of the OMRs with Mecanum wheel is shown in Fig. 2. The forward kinematics is derived as follows.

$$\begin{bmatrix} v_x \\ v_y \\ \omega \end{bmatrix} = \frac{R}{4}\begin{bmatrix} 1 & 1 & 1 & 1 \\ -1 & 1 & -1 & 1 \\ \frac{-2}{l+h} & \frac{-2}{l+h} & \frac{-2}{l+h} & \frac{-2}{l+h} \end{bmatrix}\begin{bmatrix} \omega_1 \\ \omega_2 \\ \omega_3 \\ \omega_4 \end{bmatrix} = \boldsymbol{J}_{od}\begin{bmatrix} \omega_1 \\ \omega_2 \\ \omega_3 \\ \omega_4 \end{bmatrix} \tag{1}$$

where $\omega_i (i = 1, 2, 3, 4)$ is the speed of the Mecanum wheels.

Then the state equation is obtained as

$$\begin{cases} \dot{x} = v_x \cos\varphi - v_y \sin\varphi \\ \dot{y} = v_x \sin\varphi + v_y \cos\varphi \\ \dot{\varphi} = \omega \end{cases} \tag{2}$$

where v_x, v_y, φ and ω are described in Fig. 2.

By substituting Eq. (1) into Eq. (2), then we have

$$\begin{cases} \dot{x} = \frac{R}{4}[(\omega_1 + \omega_2 + \omega_3 + \omega_4)\cos\varphi + (\omega_1 - \omega_2 + \omega_3 - \omega_4)\sin\varphi] \\ \dot{y} = \frac{R}{4}[(\omega_1 + \omega_2 + \omega_3 + \omega_4)\sin\varphi - (\omega_1 - \omega_2 + \omega_3 - \omega_4)\cos\varphi] \\ \dot{\varphi} = -\frac{R}{2(l+h)}(\omega_1 - \omega_2 - \omega_3 + \omega_4) \end{cases} \tag{3}$$

Let $\boldsymbol{X} = [x, y, \varphi]^T$ and $\boldsymbol{U} = [\omega_1, \omega_2, \omega_3, \omega_4]^T$, which denote the state and control variables, respectively. Then, Eq. (3) is changed to Eq. (4).

$$\dot{\boldsymbol{X}} = f(\boldsymbol{X}, \boldsymbol{U}) \tag{4}$$

Perform a Taylor expansion of $\dot{\boldsymbol{X}} = f(\boldsymbol{X}, \boldsymbol{U})$ referred to point $(\boldsymbol{X_r}, \boldsymbol{U_r})$, we obtain

$$\dot{\boldsymbol{X}} = f(\boldsymbol{X_r}, \boldsymbol{U_r}) + \left.\frac{\partial f}{\partial \boldsymbol{X}}\right|_{\boldsymbol{X_r}} (\boldsymbol{X} - \boldsymbol{X_r}) + \left.\frac{\partial f}{\partial \boldsymbol{U}}\right|_{\boldsymbol{U_r}} (\boldsymbol{U} - \boldsymbol{U_r}) \tag{5}$$

$$\dot{\boldsymbol{X}} - \dot{\boldsymbol{X}}_{\boldsymbol{r}} = \left.\frac{\partial f}{\partial \boldsymbol{X}}\right|_{\boldsymbol{X_r}} (\boldsymbol{X} - \boldsymbol{X_r}) + \left.\frac{\partial f}{\partial \boldsymbol{U}}\right|_{\boldsymbol{U_r}} (\boldsymbol{U} - \boldsymbol{U_r}) \tag{6}$$

Then, Eq. (6) is written as

$$\dot{\tilde{\boldsymbol{X}}} = \boldsymbol{A}\tilde{\boldsymbol{X}} + \boldsymbol{B}\tilde{\boldsymbol{U}} \tag{7}$$

$$\frac{\tilde{\boldsymbol{X}}(k+1) - \tilde{\boldsymbol{X}}(k)}{T} = \boldsymbol{A}(k)\tilde{\boldsymbol{X}} + \boldsymbol{B}(k)\tilde{\boldsymbol{U}} \tag{8}$$

in which, T represents the sampling time,

$$\boldsymbol{A}(k) = \begin{bmatrix} 1 & 0 & \frac{TR}{4}[(\omega_{1r} - \omega_{2r} + \omega_{3r} - \omega_{4r})\cos\varphi_r - (\omega_{1r} + \omega_{2r} + \omega_{3r} + \omega_{4r})\sin\varphi_r] \\ 0 & 1 & \frac{TR}{4}[(\omega_{1r} + \omega_{2r} + \omega_{3r} + \omega_{4r})\cos\varphi_r - (\omega_{1r} - \omega_{2r} + \omega_{3r} - \omega_{4r})\sin\varphi_r] \\ 0 & 0 & 1 \end{bmatrix},$$

$$\begin{cases} \boldsymbol{B}(k) = \begin{bmatrix} \mu + \theta & \mu - \theta & \mu + \theta & \mu - \theta \\ -\mu + \theta & \mu + \theta & \mu + \theta & \mu + \theta \\ -\frac{2}{l+h} & \frac{2}{l+h} & \frac{2}{l+h} & -\frac{2}{l+h} \end{bmatrix}. \\ \mu = \cos\varphi_r \quad \theta = \sin\varphi_r \end{cases}$$

As well, Eq. (8) is rewritten as

$$\tilde{\boldsymbol{X}}(k+1) = \boldsymbol{A_1}(k)\tilde{\boldsymbol{X}} + \boldsymbol{B_1}(k)\tilde{\boldsymbol{U}} \tag{9}$$

In this case, $\boldsymbol{A_1} = T\boldsymbol{A} + \boldsymbol{I}$, $\boldsymbol{B_1} = T\boldsymbol{B}$.

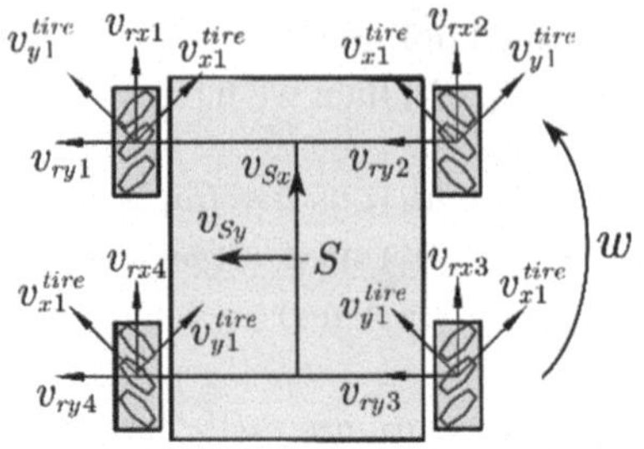

Fig. 3. Analysis of the slip velocity of the Mecanum wheels

2.2 The Wear Model for Mecanum Wheel Tires

The slippage speed model of the Mecanum wheel is shown in Fig. 3. The slippage speed of the Mecanum wheel V_i^{tire} is

$$V_i^{tire} = \begin{bmatrix} v_{x_i}^{tire} \\ v_{y_i}^{tire} \end{bmatrix} = D_i \begin{bmatrix} v_x \\ v_y \\ \omega \end{bmatrix}, (i = 1, 2, 3, 4) \tag{10}$$

where D_i is the transformation matrix for the movement speed of the ith Mecanum wheel.

The rolling speed of the Mecanum wheel V_i^{roll}, is calculated as

$$V_i^{roll} = Z_i U, (i = 1, 2, 3, 4) \tag{11}$$

where Z_i is the transformation matrix for the rotational speed of the ith Mecanum wheel.

The moving speed of the Mecanum wheel, V_i^{slip}, can be composed of V_i^{roll} and V_i^{tire}, forming the following relationship.

$$\begin{aligned} V_i^{slip} &= V_i^{tire} - V_i^{roll} = D_i J_{od} U - Z_i U \\ &= (D_i J_{od} - Z_i) U \end{aligned} \tag{12}$$

Assuming that the pressure exerted on the roller wheel is $\mathbf{N}$, and the sliding friction coefficient of the roller wheel is μ, then the tire friction energy can be expressed as E_{wi}.

$$E_{wi} = \mu \mathbf{N}_i \int_0^t \left(\left\| V_{xi}^{slip} \right\| + \left\| V_{yi}^{slip} \right\| \right) dt \tag{13}$$

Derivative both side of Eq. (13) with respect to time, then we have

$$\begin{aligned} \frac{\partial E_{wi}}{\partial t} &= \mu N_i \left(\left\| V_{xi}^{slip} \right\| + \left\| V_{yi}^{slip} \right\| \right) = \left[(\mu N_i)^2 \left(V_i^{slip} \right)^T V_i^{slip} \right]^{\frac{1}{2}} \\ &= \left[\rho^2 U^T (D_i J_{od} - Z_i)^T (D_i J_{od} - Z_i) U \right]^{\frac{1}{2}} \end{aligned} \tag{14}$$

where ρ denotes the coefficient of road friction constant.

Calculate the tire wear index J_f^{tire}, which reflects the overall tire wear of the omnidirectional robot with Mecanum wheels per unit time, as

$$\begin{aligned} J_f^{tire} &= \sum_{i=1}^{4}\left(\frac{\partial E_{w_i}}{\partial t}\right)^2 = \sum_{i=1}^{4}\left[\rho^2 \boldsymbol{U}^T(\boldsymbol{D}_i\boldsymbol{J}_{od}-\boldsymbol{Z}_i)^T(\boldsymbol{D}_i\boldsymbol{J}_{od}-\boldsymbol{Z}_i)\boldsymbol{U}\right] \\ &= \rho^2\boldsymbol{U}^T\left[\sum_{i=1}^{4}(\boldsymbol{D}_i\boldsymbol{J}_{od}-\boldsymbol{Z}_i)^T(\boldsymbol{D}_i\boldsymbol{J}_{od}-\boldsymbol{Z}_i)\right]\boldsymbol{U} = \boldsymbol{U}^T\boldsymbol{G}\boldsymbol{U} \end{aligned} \tag{15}$$

where $\boldsymbol{G} = \sum_{i=1}^{4}\left[\rho^2(\boldsymbol{D}_{xi}\boldsymbol{J}_{od}-\boldsymbol{Z}_i)^T(\boldsymbol{D}_{xi}\boldsymbol{J}_{od}-\boldsymbol{Z}_i)\right]$.

3 Design of Trajectory-Tracking Controller

3.1 Overall Framework of the Controller

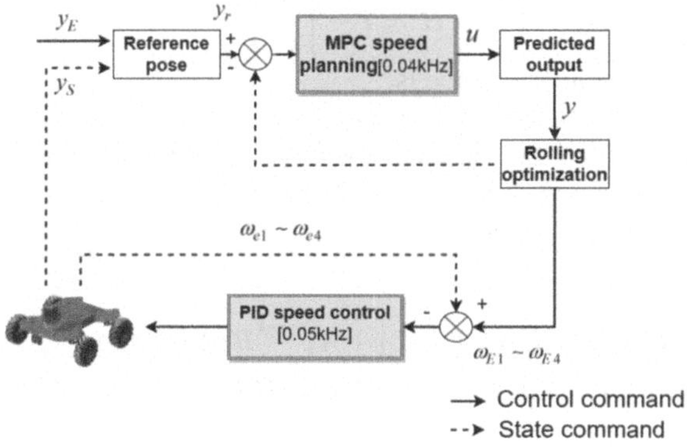

Fig. 4. Flowchart of the controller framework

As shown in Fig. 4, the controller is divided into two layers. In the upper-level controller, a MPC algorithm is employed to utilize the kinematics model of the OMRs, thereby tracking path information to minimize a cost function and generate the desired rotational speeds for the four Mecanum wheels. In the lower-level controller, the speed errors are then input into four PID controllers. This allows for precise control of the rotational speeds of the Mecanum wheels, enabling the OMRs to successfully track the desired path.

3.2 Design of Model Predictive Controller

Compared to the traditional path tracking control algorithms, in which only factors such as tracking error and motion power consumption are typically considered, while the impact of tire wear on system performance is ignored; this paper introduces a novel cost function design method that incorporates tire wear as an important metric into the cost function.

Define new control variables ξ,let $\boldsymbol{\xi}(k) = \begin{bmatrix} \boldsymbol{X}(k) \\ \boldsymbol{U}(k-1) \end{bmatrix}$.

By transforming the linear discrete state equation in Eq. (9), we obtain

$$\begin{aligned} \boldsymbol{\xi}(k+1) &= \begin{bmatrix} \boldsymbol{X}(k+1) \\ \boldsymbol{U}(k) \end{bmatrix} = \begin{bmatrix} \tilde{\boldsymbol{X}}(k+1) \\ \tilde{\boldsymbol{U}}(k) \end{bmatrix} + \begin{bmatrix} \tilde{\boldsymbol{X}}_r(k+1) \\ \tilde{\boldsymbol{U}}_r(k) \end{bmatrix} \\ &= \begin{bmatrix} \boldsymbol{A}\tilde{\boldsymbol{X}}(k) + \boldsymbol{B}\tilde{\boldsymbol{U}}(k) \\ \tilde{\boldsymbol{U}}(k) \end{bmatrix} + \boldsymbol{\xi}_r \\ &= \begin{bmatrix} \boldsymbol{A} & \boldsymbol{B} \\ \boldsymbol{O} & \boldsymbol{I} \end{bmatrix} \begin{bmatrix} \tilde{\boldsymbol{X}}(k) \\ \tilde{\boldsymbol{U}}(k-1) \end{bmatrix} + \begin{bmatrix} \boldsymbol{B} \\ \boldsymbol{I} \end{bmatrix} \Delta\tilde{\boldsymbol{U}}(k) + \boldsymbol{\xi}_r \\ &= \begin{bmatrix} \boldsymbol{A} & \boldsymbol{B} \\ \boldsymbol{O} & \boldsymbol{I} \end{bmatrix} \boldsymbol{\xi}(k) - \begin{bmatrix} \boldsymbol{A} & \boldsymbol{B} \\ \boldsymbol{O} & \boldsymbol{I} \end{bmatrix} \boldsymbol{\xi}_r + \begin{bmatrix} \boldsymbol{B} \\ \boldsymbol{I} \end{bmatrix} \Delta\tilde{\boldsymbol{U}}(k) + \boldsymbol{\xi}_r \\ &= \boldsymbol{A}_1\boldsymbol{\xi}(k) + \boldsymbol{B}_1\Delta\tilde{\boldsymbol{U}}(k) + \boldsymbol{H}\boldsymbol{\xi}_r \end{aligned} \tag{16}$$

wherein, $\boldsymbol{A}_1 = \begin{bmatrix} \boldsymbol{A} & \boldsymbol{B} \\ \boldsymbol{O} & \boldsymbol{I} \end{bmatrix}$, $\boldsymbol{B}_1 = \begin{bmatrix} \boldsymbol{B} \\ \boldsymbol{I} \end{bmatrix}$, $\boldsymbol{H} = \boldsymbol{I} - \begin{bmatrix} \boldsymbol{A} & \boldsymbol{B} \\ \boldsymbol{O} & \boldsymbol{I} \end{bmatrix}$.

Then, the predicted state sequence is

$$\begin{cases} \boldsymbol{\xi}(1|k) = \boldsymbol{A}_1\boldsymbol{\xi}(0|k) + \boldsymbol{B}_1\Delta\boldsymbol{U}(0|k) + \boldsymbol{H}\boldsymbol{\xi}_r \\ \boldsymbol{\xi}(2|k) = \boldsymbol{A}_1^2\boldsymbol{\xi}(0|k) + \boldsymbol{A}_1\boldsymbol{B}_1\Delta\boldsymbol{U}(0|k) + \boldsymbol{B}_1\Delta\boldsymbol{U}(1|k) \\ +(\boldsymbol{A}_1\boldsymbol{H} + \boldsymbol{H})\boldsymbol{\xi}_r \\ \vdots \\ \boldsymbol{\xi}(N_p|k) = \boldsymbol{A}_1^{N_p}\boldsymbol{\xi}(0|k) + \boldsymbol{A}_1^{N_p-1}\boldsymbol{B}_1\Delta\boldsymbol{U}(0|k) + \cdots \\ +\left(\boldsymbol{A}_1^{N-1} + \boldsymbol{A}_1^{N-2} + \cdots + \boldsymbol{I}\right)\boldsymbol{H}\boldsymbol{\xi}_r \end{cases} \tag{17}$$

Define the output equation as

$$\boldsymbol{\eta}(k) = \begin{bmatrix} \boldsymbol{I}_{3\times 3} & \boldsymbol{O} \end{bmatrix} \begin{bmatrix} \boldsymbol{X}(k) \\ \boldsymbol{U}(k-1) \end{bmatrix} = \boldsymbol{C}\boldsymbol{\xi}(k) \tag{18}$$

Then, the predicted output sequence is

$$\begin{cases} \boldsymbol{\eta}(1|k) = \boldsymbol{C}\boldsymbol{\xi}(1|k) \\ \boldsymbol{\eta}(2|k) = \boldsymbol{C}\boldsymbol{\xi}(2|k) \\ \vdots \\ \boldsymbol{\eta}(N_p|k) = \boldsymbol{C}\boldsymbol{\xi}(N_p|k) \end{cases} \tag{19}$$

Select,

$$\boldsymbol{X}(k) \triangleq \left[\boldsymbol{\xi}(1|k)\,\boldsymbol{\xi}(2|k)\,\cdots\,\boldsymbol{\xi}(N_p-1|k)\right]^T$$
$$\boldsymbol{Y}(k) \triangleq \left[\boldsymbol{\eta}(1|k)\,\boldsymbol{\eta}(2|k)\,\cdots\,\boldsymbol{\eta}(N_p-1|k)\right]^T$$

$$\boldsymbol{u}(k)=\left[\boldsymbol{U}(0|k)\,\boldsymbol{U}(1|k)\,\cdots\,\boldsymbol{U}\left(N_p-1|k\right)\right]^T$$
$$\Delta\boldsymbol{u}(k)=\left[\Delta\boldsymbol{U}(0|k)\,\Delta\boldsymbol{U}(1|k)\,\cdots\,\Delta\boldsymbol{U}\left(N_p-1|k\right)\right]^T$$

Equation (17) and Eq. (19) are represented in matrix form as

$$\begin{cases}\boldsymbol{X}(k)=\boldsymbol{F}\boldsymbol{\xi}_0+\boldsymbol{\Phi}\Delta\boldsymbol{u}(k)+\boldsymbol{K}\boldsymbol{\xi}_r\\ \boldsymbol{Y}(k)=\boldsymbol{C}_k\boldsymbol{X}(k)\end{cases}\tag{20}$$

wherein,

$$\boldsymbol{F}=\begin{bmatrix}\tilde{C}\tilde{A}\\ \tilde{C}\tilde{A}^2\\ M\\ \tilde{C}\tilde{A}^N\end{bmatrix}\quad \boldsymbol{\Phi}=\begin{bmatrix}\tilde{C}\tilde{B} & O & \cdots & O\\ \tilde{C}\tilde{A}\tilde{B} & \tilde{C}\tilde{B} & \cdots & O\\ \vdots & \vdots & \ddots & \vdots\\ \tilde{C}\tilde{A}^{N-1}\tilde{B} & \tilde{C}\tilde{A}^{N-2}\tilde{B} & \cdots & \tilde{C}\tilde{B}\end{bmatrix}$$

$$\boldsymbol{C_k}=\begin{bmatrix}C & & \\ & \ddots & \\ & & C\end{bmatrix}\ \boldsymbol{K}=\begin{bmatrix}I\\ A_1+I\\ \vdots\\ A_1^{N_p-1}+A_1^{N_p-2}+\cdots+I\end{bmatrix}\boldsymbol{H}$$

Noting that $U(k)=U(k-1)+\Delta U(k)$, the following conclusion can be drawn through recursive calculations as

$$\begin{aligned}\boldsymbol{u}(k)&=\begin{bmatrix}U(0|k)\\ U(1|k)\\ \vdots\\ U\left(N_p-1|k\right)\end{bmatrix}\\ &=\begin{bmatrix}I\\ I\\ \vdots\\ I\end{bmatrix}U(-1|k)+\begin{bmatrix}I & O & O & O\\ I & I & O & O\\ \vdots & \vdots & \ddots & O\\ I & I & I & I\end{bmatrix}\begin{bmatrix}\Delta U(0|k)\\ \Delta U(1|k)\\ \vdots\\ \Delta U\left(N_p-1|k\right)\end{bmatrix}\\ &=\boldsymbol{P}_1U_0+\boldsymbol{P}_2\Delta\boldsymbol{u}(k)\end{aligned}\tag{21}$$

wherein, $\boldsymbol{P}_1=\begin{bmatrix}I\\ I\\ \vdots\\ I\end{bmatrix}$,$\boldsymbol{P}_2=\begin{bmatrix}I & O & \cdots & O\\ I & I & \cdots & O\\ \vdots & \vdots & \ddots & \vdots\\ I & I & \cdots & I\end{bmatrix}$.

The constraint on the rate of change of control action can be expressed as

$$\begin{bmatrix}-\boldsymbol{I}\\ \boldsymbol{I}\end{bmatrix}\Delta\boldsymbol{u}(k)\le\begin{bmatrix}-\Delta\boldsymbol{u}_{\min}\\ \Delta\boldsymbol{u}_{\max}\end{bmatrix}\tag{22}$$

Then,

$$\begin{bmatrix}-\boldsymbol{P_2}\\ \boldsymbol{P_2}\end{bmatrix}\Delta\boldsymbol{u}(k)\le\begin{bmatrix}-\boldsymbol{u}_{\min}+\boldsymbol{P}_1U_0\\ \boldsymbol{u}_{\max}-\boldsymbol{P}_1U_0\end{bmatrix}\tag{23}$$

Apply the following constraints

$$A_Y Y \le B_Y \tag{24}$$

Substitute Eq. (20) into Eq. (24), the constraint on the output of the controlled system is

$$A_Y C_k \Phi \Delta u(k) \le B_Y - A_Y C_k (K + F)\xi_0 \tag{25}$$

Compile into a unified format, we have

$$\begin{bmatrix} -I \\ I \\ -P_2 \\ P_2 \\ A_Y C_k \Phi \end{bmatrix} \Delta u(k) \le \begin{bmatrix} -\Delta u_{\min} \\ \Delta u_{\max} \\ -\Delta u_{\min} + P_1 U_0 \\ \Delta u_{\max} - P_1 U_0 \\ B_Y - A_Y C_k (K + F)\xi_0 \end{bmatrix} \tag{26}$$

The following cost function expression is established as

$$\begin{aligned} J(X(k), \mathrm{U}(k-1), \Delta\mathrm{U}(k)) &= \sum_{i=1}^{X} \|Y(i|k)\|_Q^2 \\ &+ \|\Delta U(i-1)|k\|_R^2 + \|U(i-1)|k\|_E^2 \\ &+ \gamma \sum_{i=1}^{N} J_I^{tire}(i-1|k) + \rho\varepsilon^2 \end{aligned} \tag{27}$$

where Q is a positive definite matrix representing the weight of error, R a positive definite matrix indicating the weight of the penalty term for the change in rotational speed. as well, E is a positive definite matrix denoting the weight of the penalty term for rotational speed; while γ, ρ, and ε being the weight of tire wear, the weight of the slack factor, and the slack factor, respectively.

Substitute both the prediction and the Mecanum wheel wear models into Eq. (27), then we obtain

$$\begin{aligned} \Delta u^*(k) &= \arg\min_{\Delta u}\{\sum_{i=1}^{N} [\|X(i|k) - X_g(i|k)\|_Q^2 \\ &+ \|\Delta U(i-1|k)\|_R^2 + \|U(i-1|k)\|_E^2] \\ &+ \gamma \sum_{i-1}^{N} J_f^{tire}(i-1|k) + \rho\varepsilon^2\} \\ &= \arg\min_{\Delta u}[\Delta u(k)^T(\Phi^T Q \Phi + P_2^T(\varepsilon + \gamma\varsigma)P_2 \\ &+ R)\Delta u(k) + 2(\xi_0^T F^T Q \Phi + U_0^T P_1^T(\varepsilon + \gamma\varsigma)P_2)\Delta u(k) + \rho\varepsilon^2] \\ &= \arg\min_{\Delta u}[\Delta u(k)^T M \Delta u(k) + N\Delta u(k) + \rho\varepsilon^2] \end{aligned} \tag{28}$$

wherein, $M = \boldsymbol{\Phi}^T \boldsymbol{Q} \boldsymbol{\Phi} + \boldsymbol{P}_2^T(\varepsilon + \gamma\varsigma)\boldsymbol{P}_2 + \boldsymbol{R}$, $N = \xi_0^T \boldsymbol{F}^T \boldsymbol{Q} \boldsymbol{\Phi} + U_0^T \boldsymbol{P}_1^T(\varepsilon + \gamma\varsigma)\boldsymbol{P}_2$.

By converting the cost function into a standard quadratic form and adding the constraint conditions as shown in Eq. (26), the final constrained quadratic programming problem is solved as

$$\begin{cases} \min\limits_{\Delta \boldsymbol{u}} \frac{1}{2} \begin{bmatrix} \Delta \boldsymbol{u}(k) \\ \varepsilon \end{bmatrix}^T \begin{bmatrix} \boldsymbol{M} & \boldsymbol{O} \\ \boldsymbol{O} & \rho \end{bmatrix} \begin{bmatrix} \Delta \boldsymbol{u}(k) \\ \varepsilon \end{bmatrix} + \begin{bmatrix} \boldsymbol{N} \\ \boldsymbol{O} \end{bmatrix}^T \begin{bmatrix} \Delta \boldsymbol{u}(k) \\ \varepsilon \end{bmatrix} \\ s.t. \begin{bmatrix} -\boldsymbol{I} \\ \boldsymbol{I} \\ -\boldsymbol{P}_2 \\ \boldsymbol{P}_2 \\ \boldsymbol{A}_Y \boldsymbol{C}_k \boldsymbol{\Phi} \end{bmatrix} \Delta \boldsymbol{u}(k) \le \begin{bmatrix} -\Delta \boldsymbol{u}_{\min} \\ \Delta \boldsymbol{u}_{\max} \\ -\Delta \boldsymbol{u}_{\min} + \boldsymbol{P}_1 U_0 \\ \Delta \boldsymbol{u}_{\max} - \boldsymbol{P}_1 U_0 \\ \boldsymbol{B}_Y - \boldsymbol{A}_Y \boldsymbol{C}_k (\boldsymbol{K} + \boldsymbol{F})\xi_0 \end{bmatrix} \end{cases} \tag{29}$$

By solving Eq. (29) using quadratic programming methods, a feasible solution $\Delta \boldsymbol{u}(k)$ is obtained. In each control cycle, the controller performs rolling optimization based on $\Delta \boldsymbol{u}(k)$ to complete a control loop. This process is continuously repeated, thereby achieving control of the OMRs.

4 Simulation Analysis and Experimental Results

To verify the effectiveness of the controller, this paper utilizes the V-rep dynamics simulation software and MATLAB to conduct joint simulation experiments. The vehicle and control parameters are shown in Table 1.

Table 1. Vehicle and Control Parameters

Parameter	Parameter value
Mass of the vehicle platform(kg)	15
Front-to-back distance of the vehicle platform(m)	0.4
Left-to-right distance of the vehicle platform(m)	0.3
Height of the vehicle platform(m)	0.05
Distance between the front and rear wheels(m)	0.26
Distance between the left and right wheels(m)	0.4
Radius of the Mecanum wheel(m)	0.47
Mass of the Mecanum wheel(kg)	0.5
Sampling time T(s)	0.01

The simulation experiment validates the controller using the trajectory expressed in Eq. (30). Additionally, high-frequency disturbances are applied to the heading angle of the OMR to induce oscillations during its movement to verify the anti-interference capability of the controller. The formula for the reference trajectory is:

$$\begin{cases} x(t) = 10\cos(t) \\ y(t) = 10\sin(t) \end{cases} \tag{30}$$

To test the effectiveness of the proposed MPC algorithm based on minimizing tire wear in this paper, a comparison among the algorithm proposed in this paper, the LQR algorithm, and the MPC algorithm. Figure 5 shows the tracking performance of the three controllers: LQR, MPC, and the algorithm proposed in this paper, for the referred trajectory.

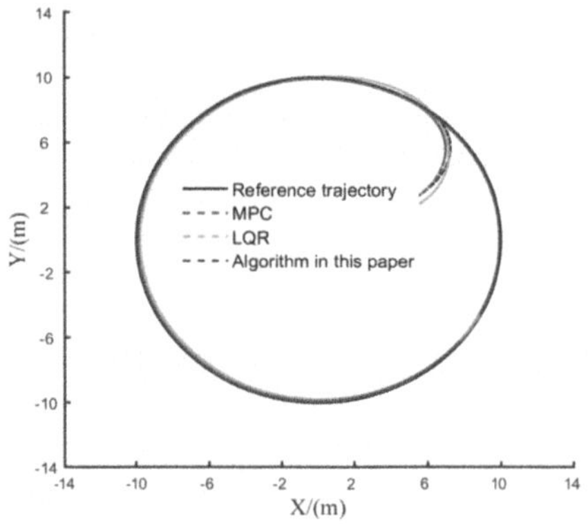

Fig. 5. Trajectory tracking effect

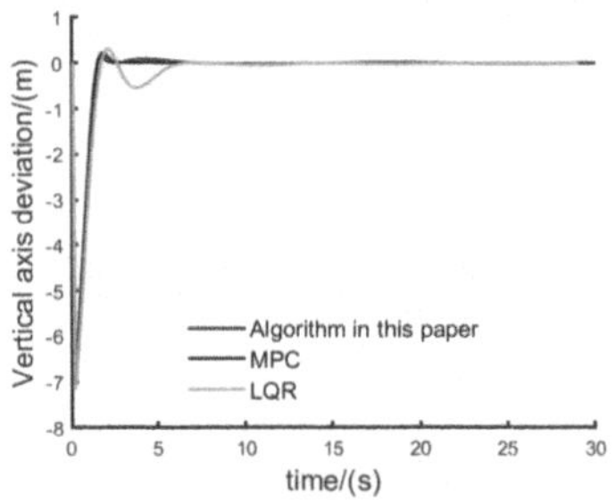

Fig. 6. Longitudinal axis deviation

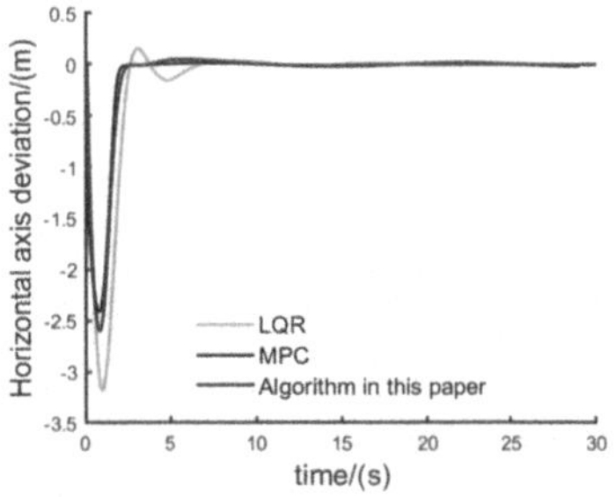

Fig. 7. Lateral axis deviation

Figure 6 and Fig. 7 show the lateral and longitudinal errors of the vehicle's actual motion trajectory relative to the reference trajectory, respectively. As can be seen from the figures, the tracking performance of MPC and the algorithm proposed in this paper is relatively good and basically consistent, while the tracking performance of the LQR algorithm is poorer.

Figure 8, Fig. 9, and Fig. 10 show the rotational speed diagrams of the Mecanum wheels when using the LQR algorithm, the MPC algorithm, and the algorithm proposed in this paper, respectively, to track the reference trajectory. As can be seen from the

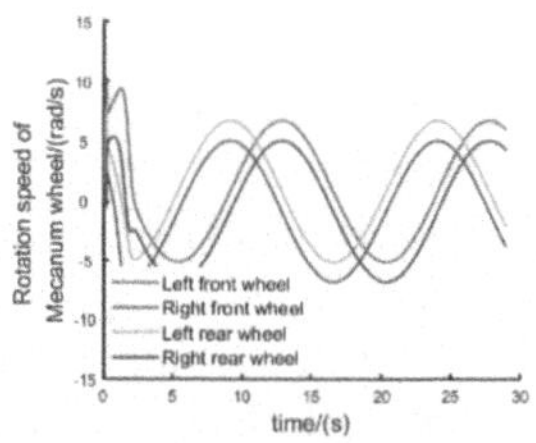

Fig. 8. LQR algorithm

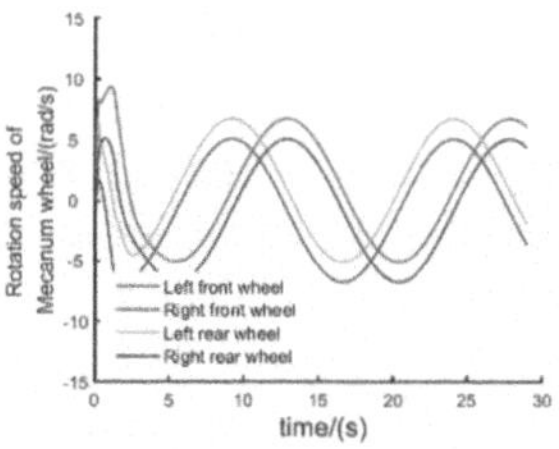

Fig. 9. MPC algorithm

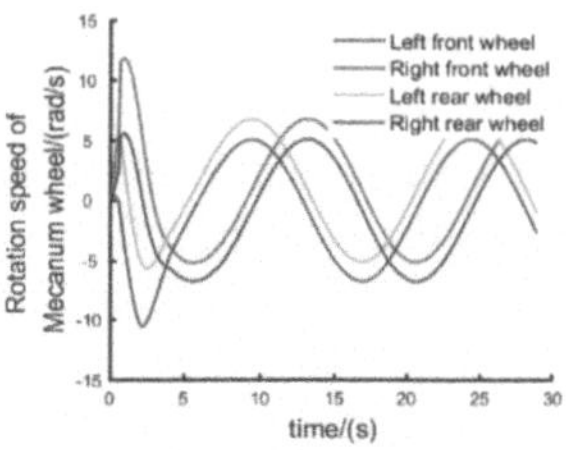

Fig. 10. Algorithm in this paper

figures, the rotational speed of the Mecanum wheels changes more dramatically within 0 to 5 s, which is due to the relatively chaotic collaboration between the Mecanum wheels at the beginning of the tracking control. As the OMRs gradually follows the reference trajectory, the rotational speed of the Mecanum wheels also gradually becomes smoother and more stable. Figure 11 compares the tire wear of the three algorithms, and it can be seen that after 5 s, when the collaboration between the Mecanum wheels reaches stability, there is a very significant decrease in tire wear. Furthermore, it can be observed from the figure that compared to the LQR and MPC algorithms, the algorithm proposed in this paper has a significant advantage in reducing tire wear.

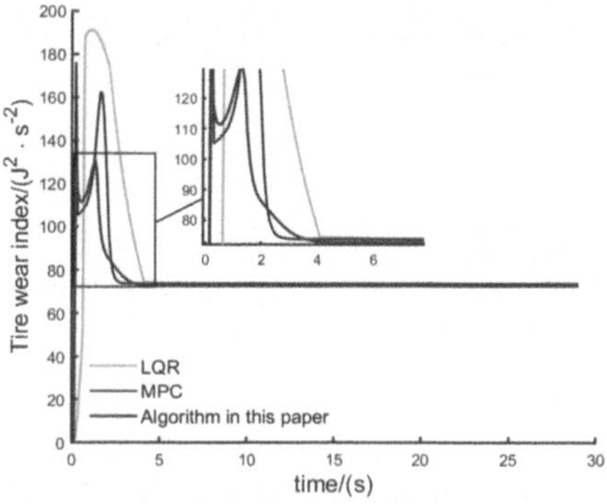

Fig. 11. Tire wear comparison chart

Table 2. Comparison of tire wear

Algorithm	Tire wear $/J^2s^{-2}$	
	Within the first 5 s	Throughout the entire process
LQR	5874	23481
MPC	4720	22489
Algorithm in this paper	4294	20719

During simulations with different algorithms, the tire wear generated by the vehicle during trajectory tracking is shown in Table 2. It can be seen that during the initial 5 s of vehicle acceleration, the application of the algorithm proposed in this paper can reduce tire wear by 8.02% compared to the conventional MPC algorithm and by 26.03% compared to the LQR algorithm. Throughout the entire simulation process, the application of the algorithm proposed in this paper can reduce tire wear by 5.87% compared to the conventional MPC algorithm and by 11.76% compared to the LQR algorithm. The results indicate that the controller designed in this paper exhibits accurate and rapid path tracking and yaw angle tracking performance in simulation conditions, ensuring precise path tracking. Additionally, by incorporating tire wear control indicators, the tire wear and operational power consumption are significantly reduced compared to the LQR and MPC algorithms.

5 Conclusion

In this paper, a tire wear model for the OMRs with Mecanum wheels is first established, a novel trajectory-tracking control algorithm thereafter being proposed. The MPC designed in this paper can improve control precision by correcting errors online during the control process of the Mecanum wheel mobile robot, meeting the stability requirements of the vehicle, and thus providing powerful control capabilities for its application. Through simulation experiments, it is demonstrated that, compared to the LQR and MPC algorithms, the algorithm proposed in this paper effectively reduce tire wear generated during the operation of the OMRs.

References

1. Zhou, Z., Liu, X.: Research on automobile tire wear mechanism and mathematical model. J. Northeast Forestry Univ. **20**(2), 55–60 (1992)
2. Das, R.K., et al.: Effect of tire inflation pressure and wheel front toe angle on fuel consumption of a light-duty vehicle. Int. J. Automot. Technol. **24**(5), 1459–1473 (2023)
3. Meena, K.K., et al.: 3D-printed stretchable hybrid piezoelectric-triboelectric nanogenerator for smart tire: onboard real-time tread wear monitoring system. Nano Energy **115** (2023)
4. Chen, X., Xu, N., Guo, K.H.: Tire wear estimation based on nonlinear lateral dynamic of multi-axle steering vehicle. Int. J. Automotive Technol. **19**(1) (2018)
5. Shojaei, K., Shahri, M.A., Tarakameh, A., et al.: Adaptive trajectory tracking control of a differential drive wheeled mobile robot. Robotica **29**(3), 391–402 (2011)
6. Lu, X., Zhang, X., Zhang, G., et al.: Neural network adaptive sliding mode control for omnidirectional vehicle with uncertainties. ISA Trans. 86201–8214 (2018)
7. Che, H.: Research on trajectory tracking of omnidirectional mobile robots based on dual loop sliding mode control. High Tech Commun. **32**(07), 756–762 (2022)
8. Shui, Y., Yang, Y., Xiang, G., et al.: OMR trajectory tracking predictive control based on ESO. Comput. Simul. **39**(08), 415–419 (2022)
9. Huang, X., Sun, Y., Li, J., et al.: Trajectory tracking control of McNamm wheel mobile platform based on MPC. Mech. Transmission **47**(11), 22–29 (2023)
10. Mohammad, R., Navid, M., Saeid, N.: Effective adoption of vehicle models for autonomous vehicle path tracking: a switched MPC approach. Vehicle Syst. Dyn. **61**(5), 1236–1259 (2023)

11. Du, R., Hu, H., Gao, K., et al.: Research on trajectory tracking control of autonomous vehicle based on variable predictive time domain MPC. J. Mech. Eng. **58**(24), 275–288 (2022)
12. Wang, Y., Zheng, Y., Yang, J., et al.: Robust compensation trajectory tracking control for omnidirectional mobile robots based on energy conservation considerations. Control Decision Making **37**(11), 3065–3072 (2022)
13. Zheng, Z.D.: Optimal energy consumption trajectory planning for mobile robot based on motion control and frequency domain analysis. Acta Automatica Sinica **46**(5), 934–945 (2020)
14. Hongwen, H., Mo, H., Wei, L., et al.: MPC-based longitudinal control strategy considering energy consumption for a dual-motor electric vehicle. Energy **253** (2023)

Conceptual Design, Control System Development and Prototype Fabrication of a 5-Axis Hybrid Machining Robot for Handicraft Carving

Wenlong Chen[1], Zhen He[1], Yulu Li[1], Hanliang Fang[2], Fufu Yang[1], and Jun Zhang[1](✉)

[1] School of Mechanical Engineering and Automation, Fuzhou University, Fuzhou 350116, China
zhang_jun@fzu.edu.cn

[2] School of Advanced Manufacturing, Fuzhou University, Jinjiang 362251, China

Abstract. This paper aims to propose a cost-efficient 5-axis hybrid machining robot for handicraft carving. For this purpose, a conceptual design is performed with a hierarchical design strategy which consists of a 2UPR&2RPS parallel manipulator (PM) and an orthogonal sliding gantry. Based on the conceptual design scheme, a kinematic analysis is conducted to yield the inverse/forward position formulations and the predicted reachable workspace. Meanwhile, an open-architecture numerical control system is developed for the proposed hybrid machining robot, which includes hardware construction, post processing and human-machine interface (HMI) development. Finally, a laboratory prototype is fabricated and integrated with the developed control system to construct a 5-axis machining unit. A set of test is performed on the robot to verify its 5-axis machining capability. The test results indicate that the proposed hybrid machining robot provide a promising solution for handicraft carving.

Keywords: Hybrid machining robot · Conceptual design · Kinematic analysis · Control system · handicraft carving

1 Introduction

Traditional hand carving has been gradually replaced by 5-axis machining devices due to the harsh working conditions as well as the shortage of experienced carving craftsman [1, 2]. These 5-axis machining devices can be roughly divided into three categories, i.e., stacked machine tools [3], articulated robots [4] and hybrid machining robots [5–7]. Compared with stacked machine tools and articulated robots, hybrid machining robots have conceptual advantages of larger stiffness-mass ratio [8], higher manipulate dexterity [9], and better dynamic characteristics [10]. These comparative advantages make hybrid machining robots promising alternative solutions for high efficiency 5-axis machining tasks. This has been evidenced by commercial applications of Tricept, Eco-speed, and Exechon in the past decades [11–13]. Despite their commercial success, the aforementioned hybrid machining robots are very expensive and comprehensive, making them

X. Lan et al. (Eds.): icira 2024, LNAI 15201, pp. 68–82, 2025.
https://doi.org/10.1007/978-981-96-0771-6_6

not suitable for those cost-efficient manufacturing scenarios such as handicraft carving. To realize cost-efficient handicraft carving with hybrid machining robot, two critical issues must be solved. The first issue is how to construct a 5-axis machining unit with an easy-assembled structure. The second issue is how to perform a 5-axis machining motion with a low-cost control system.

For the first issue, literature survey indicates that a typical hybrid machining robot with 5-axis machining capability usually consists of a three degree-of-freedom (3-DOF) parallel mechanism and a 2-DOF serial mechanism. For example, the topological architecture behind the Tricept is 3-RPS&UP, where 'U', 'P', 'R' and 'S' represent a universal joint, a prismatic pair, a revolute pair, and a spherical pair, respectively. The Eco-speed integrates a 3-PRS parallel module named Sprint Z3 spindle head with an orthogonal sliding gantry. The Exechon realizes 5-axis machining by hybridizing a 2UPR-SPR parallel module and a 2R (two-rotation) rotational wrist joint. Inspired by these hybrid machining robots, some variational 5-axis machining robots have been proposed. For example, the VERNE forms a 5-axis machining unit by integrating a 3T (three-translation) parallel mechanism with a 2-DOF tilting table [14]. Huang et al. proposed a hybrid 5-axis machining unit by integrating a 3-RPS spindle head named TJU-A3 with a 2T sliding gantry [15]. As can be seen, a combination of 3-DOF parallel mechanism and 2-DOF serial mechanism is a preferable scheme to construct a 5-axis hybrid machining robot. Following this track, the authors proposed a new hybrid machining robot by hybridizing a redundantly actuated parallel mechanism with a topology of 2UPR&2RPS and an orthogonal sliding gantry assembly. Our previous research indicates that such a construction scheme claims two distinct merits [16]. The first merit is that the redundant actuation of 2UPR&2RPS parallel mechanism helps to eliminate singularity and to improve dexterity. The second merit is that the symmetrical arrangement of limbs in 2UPR&2RPS brings significant enhancement of kinematic as well as dynamic performance. This is very suitable for 5-axis machining of complex component such as handicraft carving that requires high dexterity and stability.

For the second issue, there are two common methods to perform a 5-axis machining motion: (1) customizing a commercial numerical control (NC) system; (2) developing an open-architecture NC system based on motion control units. Following the first method, the commercial Exechon XMini robot [17] and Tricept T9000 robot [18] use Siemens 840D NC system; Tricept 606 robot adopts ABB's fifth generation robot controller IRC5 [19]. Although commercial 5-axis NC systems offer the advantages of standardization, reliability and stability, details of their key algorithms have not been fully disclosed and software access rights as well as hardware transformation are limited. Besides, customizing a commercial NC system is expensive, making it not suitable for low-cost product manufacturing such as handicraft carving. These issues can be avoided by following the second method. For example, Li et al. [20] proposed an open-architecture NC system based on "PC + PAMC". Jonatan et al. [21] developed a NC system for a SPIDETR4 5-axis parallel robot based on Automation PC 910 and X20 system. Xie et al. [22] developed a control system for a DiaRoM-300 parallel machine tool by using a BeckHoff controller. These investigations prove that open-architecture NC system based on motion control units can perform the 5-axis machining motion. Following this track, the authors aim to develop an open-architecture NC system by using a Leadshine motion controller. Under the framework of this NC system, a kinematic analysis is conducted to provide necessary information for motion control. Due to the content limitation, the present study only introduces the inverse/forward position formulations and the predicted reachable workspace.

The rest of this paper is organized as follows: in Sect. 2, the conceptual design of the 5-axis hybrid machining robot is described in detail by adopting a hierarchical design strategy. In Sect. 3, a kinematic analysis is conducted to yield the inverse/forward position formulations and predicted reachable workspace of the proposed hybrid machining robot. In Sect. 4, an open-architecture NC system is developed for the hybrid machining robot. In Sect. 5, a laboratory prototype is fabricated and a set of handcraft craving is performed to prove the effectiveness of the conceptual design as well as the NC system development.

2 Conceptual Design

Figure 1 illustrates the hierarchical design process of the proposed 5- axis hybrid machining robot. As can be seen, the conceptual design is hierarchically decomposed into five levels, namely, components, kinematic joints, kinematic limb assemblies, kinematic modules and hybridized system.

As shown in Fig. 1(a), at the components level, some critical non-standard components are designed. With these components, two typical kinematic joints are constructed as shown in Fig. 1(b). To be specific, the 'S' joint is made up of three crossed pin-shafts whose axes being perpendicular to each other; the 'U' joint is formed by two rotating joints with mutually perpendicular axes combined through a pin shaft. The prismatic pair is formed through a standard lead-screw module driven by a servo motor. By combining it with the aforementioned kinematic joints, two critical kinematic limb assemblies with UPR and RPS configurations are constructed as shown in Fig. 1(c). Then, two identical UPR limbs and RPS limbs are symmetrically arranged to form a 2UPR&2RPS parallel module. Two orthogonal lead-screw assemblies are stacked to form a serial sliding gantry. By integrating the parallel module and the serial module with a simple frame, a novel hybrid machining robot is hybridized. As shown in Fig. 1(e), the 2UPR&2RPS parallel module has the motion ability of 1T2R while the sliding gantry can achieve the motion ability of 2T, thus realizing a 5-axis machining capability.

3 Kinematic Analysis

In this section, a kinematic analysis is conducted to provide necessary information for motion control of the proposed hybrid machining robot. The inverse/forward position formulations are yielded and the reachable workspace is predicted, which will be embedded into the NC system.

For the convenience of subsequent analysis, a kinematic diagram of the proposed robot is depicted in Fig. 2. Herein, A_i (i = 1, 2,…,4) represents the geometric center of the joints installed on the fixed base, which forms a square with o_1 being its geometric centroid. Similarly, B_i (i = 1, 2,…,4) represent the geometric center of the joints on the moving platform, which also forms a square with o_2 being its geometric centroid.

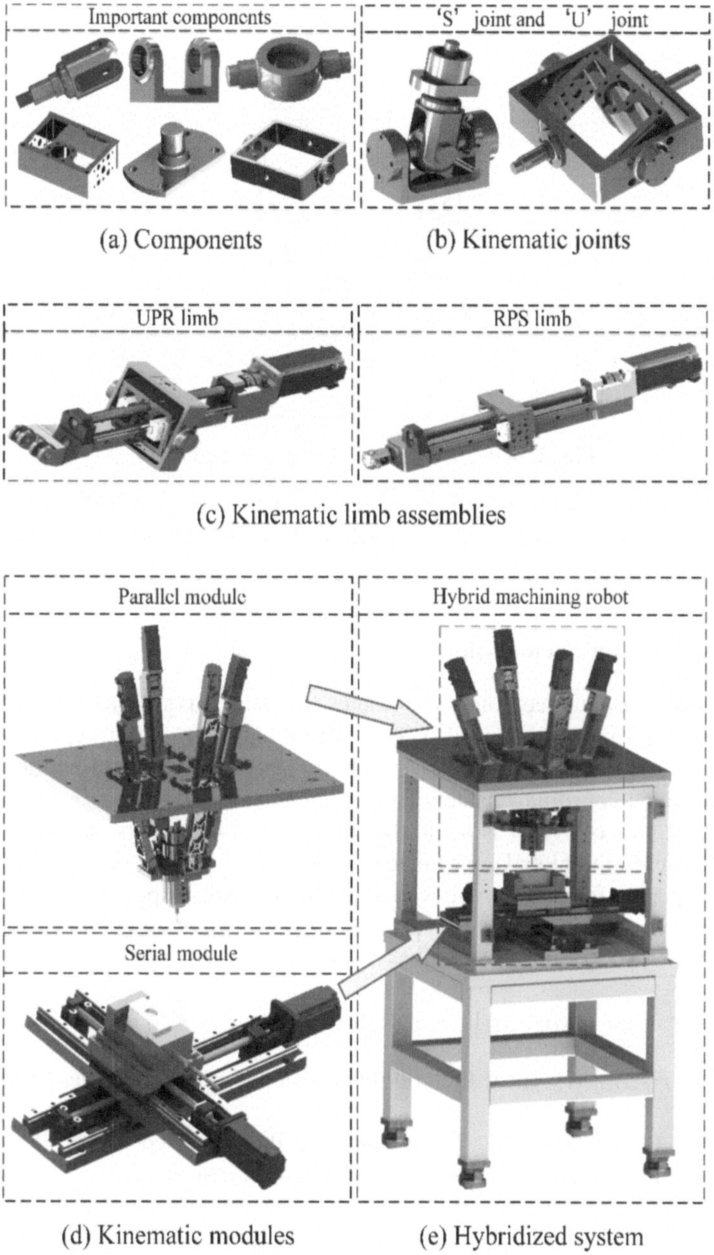

Fig. 1. Hierarchical decomposition scheme for proposed hybrid machining robot.

For derivation simplicity, the following screw definitions are set. The fixed base and the moving platform are connected through four limbs driven by corresponding prismatic pairs denoted as $S_{1,3}$, $S_{3,2}$, $S_{2,3}$ and $S_{4,2}$. The rotational axes in the kinematic

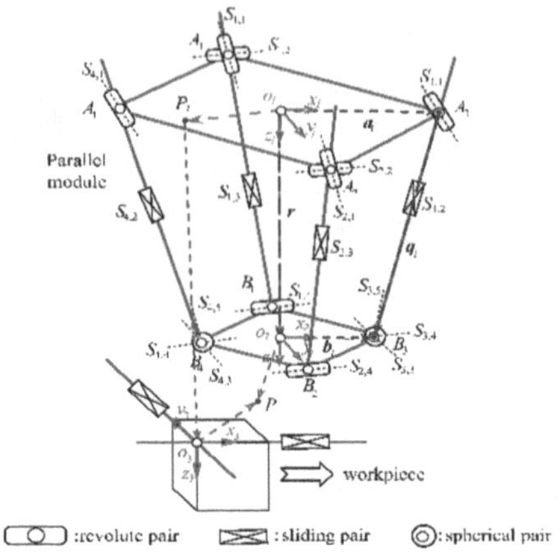

Fig. 2. Kinematic sketch of the proposed robot.

joints have the following positional relationships: $S_{1,1} \perp S_{1,2}$, $S_{2,1} \perp S_{2,2}$, $S_{3,3} \perp S_{3,4} \perp S_{3,5}$, $S_{4,3} \perp S_{4,4} \perp S_{4,5}$, and $S_{1,2} \| S_{1,4} \| S_{2,2} \| S_{2,4}$, $S_{3,1} \| S_{4,1} \| S_{4,3} \| S_{3,3}$.

3.1 Inverse Position Formulation

For formulation convenience, some coordinates are defined as shown in Fig. 2. To be specific, a global coordinate system $o_1 - x_1y_1z_1$ is established at o_1, with x_1 axis coincident with A_4A_3, y_1 axis coincident with A_1A_2, while z_1 being determined by the right-hand rule. A body-fixed coordinate system $o_2 - x_2y_2z_2$ is established at o_2 and a workpiece coordinate system $o_3 - x_3y_3z_3$ is set at the lower left corner of the workpiece surface. They are parallel to the global coordinate system.

Denote the transformation matrix of o_2 - $x_2y_2z_2$ with respect to o_1 - $x_1y_1z_1$ as $\boldsymbol{R}$ [8]. In the coordinate system o_1 - $x_1y_1z_1$, the vectors $\boldsymbol{r}$ pointing from o_1 to o_2, and the direction vectors $\boldsymbol{S}_{i,1}$ $(i = 3, 4)$ as well as $\boldsymbol{S}_{j,4}$ $(j = 1, 2)$ are expressed as

$$\boldsymbol{r} = [x_{O2}, y_{O2}, z_{O2}]^T, \boldsymbol{s}_{i,1} = [0, 1, 0]^T, \boldsymbol{s}_{j,4} = \boldsymbol{R} \cdot [1, 0, 0]^T, \tag{1}$$

where $[x_{O2}, y_{O2}, z_{O2}]$ represent the coordinates of the point o_2 in the fixed frame of o_1 - $x_1y_1z_1$.

According to the geometrical constraints of the proposed machining robot, the parasitic motion of the parallel machine can be determined as

$$\alpha = 0, x_{O2} = z_{O2} \cdot \tan\beta, y_{O2} = 0 \tag{2}$$

where α and β represent Euler angles of the moving platform in terms of nutation, precession.

According to Fig. 2, points A_i, B_i, o_1, and o_2 can form a closed-loop vector. The closed-loop vector equation can be expressed as

$$\boldsymbol{q}_i + \boldsymbol{a}_i = \boldsymbol{r} + \boldsymbol{R} \cdot \boldsymbol{b}_i (i = 1, 2, 3, 4) \tag{3}$$

where $\boldsymbol{a}_i$ represents the distance from point o_1 to point A_i; $\boldsymbol{b}_i$ represent the distance from point o_2 to point B_i.

By substituting the known parameters into Eq. (3), the length q_i of the limbs can be determined as

$$q_i = |\boldsymbol{r} + \boldsymbol{R} \times \boldsymbol{b}_i - \boldsymbol{a}_i| (i = 1, 2, 3, 4) \tag{4}$$

Assume the o_3 measured in o_1 - $\mathrm{x}_1\mathrm{y}_1\mathrm{z}_1$ is expressed as $\boldsymbol{o}_1\boldsymbol{o}_3 = [x_3, y_3, z_3]^\mathrm{T}$, while the transformation matrix of o_3 - $\mathrm{x}_3\mathrm{y}_3\mathrm{z}_3$ with respect to o_1 - $\mathrm{x}_1\mathrm{y}_1\mathrm{z}_1$ is represented as $\boldsymbol{R}_1$ [8]. The position vector of the tool tip measured in o_3 - $\mathrm{x}_3\mathrm{y}_3\mathrm{z}_3$ is $\boldsymbol{o}_3\boldsymbol{P} = [x_{p1}, y_{p1}, z_{p1}]^\mathrm{T}$, and its orientation angles are $\alpha_{\mathrm{p}1}$ and $\beta_{\mathrm{p}1} (\alpha_{\mathrm{p}1} = \alpha, \beta_{\mathrm{p}1} = \beta)$. Therefore, the unit direction vector $\boldsymbol{e}_{\mathrm{t}1}$ of the tool and the orientation angles measured in o_3 - $\mathrm{x}_3\mathrm{y}_3\mathrm{z}_3$ can be expressed as

$$\boldsymbol{e}_{\mathrm{t}1} = [\sin\beta_{\mathrm{P}1} \cos\alpha_{\mathrm{P}1}, -\sin\alpha_{\mathrm{P}1}, \cos\beta_{\mathrm{P}1}\cos\alpha_{\mathrm{P}1}]^\mathrm{T}, \boldsymbol{e}_\mathrm{t} = \boldsymbol{R}_1 \cdot \boldsymbol{e}_{\mathrm{t}1} \tag{5}$$

where $\boldsymbol{e}_\mathrm{t}$ represents the unit direction vector of the tool measured in o_1 - $\mathrm{x}_1\mathrm{y}_1\mathrm{z}_1$.

Note that there is the following relationship.

$$\mathbf{o}_1\boldsymbol{P} = \mathbf{o}_1\mathbf{o}_3 + \mathbf{o}_3\boldsymbol{P} \tag{6}$$

where $\boldsymbol{o}_1\boldsymbol{P} = [x_p, y_p, z_p]^\mathrm{T}$.

Form Eq. (6), the coordinates of P can be determined as

$$x_\mathrm{P} = x_3 + x_{\mathrm{P}1}, y_\mathrm{P} = y_3 + y_{\mathrm{P}1}, z_\mathrm{P} = z_3 + z_{\mathrm{P}1} \tag{7}$$

Substituting $\alpha_{\mathrm{p}1}, \beta_{\mathrm{p}1}$, and $z_{\mathrm{p}1}$ into Eq. (6) and Eq. (7) leads to

$$q_5 = x_\mathrm{P} - x_{\mathrm{P}1}, q_6 = y_\mathrm{P} - y_{\mathrm{P}1}, \tag{8}$$

where q_i $(i = 5, 6)$ is the driven length of the two orthogonal sliding gantries

3.2 Forward Position Formulation

From Eq. (4), the following equations can be derived

$$(q_2^2 - q_1^2)\cos\beta = 4 \cdot b \cdot z_{O2} \cdot \sin\alpha \tag{9}$$

$$q_4^2 - q_3^2 = 4 \cdot a \cdot z_{O2} \cdot \tan\beta \tag{10}$$

$$\begin{aligned} q_4^2 + q_3^2 \cdot 16 \cdot a^2 = {} & 2 \cdot (q_4^2 - q_3^2)^2 + 32 \cdot a^4 + 32 \cdot a^2 b^2 \\ & + 32 \cdot a^2 \cdot z_{O2}^2 - 64 \cdot a^3 \cdot b \cdot \cos\beta \end{aligned} \tag{11}$$

As can be seen, there are two unknown values of z_{O2} and β in Eq. (10) and Eq. (11). By simplifying them, the following equation can be obtained

$$m_1 \cdot \tan^2\beta \cdot \cos\beta - m_2 \cdot \sin^2\beta - m_3 = 0 \tag{12}$$

where

$$m_1 = q_4^2 + q_3^2 - 2 \cdot (\frac{q_4^2 - q_3^2}{4 \cdot a})^2 + 2 \cdot a^2 + 2 \cdot b^2, m_2 = -4 \cdot a \cdot b, m_3 = 2 \cdot (\frac{q_4^2 - q_3^2}{4a})^2 \quad (13)$$

By simplifying Eq. (12), one may obtain the following equation

$$t^3 + m_5 \cdot t + m_6 = 0 \quad (14)$$

where

$$m_4 = -\frac{m_1 + m_3}{m_2}, \cos\beta = t_0 = t - \frac{m_4}{3}, m_5 = -\frac{m_4^2}{3} - 1, m_6 = -(\frac{m_4}{3})^3 + \frac{m_4^3}{9} + \frac{m_4}{3} + \frac{m_1}{m_2} \quad (15)$$

After solving Eq. (14), three roots can be determined as

$$t_1 = \sqrt[3]{m_7} + \sqrt[3]{m_8}, t_2 = \sqrt[3]{m_7} \cdot \omega + \sqrt[3]{m_8} \cdot \omega^2, t_3 = \sqrt[3]{m_7} \cdot \omega^2 + \sqrt[3]{m_8} \cdot \omega \quad (16)$$

where

$$\omega = \frac{-1 + \sqrt{3}i}{2}, m_7 = -\frac{m_6}{2} - \sqrt{(\frac{m_6}{2})^2 + (\frac{m_5}{3})^3}, m_{12} = \sqrt{-\frac{m_6}{2} + (\frac{m_6}{2})^2 + (\frac{m_5}{3})^3} \quad (17)$$

The discriminant of Eq. (14) is $\Delta = (\frac{m_6}{2})^2 + (\frac{m_6}{3})^3$. When $\Delta > 0$, t_1 is a real root, t_2 and t_3 are imaginary roots, therefore $t = t_1$; When $\Delta \leq 0$, t_1, t_2 and t_3 are real roots, the value of t needs further confirmation by determining whether they satisfy the equation $t - \frac{m_4}{3} \in [0, 1][0, 1]$.

According to the motion of the parallel module, it can be determined that β and $(q_4 - q_3)$ have the same plus-minus sign. Therefore, the orientation angle β can be determined as

$$\beta = \mathrm{sign}(q_4 - q_3) \cdot \cos^{-1}(t_0) \quad (18)$$

Substituting Eq. (18) into Eq. (10), z_{O2} can be determined as

$$z_{O2} = \sqrt{\frac{q_4^2}{2} + \frac{q_3^2}{2} + 2 \cdot a \cdot b \cdot \cos\beta - \frac{1}{16}(\frac{q_4^2 - q_3^2}{a})^2 - a^2 - b^2} \quad (19)$$

Substituting Eq. (18) and Eq. (19) into Eq. (9), angle α can be determined as

$$\alpha = \arcsin(q_2^2 - q_1^2) \cdot \cos\beta / (4 z_{O2} b) \quad (20)$$

Combining with Eq. (6), the tool pose measured in the global coordinate system can be determined. Finally, by substituting $\boldsymbol{o_1 o_3}$ into Eq. (6) and Eq. (7), the coordinates of tool tip measured in o_3 - $x_3y_3z_3$ can be determined as

$$x_{P1} = x_P - q_5, y_{P1} = y_P - q_6 \quad (21)$$

3.3 Reachable Workspace Prediction

In this paper, a 'sliced-partition' searching algorithm [7] is adopted to identify the reachable workspace.

The search of the reachable workspace can be divided into the following steps:

Step 1: the end-effector is set as the target for searching the workspace. Next, the target space is divided equally into a finite number of sub-planes with thickness Δz by using a plane parallel to the fixed base. The search is started from the plane of the fixed base;

Step 2: When the end-effector reaches the corresponding sub-plane, the movement of six prismatic pairs and the corresponding rotation angles of passive joints are calculated through the inverse position formulation. If the calculated results fall within their allowable values, the results will be saved. Conversely, the results will be rounded off;

Step 3: When the distance reaches the maximum value of z, the search will be terminated. By recording all valid results, the reachable workspace of the proposed machining robot can be depicted.

According to the conceptual design of the hybridized system, its major dimensional parameters can be determined and are listed in Table.1.

Table 1. The kinematic ranges of each joint.

Parameter	Value	Parameter	Value
$d_{1,2}$/mm	140 ~ 340	$U_{h1,2}$/	52~128
$d_{3,4}$/mm	140 ~ 400	$U_{z1,2}$/	45~135
$R_{1,2}$/°	60~150	$S_{h3,4}$/	60~150
$R_{3,4}$/°	50~130	$S_{z3,4}$/	58~122

As shown in Table 1, d1, 2 and d3,4 represents the allowable movement ranges of L1, L2, L3 and L4. $R_{1,2}$ and $R_{3,4}$ represents the allowable rotation ranges of 'R' joints on L1, L2, L3 and L4. $U_{h1,2}$ and $U_{z1,2}$ represent the allowable rotation ranges of 'U' joints. $S_{h3,4}$ and $S_{z3,4}$ represent the allowable rotation ranges of 'S' joints.

For expressing the reachable workspace of the machining robot specifically, two types of workspace are defined in terms of orientation workspace and position workspace[19]. They are defined in the global coordinate system and depicted in Fig. 3.

For clarity, the machining ranges of the proposed machining robot are listed in Table 2.

4 NC System Development

An open-architecture NC system is developed for the proposed machining robot in this section. The present study focuses on design and construction of the NC system for motion control of the proposed machining robot. For this purpose, the following three issues are clarified to provide necessary foundation for NC system design: the structure construction, the hardware configuration and the software development.

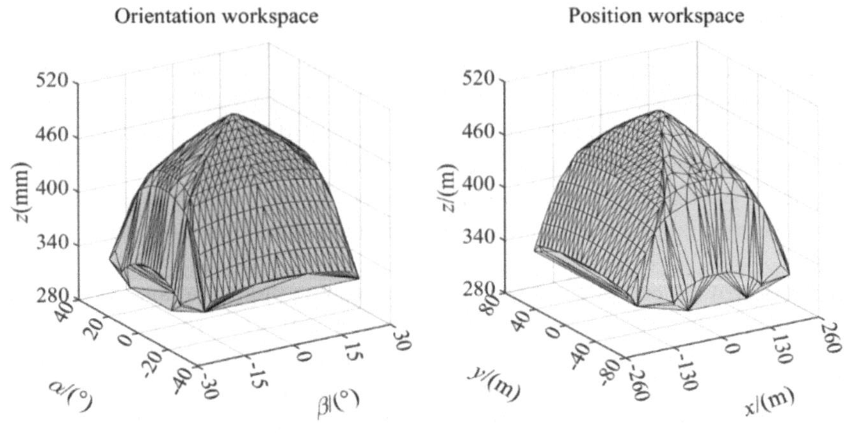

Fig. 3. Reachable workspace of the proposed machining robot.

Table 2. Machining ranges of the machining robot.

z/mm	*x/mm*	*y/mm*	$\alpha/°$	$\beta/°$
[130, 260]	[−217, 217]	[−70, 70]	[−36,36]	[−30,30]

4.1 System Construction

Based on the kinematic characteristics of the proposed machining robot, the structure of the developed NC system is constructed as shown in Fig. 4.

As shown in Fig. 4, the NC system uses a "PC + MCU (motion control units)" hybrid hardware architecture. It includes an upper computer, a MCU, a set of servo control system and other important electronic components. The functions of these modules are as follows:

- Upper Computer: on the one hand, postprocessor converts toolpath files generated by commercial software such as MasterCAM into NC code toolpath files suitable for the machining robot; On the other hand, the HMI transmits signals to MCU to control the motion of the machining robot and display the status of the system.
- MCU: receives and feedbacks control signals; realizes the real-time detection and control of the position as well as the speed of each limb.
- Servo systems: receives control commands from the MCU; converts pulse signals into current signals; feeds back the encoder position of the servo motor; realizes the linear motion of each limb.
- Other Electronic Components: detect position signals; control circuit switchings; amplify digital signals, etc.

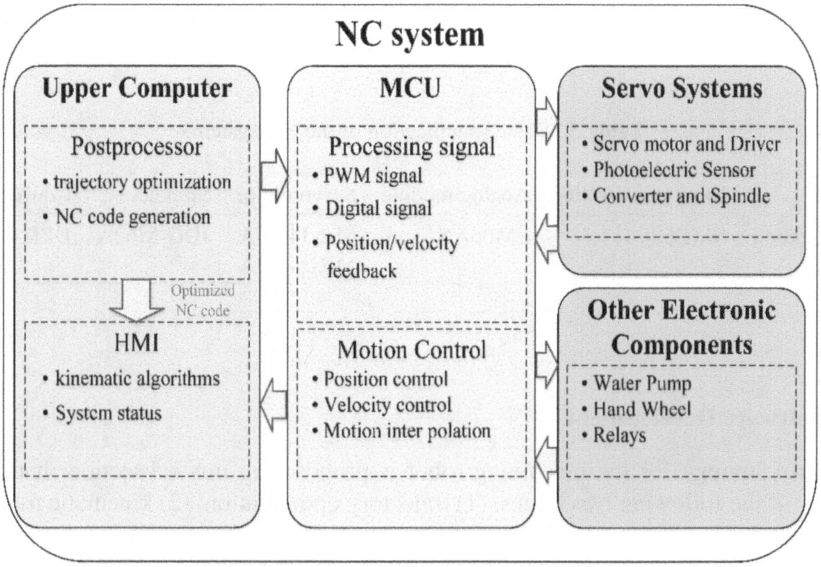

Fig. 4. Structure diagram of the NC system.

4.2 Hardware Configuration

Based on the structure of the NC system, a 6-axis motion controller (Leadshine SMC606) is chosen as the core of the NC system. The remaining hardware configurations of the NC system are constructed in Fig. 5.

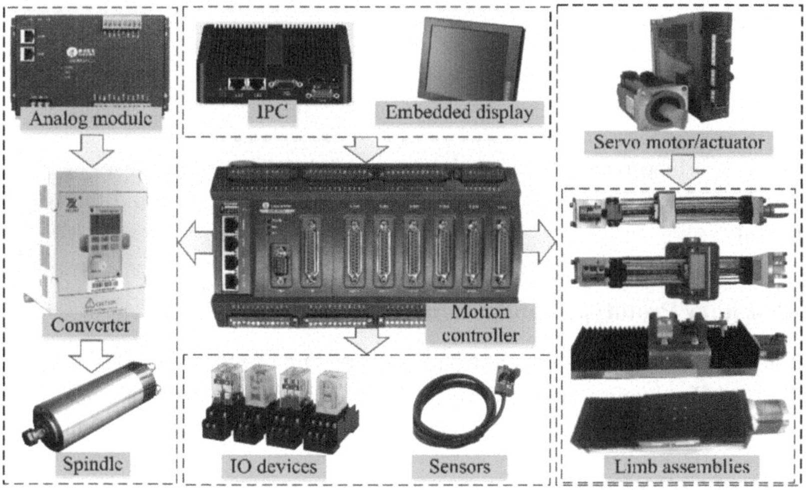

Fig. 5. Core hardware components of the NC system.

For clarity, technical specifications of the above core electronic components are listed in Table 3.

Table 3. Some specification of the NC system.

Object	Motion controller	Analog module	Servo motor	Spindle	Converter
specification	SMC606	EM06AX	MR-J4-40A MR-J4-70A	JDG-M62A	DZB200M

4.3 Software Development

A control strategy for the machining robot is proposed in this subsection. It mainly consists of the following two stages: (1) trajectory optimization; (2) kinematic transformation.

In the stage of trajectory optimization, firstly, commercial CAM software are used to obtain a set of original toolpath. Next, a set of smooth toolpath is calculated by using the postprocessing strategy. Finally, NC code for machining is generated.

In the stage of kinematic transformation, firstly, the position of o_2 relative to the global coordinate system is determined based on the forward kinematics formulation. Secondly, the proposed kinematic analysis is conducted to convert the generated NC code into the trajectory and the velocity of six servo motors. Finally, the six servo motors are driven based on the obtained signals to realize 5-axis machining of the proposed machining robot.

Based on the control strategy, the postprocessing software and HMI have been developed and depicted in Fig. 6.

5 Experimental Text

In this section, a laboratory prototype is constructed to accomplish a set of machining test to verify the effectiveness of the proposed conceptual design and the NC system development.

5.1 Laboratory Prototype Fabrication

A laboratory prototype is fabricated based on the hierarchical design strategy illustrated in Fig. 1. By integrating the developed NC system with the fabricated laboratory prototype, a 5-axis hybrid machining robot system is constructed and demonstrated in Fig. 7.

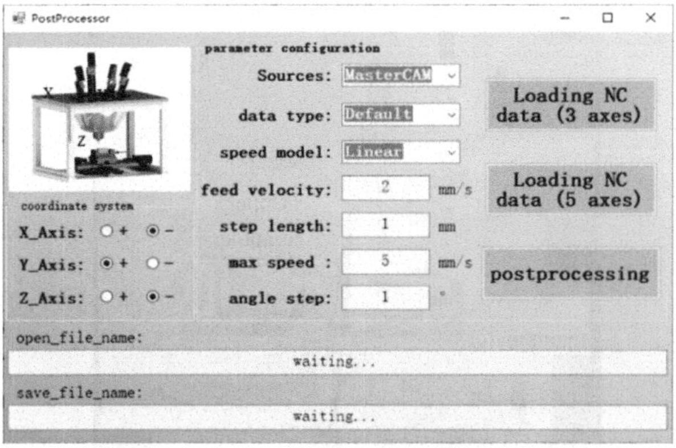

(a) Postprocessing software

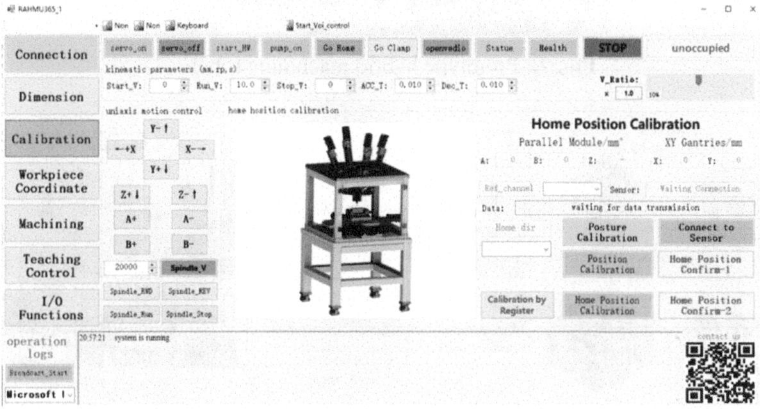

(b) HMI software

Fig. 6. Software development.

5.2 Machining Text

To validate the ability of machining complex handicraft carving, a set of machining test for ‘S’-shaped workpiece (ISO 10791-7) is carried out on the constructed hybrid machining robot. The machining test is mainly divided into three stages, i.e. preprocessing, postprocessing and machining. For clarity, the machining steps are summarized and depicted in Fig. 8.

To evaluate the machining performance of the proposed machining robot, the MarSurf PS 10 roughness tester is employed to conduct surface roughness tests on the specimens in this section. The surface roughness values Ra and Rz of the specimens are measured and depicted in Fig. 9. According to the workpiece surface cleanliness grades, the finished ’S’-shaped test specimens achieved a cleanliness grade of six (Ra: ≤ 3.2 μm; Rz: ≤ 6.3 μm).

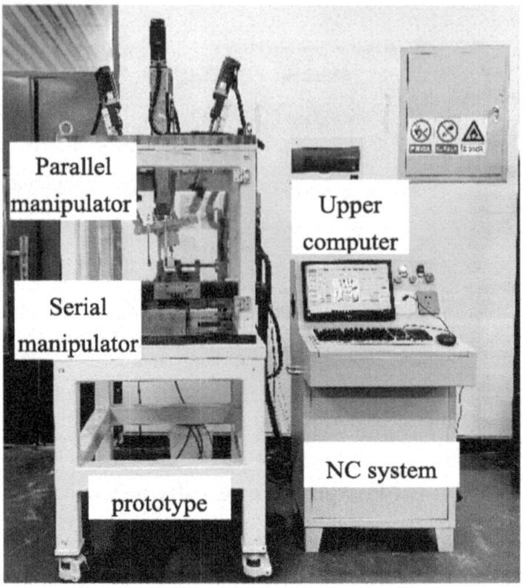

Fig. 7. Prototype hybrid machining robot.

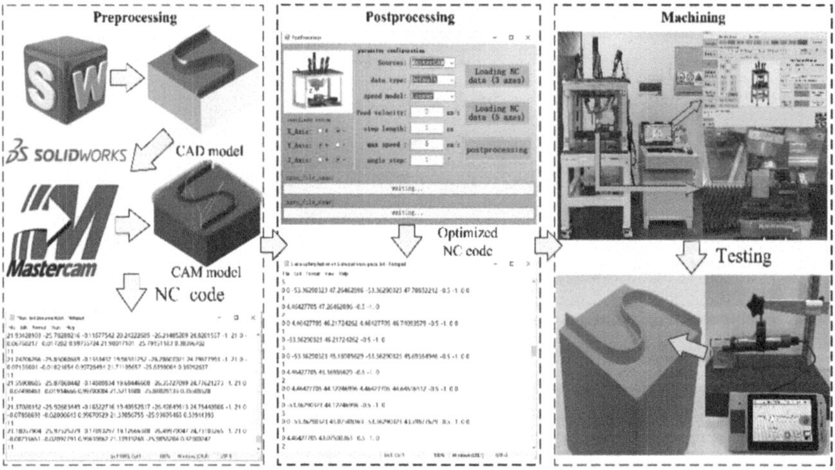

Fig. 8. Cutting text process diagram

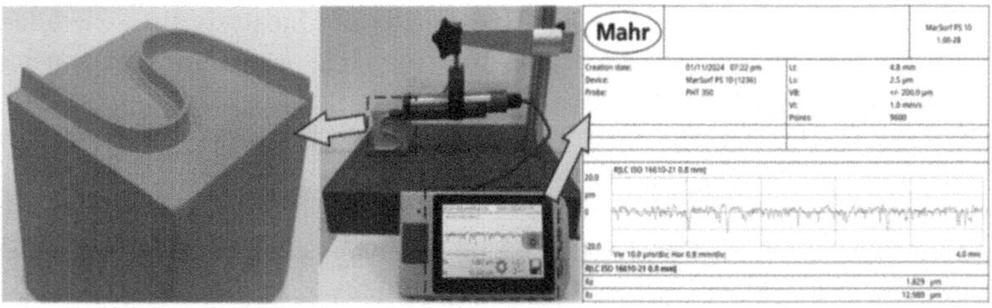

Fig. 9. Schematic diagram of text results.

6 Conclusion

Based on the work in this paper, the following conclusions can be drawn:

1) A novel conceptual design of 5-axis hybrid machining robot is addressed by using the hierarchical design strategy. Based on the hierarchical design strategy, a laboratory prototype is fabricated.
2) The inverse/forward position formulations and the reachable workspace prediction of the constructed machining robot are investigated to reveal its fundamental kinematic properties.
3) By adopting a "PC + MCU" hybrid hardware architecture, an open-architecture NC system with a postprocessing system and an HMI system is developed. It can be extended to other hybrid machining robots.
4) By integrating the NC system with the fabricated laboratory prototype, a hybrid machining robot system with 5-axis machining capability is constructed. The machining test shows that Class 6 surface finish (Ra: $\leq 3.2\ \mu m$; Rz: $\leq 6.3\ \mu m$) can be achieved for handicraft carving.
5) Our further investigations will be focused on the issues of dynamic calibration and contour error compensation algorithm.

Funding. This work is jointly supported by the National Natural Science Foundation of China [Grant No. 52375009], and the Natural Science Foundation of Fujian Province [Grant No. 2024J08147, 2024J02007].

References

1. Jan-Erilk, A., Gert, J.: Robot control for wood carving operations. Mechatronics **11**(4), 475–490 (2001)
2. Leng, Y., Shi, X., Hiroatsu, F., Kalachev, A., Wan, D.: Automated construction for human-robot interaction in wooden buildings: integrated robotic construction and digital design of iSMART wooden arches. J. Field Rob. **40**(4), 810–827 (2023)
3. Li, H., Zhang, P., Deng, M., et al.: Thermally induced comprehensive error modeling and compensation for gantry machine tools with grating scale in large structure machining. Int. J. Adv. Manuf. Tech. **107**(3–4), 1367–1376 (2020)
4. Spyrakos-Papastavridis, E., Dai, J.: Minimally model-based trajectory tracking and variable impedance control of flexible-joint robots. IEEE Trans. Ind. Electron. **68**(7), 6031–6041 (2021)

5. Tang, T., Zhang, J.: Conceptual design and kinetostatic analysis of a modular parallel kinematic machine-based hybrid machine tool for large aeronautic components. Robot Comput.-Integr. Manuf. **57**, 1–16 (2019)
6. Fang, H., Tang, T., He, Z., et al.: A novel hybrid machine tool integrating a symmetrical redundantly actuated parallel mechanism: design, kinematics, prototype and experiment. Mech. Mach. Theory **176**, 105013 (2022)
7. López-Custodio, P., Fu, R., Dai, J., et al.: Compliance model of Exechon manipulators with an offset wrist. Mech. Mach. Theory **167**, 104558 (2022)
8. Sun, C., Chen, L., Liu, J., et al.: A hybrid continuum robot based on pneumatic muscles with embedded elastic rods. Proc. Inst. Mech. Eng., Part C: J. Mech. Eng. Sci. **234**(1), 318–328 (2020)
9. Ma, X., Wang, X., Zhao, Z., et al.: Design and experiment validation of a novel hybrid continuum robot with enhanced dexterity and manipulability in confined space. IEEE-ASME T. Mech. **28**(4), 1–10 (2023)
10. Wang, S., Mei, Y., Li, R.: Solving dynamics for a novel 3T2R gantry hybrid machine tool. Chin. J. Mech. Eng. **52**(15), 81–90 (2016)
11. Caccavale, F., Siciliano, B., Villani, L.: The tricept robot: dynamics and impedance control. IEEE/ASME Trans. Mechatron. **8**(2), 263–268 (2003)
12. Hennes, N., Staimer, D.: Application of PKM in aerospace manufacturing-high performance machining centers ECOSPEED, ECOSPEED-F and ECOLINER. In: Proc. 4th Chemnitz parallel kinematics semin, pp. 557–577. Verlag Wissenschaftliche Scripten, Chemnitz, Germany (2004)
13. Zhao, Y., Jin, Y., Zhang, J.: Kinematic modeling of Exechon parallel kinematic machine. Robot Comput.-Integr. Manuf. **27**(1), 186–193 (2011)
14. Kanaan, D., Wenger, P., Chablat, D.: Kinematic analysis of a serial–parallel machine tool: the VERNE machine. Mech. Mach. Theory **44**(2), 487–498 (2009)
15. Li, Y., Liu, H., Zhao, X., et al.: Design of a 3-DOF PKM module for large structural component machining. Mech. Mach. Theory **45**(6), 941–954 (2010)
16. Tang, T., Fang, H., Zhang, J.: Hierarchical design, laboratory prototype fabrication and machining tests of a novel 5-axis hybrid serial-parallel kinematic machine tool. Robot Comput.-Integr. Manuf. **64**, 101944 (2020)
17. Exechon XMini XMobile. https://exechon.com/xmobile/. Accessed 11 May 2024
18. Olazagoitia, J., Wyatt, S.: New PKM Tricept T9000 and its application to flexible manufacturing at aerospace industry. In: SAE International, pp. 94–106. AeroTech Congress Exhibition, Los Angeles, USA (2007)
19. Liu, Q., Liu, H., Xiao, J., et al.: Open-architecture of NC system and mirror milling technology for a 5-axis hybrid robot. Robot Comput.-Integr. Manuf. **81**, 102504 (2023)
20. Li, P., Gao, T., Wang, J., et al.: Open architecture of NC system research based on CAD graph-driven technology. Robot Comput.-Integr. Manuf. **26**(6), 720–724 (2010)
21. Escorcia-Hernández, J., Chemori, A., Aguilar-Sierra, H., et al.: A new solution for machining with RA-PKMs: Modelling, control and experiments. Mech. Mach. Theory **150**, 103864 (2020)
22. Xie, Z., Xie, F., Liu, X., et al.: Tracking error prediction informed motion control of a parallel machine tool for high-performance machining. Int. J. Mach. Tools Manuf. **164**, 103714 (2021)

Twin Mushroom Picker Suspension Chassis Design Facing the Narrow Space

Sheng Ye, Chunyan Zhang(✉), Wenqian Li, and Yuhang Liu

School of Mechanical and Automotive Engineering, Shanghai University of Engineering Science, Shanghai 201620, China
1839295798@qq.com

Abstract. With the development of science and technology, robot technology has been widely used in the field of agriculture, in order to solve the stability problem of the twin mushroom picking machine in the picking process, a suspension chassis is designed in this paper, so as to prevent the machine from bumping due to uneven track caused by soil and external factors during the picking process. In this paper, the chassis is modeled in 3D based on SolidWorks, and the chassis structure designed must adapt to the narrow space of the mushroom rack to ensure that it does not interfere with the picking area and the mushroom rack. Secondly, in order to ensure that the chassis can bear a certain load, the finite element analysis of each part of the suspension chassis is carried out to verify whether each part meets the strength requirements, and finally the designed suspension chassis is simulated and verified.

Keywords: suspension chassis · 3D modeling · finite element analysis · Motion simulation

1 Introduction

In modern times, with the development of science and technology, machines have replaced traditional human labor. Whether it is manufacturing, the military industry, or daily life, all kinds of machines are everywhere. These machines have high efficiency, low cost, continuous and stable work, reduce production costs, and improve profits. In recent years, the use of machines in the agricultural field has become more and more frequent, especially for a large agricultural country like China, where some agricultural machines are urgently needed to replace traditional manual planting, cultivation and harvesting to improve production efficiency. Yu Jiawei of Changchun Normal University designed the mechanical system of the durian picking machine [1], Huang Baosai of Liaocheng University designed a tree-borne fruit picking machine [2], and Pan Xiaonan of Longdong University designed and analyzed the structure of the apple picking robot [3]. Due to the short cultivation cycle of twin mushrooms, in view of the need to invest a lot of manpower and capital in the picking and collection process, the continuous working time of workers is short and the work is unstable, this paper designs a twin mushroom picking machine, first laying a track on the mushroom culture rack, and then

X. Lan et al. (Eds.): ICIRA 2024, LNAI 15201, pp. 83–94, 2025.
https://doi.org/10.1007/978-981-96-0771-6_7

installing a picking mechanical arm on the trolley to complete the picking task of each layer with the trolley movement. In the early experimental process, we found that due to the uneven growth of mushrooms on the culture rack and the position of the nutrient soil on the culture rack is higher than the track, the nutrient soil and foreign matter are attached to the track, and some tracks also have some corrosion and deformation with the use time, causing the trolley to shake often during operation, affecting the picking efficiency and stability [4]. In response to these problems, we designed a chassis with suspension.

2 Suspension Development History

The suspension can be traced back to the Warring States period, and we found that the wheels of the ancient carriages were made of wood, and the road conditions were not very good at that time, so the carriage was very bumpy to sit on. Therefore, in order to "shock absorption", the ancients added something called "Fu Rabbit" between the body (called "Yu" in ancient times) and the axle, which is probably the earliest "shock absorption system" of human beings; In 1776, leaf springs for horse-drawn carriages were patented, and they were used until the thirties of the 20th century, when leaf springs were gradually replaced by coil springs [5]. Its carrying capacity is strong, the structure is simple, heavy vehicles, cheap small noodles are basically used, when the bearing capacity is not enough, just add the number of pieces. However, the disadvantage of leaf springs is their self-weight, and their comfort is poor (Fig. 1).

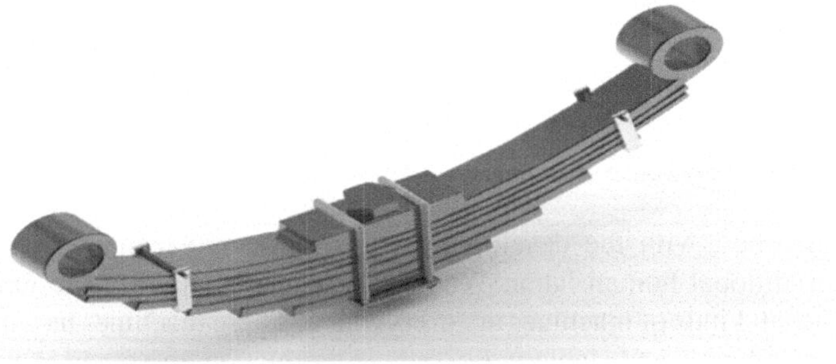

Fig. 1. Blade spring suspension

In 1906, two brothers, Alnson and William Brush, installed coil springs and shock absorbers on the wooden front axle of the Brush Runabout, and the first generation of coil spring suspension coil springs was finally manufactured and used [6]. In 1922, the Lambda was the first to adopt a spring-based independent suspension that allowed the left and right front wheels to be raised and lowered independently. Instead of a fixed axle connecting the two wheels, the independent suspension replaced it with two axles that could oscillate independently, with the left and right wheels connected to the frame by suspension, and the coil springs on both sides were responsible for the shock absorption of the respective wheels [7]. Independent suspension makes the movement between the wheels do not affect each other, which greatly improves the driving stability and ride comfort of the car. Up to now, the suspension technology has been very mature, hydraulic suspension, air suspension, electromagnetic suspension, etc., greatly improve the stability and comfort of the chassis, people can manufacture a variety of different suspension chassis according to the use environment and performance requirements of the machine.

3 Chassis Structure Design

3.1 Narrow Workspace Analysis

According to the actual investigation experiment, as shown in Fig. 2, the artificial planting of twin mushrooms is cultivated on the mushroom shelf, in order to reduce the production cost, improve the space utilization, each mushroom room is equipped with six groups of mushroom racks, each group of mushroom racks is 1 m apart, the mushroom rack is 2 m away from the mushroom room outlet, each group of mushroom shelves is divided into six layers, the height of each layer is 600 mm, assuming that the soil layer is consistent with the track height, the distance between the track and the bottom of the layer is 270 mm, except the part that the track and the wheel fit, the effective height of each layer is 340 mm; In addition to the height, its width is also limited, the width of each layer is 1400 mm, and enough redundant space should be reserved on the side to prevent the twin mushroom picker from interfering with the side columns, and at the same time ensure that the inner picking area is sufficient when the wheels fit with the track.

Fig. 2. Diagram of the working space of the mushroom picker

Because the column and the bottom plate of each layer of the actual mushroom rack are bolted together, in order to prevent the protruding bolts from interfering with the edge of the trolley, the height of the trolley must be reduced by 30 mm when designing, and the height of the mushroom picker must be controlled within 310 mm. At the same time, in order to ensure a large picking area, facilitate visual scanning and robotic arm picking, and improve the production efficiency of twin mushrooms, the outermost side of the track is only 10 mm redundant part from the two side columns of the mushroom rack, and the wheels on the two sides can not interfere with the column while ensuring that they fit with the track. As shown in Fig. 3, according to the above requirements, the design of the wheel must ensure that the outermost side of the wheel is the outermost side of the whole picking machine, so the matching mode of the wheel is very important, and it is necessary to ensure that the axial fixing and circumferential fixing parts of the wheel when the wheel is matched with the short shaft can not exceed the outermost side of the wheel, so as to avoid interference with the mushroom frame.

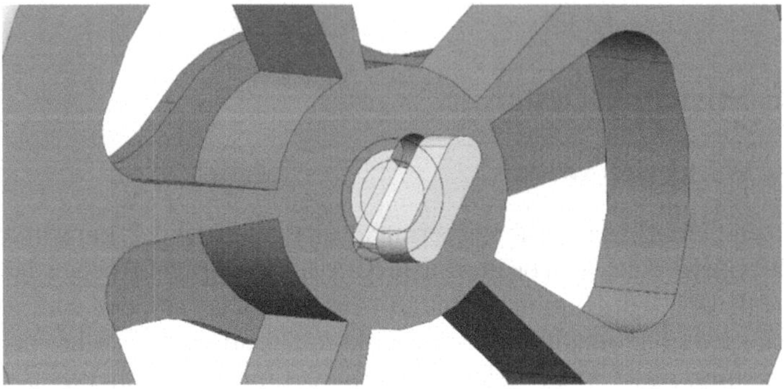

Fig. 3. Wheel connection coordination diagram

First, the thread is cut at the end of the shaft, and the length of the thread is exactly the same as the width of the wheel, so that it can be ensured that after the shaft and the wheel are matched, the end face of the shaft coincides with the outer side of the wheel, and the wheel will not be affected to be on the outermost side; in order to prevent the thread from loosening due to the backward of the trolley, the keyway is cut on the end face of the shaft and the outside of the wheel, and the key and the keyway are an interference fit, which can not only ensure that the thread will not loosen, but also provide better circumferential fixation. Finally, the arc surface of the wheel is cut to match with the track, the wheel is hollowed out to reduce the weight of the wheel, and a layer of rubber structure is wrapped on the arc surface, which can not only improve the stability of the wheel, but also reduce the wear and noise of the wheel.

3.2 The Overall Frame of the Twin Mushroom Picker

Combined with the twin mushroom culture rack standard design of a twin mushroom picking robot, as shown in Fig. 4, it is respectively composed of a chassis part, a picking part, a visual part and an electrical component part, wherein the chassis as the basis of the whole robot, used for the later mechanical picking parts, visual parts and control parts to provide assembly space, plays a very important role, this article will focus on the introduction.

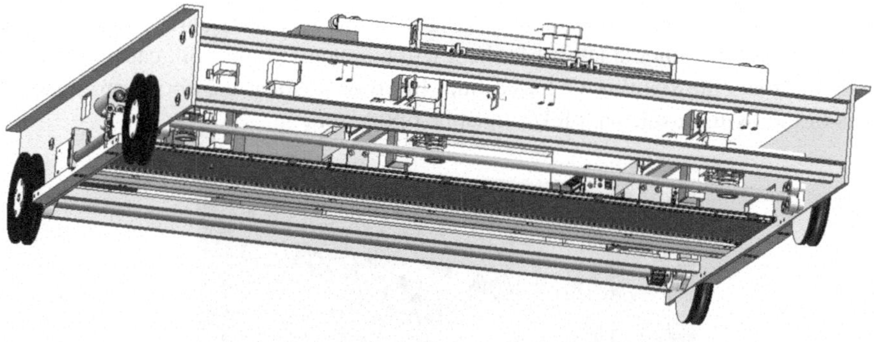

Fig. 4. General assembly drawing of twin mushroom picker

3.3 Chassis Design

The chassis structure is shown in Fig. 5, the overall height is 300 mm, the width is 1380 mm, and the length is 1460 mm, which meets the narrow space requirements of the mushroom rack. Its structure is to install flange bearings on 2 side outer plates, then connect 2 side outer plates through a long optical shaft, and finally install wheel sets on 2 sides of the optical axis. A number of beams are installed in the middle of the two outer plates, which are used for installing mechanical picking arms and some electrical components. The middle notch of the outer plate is used for the installation of a belt drive for transporting the harvested mushrooms to the collection unit. Such a chassis design can not only meet the narrow space of the mushroom culture rack, but also make the chassis design compact and stiff because the middle long axis has a fixed and supporting effect on the wheel.

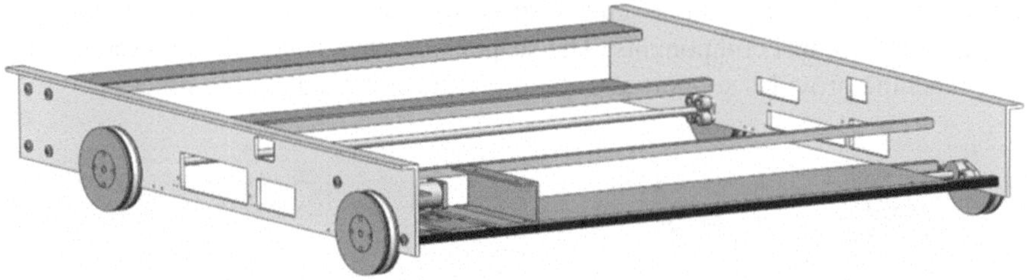

Fig. 5. Chassis assembly drawing

3.4 Optimized Design of the Chassis of the Twin Mushroom Picker

In the process of experiment, we found that the height of the nutrient soil on the mushroom shelf is not below the track, more often as shown in Fig. 6, the nutrient soil layer will be higher than the track, and the height of the nutrient soil will be higher, which will lead to the actual position of the actual twin mushroom becoming higher, and the result is that in the actual experimental process, the intermediate axis will interfere with some larger twin mushrooms, and as shown in Fig. 6, some soil and debris will be attached to the track, and the inner side of the wheel will contact with the soil, causing the body to shake. Affects the stability of harvesting. In order to solve the above problems, the chassis of the twin mushroom picker must be optimized.

Fig. 6. Actual experimental soil layer height map

The new chassis assembly drawing is shown in Fig. 7 and consists of a chassis frame and four suspension wheels. The change in this structure compared to the previous chassis structure is that the long axle in the middle is replaced with two short axles. This improvement not only eliminates the problem of interference with the twin mushrooms, but also allows the structure to form four sets of suspension wheels with independent suspension functions. The elastic force generated by these suspension wheels can effectively reduce the sway caused by debris and deformation on the track. The function of the chassis frame is to provide assembly space for the later mechanical picking parts, visual parts and control components; The suspension wheels are mainly used to ensure that the machine provides support and stability during the harvesting process.

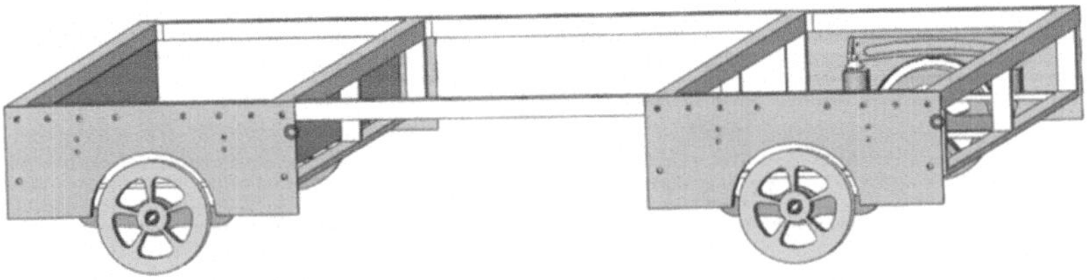

Fig. 7. Assembly drawing of suspension wheel chassis

3.5 Suspension Wheel Structure Design

The suspension wheel structure is shown in Fig. 8, which is composed of a frame, an outer plate, a spring cover, a rolling bearing, a wheel, a connecting piece 1, a suspension spring, a connecting piece 2, and a connecting shaft.

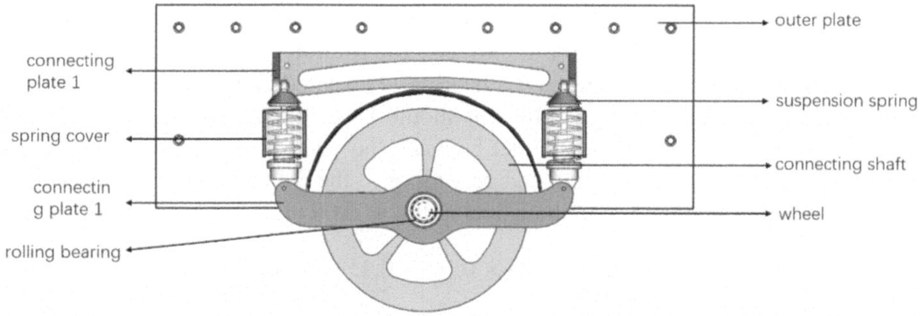

Fig. 8. Assembly drawing of suspension wheels

Where in the outer plate connects the connecting piece 1 with the upper plate, and the spring cover not only has a guiding effect on the spring, but also has a sealing effect on the spring at the same time, prevents the soil and other objects from entering the suspension spring during picking, and ensures that the spring has good working conditions; The connecting plate 1 and the connecting plate 2 are responsible for connecting the two ends of the suspension spring, and while being fixed, one side is suspended, and the suspension mechanism is formed; The outer ring of the bearing is fixed on the connecting plate 2, and the inner ring is matched with the interference of the connecting shaft, and the wheel is fixed with the connecting shaft, so that the wheel rotates.

4 Finite Element Analysis

The basic idea of the finite element method is to discretize the continuously changing geometry into elements, and then obtain the strain and stress fields of the entire solution domain by solving for the unknown quantities of the elements [8]. In order to ensure that the mechanism can work stably, finite element analysis is carried out on each part of the suspension chassis to verify whether each part has sufficient stiffness and bearing capacity. Select the appropriate material according to the actual use conditions of each part, apply the external load according to the force of the part, select the appropriate parameters, and finally mesh the part, and calculate the result.

4.1 Load Calculation

Cording to the actual measurement, except for the suspension wheel, the total mass of the rest of the parts is about 25 kg, according to the relationship between external force and gravity, it can be obtained:

$$F = 10G = 10 \times 25N = 250N \tag{1}$$

$$F1 = F2 = F3 = F4 = F/n = 250/4 = 75N \tag{2}$$

$$Fz = \varepsilon \cdot F1 = 2 \times 75 = 150N \tag{3}$$

In order to select the right motor to drive the trolley to move, it is necessary to calculate the torque required to drive the wheels. The friction state of the wheel designed in this paper is rolling friction [9], and a bearing is installed between the shaft and the connecting plate, and its rolling coefficient should be $\mu = 0.09$, but because we wrap a layer of rubber structure at the contact between the wheel and the track, the rolling friction coefficient should be calculated according to the rolling friction coefficient of the rubber material $\mu = 0.15$, and the wheel radius is 0.09 m.

$$T = F1L\mu = 150 \times 0.09 \times 0.15 = 2.025N \tag{4}$$

thereinto F—the overall load of the body; F_1—the load on the first wheel; T—the torque required to drive the wheel; Fz—Calculate the load; L—force arm; μ—rolling friction coefficient; ε—safety factor.

4.2 Finite Element Analysis of Each Part

According to the calculation of 4.1, each wheel needs to bear a workload of 150 N, we set the material of the connector to be aluminum alloy, and its force mainly occurs at the junction with the hole position of the suspension spring, the connector 1 has 2 hole positions, so we apply an external load of 75 N to each hole position for calculation, as shown in Table 1a, the yield strength of the connector 1 is 2.757e + 07pa, and the maximum stress of the test is 1.647e + 07pa, so it can be seen that the strength of the connector 1 meets the requirements.

According to the above, each wheel is subjected to an external load of 150 N, and each wheel is equipped with two suspension springs, so each of our suspension springs should be subjected to a pressure of 75 N, the spring material is spring steel, and the rest of the suspension spring material parts are set to alloy steel. As shown in Table 1b, the yield strength of the suspension spring is 6.204e + 08 pa, and the maximum stress is 2.690e + 05 pa, so it can be seen that the strength of the suspension spring meets the requirements. As shown in Table 1c, the yield strength of connector 2 is 2.757e + 07 pa, and the maximum stress of the test is 4.763e + 02 pa, so it can be seen that the strength of connector 2 meets the requirements.

Each wheel bears an external load of 150 N, the bearing is a single piece, and its surface is also subjected to an external load of 150 N, the material of the bearing is generally high carbon steel, alloy steel and stainless steel, and we set the bearing material to be alloy steel. As shown in Table 1d, the yield strength of the suspension spring is 6.204e+08 pa, and the maximum stress is 1.754e+06 pa, so it can be seen that the strength of the suspension spring meets the requirements. The main state of force in the operation of the shaft is torque, we according to the torque formula:

$$M = FL = 150 \times 0.09 = 13.5 \text{ N/m} \tag{5}$$

The shaft surface is subjected to an external torque of 13.5 N/m, and alloy steel is selected as the material of the shaft. As shown in Table 1e, the yield strength of the shaft is 6.204e+08 pa, and the maximum stress is 3.226e+07 pa, so it can be seen that the strength of the suspension spring meets the requirements. The main stress state of the wheel during operation is torque, and its torque size is 13.5 N/m, and we choose alloy steel as the material of the shaft. As shown in Table 1f, the yield strength of the shaft is 2.757e+07 pa, and the maximum stress is 2.966e+06 pa, so it can be seen that the strength of the suspension spring meets the requirements.

Table 1. Finite element analysis diagram of components

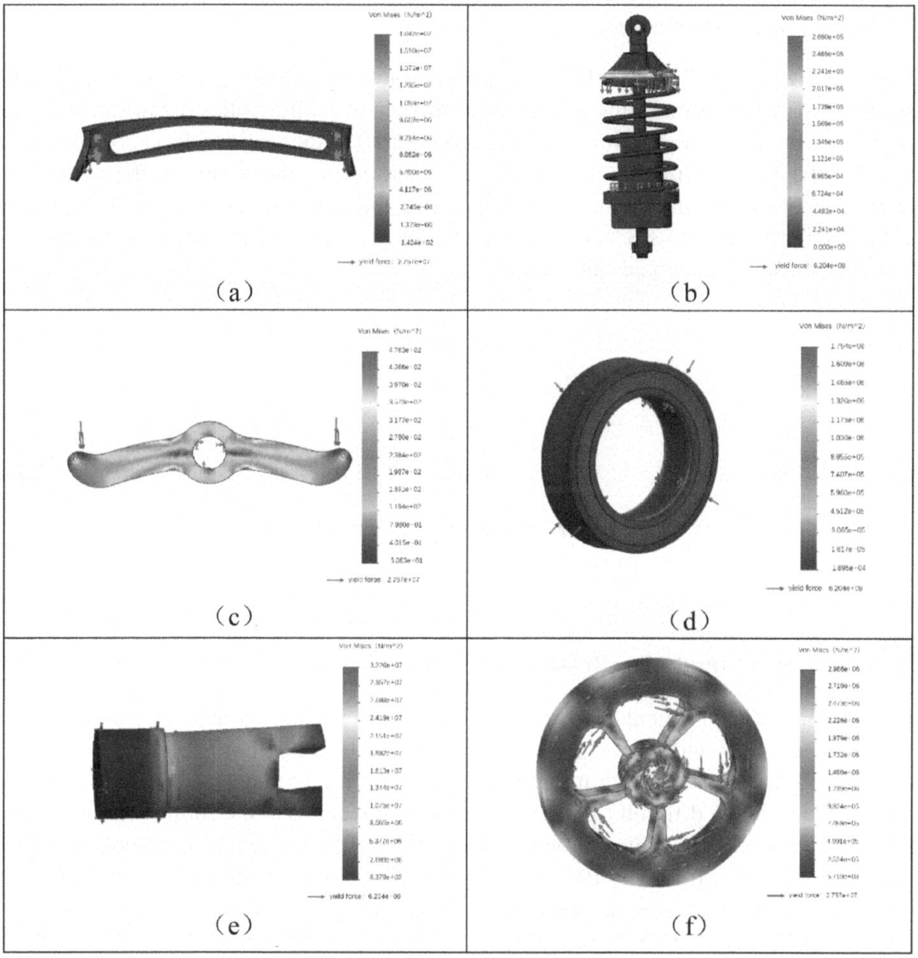

5 Simulation of Suspension Chassis

In order to verify that the designed suspension chassis can increase the stability of trolley movement, simulation experiments were carried out on the mechanism to simulate the motion process of the entity and draw the displacement mass curve [10]. We import the model in SolidWorks, and design a terrain with uneven pavement, test the vibration of the trolley when passing through the road, so as to obtain the vibration curve of the wheels and frame of the trolley, compared with the two sets of curves, if the frame curve tends to be smooth or compared with the vibration curve of the tire has been greatly improved, it means that the designed suspension chassis can increase the stability of the trolley.

5.1 Simulation Experiments

As shown in Fig. 9, in SolidWorks, the concave-convex road surface and the trolley with a suspension chassis are put into an assembly, the wheels of the trolley are in contact with the ground, the dynamic friction coefficient is set to 0.6, the static friction coefficient is set to 0.8, the gravity direction is set to the Y-axis direction, the spring coefficient [11] is 4 N/mm according to the purchased spring model, the wheel speed is set to 20 rpm, and the simulation time is 55 s. Once the data was set, we started the simulation to observe the deformation of the wheels and frame.

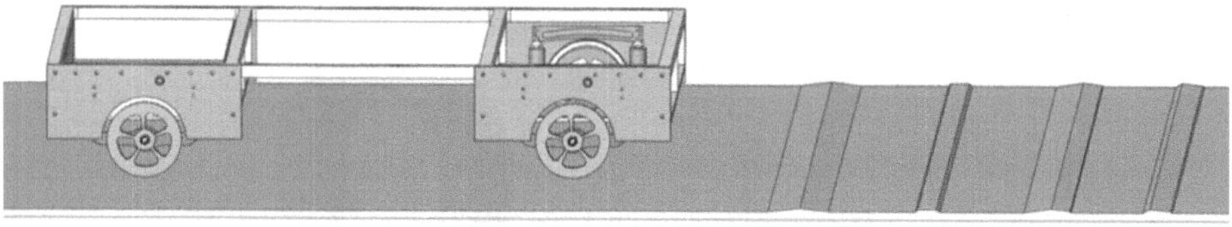

Fig. 9. Simulation experiment

5.2 Analysis of Simulation Results

After simulation experiments, we selected the central mass displacement curves of the Y-axis of the wheel and frame as the simulation results, and compared the two sets of curves to observe their vibration degree. Comparing the two sets of curves in Fig. 10 and Fig. 5-3, it is not difficult to find that the vibration curve of the frame is more gentle than that of the wheels, which shows that the designed suspension device plays a role in shock absorption. In 4–7 s, 10–13 s, 18–26 s, 32–39 s the trolley passes through the concave and convex surface, the maximum vibration degree is the largest, the maximum vibration of the frame is 5–6 mm, and the maximum vibration of the wheel is about 12 mm, indicating that the suspension device reduces the vibration by half, and the stability of the trolley is significantly improved.

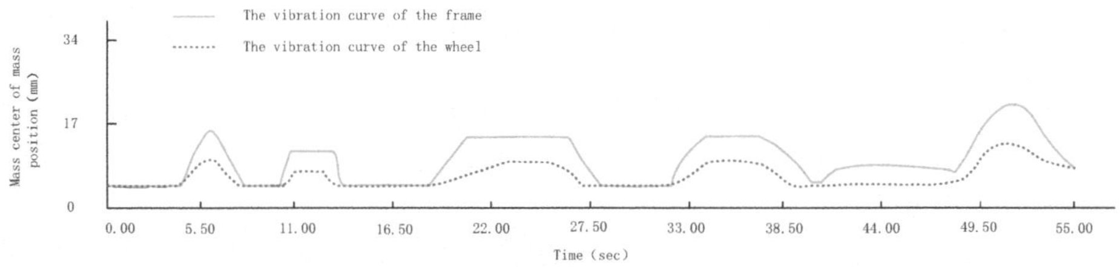

Fig. 10. Vibration curve

6 Conclusion

1. Firstly, based on the use requirements of the mushroom picking machine, with the goal of improving the stability of the machine and adapting to the needs of narrow space, a suspension chassis of the mushroom picking machine was designed.
2. According to the actual use and the size of the load, the finite element analysis was carried out on the parts of the suspension chassis wheel block, and its stiffness and reliability were analyzed to meet the requirements of use.
3. The suspension chassis is simulated and verified, and the vibration curves of the frame and the wheel are obtained, and the comparison curves prove that the designed chassis has the functions of reducing vibration and improving the stability of the mushroom picker Book Metrics.

The book metrics for Springer publications are now available on Springer.com and SpringerLink. These give details on the number of citations, downloads, and readers at paper level and at book level. Please see Springer.com/bookmetrix for more details.

References

1. Yu, J., Jiang, D., Pei, Q., et al.: Durian picking machine mechanical system design. Mech. Manage. Develop. **38**(10), 71–73+76. (2023). https://doi.org/10.16525/j.carol carrollnkicn14-1134/th
2. Huang, B., Zhao, D., Zhang, W., et al.: Structural design of a tree-borne fruit picking robot. J. South. Agric. Mach. **54**(12), 47–50 (2023)
3. Pan, X., Zhang, Y., Geng, B., et al.: Structural design and analysis of apple picking robot. J. China Equip. Eng. (18), 38–40 (2023)
4. Chen, X.: Research on the motion planning method of serpentine manipulator for complex and narrow space (2023)
5. Xu, G.: Research status and development trend of automobile suspension. J. High-Tech Enterp. China (22), 35–6 (2010)
6. Yang, F.: Optimal design and CAE study of automobile suspension coil springs (2009)
7. Cao, Y., Zhao, Y., Fu, Z.: Design and simulation of independent suspension system for unmanned vehicles. J. Mechatron. **19**(02), 17–21 (2012)
8. Zhao, Y.: Finite element analysis and lightweight study of a frame based on ANSYS Workbench (2018)

9. Zhu, A., Zhu, C., Zhang, W.: Calculation and analysis of frictional torque of rolling bearing. J. Bear. (07), 1–3 (2008)
10. Wei, J.: Motion analysis and simulation of connecting rod mechanism based on SolidWorks (2006)
11. Zheng, Y.: Calculation model of automobile leaf spring (2005)

Kinematic Calibration Method Based on Point Cloud Measurement for 3-RPS Parallel Robot

Lingyun Sheng[1], Xingwei Zhao[1,2](✉), Yajun Fan[1], Lei Xue[3], and Bo Tao[1]

[1] School of Mechanical Science and Engineering, Huazhong University of Science and Technology, Wuhan 430074, Hubei, China
zhaoxingwei@hust.edu.cn

[2] Huazhong University of Science and Technology-Wuxi Research Institute, Wuhan, China

[3] Shanghai Aircraft Manufacturing Co., Ltd., Shanghai, China

Abstract. In order to control the end-effector to achieve accurate and suitable posture for high-precision processes in complex industrial environments, a mechanism is often added to make secondary adjustment of the tool end posture. The 3-RPS parallel connection is widely used for target posture control in small workspaces due to its features of high control accuracy, large load, and small size and mass. In order to avoid the influence of process error and assembly error on the control accuracy of the parallel system, it is necessary to identify its parameters with high accuracy before use. However, the traditional non-contact calibration methods, such as position sensors and cameras, have the disadvantages of complex system, difficult to build, lower accuracy and cumbersome operation. To address the above problems, this paper proposes a non-contact measurement calibration method based on facial laser scanner, and establishes a calibration system based on a self-designed and fabricated 3-RPS parallel robot, realizes the high-precision measurement of the overall position and attitude information of the robot through the splicing of multi-segmented point clouds and feature extraction algorithms, establishes an inverse kinematic model of the robot, combines the 3D model with the parameter identification equations, realizes the parallel robot kinematic calibration, and designs the accuracy verification method. The effectiveness of the parameter calibration and the control algorithm of the parallel robot are verified by experiments.

Keywords: 3-RPS Parallel Robot · Kinematic Calibration · Computer Vision

1 Introduction

Parallel robots are characterized by high load capacity and high control accuracy in a small workspace, and can perform precise position adjustment at the end of the robot [1]. However, the parameter deviation of the device caused by the manufacturing process and assembly error will greatly affect the control accuracy of the system. Considering the motion characteristics and calibration accuracy of parallel robots, the conventional parameter calibration scheme is not applicable, so many researchers have invested in the research of position measurement and parameter calibration methods for parallel robots [2, 3].

X. Lan et al. (Eds.): ICIRA 2024, LNAI 15201, pp. 95–107, 2025.
https://doi.org/10.1007/978-981-96-0771-6_8

The kinematic calibration of parallel robots is usually performed by measuring the position information of the parallel robots under different conditions and then identifying the unknown parameters with the help of the robot's kinematic model. Currently, the measurement schemes for parallel robots are mainly classified into contact and non-contact; G. Rubio-Gómez et al. [4] indirectly obtained the end-position information by obtaining the strain of multiple sets of cables connected to the end, and X. Ren et al. [5] partially constrained the parallel robot, and then used a dual-axis inclinometer to measure the end-position, and then performed the optimal combination. However, the contact measurement is less accurate and less flexible, while the non-contact measurement mainly based on computer vision is more widely used [6–8]. A. Traslosheros et al. [9] mounted a camera on the end of the robot and used a standard ball as a datum to obtain the relative robot position. I. Tyapin et al. [10]achieved an actuator attitude measurement accuracy of about 20 μm using laser tracker measurements and least squares estimation of polynomial functions. M.R. Dindarloo et al. [11] proposed a method to measure relative position and achieve calibration of a spherical parallel robot based on a laser tracker with improved repeatability and trajectory tracking after calibration. T. Sun et al. [12] proposed a general error modelling method for tandem robots and extended the finite instantaneous spiral (FIS) theory to parallel robots, using a laser tracker to achieve the construction of the error model and parameter identification for parallel robots [13–15].

This paper describes a methodology for position measurement of a 3-RPS parallel robot based on a 3D laser scanner, and the parameter calibration of the parallel robot is achieved by means of a high-precision point cloud with a 3D model of the device, and the robot model inverse solution of the robot model and the accuracy validation scheme, and experimentally verifies the validity of the methodology. The rest of the paper is organized as follows. Section 2 describes the whole system components. Section 3 describes the principle of parallel robot position measurement and parameter calibration method as well as the principle of kinematic model optimization and accuracy verification. Experimental results are given in Sect. 4. Section 5 concludes the whole paper.

2 Faceted Laser-Based Calibration System for Parallel Robots

The parallel robot calibration system mainly consists of an industrial robot, a 3-RPS parallel unit and a laser scanner.

Due to the material properties of the parallel device and the limitation of the laser scanning principle, there is a large error in the extraction of edge features, so we need the laser scanner to obtain the point cloud information of multiple surfaces of the robot for the derivation of the position, but due to the limited field of view of the scanner, we need to scan the surfaces several times and then carry out the splicing of the point cloud. In order to minimize the measurement error of the relative positions and postures of the base and the moving platform on the parallel device, the coordinate system of each group of point clouds cannot be unified by relying on the position information of the robotic arm, and it is necessary to make the laser scanner include part of the surfaces of the base and the moving platform and as many standard points as possible in the field of view of each scanning. Therefore, the range of suitable angles for each scanning is limited, and it is necessary to adjust and record the scanning angles with the help of industrial robots by means of demonstration teaching, in order to improve the measurement efficiency, and ultimately obtain the position mapping relationship between the base and the moving stage under different parameters of the parallel robot.

In this paper, in order to make the parallel robot better meet the end position adjustment needs, the design is optimized, as shown in Fig. 1. First of all, the standard components are selected for the actual load, and the open-loop spline screw stepping linear motor is selected to reduce the overall mass and volume while ensuring the control accuracy. Adjust the structure of the linear motor rotating vice, increase the locking end cap at the bearing, which will make the actual assembly position have a small difference with the 3D model, but will eliminate the assembly gap and avoid the system shaking.

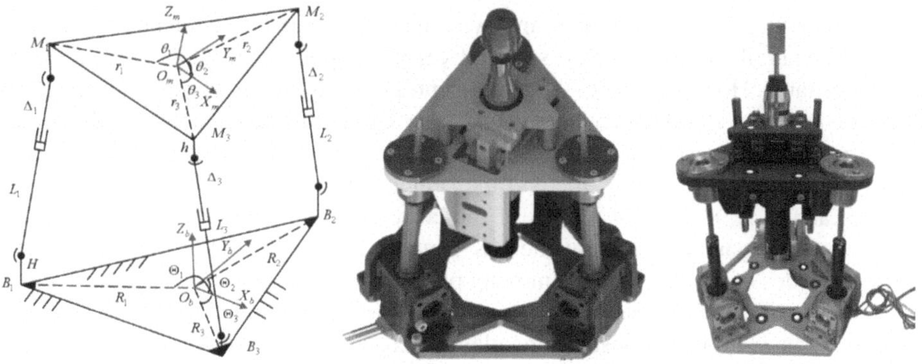

(a) (b) (c)

Fig. 1. (a) Schematic diagram of the parallel robot (b) 3D model of the robot (c) Physical drawing of the robot.

Subsequently, the parameter errors to be identified in the parallel robot are analyzed, firstly, the way the ball hinge is connected to the moving platform causes the center of motion of the ball hinge $[M_1, M_2, M_3]$ to be shifted in the $X_m Y_m$ plane, the low accuracy of the initial dimensional measurements of the linear motor as well as the existence of a threaded bushing conversion between the motor end and the ball hinge causes the initial length of the connecting rods $X_b Y_b$ to be calibrated, and lastly the process of locking the slewing Finally, during the locking slewing process, the motor slewing points $[B_1, B_2, B_3]$ will be displaced in the $X_b Y_b$ plane. Other parameters such as h, H, Δ_1, Δ_2, Δ_3 are determined by the manufacturing process and design, and their process and control errors are so small that they are negligible. Therefore, assuming that the relative rotation matrix in the base coordinate system O_b and the moving platform coordinate system O_m is R_m^b, the control transformation can be expressed by Eq:

$$\begin{pmatrix} R_m^b & T_m^1 \\ 0 & 1 \end{pmatrix} = \begin{pmatrix} (f_{ij})_{3\times3} & (f_k)_{3\times1} \\ 0 & 1 \end{pmatrix} \tag{1}$$

Where f_{ij} and f_k are the conversion functions of the corresponding elements of the rotation matrix to the parameters to be identified parameters L_i, R_i, Θ_i, r_i, θ_i and the set parameters Δ_i (i = 1, 2, 3). Therefore, the key to calibration is to obtain several sets of accurate mapping relations and construct the optimized transformation equations.

3 Kinematic Calibration of Parallel Robots

After establishing the calibration system, the point cloud measurement of the parallel robot is performed. This section describes the calibration principle of the parallel robot, the optimized kinematic model and the method for accuracy verification.

3.1 Measurement of Position and Posture

After completing the face laser scanning, we can obtain a high-precision point cloud of a multi-piece parallel robot, which is spliced by marking points arranged to the robot and the carrier table. However, due to the material properties of the robots, the measurement of their edge point clouds has a large error, so we extract the face features of the robots and derive the positional relationship between the base and the moving platform. Firstly, we fit the normal vectors n_{bsi}, n_{bt} and the center points p_{bsi}, p_{bt} of the base and top surfaces and n_{bmi}, n_{mt} and p_{msi}, p_{mt} of the corresponding moving platforms to each group of spliced point clouds using the least squares method. We define the intersections of the two sides of the base and the moving platform with a top surface as three datums, and use them to construct the coordinate system $O_b - X_b Y_b Z_b$ and $O_m - X_m Y_m Z_m$. Take the base as an example to construct the plane intersection equations:

$$\left(\begin{pmatrix} P_{Bi} \\ P_{Bi} \\ P_{Bi} \end{pmatrix} - \begin{pmatrix} p_{bsi} \\ p_{bsk} \\ p_{bst} \end{pmatrix}\right)\left(n_{bsi}^T \; n_{bsk}^T \; n_{bst}^T\right) = 0 \tag{2}$$

Equation (2) in for the base of the i reference point, p_{bi}, p_{bk} and n_{bi}, n_{bk} and denote the center point of the plane adjacent to the datum and the normal vector, the definition of the camera coordinate system under the base of the coordinate system:

$$X_b^c \triangleq (P_{B3} - P_{B1}) / \| P_{B3} - P_{B1} \| \tag{3}$$

$$Y_b^c \triangleq \hat{P}_2 \tag{4}$$

$$Z_b^c \triangleq X_b^c \times Y_b^c \tag{5}$$

Define the origin of the coordinate system as the center of the circle outside the datum and solved by the midline method:

$$d_s = \det\begin{pmatrix} N'_{12} \\ (P'_{12} - P'_{23}) \end{pmatrix}\left(\det\begin{pmatrix} N'_{12} \\ N'_{23} \end{pmatrix}\right)^{-1} \tag{6}$$

$$O_b^c = P_{23} + d_s N_{23} \tag{7}$$

In Eq. (7) $P_{23} = 0.5(P_2 + P_3)$, $N_{23} = Z_b \times (P_2 - P_3)$, In Eq. (6) $N_{12'}$, $P_{12'}$, $P_{23'}$, $N_{23'}$ is the first two terms of the corresponding function. Similarly, we can obtain the coordinate system position O_m^c and attitude of the moving platform based on the camera coordinate system R_m^c. Due to the large number of unknown parameters and nonlinear relationship, the global optimization algorithm is chosen for the solution. In order to reduce the optimization range and iteration speed, so that the optimization solution can converge to the global optimum, the parameters of the 3D model can be introduced as the reference of the initial quantities. Therefore, it is necessary to transform the position relation based on the camera coordinate system to the base coordinate system. Then the displacement and rotation expressions of $O_b - X_bY_bZ_b$ with respect to $O_m - X_mY_mZ_m$ are:

$$T_m^b = \left(X_b^T \; Y_b^T \; Z_b^T\right)^{-1}\left(O_m^c - O_b^c\right) \tag{8}$$

$$R_m^b = \left(X_b^{cT} \; Y_b^{cT} \; Z_b^{cT}\right)^{-1}\left(X_m^{cT} \; Y_m^{cT} \; Z_m^{cT}\right) \tag{9}$$

Adjust the output of the linear motor and obtain the coordinate points and rotation matrix corresponding to the $O_b - X_bY_bZ_b$ coordinate system with respect to $O_m - X_mY_mZ_m$.

3.2 Kinematic Calibration

Unlike cameras and position sensors, surface laser scanning can directly calculate the spatial position of the moving platform, so only a simple transformation is required before parameter identification. To facilitate comparison with the parameters of the 3D model, the coordinates of the center of the ball hinge under the coordinate system $O_m - X_mY_mZ_m$ are defined:

$$\left(M_1^m \; M_2^m \; M_3^m\right) = \begin{pmatrix} r_1\cos\theta_1 & r_2\cos\theta_2 & r_3\cos\theta_3 \\ r_1\sin\theta_1 & r_2\sin\theta_2 & r_3\sin\theta_3 \\ -h & -h & -h \end{pmatrix} \tag{10}$$

Similarly, the coordinates of the center of gyration in coordinate system $O_b - X_bY_bZ_b$ are:

$$\left(B_1^b \; B_2^b \; B_3^b\right) = \begin{pmatrix} R_1\cos\Theta_1 & R_2\cos\Theta_2 & R_3\cos\Theta_3 \\ R_1\sin\Theta_1 & R_2\sin\Theta_2 & R_3\sin\Theta_3 \\ H & H & H \end{pmatrix} \tag{11}$$

The coordinates of the center of the ball hinge are then transformed to the coordinate system $O_b - X_bY_bZ_b$ as:

$$\left(M_1^b \; M_2^b \; M_3^b\right) = R_m^b\left(M_1^m \; M_2^m \; M_3^m\right) + T_m^b \tag{12}$$

The kinematic model is constructed from the parallel robot schematic as:

$$\begin{cases} \left\|B_1^b - R_m^b M_1^m - T_m^b\right\| = L_1 + \Delta_1 \\ \left\|B_2^b - R_m^b M_2^b - T_m^b\right\| = L_2 + \Delta_2 \\ \left\|B_3^b - R_m^b M_3^b - T_m^b\right\| = L_3 + \Delta_3 \end{cases} \tag{13}$$

From the kinematic model can be, the 15 unknown parameters can be divided into three groups to identify separately, in this paper, the general particle swarm optimization algorithm is used to optimize the solution. Then the five independent variable equations are overdetermined, so the optimization equation is constructed as:

$$f\left(r_i\ \theta_i\ R_i\ \Theta_i\ L_i\right) \triangleq \sum_{j=1}^{n} \left| \left\| B_{ij}^b - \left(R_{mj}^b M_{ij}^m + T_{mj}^b\right) \right\| - L_{ij} - \Delta_{ij} \right| \tag{14}$$

Due to the large number of unknowns, in order to ensure the convergence of the equations and avoid convergence to a local optimum, the particle range is limited by combining the 3D model and the maximum deviation in the assembly process for estimation. In addition, the core equation of particle swarm optimization is:

$$v_i = v_{i-1} w + c_1 \lambda_1 p_a + c_2 \lambda_2 p_b \tag{15}$$

In Eq. (15) v_i denotes the step factor, w denotes the inertia weight, p_a and c_1 denote the local optimal directional quantities and their corresponding weights, and p_b and c_2 denote the global optimal directional quantities and their corresponding weights In the case that the optimal solution range is determined as well as the error range is small, the inertia weight is reduced, and the learning weights of the locally and globally optimal solutions are increased in order to increase the rate of convergence and to avoid converging to the wrong optimal solution.

3.3 Optimized Kinematic Model

When performing attitude adjustment, we can obtain the normal vector of the target surface in the camera coordinate system through the camera, radar, etc. The new normal unit vector is obtained by transforming the vector through the calibrated coordinate system transformation matrix, and then representing the vector to the base coordinate system of the parallel robot:

$$\hat{n} \triangleq \left(x_n\ y_n\ z_n\right) \tag{16}$$

The normal vectors then need to be converted into a rotation matrix from $O_b - X_b Y_b Z_b$ to $O_m - X_m Y_m Z_m$. Theoretically, the three degrees of freedom of a standard 3-RPS parallel robot are movement along the z-axis and rotation around the x-axis and y-axis, respectively, and the planes defined by the three sets of rotating subsets on the base pass through the coordinate origin of the base, so that the rotation of the moving platform around the z-axis during its movement is always 0. However, due to the mounting error, the positions of the three planes are shifted, which results in the rotations of the moving platform around the z-axis as well, and the specific value is determined by the mounting offset and motor telescoping length. The exact value is determined by the mounting offset and the motor telescoping length.

If only the unknowns are set to solve the equations, the arithmetic process is more complicated, in order to facilitate the continuation of the derivation, this paper adopts the rotation matrix corresponding to the sequential Euler angles in order to eliminate the variable γ in the third column:

$$R_m^b = \begin{pmatrix} c\beta c\gamma & -c\beta s\gamma & s\beta \\ c\alpha s\gamma + s\alpha s\beta c\gamma & c\alpha c\gamma - s\alpha s\beta s\gamma & -s\alpha c\beta \\ s\alpha s\gamma - c\alpha s\beta c\gamma & s\alpha c\gamma + c\alpha s\beta s\gamma & c\alpha c\beta \end{pmatrix} \tag{17}$$

α, β and γ in Eq. (17) are the angles of rotation of the coordinate system O about the axes X,Y and Z, respectively. Let the normal coincide with the Z-axis of the coordinate system $O_m - X_m Y_m Z_m$ to obtain the result:

$$\begin{cases} x_n = s\beta \\ y_n = -s\alpha c\beta \\ z_n = c\alpha c\beta \end{cases} \tag{18}$$

Considering the range of variation α, β and γ, Eq. (18) is simplified by substituting into Eq. (17):

$$R_m^b = \begin{pmatrix} \cos\gamma\sqrt{1-x_n^2} & -\sin\gamma\sqrt{1-x_n^2} & x_n \\ \frac{z_n \sin\gamma - y_n x_n \cos\gamma}{\sqrt{1-x_n^2}} & \frac{z_n \cos\gamma - y_n x_n \sin\gamma}{\sqrt{1-x_n^2}} & y_n \\ \frac{-y_n \sin\gamma - z_n x_n \cos\gamma}{\sqrt{1-x_n^2}} & \frac{-y_n \cos\gamma + z_n x_n \sin\gamma}{\sqrt{1-x_n^2}} & z_n \end{pmatrix} \tag{19}$$

At the same time the plane on the base determined by the rotating sub is necessarily parallel to the direction of the Z-axis of the base coordinate system, so that the equations of the ball-hinge plane of motion can be determined by using the calibrated coordinate points of the slewing center and the measured center points of the N sets of ball-hinge center motions:

$$B_c \triangleq \frac{1}{N}\sum_{i=1}^{N}\left(R_{mi}^b\left(M_1^m\ M_2^m\ M_3^m\right) + T_{mi}^b\right) \tag{20}$$

$$n_p \triangleq \begin{pmatrix} 0 \\ 0 \\ 1 \end{pmatrix} \times \left(B_c - \left(B_1^b\ B_2^b\ B_3^b\right)\right) \tag{21}$$

Equation (21) where n_p is the normal to the three sets of ball-hinged planes of motion as over the center of the rotating on the base, the three sets of plane equations are:

$$n_p\left(B_c - \left(B_1^b\ B_2^b\ B_3^b\right)\right) = 0 \tag{22}$$

From the degrees of freedom of the system, it is also necessary to specify the displacement z_m of the moving platform along the z-direction of the base coordinate system when performing the position adjustment, so that the point $(M_1^b M_2^b M_3^b)$ calculated by Eq. (12) satisfies the plane equation in Eq. (22). From this, the offsets x_m, y_m and the rotation angle γ of the moving stage around the Z_m are solved. The linear motor output parameters are then calculated:

$$\begin{cases} \Delta_1 = \left\|B_1^b - R_m^b M_1^b + T_m^b\right\| - L_1 \\ \Delta_2 = \left\|B_2^b - R_m^b M_2^b + T_m^b\right\| - L_2 \\ \Delta_3 = \left\|B_3^b - R_m^b M_2^b + T_m^b\right\| - L_3 \end{cases} \tag{23}$$

and return the offsets x_m, y_m to the control program for offset compensation. In order to demonstrate the effectiveness of the calibration and following methods for parallel robots, a comparison is performed for a standard parallel robot with 3-RPS. The motion platform of the parallel robot does not rotate around the Z_m when assembly clearance and errors are not considered, i.e., $\gamma = 0$. When the surface normal is obtained, the rotation matrix can be calculated directly from (19) and the kinematic limiting plane of the ball joint is as follows:

$$\begin{cases} M_1^x - \sqrt{3}M_1^y = 0 \\ M_2^x = 0 \\ -M_1^x - \sqrt{3}M_1^y = 0 \end{cases} \tag{24}$$

The remaining parameters are set according to the 3D model, and the output of each linear motor can be solved from Eqs. (19), (24), and (23). Error comparisons are made by measuring the data in the experiment as the true value [16–18].

4 Experiment

In this paper, we built the parallel robot calibration system shown in Fig. 2 based on the calibration principle, and chose the PowerScan_5M laser 3D measuring instrument from VISION3D, whose proximal field of view range is $250 \times 215 - 440$ mm, and the distal field of view range is $345 \times 345 - 740$ mm, and the accuracy of the point cloud of a single frame is ± 0.02 mm, which meets the experimental requirements.

Fig. 2. Calibration system device composition

4.1 Kinematic Calibration

In this paper, we adjust the shooting angle of the industrial robot carrying the surface laser to the parallel robot by means of demonstration. In order to avoid excessive point cloud splicing error, we need to make sure that there are enough marking points under the field of view of the surface laser each time as well as covering the surface point cloud of the base and the movable platform part at the same time. After determining the shooting angles of multiple sets of surface lasers, the output of linear motors starts to be randomly adjusted, and every time the platform attitude adjustment is completed, a multi-angle measurement is carried out, followed by point cloud stitching and feature extraction, as shown in Fig. 3. In order to ensure the convergence of the optimization equations during parameter identification as well as to improve the accuracy of parameter identification, we carried out 30 sets of point cloud measurements with different attitudes and extracted the point cloud set of the required feature surfaces, and fitted the normal vectors and the plane centroids of the feature surfaces with the least-squares method. With the 3D model, we can initially determine the desired values of the parameters to be identified, as shown in Table 1. Since the fit gap determines the maximum range of assembly error, the parameters to be identified can be roughly estimated.

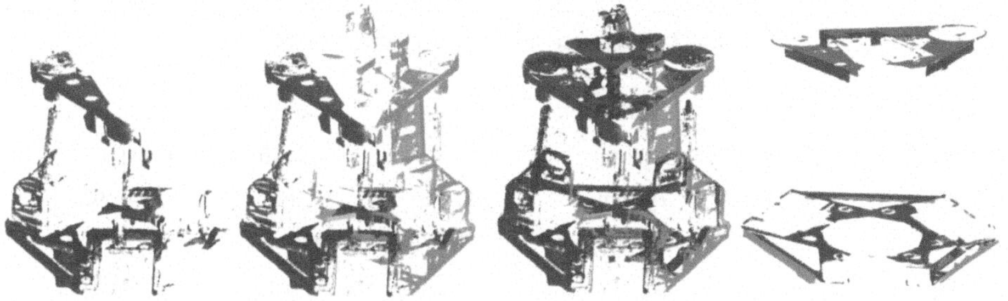

Fig. 3. Point cloud measurement and feature extraction for parallel robots.

Table 1. Expected value of the parameter to be identified

Parameter	Value	Parameter	Value	Parameter	Value
L_1/mm	60	L_2/mm	60	L_3/mm	60
r_1/mm	50	r_2/mm	50	r_3/mm	50
θ_1/rad	3.665	θ_2/rad	1.571	θ_3/rad	5.759
R_1/mm	54	R_2/mm	54	R_3/mm	54
Θ_1/rad	3.665	Θ_2/rad	1.571	Θ_3/rad	5.759

The range of the initial length value L from the center of the ball hinge to the corresponding rotation center is large, so it is defined as ± 6 mm. While the fit gap between the hole and the screw is small, and the positioning errors for the center of the ball hinge and the rotation center are defined as ± 3 mm for r and R, and $\pm 3°$ for θ and Θ. And modify the generation of particle swarm in the optimization algorithm, modify the range class of random distribution of the Positive-Taiwanese distribution, in order to avoid the convergence of the parameters to the vicinity of the non-expected value.

In Eq. (14), 20 sets of measurements are introduced for optimization, the number of optimization populations is set to be 100, the number of iterations is set to be 20, and the inertia weights, local optimal learning factor and global optimal learning factor are set to be 0.3, 0.5, 0.5. The final optimization results are shown in Fig. 4 and Table 2.

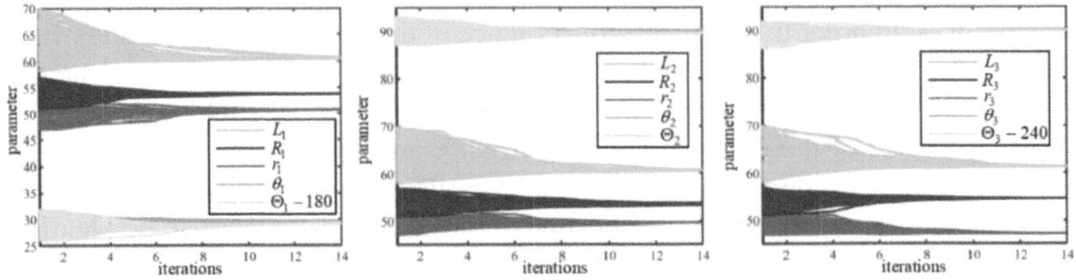

Fig. 4. Parameter identification results

Table 2. Parameter identification results table

Parameter	Value	Parameter	Value	Parameter	Value
L_1/mm	60.55	L_2/mm	60.58	L_3/mm	60.69
r_1/mm	50.21	r_2/mm	49.96	r_3/mm	49.92
θ_1/rad	3.658	θ_2/rad	1.570	θ_3/rad	5.763
R_1/mm	53.66	R_2/mm	53.54	R_3/mm	54.01
Θ_1/rad	3.663	Θ_2/rad	1.564	Θ_3/rad	5.774

4.2 Kinematic Model Accuracy Validation

The kinematic model of the parallel robot is built using the calibrated parameters and compared with the uncalibrated model. Using the remaining results of the measurements for the control experiments, the measured displacements of the moving platform along the axis Z_b and the Euler angles α and β around the X_m and Y_m axes for each set of poses are used as inputs. The actual values of the three sets of linear motors were used as standard value outputs to compare the output errors of the kinematic models before and after calibration. At the same time, in order to accurately compensate for the coupled motion of the moving platform, it is also necessary to calculate the displacements of the platform along the X_b and Y_b (x_m, y_m) by means of the model, and finally compare the accuracy of the model calculations by using the measured values as the standard results.

It can be seen that the direct use of uncalibrated kinematic model, the average error of the output of the control linear motor is about +0.5 mm or more, and the model calculated the compensation amount of x_m and y_m error in the +0.5 mm and −0.6 mm on the floating, respectively. After calibration, the control error of the output of the control linear motor is within ±0.15 mm, and the error of the compensation amount x_m

and y_m is within $+0.2$ mm and -0.18 mm respectively, so it can be tasked to improve the control accuracy and the calculation accuracy of the displacement compensation relatively high which are shown in Figs. 5 and 6.

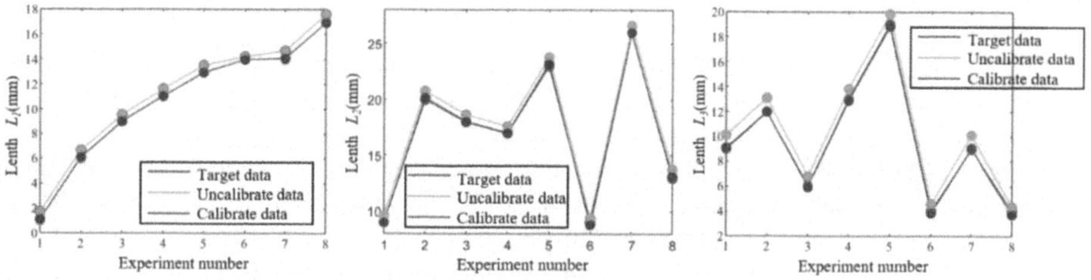

Fig. 5. Linear motor output control experiment results

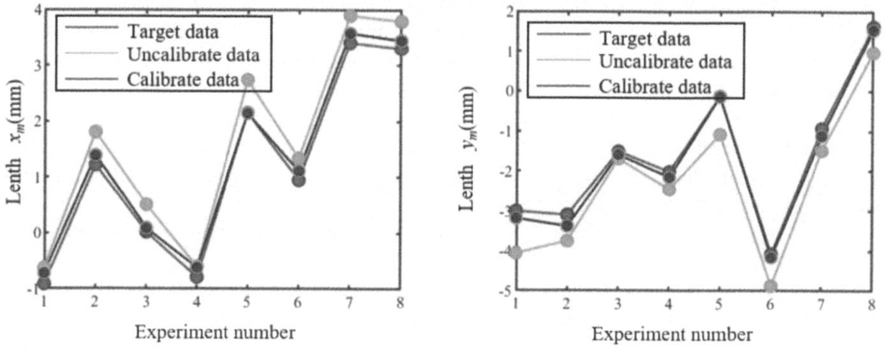

Fig. 6. Compensation x_m and y_m control experiment results

5 Conclusion

In this paper, a method related to the kinematic calibration of a 3-RPS parallel robot is investigated based on a surface laser. The article firstly restructures the parallel robot, which increases the assembly error but eliminates the assembly gap. Robot fabrication and assembly requirements are reduced and more practical. The laser 3D scanning, splicing and feature extraction process are introduced, and a parameter identification strategy is constructed for the parameters to be identified and the robot's motion characteristics to complete the calibration of the kinematic parameters of the parallel robot. Combined with the new kinematic parameters, the kinematic model is optimized and the model accuracy verification method is proposed. Finally, the kinematic parameter calibration experiment of the parallel robot is carried out, and the model accuracy verification is completed using the calibration results, which proves the effectiveness of the kinematic calibration and surface following methods.

Acknowledgement. This work was supported by the National Key Research and Development Program of China under Grant 2023YFB3408603.

References

1. Xie, F., Liu, X.-J.: Analysis of the kinematic characteristics of a high-speed parallel robot with Schönflies motion: mobility, kinematics, and singularity. Front. Mech. Eng. **11**, 135–143 (2016). https://doi.org/10.1007/s11465-016-0389-7
2. Wang, B., Cardou, P., Caro, S.: An approach for predicting the calibration accuracy in planar cable-driven parallel robots and experiment validation. Meccanica **58**, 2177–2196 (2023). https://doi.org/10.1007/s11012-023-01720-y
3. Zhang, T., Ma, G., Cao, Y., He, Y.: Accuracy calibration of a 3-CRU translational parallel robot based on the subset of error measurements. Proc. Inst. Mech. Eng. Part C J. Mech. Eng. Sci. **235**, 3737–3748 (2021). https://doi.org/10.1177/0954406220967691
4. Rubio-Gómez, G., et al.: New sensor device to accurately measure cable tension in cable-driven parallel robots, Sensors **21**, 3604 (2021). https://doi.org/10.3390/s21113604
5. Ren, X., Feng, Z., Yang, D., Wang, X., Gao, D.: Calibration of parallel robots based on orientation constraint and total least squares approach. In: 2013 IEEE International Conference on Information and Automation (ICIA), pp. 828–833. IEEE, Yinchuan, China (2013). https://doi.org/10.1109/ICInfA.2013.6720408
6. Renaud, P., Andreff, N., Lavest, J.-M., Dhome, M.: Simplifying the kinematic calibration of parallel mechanisms using vision-based metrology. IEEE Trans. Robot. **22**, 12–22 (2006). https://doi.org/10.1109/TRO.2005.861482
7. Wu, J., Wang, J., You, Z.: An overview of dynamic parameter identification of robots. Robot. Comput.-Integrat. Manufac. **26**, 414–419 (2010). https://doi.org/10.1016/j.rcim.2010.03.013
8. Sun, T., Zhai, Y., Song, Y., Zhang, J.: Kinematic calibration of a 3-DoF rotational parallel manipulator using laser tracker. Robot. Comput.-Integrat. Manufac. **41**, 78–91 (2016). https://doi.org/10.1016/j.rcim.2016.02.008
9. Traslosheros, A., Sebastian, J.M., Castillo, E., Roberti, F., Carelli, R.: A method for kinematic calibration of a parallel robot by using one camera in hand and a spherical object. In: 2011 15th International Conference on Advanced Robotics (ICAR), pp. 75–81. IEEE, Tallinn, Estonia (2011). https://doi.org/10.1109/ICAR.2011.6088594
10. Tyapin, I., Hovland, G.: Kinematic calibration method for a 5-DOF Gantry-Tau parallel kinematic machine. In: 2013 IEEE International Conference on Robotics and Automation, pp. 4665–4670. IEEE, Karlsruhe, Germany (2013). https://doi.org/10.1109/ICRA.2013.6631241
11. Dindarloo, M.R., Mirjalili, A.S., Khorrambakht, R., Khalilpour, S.A., Cardou, P., Taghirad, H.D.: Kinematic calibration of a spherical parallel robot. In: 2023 11th RSI International Conference on Robotics and Mechatronics (ICRoM), pp. 669–674. IEEE, Tehran, Iran, Islamic Republic of (2023). https://doi.org/10.1109/ICRoM60803.2023.10412613
12. Sun, T., Lian, B., Yang, S., Song, Y.: Kinematic calibration of serial and parallel robots based on finite and instantaneous screw theory. IEEE Trans. Robot. **36**, 816–834 (2020). https://doi.org/10.1109/TRO.2020.2969028
13. Stenz, U., Hartmann, J., Paffenholz, J.-A., Neumann, I.: High-precision 3D object capturing with static and kinematic terrestrial laser scanning in industrial applications—approaches of quality assessment. Remote Sens. **12**, 290 (2020). https://doi.org/10.3390/rs12020290
14. Guo, J., Wang, Q., Park, J.-H..: Geometric quality inspection of prefabricated MEP modules with 3D laser scanning. Autom. Construct. **111**, 103053 (2020). https://doi.org/10.1016/j.autcon.2019.103053

15. Li, M., Du, Z., Ma, X., Dong, W., Gao, Y.: A robot hand-eye calibration method of line laser sensor based on 3D reconstruction. Robot. Comput.-Integrat. Manufac. **71**, 102136 (2021). https://doi.org/10.1016/j.rcim.2021.102136
16. Yu, L., Yan, Y., Ren, S., Zhao,J.: Vision-based method of kinematic calibration and image tracking of position and posture for 3-RPS parallel robot. In: 2017 IEEE International Conference on Mechatronics and Automation (ICMA), pp. 1757–1762. IEEE, Takamatsu, Japan (2017). https://doi.org/10.1109/ICMA.2017.8016083
17. Dou, S., Wang, H., Jiang, Z., Zhan, X.: Design and analysis of a three-degree-of-freedom parallel robot. In: 2020 IEEE 9th Joint International Information Technology and Artificial Intelligence Conference (ITAIC), pp. 1213–1217. IEEE, Chongqing, China (2020). https://doi.org/10.1109/ITAIC49862.2020.9339173
18. Zhang, D., Wang, T., Fan, W.: Structure and machinery simulation of three degrees of freedom parallel pneumatic robot. In: 2015 International Conference on Fluid Power and Mechatronics (FPM), pp. 776–780. IEEE, Harbin, China (2015). https://doi.org/10.1109/FPM.2015.7337219

Design and Analysis of a Multi-panel Solar Array with Struts

Shouzhi Ren[1(✉)], Ying Liu[1], Wenyan Cui[1], Shuai Guan[1], Wenwen Jia[1], and Zhouyi Ren[2]

[1] Beijing Institute of Spacecraft System Engineering, Beijing 100094, China
renshouzhi@163.com

[2] School of Mechanical Engineering, University of Science and Technology Beijing, Beijing 100083, China

Abstract. The solar array is a crucial energy source for satellites. Considering the trend towards miniaturization and rapid maneuverability in satellite technology, solar arrays must balance stowage efficiency and stiffness. This study first conducted an analysis of the structural features of high-stiffness solar arrays. Then, based on the practical requirements of a specific satellite, an innovative solar array design was proposed. This design incorporates a multi-panel Solar Array with Struts, specifically using three struts and two springs to stabilize and reinforce the outer panel among the two solar panels, thereby significantly enhancing the stiffness of the solar array. This paper conducts a finite element analysis model of the solar array to analyze its fundamental frequency in the deployed state. Additionally, a rigid-flexible multibody dynamics simulation model was established to facilitate a comprehensive understanding of the solar array deployment process. The simulation results validate the rationality and superiority of the design. Furthermore, this paper provides a comprehensive summary of the research and presents professional recommendations for designing high-stiffness solar arrays, to offer valuable references and insights for future related studies .

Keywords: solar array · multi-panel · strut · high stiffness

1 Introductory

With the continuous advancement of technology, high-resolution agile remote sensing satellite technology is increasingly moving towards miniaturization and rapid maneuverability. Considering this trend, the design of satellite solar arrays is facing unprecedented challenges. On the one hand, as the overall satellite power consumption has not decreased, the solar array needs to achieve a larger deployment area under the limited installation size to ensure the energy supply of the satellite; on the other hand, to meet the rapid maneuvering needs of the satellite, the solar array must maintain high stiffness in the deployed state to respond various complex space environments.

The existing agile satellite high-stiffness deployable solar arrays usually adopt a configuration of a single solar panel with struts, such as the Pleiades-1A satellite developed

X. Lan et al. (Eds.): ICIRA 2024, LNAI 15201, pp. 108–125, 2025.
https://doi.org/10.1007/978-981-96-0771-6_9

by the European company Astrium, as shown in Fig. 1. A single satellite includes three solar arrays, each supported by two struts arranged on the side to improve its stiffness in the deployed state. The KOMPSAT-3 developed by the Korean Aerospace Research Institute adopts a similar configuration with Pleiades-1A. However, the solar array of KOMPSAT-3 adopts a single strut configuration. The strut consists of two sections, the strut is connected by a spring hinge and located in the middle of the solar panel [3]. The composition and deployment configuration of solar array are shown in Fig. 2. Liu introduced a design for high-rigidity solar arrays whose configuration is similar to the configuration of the KOMPSAT-3 solar arrays. They optimized the support points to attain a higher support rigidity [4]. These agile satellite high-rigidity solar array designs meet the requirements of the satellites by utilizing a single solar panel with struts. However, this particular design has limitations, especially for the satellite with smaller size or needing larger deployment area. Based on above, this paper proposes a design proposal for solar arrays featuring a multi-panel configuration reinforced with struts. This innovative approach is geared towards overcoming the aforementioned technical obstacles, to achieve both the miniaturization and enhanced rigidity of solar arrays. Furthermore, this paper delves the dynamic modeling and examination of these solar arrays, exploring their structural characteristics, deployment process, and dynamic performances by theoretical derivations and simulation verifications.

Apart from this introduction, this paper includes three chapters, outlined as follows: Sect. 2 proposes the design of the multi-panel solar arrays with struts, formulates a finite element analysis model for these solar arrays, and scrutinizes their fundamental frequencies in the deployed state. Section 3 constructs a rigid-flexible coupled dynamic simulation model to offer an insightful analysis of the deployment process of the solar arrays. Lastly, Sect. 4 generalizes the entire paper and provides recommendations for designing high-rigidity solar arrays.

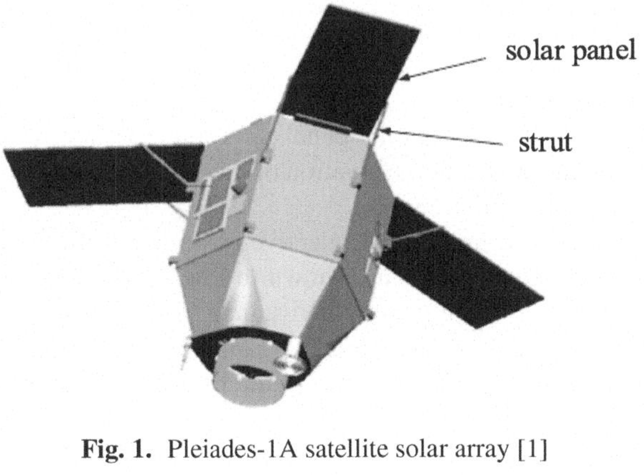

Fig. 1. Pleiades-1A satellite solar array [1]

Fig. 2. The composition and deployment configuration of solar array of KOMPSAT-3

2 Design of a Multi-panel Solar Array with Struts

2.1 Analysis of the Design Requirement

The agile satellite has a relatively small size but high requirements of power. The design scheme of a single solar panel for the solar array cannot meet the overall satellite requirements of power. Upon analysis, it was determined that two solar panels, each with dimensions of 1500 mm × 1080 mm, are required for a single solar array to meet the power demands of the entire satellite. On the other hand, this satellite has high requirements for the stiffness of the solar array in its deployed state, demanding that the fundamental frequency of the solar array in the deployed state should not be less than 5 Hz. However, upon analysis, it was found that the maximum fundamental frequency of a solar array without struts is only 1.5 Hz, which does not meet the design requirements.

Therefore, this paper proposes a design scheme that incorporates struts to enhance the stiffness of the solar array. The deployed state of the solar array is shown in Fig. 3.

2.2 Configuration Design of Solar Array

Selection of Support Points

The support points of the struts and solar panels of a single solar array can be located on either the inner or outer panel, and the position of the support points has been optimized to meet the development requirements.

Based on the design constraints, the selective positions of the support points of the solar array struts on the solar panels are shown in Fig. 4. The total length of the solar array after deployment is 2400 mm, and the distance from the support point to the root of the solar array is denoted as s. The selectable range for s is [500 mm, 2400 mm]. The support position is optimized, to increase the frequency of the solar array in its deployed state.

Initially, an analysis of the fundamental frequency of the solar array is conducted. The torsion and bending frequency vibration modes of the solar array in its deployed state are shown in Figs. 5 and 6 respectively [5]. When the solar panel of the solar array vibrates freely in the transverse direction, its deflection function is expressed as:

$$w_1(\xi, \zeta, t) = W_1(\xi, \zeta)\sin(\omega t) \tag{1}$$

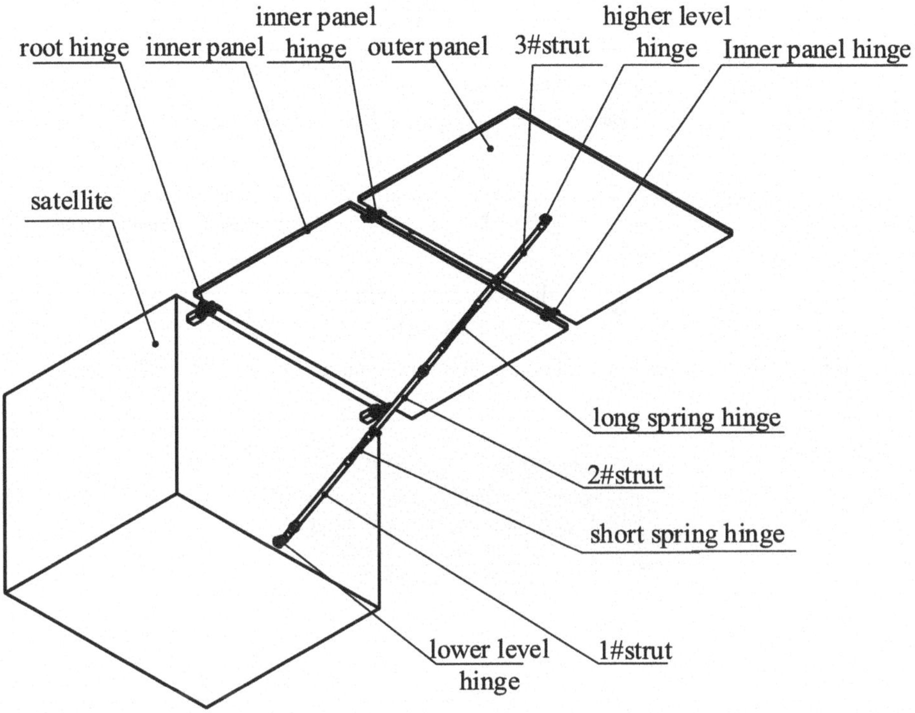

Fig. 3. The composition and deployment configuration of Multi-panel Solar Array with Struts

Based on Eq. (1), the kinetic energy and potential energy expressions of the solar array are established, and further derivation can obtain the natural frequency of the system [5]:

$$f = \frac{\omega}{2\pi} = \frac{1}{2\pi a^2}\sqrt{\frac{\eta D}{\rho h}} \tag{2}$$

When the material and structure of the solar array are determined, the natural frequency of the solar array can be obtained from Eq. (2).

Based on the above analysis, a finite element model of the solar array in its deployed state was established, and the relationship between the bending frequency and torsion frequency of the solar array in its deployed state and the position of the support point is shown in Fig. 7.

As can be seen from Fig. 7, the outer bending frequency of the solar array is highest when the support point of the solar array is at s = 1800 mm. Since this position is located at the center of the outer panel, the solar array configuration with a single strut cannot be used [1, 4]. Therefore, this paper designs a special configuration of struts, which consist of 3 short struts and 2 spring hinges. The strut and spring hinge structures are identical to those proposed by Liu et al. [4] in terms of form, differing only in length. The inner

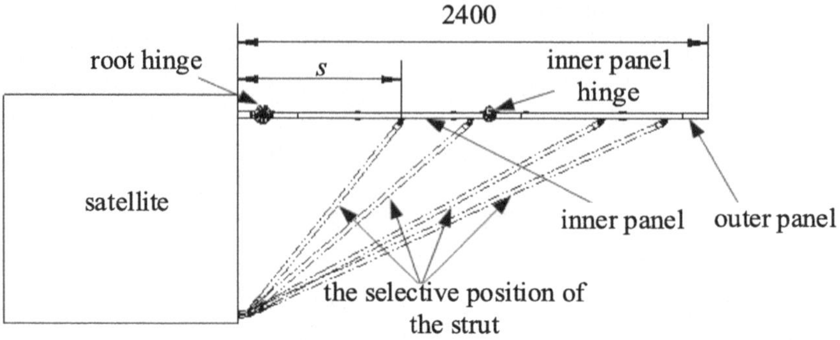

Fig. 4. The position of the support point of the solar array strut on the substrate

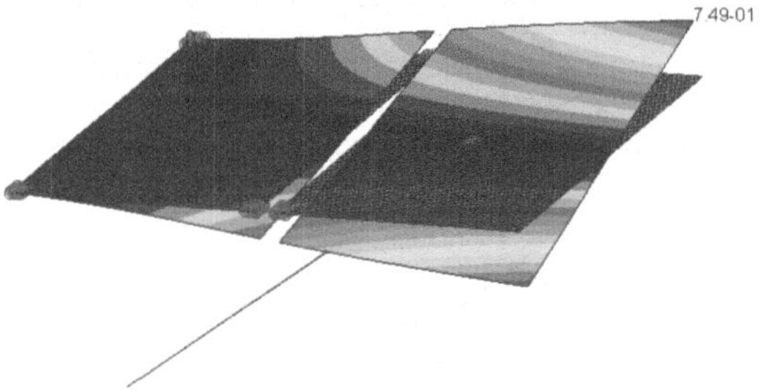

Fig. 5. Torsional frequency of solar array (first order)

Fig. 6. Bending frequency of solar array (second order)

and outer panels are connected by two hinged joints, and the two hinge lines are linked through a linkage device. The detailed composition of the solar array is shown in Fig. 3 [4].

Degrees of Freedom of the System

The motion of the solar array is a typical platform mechanism, with the connection between each component achieved through hinges. The hinge relationships between the components are shown in Fig. 8.

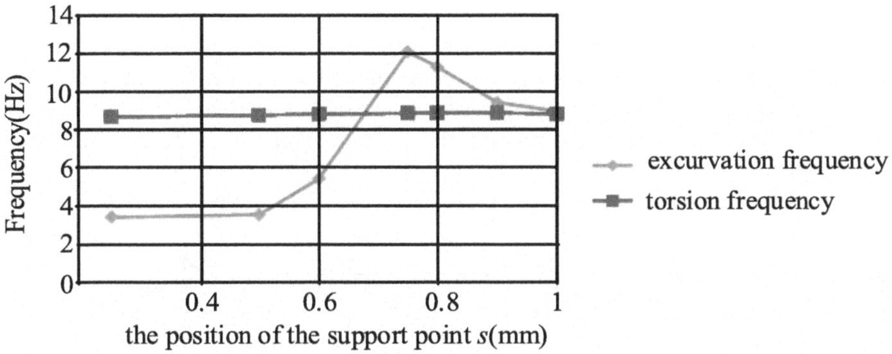

Fig. 7. Relationship between the frequency of the solar array in its deployed state and the position of the support point

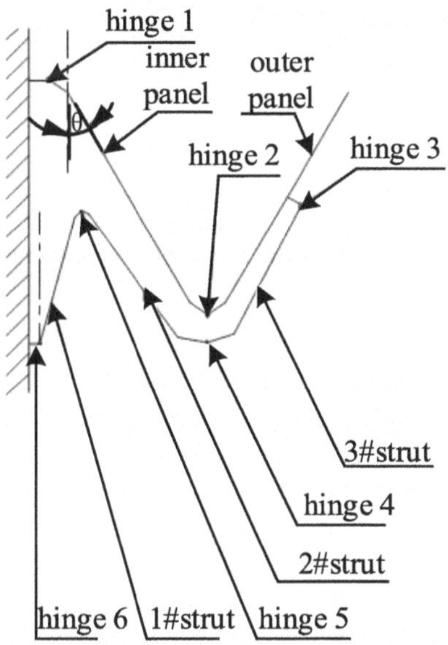

Fig. 8. The hinge relationships between the components of solar array

The system consists of 5 moving components, 6 rotational pairs, and a constraint introduced by a linkage device. Therefore, the degrees of freedom of the system can be calculated as follows:

$$f = \frac{\omega}{2\pi} = \frac{1}{2\pi a^2}\sqrt{\frac{\eta D}{\rho h}} \tag{3}$$

$$F = 3 \times n - 2 \times P_L - 1 = 3 \times 5 - 2 \times 6 - 1 = 2 \tag{4}$$

Determination of Component Sizes

The lengths of the three sections of the solar array strut component must be coordinated with the solar array configuration in both the deployed and retracted states, otherwise the solar array will lose the ability to deploy or retract. The connection relationships and dimensions of the components in both the deployed and retracted states of the solar array are shown in Fig. 9.

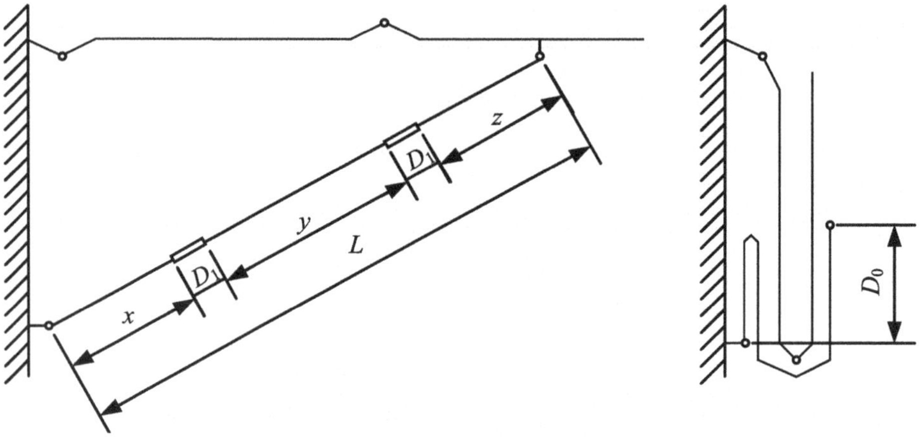

Fig. 9. The connection relationships and dimensions of the components in both the deployed and retracted states of the solar array

Once the solar array configuration is determined, the installation position and length of the struts can also be determined. In Fig. 9, L represents the total length of the strut after deployment, D_1 and D_2 represent the lengths of the two spring hinges after deployment, and D_0 represents the difference in projection distance between the connection points of the strut and the satellite body as well as the outer panel on the satellite body after the solar array is retracted. Connection relationship of various components in the folded state of solar arrays is shown in Fig. 10. All of these values are fixed. Let the lengths of the three struts be x, y, and z respectively. Based on Fig. 8, the relationship between these dimensions can be expressed as follows [6]:

$$\mathrm{x} + y + z = L - D_1 - D_2 \tag{5}$$

$$\mathrm{x} + z - y = D_0 \tag{6}$$

Based on Eqs. (5) and (6), it can be observed that there are three design variables for the struts but only two equations. From a mathematical perspective, there are countless solutions for the lengths x, y, and z of the three struts. However, from an engineering perspective, the length of the third strut can be determined based on constraints such as envelope size and force distribution. The dimensions of each component of the solar array can be determined based on the requirements of the satellite for solar array area, interfaces, and envelope size, as shown in Fig. 11.

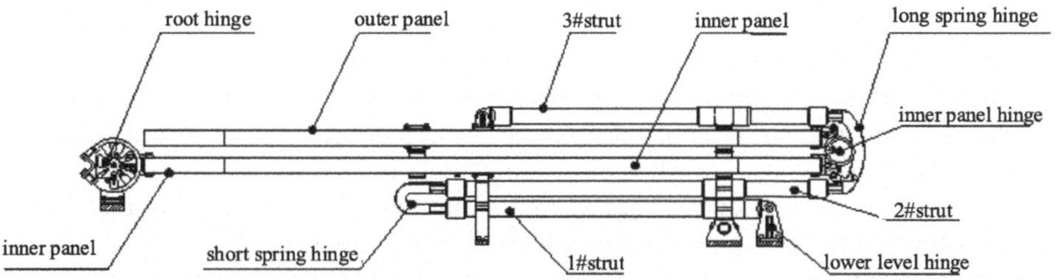

Fig. 10. Connection relationship of various components in the folded state of solar arrays

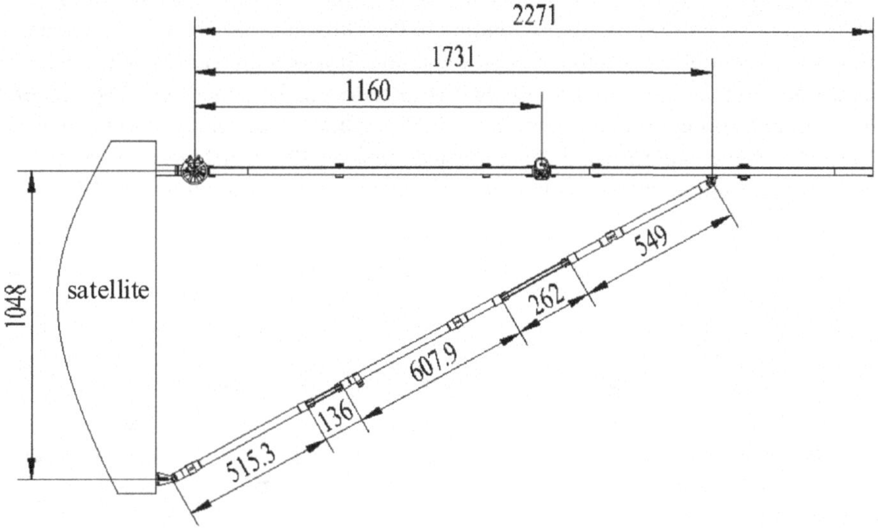

Fig. 11. Connection Relationships and Dimensional Relationships of Various Components in the Deployed State of Solar Arrays

3 Dynamic Modelling and Analysis of Solar Array Deployment Process

3.1 Sample Point Selection Method

The solar array designed in this paper is in a complex working condition with difficult dynamic analysis and solution. Therefore, the design method based on computer simulation experiments is applied to the dynamic analysis process of solar array deployment. Design of Experiments (DOE) is a mathematical statistical method for arranging experiments and analyzing experimental data. It selects a set of samples from the input variable space according to certain rules to form an experimental matrix. Based on this matrix, a series of structured and systematic experiments are conducted to obtain maximized information about system behavior with a smaller experiment scale, shorter experiment cycle, and lower experiment cost, and to draw scientific conclusions [14]. Latin hypercube sampling is applied for typical working condition sampling analysis.

The specific approach of Latin hypercube sampling is to divide the value range of each factor in the k-dimensional design space evenly into n equal parts, thus dividing the entire design space into n_k uniform hypercubic subspaces. Then, n sample points are randomly selected from these subspaces to form a design matrix. The generated n sample points must satisfy that when projecting them onto the value range of any factor in one dimension, there is only one projection point in each sub-interval of that factor. The algorithm for Latin hypercube sampling is shown in Eq. (7) [15].

Where n represents the number of sample points, k represents the number of factors, $\pi^j(1), \ldots, \pi^j(n)$ is an independent and uniformly distributed random sequence of integers from 1 to n, and ${U_j}^i$ is a random number uniformly distributed in the interval [0, 1]. Since the sampling process within each subspace is random, the sample points obtained by Latin hypercube sampling, although tending to be uniformly distributed overall, are not locally the best sample points that meet the spatial filling design requirements. Thus, the optimal Latin hypercube sampling method is introduced. This method adds a criterion to the random Latin hypercube sampling, which further optimizes the order of levels in each column of the experimental design matrix, making the distribution of factor levels among various sample points in the matrix more uniform, as shown in Fig. 12.

$$X_i^j = \frac{\pi^j(i) - U_j^i}{n}, 1 \leq i \leq n, 1 \leq j \leq k \tag{7}$$

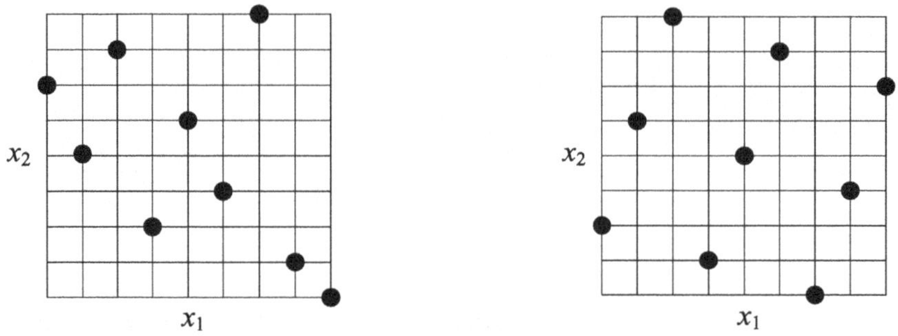

(a) Random Latin hypercube sampling (b) Optimal Latin hypercube sampling

Fig. 12. Distribution of Latin hypercube sampling points

The most commonly used optimization criterion nowadays is the ϕ_p criterion, which is defined based on the maximin distance criterion. The maximin distance criterion aims to maximize the minimum inter-site distance between sample points [16], which is expressed as follows:

$$\min_{1 \leq i,j \leq n, i \neq j} d(x_i, x_j) \rightarrow \max \tag{8}$$

where $d(\boldsymbol{x}_i, \boldsymbol{x}_j)$ represents the Euclidean distance between sample points $\boldsymbol{x}_i$ and $\boldsymbol{x}_j$, defined as [17]:

$$d\left(x_i, x_j\right) = d_{ij} = \left[\sum_{m=1}^{k} \left|x_{im} - x_{jm}\right|^{i}\right]^{1/t}, t = 1or2 \tag{9}$$

If we categorize all inter-site distances d_{ij}, we obtain s distinct distance values. Arranging these values in ascending order gives a distance list (d_1, d_2, ..., d_s) and an index list (J_1, J_2, ..., J_s), where J_i represents the number of sample point pairs with a distance equal to d_i. In this context, the maximin distance criterion can be stated as maximizing d_1 while minimizing J_1. Extending this criterion further, for all $i(i = 1, 2, \ldots, s)$, we aim to maximize di and minimize J_i, leading to the ϕ_p criterion [18] as shown in Eq. (8):

$$\min \phi_p = \left[\sum_{i=1}^{s} J_i d_i^{-p}\right]^{1/p} \tag{10}$$

where p is a positive integer. When p is sufficiently large, the ϕ_p criterion becomes equivalent to the maximin distance criterion. In this paper, we apply this method for sample point selection, laying a foundation for more targeted analysis.

3.2 Establishment of Solar Array Simulation Model

Based on the method in the previous section, sample points are selected first, followed by the establishment of a simulation analysis model for the solar array. As shown in Figs. 10 and 11, the inner and outer panel of the solar array are connected by a linkage device, allow them to deploy simultaneously during deployment. However, the strut contains two spring hinges without linkage between them. Therefore, it is necessary to reasonably set the torque of the spring hinge during the deployment of the solar array to ensure a relatively orderly deployment of the strut through torque control.

To establish a flexible dynamic analysis model for the solar array, the orthogonal Craig-Bampton modes of three struts and two solar panels were calculated using NASTRAN finite element software, and the modal analysis results were imported into ADAMS software. The rope linkage device of the solar array was simulated with corresponding torques. Sensors automatically detect the deployment angle of each component, and when the locking angle of the solar panel is reached, a locking torque is triggered to lock the corresponding hinge line [7–13]·

The stiffness of the spring hinge during locking is provided based on measured data and plotted in the form of a curve. The deployment torque of the two spring hinges is simulated using the measured torque curve. The torque and angle curve for the spring hinge during deployment and locking is shown in Fig. 13. As locking approaches, the driving torque rises sharply and then drops sharply. When the deployment angle reaches 180°, the driving torque is 0 N·m.

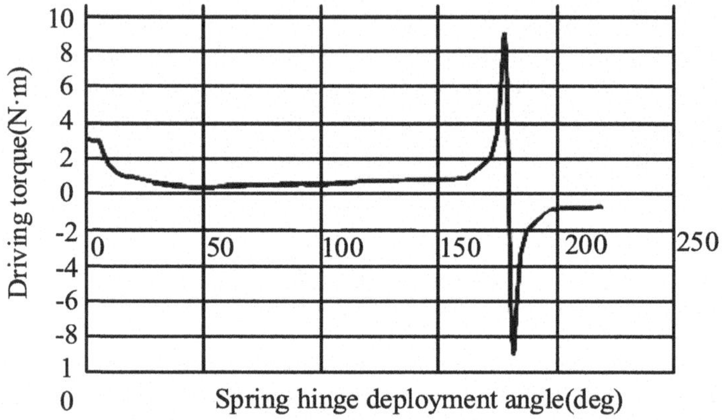

Fig. 13. Relationship between spring hinge torque and deployment angle

The hinges between solar array panels and at the root are driven by ordinary spiral springs. After deployment is in place, the locking impact torque is simulated using the BISTOP double-sided contact function. The established flexible dynamic model of the solar array is shown in Fig. 14.

Fig. 14. Flexible dynamic model of solar arrays

The initial driving torque of the hinge at the base of the solar array and the hinge between panels is 0.25 N·m, and the spring stiffness is 1×10^{-3} N·m/deg. The solar array deployment process is as follows: After the pressing and releasing device releases the restraint on the solar array and struts, the inner panel, outer panel, and strut components are driven by the hinge to deploy. The inner and outer panels are linked and deployed through a linkage mechanism. The linkage mechanism is simulated by designing rope preset tension [14].

According to the connection relationship of the various components of the solar array shown in Figs. 9, 10 and 11, the solar array consists of 5 moving parts and 6 revolute pairs. A set of linkage mechanisms is used to restrict the rotation angles of the hinge at the base and the hinge between panels to make them the same. The total degree of freedom during the solar array deployment process is 2. Therefore, the deployment trajectories of the various components during the solar array deployment process will change with the driving torque on the hinge, that is, the deployment trajectories of the components are not only one.

3.3 Result Analysis

To prevent interference during the deployment of various components of the solar array, the number of reeds in the spring hinges on the solar array struts has been optimized. Since the driving torque of the spring hinge is related only to the number of reeds and not their length, adjustments to the product can be made simply by varying the number of reeds based on the required driving torque. The deployment trajectories of the solar array were calculated based on three working conditions, with varying driving torques set for both short and long spring hinges. The driving torques for the spring hinges in these three working conditions are shown in Table 1.

Table 1. Driving torque in the spring hinge in three working conditions

Working condition	Short spring hinge driving torque	Long spring hinge driving torque
Working condition 1	0.6 Nm	0.6 Nm
Working condition 2	0.7 Nm	0.6 Nm
Working condition 3	0.6 Nm	0.7 Nm

The configurations of the solar array at different deployment states in the three working conditions are shown in Table 2. Based on the above analysis, it is evident that the deployment trajectories of the two spring hinges in the struts differ when they have varying driving torques. When the driving torque of the long spring hinge is less than that of the short one, the struts come into contact with the inner panel during deployment, and the short spring hinge locks first. However, when the driving torque of the long spring hinge is greater than or equal to that of the short one, no contact occurs between the strut components and the inner panel during deployment.

Working condition 1 was selected as the design state for the solar array, and further dynamic analysis was conducted on the deployment process. The locking torque curves of various hinges and the deployment angle curves of the spring hinges during the deployment and locking process of the solar array are shown in Figs. 15, 16, 17, 18, 19 and 20.

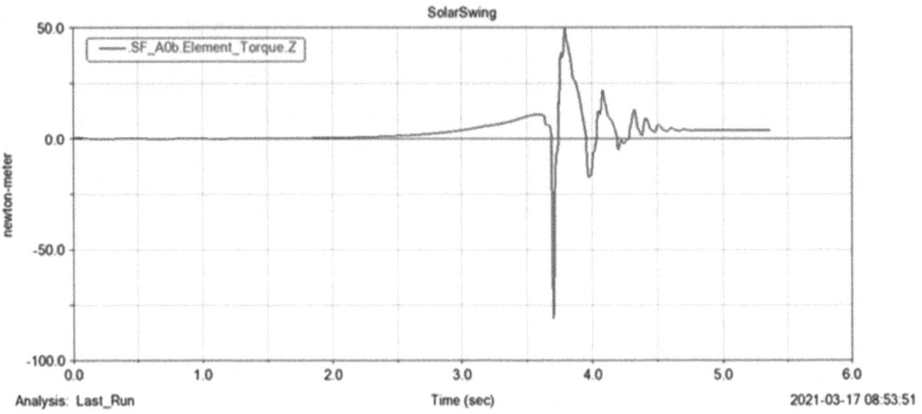

Fig. 15. Root hinge deployment locking torque

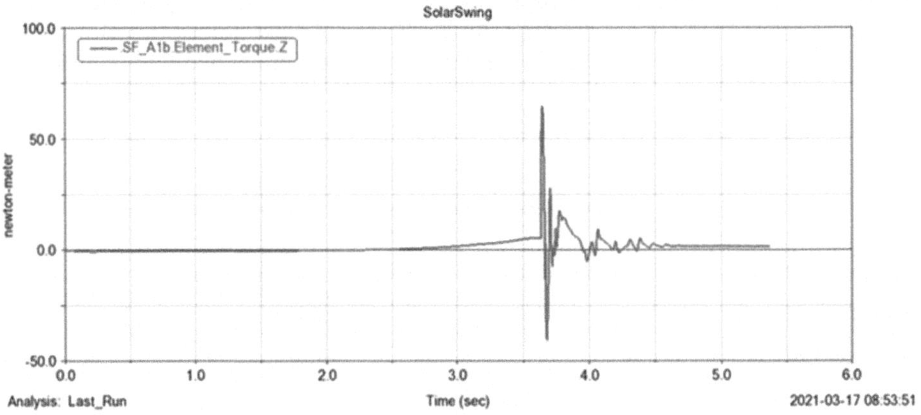

Fig. 16. Inner panel hinge locking impact torque

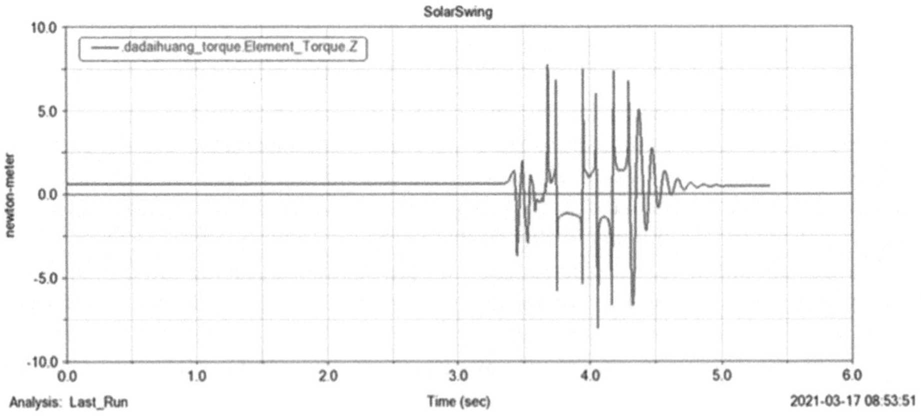

Fig. 17. Long spring hinge deployment locking torque

From the above analysis, the conclusions are as follows:

The solar array possesses two degrees of freedom. However, during the deployment process, the inner and outer panels are constrained by a linkage device, ensuring synchronous deployment and locking. The struts contain two hinges that are not directly connected, resulting in non-unique positions. The deployment trajectory of the solar array is determined by the driving torque of the hinges. When the driving torque in the long spring-hinge exceeds that of the short one, the #3 strut avoids contact with the inner panel during deployment.

Table 2. Configurations of solar arrays at different deployment times in three working conditions

deployment times	Working condition 1	Working condition 2	Working condition 3
0s		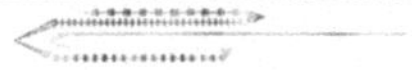	
1.7s			
3s			
3.4s			

(1) The maximum locking impact torque at the root hinge and inter-panel hinge during solar array deployment and locking is 86 N·m, which is far less than the hinge's load-bearing capacity.
(2) Based on the locking torque curve of the long spring-hinge (see Fig. 17) and the angle changes during the deployment and locking process (see Fig. 19), it can be

observed that when the locking impact torque exceeds its instability torque, the long spring-hinge can undergo multiple folding-back phenomena. However, the short spring hinge does not exhibit this reflex behavior. This is because the instability torque of the long spring is lower than that of the short spring. When the long spring becomes unstable, the torque exerted on the short spring decreases, preventing it from becoming unstable.

(3) During the solar array deployment and locking process, the maximum tensile force in the strut reaches 936 N, as shown in Fig. 21. This relatively high tensile force directly acts on the connection points of the solar array's outer panel. Therefore, reinforcement design, such as adding more honeycomb structures, increasing the bonding area between the embedded parts and the honeycomb, is necessary around the embedded parts at the outer panel connection points.

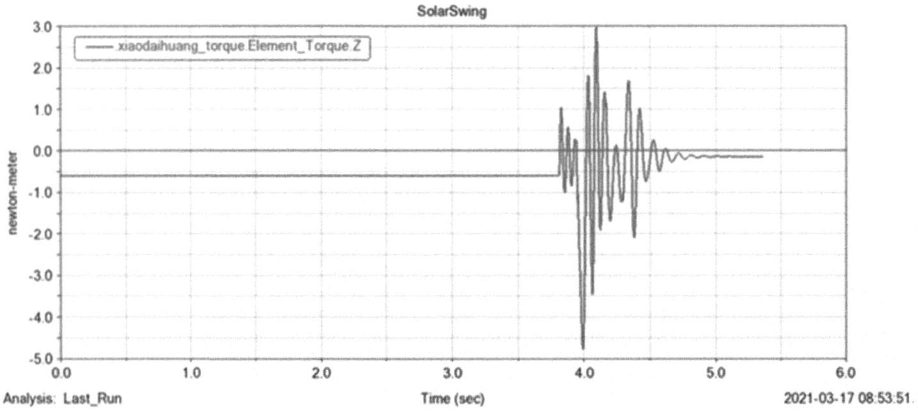

Fig. 18. Short spring hinge deployment locking torque

(4) The solar array configuration described in this paper can smoothly achieve on-orbit deployment and locking, and no collision occurs between components during the deployment process.

Please note that the first paragraph of a section or subsection is not indented. The first paragraphs that follows a table, figure, equation etc. does not have an indent, either.

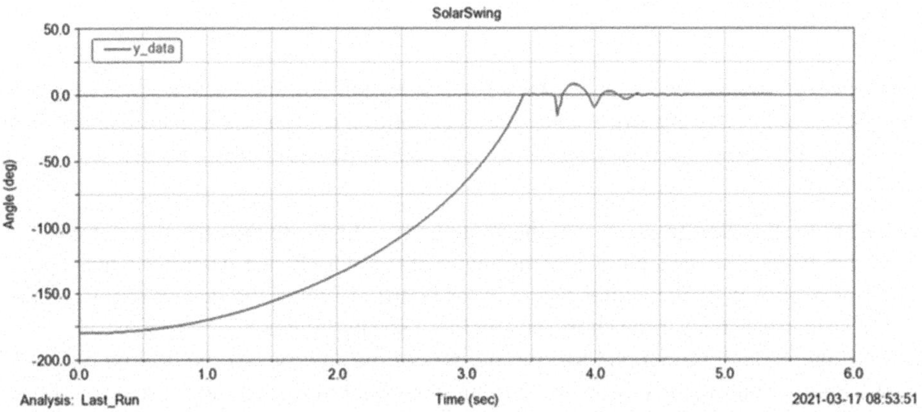

Fig. 19. Long spring hinge deployment angle curve

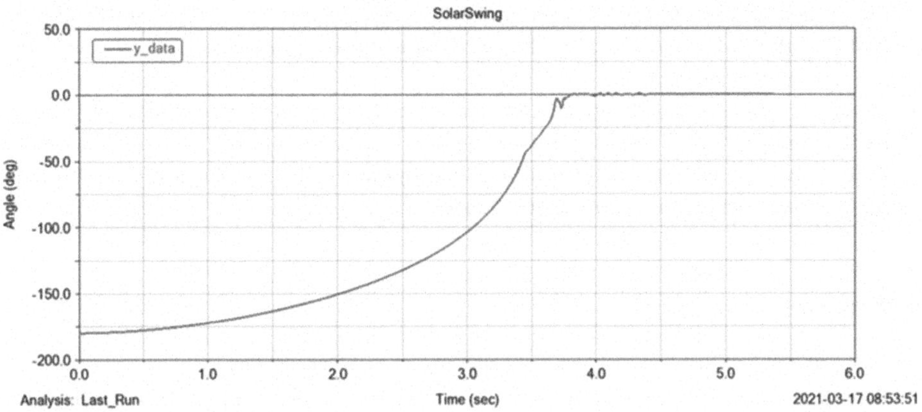

Fig. 20. Short spring hinge deployment angle curve

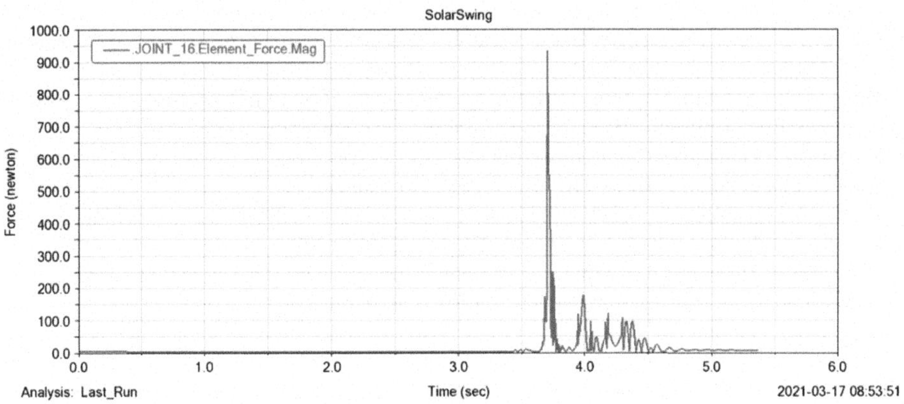

Fig. 21. Maximum tensile force in the strut

4 Conclusion

This paper proposes a new high-stiffness solar array configuration scheme with multiple solar panels supported by struts, and conducts optimal design and dynamic analysis of the deployment process. Based on the design and analysis results, the conclusions are as follows:

(1) The outer bending frequency of the solar array is highest when the support position of the strut on the solar panel is at the center of the outer board. Therefore, the support point is chosen at the center of the outer board. To meet the design requirements, the strut consists of three short rods and two spring hinges;
(2) During the deployment and locking process of the solar array, the driving torque of the long spring hinge should be more than or equal to that of the short spring hinge to ensure that the strut does not come into contact with the inner board during the deployment of the solar array;
(3) When the solar array is locked, the tension on the strut is relatively high, with a maximum value of 936N. It is recommended to reinforce the design at the support point of the solar array's outer board during the design phase and to verify the production test pieces;
(4) When the solar array is deployed and locked, the long spring hinge exhibits a folding-back phenomenon. Therefore, it is necessary to pay attention to the surface condition of the spring hinge after multiple deployments of the solar array, and timely replacement is required if there are creases.

References

1. Baker, D.: Jane's space systems and industry. Spaceflight **56**(1), 31 (2014)
2. Kim, K.W., Kim, S.W., Lim, J.H., et a1.: Solar array deployment mechanism development for LEO EO satellite. In: The 60th International Astronautical Congress, Daejoen, South Korea12–16 OCt 2009
3. Kim, K.W., Kim, S.H., Hwang, D.S., et al.: Design of tape spring hinges for solar array considering deployment performances. In: 65th International Astronautical Congress 2014: Our World Needs Space, IAC 2014, pp. 5591–5594. International Astronautical Federation, IAF (2014)
4. Zhiquan, L., Yuemin, W., Jingya, M.: Design and verification of high-stiffness solar wing on agile satellites. J. Astron. **40**(6), 621–627 (2019). (in Chinese)
5. Zhengfa, L., Dengqing, C.: Optimization analysis of supporting point distribution for folding solar panels. J. Astron. **36**(6), 661–666 (2015). (in Chinese)
6. Kaijie, D., Duanling, L., Qiuhong, L., et al.: Design and analysis of a novel hinged boom based on cable drive. Chin. J. Aeronaut. **35**(3), 592–606 (2022)
7. Shouzhi, R., Hongjun, S., Hailing, P.: Dynamic simulation for deployment of a 2-dimension solar array. Spacecraft Eng. **21**(4), 32–36 (2012). (in Chinese)
8. Tianzhi, C., Hailing, P., Liping, L., et al.: Simulation and test of solar array deployment and locking. In: Beijing: Communication Conference by Committee of Structure Strength and Environment Engineering, China Society of Astronautics and the Eighth Specialty Information Web. CASC (2007). (in Chinese)

9. Guangji, Q., Dengyun, Y., Fengnian, L., et al.: The flexible multi-body shock dynamics finite analysis for the deployment and locking of the solar array. Spacecraft Eng. **6**(1,2), 10–17 (1997). (in Chinese)
10. Xian, W., Tianzhi, C., Hongyou, C.: Dynamics simulation analysis of solar array ground deployment and locking. Spacecraft Eng. **20**(3), 86–92 (2011). (in Chinese)
11. Liemin, C.: The deployment analysis of satellite solar array. China Space Sci. Technol. **2**, 21–26 (1992). (in Chinese)
12. Tianzhi, C., Xian, W., Hongyou, C.: Method of modifying maximum impact load on solar array deployment and locking process. Spacecraft Eng. **20**(6), 55–62 (2011). (in Chinese)
13. Weituo, L.: The design and analyses of close cable loop of solar array. Chin. Space Sci. Technol. **2**, 52–57 (2006). (in Chinese)
14. Weissman, S.A., Anderson, N.G.: Design of experiments (DoE) and process optimization. A review of recent publications. Organic Process Res. Develop. **19**(11), 1605–1633 (2015)
15. Shields, M.D., Zhang, J.: The generalization of Latin hypercube sampling. Reliab. Eng. Syst. Saf. **148**, 96–108 (2016)
16. Jing, Z., Jin, X., Kai, J., et al.: Optimal sliced latin hypercube designs with slices of arbitrary run sizes. Mathematics **7**(9), 854 (2019)
17. Krislock, N., Wolkowicz, H.: Euclidean distance matrices and applications. Springer, US (2012)
18. Johnson, M.E., Moore, L.M., Ylvisaker, D.: Minimax and maximin distance designs. J. Statist. Plan. Inferen. **26**(2), 131–148 (1990)

Design and Analysis of a Consecutive Aquatic Jumping Robot Inspired by Water-Dwelling Frog Hind Legs

Qianqian Chen, Jiawei Dong, Wei Wang, Lin Zhong, Huan Peng, Xiongqian Wu, Haifei Zhu, Yisheng Guan, and Tao Zhang(✉)

School of Electromechanical Engineering, Guangdong University of Technology, Guangzhou 510006, China
tzhang@gdut.edu.cn

Abstract. Frogs dwelling in water possess an extraordinary ability for explosive power, which enables them to leap out of the water from a floating position. The energy storage and release of the hind leg tendons and muscles are crucial for their jumping in water. To emulate the bone structure of frog hind legs and their unique jumping movement behavior, this paper proposes a consecutive aquatic jumping robot (CAJR). The CAJR comprises a four-link mechanism, two bionic water-pushing flippers and a streamlined head, which stores energy through rubber bands and employs a release mechanism and a drive rope to achieve the effect of consecutive energy storage and instantaneous release. The structure of the CAJR was initially analysed statically and dynamically. Subsequently, the energy storage capacity of the CAJR was investigated, and the maximum tension of the drive rope is 63 N. Thereafter, the terrestrial jumping process was simulated by ADAMS, revealing a jumping height to 1372 mm. The trigger was optimally designed by ANSYS to analyze the maximum equivalent stress at triggering. The relationship between the velocity and static pressure of the fluid during the process of streamlined head water discharge was simulated by Fluent. The design of this frog-inspired aquatic jumping robot offers a novel approach, with broad potential for rescue or exploration in complex terrain.

Keywords: Jumping robot · biomimetic · aquatic jumping · fluid simulation · hydrostatic analysis · dynamics analysis

1 Introduction

Over millions of years, animals in nature have evolved highly agile modes of movement. As a typical amphibian, water-dwelling frogs have excellent cross-domain jumping ability and environmental adaptability, which enables them to adapt to survival

Supported by the National Natural Science Foundation of China (Grant No. 52275011), the Natural Science Foundation of Guangdong Province (Grant No. 2023B1515020080), the Young Elite Scientists Sponsorship Program by CAST (Grant No. 2021 QNRC001), and the Natural Science Foundation of Guangzhou (Grant No. 2024A04J2552).

X. Lan et al. (Eds.): ICIRA 2024, LNAI 15201, pp. 126–138, 2025.
https://doi.org/10.1007/978-981-96-0771-6_10

activities such as feeding and avoiding natural enemies in complex environments [1]. Bionics involves designing and fabricating artificial systems with biological properties or functions inspired by nature [2]. The frog-inspired robot is a kind of representative biomimetic robots, primarily move by jumping or swimming [3]. But compared with swimming, jumping has greater flexibility and better adapts to unstructured terrain.

Frog-inspired jumping robots (FIJR) typically utilise motors, hydraulics and explosive actuators for energy conversion [4]. The most direct way to convert mechanical and elastic potential energy into driving energy is by using a motor. In 2014, Ahn et al. [5] proposed a small FIJR based on motor torsion and elastomer energy storage. The robot employed a four-link mechanism to mimic the movement of the hind legs of frog and achieve high jumps through instant elastic release. In 2020, Hong Chong et al. [6] designed a FIJR by combining series-connected elastic actuator with a parallel elastic four-link mechanism. Compared with motors, hydraulic linear actuators have a higher power-to-weight ratio. In 2017, Yang Li et al. [2] designed a hydraulically-driven FIJR. The leg mechanism resembles a diamond-shaped four-link spring mechanism. However, the velocity response of the hydraulic linear actuator is nonlinear, and the fluid compressor or energy storage device is not favourable for mounting on the robot. From 2019 to 2021, the HIT developed two FIJRs utilising explosively driven soft actuators, achieving a jump distance of 1.4 m and a jump height of 0.6 m [7,8]. The chemical fuel drive offers high energy density but lacks the continuous fuel supply and safety compared to motors. The current FIJRs have limitations, including limited ability to traverse different terrains, inability to achieve consecutive jumping, and drive optimization in certain designs.

The consecutive aquatic jumping robot (CAJR) inspired by water-dwelling frog hind legs, is driven by a combination of motors and elastic units. The motor drive mode boasts a simple structure, easy to control, and reliable in operation. Elastic units such as rubber bands meet the demand for miniaturization and lightweighting of FIJRs [5]. The novel aquatic jumping movement mode of the CAJR enables consecutive jumps and adjustable angle in water, offering environmental adaptability. Its suitability for exploration and communication system carriers in complex terrains [4]. It can provide certain value for the design and research of aquatic consecutive jumping robots.

2 Electro-Mechanical System Design

The movement of water-dwelling frog is characterized by using their strong hind legs to propel themselves out of the water. Consequently, we bionically map and simplify its skeleton, and a CAJR inspired by the hind legs of frog is shown in Fig. 1(a-b). The CAJR has a streamlined head for breaking the surface tension of the water, a four-link mechanism as the kinematic structure [2], eight rubber bands as the elastic potential energy storage unit, and two bionic water-pushing flippers to provide kinetic energy for the CAJR to aquatic jumping. The streamlined head reduces the resistance of water by streamlining the design, which in turn improves the motion performance. The CAJR employs Kevlar rope as the drive rope to control the energy storage and release of the elastic potential energy storage units, which are made of a material with high strength, good abrasion resistance, and can withstand high tensile force. A trigger is fixed on the drive rope to unlock the release mechanism, thereby instantaneously releasing the elastic potential energy. The control system manages elastic potential energy storage unit and controls the center of gravity adjustment mechanism to achieve jumping posture adjustment of the CAJR in water.

Table 1. Design parameters of each component and the overall design of the CAJR.

Components	Mass (g)	Length (mm)	Material
Head	41.1	80.00	PLA
Frog-inspired Thigh Rods	3.9	54.23	PLA
Frog-inspired Crus Rods	4.1	54.23	PLA
Bionic Water-pushing Flippers	7.2	124.00	PLA
Center of Gravity Adjustment Mechanism	48.0	44.40	PLA
CAJR	119.2	318.66	PLA

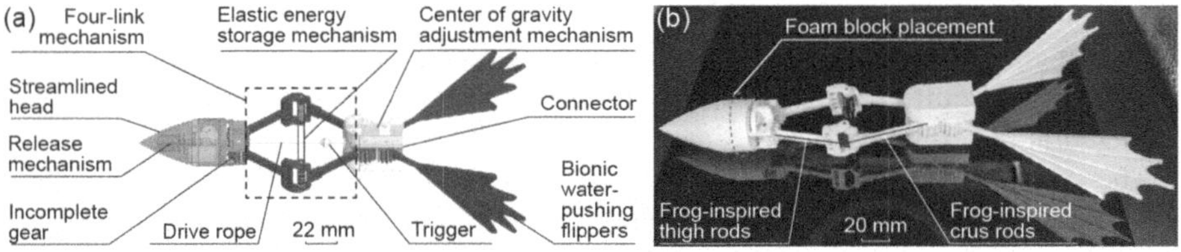

Fig. 1. Mechanism design of the CAJR. (a) 3D model. (b) Prototype.

The four-link mechanism (Fig. 1(a)) mimicked the structure of a thigh and crus of frog following biomimetic principles, with elliptical cross-sections for the links. The mechanism utilized PLA material for high strength and excellent toughness. The frog-inspired thigh and crus rods are connected by aluminium alloy metal pins, and an elastic potential energy storage unit is provided, and eight rubber bands are placed in the groove. With the rubber bands, the four-link mechanism expands transversely for energy storage and lengthwise for energy release. A water filter at the connection of the rod reduces resistance for the CAJR during aquatic jumps. Gear meshing drives the rods, enabling them to possess a dual degree-of-freedom (DOF) and enhancing structural stability. The end of frog-inspired thigh rods are incomplete gears, fixed to the lower end of the head by a metal pin, and the middle 3/4 of the skeleton is driven by the drive rope and drop-shaped trigger. The frog-inspired crus rods are complete gears being fixed in the connector.

The release mechanism based on the latch mechanism is designed (Fig. 2(a)). The CAJR is equipped with a DC gear motor at the head, whose output shaft is connected to drive the drive rope winding on the inclined sleeve. The baffle of latch mechanism secures the pendulum horizontally, while the drive rope wraps around the rotating of pendulum axis to alter its winding direction. When the trigger on the drive rope pushes the baffle, it opens, unlocking the pendulum. The drive rope experiences tension in the negative y-axis direction. The beveled surface allows the drive rope to naturally wrap around the top. Instantly, the four-link mechanism loses its binding force in the y-axis direction, releasing the elastic potential energy (Fig. 2(b)) of the rubber bands [7]. After completing the jump, the pendulum and frame are fixed, enabling the tension spring to drive the rope upward. Sufficient tension pulls the pendulum onto the baffle, where it re-locks, and the drive rope is rewound on the beveled sleeve, repeating the energy storage and release process.

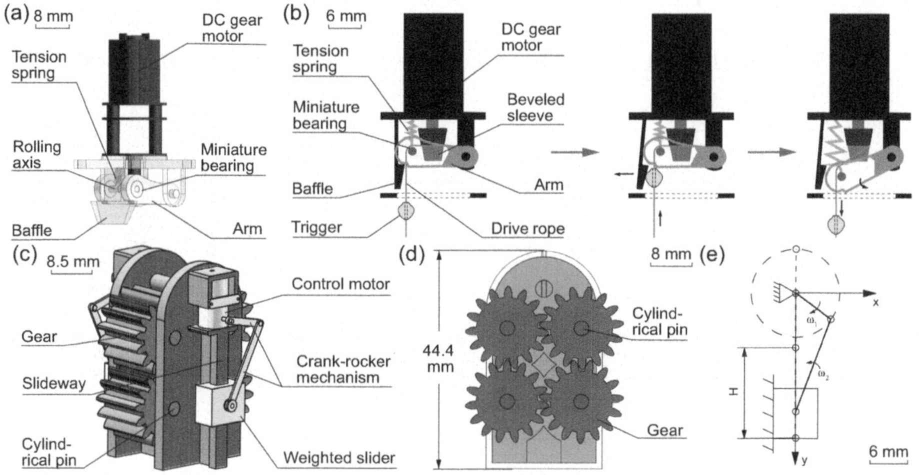

Fig. 2. Design of release mechanism and center of gravity adjustment mechanism. (a) Structure of release mechanism. (b) Schematic diagram of the release process. (c) Structure of center of gravity adjustment mechanism. (d) Sectional view. (e) Schematic diagram.

A symmetrically distributed center of gravity adjustment device was designed (Fig. 2). The motor drives the crank linkage mechanism to drive the heavy slider for sliding with a maximum adjustment distance H = 10 mm (Fig. 2(e)), thus achieving the effect of adjusting attitude of the CAJR. The center of gravity is adjusted by encircling the foam block around its head (Fig. 1(b)), so that the top of its head is located on the water surface and the overall attitude of the CAJR is perpendicular to the water surface. The mechanism ensures that center of gravity of the CAJR is at the connector and maintains a head-up attitude in the water. When energy is stored, the gyroscope in the control system provides feedback on current attitude of the CAJR. This information is used by the main control board to adjust the motor angle. The output shaft of motor drives the crank-rocker mechanism, adjusting the positions of heavy sliders to shift the center of gravity of the CAJR, adjusting its attitude before aquatic jumping.

The bionic water-pushing flippers, mimicking frog fins skeletal structure (Fig. 3(a)), are the primary driving unit during aquatic jumping, significantly impacting overall motion efficiency of the CAJR. The bionic water-pushing flippers with the fin plates and tarsometatarsal joints being open [8] when pushing water (Fig. 3(b)). Constructed from PLA material, they withstand deformation and convert downward thrust into water reaction force. This skeleton-like design strengthens flipper edges, reduces energy loss from deformation, and prevents water flow to sides, maximizing driving force.

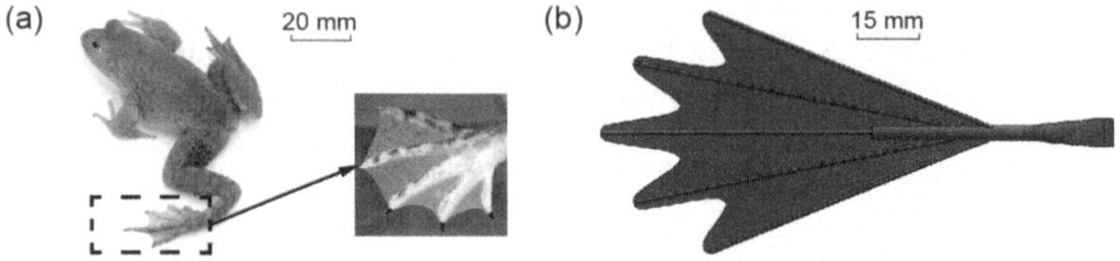

Fig. 3. Bionic Mapping of frog flippers. (a) Entities with frog flippers. (b) 3D model.

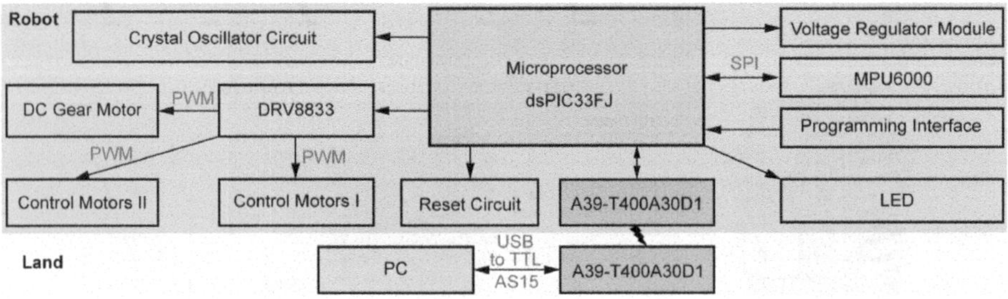

Fig. 4. Block diagram of controller.

To enhance the autonomy and reliability of the CAJR, a control system was designed. The system structure frame diagram was shown in Fig. 4. The control circuit board of the CAJR is fixed in the head, taking into account the high quality characteristics of the dsPIC33FJ such as low cost, low power consumption, high performance of digital signal processing, an external wireless serial communication module (A39-T400A30D1) is connected to the motor drive module (DRV8833) through the IO port to generate PWM to drive the three-way DC gear motors, one way to control the motor to pull the drive rope, and two ways to control the motors on the connector for the adjustment of the center of gravity of the mechanism. The gyroscope and accelerometer MPU6000 are connected through SPI bus interface [11].

3 Static and Dynamic Analysis

3.1 Static Analysis of Links

The biomimetic design based on the structure of frog hind legs simplified the jumping mechanism into four links with four joints and underwent modeling and static analysis. The storage of elastic potential energy was also taken into account (Fig. 5(a)).

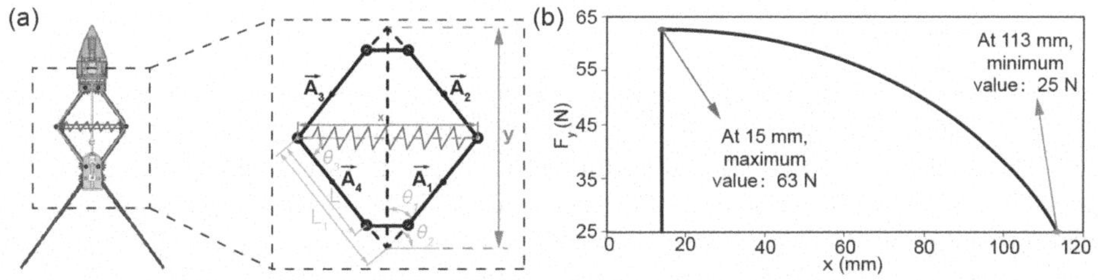

Fig. 5. Mechanism schematic and tensile force calculation results. (a) Simplified mechanism. (b) Calculation results of tensile force with x-direction data.

The rubber bands are employed as the energy storage unit. Energy storage is achieved through a DC gear motor, which rotates to wind the drive rope, shortening the distance between the streamlined head and the connector. This results in an increase in the transverse distance of the four-link mechanism, thereby stretching the rubber bands to store elastic potential energy. By analysing the relationship between force and displacement in the transverse and longitudinal directions can be obtained (Fig. 5(a)). The transverse and longitudinal distances of the four-link mechanism are represented by x and y respectively. The displacement relationship [12] between x and y can be expressed as:

$$y = 2\sqrt{L_1^2 - x^2/4}, x = \sqrt{4L_1^2 - y^2} \tag{1}$$

where $L_1 = 54x/(x - 15)$ is the length of one side of the rhombus.

Following the principle of virtual work, it can be concluded that for the infinitesimal displacement of the mechanism ($F_x dx = F_y dy$). F_x is the spring force along the x-axis, whereas F_y is the longitudinal tension of the drive rope along the y-axis. The relationship between the F_y of the drive rope and the F_x can be expressed as:

$$F_y = \frac{F_x}{dy/dx} = \frac{2k\left(x - x_0\right)\sqrt{L_1^2 - x^2/4}}{x} \tag{2}$$

where $k = 0.084$ N/mm and $x_0 = 15$ mm (as determined by experiments) are the elasticity constants and the undeformed lengths of rubber bands.

The relationship between the longitudinal length of the drive rope and the spring length was shown in Eqs. 1 and 2, and considering the rubber bands, F_x can be expressed as:

$$F_x = \frac{F_y}{dx/dy} = ky\left(1 - \frac{x_0}{\sqrt{4L_1^2 - y^2}}\right) \tag{3}$$

During the process of elastic potential energy storage (Fig. 5(b)), the value of x within the range of 0 to 15 mm (as the undeformed length of the rubber band) is 0. As x exceeds 15 mm, the tension force of the drive rope decreases continuously as the transverse coordinate increases. Meanwhile, the decreasing angle between the frog-inspired thigh rods and the frog-inspired crus rods increases the transverse tension of the drive rope, gradually reducing the required longitudinal tension.

3.2 Dynamic Analysis

The model has only 2-DOF and employed a generalised coordinate. The angle θ_1 (in the global coordinate) between the frog-inspired crus rods and the frog-inspired thigh rods. The angle θ_2 (in the global coordinate) between the frog-inspired crus rods and the horizontal plane. The position of the center of mass of the rods are as shown in the following equation:

$$\overrightarrow{A_1} = (0.5\,L\cos\theta_2, 0.5\,L\sin\theta_2)^{\mathsf{T}} \tag{4}$$

where $\boldsymbol{A}_i$ is the position vector of each rod and L is the length of each rod:

$$\overrightarrow{A_2} = (\,L\cos\theta_2 + 0.5\,L\cos(\theta_1+\theta_2)\,, L\sin\theta_2 + 0.5\,L\sin(\theta_1+\theta_2)\,)^{\mathsf{T}} \tag{5}$$

$$\overrightarrow{A_3} = (\,L\cos(\theta_1+\theta_2) + 0.5\,L\cos\theta_2, L\sin(\theta_1+\theta_2) + 0.5\,L\sin\theta_2\,)^{\mathsf{T}} \tag{6}$$

$$\overrightarrow{A_4} = (0.5\,L\cos(\theta_1+\theta_2)\,, 0.5\,L\sin(\theta_1+\theta_2))^{\mathsf{T}} \tag{7}$$

Dynamics analysis of the model treats each component as a separate part of the overall mechanics (which aids in jumping), giving the dynamics equations as [13]:

$$\begin{aligned} &\left[(2M_B + M_S + 5M_L)\cot\theta_3 + M_L\tan\theta_3 + \left(\frac{4I_L}{L^2\cos\theta_3\sin\theta_3}\right)\right]\ddot{\theta}_3 \\ &- [2M_B + M_S + 4M_L]\,\dot{\theta}_3^{\,2} - \left[\sum_{i=1}^{2} k\left(2 - \frac{x_0}{L\cos\theta_3}\right)\right] = \left[\frac{1}{2\,L^2\cos\theta_3\sin\theta_3}\right]Q_k \end{aligned} \tag{8}$$

where angle θ_3 between the frog-inspired thigh rods and the frog-inspired crus rods.

The body mass is represented as M_B, the spring mass as M_S, and the leg mass as M_L. The specific values are shown in Table 1. I_L and L are the moment of inertia (g.mm^2) and the leg length, respectively. The non-conservative forces, such as the shape resistance of all components, are represented by Q_k, provided that friction is neglected. When the CAJR is in a fully stored energy state, the clamp angle θ_3 is approximately 9.96°, which gives the maximum jump energy. As the four-link mechanism restricts the direction of motion to the y-axis during the jumping, the 2-DOF model is an effective in dynamics.

3.3 Gravity and Elastic Potential Energy

The potential energy of the CAJR is mainly composed of gravitational potential energy and elastic potential energy stored in the rubber bands. Taking the ground as the zero point, the gravitational potential energy of the CAJR was represented as:

$$V_G = \sum_{i=1}^{4} M_{Li} g \overrightarrow{A_{iy}} \tag{9}$$

where M_{Li} is the mass of each frog-inspired hind leg rod; g = 9.8 N/kg is the acceleration of gravity; $\overrightarrow{A_{iy}}$ is the position vector in the vertical direction of each rod.

The rubber bands are mounted on a metal pin between the frog-inspired thigh rods and the frog-inspired crus rods assembly with an elastic potential energy expression:

$$V_P = 1/2k\left(x - x_0\right) \tag{10}$$

where k and x_0 are the elastic constant and the undeformed length, respectively.

4 Experiments and Simulation Verification

4.1 Tensile Force Test Experiment

To guarantee that the drive rope and release mechanism can withstand the requisite pulling force of the rubber bands when storing energy, as well as to validate the pulling force analysis presented in Sect. 3, the design of the tensile force experiment for the robot energy storage is presented here.

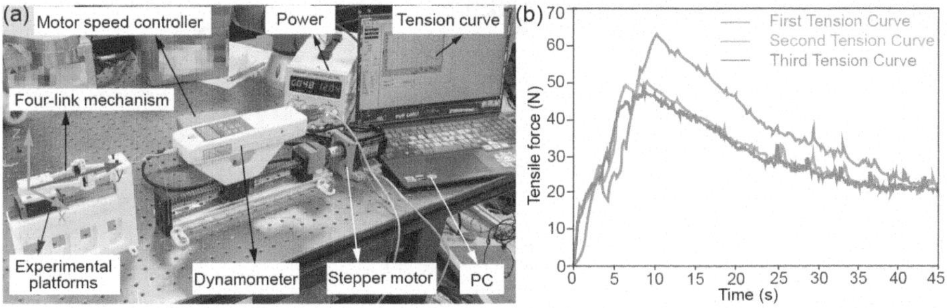

Fig. 6. Tension test experiment. (a) Experimental platform. (b) Experimental data.

Firstly, the experimental platform consisted of a base and a slider. The gear portion of the four-link mechanism were fixed separately on the base and slider, and the two are connected by metal pins to the groove. The four rubber bands were secured onto the fixture to simulate the stretching process of the CAJR. To ensure accurate force measurement and prevent damage to the beam caused by external forces, we ensured that the dynamometer, base, and slider remained within the xy-plane (Fig. 6(a)). Secondly, a 150-mm slide rail is installed on the base to match the square slide base with built-in ball bearings, reducing friction, and is then bolted to the slider. Finally, the stepper motor drive ensures the dynamometer moves uniformly along the y-axis, and the data of tension force is obtained through the host computer.

The maximum tension values measured in the three experiments were 63.11 N, 50.15 N, and 47.45 N (Fig. 6(b)) respectively. The initial experiment corresponds to the theoretical calculation in the Sect. 3 with a matching degree of 99.82% for the maximum tension, and the trends align. As the number of jumps increases, the material characteristics of rubber bands will lead to fatigue. The energy losses of the second and third experimental were 20.54% and 25.92%, respectively, in comparison to the first.

4.2 Kinematics Simulation of Mechanism Simplified Model

To investigate the jumping performance of the CAJR, the dynamics study is carried out in this section using automatic dynamic analysis of mechanical system (ADAMS).

Firstly, the 'x_t' file is generated by Solidworks and imported into ADAMS. The material properties of each component of the model were set to be the same as those of the actual objects (The density of PLA is 1.668e-3 g/mm^3) was shown in Table 1. Secondly, the connection relationships between components and contact friction have been configured. Then, a movable joint was added to the streamlined head. Finally, by adding a movable driver to the head, the motion of consecutive jumping of the CAJR driven by a DC gear motor was simulated, and the motion process lasts for 50 s.

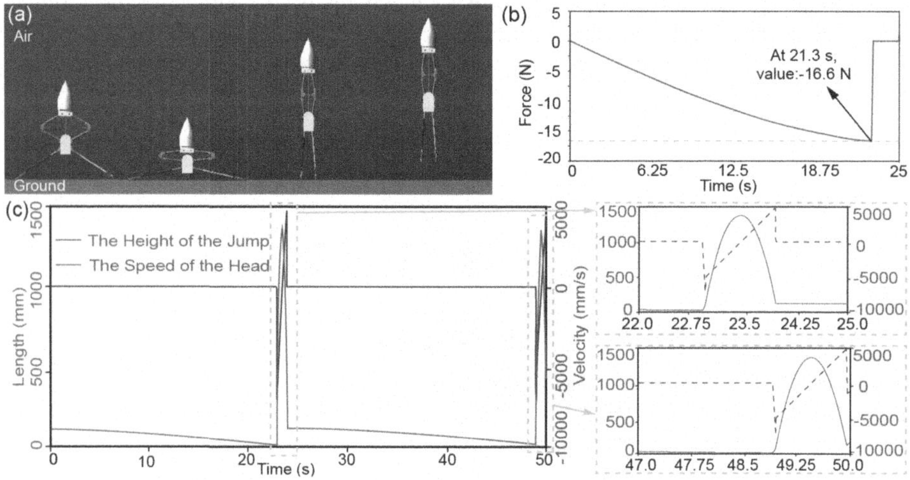

Fig. 7. Jumping process simulation by ADAMS. (a) Simulation results. (b) Tension change of rubber bands. (c) Variation curve of jump height and head velocity.

The posture during the simulated jumping process was shown in Fig. 7(a). Based on the actual rotational speed of motor, the speed of rope ascent during the energy storage process was calculated to be approximately 7.995 mm/s, and this was used to set the speed of the head movement drive. In addition, The stiffness coefficient of each individual rubber band is set to 0.084 N/mm, with a damping coefficient of 5×10^{-4} N.s/mm, matching the actual conditions. There are eight rubber bands in total. The relationship between the two rubber bands elastic forces and time during the simulation of the robot in the primary energy storage phase is shown in Fig. 7(b). The maximum elasticity of two rubber bands is 16.6 N, differing from the measured elasticity at final energy storage of the CAJR by only 0.2 N, confirming the validity of the rubber bands parameter settings.

The variation in the center of mass height and head velocity during one jump simulation of the CAJR was shown in Fig. 7(c). The red solid line is the height of the center of mass (corresponding to the left y-axis) and the blue dashed line is the velocity of the head (corresponding to the right y-axis). During this simulation, from 0 to 22.9 s, the CAJR started to accumulate energy for the first jump, and its center of mass gradually drops to the lowest point under the action of the drive rope. From 22.9 to 22.95 s, the CAJR released energy to initiate the jump and gradually accelerated to reach the highest point. During this process, the elastic potential energy accumulated by the CAJR is fully converted into kinetic energy, and the height of the highest point of the jump is about 1372 mm. From 25 to 48.9 s, the CAJR accumulates energy for the second jump. From 48.9 to 48.95 s, the CAJR released its energy and started jumping, and the height of the highest point of the jump is 1356 mm. The relationship between elastic potential energy, kinetic energy, and gravitational potential energy is shown in Fig. 7(c).

4.3 Structural Dynamics Analysis

In the trigger-release stage, the trigger opens the baffle to release the drive rope, the baffle will be subjected to a large impact force, and the shape of the trigger will also affect the mechanical properties of the baffle. Three shapes of triggers were designed, including conical, right-angled, and drop-shaped ones. ANSYS was utilized to investigate the mechanical properties of the three different trigger during the process of opening the baffle of the trigger to release the drive rope (Fig. 8).

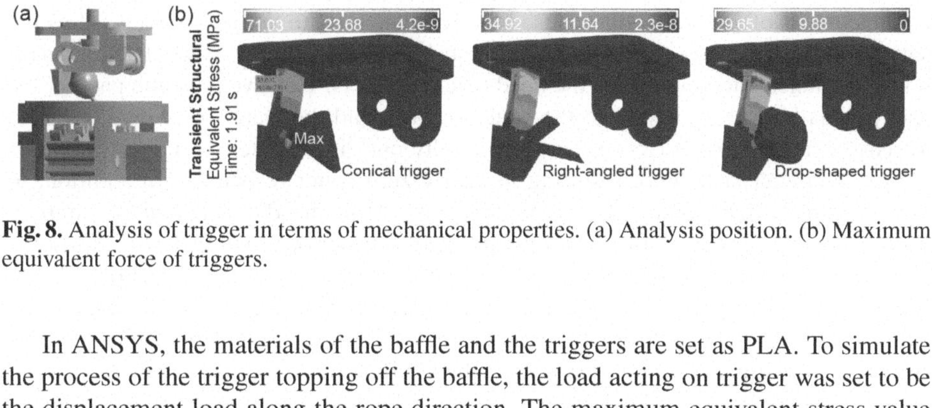

Fig. 8. Analysis of trigger in terms of mechanical properties. (a) Analysis position. (b) Maximum equivalent force of triggers.

In ANSYS, the materials of the baffle and the triggers are set as PLA. To simulate the process of the trigger topping off the baffle, the load acting on trigger was set to be the displacement load along the rope direction. The maximum equivalent stress value of the conical trigger when the baffle is opened to the critical state of the drive rope release is 71.210 MPa, and the stress concentration occurs at the contact point between the conical trigger and the baffle because the top of the conical trigger has not been rounded. Ignoring the stress concentration, the maximum equivalent stress is 34.325 MPa, which occurs at the root of the baffle and is smaller than the yield strength of PLA (42 MPa), which is consistent with the actual situation. The equivalent stress values of the angular trigger and the drop-shaped trigger when the baffle is opened to the critical state of the drive rope release are 34.919 MPa and 29.645 MPa, respectively, which are smaller than the yield strength of PLA. The drop-shaped trigger facilitated the drive rope release process, kept baffle stress within the safe range, and resulted in a smaller maximum equivalent force on the baffle compared to the right-angle trigger. Therefore, the drop-shaped trigger design is the most reasonable.

4.4 Fluid Simulation of Head Jumping Process

When the CAJR leaps out of the water, its streamlined head will be the first to make contact and break the water surface. To explore this critical process in depth, we used Fluent to simulate and analyse the streamlined head of the CAJR. The analysis focused on the water-breaking process starting from the point where the streamlined head was tangent to the water surface. The head has a bottom circle radius of 18 mm and a density of 1044.61 kg/mm^3. In simulating the release of elastic potential energy through the energy storage mechanism, a vertical upward initial velocity was assigned to the head, accurately targeting its center of gravity to reproduce the actual scenario of the aquatic jumping of the CAJR. We constructed a $400 \times 300 \times 650\,\text{mm}^3$ rectangular computational domain, in which the water depth is set to 220 mm to simulate the environment of water, and the rest is set to air. We used tetrahedral cells for meshing to ensure the accuracy and efficiency of the simulation. The overall grid size is 10 mm and the skewness is set to 0.74 to ensure the accuracy and enhance the stability of the simulation. During the leap, water surface tension and inertia cause a film of water to adhere to the surface of head, persisting as it rises [14]. The streamlined head design reduces resistance during aquatic jumping, minimizing its impact on the CAJR.

The head was considered a rigid body for transient analysis and processing, capturing its dynamic changes during the jumping process. The time step was set to 5×10^{-4} s, and 345 steps in 0.1725 s. As the head broke through the water surface, the attachment of the water film caused the resistance (with vertical downward as the negative direction) it experienced to continuously increase (Fig. 9). At 0.018 s, the maximum resistance encountered by the head reaches 3.62 N. However, as time passed, the head gradually broke away from the water surface, and the water resistance began to decrease gradually. At 0.12 s, the head was fully out of the water, with the water film almost completely ruptured, resulting in nearly zero water resistance. In addition, to more intuitively demonstrate the dynamic changes of the head during aquatic jumping process, we also generated the fluid velocity field distribution cloud map (Fig. 9(a)), the hydrostatic pressure cloud map (Fig. 9(c)) and the velocity cloud map (Fig. 9(d)). These figures can clearly present the fluid flow, velocity distribution, and hydrostatic pressure changes of the head during the jumping process, which provided us with intuitive support for the aquatic jumping process of the CAJR.

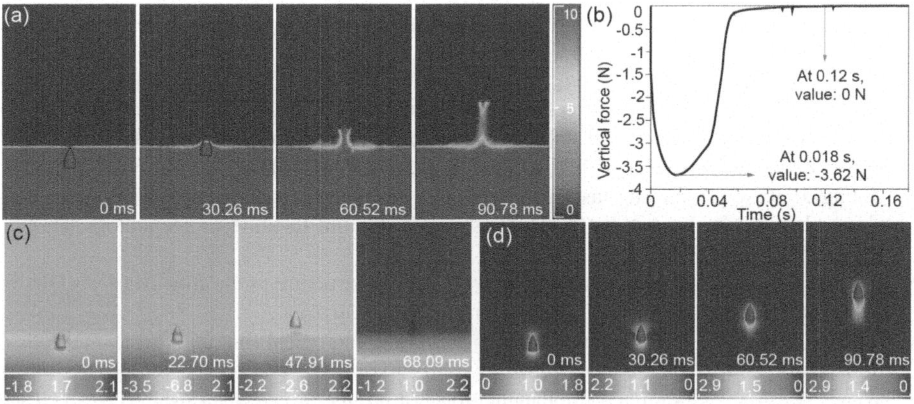

Fig. 9. Fluent fluid simulation analysis of the head breaking process. (a) Fluid velocity fraction field distribution cloud (volume fraction (water)). (b) Water resistance variation data. (c) Static pressure cloud diagram (Pa). (d) Distribution of fluid velocity field (m/s).

5 Conclusion

In our research, we initially utilized bionic design principles to model the bones and muscles of the water-dwelling frog hind legs, as well as the flippers, in order to propose a 2-DOF consecutive aquatic jumping robot (CAJR). Then, the variation of the required tension of the drive rope in the energy storage phase was theoretically analyzed (63.00 N) and experimentally measured (63.11 N), and the calculated results agreed with the experimental results by 99.82%. Moreover, the jumping process of the CAJR was simulated by ADAMS, and the maximum jumping height on land could reach 1372 mm. In addition, the optimal design and analysis of various shapes of triggers were carried out, and the maximum equivalent force of the water-drop type trigger in pushing the baffle is 29.645 MPa. Next, Fluent was used to simulate the water breaking process of streamlined head, and the maximum water resistance of the head is 3.62 N. Finally, a CAJR prototype with a maximum length of 318.66 mm and a weight of 119.2 g was fabricated. The future works will be the consecutive aquatic jumping experiments of the CAJR, and the proposed theoretical method and simulation results will be verified.

References

1. Azizi, E., Roberts, T.J.: Muscle performance during frog jumping: influence of elasticity on muscle operating lengths. Proc. Roy. Soc. B Biol. Sci. **277**(1687), 1523–1530 (2010)
2. Chong, H., Dewei, T., Qiquan, Q., Zhuoqun, C., Zongquan, D.: A combined series-elastic actuator & parallel-elastic leg no-latch bio-inspired jumping robot. Mech. Mach. Theory **149**, 103814 (2020)
3. Fan, J., Du, Q., Dong, Z., Zhao, J., Xu, T.: Design of the jump mechanism for a biomimetic robotic frog. Biomimetics **7**(4), 142 (2022)
4. Wang, S., Fan, J., Liu, G.: Research status and development trend of frog-inspired robots. Robotica **41**(7), 2228–2248 (2023)

5. Ahn, J., Park, J., Kim, K. S., Kim, S.: Frog-inspired jumpping robot for overcoming high obstacles. In: IEEE ISR, pp. 1–4 (2013)
6. Zhang, W., Fan, J., Cai, H.: Design of a novel frog-inspired hopping leg. In: IEEE International Conference on Information and Automation, pp. 277–282 (2012)
7. Li, Y.: Trajectory planning and stability analysis of bio-frog jumping robot. Master's Dissertation, Zhejiang University of Technology, Hangzhou, China (2018)
8. Zhong, J.: Research on frog-inspired biomimetic jumping robot actuated by pneumatic muscles and its key technologies. Ph. D. Dissertation, Harbin Institute of Technology, Harbin, China (2015)
9. Fan, Z.: Research on jumping robot based on skeletal structure of the frog. Master's Dissertation, Harbin Institute of Technology, Harbin, China (2016)
10. Hawkes, E.W., et al.: Engineered jumpers overcome biological limits via work multiplication. Nature **604**(7907), 657–661 (2022)
11. Wang, W., et al.: Design and implementation of a miniature jellyfish-inspired robot. IEEE Robot. Autom. Lett. **8**(6), 3134–3141 (2023)
12. Woodward, M.A., Sitti, M.: Multimo-bat: a biologically inspired integrated jumpping-gliding robot. Int. J. Robot. Res. **33**(12), 1511–1529 (2014)
13. Wang, M., Zang, X., Fan, J., Zhao, J.: Biological jumpping mechanism analysis and modeling for frog robot. J. Bionic Eng. **5**(3), 181–188 (2008)
14. Zhong, L., et al.: Dynamical modeling and numerical simulation of water discharge process of spherical objects. In: 2023 IEEE International Conference on Mechatronics and Automation (ICMA), Harbin, Heilongjiang, China, pp. 1551–1556 (2023)

Design of Multi-Mode Morphing Wings Based on Multi-Stable Beam-Type Metastructures

Jieyu Wang[1,2], Yadong Wang[1,2], Yingzhong Tian[1,2], Guangbo Hao[3], Fengfeng Xi[4], and Yinjun Zhao[5](✉)

[1] School of Mechatronic Engineering and Automation, Shanghai University, Shanghai 200444, China
[2] Shanghai Key Laboratory of Intelligent Manufacturing and Robotics, Shanghai 200444, China
[3] School of Engineering and Architecture, Electrical and Electronic Engineering, University College Cork, Cork T12 K8AF, Ireland
[4] Department of Aerospace Engineering, Toronto Metropolitan University, Toronto, ON M5B 2K3, Canada
[5] School of Mechanical Engineering, University of Shanghai for Science and Technology, Shanghai 200093, China
zhaoyinjun@usst.edu.cn

Abstract. The morphing wing can change its shape through mechanism deformation, to improve the aerodynamic performance of the aircraft and save energy. Based on the multi-stable beam-type metastructures, a morphing wing structure with lightweight, large deformation, multiple stable states is designed in this paper. The overall structure can achieve two different deformation modes and maintain the profile shapes without the need for continuous external driving forces. Additionally, carbon-fiber materials are utilized for the flexible skin and actuation of the morphing structure. Finally, a prototype is constructed to demonstrate the multiple morphing modes, thereby validating the feasibility of the proposed structure.

Keywords: Multi-Stability · Beam-Type Metastructure · Morphing Wing · Flexible Skin Driving

1 Introduction

Aerodynamic performance is a key indicator of aircraft performance. The shape of aircraft wings is often tailored to specific flight environments and needs to be optimized for particular flight scenarios to meet operational needs. However, wings designed with a single configuration can excel in specific flight conditions but may struggle to adapt swiftly to unexpected situations. Morphing wings address this limitation by offering adaptable wing geometries that can significantly enhance aircraft aerodynamics. Consequently, the ability to achieve multiple wing configurations through multi-mode morphing mechanisms holds considerable promise in the future of aviation and has become a focal point of research among numerous scholars.

The deformation modes of morphing wings primarily fall into two categories: internal wing deformation and external wing deformation. Internal wing deformation includes

X. Lan et al. (Eds.): ICIRA 2024, LNAI 15201, pp. 139–153, 2025.
https://doi.org/10.1007/978-981-96-0771-6_11

variations in sweep angle, spanwise length, and chord length. External wing deformation encompasses changes in twist, spanwise bending, chordwise bending, and thickness variations in airfoil shape. Yang et al. [1] proposed a morphing wing skeleton (MWS) mechanism that can achieve continuously variable spanwise bending, spanwise twisting and sweep; Luo et al. [2] proposed an active twisting morphing (ATM) wings, each rib is driven to swing in a separate plane perpendicular to the axis thus form active wing twisting; Wang et al. [3] proposed a composed of *n* planar mechanism units length-wise morphing structure. The aforementioned morphing wing designs all utilize mechanism-based deformations to achieve various wing configurations. To meet the growing demands for compactness and lightweight construction, many scholars have also explored novel morphing structures to enable wing deformation in aircraft.

Boston et al. [4] introduced a novel compliant structure composed of cellular metastructures with multiple stable shapes, enabling spanwise wing morphing; Jia et al. [5] proposed a novel variable camber wing, which achieves a large deflection range and exhibits robustness. While the aforementioned morphing wings achieve their deformations through structural changes, fulfilling the requirements for significant deformations and lightweight construction, these structures typically offer limited variations and cannot satisfy diverse flight conditions through multiple deformations alone; Xi et al. [6] designed a grid patch multi-stable composite, which can be used to create a large multistable surface and provide guidance for the flexible skin of morphing wings. This paper introduces beam-type metastructures with phase deformation characteristics, enabling wings to simultaneously achieve variable chord length and camber angle deformations. This structure exhibits two stable states, transiting from one stable state to another when the applied force reaches a critical threshold. Additionally, its elastic properties allow for significant deformations and controllable reversible shape changes. Unlike translational state transitions, rotational state transitions require less energy, making it possible to meet the requirements for multiple deformation modes and minimal actuation in morphing wings.

The rest of the paper is structured as follows: Sect. 2 provides an overview of beam-type metastructures and outlines the design principles for the multi-stable structure. Section 3 presents the geometric configuration of morphing wings based on beam-type metastructures, enabling variable chord length and camber angle deformations. Section 4 details the design of a flexible skin actuation system and describes the fabrication of a prototype. Some concluding remarks and future works are given in Sect. 5.

2 Beam-Type Metastructures

2.1 Beam Structure Module

The beam structure module consists of curved beams with snap-through behavior, initially investigated by Vangbo [7]. Each beam module comprises a curved beam and upper and lower stiffer walls, as illustrated in Fig. 1. The curved beam is an elastic structure, allowing for deformations to achieve different bending states. Connection to stiffer walls with a thickness of s provides local support to the curved beam and prevents lateral displacement.

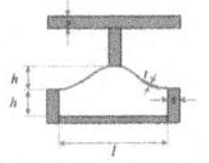

Fig. 1. Beam structure module

Curved beams evolve from elastic straight beams, typically with a length of $l + a$ (a>0). The initial state of a beam module is a stable curved state maintained by axial lateral forces exerted by stiffer walls at both ends. The equilibrium equation describing the stable state of the curved beam at this moment can be expressed as follows:

$$EI\frac{d^4u}{dx^4} + f\frac{d^2u}{dx^2} = 0 \tag{1}$$

where u represents the lateral deflection of the elastic beam, E is the Young's modulus of the material used for the curved beam, I is the moment of inertia of the beam, and f denotes the axial lateral force exerted on the curved beam by the stiffer walls at both ends. The boundary conditions of the beam structure, when the curved beam is constrained and maintained stable, can be expressed as follows:

$$u(0) = u(l) = 0, \quad \left(\frac{du}{dx}\right)_{u=0} = \left(\frac{du}{dx}\right)_{u=l} = 0 \tag{2}$$

Afterward, the axial force N can be normalized and represented as follows:

$$N^2 = \frac{fl^2}{EI} \tag{3}$$

In order to let the equation have a nontrivial solution, N must satisfy the following condition:

$$\sin\left(\frac{N}{2}\right)\left[\tan\left(\frac{N}{2}\right) - \frac{N}{2}\right] = 0 \tag{4}$$

which allows two kinds of non-trivial eigenfunctions:

$$\left.\begin{matrix} u_i(x)=A_i\left[1-\cos\left(N_i\frac{x}{l}\right)\right] \\ N_i=(i+1)\pi\ldots \end{matrix}\right\}, i = 1, 3, 5\ldots \tag{5}$$

and

$$\left.\begin{matrix} u_i(x)=A_i\left[1-2\frac{x}{l}-\cos\left(N_i\frac{x}{l}\right)+\frac{2\sin\left(N_i\frac{x}{l}\right)}{N_i}\right] \\ N_i=2.86\pi, 4.92\pi, 6.94\pi\ldots \end{matrix}\right\}, i = 2, 4, 6\ldots \tag{6}$$

Here, A_i represents the amplitude of the function $u_i(x)$ and can be any constant. According to the mathematical analysis of the curved beam mentioned above, guided by the principle of minimum potential energy, a curved beam, when not disturbed externally, exhibits stability only in the first mode of Euler Buckling [8]. In this case, $i = 1, N_1 = 2\pi$ are satisfied in Eq. 5. Thus, the initial shape of the curved beam can be expressed as the following cosine function [9–12]:

$$y = \left(\frac{h}{2}\right)\left[1 - \cos\left(\frac{2\pi x}{l}\right)\right] \tag{7}$$

where h is the initial height of the beam, and l is the total length of the curved beam projected in the vertical direction.

The stable state characteristics of a beam module stem from the geometric structure of the curved beam. The attainment of stability in curved beams is closely associated with several parameters of the beam module. Apart from the geometric shape, denoted by y, other parameters such as the thickness t, initial height h, and the total length l of the curved beam's projection in the vertical direction play crucial roles. The parameter k, representing the ratio between the initial height h and the thickness t of the curved beam, is expressed as $k = \frac{h}{t}$. Qiu et al. utilized the mode superposition method to analyze beam deflection and validated that curved beams exhibit two stable forms only when the ratio $k>2.31$ [11]. Additionally, the maximum stress in the material used for the curved beam during deflection must satisfies the condition $\varepsilon_{max} = 2\pi^2\frac{ht}{l^2}$ [13].

Upon satisfying the aforementioned design criteria, curved beams can achieve two stable states. Additionally, curved beams typically exhibit three states: the initial state, transitional state, and compressed state, as illustrated in Fig. 2. When no external load is applied, the curved beam is in its initial state, depicted as State 1 in Fig. 2. As a gradually increasing longitudinal load is applied to the curved beam, reaching a sufficiently large magnitude at $l/2$ distance, the beam begins to deform. At the point where the applied force reaches its maximum value, the curved beam transits to State 2. In this state, the beam is in a transitional phase, yet it has not reached the critical condition for snap-through behavior. Compression energy is stored within the curved beam and gradually reaches its maximum. As the load continues to act, upon reaching the critical value, all compression energy is released, leading to snap-through behavior, and the curved beam rapidly deforms to State 3, completing the entire phase transition process. In other words, the phase transition of the curved beam does not require continuous external force participation. Once an external load is applied, causing the beam's deformation to reach a certain threshold, the curved beam can autonomously reach the second stable state. Therefore, this bistable beam structure with snap-through behavior meets the requirements for significant deformations without the need for continuous force and maintains stability through its inherent structural characteristics. This deformation characteristic reduces the need for energy supply during large structural deformations.

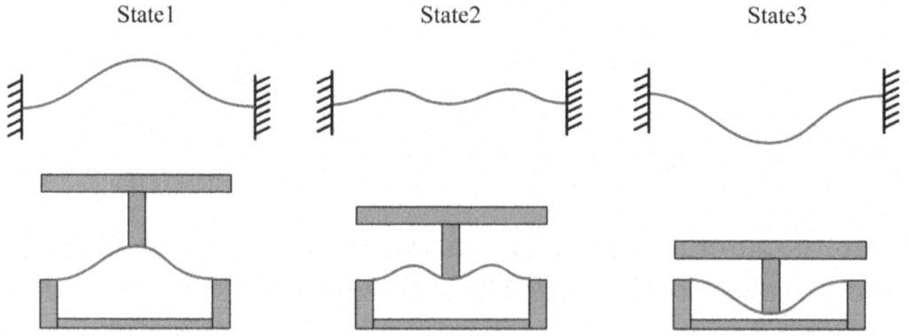

Fig. 2. Three state of curve beam and corresponding beam structure modules

2.2 Double-Beam Structure

In Sect. 2.1, the beam module is introduced, showcasing its ability to achieve two stable states through its unique configuration and the judicious arrangement of parameters, demonstrating translational state transition characteristics. Moreover, the beam module may possess various deformation capabilities. By combining double modules side by side, they may simultaneously exhibit two transformation properties, as depicted in Fig. 3, where each parameter remains consistent with those of a single module. Additionally, the multi-stable beam structure formed by the combination of double-beam modules can undergo both translational state transition and rotational state transition. Furthermore, rotational state transition requires less energy compared to translational state transition [10].

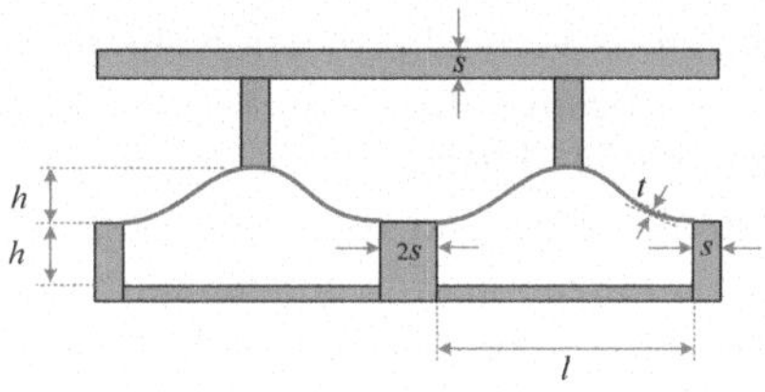

Fig. 3. Double-beam structure

The two transition states achievable by the double-beam structure are illustrated in Fig. 4.

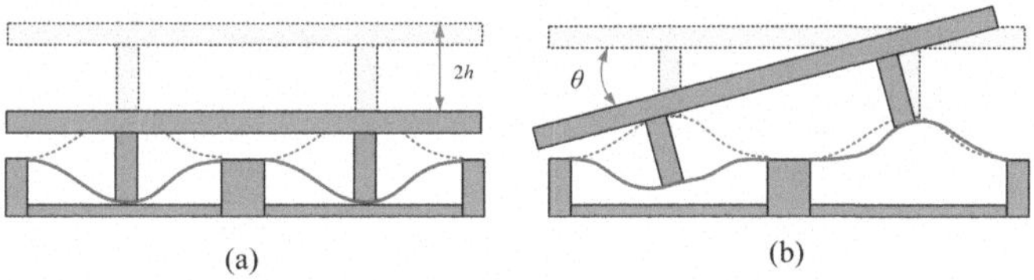

Fig. 4. Two transition states of double-beam structure: (a) translational state; (b) rotational state. In translational state, the maximum translation length is $2h$; in rotational state, the maximum rotation angle is θ.

During translational state transition, the two curved beams undergo three synchronous states: the initial state, transitional state, and compressed state. In this process, the two parallel beam modules maintain a symmetric structure, experiencing deformation on both sides simultaneously and reaching the respective conditions for snap-through behavior. As discussed in the previous section, beam modules can undergo phase transitions and maintain two stable states. However, during rotational state transition, the deformation of the two curved beams changes. As depicted in Fig. 4b, the curved beam on the left undergoes snap-through, while the deformation of the curved beam compresses to an irregular shape. At this point, the symmetry of the two parallel beam modules is disrupted, making it more challenging to maintain stability in the rotational state.

The three primary parameters of the curved beam, namely thickness t, initial height h, and the total length l of its vertical projection, can determine whether the structure can maintain rotational stability and may also affect the maximum rotation angle θ during rotational state transition. With variations in these key parameters, the double-beam structure may exhibit stability under rotational conditions or experience self-rebound effects. Specifically, certain design parameters under specific conditions may fail to maintain stability in the rotational state, causing the beam on the side experiencing snap-through to rebound to the initial stable state of the curved beam, as illustrated in Fig. 3. k_1 can be represented as the ratio between the initial height h of the curved beam and the total length l of its vertical projection, while k_2 can be represented as the ratio between the thickness t of the curved beam and the total length l of its vertical projection. By setting appropriate values for these two ratio coefficients, the double-beam structure can exhibit rotational stability. Generally, the ratio coefficient of the curved beam's initial height h to the total length l of its vertical projection should satisfy $k_1 > 0.075$, and the ratio coefficient of the curved beam's thickness t to the total length l of its vertical projection should satisfy $k_2 > 0.0275$ [10].

To validate the translational state and rotational state of the multi-stable curved beam structure, parameter optimization was conducted based on the aforementioned criteria. The sample parameters are presented in Table 1. Subsequently, Thermoplastic Polyurethane (TPU) was used as the base material, and multiple samples were fabricated using 3D printing technology.

Table 1. Test sample parameter

Parameters	Value
The thickness of wall s	4 mm
The thickness of curve beam t	1.2 mm
The initial height of curve beam h	8 mm
The projected length of the beam l	41 mm
Proportional coefficient $k = \frac{h}{t}$	6.66
Proportional coefficient $k_1 = \frac{h}{l}$	0.195
Proportional coefficient $k_2 = \frac{t}{l}$	0.02927

Two kinds of materials were chosen for the fabrication of the samples, TPU and Polylactic Acid (PLA). TPU is selected to fulfill the requirement of the curved beam's elastic properties for repeatable deformation, while PLA is chosen to provide stiffness for clamping the curved beam. Additionally, PLA exhibits higher strength compared to TPU. Let PLA effectively bond with TPU, enabling the integration of the overall structure in printing. The printed samples are depicted in Fig. 5. Figure 5a represents the initial state of the double-beam structure, where the curved beam is not subjected to any external forces and remains in a stable state. As shown in Fig. 5b, the curved beam has been subjected to an external downward force, leading to snap-through behavior, maintaining the second stable state and achieving translational state. The two different curved states are represented in Figs. 5c and d. Figure 5c illustrates rotational state anticlockwise, where the left curved beam undergoes snap-through, while the right curved beam experiences compression. Conversely, Fig. 5d depicts rotational state clockwise, with the left curved beam undergoing compression and the right curved beam snapping. Additionally, double-beam structures can maintain corresponding stable states after undergoing the respective rotational state transitions. This multi-stable property provides a solid design foundation for the subsequent multi-mode variable geometry wing.

2.3 Quadruple-Beam Structure

In the preceding sub-sections, we discussed a beam module capable of exhibiting multiple stable states, as well as a double-beam structure capable of snap-through behavior, achieving translational state and rotational state. By incorporating these beam-type metastructures with multi-stable characteristics into the design of multi-mode variable geometry wings, multiple deformation effects can be achieved. Based on the deformation characteristics of the double-beam structure, a geometric structure capable of achieving variable chord length and camber angle deformation for the quadruple-beam structure has been designed. This quadruple-beam structure comprises two double-beam structures combined as a single unit, as depicted in Fig. 6.

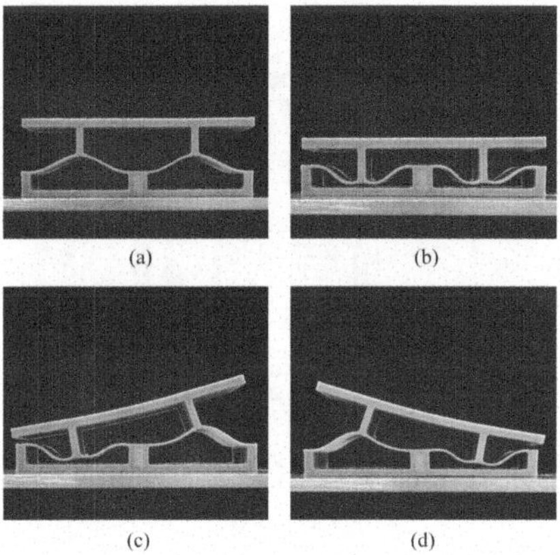

Fig. 5. Test sample with different stable states: (a) the initial state of double-beam structure; (b) translational state and remain stable; (c) rotational state towards left side; (d) rotational state towards right side.

The design parameters remain consistent with those outlined in the preceding sections, as shown in Table 1. The reason for employing two symmetrical double-beam structures is that the double-beam structure alone can only achieve relatively minor translational state transition and rotational state transition. To meet various deformation requirements, combining two symmetrical double-beam structures into a quadruple-beam structure enables greater translational state transition and rotational state transition compared to a single double-beam structure. Additionally, by inducing deformation on

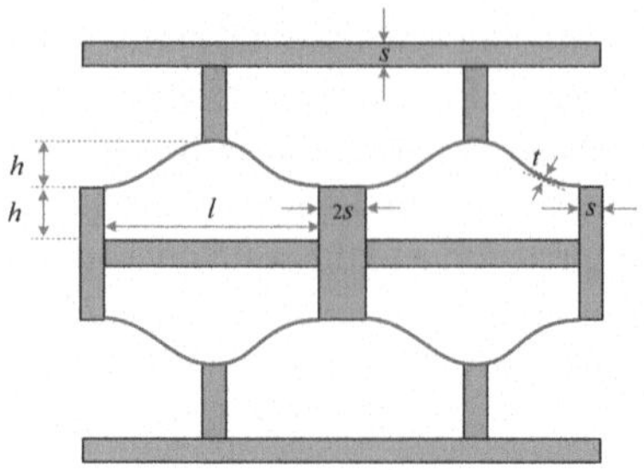

Fig. 6. Quadruple-beam structure

one side or both sides simultaneously, the extent of translational or rotational deformation can be adjusted, facilitating more precise deformation control, as illustrated in Fig. 7.

The initial structure of the quadruple-beam structure remains in a contraction state, as illustrated on the left side of Fig. 7. Subsequently, two arrows point to two different transition modes. The upper arrow indicates translational state transition, corresponding to unilateral deformation and bilateral deformation.

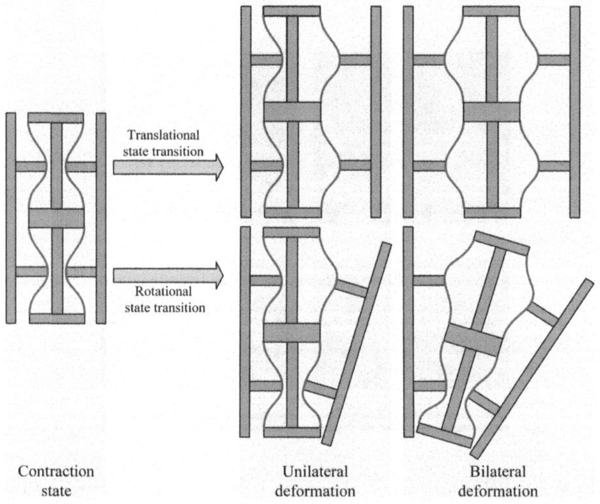

Fig. 7. Deformed form of quadruple-beam structure

When deformation occurs on only one side, the displacement is $2h$, as illustrated in Fig. 4a. However, when both curved beams deform simultaneously, the displacement is doubled, resulting in $4h$. The lower arrow points to rotational state transition, similarly corresponding to unilateral deformation and bilateral deformation. When deformation occurs on only one side, the rotation angle is θ, as depicted in Fig. 4b. Correspondingly, with bilateral deformation, both left and right sides undergo rotational state transition simultaneously and maintain stability when reaching their maximum rotation angle. At this point, the maximum rotation angle is twice that of unilateral deformation, reaching $2\,\theta$. By controlling the magnitude of the driving force or the length of displacement, the structure can achieve various ranges of deformation while maintaining stability through its multi-stable configuration. This facilitates meeting the diverse deformation requirements of the morphing wing and will be further elaborated upon in Sect. 4 regarding the design of the driving device and the construction of prototypes.

3 Design of the Morphing Wing Structure

3.1 Chord Morphing of the Wing

The chord morphing of the wing primarily includes changing chord length and camber angle, as illustrated in Fig. 8. The chord morphing of the wing can effectively increase the overall wing area and lift coefficient [14], thus enabling effective deformation in response to different flight environments and enhancing the aerodynamic performance of the aircraft.

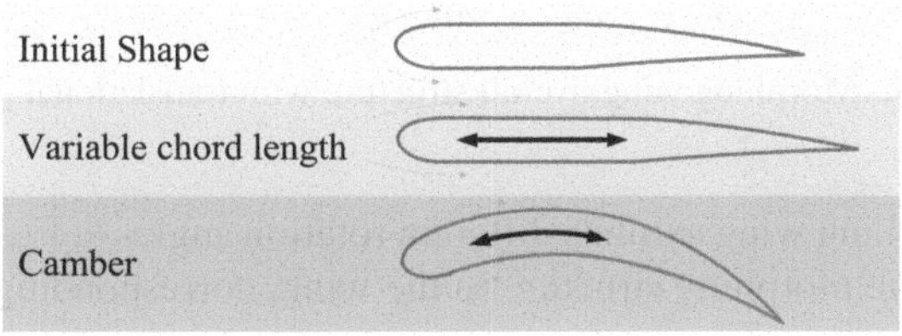

Fig. 8. Wing deformation

In Sect. 2.3, the unit structures constituting the morphing wing were introduced. This section will discuss the application of unit structures in chordwise wings. For a larger workspace, multiple quadruple-beam structures are combined. The schematic diagram of the morphing wing structure and its application to chordwise sections are illustrated in Fig. 9.

Figure 9a corresponds to the initial shape, Figs. 9b and c represent variable chord lengths, corresponding to unilateral deformation and bilateral deformation, respectively, with different translation lengths h. Figure 9d represents the application of the morphing structure to the wing, corresponding to three different states with different translation lengths.

3.2 Camber Morphing of the Wing

The morphing wing structure capable of achieving rotational state maintains consistency with the initial state and translational state of the morphing wing and is also comprised of three quadruple-beam structures. The schematic diagram of the morphing wing structure and its application to chordwise sections is depicted in Fig. 10.

Figure 10a corresponds to the initial shape, while Figs. 10b and c represent chord camber, corresponding to unilateral deformation and bilateral deformation, respectively.

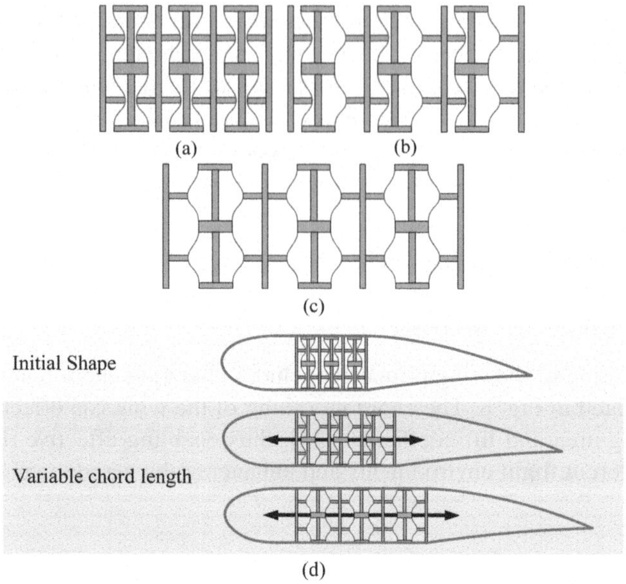

Fig. 9. Morphing wing overall structure with translational state

Therefore, the morphing wing exhibits different rotation angles θ. Figure 10d represents the application of the morphing structure to the wing, corresponding to three different states with different rotation angles.

3.3 Prototype of the Morphing Wing Structure

Based on the morphing wing overall structure proposed above and the design parameters in Table 1, samples of the morphing wing structure were fabricated using TPU as the base material and PLA as the auxiliary material, utilizing a 3D printing device, as shown in Fig. 11. Figure 11a depicts the initial state of the morphing wing structure, with the minimum overall length. Figures 11b and c represent translational states with unilateral and bilateral deformations, respectively. Figures 11d and e depict rotational states with unilateral and bilateral deformations, respectively. Figure 11f illustrates a mixed state of translational and rotational deformations, with both unilateral and bilateral deformations occurring simultaneously. According to the fundamental design theory outlined earlier and the relevant design parameters, the samples can maintain their stable state characteristics in the aforementioned states.

4 Morphing Wing with Flexible Skin

Based on the design of the morphing wing structure, this section explores control strategies for the different deformation modes of the morphing wing to achieve the expected performances. The following sections correspond to the fabrication of skin-driven design, and the final assembly of the overall prototype.

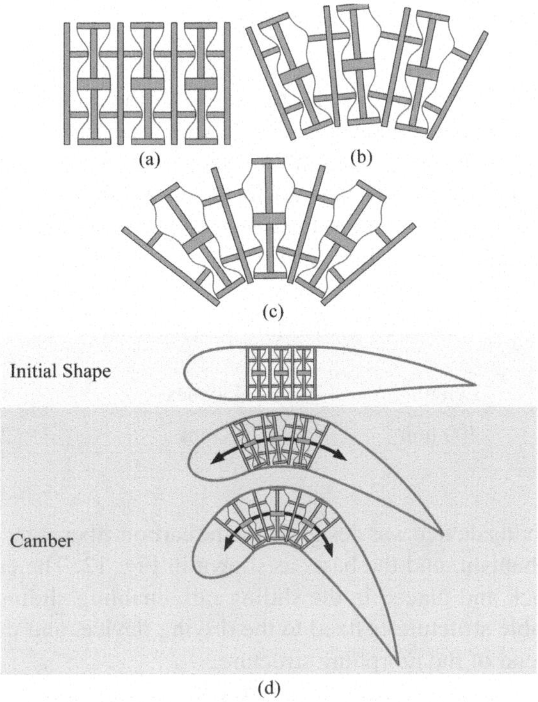

Fig. 10. Morphing wing overall structure with rotational state

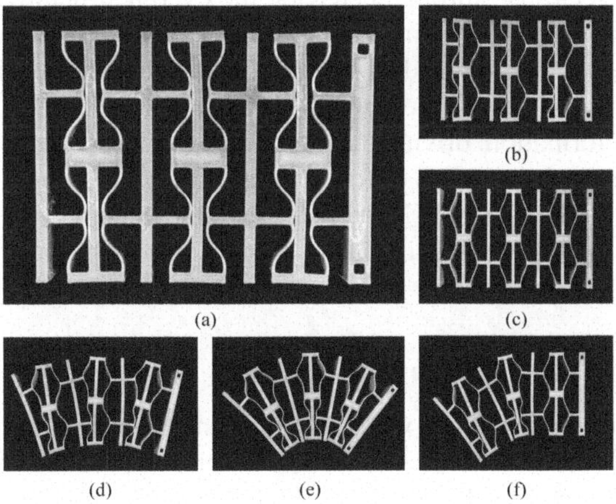

Fig. 11. Samples of morphing wing structure: (a) the initial state of morphing structure; (b) the translational state with unilateral deformation; (c) the translational state with bilateral deformation; (d) the rotational state with unilateral deformation; (e) the rotational state with bilateral deformation; (f) translational and rotational mixed state with both unilateral and bilateral deformation.

4.1 Fabricated of the Flexible Skin Driving

Carbon-fiber skin provides higher strength to meet the load-bearing requirements of aircraft. Additionally, by controlling the thickness of the carbon-fiber skin, different bending performances can be achieved. Some flexible material skin has also been considered, but it seems that it is difficult to fill the need to drive [15]. In this paper, 0.5 mm carbon-fiber skin is used as the driving part for the morphing structure, providing both deformation capabilities and excellent load-bearing performance. Other parameters of the carbon fiber skin are listed in Table 2.

Table 2. Carbon-fiber skin parameter

Parameters	Length	Thickness	Width
Value	300 mm	0.5 mm	25 mm

Afterward, a driving device was designed for the carbon-fiber skin, including a sliding rail, gear rack mechanism, and the base, as shown in Fig. 12. The carbon-fiber skin is fixed to the gear rack and placed in the sliding rail, enabling sliding motion. The left side of the deformable structure is fixed to the driving device, and the right side of the skin is fixed to the end of the morphing structure.

Through the rotation of gears, the overall structure can undergo various deformations to achieve different stable states. When both gears rotate simultaneously, the upper and lower gear racks drive the skin to move, enabling different translational states. After the curved beam undergoes snap-through behavior, the overall structure remains relatively stable and no longer requires continuous driving force. When rotating only the upper gear, one side of the skin is stretched by the gear rack. At this point, since the lower gear remains fixed when the upper skin reaches its maximum stretchability, the skin begins to undergo bending deformation, driving the morphing structure to achieve rotational state transition. Depending on the skin's different elongation values, the morphing structure can reach different rotation angles. Moreover, when the bending beam reaches a stable state, the overall structure can maintain its shape without the need for a continuous driving force.

4.2 Prototype with Flexible Skin Driving

Based on the described morphing wing structure and skin driving device, a physical prototype was fabricated. The main structure of the prototype and different deformation modes are illustrated in Fig. 13. Figures 13a and b depict the initial state when not subjected to any external force. Figures 13c and f correspond to different lengths of translational state transition. Specifically, Fig. 13c represents a morphing structure with unilateral deformation, characterized by a smaller translation length, while Fig. 13f corresponds to the maximum translation length, accompanied by a morphing structure with bilateral deformation. The red arrows indicate the movement directions of the gears and deformable structure. Similarly, Figs. 13d and e respectively illustrate smaller and larger rotation angles.

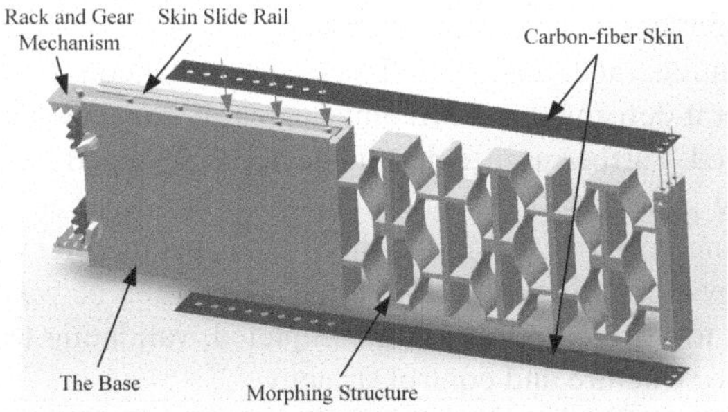

Fig. 12. Carbon-fiber skin driving device

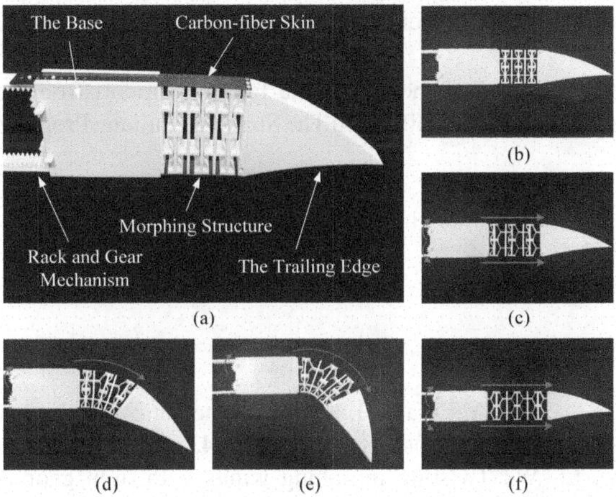

Fig. 13. Prototype of multi-mode morphing wing with flexible skin driving: (a) the structure of each part; (b) the initial state of morphing wing; (c) the translational state with unilateral deformation; (d) the rotational state with unilateral deformation; (e) the rotational state with both unilateral and bilateral deformation; (f) the translational state with bilateral deformation.

Through the outlined driving control strategy and the fabrication of the prototype, the multi-stable deformable structure proposed in this paper can achieve multiple modes for morphing wings. Moreover, it allows precise control over different translation lengths and rotation angles. Additionally, once the deformable structure reaches a stable state, no external driving force is required to maintain the overall shape of the morphing wing structure.

5 Conclusion

This paper proposes a multi-mode morphing wing structure capable of simultaneous chord length variation and camber angle deformation. The structure comprises a multi-stable beam with snap-through behavior, enabling both translational state and rotational state. Stability is maintained before and after snap-through behavior occurs. Additionally, by controlling unilateral deformation, bilateral simultaneous deformation, or mixed unilateral and bilateral deformation, different ranges of translation length and rotation angles can be achieved. Furthermore, a driving device is designed for the morphing wing structure, employing gear rack drive and utilizing carbon fiber as its skin structure to accommodate bending deformation and higher load capacity. Precise control of deformation is achieved by elongating the skin. Finally, the prototype was fabricated and the deformation control to different scales was completed, validating the feasibility of the proposed deformable structure and control strategy.

In future work, we will delve deeper into the relationship between stress and configuration. Additionally, the aerodynamics of the overall morphing wing structure will be analyzed through finite element modeling, and the structure then will be optimized to achieve optimal aerodynamic performance for the morphing wing. Furthermore, the driving control strategy and lightweight design will also be considered.

Acknowledgments. The authors acknowledge the funding support from the National Natural Science Foundation of China No. 52105002 and The Shanghai Pujiang Programme No. 23PJD069.

Disclosure of Interests. The authors have no competing interests to declare that are relevant to the content of this article.

References

1. Yang, H., Jiang, S., Wang, Y., Xiao, H.: Design, kinematic and fluid-structure interaction analysis of a morphing wing. Aerosp. Sci. Technol. **143**, 108721 (2023)
2. Luo, B., Cui, W., Li, W.: Twisting morphing wings with tight geometric constraints for biomimetic swimming or flying robotic vehicles. J. Eng. Res. (2023)
3. Wang, J., Zhao, Y., Xi, F., Tian, Y.: Design and analysis of a configuration-based lengthwise morphing structure. Mech. Mach. Theory **147**, 103767 (2020)
4. Boston, D.M., Phillips, F.R., Henry, T.C., Arrieta, A.F.: Spanwise wing morphing using multistable cellular metastructures. Extreme Mech. Lett. **53**, 101706 (2022)
5. Jia, S., Zhang, Z., Zhang, H., Song, C., Yang, C.: Wind tunnel tests of 3d-printed variable camber morphing wing. Aerosp. **9**(11), 699 (2022)
6. Algmuni, A., Xi, F., Alighanbari, H.: Design and analysis of a grid patch multi-stable composite. Compos. Struct. **246**, 112378 (2020)
7. Vangbo, M., Bäcklund, Y.: A lateral symmetrically bistable buckled beam. J. Micromech. Microeng. **8**(1), 29–32 (1998)
8. Vangbo, M.: An analytical analysis of a compressed bistable buckled beam. Sens. Actuat. A.-Phys. **69**(3), 212–216 (1998)
9. Yang, H., Ma, L.: 1D to 3D multi-stable architected materials with zero Poisson's ratio and controllable thermal expansion. Mater. Des. **188**, 108430 (2020)
10. Zhang, Y., Tichem, M., Keulen, F.: Rotational snap-through behavior of multi-stable beam-type metastructures. Int. J. Mech. Sci. **193**, 106172 (2021)
11. Qiu, J., Lang, J.H., Slocum, A.H.: A curved-beam bistable mechanism. J. Microelectromech. Syst. **13**(2), 137–146 (2004)
12. Montalbano, A., Fadel, G.M., Li, G.: Design for energy absorption using snap-through bistable metamaterials. Mech. Based Des. Struc. **51**(3), 1368–1386 (2023)

13. Restrepo, D., Mankame, N.D., Zavattieri, P.D.: Phase transforming cellular materials. Extreme Mech. Lett. **4**, 52–60 (2015)
14. Bilgen, O., Friswell, M.I.: Piezoceramic composite actuators for a solid-state variable-camber wing. J. Intel. Mat. Syst. Str. **25**(7), 806–817 (2014)
15. Zhao P., Wu. C. and Li. Y.: Design and application of solar sailing: a review on key technologies. Chin. J. Aeronaut. **36**(5), 125–144 (2023)

Kinematic Modeling and Analysis of Robotic Axial Tilt Errors

Xinyu Feng, Xu Zhang, and Dawei Tu(✉)

School of Mechatronic Engineering and Automation, Shanghai University, Shanghai 200072, China
tdw@shu.edu.cn

Abstract. Collaborative robots boast high flexibility, reliable safety, and strong human-machine collaboration capabilities. However, in practical operations, axis tilt errors can lead to decreased end-effector positioning accuracy, thereby affecting work performance and quality. To address this issue, this paper presents a kinematic model for collaborative robots that integrates Denavit-Hartenberg (DH) parameter errors with axis tilt errors. Initially referencing the DH method, the model establishes both the robot's kinematic model and a parameter error model. It addresses issues unresolved by traditional non-geometric error compensation methods, namely the inability to establish a mapping relationship between the axis tilt joint positions in the calibration coordinate system and the end-effector positional errors. By utilizing the DH method and incorporating a generalized error matrix model, an improved kinematic model that includes tilt errors is proposed. This paper conducts forward kinematic analysis and employs the Newton-Raphson iteration method for inverse kinematics solutions. Simulation and experimental results demonstrate that, regardless of the influence of the tilt error matrix, the model accurately and effectively determines the end-effector pose and joint angles of the collaborative robot.

Keywords: Collaborative robot · axis tilt error · error model · kinematics

1 Introduction

Currently, collaborative robots have become indispensable tools in modern factories and service industries. Precision, as one of the key indicators for evaluating the performance of collaborative robots, receives considerable attention [1]. Both the academic community and the industrial sector widely acknowledge that establishing accurate kinematic models and conducting kinematic calibration are effective approaches to enhancing the positioning accuracy of robots.

Traditional kinematic calibration of robots [2] typically involves two steps. Initially, geometric parameter errors in the robot's kinematic model are calibrated [3] based on a parametric model, primarily addressing deviations such as joint angle offsets, link twist errors, link length discrepancies, and link offset

X. Lan et al. (Eds.): ICIRA 2024, LNAI 15201, pp. 154–165, 2025.
https://doi.org/10.1007/978-981-96-0771-6_12

errors caused by machining and assembly [4]. Subsequently, non-parametric models [5] (such as neural networks, support vector machines, fuzzy algorithms, and other intelligent methods) are employed to compensate for non-geometric errors induced by joint flexibility, joint play, and gear backlash. Although the combined parametric and non-parametric calibration methods are straightforward, effective, and easy to implement, traditional calibration approaches within the parametric model have predominantly focused on errors caused by DH model parameters under calibration coordinate systems [6], overlooking the impact of axial tilt errors under operational conditions on DH modeling, leading to model failure. Numerous researchers have proposed various methods for establishing the kinematic models of robots to enhance the kinematic accuracy of collaborative robots. The Denavit-Hartenberg (DH) model [7] is considered the most classical kinematic model for robots. Hayati et al. [8] introduced an improved four-parameter DH formula that addresses the ill-conditioned issues arising when two adjacent joint axes are parallel or nearly parallel. Veitschegger [9] proposed another modified DH formula type that includes a post-multiplication rotation about the Y-axis in the standard DH convention, improving the condition when two adjacent joint axes are parallel or nearly parallel. To adhere to the three principles of the robotic arm kinematic model—parameterization, continuity, and completeness—Hamano [10] and others proposed a complete, parameterized, continuous kinematic model by adding two parameters to Roberts' line parameters. Recently, some researchers have also suggested a generalized geometric error model [11] method that considers both geometric and non-geometric errors. In the field of articulated arm measurement machines, Lian-Dong Yu et al. [12] proposed a new kinematic model for a Portable Articulated Coordinate Measuring Machine (PACMM) aimed at addressing the ill-conditioned problems encountered by the traditional Denavit-Hartenberg (DH) model when continuous joint axes are parallel or nearly parallel. This new model, based on the generalized geometric error model, eliminates the shortcomings of the DH model and optimizes the generalized geometric error parameters of PACMM using the Levenberg-Marquard (L-M) algorithm, reducing the standard deviation of measurement values from 0.0627 mm to 0.0452 mm, showing an improvement over the DH model. Inspired by the aforementioned work, we integrate the traditional DH model with a tilt error model [13], aiming to achieve an enhancement in the accuracy of the kinematic model of collaborative robots, thereby effectively improving the motion performance of collaborative robots in various complex application scenarios.

2 Kinematic Error Modeling

2.1 Comprehensive Error Model Combining DH Parameters and Axial Tilt Errors

The DH parameter model is considered one of the most classic relational models for the joints of robots. However, due to factors such as machining errors, assembly errors, and linkage deformation, when the axis system is tilted, there are deviations in the actual geometric parameters of the coordinate system f_i^{ideal} with respect to f_i^{real}. Therefore, the coordinate system f_{i-1}^{real} is transformed to f_i^{ideal} through the homogeneous transformation matrix A_i [14]. Due to the deviation matrix E_i, it is further transformed to f_i^{real}. The transformation relationship between the coordinate systems f_{i-1}^{real} and f_i^{real} is illustrated in Fig. 1.

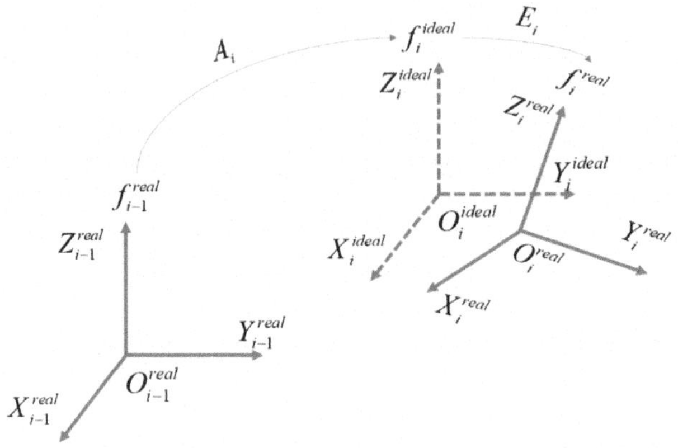

Fig. 1. Coordinate system pose transformation caused by errors in the ith link.

The transformation matrix A_i from the coordinate system f_{i-1}^{real} to f_i^{ideal} is represented by Eq. (1):

$$Ai = \mathrm{Rot}(x, \alpha_{i-1})\mathrm{Trans}(x, \alpha_{i-1})\mathrm{Rot}(z, \theta_i)\mathrm{Trans}(z, d_i) \tag{1}$$

According to the principles of DH parameter modeling, exchanging the last two terms involving rotation and translation about the z-axis in matrix A_i does not alter the result. Therefore, A_i can be rewritten as Eq. (2):

$$\begin{aligned} Ai &= \mathrm{Rot}(x, \alpha_{i-1})\mathrm{Trans}(x, a_{i-1})\mathrm{Trans}(z, d_i)\mathrm{Rot}(z, \theta_i) \\ &= \begin{bmatrix} c\theta_i & -s\theta_i & 0 & a_{i-1} \\ s\theta_i c\alpha_{i-1} & c\theta_i c\alpha_{i-1} & -s\alpha_{i-1} & -s\alpha_{i-1} d_i \\ s\theta_i s\alpha_{i-1} & c\theta_i s\alpha_{i-1} & c\alpha_{i-1} & c\alpha_{i-1} d_i \\ 0 & 0 & 0 & 1 \end{bmatrix} \end{aligned} \tag{2}$$

The transformation matrix E_i from the coordinate system f_i^{ideal} to f_i^{real} is represented by Eq. (3):

$$E_i = Rot(x_i, \varepsilon_{i4})Rot(y_i, \varepsilon_{i5})Rot(z_i, \varepsilon_{i6})\mathrm{Trans}(x_i, \varepsilon_{i1})\mathrm{Trans}(y_i, \varepsilon_{i2})\mathrm{Trans}(z_i, \varepsilon_{i3}) \tag{3}$$

In this, the three parameters $\varepsilon_{i1}, \varepsilon_{i2}, \varepsilon_{i3}$ represent the translational values from the origin of the coordinate system f_i^{ideal} to the origin of the coordinate system

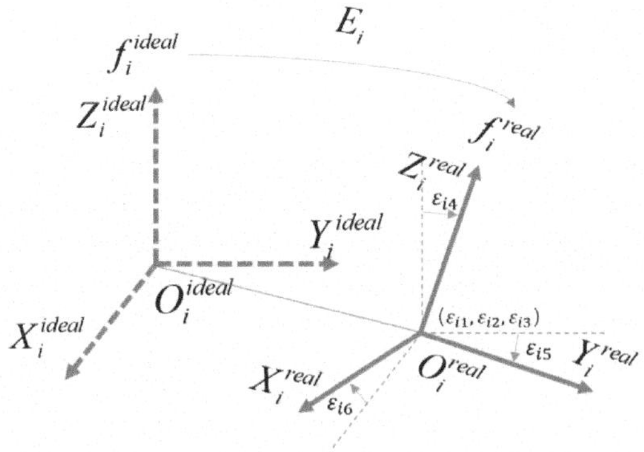

Fig. 2. The transformation of the i-th link coordinate system f_i^{real} relative to f_i^{ideal}.

f_i^{real} along the X, Y, and Z axes, respectively. The other three parameters $\varepsilon_{i4}, \varepsilon_{i5}$, and ε_{i6} represent the Euler angles of the coordinate system f_i^{real} relative to f_i^{ideal}, as shown in Fig. 2.

In matrix multiplication, if the order of multiplication is changed, the result will also change. Multiplying two differential motions in different orders will yield two different results, as shown in Eqs. (4) and (5).

$$\begin{aligned} Rot(x,\delta x)Rot(y,\delta y) &= \begin{bmatrix} 1 & 0 & 0 & 0 \\ 0 & 1 & -\delta x & 0 \\ 0 & \delta x & 1 & 0 \\ 0 & 0 & 0 & 1 \end{bmatrix} \begin{bmatrix} 1 & 0 & \delta y & 0 \\ 0 & 1 & 0 & 0 \\ -\delta y & 0 & 1 & 0 \\ 0 & 0 & 0 & 1 \end{bmatrix} \\ &= \begin{bmatrix} 1 & 0 & \delta y & 0 \\ \delta x\delta y & 1 & -\delta x & 0 \\ -\delta y & \delta x & 1 & 0 \\ 0 & 0 & 0 & 1 \end{bmatrix} \end{aligned} \tag{4}$$

$$\begin{aligned} Rot(y,\delta y)Rot(x,\delta x) &= \begin{bmatrix} 1 & 0 & \delta y & 0 \\ 0 & 1 & 0 & 0 \\ -\delta y & 0 & 1 & 0 \\ 0 & 0 & 0 & 1 \end{bmatrix} \begin{bmatrix} 1 & 0 & 0 & 0 \\ 0 & 1 & -\delta x & 0 \\ 0 & \delta x & 1 & 0 \\ 0 & 0 & 0 & 1 \end{bmatrix} \\ &= \begin{bmatrix} 1 & \delta x\delta y & \delta y & 0 \\ 0 & 1 & -\delta x & 0 \\ -\delta y & \delta x & 1 & 0 \\ 0 & 0 & 0 & 1 \end{bmatrix} \end{aligned} \tag{5}$$

If the higher order derivatives are set to zero, then the results of the above two equations are exactly the same. Therefore, in differential motion, it can be considered that the order of multiplication is not important, and this conclusion is also true for other combinations (including differential rotations about the z-axis, or differential translations about any axis).

Therefore, Eq. (3) can be rewritten as:

$$E_i = Rot(z_i, \varepsilon_{i6})Trans(z, \varepsilon_{i3})Rot(x_i, \varepsilon_{i4})Rot(y_i, \varepsilon_{i5})Trans(x, \varepsilon_{i1})Trans(y, \varepsilon_{i2}) \tag{6}$$

In Eq. (6), the six parameters $\varepsilon_{i1}, \varepsilon_{i2}, \varepsilon_{i3}, \varepsilon_{i4}, \varepsilon_{i5}, \varepsilon_{i6}$ are commonly referred to as generalized geometric error parameters. To simplify the computational process, matrix E_i is approximated using the Taylor expansion of Eq. (6). Since the coordinate system f_i^{real} deviates from f_i^{ideal}, only the first-order terms of the expansion are retained. Therefore, matrix E_i can be rewritten as Eq. (7):

$$Ei = \begin{bmatrix} 1 & -\varepsilon_{i6} & \varepsilon_{i5} & \varepsilon_{i1} \\ \varepsilon_{i6} & 1 & -\varepsilon_{i4} & \varepsilon_{i2} \\ -\varepsilon_{i5} & \varepsilon_{i4} & 1 & \varepsilon_{i3} \\ 0 & 0 & 0 & 1 \end{bmatrix} \tag{7}$$

Thus, the transformation matrix B_i that includes the axial inclination errors of the coordinate system f_i^{real} relative to f_{i-1}^{real} can be represented, as shown in Eq. (8):

$$\begin{aligned} B_i &= A_i E_i \\ &= \text{Rot}(x, \alpha_{i-1}) \cdot \text{Trans}(x, a_{i-1}) \cdot \text{Trans}(z, d_i) \cdot \text{Rot}(z, \theta_i) \cdot \text{Rot}(z_i, \varepsilon_{i6}) \\ &\cdot \text{Trans}(z, \varepsilon_{i3}) \cdot \text{Rot}(x_i, \varepsilon_{i4}) \cdot \text{Rot}(y_i, \varepsilon_{i5}) \cdot \text{Trans}(x_i, \varepsilon_{i1}) \cdot \text{Trans}(y_i, \varepsilon_{i2}) \end{aligned} \tag{8}$$

Among them, $\text{trans}(z, d_i)\text{Rot}(z, \theta_i)\text{Rot}(z_i, \varepsilon_{i6})\text{Trans}(z, \varepsilon_{i3})$ represents a translation along the z-axis by d_i, followed by a rotation around the z-axis by θ_i, then a rotation around the z-axis by ε_{i6}, and finally a translation along the z-axis by ε_{i3}. In geometric transformations, the order of these four can be interchanged without altering the final result. Therefore, we can combine them, which yields B_i as shown in Eq. (9):

$$\begin{aligned} B_i &= A_i E_i \\ &= \text{Rot}(x, \alpha_{i-1}) \cdot \text{Trans}(x, a_{i-1}) \cdot \text{Trans}(z, d_i + \varepsilon_{i3}) \cdot \text{Rot}(z, \theta_i + \varepsilon_{i6}) \\ &\cdot \text{Rot}(x_i, \varepsilon_{i4}) \cdot \text{Rot}(y_i, \varepsilon_{i5}) \cdot \text{Trans}(x_i, \varepsilon_{i1}) \cdot \text{Trans}(y_i, \varepsilon_{i2}) \end{aligned} \tag{9}$$

Thus, it can be observed that the error factors affecting B_i can be categorized into 24(4 × 6) terms of D-H parameter errors $\{\alpha_{i-1}, a_{i-1}, d_i, \theta_i\}$ and 36(6 × 6) terms of inclination errors due to rotation angles $\{\varepsilon_{i1}, \varepsilon_{i2}, \varepsilon_{i3}, \varepsilon_{i4}, \varepsilon_{i5}, \varepsilon_{i6}\}$.

Due to potential zero position errors at the zero position of the angle encoder, which are caused by manufacturing and assembly errors of the angle encoder, θ_{i0} is considered to be the zero position error of the joint variable θ_i at its zero position. The actual joint variable is denoted by Θ:

$$\Theta = \theta_{i0} + \theta_i \tag{10}$$

The homogeneous transformation matrix A_i is rewritten as Eq. (11):

$$Ai = \begin{bmatrix} c\Theta_i & -s\Theta_i & 0 & a_{i-1} \\ s\Theta_i c\alpha_{i-1} & c\Theta_i c\alpha_{i-1} & -s\alpha_{i-1} & -s\alpha_{i-1} d_i \\ s\Theta_i s\alpha_{i-1} & c\Theta_i s\alpha_{i-1} & c\alpha_{i-1} & c\alpha_{i-1} d_i \\ 0 & 0 & 0 & 1 \end{bmatrix} \tag{11}$$

Therefore, the relationship matrix T from the base coordinate system to the origin of the tool coordinate system is represented by Eq. (12):

$$T = \prod_{i=1}^{6} B_i = \prod_{i=1}^{6} A_i E_i \tag{12}$$

In the actual kinematic model, all axial inclination error parameters are represented by the vector $\varepsilon = [\varepsilon_{11}, \varepsilon_{12}, \ldots, \varepsilon_{ij}, \ldots, \varepsilon_{66}]$ where $i, j = 1, 2, \ldots, 6$.

2.2 Inverse Kinematics

Given the target pose T^{ideal}, through inverse kinematics, the theoretical values of the six joint angles $\theta_1^{\text{ideal}}, \theta_2^{\text{ideal}}, \theta_3^{\text{ideal}}, \theta_4^{\text{ideal}}, \theta_5^{\text{ideal}}, \theta_6^{\text{ideal}}$ can be obtained. However, the actual pose T^{real} is not the same as the ideal target pose T^{ideal}, and there is an error matrix E_i between them. By comparing the two homogeneous transformation matrices, the actual robot pose can be iteratively moved to the true target pose, thereby solving for the actual joint angles at the target pose θ_i^{real}.

The Newton-Raphson iteration method [15] is a numerical technique for solving nonlinear equations, which can be applied to solve inverse kinematics problems [16]. In robotics, inverse kinematics [17] refers to the calculation of the angles of the joints of a robotic arm based on the known position (pose) of the end-effector, so that the arm's end can reach a specified location. Below are the specific steps for using the Newton-Raphson iteration method for compensation:

Step 1: Set an initial guess value.

To begin the iteration process, an initial guess of the joint angles is required. This can be any reasonable value, but it is best to start with a value close to the solution. Here, we use the theoretical joint angles at the target pose as the initial values.

Step 2: Calculate the forward kinematics including the inclination errors.

Using the initial guessed values, calculate the forward kinematics to obtain the current position and orientation of the end effector. The homogeneous transformation matrix between coordinate systems that includes inclination errors is given by Eq. (9). Due to the presence of errors, to have the robot's actual end pose reach the ideal pose, a joint angle correction $\Delta\theta_i$ must be applied. Therefore, the joint angles under the actual pose are given by Eq. (13):

$$\theta_i^{real} = \theta_i^{ideal} + \Delta\theta_i \tag{13}$$

Determine the actual homogeneous transformation matrix between coordinate systems:

$${}^{i-1}_{\ \ i}T^{real} = \begin{bmatrix} c\theta_i^{real} & -s\theta_i^{real} & 0 & a_{i-1} \\ s\theta_i^{real} c\alpha_{i-1} & c\theta_i^{real} c\alpha_{i-1} & -s\alpha_{i-1} & -s\alpha_{i-1} d_i \\ s\theta_i^{real} s\alpha_{i-1} & c\theta_i^{real} s\alpha_{i-1} & c\alpha_{i-1} & c\alpha_{i-1} d_i \\ 0 & 0 & 0 & 1 \end{bmatrix} \begin{bmatrix} 1 & -\varepsilon_{i6} & \varepsilon_{i5} & \varepsilon_{i1} \\ \varepsilon_{i6} & 1 & -\varepsilon_{i4} & \varepsilon_{i2} \\ -\varepsilon_{i5} & \varepsilon_{i4} & 1 & \varepsilon_{i3} \\ 0 & 0 & 0 & 1 \end{bmatrix} \tag{14}$$

Establishing the homogeneous transformation matrices for each joint:

$$ {}_{1}^{0}T = \begin{bmatrix} c_1 & -s_1 & 0 & a_0 \\ s_1 & c_1 & 0 & 0 \\ 0 & 0 & 1 & d_1 \\ 0 & 0 & 0 & 1 \end{bmatrix} E_1 \tag{15} $$

$$ {}_{2}^{1}T = \begin{bmatrix} c_2 & -s_2 & 0 & a_1 \\ 0 & 0 & -1 & -d_2 \\ s_2 & c_2 & 0 & 0 \\ 0 & 0 & 0 & 1 \end{bmatrix} E_2 \tag{16} $$

$$ {}_{3}^{2}T = \begin{bmatrix} c_3 & -s_3 & 0 & a_2 \\ s_3 & c_3 & 0 & 0 \\ 0 & 0 & 1 & d_3 \\ 0 & 0 & 0 & 1 \end{bmatrix} E_3 \tag{17} $$

$$ {}_{4}^{3}T = \begin{bmatrix} c_4 & -s_4 & 0 & a_3 \\ s_4 & c_4 & 0 & 0 \\ 0 & 0 & 1 & d_4 \\ 0 & 0 & 0 & 1 \end{bmatrix} E_4 \tag{18} $$

$$ {}_{5}^{4}T = \begin{bmatrix} c_5 & -s_5 & 0 & a_4 \\ 0 & 0 & -1 & -d_5 \\ s_5 & c_5 & 0 & 0 \\ 0 & 0 & 0 & 1 \end{bmatrix} E_5 \tag{19} $$

$$ {}_{6}^{5}T = \begin{bmatrix} c_6 & -s_6 & 0 & a_5 \\ 0 & 0 & 1 & d_6 \\ -s_6 & -c_6 & 0 & 0 \\ 0 & 0 & 0 & 1 \end{bmatrix} E_6 \tag{20} $$

$$ {}_{6}^{0}T = {}_{1}^{0}TE_1{}^{1}{}_{2}TE_2{}^{2}{}_{3}TE_3{}^{3}{}_{4}TE_4{}^{4}{}_{5}TE_5{}^{5}{}_{6}TE_6 \tag{21} $$

Step 3: Calculate the error.

Compare the target position and orientation of the end effector with the currently calculated position and orientation of the end effector to compute the error.

It is necessary to construct a system of nonlinear equations:

$$ F(\theta) = 0, F(\theta) = (f_1, f_2, \cdots, f_{12})^{\mathrm{T}}, \theta = (\theta_1, \theta_2, \cdots, \theta_6)^{\mathrm{T}} \tag{22} $$

Given the target pose homogeneous transformation matrix T from the base coordinate system $\{0\}$ to the end effector coordinate system $\{6\}$, a homogeneous transformation matrix ${}_{6}^{0}T_\theta(\theta_1^i, \theta_2^i, \theta_3^i, \theta_4^i, \theta_5^i, \theta_6^i)$ can also be obtained for each iteration, where i is the iteration number, $i = 0, 1, 2, \ldots$. Subtract the elements of the two matrices element-wise to form the equation:

$$ F(\theta) = [{}_{6}^{0}T_\theta(a, b) - T(a, b)] = \theta \tag{23} $$

In the expression, ${}_6^0T_\theta(a,b)$ is the element in the a-th row and b-th column of the homogeneous transformation matrix ${}_6^0T_\theta$; $T(a,b)$ is the element in the a-th row and b-th column of the homogeneous transformation matrix T.

Step 4: Calculate the Jacobian matrix.

Based on the geometric model of the robot, calculate the Jacobian matrix. The Jacobian matrix describes the rate of change of the position and orientation of the end effector with respect to changes in the joint angles.

From Eq. (23), the Jacobian matrix of this equation can be determined as:

$$J_i(\theta^i) = \begin{bmatrix} J_{1,1} & J_{1,2} & \cdots & J_{1,6} \\ J_{2,1} & J_{2,2} & \cdots & J_{2,6} \\ \vdots & \vdots & \cdots & \vdots \\ J_{12,1} & J_{12,2} & \cdots & J_{12,6} \end{bmatrix} = \begin{bmatrix} \frac{\partial f_1}{\partial \theta_1^i} & \frac{\partial f_1}{\partial \theta_2^i} & \cdots & \frac{\partial f_1}{\partial \theta_6^i} \\ \frac{\partial f_2}{\partial \theta_1^i} & \frac{\partial f_2}{\partial \theta_2^i} & \cdots & \frac{\partial f_2}{\partial \theta_6^i} \\ \vdots & \vdots & \vdots & \vdots \\ \frac{\partial f_{12}}{\partial \theta_1^i} & \frac{\partial f_{12}}{\partial \theta_2^i} & \cdots & \frac{\partial f_{12}}{\partial \theta_6^i} \end{bmatrix} \tag{24}$$

Step 5: Calculate the update for the joint angles.

The Newton iteration formula for solving the system of equations is:

$$\theta^{i+1} = \theta^i - J^{-1}F(\theta^i) \tag{25}$$

However, since the Jacobian matrix is a 12×6 matrix, it is only possible to calculate its pseudoinverse. Therefore, the iteration formula becomes:

$$\theta^{i+1} = \theta^i - (J_i^T J_i)^{-1} J_i^T(\theta^i)F(\theta^i) \tag{26}$$

Thus, obtaining the new joint update values.

Step 6: Repeat the iteration.

Repeat steps 2 to 5 until the error converges to a sufficiently small value, or the predetermined number of iterations is reached.

Step 7: Output the results.

When the error is sufficiently small or the predetermined number of iterations is reached, output the final calculated joint angles $\theta_1^{\mathrm{real}}, \theta_2^{\mathrm{real}}, \theta_3^{\mathrm{real}}, \theta_4^{\mathrm{real}}, \theta_5^{\mathrm{real}}, \theta_6^{\mathrm{real}}$.

3 Simulation and Experimental Analysis

In the simulation experiment, 50 sets of random error matrices are generated and incorporated into the new model of the collaborative robot to verify whether the model can accurately and effectively determine the end effector's pose and joint angles of the collaborative robot. To make the experimental results closer to real conditions, the error values are drawn from a Gaussian distribution. The error term for each joint follows a Gaussian distribution with a mean of 0 and a standard deviation of 1 mm.

For the six error terms of each joint $[\varepsilon_{i1}, \varepsilon_{i2}, \varepsilon_{i3}, \varepsilon_{i4}, \varepsilon_{i5}, \varepsilon_{i6}]$, random numbers will be drawn from a Gaussian distribution with a mean of 0 and a standard deviation of 1mm. This ensures that each error term is randomly generated around a mean of 0, with most values concentrated within 2 mm.

Using the six generated random error terms $[\varepsilon_{i1}, \varepsilon_{i2}, \varepsilon_{i3}, \varepsilon_{i4}, \varepsilon_{i5}, \varepsilon_{i6}]$, construct the random error matrix for each joint in the form of an error matrix, as specified in Eq. (7).

The simulation experiment is conducted in a MATLAB environment, where the kinematic structure model of the robot is built based on the provided DH parameters. The specific DH parameters are as follows (Table 1):

Table 1. Denavit-Hartenberg parameters for collaborative robot.

link	θ_i	α_{i-1}	a_i	d_i	offset
1	$q1$	0°	0	148	0°
2	$q2$	−90°	0	0	−90°
3	$q3$	0°	663	0	0°
4	$q4$	0°	547.5	185	−90°
5	$q5$	−90°	0	122.5	0°
6	$q6$	90°	0	106.5	0°

where:

- link: Joint number.
- θ: Joint angle.
- d: Joint offset (link length).
- a: Joint length (link length).
- α: Joint twist angle (rotation around the z-axis).
- offset: Offset of the joint angle.

A total of 50 simulation experiments were conducted, with each set using a different random set of inclination error matrices. Within the same set of experiments, 50 different end effector positions were randomly selected using the Monte Carlo method. For each set of experiments, the kinematic inverse solution for the robot's end effector pose was calculated using the axial inclination error model, resulting in 50 sets of robot joint angles for each experiment.

The 50 sets of joint angles are solved using forward kinematics to obtain the corresponding end effector poses. Using the first position generated by the Monte Carlo method as a reference, the distances from the other generated points to this reference point are calculated and recorded as standard values. The distances from the points obtained through forward kinematics solutions to the reference point are also calculated. These 50 sets of distances are compared to the standard values, aiming to observe whether the axial inclination error model can effectively solve for spatial points, thereby evaluating the accuracy of the model. By comparing the true values of the positions generated by the Monte Carlo method, the performance of the model under different error conditions can be assessed.

Data analysis results indicate that, through 50 sets of experiments, an analysis was conducted on the solution results for the robot's end effector position. This included calculating the distances from the position points generated by the Monte Carlo method to the reference point and from the points obtained by the forward kinematics solution to the generated reference point for each experiment. Statistical analysis of these distances was carried out, including the calculation of mean values and standard deviations (Fig. 3).

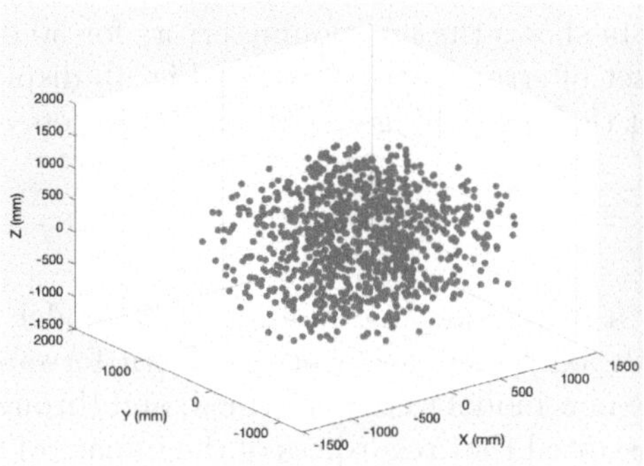

Fig. 3. The position of the robot's end effector is generated using the Monte Carlo method.

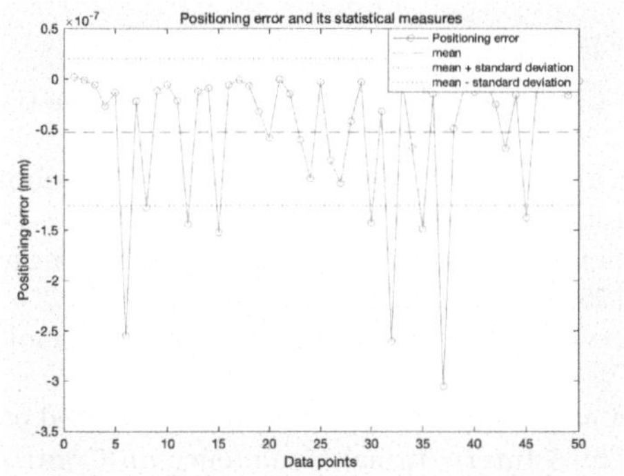

(a) The positioning error and statistical measures for a particular set of experiments.

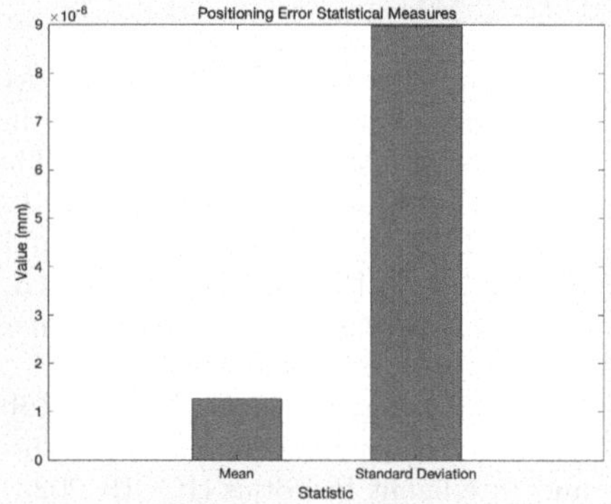

(b) Statistical measures of positioning errors for 50 sets of experiments.

Fig. 4. Experimental Error and Statistical Measures.

Data analysis results from 50 sets of experiments show that we analyzed the robot's end effector position solutions, including calculating the distances from the Monte Carlo-generated position points to the reference point and from other forward kinematics solution points to the generated reference point for each set of experiments. We conducted statistical analysis on these distances, calculating the mean and standard deviation.

The results show that the average distance is -1.267×10^{-8} mm, which is close to the set standard value of 0, and the standard deviation is also small, indicating that the distribution of distance values is relatively concentrated. This demonstrates that the tilt error model established in this paper is effective in solving the robot's end effector position, and can accurately predict the robot's motion state. Figure 4a shows the positioning errors for 50 different end effector positions under one set of error matrices, while Fig. 4b displays the average and standard deviation of the positioning errors for the 50 sets of experiments.

4 Conclusion

This study proposes a comprehensive motion error model that combines D-H parameter errors with axial inclination errors. Both forward and inverse kinematics analyses of the new model were performed, and through simulation experiments, it was demonstrated that regardless of the impact of the inclination error matrix, the model can accurately and effectively determine the end effector position and joint angles of the collaborative robot.

Acknowledgements. This research was supported by the National Natural Science Foundation of China (Nos. 62176149 and 61673252).

References

1. Riedl, M., Danzl, R., Felberbauer, M., Lankmair, T.: High-resolution geometry measurement with a collaborative robot. MM Sci. J. (2019)
2. Hollerbach, J.M., Wampler, C.W.: The calibration index and taxonomy for robot kinematic calibration methods. Int. J. Robot. Res. **15**(6), 573–591 (1996)
3. Xuan, J.-Q., Xu, S.-H.: Review on kinematics calibration technology of serial robots. Int. J. Precis. Eng. Manuf. **15**, 1759–1774 (2014)
4. Roth, Z., Mooring, B., Ravani, B.: An overview of robot calibration. IEEE J. Robot. Autom. **3**(5), 377–385 (1987)
5. Wang, E., Feng, X., Su, C., Ma, C.: Robot autonomous calibration method based on machine vision. In: Proceedings of the Third International Conference on Control and Intelligent Robotics (ICCIR 2023). SPIE (2023)
6. Lee, J.-W., Park, G.-T., Shin, J.-S., Woo, J.W.: Industrial robot calibration method using Denavit-Hartenberg parameters. In: Proceedings of the 2017 17th International Conference on Control, Automation and Systems (ICCAS). IEEE (2017)
7. Denavit, J., Hartenberg, R.S.: A kinematic notation for lower-pair mechanisms based on matrices. J. Appl. Mech. **22**(2), 215–221 (1955)
8. Hayati, S.A.: Robot arm geometric link parameter estimation. In: Proceedings of the The 22nd IEEE Conference on Decision and Control. IEEE (1983)
9. Veitschegger, W.K., Wu, C.-H.: Robot calibration and compensation. IEEE J. Robot. Autom. **4**(6), 643–656 (1988)

10. Zhuang, H., Roth, Z.S., Hamano, F.: A complete and parametrically continuous kinematic model for robot manipulators. In: Proceedings of the IEEE International Conference on Robotics and Automation. IEEE (1990)
11. Eman, K., Wu, B., Devries, M.: A generalized geometric error model for multi-axis machines. CIRP Ann. **36**(1), 253–256 (1987)
12. Zhao, H.N., Yu, L.D., Jia, H.K., Li, W.S., Sun, J.Q.: A new kinematic model of portable articulated coordinate measuring machine. Appl. Sci. **6**(7), 181 (2016)
13. Daulay, B., Lydia, M.S., Sembiring, R.: Robot arm inverse kinematics wrist tilt repair using PID control system (proportional, integrative, derivative). In: Proceedings of the Journal of Physics: Conference Series. IOP Publishing (2021)
14. Seng Yee, C., Lim, K.-B.: Forward kinematics solution of stewart platform using neural networks. Neurocomputing **16**(4), 333–349 (1997)
15. Sherman, A.H.: On Newton-iterative methods for the solution of systems of non-linear equations. SIAM J. Numer. Anal. **15**(4), 755–771 (1978)
16. Aristidou, A., Lasenby, J.: Inverse kinematics: a review of existing techniques and introduction of a new fast iterative solver (2009)
17. Shamma, J.S., Whitney, D.: A method for inverse robot calibration. J. Dyn. Sys. Meas. Control **109**(1), 36–43 (1987)

Minimum Jerk Trajectory Planning for a Redundant Actuated Three-DOF Cable-Suspended Parallel Robot with Parallelogram Architecture

Sheng Xiang[1(✉)], Wenlong Lu[1], Weikun Bian[1], Zhang Wei[1], Cong Sun[2], and Zhen Liu[3]

[1] School of Automation, Nanjing University of Information Science and Technology, Nanjing 210044, Jiangsu, China
xiangsheng@nuist.edu.cn

[2] School of Mechanical Engineering and Automation, Northeastern University, Shenyang 110819, Liaoning, China

[3] State Key Laboratory of Robotics and System, Harbin Institute of Technology, Harbin 150001, China

Abstract. This paper presents the design of a redundant actuated three-DOF Cable-Suspended Parallel Robot (CSPR) with parallelogram architecture and its minimum jerk trajectory planning method. The moving platform of the designed CSPR is supported by eight redundant cables to enable three translational motion degrees. These cables are organized in four sets arranged in parallelogram configurations, with each set driven synchronously by a single motor. To achieve smooth robot motion and avoid abrupt changes in cable tensions, a trajectory planning method is proposed that utilizes seventh degree polynomial curves for minimum jerk in the Cartesian space of the moving platform. A dynamic simulation model of the redundantly actuated CSPR is developed, and point-to-point simulations are conducted. The simulation results indicate that the optimized trajectories exhibit reduced sudden cable tension changes and decreased position tracking errors. Compared to third degree polynomial and seventh degree polynomial trajectory before optimized, the average trajectory errors decreased by 3.6% and 2.3%, respectively, and the maximum trajectory errors are below 3.2 mm.

Keywords: Cable-Suspended Parallel Robot · Redundancy Actuated · Trajectory Planning · Dynamical Simulation

1 Introduction

Parallel robots have advantages such as high load capacity, high stiffness, and high speed and have been widely studied and applied. A series of three-degree-of-freedom parallel robots, represented by the Delta robot [1], have been widely used in pick-and-place tasks. However, traditional parallel robot mechanisms are complex, with limited workspace [2,

X. Lan et al. (Eds.): icira 2024, LNAI 15201, pp. 166–181, 2025.
https://doi.org/10.1007/978-981-96-0771-6_13

3], and high energy consumption due to rigid link connections between joints resulting in a large self-weight of the robot. Cable-suspended parallel robots use flexible cables instead of rigid components, making them advantageous in terms of large workspace, low inertia, and reconfigurability. They have been widely applied in various fields such as large-scale lifting and transportation [4–6], large radio telescopes [7, 8], high-speed cameras [9], and wind tunnel experiments [10].

According to the relationship between the degrees of freedom n and the number of driving cables m of CSPR, they can be classified into three types: unconstrained ($m < n + 1$), fully constrained ($m = n + 1$), and redundancy constraint ($m > n + 1$) [11]. Compared to unconstrained and fully constrained types, redundancy constraint types increase the workspace and improve the end effector load capacity by adding redundant driving cables. As described in [12], the designed three-degree-of-freedom CSPR uses redundant driving mode with six cables to drive the moving platform for three-degree-of-freedom translational motion. Meanwhile, three sets of cables are arranged in a parallelogram structure to restrict the rotational degrees of freedom of the moving platform, thereby improving the stability of the moving platform. Considering the unidirectional force characteristics of the cables, it is necessary to ensure that the cables are always tensioned during the motion of the moving platform. However, the constraint of cable tension [13–15] adds complexity to trajectory planning and motion control, leading to the inapplicability of traditional robot planning methods to CSPR. In [16], a point-to-point dynamic trajectory planning method for a planar two-degree-of-freedom CSPR is proposed. Based on the CSPR's dynamic model, the constraint conditions of cable tension are derived, and experimental verification shows that the proposed trajectory planning method not only satisfies the cable tension constraint but also achieves stable point-to-point motion.

However, as the complexity of operational tasks increases, reasonable trajectory planning can reduce jerk and trajectory tracking errors, thereby improving the accuracy of robots. Cubic polynomial curves can be used for trajectory planning. Alessandro et al. [17] proposed a cubic spline curve trajectory planning method to optimize jerk, which has fewer kinematic constraint conditions and ensures continuous joint velocity and acceleration but exhibits significant discontinuities due to jerk at intermediate points. Kong et al. [18] proposed cubic B-spline trajectory interpolation, which results in relatively smooth trajectory curves but does not constrain the accelerations and jerks at the starting and ending points. In [19], a combination of quintic polynomial trajectory and minimum jerk theory was used to create smooth motion for assisting robots. However, this study did not consider kinematic constraints. As mentioned in [20], quintic polynomial trajectories with unfavorable jerk at the starting and ending points adversely affect the positioning accuracy of robots. In order to reduce the adverse effects of jerk and obtain smoother and continuous trajectories, some research works attempt to construct trajectories by increasing the order of polynomials [21]. For example, in robot pick-and-place operations [22, 23] and high-precision positioning [24], seventh degree polynomial trajectory planning is performed, which can satisfy the constraints of jerk boundary conditions. Kucuk et al. [25] combined third degree polynomial curves and seventh degree polynomial curves to ensure zero acceleration at the starting and ending points of joint motion. Based on the above research, this paper proposes a minimum jerk trajectory planning method for CSPRs.

The content arrangement of this paper is as follows: Section 2 introduces the mechanical structure design of the three-DOF CSPR designed in this paper and the kinematic model considering the universal guide pulley. Section 3 proposes a trajectory planning method based on jerk minimization using seventh degree polynomial curves by solving a constrained quadratic optimization problem. Section 4 builds a simulation model in the Simulink simulation environment and conducts simulation experiments. Section 5 is the conclusion of the paper.

2 Modeling of the Three-DOF CSPR

2.1 Kinematic Modeling Considering Universal Guide Pulley Mechanisms

The overall configuration of the CSPR is illustrated in Fig. 1(a). The moving platform of the CSPR designed in this paper is connected to the main frame through four sets of parallel cables. One set of parallel cables, drawn out by spools, is synchronously controlled by the same motor. The arrangement of cables in parallelogram restricts the rotational degrees of freedom of the moving platform, thereby ensuring that the platform can only perform three degrees of translational motion. Simultaneously, redundant driving is employed to enhance the load capacity and reliability of the moving platform. Cross-connections of cables on the moving platform increase the workspace while minimum interference between cables.

Two coordinate systems are primarily defined: the global coordinate system *O-XYZ* established at the center of the positioning plate in the main frame, where the *Z*-axis is parallel to the direction of gravity, and the dynamic coordinate system $O_p - x_p y_p z_p$ fixed on the moving platform. The global coordinate system serves as a stationary reference fixed to the CSPR's main frame, while the dynamic coordinate system fixed on the moving platform moves relative to the global coordinate system to describe the motion state of the platform. Additionally, as shown in Fig. 1(c). a local coordinate system $B_i - x_i y_i z_i$ is established at the entry point B_i of the universal guide pulley mechanism, Fig. 1(b) depicts the coordinate transformation from the local coordinate system $B_i - x_i y_i z_i$ to the global coordinate system *O-XYZ*.

When using the universal guide pulley mechanism for cable guiding, the cable enters the pulley at point A_i, exits at another point C_i, and ultimately connects to the cable attachment point on the moving platform. The spatial orientation of the cable changes with the motion of the platform, accompanied by changes in the position of the point C_i where the cable leaves the pulley. Therefore, when using the universal guide pulley mechanism, the actual position of point C_i changes in real-time during the motion process. M_i is the center of the universal guide pulley, the universal guide pulley mechanism can be equivalently represented as an RP motion chain (where R and P represent rotary and prismatic joints, respectively), as shown in Fig. 1(d).

Along the direction of the Z-axis in the global coordinate system, the unit vector is denoted as K_i. α_i represents the rotation angle of the universal guide pulley, β_i is the wrapping angle of the cable on the universal guide pulley, and r_p is the radius of the universal guide pulley. The position vector p of the moving platform points from the

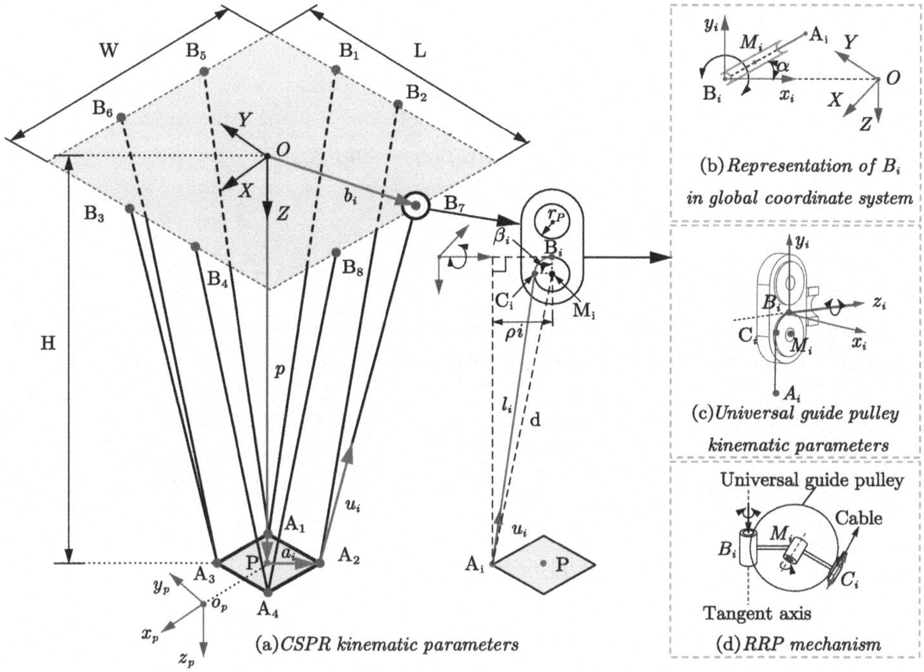

Fig. 1. Kinematic diagram of CSPR considering universal guide pulley mechanisms

origin O to point P. The rotation matrix of the dynamic coordinate system $O_p - x_p y_p z_p$ relative to the global coordinate system $O - XYZ$ is denoted as ${}^oR_p$, and the rotation matrix of the local coordinate system $B_i - x_i y_i z_i$ relative to the global coordinate system $O - XYZ$ is denoted as ${}^oR_i$. p is the position vector of point P in the global coordinate system $O - XYZ$, and the unit directional vector along the cable is denoted as α_i, with the length of the cable denoted as $\|l_i\|$.

The position of the cable connection point A_i in the local coordinate system $B_i - x_i y_i z_i$ is denoted B_{a_i},

$$\mathbf{a}_i^B = {}^o R_i^T (p + {}^o R_p^u r_i - b_i) = \left[x_i \; y_i \; z_i \right]^T \tag{1}$$

The swivel pulley's rotation angle can be calculated using inverse trigonometric functions.

$$\alpha_i = \tan 2(y_i, x_i) \tag{2}$$

The unit vector on $B_i M_i$ is denoted as e_i, and its expression in the local coordinate system $B_i - x_i y_i z_i$ is:

$$e_i = {}^o R_i^B e_i \tag{3}$$

$${}^B e_i = \left[\cos\alpha_i \; \sin\alpha_i \; 0 \right]^T \tag{4}$$

Then, we can obtain:

$$B_iM_i = r_p e_i \tag{5}$$

$$\overrightarrow{M_iC_i} = r_p(-\cos\beta_i e_i - \sin\beta_i k_i) \tag{6}$$

From this, we can derive:

$$l_i u_i = b_i + r_p e_i - r_p(\cos\beta_i e_i + \sin\beta_i k_i) - a_i \tag{7}$$

Considering the motion of the universal guide pulley in modeling the CSPR kinematics, the actual length of a single cable is obtained as::

$$\|L_i\| = \|l_i u_i\| + r_p\beta_i = \left\|\alpha_i + r_p e_i - r_p(\cos\beta_i e_i + \sin\beta_i k_i) - b_i\right\| + r_p\beta_i \tag{8}$$

By taking the dot product of Eq. (1) and the unit vector u_i, we can obtain the velocity of the cable, as shown in Eq. (10):

$$\|l_i\| = u_i \cdot \dot{l}_i = -u_i \cdot \dot{p} \tag{9}$$

$$\dot{L}_i = \begin{bmatrix} \dot{l}_1\ \dot{l}_2 \ldots \dot{l}_7\ \dot{l}_8 \end{bmatrix}^T = \begin{bmatrix} -u_1\ -u_2 \ldots -u_6\ -u_8 \end{bmatrix}^T \dot{p} = J\dot{p} \tag{10}$$

where $J = \begin{bmatrix} -u_1\ -u_2 \ldots -u_6\ -u_8 \end{bmatrix}^T$ is the inverse Jacobian matrix of the CSPR.

2.2 Detailed Mechanical Design of the Three-DOF CSPR

As shown in Fig. 2(a). The CSPR consists of the main frame, drive motors, cables, pulley mechanisms, and the moving platform. The cables wind around spools and are guided through pulleys to traverse the robot. The cables depart from the main frame at the exit points of the universal guide pulleys and reach the moving platform. The winding spools rotate in both directions to control the extension and retraction of the cables, thereby controlling the motion of the moving platform.

Each winch module is driven by a motor, and a spool winds a set of parallel cables in the opposite direction. Moreover, the winch modules are equipped with force sensors for real-time monitoring of cable tension states. As depicted in Fig. 2(c), one end of the cable is fixed to the spool and passes through a guiding pulley connected to the force sensor. The force sensor measures cable tension in real-time, with the measuring end of the force sensor being an S-type load cell. The cables are ultimately led out by universal guide pulleys and connected to the cable attachment points on the moving platform. Four cable attachment points symmetrically distributed on the moving platform, with adjacent pairs of cables cross-connected at the same point, are illustrated in Fig. 2(b).

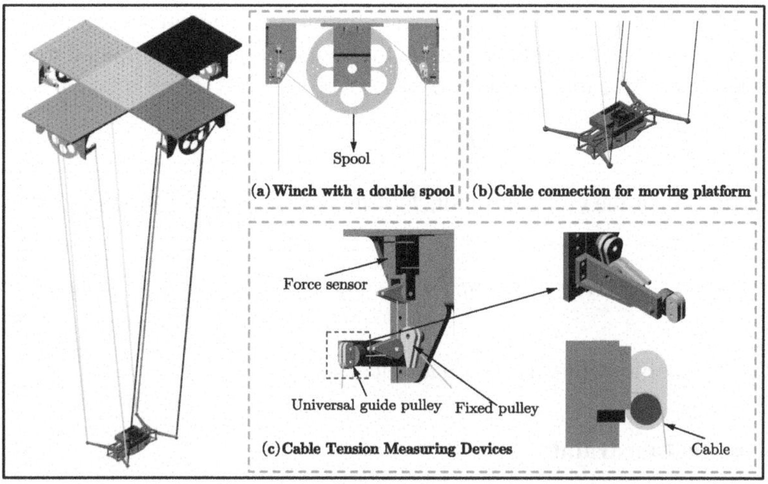

Fig. 2. Mechanical design and cable arrangement of the Three-DOF CSPR

3 Minimum Jerk Trajectory Planning Based on Seventh Degree Polynomials

Based on the initial target position and final position to be placed by the CSPR, different trajectory with different motion parameters by the moving platform tracked can be generated. Suppose there are n + 1 target points on the trajectory to connect multiple segments. The entire trajectory can be represented using a polynomial consisting of k segments, where each individual segment is represented by a seventh degree polynomial:

$$f(t) = a_0 + a_1 t + a_2 t^2 + a_3 t^3 + a_4 t^4 + a_5 t^5 + a_6 t^6 + a_7 t^7 \tag{11}$$

Writing the nth-order coefficients in vector form as $p = \left[p_0, p_1, \ldots, p_n\right]^T$, a single segment of the trajectory can be represented as follows:

$$f(t) = [1, t, t^2, \ldots, t^n] \cdot p \tag{12}$$

The derivative of Eq. (11) with respect to time yields the velocity, acceleration, and jerk functions. The expressions are as follows:

$$\begin{aligned} v(t) &= f'(t) = [0, 1, 2t, 3t^2, 4t^3, 5t^4, 6t^5, \ldots, nt^{n-1}] \cdot p \\ a(t) &= f''(t) = \left[0, 0, 2, 6t, 12t^2, 60t^3, 30t^4, \ldots, \frac{n!}{(n-2)!}t^{n-2}\right] \cdot p \\ jerk(t) &= f'''(t) = \left[0, 0, 0, 6, 24t, 60t^2, 120t^3, \ldots, \frac{n!}{(n-3)!}t^{n-3}\right] \cdot p \end{aligned} \tag{13}$$

3.1 Principle of Jerk Minimization

To reduce the jerk during the motion of the CSPR's moving platform, the optimization objective of the planned seventh degree polynomial trajectory in this paper is to achieve minimum jerk, thereby reducing the jerk and vibration of the platform. Considering that the sum of multiple jerks may be negative, the square of jerk is computed to obtain the minimum jerk objective function as follows:

$$minf(t) = min(f'''(t))^2 \tag{14}$$

The integral over the entire duration T of its operation is as follows:

$$min\int_0^T (f'''(t))^2dt = min\sum_{i=1}^{k}\int_{t_{i-1}}^{t_i}(f'''(t))^2dt = min\sum_{i=1}^{k}p^TQ_ip \tag{15}$$

where Q is the coefficient matrix of quadratic terms.

3.2 Kinematic Constraints

To ensure the continuity of the trajectory, certain constraints must be satisfied regarding the position, velocity, acceleration, and jerk of the moving platform at the start and end points of the trajectory. It is defined that at the beginning of the trajectory, the initial position, velocity, and acceleration are denoted as p_0, v_0, and a_0 respectively. For continuous trajectories, at the end of the current segment, the position, velocity, acceleration, and jerk are equal to the position, velocity, acceleration, and jerk at the beginning of the next segment. The corresponding kinematic constraint conditions are expressed as follows:

$$\begin{cases} p_j(t_i) = p_{j+1}(t_i) \\ v_j(t_i) = v_{j+1}(t_i) \\ a_j(t_i) = a_{j+1}(t_i) \\ j_j(t_i) = j_{j+1}(t_i) \end{cases} \tag{16}$$

The first segment calculates the constraint as follows:

$$\begin{gathered} p_{(0)} = 0 \quad p'_{(0)} = 0 \quad p''_{(0)} = 0 \quad p'''_{(0)} = 0 \\ p_1(t_1) = p_1 = p_2(t_1) \quad p'_1(t_1) = v_1 = p'_2(t_2) \\ p'''_1(t_1) = a_1 = p''_2(t_2) \quad p'''_1(t_1) = j_1 = p'''_2(t_1) \end{gathered} \tag{17}$$

The constraints for the last segment are calculated as follows:

$$\begin{gathered} p_{k-1}(t_{k-1}) = p_{k-1} = p_k(t_{k-1}); p'_{k-1}(t_{k-1}) = v_{k-1} = p'_k(t_{k-1}) \\ p''_{k-1}(t_{k-1}) = a_{k-1} = p''_k(t_{k-1}); p'''_{k-1}(t_{k-1}) = j_{k-1} = p'''_k(t_{k-1}) \\ p_k(t_k) = 0; p'_k(t_k) = 0; p''_k(t_k) = 0; p'''_k(t_k) = 0 \end{gathered} \tag{18}$$

The constraints for the middle segments are calculated as follows:

$$\begin{gathered} p_{n-1}(t_{n-1}) = p_{n-1} = p_n(t_{n-1}); p'_{n-1}(t_{n-1}) = a_{n-1} = p'_n(t_{n-1}) \\ p''_{n-1}(t_{n-1}) = v_{n-1} = p''_n(t_{n-1}); p'''_{n-1}(t_{n-1}) = j_{n-1} = p'''_n(t_{n-1}) \\ p_n(t_n) = a_n = p_{n+1}(t_n); p'_n(t_n) = v_n = p'_{n+1}(t_n) \\ p''_n(t_n) = a_n = p''_{n+1}; p'''_n(t_n) = j_n = p'''_{n+1}(t_n) \end{gathered} \tag{19}$$

Combining all the kinematic constraint equations for the target points mentioned above with Eqs. (14) and (15), the optimization problem for minimum jerk can be expressed in the quadratic form as shown in Eq. (20). Since the objective function is a quadratic programming problem, it can be solved by using a quadratic solver in MATLAB to optimize the polynomial coefficients for each part of the trajectory to minimize jerk.

$$f(x) = \frac{1}{2}x^T Hx + f^T x \tag{20}$$

4 Dynamical Simulation of the CSPR

Due to the elasticity and deformation of flexible cables, adding telescoping joints at cable attachment points is necessary to better simulate the motion state of the cables in real scenarios. These joints mimic the stiffness of the cables and the oscillations generated during cable motion. As illustrated in Fig. 3, the telescoping joint consists of a spherical joint and a prismatic joint moving along the Z-axis, forming a four-DOF joint. The prismatic joint is equipped with stiffness K and damping coefficient ζ to simulate the mechanical properties of the cables. The detailed simulation parameters are shown in Table 1 below. As the moving platform moves with the cables, the spherical joint rotates accordingly to ensure that the cables are always aligned with the Z-axis of the joint. The diagram in Fig. 3 illustrates the mechanism of a telescoping joint. Figure 3(a) depicts the initial state of the telescoping joint, while Fig. 3(b) and 3(c) respectively illustrate schematic diagrams of its rotational and translational states.

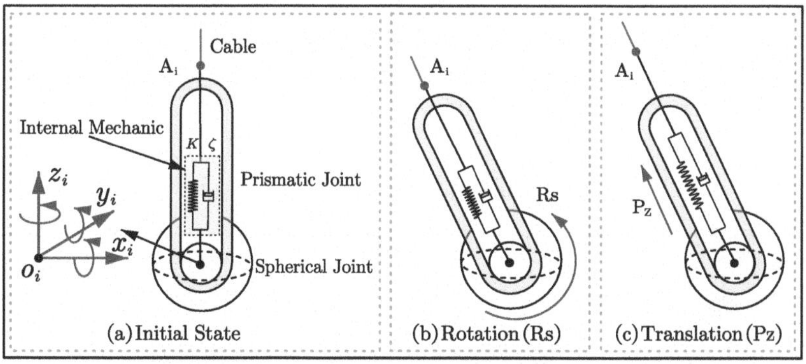

Fig. 3. Schematic diagram of the Telescoping Joint mechanism

Based on the constraints and relative positions of each component, settings were made for the corresponding spools, pulleys, cables, rotary joints, prismatic joints, and coordinate transformation modules. The model was imported into the Simulink simulation environment using the Multibody-Link plugin to perform dynamical simulation for the moving platform trajectory planning. Detailed simulation model parameters are presented in Table 1 (Fig. 4).

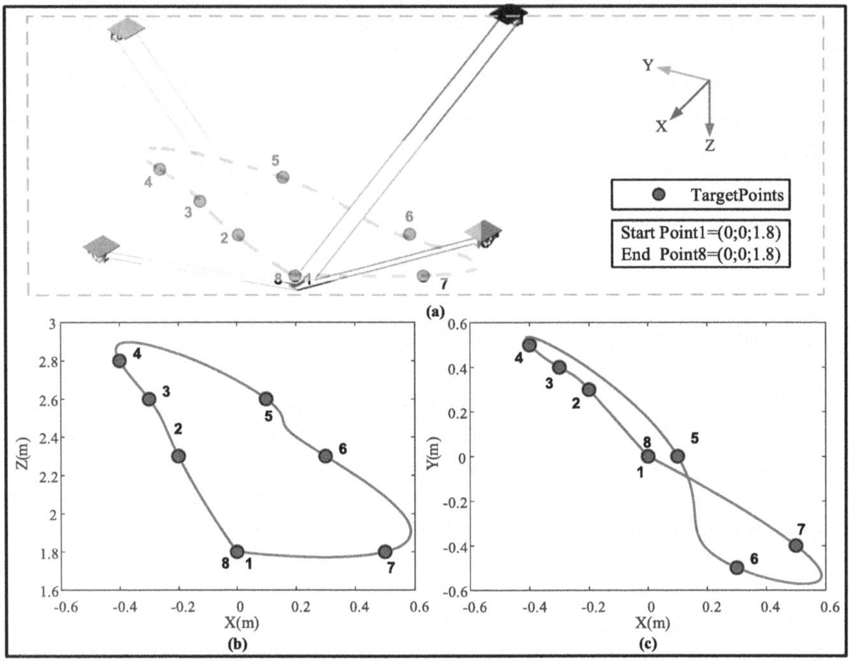

Fig. 4. Distribution of target points in the simulated trajectory, (a) represents the spatial trajectory and distribution of target points of the moving platform, (b) represents the trajectory and distribution of target points in the OXZ plane, and (c) represents the trajectory and distribution of target points in the OXY plane.

A series of target points with position coordinates denoted as $p_i = \left[x_i, y_i, z_i\right], i \in [0, 1 \cdot \cdot\cdot, n]$, The moving platform sequentially reaches these target points. The target points for trajectory planning are listed in Table 2.

Table 1. Simulation Model Parameter Table

Parameter items	Unit	Parameter value
Body frame length L	mm	7850
Body frame width W	mm	6550
Initial height of moving platform H	mm	1800
Radius of cable Spool R	mm	80
Radius of guide pulley r	mm	5
Radius of universal guide wheel r_p	mm	4
Mass of moving platform M	kg	5
Cable stiffness K	N/m	1.8e4
Damping coefficient ζ	N/(m/s)	100

Table 2. Distribution of target points for trajectory planning

Target point	Position	Target point	Position
1	[0, 0,1.8]	5	[0.1, 0, 2.6]
2	[−0.2, 0.3, 2.3]	6	[0.3, −0.5, 2.3]
3	[−0.3, 0.4, 2.6]	7	[0.5, −0.4, 1.8]
4	[−0.4, 0.5, 2.8]	8	[0, 0,1.8]

Figure 5 illustrates the variation in cable lengths and the cable length error for the trajectory simulated using the polynomial optimized for minimum jerk. It can be observed that the lengths of the same set of cables vary consistently, and the cable length errors are all controlled within the range of 0–3 mm. Relative to the cable length of 3000 mm, the cable length error is controlled within a range of 0 to 3 mm, with the maximum error accounting for approximately 0.1% of the cable length.

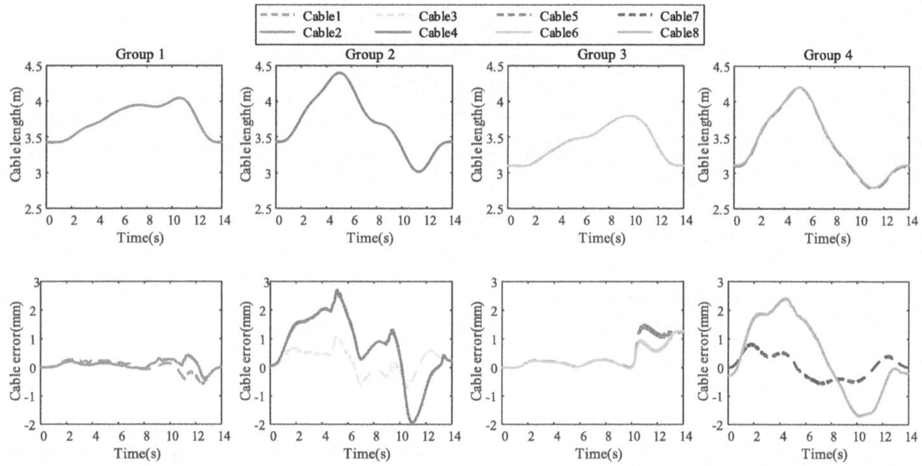

Fig. 5. Variation of cable length for minimum jerk optimized seventh degree polynomial based trajectory and cable length error

Figure 6 compares the changes in tension for the three sets of cables. From Fig. 6(a) and 6(b), it can be observed that the tension fluctuations of the cables under the third polynomial trajectory and seventh degree polynomial trajectory before jerk optimization are relatively large. Additionally, there is a noticeable difference in tension among cables drawn out by the same spool, attributed to cable oscillations caused by high jerk. As shown in Fig. 6(c), for minimum jerk optimized seventh degree polynomial based trajectory, there is no significant fluctuation in cable tension throughout the simulation process. The tension of all eight cables remains continuous, with tension values greater than zero, satisfying the unidirectional tensile force characteristics of the cables. Moreover, the tension among cables drawn out by the same spool is evenly distributed. This further confirms the feasibility of the trajectory planning method using seventh degree polynomial optimized for minimum jerk.

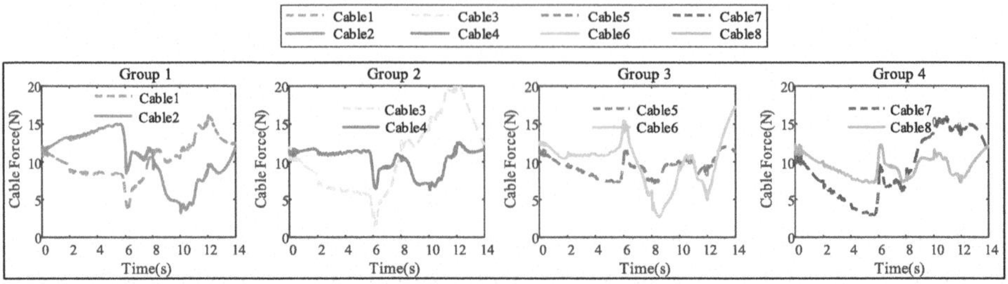

(a)Third degree polynomial trajectory

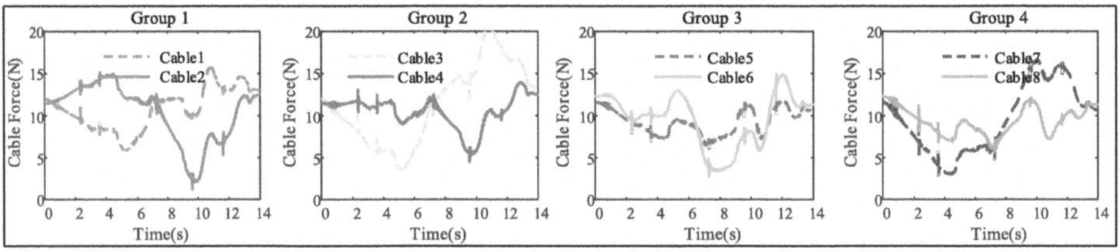

(b)Seventh degree polynomial trajectory

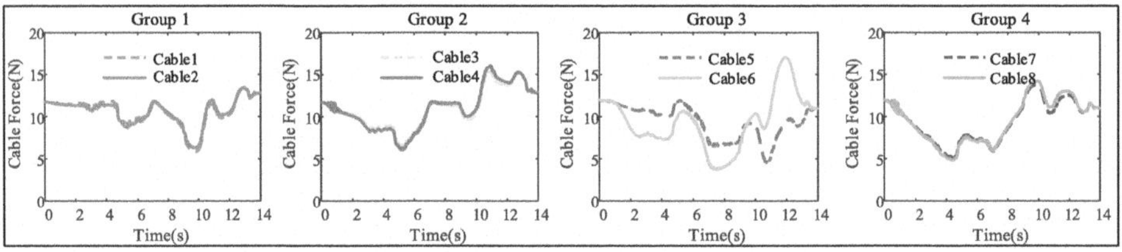

(c)Optimized sevth degree polynomial trajectory

Fig. 6. Comparison of cable tensions

As shown in Fig. 7, minimum jerk optimized seventh degree polynomial trajectory appears smoother compared to third degree polynomial trajectory and seventh degree polynomial trajectory before optimization. Figure 8 presents a comparison of trajectory errors among the three trajectories, with the errors predominantly concentrated in the Z-direction. As shown in Fig. 8(a), the optimized seventh degree polynomial trajectory exhibits an average trajectory error reduction of approximately 3.6% and 2.3% compared to third degree polynomial and seventh degree polynomial trajectory before optimization, respectively. Figure 8(b) illustrates the maximum trajectory error comparison, where the minimum jerk optimized seventh degree polynomial trajectory outperforms the other two trajectories in all three XYZ directions. The maximum trajectory error in the Z-direction for the optimized seventh degree polynomial trajectory is approximately 2.9% and 2.2% lower than the other two trajectories, respectively (Fig. 7).

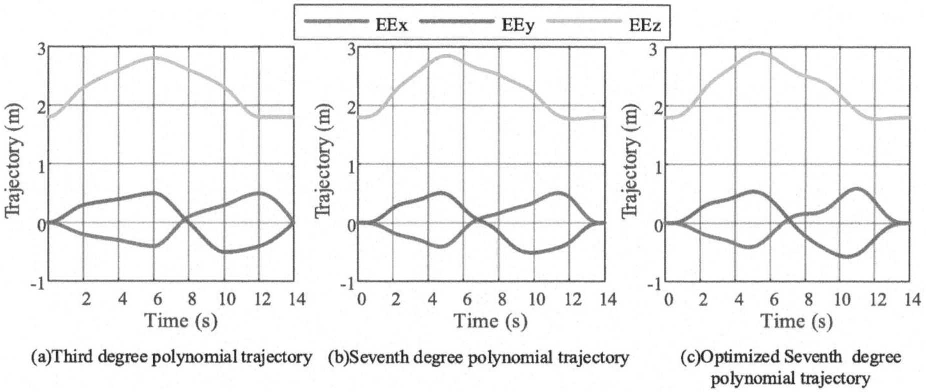

Fig. 7. Comparison of trajectory for the moving platform

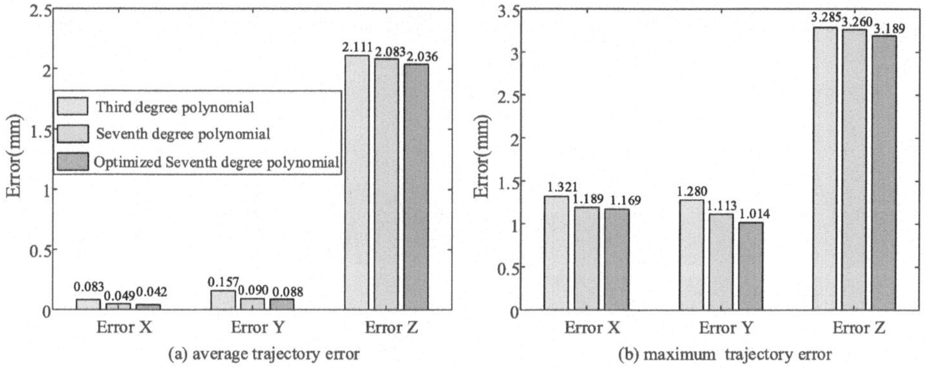

Fig. 8. Comparison of trajectory errors of the moving platform

The first group comprises third degree polynomial trajectories. Figure 9(a1) and Fig. 9 (a2) depict the variations in the velocity and acceleration of the moving platform. At the beginning of the simulation, there is a significant acceleration spike, accompanied by considerable jerk. Throughout the simulation, the acceleration exhibits significant fluctuations, with varying degrees of jerk. The second group comprises seventh degree polynomial trajectories before optimization. Figure 9(b1) and Fig. 9(b2) illustrate the changes in the velocity and acceleration of the moving platform. Compared to third degree polynomial trajectories, the velocity profile of seventh degree polynomial trajectories is smoother. There are no abrupt changes in acceleration at the beginning of the simulation, but there are regions with significant jerk throughout the simulation. The third group consists of seventh degree polynomial trajectories optimized for minimal jerk. The velocity, acceleration, and jerk profiles of the optimized seventh degree polynomial trajectories are depicted in Fig. 9(c1), Fig. 9(c2), and Fig. 9(c3), respectively, all of which are continuous and smooth. At the beginning and end of the simulation, the velocity, acceleration, and jerk of the moving platform are all zero. Compared to the trajectories before optimization, the maximum magnitudes of acceleration and jerk of the moving platform are significantly reduced in the optimized trajectories. Therefore, the proposed minimum jerk optimized seventh degree polynomial based trajectories result in more stable motion of the moving platform with reduced jerk.

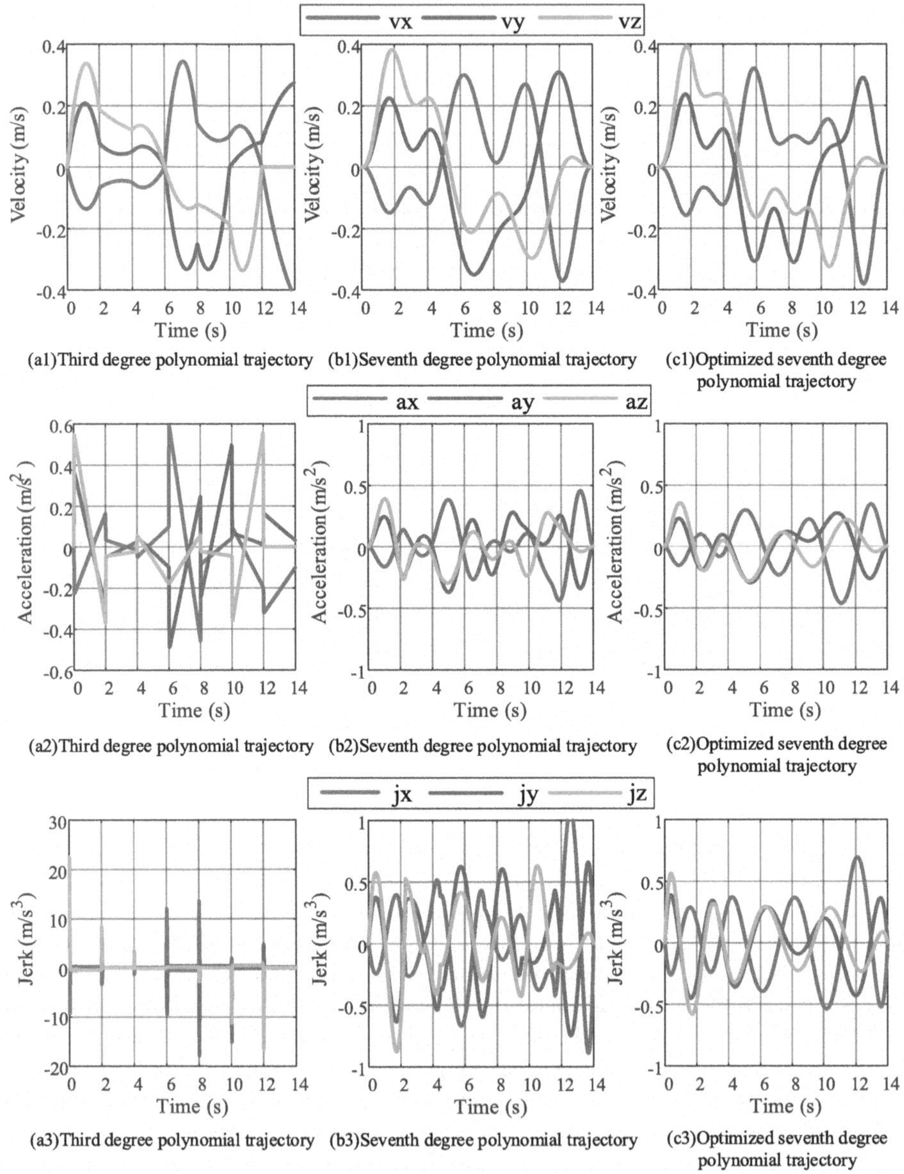

Fig. 9. Comparison of moving platform velocity, acceleration, and jerk Variations

Additionally, to validate that the designed three-DOF CSPR can constrain the rotational degrees of freedom of the moving platform under the constraints of parallel cables, the angular errors of the moving platform were measured in Cartesian space. The angular errors in three directions are shown in Fig. 10, all of which are less than 6×10^{-3} degrees. This demonstrates that the designed parallel cable arrangement can effectively constrain the rotational degrees of freedom of the moving platform.

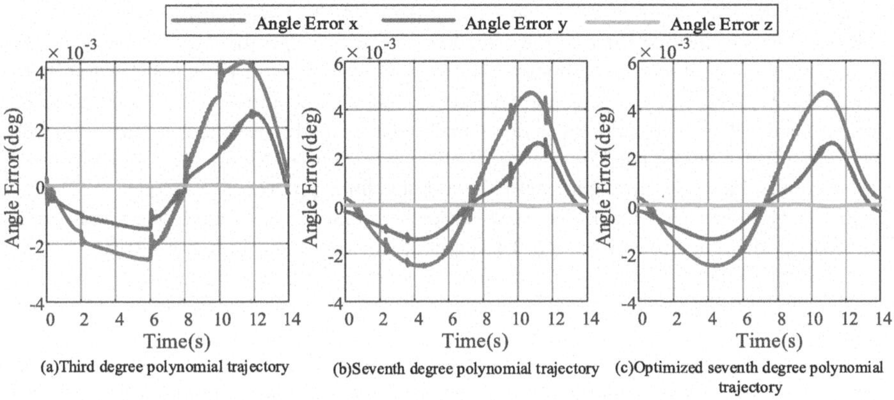

Fig. 10. Rotation errors of the moving platform

5 Conclusions

This paper presents the design of a redundant actuated three-DOF Cable-Suspended Parallel Robot (CSPR) with parallelogram architecture and its minimum jerk trajectory planning method. To validate the effectiveness of the proposed minimum jerk trajectory planning, simulation experiments are conducted in the Simulink simulation environment. The simulation results indicate that the optimized trajectories exhibit reduced sudden cable tension changes and decreased position tracking errors. The average trajectory errors in the Z-direction for the minimum jerk optimized seventh degree polynomial trajectory decreased below 2.1 mm. Compared to third degree polynomial and seventh degree polynomial trajectory before optimized, it decreased by 3.6% and 2.3%, respectively. Additionally, the maximum trajectory error decreased below 3.2 mm. Compared to the other two trajectories, it decreased by 2.9% and 2.2%, respectively. Furthermore, compared to third degree polynomial trajectory and the unoptimized seventh degree polynomial trajectory, the minimum jerk optimized seventh degree polynomial based trajectory significantly reduces the acceleration and jerk of the moving platform, making the trajectory smoother and thereby improving the mechanical performance of the robot. This validates the effectiveness of the proposed trajectory planning method based on seventh degree polynomial jerk minimization.

Acknowledgment. The work was supported by the Foundation for the National Natural Science Foundation of China (Grant No.52105024 and 52305011) and the Open Project of State Key

Laboratory of Robotics and System (HIT) (Grant No. SKLRS-2023-KF-23 and SKLRS-2024-KF-06).

References

1. Shen, H., Meng, Q., Li, J., et al.: Kinematic sensitivity, parameter identification and calibration of a non-fully symmetric parallel Delta robot. Mech. Mach. Theory **161**, 104311 (2021)
2. Merlet, J.P.: On the workspace of suspended cable-driven parallel robots. In: 2016 IEEE International Conference on Robotics and Automation (ICRA). IEEE, pp.841–846 (2016)
3. Yu, J., Li, X., Tao, J., et al.: Workspace quality evaluation and optimal design of a redundantly constrained 6-DoF cable-driven parallel manipulator. In: Intelligent Robotics and Applications: 14th International Conference, ICIRA 2021, Yantai, China, 22–25 October 2021, Proceedings, Part I 14. Springer International Publishing, pp. 575–585 (2021)
4. Pott, A., Mütherich, H., Kraus, W., et al.: IPAnema: a family of cable-driven parallel robots for industrial applications. In: Cable-Driven Parallel Robots, pp. 119–134 (2013)
5. Zi, B., Lin, J., Qian, S.: Localization, obstacle avoidance planning and control of a cooperative cable parallel robot for multiple mobile cranes. Robot. Comput. Integr. Manuf. **34**, 105–123 (2015)
6. Scalera, L., Gallina, P., Seriani, S., et al.: Cable-based robotic crane (CBRC): design and implementation of overhead traveling cranes based on variable radius drums. IEEE Trans. Robot. **34**(2), 474–485 (2018)
7. Yao, R., Tang, X.Q., Wang, J.S., et al.: Dimensional optimization design of the four-cable-driven parallel manipulator in FAST. IEEE/ASME Trans. Mechatron. **15**(6), 932–941 (2010)
8. Tang, X.Q., Yao, R.: Dimensional design on the six-cable driven parallel manipulator of FAST. J. Mech. Des. **133**(11), 111012 (2011)
9. Wang, L., Sheng, Y., Qiu, Y.Y., et al.: Design and implementation of the control device for a cable-driven camera robot. Appl. Mech. Mater. **373**, 225–230 (2013)
10. Wang, X.G., Ma, S.Y., Lin, Q.: Hybrid pose/tension control based on stiffness optimization of cable-driven parallel mechanism in wind tunnel test. In: 2016 2nd International Conference on Control, Automation and Robotics (ICCAR), Hong Kong, China, April 28–30, pp. 75–79 (2016)
11. Zi, B., Qian, S.: Design, Analysis and Control of Cable-Suspended Parallel Robots and It's Applications, pp. 978–981. Springer (2017). https://doi.org/10.1007/978-981-10-1753-7
12. Vu, D.S., Barnett, E., Gosselin, C.: Experimental validation of a three-degree-of-freedom cable-suspended parallel robot for spatial translation with constant orientation. J. Mech. Robot. **11**(2), 024502 (2013)
13. Trevisani, A.: Underconstrained planar cable-direct-driven robots: a trajectory planning method ensuring positive and bounded cable tensions Mechatronics **20**(1), 113–127 (2010)
14. Xiang, Y., Li, Q., Jiang, X.: Dynamic rotational trajectory planning of a cable-driven parallel robot for passing through singular orientations. Mech. Mach. Theory **158**, 104223 (2021)
15. Ueland, E., Sauder, T., Skjetne, R.: Optimal force allocation for overconstrained cable-driven parallel robots: Continuously differentiable solutions with assessment of computational efficiency. IEEE Trans. Robot. **37**(2), 659–666 (2020)
16. Gosselin, C., Foucault, S.: Dynamic point-to-point trajectory planning of a two-DOF cable-suspended parallel robot. IEEE Trans. Robot. **30**(3), 728–736 (2014)
17. Gasparetto, A., Zanotto, V.: A technique for time-jerk optimal planning of robot trajectories. Robot. Comput. Integr. Manuf. **24**, 415–426 (2008)

18. Kong, M., Ji, C., Chen, Z., et al.: Smooth and near time-optimal trajectory planning of robotic manipulator with smooth constraint based on cubic B-spline. In: 2013 IEEE International Conference on Robotics and Biomimetics (ROBIO). IEEE, pp. 2328–2333 (2013)
19. Seki, H., Tadakuma, S.: Minimum jerk control of power assisting robot on human arm behavior characteristic. In: 2004 IEEE International Conference on Systems, Man and Cybernetics (IEEE Cat. No. 04CH37583). IEEE, pp. 722–727 (2004)
20. Visioli, A.: Trajectory planning of robot manipulators by using algebraic and trigonometric splines. Robotica **18**, 611–631 (2000)
21. Huang, M.S., Hsu, Y.L., Fung, R.F.: Minimum-energy point-to-point trajectory planning for a motor-toggle servomechanism. IEEE/ASME Trans. Mechatron. **17**, 337–344 (2012)
22. Fang, S., Ma, X., Zhao, Y., et al.: Trajectory planning for seven-DOF robotic arm based on quintic polynormial. In: 2019 11th International Conference on Intelligent Human-Machine Systems and Cybernetics (IHMSC). IEEE, pp. 198–201 (2019)
23. Xie, Z., Wu, P., Ren, P.: A comparative study on the pick-and-place trajectories for a delta robot. In: Proceedings of the ASME Design Engineering Technical Conferences American Society of Mechanical Engineers Digital Collection (2016)
24. Chang, B.H., Hori, Y.: Trajectory design considering derivative of jerk for head-positioning of disk drive system with mechanical vibration. IEEE/ASME Trans. Mechatron. **11**(3), 273–279 (2006)
25. Kucuk, S.: Optimal trajectory generation algorithm for serial and parallel manipulators. Robot. Comput. Integr. Manuf. **48**, 219–232 (2017)

Kinematic Analysis and Control Strategy Research of Hydraulic Robotic Arm Drive Module 2-UPS+U Parallel Mechanism

Shenglong Nie[1], Bo Chen[1], He Liu[1], Yichao Li[1], Yundou Xu[1,2](✉), Jiantao Yao[1,2], and Yongsheng Zhao[1,2]

[1] Parallel Robot and Mechatronic System Laboratory of Hebei Province, Yanshan University, Qinhuangdao 066004, China
ydxu@ysu.edu.cn

[2] Key Laboratory of Advanced Forging and Stamping Technology and Science of Ministry of National Education, Yanshan University, Qinhuangdao 066004, China

Abstract. In this article, we propose a low degree-of-freedom parallel mechanism known as the 2-UPS+U parallel structure. This mechanism features a double-triangle configuration and exhibits unique structural properties, resulting in a coupled system with multivariable input and output. In terms of kinematic analysis, Firstly, we establish the closed-loop directed transformation graph of the mechanism. Then, using the D-H method, we determine the position and orientation of the end-effector. Finally, we solve the inverse position problem of the mechanism through a geometric approach. Aiming at the common synchronous loop problem in hydraulic system, the control strategy of double hydraulic cylinder drive is designed. The validity of our kinematic analysis is confirmed by simulation models constructed in Adams simulation software which demonstrate consistent results with theoretical calculations, thus affirming its accuracy. The 2-UPS+U parallel mechanism finds common application in hydraulic drive units for hydraulic robotic arms. The findings from this research are highly significant as they contribute to enhancing control precision in hydraulic-driven joints.

Keywords: The 2-UPS+U Parallel Mechanism · Kinematics · Double hydraulic cylinder drive · Synchronizing loop · Hydraulic Robotic Arm

1 Introduction

The parallel mechanism with fewer degrees of freedom is a kind of parallel mechanism with less than six degrees of freedom. Compared with the parallel mechanism with six degrees of freedom, the parallel mechanism with fewer degrees of freedom has the advantages of simple mechanism configuration, fewer driving parts, convenient control, easy manufacturing and lower cost. In many applications, a fully 6-DOF parallel mechanism is not required, so the less-DOF parallel mechanism is more advantageous in such applications. Because of its special structural characteristics, the modeling and analysis of kinematics, singularity and stiffness of the low-degree-of-freedom parallel mechanism

X. Lan et al. (Eds.): ICIRA 2024, LNAI 15201, pp. 182–194, 2025.
https://doi.org/10.1007/978-981-96-0771-6_14

are more special than those of the six-degree-of-freedom parallel mechanism, and it is difficult to find a general analysis method for the low-degree-of-freedom mechanism [1–3]. For the kinematic analysis of the parallel mechanism with fewer degrees of freedom, Huang Zhen et al. [4] put forward the method of dummy mechanism, which transforms the branches with less than six degrees of freedom into six degrees of freedom branches to realize the full rank processing of the matrix, so that the analysis process with fewer degrees of freedom is the same as that of the parallel mechanism with six degrees of freedom. The characteristic of this method is that the more complex the mechanism, the more obvious its superiority, but for different mechanisms, different dummy processing is needed, and this processing method increases the rank of the Jacobian matrix, thus increasing the calculation amount. In order to solve this problem, Huang Zhen et al. [5] also proposed a new direct method based on the influence coefficient method, which is suitable for the parallel mechanism with few degrees of freedom. Based on the dual spinor theory, JOSHI et al. [6] established a complete Jacobian matrix of three free mechanisms. RICO et al. [7, 8] combined spiral theory and Lie group Lie algebra system to establish the velocity and acceleration models of series mechanism and parallel mechanism. Based on the dual helix theory, Li Yonggang et al. [9] derived the moving helix system and the anti-helix system in the constrained branch chain, obtained the constraint submatrix of the mechanism by using the reciprocal product, and combined the constraint submatrix and the motion submatrix to establish the complete Jacobian of the mechanism, but they did not construct the second-order acceleration influence coefficient and acceleration constraint matrix of the mechanism with few degrees of freedom.

The positive position solution of parallel mechanism is always difficult to solve, the key is to solve a set of nonlinear constraint equations. The solutions are mainly numerical method and analytical method. The numerical method has the advantages of simple mathematical modeling, no complicated mathematical derivation, and is suitable for general parallel mechanism. However, the numerical method is slow, and when the mechanism is close to the singular configuration, it is difficult to converge, and it is difficult to obtain all the position solutions, and the results are directly related to the initial value selection. The analytical method is mainly to eliminate the unknowns in the mechanism equation by elimination method, so that the input and output equations of the mechanism are only a high-order equation containing one unknown, which is characterized by the fact that all possible solutions of the positive solution of the position can be found without the initial value, but the mathematical derivation is extremely complex. When the degree of the unary algebraic equation to be solved is less than 4, the solution speed is faster, whereas the solution speed is lower. Shen Huiping [10, 11] carried out topological design and kinematics analysis of the traditional 2T1R parallel mechanism, and solved the forward and reverse kinematics model based on the principle of kinematic modeling by using topological features. Simplify path planning and dynamic analysis with partial decoupling. Lin Rongfu [12] and Abdullah [13] carried out kinematics analysis of the forward and backward solutions of the 2R1T parallel mechanism, and innovated the configuration and applied it to minimally invasive surgery. Torre H [14] carried out kinematic analysis of 3-CRC parallel mechanism. Zhang Dongsheng

[15] proposed a new three-degree-of-freedom planar parallel mechanism and carried out kinematics analysis on it.

The hydraulic drive component of the drilling manipulator arm is driven by double hydraulic cylinders. If the hydraulic drive unit and the joint connecting rod connected with it are isolated and analyzed, this is the 2-UPS+U parallel mechanism with less degrees of freedom involved in this paper. In structure, the 2-UPS+U parallel mechanism is a double triangle structure. As the drive system of the manipulator, it is a coupling system with multi-variable input and multi-variable output. Based on the closed directed transformation graph, the D-H method is used to determine the pose of the terminal point, and then the P-pair length driven by the geometric method is obtained.

2 Kinematics Analysis of 2-UPS+U

For the drilling robot arm [16–18], this large hydraulic robot arm is usually considered as a series robot arm, and when conducting kinematic analysis and calculation, it is also analyzed according to the series mechanism. However, if the hydraulically driven joint connecting rod is taken out separately, its essence may be a parallel mechanism, and the analysis of the kinematic accuracy of the parallel mechanism directly affects the control accuracy of the robot arm. This paper takes a certain type of rock drilling robot arm as the research object. The robot arm has 9 joints and its configuration is RRPRRRRPP. The upper arm joints 1 and 2 and the lower arm joints 4 and 5 are driven by double hydraulic cylinders. Its configuration is 2-UPS+U parallel mechanism (Fig. 1).

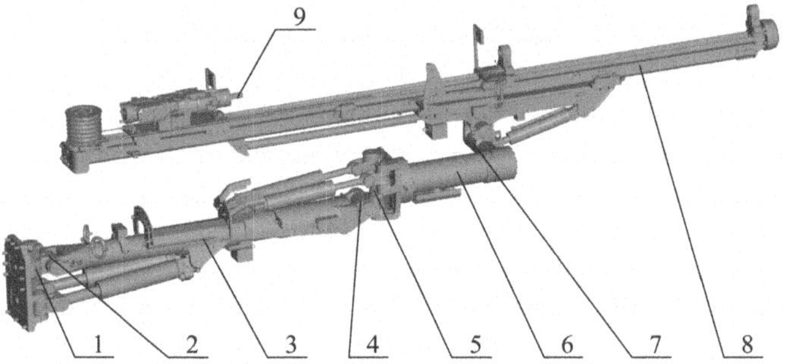

Fig. 1. Hydraulically driven 9-joint drilling mechanical arm, in which the swing of the upper and lower arms is driven by double hydraulic cylinders, that is, the 2-UPS + U parallel mechanism. In this manipulator system, the 2-UPS + U parallel mechanism is a coupling system with multi-variable input and multi-variable output.

In the manipulator, the 2-UPS+U parallel mechanism drives the big arm and the small arm in the same way. The 2-UPS+U mechanism driving the big arm is analyzed below. The schematic diagram of the 2-UPS+U parallel mechanism is shown in Fig. 2.

According to the modified G-K formula, the degree of freedom of the 2-UPS+U parallel mechanism is calculated:

$$K = d(n - g - 1) + \sum_{i=1}^{g} f_i + v$$

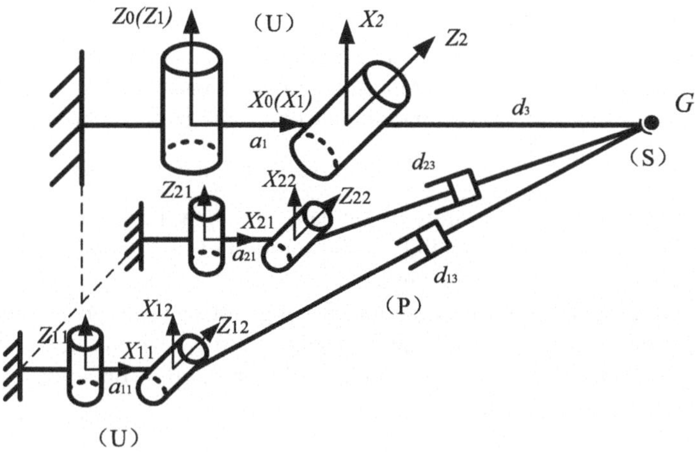

Fig. 2. The 2-UPS+U parallel mechanism driving the big arm movement, and the G-point in the figure can be regarded as the moving platform of the parallel mechanism.

$$
\begin{aligned}
&= 6 \times (6 - 7 - 1) + 14 + 0 \\
&= 2
\end{aligned}
\tag{1}
$$

As shown in Fig. 2, d3 is the length of the connecting rod of the big arm of the main body of the drilling mechanical arm, which plays a role in carrying other components and moving the end in a large range in the drilling mechanical arm. It is connected with the base through joint 1 and joint 2. d13 and d23 are the lengths of two hydraulic cylinders, whose function is to support the connecting rod of the big arm and adjust the Angle of joint 1 and joint 2. They are also connected with the base by two vertical rotating shafts with different spatial surfaces. By driving the two hydraulic cylinders, the G-point can move in a wide range in space and coordinate with other joints to control the end of the robot arm to reach the specified attitude.

The 2-UPS+U parallel mechanism with double hydraulic cylinders as the main driving mode of the drilling manipulator has the following characteristics:

(1) Aiming at the problem of synchronous circuit in hydraulic system, the two degrees of freedom movement of the end G-point is realized by the synchronous movement of the two hydraulic cylinders in the same direction and the reverse synchronous movement. Ensure that the G spot can move in a large range of space and meet the control requirements of the hydraulic system.
(2) The double hydraulic cylinders are arranged under the big arm to support the big arm to improve the bearing capacity of the mechanical arm and enhance the reliability of the mechanical arm.

2.1 Positive Solution and Inverse Solution

For a single UPS+U mechanism, according to the closed directed transformation diagram shown in Fig. 3, point *J* is the coordinate system formed by the output end of the drive, and point *A* is the base marking system. The pose of the *J* system under the *A* system can be represented by three paths: Path 1: A, A_1, A_2, J; Path 2: A, A_{10}, A_{11}, A_{12}, A_{13}, J; and path 3: A, A_{20}, A_{21}, A_{22}, A_{23}, J. According to the kinematics, the pose transformation of J system under A system can be represented by a 4-order matrix, and the product $\prod A_i$ of the connecting rod transformation matrix for any path can be expressed as the block moment $\begin{bmatrix} \boldsymbol{H}_{11} & \boldsymbol{H}_{12} \\ 0 & 1 \end{bmatrix}$. For a given joint Angle 1 and 2, the pose of J point can be calculated through a positive solution of the path, and then the length of the hydraulic cylinder can be calculated through the inverse solution of other paths, so as to achieve accurate control of the Angle of the big arm.

The analysis process adopts the combination of geometric method and inverse transformation method, that is, when the Angle of joint 1 and 2 is given, the J -point pose is calculated by D-H method, and the hydraulic cylinder length is obtained by geometric method for the other two paths.

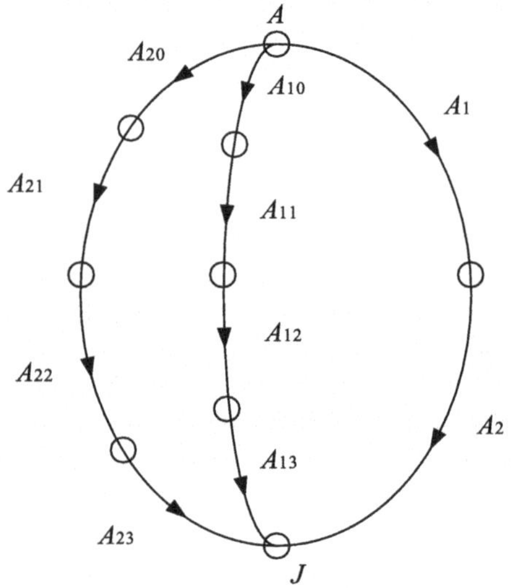

Fig. 3. A closed directed transformation graph from the base coordinate system to the output coordinate system

The D-H coordinate system constructed with the front two joints of the upper arm is shown in Fig. 4.

The D-H coordinate link parameters of the front two joints of the big arm are shown in Table 1.

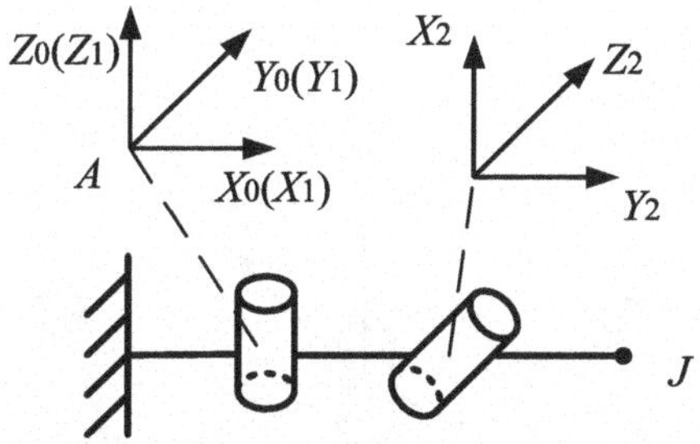

Fig. 4. The first two joints D-H coordinate system

Table 1. Parameters of connecting rod in D-H coordinate system for the first two joints

$a_{i\text{-}1}$ (mm)	$\alpha_{i\text{-}1}$ (°)	d_i (mm)	θ_i (°)	θ_i (°)	Value range (°)	Initial value (°)
0	0	0	θ_1	θ_1	(−30,30)	0
a_1(160)	90	d_2	θ_2	θ_2	(−180,0)	0
a_2(300)	0	Δd	0	——	——	——

Calculate the connecting rod transformation matrix:

$$\begin{cases} {}_1^0\boldsymbol{T} = \begin{bmatrix} \cos\theta_1 & -\sin\theta_1 & 0 & 0 \\ \sin\theta_1 & \cos\theta_1 & 0 & 0 \\ 0 & 0 & 1 & 0 \\ 0 & 0 & 0 & 1 \end{bmatrix} \\ {}_2^1\boldsymbol{T} = \begin{bmatrix} \cos\theta_2 & -\sin\theta_2 & 0 & a_1 \\ 0 & 0 & 1 & 0 \\ -\sin\theta_2 & -\cos\theta_2 & 0 & 0 \\ 0 & 0 & 0 & 1 \end{bmatrix} \\ {}_J^2\boldsymbol{T} = \begin{bmatrix} 1 & 0 & 0 & a_2 \\ 0 & 1 & 1 & 0 \\ 0 & 0 & 1 & \Delta d \\ 0 & 0 & 0 & 1 \end{bmatrix} \end{cases} \tag{2}$$

According to the forward kinematics knowledge of the series mechanism, the pose of J-point in the 0 system is obtained as ${}_J^0\boldsymbol{T}$:

$${}_J^0\boldsymbol{T} = {}_1^0\boldsymbol{T}(q_1){}_2^1\boldsymbol{T}(q_2){}_J^2\boldsymbol{T} \tag{3}$$

Taking the pose matrix as a known parameter, the length of the two hydraulic cylinders is obtained by geometric method, as shown in Fig. 5, θl_1 is the vertical axis declination Angle of the hydraulic cylinder drive group, θl_2 is the horizontal axis declination Angle, NJ is the distance from the horizontal axis center to point J, expressed as:

$$NL = D_{const} + dl \tag{4}$$

Where, D_{const} is the fixed value, dl is the expansion of the hydraulic cylinder in the hydraulic cylinder drive group.

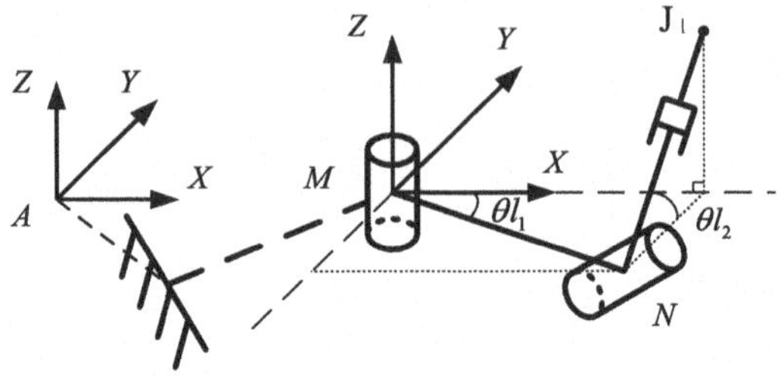

Fig. 5. Hydraulic cylinder drive group D-H coordinate system diagram

According to the special geometric relationship between the M axis and the N axis, it is assumed that when the Angle of the M axis is fixed, the space plane formed by the whole rotation of the N axis is S, and the three points M, N and J are on the S plane. At this time, the M axis is rotated around the axis center for the whole cycle, and the space geometry V based on the S plane is formed. In the process of geometric analysis, the M-axis is rotated first, and an appropriate section is selected on the space geometry so that the J point of the big arm is located on the S plane. At this time, the value of θl_1 can be expressed as:

$$\theta l_1 = \text{atand}(p_y / p_x) \tag{5}$$

At this time, the J point is on the S plane, and connecting JN means rotating the n-axis so that the end is on the line JN. The absolute value of θl_2 is as follows:

$$|\theta l_2| = \text{atand}\big(\text{abs}(p_z) / (\text{abs}(p_x/\text{sind}(90 - \theta l_1)) - a_1)\big) \tag{6}$$

When $p_z \geq 0$, there are:

$$\theta l_2 = 90 + |\theta l_2| \tag{7}$$

When $p_z < 0$, there are:

$$\theta l_2 = 90 - |\theta l_2| \tag{8}$$

In the default initial state, the expansion of the hydraulic cylinder is 0, and the scalar value of NJ is obtained:

$$NJ = \big(\text{abs}\big(p_x / \text{sind}(90 - \theta l_1)\big) - a_1\big) / \text{cosd}(\theta l_2) \tag{9}$$

The final expansion of the hydraulic cylinder is:

$$dl = NL - D_{const} \tag{10}$$

Where p_x, p_y and p_z are the position of point J, and a_1 is the spatial distance between the M axis and the N axis.

There are two hydraulic drive groups for the 2-UPS+U parallel mechanism, and the structure of both is exactly the same. The above method is for the left hydraulic cylinder to obtain its expansion, and the same approach can be obtained for the right hydraulic cylinder expansion.

2.2 Control Strategy

The solutions for hydraulic cylinder expansion in the previous section are in their respective branch coordinate systems. In this section, when the left and right hydraulic cylinders are controlled in the same direction and in the reverse direction, the coordinates of G point are expressed in the base coordinate system. Now we need to convert the G-point coordinates to their respective branch coordinate systems.

As shown in Fig. 6, coordinate systems B and C are the coordinate systems of the UPS branches on the left and right sides respectively, and A is the base coordinate system.

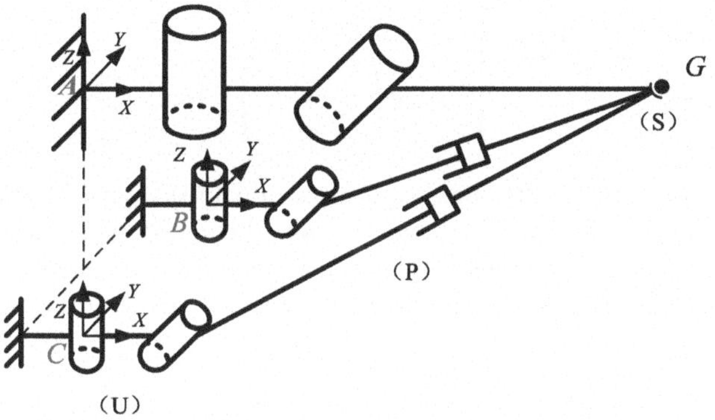

Fig. 6. UPS branch coordinates and base coordinates

When two coordinate systems have the same orientation but the origin of coordinates are not identical, according to the translation transformation formula between coordinates:

$$^{A}p = {}^{B}p + {}^{A}p_{B_O} \tag{11}$$

Among:
^{A}P—The position of point P in the coordinate system $\{A\}$.
^{B}P—The position of point P in the coordinate system $\{B\}$.
$^{A}P_{B_O}$—Translation vector of the coordinate system $\{B\}$ with respect to $\{A\}$.

The position of the G-point in the coordinate system $\{A\}$ and $\{B\}$ is obtained:

$$\begin{cases} {}^{B}p_{A_O} = \begin{pmatrix} -d_x \\ -d_y \\ d_z \end{pmatrix} \\ {}^{C}p_{A_O} = \begin{pmatrix} -d_x \\ d_y \\ d_z \end{pmatrix} \\ {}^{B}p = \begin{pmatrix} p_x - d_x \\ p_y - d_y \\ p_z + d_z \end{pmatrix} \\ {}^{C}p = \begin{pmatrix} p_x - d_x \\ p_y + d_y \\ p_z + d_z \end{pmatrix} \end{cases} \tag{12}$$

Where d_x, d_y and d_z are the distances of the coordinate system $\{A\}$ relative to $\{B\}$ in the X, Y, and Z directions. The UPS branch where the coordinate system $\{B\}$ and $\{C\}$ are located is planar symmetric with respect to the intermediate plane.

Therefore, the formula of the left hydraulic cylinder can be arranged as:

$$\begin{cases} \theta l_1 = \text{atand}((p_y - d_y)/(p_x - d_x)) \\ \theta l_2 = \text{atand}\big(\text{abs}(p_z + d_z)/(\text{abs}((p_x - d_x)/\text{sind}(90 - \theta l_1)) - a_1)\big) \\ NJ = \big(\text{abs}\big((p_x - d_x)/\text{sind}(90 - \theta l_1)\big) - a_1\big)/\text{cosd}(\theta l_2) \\ dl_l = NJ - D_{const} \end{cases} \tag{13}$$

The formula of the right hydraulic cylinder can be sorted out as:

$$\begin{cases} \theta l_1 = \text{atand}((p_y + d_y)/(p_x - d_x)) \\ \theta l_2 = \text{atand}\big(\text{abs}(p_z + d_z)/(\text{abs}((p_x - d_x)/\text{sind}(90 - \theta l_1)) - a_1)\big) \\ NJ = \big(\text{abs}\big((p_x - d_x)/\text{sind}(90 - \theta l_1)\big) - a_1\big)/\text{cosd}(\theta l_2) \\ dl_r = NJ - D_{const} \end{cases} \tag{14}$$

The 2-UPS+U parallel mechanism applied to the drilling robot arm is driven by double hydraulic cylinders. In the hydraulic system with one pump and multiple cylinders, the application of double hydraulic cylinder drive involves the problem of synchronous loop. The so-called synchronous loop: that is, in the hydraulic system, the loop that enables two or more hydraulic cylinders to maintain the same displacement or the same speed in motion. In this paper, the two degrees of freedom motion requirements of the end G-point are realized by the simultaneous and reverse synchronous motion of the two hydraulic cylinders.

In the 2-UPS+U parallel mechanism, the expansion and contraction of the two hydraulic cylinders are generally different for a certain pose of the end G-point. At this time, the problem of synchronous circuit driven by double hydraulic cylinders is considered. As a driving hydraulic cylinder, its expansion length can not reach the target length through one movement, and it needs to be broken down into two expansion movements to complete. The control algorithm is as follows:

Step 1: According to the target pose of the G point, the expansion length of the left and right hydraulic cylinder dl_l and dl_r are inverse solved, and then the average value of the two is calculated:

$$\mu_{dl} = \frac{dl_l + dl_r}{2} \tag{15}$$

Step 2: Drive the left and right hydraulic cylinders to move synchronously in the same direction, and the telescopic length is μ_{dl}.

Step 3: Calculate the difference between dl_l and dl_r.

$$\Delta dl = \frac{|dl_l - dl_r|}{2} \tag{16}$$

Step 4: Drive the left and right hydraulic cylinders to reverse synchronous movement, one hydraulic cylinder to extend the length of Δdl, the other hydraulic cylinder to shorten the length of Δdl. At this point, the end G-spot reaches the target pose.

After the above four steps to this point, the two sides of the hydraulic cylinder expansion length of different needs, through a synchronous movement in the same direction and a reverse synchronous movement to achieve. It is worth mentioning that when dl_l and dl_r are the same, only one synchronous movement in the same direction can be done.

3 Simulation Verification

In order to ensure the accuracy of the inverse kinematics analysis of the drilling robot arm, it is necessary to verify the 2-UPS+U hydraulic drive assembly. According to the analysis of the 2-UPS+U parallel mechanism in the previous section, the mechanism is a complex coupled system with multi-variable input and multi-variable output. In order to verify the accuracy of its calculation process, different output values are set at different time points, namely, the Angle values of joints 1 and 2 and joints 4 and 5, and the inverse solution algorithm of the 2-UPS+U parallel mechanism is called. The input value of the parallel mechanism, that is, the expansion and expansion of the hydraulic cylinder, is obtained. Since the same 2-UPS+U parallel mechanism is used before and after, we can analyze the front-end hydraulic cylinder drive part separately and verify the accuracy of the algorithm through simulation.

Set the Angle values of joint 1 and 2 in the corresponding time period as shown in Table 2. Through the inverse solution algorithm of the 2-UPS+U parallel mechanism, the expansion length of the hydraulic cylinder at the corresponding time point is obtained as shown in Table 3:

Table 2. The angular values of joints 1 and 2

——	0.1(s)	0.3(s)	0.5(s)	0.7(s)	0.9(s)	1.1(s)
Joint 1 (°)	0	5	10	15	10	5
Joint 2 (°)	−90	−100	−110	−100	−95	−90

Table 3. The expansion length of the hydraulic cylinder at the same time

——	0.1(s)	0.3(s)	0.5(s)	0.7(s)	0.9(s)	1.1(s)
Left side hydraulic cylinder (mm)	0	33.31	66.29	4.13	−5.78	15.13
Right side hydraulic cylinder (mm)	0	62.73	121.63	91.52	53.95	-15.20

The telescopic length of the hydraulic cylinder calculated by the algorithm is input into Adams software for simulation, and the post-processing function of the software is used to generate the curve of the Angle change of joint 1 and joint 2 with time. As is shown in Fig. 7.

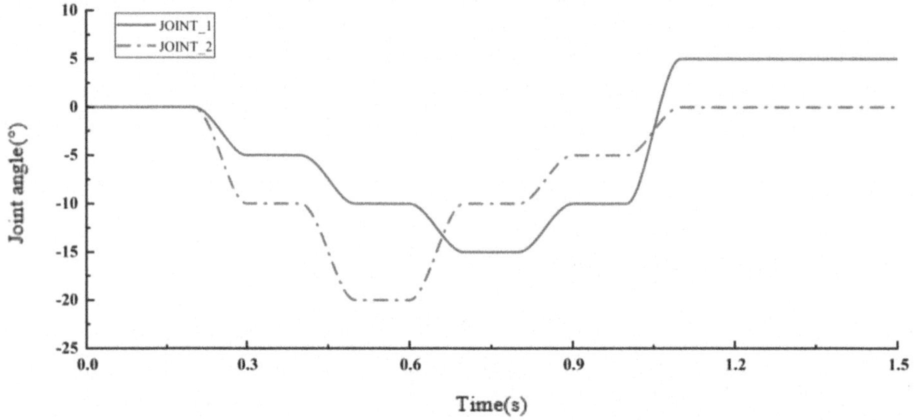

Fig. 7. Angular changes in joints 1 and 2

It is worth noting that the longitudinal coordinate of the curve generated by the post-processing function is the change of the joint value, and the initial value of each joint is shown in Table 4.

Table 4. Parameter table of D-H method connecting rod of drilling mechanical arm

Serial number	$a_{i\text{-}1}$ (mm)	$\alpha_{i\text{-}1}$ (°)	di (mm)	θ_i (°)	θ_i/d_i (°/mm)	Value range (°/mm)	Initial value (°)
1	0	0	0	θ_1	θ_1	(−30, 30)	0
2	a_1(160)	−90	0	θ_2	θ_2	(−180, 0)	−90
3	0	−90	d_3	180	d_3	(2590, 4200)	2590
4	a_3(−70)	90	0	θ_4	θ_4	(0, 180)	90

(*continued*)

Table 4. (*continued*)

Serial number	$a_{i\text{-}1}$ (mm)	$\alpha_{i\text{-}1}$ (°)	di (mm)	θ_i (°)	θ_i/d_i (°/mm)	Value range (°/mm)	Initial value (°)
5	$a_4(134.4)$	−90	$d_5(96)$	θ_5	θ_5	(−180, 0)	−90
6	0	−90	$d_6(1045)$	θ_6	θ_6	(−180, 180)	0
7	$a_6(150)$	90	$d_7(520)$	θ_7	θ_7	(−10, 5)	0
8	$a_7(567.5)$	−90	d_8	0	d_8	(2002.5, 4052)	2002.5

In the above analysis, the unit of Angle is degree, the unit of time is second, the unit of hydraulic cylinder expansion is millimeter, 0 s to 0.1 s, 0.2 s to 0.3 s, 0.4 s to 0.5 s, 0.6 s to 0.7 s, 0.8 s to 0.9 s, 1.0 s to 1.1 s, which is the transition process of each joint from the current Angle value to the next Angle value. The remaining time is the time for each joint Angle to remain in the current state. According to the images generated by Adams software, it can be seen that the Angle changes of joint nodes at each time node are completely consistent with the set input values, which verifies the correctness of the algorithm of the 2-UPS+U parallel mechanism.

4 Conclusion

In previous articles, the analysis of large hydraulic robotic arms is often simply classified as series robotic arms, and its kinematic analysis is simply carried out according to series robotic arms. It is usually neglected that the hydraulic drive cylinder and the joint connecting rod connected to it are composed of parallel mechanism. Furthermore, the analysis of hydraulic drive components is ignored, but the analysis of this part directly affects the control accuracy of the joint connected with the hydraulic cylinder.

In this paper, the common double hydraulic cylinder drive in large hydraulic robot arm is taken as an example, the hydraulic drive joint is isolated, the kinematics of the parallel mechanism is analyzed, and the control strategy of the double hydraulic cylinder drive is designed in view of the common synchronous loop problem in the hydraulic system. This paper has important guiding significance for improving the control precision of hydraulic drive joint.

References

1. Liang, X., Takeda, Y.: An iterative method for the inverse kinematics of lower-mobility parallel mechanism with three RS or SR chains based on kinematically equivalent mechanism. Mechan. Mach. Theory **141**, 40–51 (2019)
2. Wang, J., Wu, C., Liu, X.J.: Performance evaluation of parallel manipulators: Motion/force transmissibility and its index. Mechan. Mach. Theory **45**(10), 1462–1476 (2010)
3. Kong, X.W., Jaime, G.A., et al.: Kinematics and singularity analyses of a 4-dof parallel manipulator using screw theory. Mech. Mach. Theory **41**(9), 1048–1061 (2006)

4. Huang, Z., Fang, Y.: Kinematic characteristics analysis of 3-DOF in-parallel actuated pyramid mechanisms. Mechan. Mach. Theory **31**(8), 1009–1018 (1996)
5. Huang, Z., Zhao, Y., Zhao, T.: Advanced spatial mechanism. Higher Education Press, Beijing (2006)
6. Joshi, S., Tsai, L.W.: Jacobian analysis of limited-DOF parallel manipulators. ASME J. Mechan. Des. **124**(2), 254–258 (2002)
7. Rico, J.M., Gallardo, J., et al.: Screw theory and higher order analysis of open serial and closed chains. Mechan. Mach. Theory **34**(4), 559–586 (1999)
8. Rico, J.M., Duffy, J.: Forward and inverse acceleration analyses of in-parallel manipulators. ASME J. Mechan. Des. **122**(3), 299–303 (2000)
9. Li, Y., Song, Y., et al.: Complete Jacobian matrix of a class of incompletely symmetrical parallel mechanisms with 4-DOF. Chin. J. Mechan. Eng. **43**(6), 37–40 (2007)
10. Shen, H., Zhao, Y., Li, J., Wu, G., Chablat, D.: A novel partially-decoupled translational parallel manipulator with symbolic kinematics, singularity identification and workspace determination. Mechan. Mach. Theory **164**, 1–15 (2021)
11. Shen, H., Tang, Y., Wu, G., Li, J., Li, T., Yang, T.: Design and analysis of a class of two-limb non-parasitic 2T1R parallel mechanism with decoupled motion and symbolic forward position solution - influence of optimal arrangement of limbs onto the kinematics, dynamics and stiffness. Mechan. Mach. Theory **172**, 1–27 (2022)
12. Lin, R., Guo, W., Cheng, S.S.: Type synthesis of 2R1T remote center of motion parallel mechanisms with a passive limb for minimally invasive surgical robot. Mechan. Mach. Theory **172**, 1–19 (2022)
13. Yaşır, A., Kiper, G., Can Dede, M.İ.: Kinematic design of a non-parasitic 2R1T parallel mechanism with remote center of motion to be used in minimally invasive surgery applications. Mechan. Mach. Theory **153**, 1–17 (2020)
14. de la Torre, H., Rodriguez-Leal, E.: Instantaneous kinematics analysis via screw-theory of a novel 3-CRC parallel mechanism. Int. J. Adv. Rob. Syst. **13**(3), 128 (2016)
15. Zhang, D., Xu, Y., Yao, J., Hu, B., Zhao, Y.: Kinematics, dynamics and stiffness analysis of a novel 3-DOF kinematically/actuation redundant planar parallel mechanism. Mechan. Mach. Theory **116**, 203–219 (2017)
16. Chen, Z., Wu, J., Liao, J., Wang, Y., Zhang, Y.: A dual-loop feedback trajectory tracking control for rock drilling hydraulically driven manipulator. J. Mech. Eng. Sci. **238**(9), 3657–3677 (2024)
17. Cheng, M., Li, L., Ding, R., Xu, B.: Real-time anti-saturation flow optimization algorithm of the redundant hydraulic manipulator. Actuators **10**(1), 11 (2021)
18. Xia, Y., Nie, Y., Chen, Z., Lyu, L., Hu, P.: Motion control of a hydraulic manipulator with adaptive nonlinear model compensation and comparative experiments. Machines **10**(3), 214 (2022)

Design and Envelope Grasping Analysis of Deployable Manipulator for Space Capture

Hui Yang[1](✉), Yi Han[1], Chuanyang Li[2], Yan Wang[1], and Rongqiang Liu[3]

[1] Parallel Robot and Mechatronic System Laboratory of Hebei Province, Yanshan University, Qinhuangdao 066004, China
huiyang_0431@163.com

[2] Laboratory of Intelligent Control, PLA Rocket Force University of Engineering, Xi'an 710025, China

[3] State Key Laboratory of Robotics and System, Harbin Institute of Technology, Harbin 150001, China

Abstract. This paper discusses a space manipulator for grasping non-cooperative objects and an envelope grasping planning method for objects of different shapes and sizes. A novel space deployable manipulator is proposed in this paper, which consist of a finger mechanism and a wrist mechanism. Then, a novel envelope planning method is proposed to make the manipulator grasp objects of different sizes more efficiently and stably. The static analysis of grasping process is carried out, the factors affecting grasping balance are analyzed, and the mathematical model of grasping balance is established. An envelope grasping optimization model with the driving rope length as variable is proposed to obtain the best grasping posture. Finally, the envelope planning simulation is carried out, which verifies that the novel manipulator proposed in this paper has good shape adaptability and size adaptability, and verifies that the envelope grasping method is feasible.

Keywords: Space manipulator · Enveloping grasp planning · Static analysis · Grasping simulation

1 Introduction

Both space debris [1] in Earth orbit and the capture of non-cooperative targets [2, 3] depend on space manipulators. However, the size and shape of space debris and non-cooperative targets are unknown, so the space manipulator is required to have good grasp stiffness and shape adaptability. In addition, the size of the space capture mechanism [4–6] is constrained by the launch rocket, its size must be optimized, and its mass must be reduced to save the launch cost.

Grasping mechanisms are mainly divided into rigid grasping mechanisms [7–9] and soft grasping mechanisms [10–15]. Because space environment is not only characterized by strong radiation, strong magnetic field, and ultralow temperature but also high mobility dust and micrometeoroids, rigid grasping manipulators show better performance in the aspect of grasping stiffness and capacity. Serial-parallel grasping manipulators are a

X. Lan et al. (Eds.): icira 2024, LNAI 15201, pp. 195–207, 2025.
https://doi.org/10.1007/978-981-96-0771-6_15

kind of rigid grasping mechanism that combine the traditional serial and parallel grasping manipulators. Serial-parallel grasping mechanisms [16–18] not only have great stiffness, strong grasping ability, but also have a large reachable workspace. However, the size of the serial-parallel grasping mechanism increases with the size of the grasped object. When the grasping target is large, multiple parallel modules need to be connected in series, which leads to the larger volume of the grasping mechanism and increases the transportation cost. Therefore, a serial-parallel grasping manipulator with small folding volume is proposed in this paper.

The structural design and size of the rigid grasping mechanism are usually determined according to the target object. As a result, the grasping mechanism has limitations in grasping. In the process of grasping objects of different shapes and sizes, multiple contact points will be formed, and a variety of different grasping positions can be used to complete the grasping. However, some grasping postures are stable and some grasping postures are unstable, which requires further analysis and optimization. Ala [19] proposed a three-dimensional (3D) grasp synthesis algorithm to achieve distinguished grasps supporting both stability and human-like grasping. Stoyanov [20] proposed a concept of grasping pose constraints, which can be obtained from the reconstructed 3D model. Gao [21] proposed an envelope grasping method based on a three-finger deployable metamorphic robot. An envelope grasping optimization model with grasping angle as variable is proposed to obtain the best grasping posture. Li [22] studied the grasp stability analysis and optimal envelope grasp planning of a deployable manipulator, and proposed an envelope planning method that can obtain the deployment length of manipulator to achieve a stable grasp. Qiao [23, 24] studied the adaptive grasping problem of underactuated manipulators and established grasping models for 2-DOF and 3-DOF manipulators. Four kinds of grasping results are analyzed, and the stable grasping condition is obtained.

Most of the methods optimize the rod length and the angle between finger joints as design variables to achieve the optimal grasping posture. For the most grasping mechanisms, the rod length of the finger joint is determined, which is difficult to change during grasping. The method of optimizing the angle between finger joints has some limitations for serial-parallel grasping mechanisms. Therefore, a novel three-finger serial-parallel grasping manipulator composed of finger mechanism and wrist mechanism is proposed in this paper, which has a large reachable workspace and a small folding volume. Taking the novel manipulator as the research object, an enveloping grasping planning method with the rope drive length as the design variable is proposed, and an optimization model of grasping results is established. For different shapes, different sizes of objects, can get the best grasping posture. Based on the static analysis of the manipulator and the proposed optimization model, the simulation of envelope grasping is carried out. The results show that the grasping planning method proposed in this paper is reliable, and the grasping mechanism has good size adaptability and shape adaptability.

This paper is arranged in the following structure. The grasping manipulator consisting of the finger mechanism and the wrist mechanism is presented in Sect. 2. The quasi-statics analysis of the manipulator and the enveloping grasping planning based on the length of the driving rope are presented in Sect. 3. The envelope grasping simulation is presented in Sect. 4. Final conclusions are drawn in Sect. 5.

2 Mechanism Design of the Space Deployable Serial-Parallel Grasping Manipulator

This work presents a modular design of finger mechanism and wrist mechanism. Multiple Parallel Finger Modules (PFMs) are connected in series to create a complete finger mechanism. The manipulator is foldable for easy transportation, while its working status allows grasping large objects.

2.1 Finger Mechanism Design

Design of the PFM

The PFM consists of a grasping sub-mechanism (GSM) and two auxiliary sub-mechanisms (ASM) as shown in Fig. 1. The grasping sub-mechanism consists of six revolute pairs. The auxiliary sub-mechanism consists of fourteen revolute pairs.

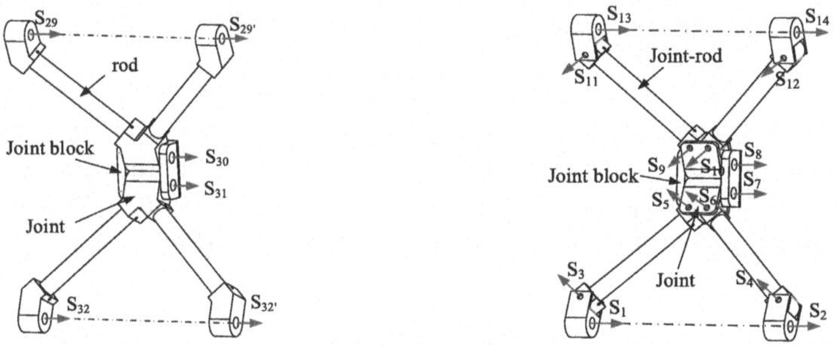

(a) Grasping sub-mechanism (b) Auxiliary sub-mechanism

Fig. 1. Two sub-mechanisms of PFM

The PFM consists of three planes distributed on the sides of the triangular prism shown in Fig. 2. After that, the PFM is constructed, consisting of the grasping sub-mechanism, the auxiliary sub-mechanism, the mobile platform, and the base platform.

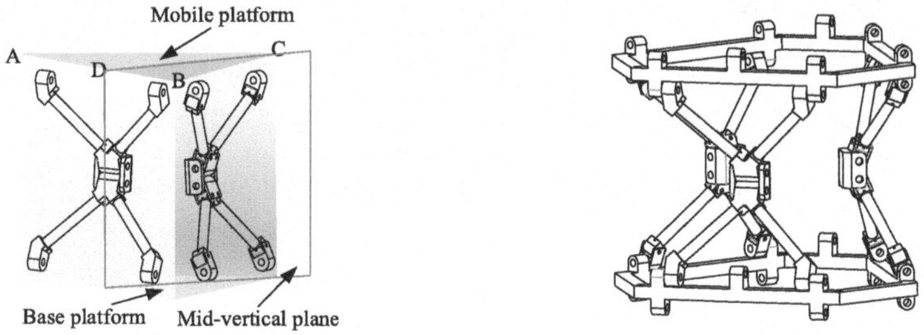

(a) Geometry of the grasping plane and auxiliary planes (b) PFM

Fig. 2. Parallel Finger Module (PFM)

The PFM has three key statuses, deployment status, bending status, folding status, as shown in Fig. 3.

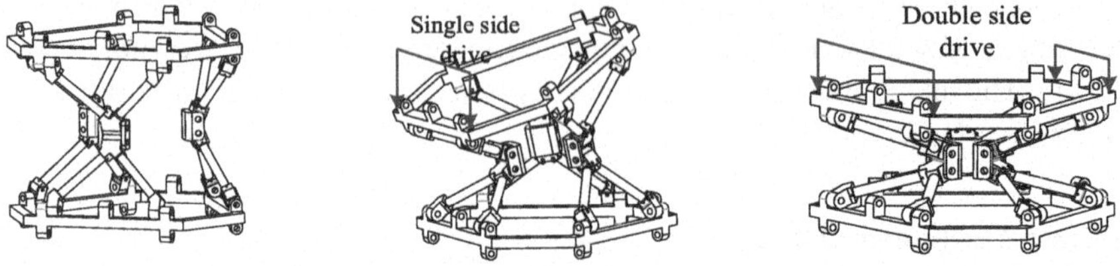

(a) PFM deployment status (b) PFM bent status (c) PFM folded status

Fig. 3. Schematic diagram of the three key status of the PFM

2.2 Finger Mechanism Design

The PFM is a parallel mechanism with three sub-chains. In order to make the finger mechanism obtain a lager reachable workspace, multiple PFMs can be connected serial, and the number of PFMs can be selected according to the size of the captured object. In this paper, finger mechanism is proposed by serially connecting three PFMs, which has three key statuses: the folded, deployed and grasping status (Fig. 4).

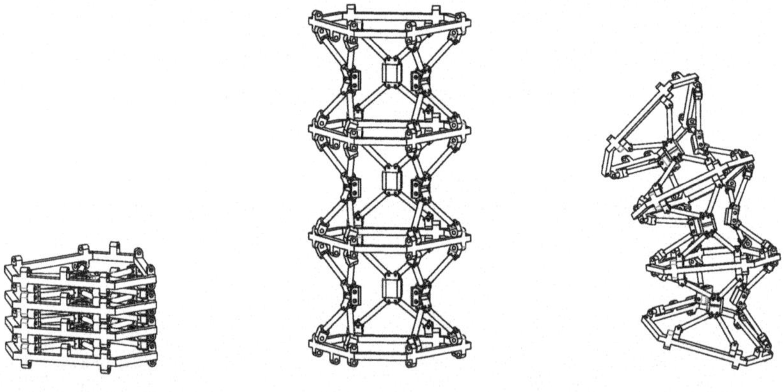

(a) Folded status (b) Development status (c) Grasping status

Fig. 4. Three status diagrams of the finger mechanism

2.3 Wrist Mechanism Design

To make the manipulator capable of more work, such as turning screws and other work that requires torsion. A novel wrist mechanism is proposed in this section, which can be twisted and has a small folding volume. The wrist mechanism consists of a platform, a base, tree moving rods and three sliding rods, and all kinematic pairs are revolute pairs. The wrist mechanism consists of two key statuses: the deploy status and the folded status, as shown in Fig. 5.

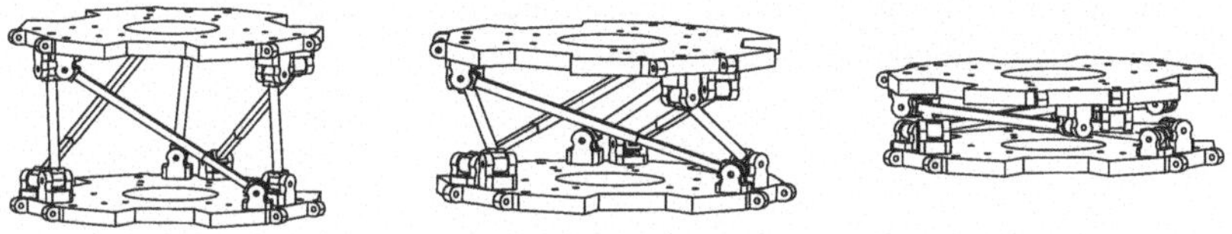

(a) Deployment status (b) Middle status (c) Folded status

Fig. 5. Schematic diagram of the folding process of the wrist mechanism

2.4 Deployable Manipulator Mechanism Design

A novel deployable grasping manipulator is proposed in this section, which consists of three serial-parallel finger mechanisms and a wrist mechanism. A two-finger manipulator encounters various problems, such as instability while grasping objects. Accordingly, this work adopts the three-finger manipulator design program. Three serial-parallel finger mechanisms are evenly distributed on the wrist mechanism. The three key statuses: folded, deployed, and captured, of the grasping manipulator are demonstrated in Fig. 6.

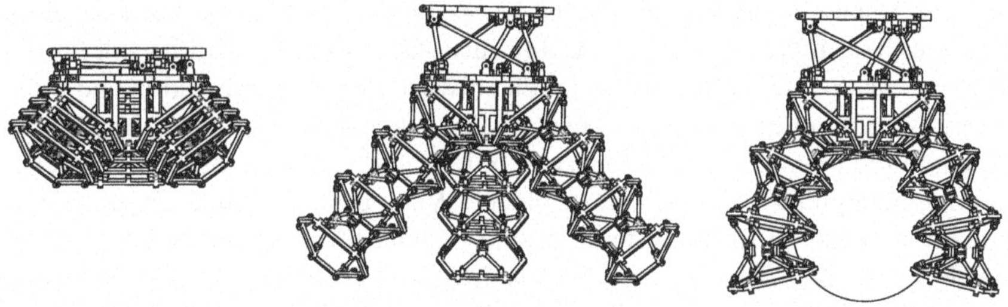

(a) Folded status (b) Deployment status (c) Grasping status

Fig. 6. Schematic diagram of the three statuses of the grasping manipulator

3 Grasping Envelope Planning for Manipulator

As shown in Fig. 7, the driving mode of the manipulator is indicated. The manipulator is driven by two sets of driving ropes. When the driving rope-1 and driving rope-2 are contracted at the same time, the manipulator is folded. When only the drive rope-2 is contracted, the manipulator can perform grasping motion. Where H represents the PFM height and ΔL represents drive rope change.

When the grasping manipulator grasps an object, it initiates an deployment motion, followed by a grasping motion. Each finger of the manipulator can be simplified to a planar 9R serial-parallel mechanism throughout the grasping process. Consequently, the manipulator can be conceptualized as a tandem dexterous manipulator with three fingers (Fig. 8). The maximum number of grasping postures for each finger can be determined based on the number of fingers with n joints, under the assumption that the end linkage of the finger remains in contact with the grasped object.

$$G_N = 2^{n-1} \tag{1}$$

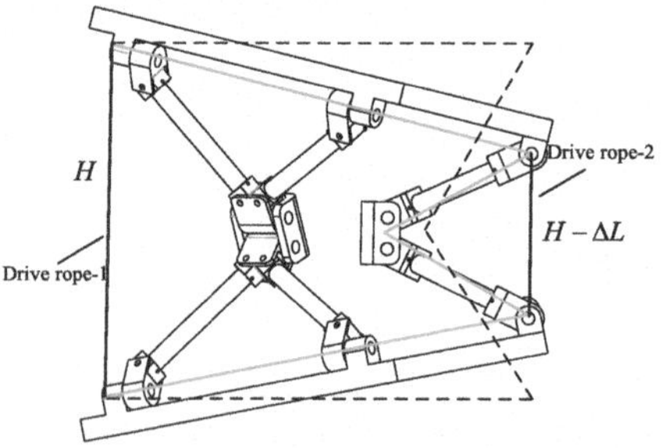

Fig. 7. Drive rope diagram of PFM

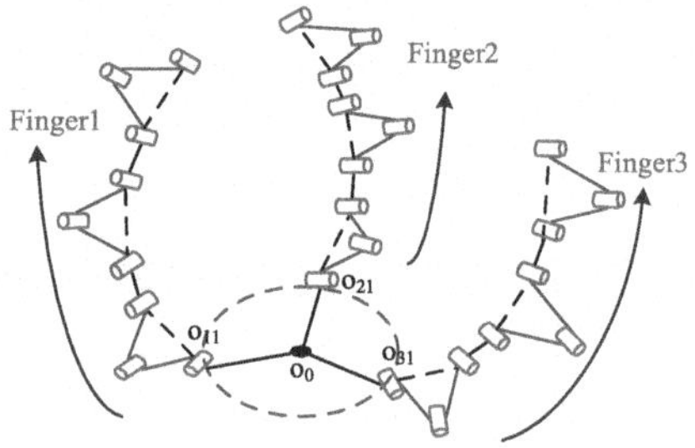

Fig. 8. Simplified diagram of a robotic finger

However, the number of grasping postures mentioned above may not always align with the task requirements, necessitating further analysis to determine the optimal grasping posture. A static analysis model must be established to address this issue (Fig. 9). This study utilizes a grasping sphere as an illustrative example, with its side view presented in Fig. 9a, to elucidate the correlation between grasping orientation and grasping force. In this configuration, finger i envelops the outer surface of the spherical object. Let R denote the diameter of the spherical object, and r_{cij} represent the contact point between the manipulator and the sphere object. When utilizing envelope grasping, certain conditions must be fulfilled: first, a point contact forms between the manipulator and the object. Second, a geometric relationship exists between the grip angle among the finger segments, the center of the spherical object, and the location of the contact points. Consequently, the coordinates of each contact point can be determined as follows:

$$\begin{cases} r_{ci1} = \left[Rs_{\theta_{i0}}, R\left(1 - c_{\theta_{i0}}\right), 0\right] \\ r_{ci2} = \left[Rs_{\theta_{i0+i1}}, R\left(1 - c_{\theta_{i0+i1}}\right), 0\right] \\ r_{ci3} = \left[Rs_{\theta_{i0+i1+i2}}, R\left(1 - c_{\theta_{i0+i1+i2}}\right), 0\right] \\ r_{ci4} = \left[Rs_{\theta_{i0+i1+i2+i3}}, R\left(1 - c_{\theta_{i0+i1+i2+i3}}\right), 0\right] \end{cases} \tag{2}$$

where $s_{\theta i1} = \sin\theta_{i1}$, $c_{\theta i1} = \cos\theta_{i1}$.

The distance between the corresponding o_{i0} and c_{i0} can be obtained through Eq. (2) and the geometric relationship in Fig. 9b:

$$l_{o_{i1}c_{i1}} = \sqrt{(R\sin\theta_{i0} - l_{o_{i0}o_{i1}})^2 + R^2(1 - \cos\theta_{i0})^2} \tag{3}$$

where l_{oi0oi1} is a constant determined by the mechanical structure. In addition, l_{oi2ci2}, l_{oi3ci3}, l_{oi4ci4} can be derived from the following equation:

$$\begin{cases} l_{o_{i2}c_{i2}} = l_{o_{i2}b_{i2}} + l_{b_{i2}c_{i2}} \\ l_{o_{i3}c_{i3}} = l_{o_{i3}b_{i4}} + l_{b_{i4}c_{i3}} \\ l_{o_{i4}c_{i4}} = l_{o_{i4}b_{i6}} + l_{b_{i6}c_{i4}} \end{cases} \tag{4}$$

where, $l_{bi2ci2} = l_{bi4ci3} = l_{bi6ci4} = d/2$, determined by the structure of the manipulator itself, $\theta_{ij} = 2\arcsin(\triangle L/2L_A)$

$$l_{o_{i2}b_{i2}} = l_{o_{i3}b_{i4}} = l_{o_{i4}b_{i6}} = (H - \Delta L) \Big/ \left(2\cos(\frac{\theta_{ij}}{2})\right) \tag{5}$$

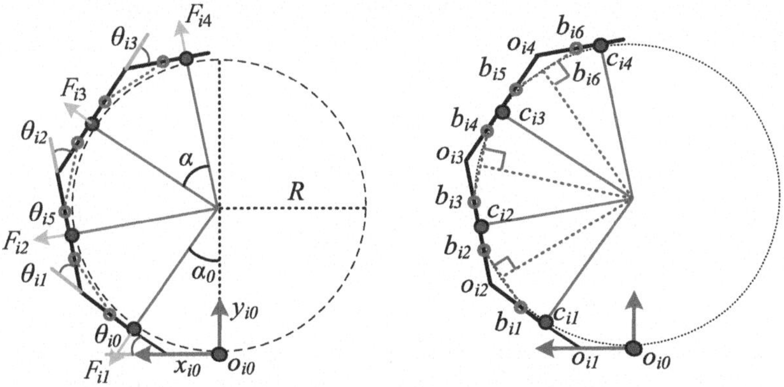

(a) The angles of a single finger (b) Side view

Fig. 9. Schematic diagram of robotic finger grasping the sphere

From Eqs. (2) to (5), the grasping posture of the manipulator is only related to variable ΔL. Considering that the manipulator contains three exactly the same fingers, only the relevant parameters of one of the fingers are derived, and the other two can be obtained from the parameters of the finger based on the transformation relationship of the D-H parameters, which is as follows:

$$^{0}T_{20} = \begin{bmatrix} \cos\zeta & 0 & \sin\xi & 0 \\ 0 & 1 & 0 & 0 \\ -\sin\xi & 0 & \cos\zeta & 0 \\ 0 & 0 & 0 & 1 \end{bmatrix} \tag{6}$$

$$^{0}T_{30} = \begin{bmatrix} \cos\zeta & 0 & \sin\xi & 0 \\ 0 & 1 & 0 & 0 \\ -\sin\xi & 0 & \cos\zeta & 0 \\ 0 & 0 & 0 & 1 \end{bmatrix} \tag{7}$$

where ξ is the angle between neighboring fingers, $\xi = 120°$.

$$\begin{cases} {}^0P_{E_1} = P_{E_1} \\ {}^0P_{E_2} = {}^0T_{20}P_{E_1} \\ {}^0P_{E_3} = {}^0T_{30}P_{E_1} \end{cases} \tag{8}$$

where, the specific form of ${}^0P_{E_1}$ is:

$${}^0P_{E_1} = \begin{bmatrix} l_{oi0oi1} + l_{oi1oi2}c\theta_{i0} + l_{oi2oi3}c\theta_{i0+i1} + l_{oi3oi4}c\theta_{i0+i1+i2} + l_{oi4ci4}c\theta_{i0+i1+i2+i3} \\ 0 \\ l_{oi1oi2}s\theta_{i0} + l_{oi2oi3}s\theta_{i0+i1} + l_{oi3oi4}s\theta_{i0+i1+i2} + l_{oi4ci4}s\theta_{i0+i1+i2+i3} \end{bmatrix} \tag{9}$$

When the manipulator securely grasps an object, it establishes a stable system. Each finger adheres to the static equilibrium condition, allowing for the calculation of the driving moment for any finger:

$$\begin{cases} \tau_{i4} = F_{i4}l_{o_{i4}c_{i4}} \\ \tau_{i3} = F_{i3}l_{o_{i3}c_{i3}} + F_{i4}\left(l_{o_{i4}c_{i4}} + l_{o_{i3}o_{i4}}c\theta_{i3}\right) \\ \tau_{i2} = F_{i2}l_{o_{i2}c_{i2}} + F_{i3}\left(l_{o_{i3}c_{i3}} + l_{o_{i2}o_{i3}}c\theta_{i2}\right) + F_{i4}\left(l_{o_{i4}c_{i4}} + l_{o_{i3}o_{i4}}c\theta_{i3} + l_{o_{i2}o_{i3}}c\theta_{i2+i3}\right) \\ \tau_{i1} = F_{i1}l_{o_{i1}c_{i1}} + F_{i2}\left(l_{o_{i2}c_{i2}} + l_{o_{i1}o_{i2}}c\theta_{i1}\right) + F_{i3}\left(l_{o_{i3}c_{i3}} + l_{o_{i2}o_{i3}}c\theta_{i2} + l_{o_{i1}o_{i2}}c\theta_{i1+i2}\right) \\ \quad + F_{i4}\left(l_{o_{i4}c_{i4}} + l_{o_{i3}o_{i4}}c\theta_{i3} + l_{o_{i2}o_{i3}}c\theta_{i2+i3} + l_{o_{i1}o_{i2}}c\theta_{i1+i2+i3}\right) \end{cases} \tag{10}$$

The manipulator not only needs to meet the above static balance conditions, but also should meet the overall balance of the manipulator during the grasping process, which can be obtained:

$$\begin{cases} \sum_{i=1}^{3} F_{i1}s\theta_{i0} + F_{i2}s\theta_{i0+i1} + F_{i3}s\theta_{i0+i1+i2} + F_{i4}s\theta_{i0+i1+i2+i3} = 0 \\ \sum_{i=1}^{3} F_{i1}c\theta_{i0} + F_{i2}c\theta_{i0+i1} + F_{i3}c\theta_{i0+i1+i2} + F_{i4}c\theta_{i0+i1+i2+i3} = 0 \end{cases} \tag{11}$$

According to Eq. (11), the grasping force can be written as follows:

$$\begin{cases} F_{i4} = \frac{\tau_{i4}}{l_{o_{i4}c_{i4}}} \\ F_{i3} = \frac{1}{l_{o_{i3}c_{i3}}}\left[\tau_{i3} - F_{i4}\left(l_{o_{i4}c_{i4}} + l_{o_{i3}o_{i4}}c\theta_{i3}\right)\right] \\ F_{i2} = \frac{1}{l_{o_{i2}c_{i2}}}\left[\tau_{i2} - F_{i3}\left(l_{o_{i3}c_{i3}} + l_{o_{i2}o_{i3}}c\theta_{i2}\right) - F_{i4}\left(l_{o_{i4}c_{i4}} + l_{o_{i3}o_{i4}}c\theta_{i3} + l_{o_{i2}o_{i3}}c\theta_{i2+i3}\right)\right] \\ F_{i1} = \frac{1}{l_{o_{i1}c_{i1}}}\begin{bmatrix} \tau_{i1} - F_{i2}\left(l_{o_{i2}c_{i2}} + l_{o_{i1}o_{i2}}c\theta_{i1}\right) - F_{i3}\left(l_{o_{i3}c_{i3}} + l_{o_{i2}o_{i3}}c\theta_{i2} + l_{o_{i1}o_{i2}}c\theta_{i1+i2}\right) \\ -F_{i4}\left(l_{o_{i4}c_{i4}} + l_{o_{i3}o_{i4}}c\theta_{i3} + l_{o_{i2}o_{i3}}c\theta_{i2+i3} + l_{o_{i1}o_{i2}}c\theta_{i1+i2+i3}\right) \end{bmatrix} \end{cases} \tag{12}$$

A uniform distribution of grasping forces must be achieved across each contact point to mitigate substantial grasping forces concentrated in specific areas during the grasping process. Hence, this principle can serve as an optimization objective, as illustrated in Eq. (13):

$$G(F_i) = \sum_{i=1}^{3}\sum_{i=1}^{3} \left| |F_{i(j+1)}| - |F_{ij}| \right| \tag{13}$$

When the function value is smaller, it indicates a more uniform distribution of grasping forces. A larger function value may result in stress concentration phenomena during the grasping process. Hence, the optimization model for the grasping manipulator's envelope grasping can be formulated as follows:

$$\begin{cases} find & \Delta L \\ min & G(F_{ij}) \\ s.t. & F_{min} < F_{ij} < F_{\max} \\ & 0 < \Delta L < H \end{cases} \tag{14}$$

Based on Eq. (14), the best grasping posture of the manipulator can be obtained when the function value is the smallest, which ensures the integrity of the object and the effectiveness of grasp during the grasp process of the manipulator.

4 Envelope Grasping Simulation of the Manipulator

The enveloping grasp simulation of manipulator is divided into two parts. In the first part, the grasping manipulator has good grasping adaptability which needs to be proved. The grasping adaptability includes two aspects: shape adaptability and size adaptability. The grasping adaptability of the manipulator was explored through experiments with two spheres of different diameters and four objects of different shapes (triangular prism, circular platform, hexagonal prism and cylinder). The above objects are used to simulate non-cooperative targets of various shapes and sizes, including those encountered in space, such as space debris and meteorites (Fig. 10a to f). Where two ball-shaped objects with different diameters and four objects with different shapes are grasped by the manipulator, and the results show that the manipulator has good size adaptability and shape adaptability.

In the second part, the envelop grasping planning method needs to be verified. The first thing to be done is to measure the key parameters through the 3D model of the grasping manipulator, $H = 517$ mm. Due to the consistency of the three fingers, one finger is used an example for explanation. In addition, we can define:

$$\begin{cases} \tau = [\tau_0, \tau_{11}, \tau_{12}, \tau_{13}, \tau_{21}, \tau_{22}, \tau_{23}, \tau_{31}, \tau_{32}, \tau_{33}] \\ \tau_0 \in [0N, 10N] \\ \tau_{ij} \in [0N, 10N](i = 1, 2, 3, j = 1, 2, 3) \end{cases} \tag{15}$$

For objects with different shapes and sizes, the grasping effect of the grasping manipulator is shown in Fig. 10. Figure 10c and d depict the grasping process of triangular prism and hexagonal objects. The contact mode between the finger mechanism of the

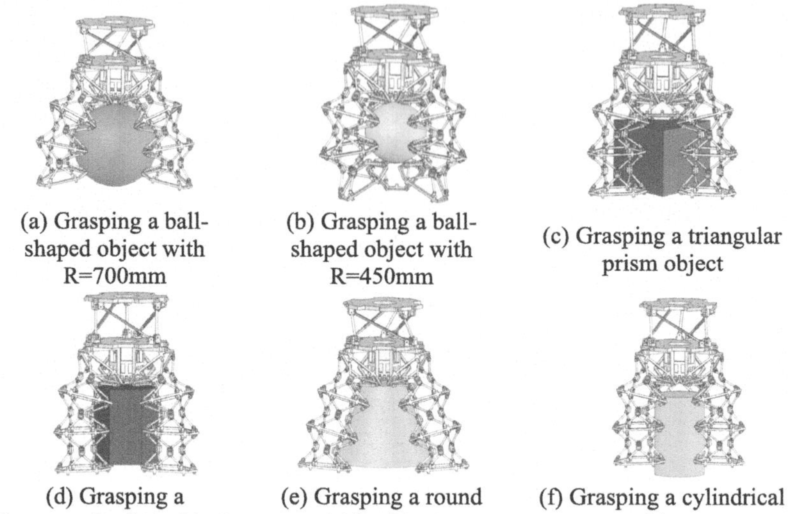

(a) Grasping a ball-shaped object with R=700mm

(b) Grasping a ball-shaped object with R=450mm

(c) Grasping a triangular prism object

(d) Grasping a hexagonal prism object

(e) Grasping a round table object

(f) Grasping a cylindrical object

Fig. 10. Schematic diagram of the grasping robot for objects of different sizes and shapes

manipulator and the grasped objects are surface contact, and the PFM sub-mechanism has uniform force, which can be seen as stable grasping. Figure 10e and f illustrate the grasping process of round table and cylindrical objects. The contact mode between the finger mechanism of the manipulator and the grasped objects are line contact, and the PFM sub-mechanism is under the uniform force, which can be seen as stable grasping. In contrast, Fig. 10a and b depict the grasping process of the ball-shaped objects. The contact mode between the finger mechanism of the manipulator and the grasped objects are point contact, and the grasping forces are all directed to the center of the ball, presenting a delicate balance. If a certain grasping force is too strong, the grasped objects may be damaged, and if a certain grasping force too small, the objects may be in an unstable state. We conduct an optimization simulation using the ball-shaped as a case study to address this challenge. We define that each PFM sub-mechanism can contact the ball-shaped object. Then, the grasping force of each finger module changes with the length of the driving rope and the driving force, as shown in Fig. 11.

The results of the envelope grasping optimization are depicted in Fig. 12. Regarding the ball-shaped object with a radius of 500 mm, the optimal grasping status is achieved when the shortening amount of the driving rope is 61.8 mm. In terms of the ball-shaped object with a radius of 300 mm, when the same analytical method is used, the optimal grasping status is attained when the shortening amount of the driving rope is 221.7 mm. Consequently, for any ball-shaped object with radius R, the corresponding optimal rope driving length under the optimal envelope status can be obtained.

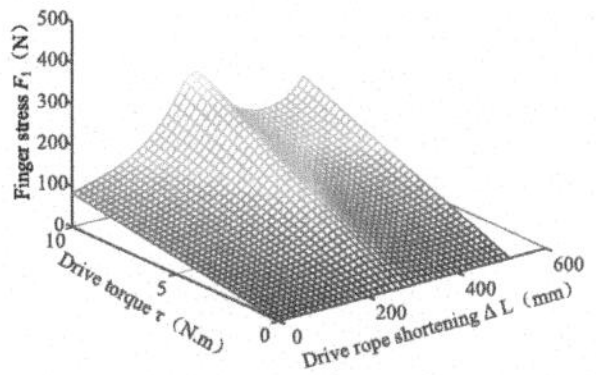

(a) First Finger Module F_{i1} Force

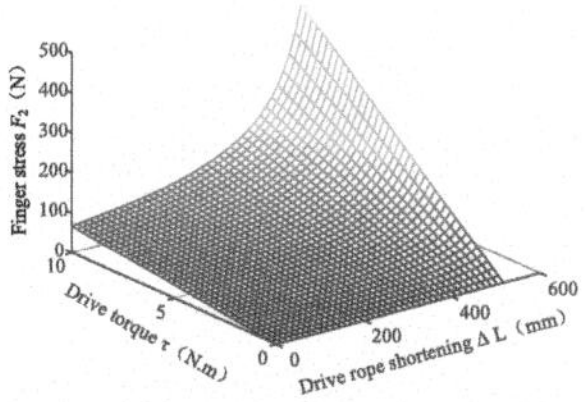

(b) Second Finger Module F_{i2} Force

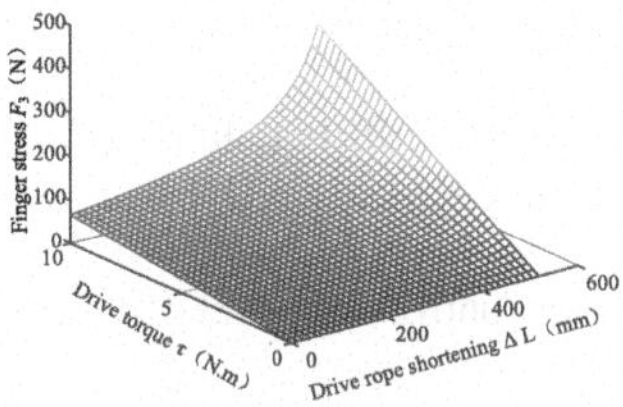

(c) Third Finger Module F_{i3} Force

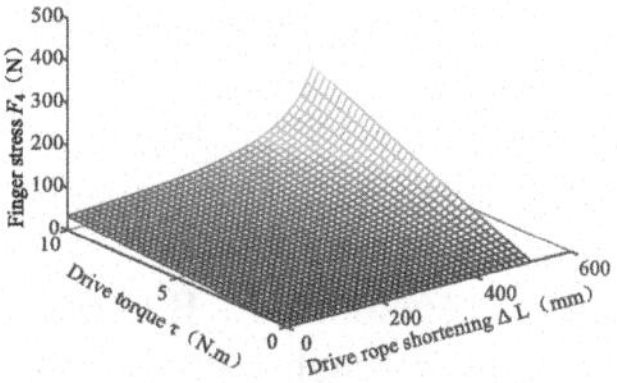

(d) Fourth Finger Module F_{i4} Force

Fig. 11. Schematic representation of the forces on the fingers

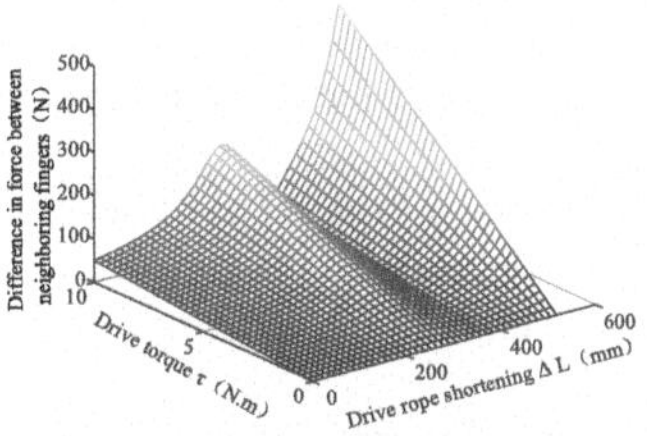

(a) Grasp R=500mm ball-shaped object results

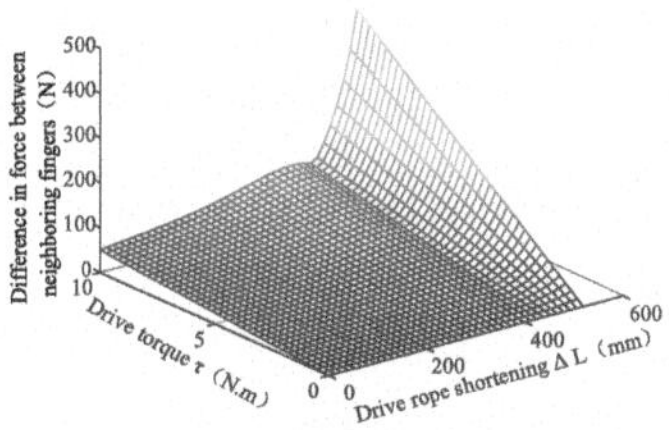

(b) Grasp R=300mm ball-shaped object results

Fig. 12. Envelope grasping optimization result schematic

5 Conclusions

In this paper, a novel space grasping manipulator is proposed, which consists of the finger mechanism and the wrist mechanism. The grasping manipulator has a large reachable workspace and a small folding volume. Taking the manipulator as the study object, a novel enveloping grasping planning method is presented to obtain the best grasp posture of the manipulator. The envelope grasping planning method proposed in this paper is different from the traditional method, which uses the length of the driving rope as the design variable and minimizes the grasping force difference between adjacent contact points as the optimization objective to establish an optimization model. By optimization, the length of the driving rope is obtained when the grasping manipulator is in the optimal grasping position. In order to verify the proposed method, envelope grasp simulation is carried out, and the results show that the proposed grasping manipulator has good dimensional adaptability and shape adaptability, and the envelope grasp planning method is reliable.

Acknowledgement. This research was support by Science and Technology Project of Hebei Education Department (Grant No. QN2023206), National Natural Science Foundation of China (Grant No. 52205040, 52375028 and 62227814), China Postdoctoral Science Foundation (Grant No. 2022M713850), Young Talent Fund of Xi'an Association for Science and Technology (Grant No. 959202313096).

References

1. Dureisseix, D.: An overview of mechanisms and patterns with origami. Int. J. Space Struct. **27**(1), 1–14 (2012)
2. Li, C., Guo, H., Tang, D., Yan, H., Liu, R., Deng, Z.: A 3-R(SRS)RP multi-loop mechanism for space manipulation: design, kinematics, singularity, and workspace. J. Mech. Robot. **12**(1), 011001–1–011001–17 (2020)
3. Li, G., Huang, H., Guo, H., Li, B.: Design, analysis and control of a novel deployable grasping manipulator. Mech. Mach. Theory **138**, 182–204 (2019)
4. Koessler, A., Goldsztejn, A., Briot, S., Bouton, N.: Dynamics-based algorithm for reliable assembly mode tracking in parallel robots. IEEE Trans. Robot. **36**(3), 937–950 (2020)
5. Zhao, C., Wang, K., Zhao, H., Guo, H., Liu, R.: Kinematics, dynamics, and experiments of n (3RRlS) reconfigurable series–parallel manipulators for capturing space noncooperative targets, J. Mech. Robot. **14**(6), 060902–1–060902–17 (2022)
6. Zhang, G., He, Y., Dai, B., Gu, F., Han, J., Liu, G.: Robust control of an aerial manipulator based on a variable inertia parameters model. IEEE Trans. Ind. Electron. **67**(11), 9515–9525 (2019)
7. Kaiser, C., Sjöberg, F., Delcura, J.M., et al.: SMART-OLEV—an orbital life extension vehicle for servicing commercial spacecrafts in GEO. Acta Astronaut. **63**(1–4), 400–410 (2008)
8. Nokleby, S.B.: Singularity analysis of the Canadarm2. Mech. Mach. Theory **42**(4), 442–454 (2007)
9. Gates, M., Johnson, L.N.: NASA's Asteroid Redirect Mission. Springer International Publishing (2014)
10. Bischof, B., Kerstein, L., Starke, J., et al.: ROGER- robotic geostationary orbit restorer. Sci. Technol. Ser. **109**, 183–193 (2004)
11. Li, Z., Kidambi, N., Wang, L., et al.: Uncovering rotational multifunctionalities of coupled Kresling modular structures. Extreme Mech. Let. **39**, 100795 (2020)
12. Lee, J.S.,. Chen, X., Li, J., et al.: A soft robotic approach to robust and dexterous grasping. In: 2018 IEEE International Conference on Soft Robotics (RoboSoft), pp. 412–417. IEEE (2018)
13. Edmondson, B.J., Bowen, L.A., Grames, C.L., et al.: Oriceps: origami-inspired forceps. Smart Materials, Adaptive Structures and Intelligent Systems. American Society of Mechanical Engineers, vol. 56031, p. V001T01A027 (2013)
14. Chen, W.H., Misra, S., Gao, Y., et al.: A programmably compliant origami mechanism for dynamically dexterous robots. IEEE Robot. Autom. Let. **5**(2), 2130–3137 (2020)
15. Cibicik, A., Egeland, O.: Kinematics and dynamics of flexible robotic manipulators using dual screws. IEEE Trans. Robot. **37**(1), 206–224 (2021)
16. Guanglu, J., Hailin, H., Bing, L., et al.: Synthesis of a novel type of metamorphic mechanism module for large scale deployable grasping manipulators. Mechan. Mach. Theory **128**, 544–559 (2018). https://doi.org/10.1016/j.mechmachtheory.2018.06.017
17. Gao, C., Wang, J., Yang, X., et al.: Design and analysis of a novel truss-shaped variable-stiffness deployable robotic grasper. IEEE Access (99), 1–1 (2020). https://doi.org/10.1109/ACCESS.2020.3002434

18. Li, G.T., Huang, H.L., Guo, H.W., Li, B.: Design, analysis and control of a novel deployable grasping manipulator. Mechan. Mach. Theory **138**, 182–204 (2019), ISSN 0094-114X, https://doi.org/10.1016/j.mechmachtheory.2019.03.043
19. Ala, R.K., Kim, D.H., Shin, S.Y., Kim, C.H., Park, S.-K.: A 3D-grasp synthesis algorithm to grasp unknown objects based on graspable boundary and convex segments. Inform. Sci. **295**, 91–106 (2015), ISSN 0020-0255
20. Stoyanov, T., Krug, R., Muthusamy, R., Kyrki, V.: Grasp envelopes: Extracting constraints on gripper postures from online reconstructed 3D models. In: 2016 IEEE/RSJ International Conference on Intelligent Robots and Systems (IROS), pp. 885–892. Daejeon, Korea (South) (2016). https://doi.org/10.1109/IROS.2016.7759155
21. Gao, C., Huang, H., Li, Y., et al.: Design and analysis of a three-fingered deployable metamorphic robotic grasper. J. Mechan. Des. (2022). https://doi.org/10.1115/1.4054115
22. Li, G., Xu, P., Qiao, S., Li, B.: Stability analysis and optimal enveloping grasp planning of a deployable robotic hand. Mech. Mach. Theory **158**, 104241 (2021)
23. Qiao, S.L., Guo, H.W., Liu, R.Q.: Self-adaptive grasp process and equilibrium configuration analysis of a 3-DOF UACT robotic finger. Mechan. Mach. Theory **133**, 250–266 (2019), ISSN 0094-114X
24. Qiao, S.L., Guo, H.W., Liu, R.Q., et al.: Configuration design of an under-actuated robotic hand based on maximum grasping space. Chin. J. Mech. Eng. **31**, 35 (2018). https://doi.org/10.1186/s10033-018-0243-4

Design, Modelling and Experiment of a Spatial Multi-locomotion Tensegrity Mobile Robot

Kaiwen Hu, Qi Yang, Binbin Lian, Yimin Song, and Tao Sun(✉)

Key Laboratory of Mechanism Theory and Equipment Design of Ministry of Education, Tianjin University, Tianjin 300350, China
stao@tju.edu.cn

Abstract. Tensegrity mobile robots, with their high stiffness-to-mass ratio and exceptional structural adaptability, have become a cutting-edge research focus in recent year. In this paper, a novel spatial multi-locomotion tensegrity mobile robot is put forward. The uniqueness of the robot lies in its ability to achieve three types of spatial locomotion modes in terms of earthworm-like, inchworm-like and turning locomotion, which endows the robot with the ability of smooth directional changing maneuvers. A general kinematic model of the spatial tensegrity robot is established, and motion planning of the three locomotion modes is carried out. On this basis, a prototype of the robot is built, and experimental results show that the tensegrity robot can effectively achieve the three spatial locomotion modes. In particular, benefit from the turning locomotion mode, the robot is capable of executing agile obstacle avoidance maneuvers and performing reverse movements with precision. This work offers valuable insights into the deployment of tensegrity structures for enhancing spatial multi-locomotion capabilities in mobile robotics.

Keywords: Spatial tensegrity robot · motion planning · obstacle avoidance · reverse movements

1 Introduction

The tensegrity robot, with its advantages of light weight, low energy consumption, and high load-bearing capacity, has become an increasing focus of research [1, 2]. After decades years of development, a variety of tensegrity mobile robots have emerged [3–5].

The concept of utilizing tensegrity robots for enhanced mobility was first introduced in a 2004 article by Masic [6]. This pioneering work presented an analytical examination of tensegrity-based locomotion, specifically through the propagation of periodic waves in a worm-like tensegrity robot. The study also showcased the innovative design of self-balanced tensegrity structures, highlighting their potential for autonomous locomotion. Building upon this foundation, Paul and colleagues [7, 8] further explored the mobility of tensegrity structures in 2006. They conducted a comprehensive analysis using a physics-based simulator and validated their findings through a hardware prototype. Their work demonstrated that tensegrity structures offer a solid foundation for the development of lightweight, robust, and fault-tolerant robots. These robots possess the versatility to

X. Lan et al. (Eds.): ICIRA 2024, LNAI 15201, pp. 208–226, 2025.
https://doi.org/10.1007/978-981-96-0771-6_16

adopt a wide array of locomotor gaits, showcasing the potential of tensegrity systems in the field of robotics. Nowadays, tensegrity mobile robots can be roughly categorized into two primary types: prismatic and spherical. Prismatic tensegrity robots, predominantly constructed from three rods and nine cables [9–11], are designed to facilitate crawling locomotion. In contrast, spherical tensegrity robots, which are largely comprised of six rods and twenty-four cables [12–14], are engineered to enable rolling locomotion.

Based on the current state of research, it is evident that the existing tensegrity mobile robots are constrained to a limited range of locomotion modes, and the majority of tensegrity robots are also constrained from performing smooth turning locomotion due to their inherent structural limitations [15]. These limitations significantly hinder the practical applications of tensegrity robots. Although our previous work introduced a novel multi-locomotion tensegrity robot [16–18], it is limited to planar structure and is unable to achieve smooth turning locomotion either. To the best of our knowledge, a spatial multi-locomotion tensegrity mobile robot with the ability of smooth directional changing maneuvers has not been reported so far. In this study, we propose a spatial multi-locomotion tensegrity mobile robot. The robot can achieve three locomotion modes in terms of earthworm-like, inchworm-like, and turning locomotion. Particularly, benefit from the turning locomotion, the robot can achieve obstacle avoidance and backward /reverse locomotion. This study fully leverages the deformability inherent in tensegrity structures, showcasing their wide range of application in the development of spatial multi-locomotion mobile robots.

The rest of this study is organized as follows. Section 2 presents the overall structure of the spatial tensegrity mobile robot. In Sect. 3, we establish a kinematic model and, utilizing this model, proceed to devise motion planning strategies for three distinct spatial locomotion modes. In Sect. 4, experiments on the prototype are carried out to show the locomotion ability of the proposed tensegrity mobile robot. Section 5 summarizes and concludes this study.

2 Mechanism Design of the Robot

The spatial multi-locomotion tensegrity mobile robot proposed in this study is based on a prismatic tensegrity structure with four rods and twelve cables (Fig. 1(a)). To independently control the motion of each rod within the tensegrity structure, the bottom of this structure is replaced with a square frame, while R pair is introduced between each rod and the frame. Under the constraints of the R pair, the motion trajectory of a single rod's end is a circle. The plane in which this circle lies is perpendicular to the frame and divides it into two equal parts. Building upon this, the four cables on the sides of the tensegrity structure are replaced with flexible cables, while the four top cables are replaced with elastic cables, resulting in a multi-motion mode tensegrity unit (Fig. 1(c)). By driving the flexible cables to change their lengths, the rods connected to them can be pulled to rotate around the R pairs, while the lengths of the elastic cables will also change. Since the endpoints of three rods form a plane, in order to achieve the required translational and rotational motion of the tensegrity unit, constraints are imposed on the lengths of the flexible cables to ensure that the endpoint of the fourth rod also lies in this plane, as shown in Fig. 1(b).

By assembling two identical tensegrity units together, a multi-locomotion tensegrity robot can be obtained, as shown in Fig. 1(d). The endpoints of the rods in the two tensegrity units are connected via S pair. The elastic cables on the end planes of the two tensegrity units are merged into one, with both ends attached to the S pairs. Each pair of flexible cables of the two tensegrity units are merged into one sliding cable, passing through the S pair. Each sliding cable is driven by an actuator to change its length, allowing the S pair to slide along the cable. Since the two tensegrity units are completely identical, when driving the sliding cables, the motions of the tensegrity units on both sides are symmetric about the plane formed by the S pairs. Combined with the motion characteristics of a single tensegrity unit, it is evident that this multi-locomotion tensegrity robot can achieve extension and contraction along the yground axis and rotation around the xground and zground axis, corresponding to the three modes of earthworm-like, inchworm-like, and turning locomotion of the robot, respectively. The specific establishment of the kinematic model and motion planning are detailed in Sect. 3.

Based on the simplified mechanism derived from Fig. 1(d), the specific structural design and 3D model of the multi-mode tensegrity mobile robot are completed, as shown in Fig. 1(e). One end of the elastic cable is anchored to one side of the frame, while the other end is wound around a wire spool. In particular, each wire spool is driven by a motor fixed on the other side of the frame. Different rotations of the four wire spools can lengthen or shorten the four sliding cables, ensuring that the robot can achieve various forms of deformation. Figure 1(g) shows the deformation of the robot under three locomotion modes. It is worth noting that to ensure smooth forward movement, unidirectional friction is provided by ratchet-based feet fixed on the two frames of the robot, which can only rotate in one direction. Taking the earthworm-like locomotion of the robot as an example, when the robot contracts, the ratchet on the front frame tends to rotate counterclockwise, while the ratchet on the rear frame tends to rotate clockwise. At this time, the ratchet on the front frame is locked, while the ratchet on the rear frame can rotate smoothly. As a result, the front frame remains stationary, and the rear frame moves forward. The situation is reversed when the robot extends. By such extension and contraction, the robot can move forward. Considering the difficulty in manufacturing S pairs and the size limitation of the robot, three R pairs (R pair-1, R pair-2, R pair-3) with axes intersecting at a point are used to equivalently replace the S pair between the two rods, as shown in Fig. 1(f). This design also has the advantage of increasing the range of robot deformation. The axis of the R pair connecting the rods to the frame and constraining the rotation of the rods is shown as Axis-RF in Fig. 1(f).

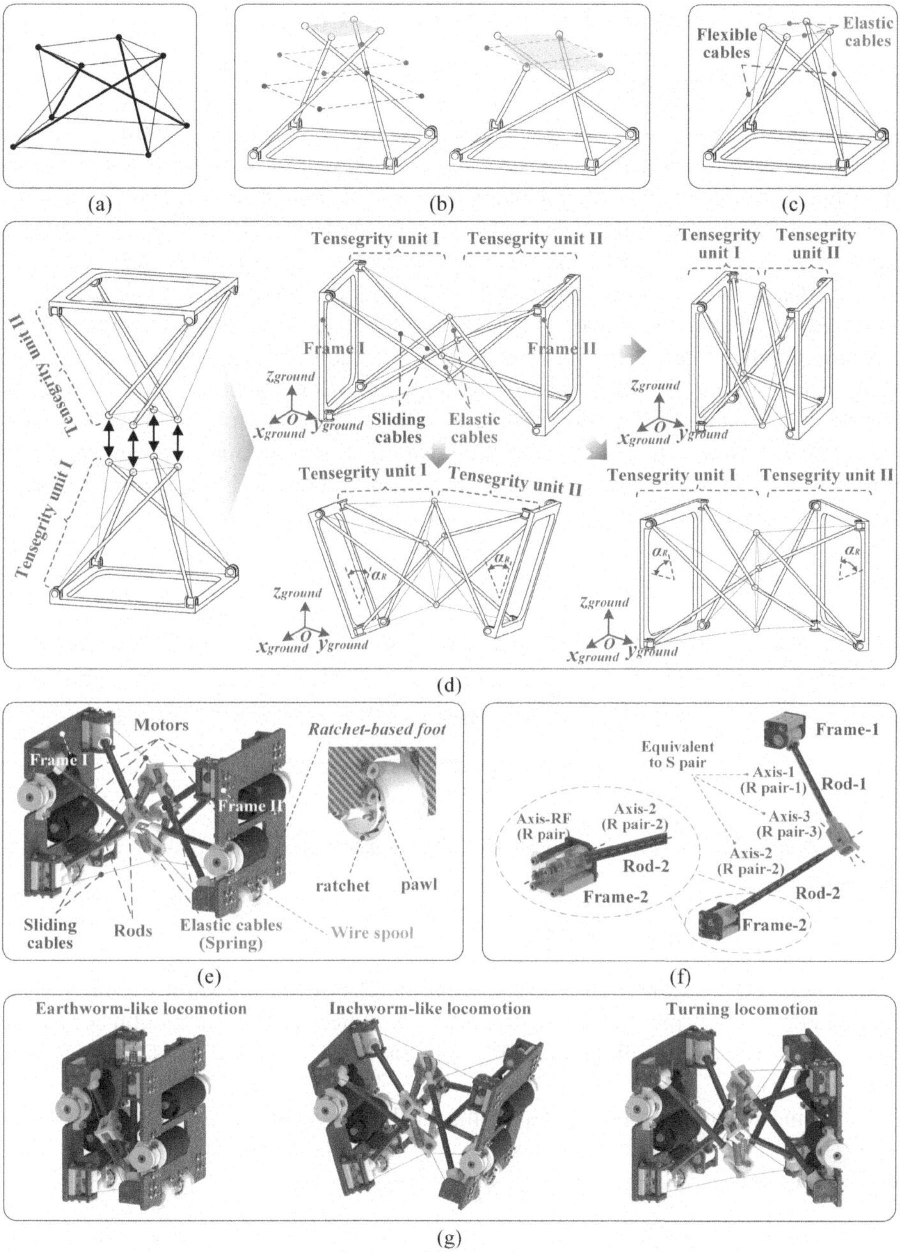

Fig. 1. Tensegrity robotic mechanism and overall structure design. (a) Prismatic tensegrity structure with four rods and twelve cables; (b) Motion of end nodes of the tensegrity unit during the translational and rotational motion process; (c) Tensegrity unit; (d) Robot based on the Tensegrity unit; (e)Structure of the robot; (f) Connection structure between two rods; (g) Different locomotion modes of robot.

3 Motion Planning for Different Locomotion Modes

3.1 Kinematic Modelling

The kinematic modeling of the proposed multi-locomotion tensegrity mobile robot aims at establishing the relationship between the driving law of each motor and the position and posture of the robot, providing a mathematical basis for subsequent motion planning of the robot. Suppose that the center of mass of each link and frame of the robot are located at its geometric center, the kinematic modeling process of the robot is shown in Fig. 2. Based on the driving angle φ_i (i = 1–4) of the robot, the total length s_i (i = 1–4) of each driving cable can be obtained according to motor-spool-cable model. Then, the position and posture of the links of the robot in the base coordinate system can be obtained on compliance with geometric relationship of the structure. Furthermore, the locomotion performance (i.e., displacement, velocity, acceleration) of the robot can be obtained. It is worth noting that given the position or locomotion performance of the robot, the input angles of each driving motor of the robot can be determined through inverse kinematics modeling process.

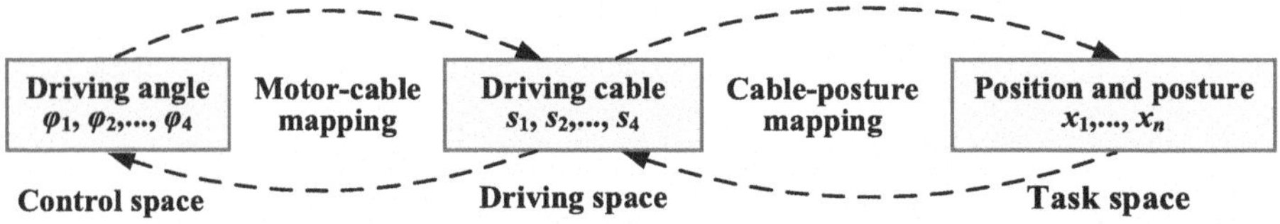

Fig. 2. Kinematic modelling process of the robot

According to motor-spool-cable model, the total length of each driving cable can be expressed as

$$s_{i\_Total} = s_{i\_0} + \varphi_i \cdot R_i = s_{i,1} + s_{i,2},\ i = 1 - 4 \tag{1}$$

where, s_{i_Total} (s_{i_0}) is the total length (initial length) of the i-th sliding cable passing through node B_i. φ_i is the driving angle of the i-th motor, and R_i is the radius of the i-th spool. s_{i_1} and s_{i_2} are the lengths of cable segments $A_{i+1}B_i$ and $B_iC_{i\text{-}1}$ of the i-th sliding cable, respectively.

According to the geometric relationship of the robot, in the coordinate system A-$x_Ay_Az_A$, the position of center of mass of each link of the tensegrity unit 1 of the robot can be expressed as

$$[\boldsymbol{O}_i]_A = \left[\, U_{1i}\cos\theta_i + U_{2i}\ V_{1i}\cos\theta_i + V_{2i}\ W_{1i}\sin\theta_i \,\right]^T,\ i{=}\ 1-4 \tag{2}$$

where, $U_{1i} = -\frac{1}{2}L_{sti}\sin\alpha_{2i}\cdot\sin\alpha_{1i}$; $V_{1i} = \frac{1}{2}L_{sti}\sin\alpha_{2i}\cdot\cos\alpha_{1i}$; $W_{1i} = \frac{1}{2}L_{sti}\sin\alpha_{2i}$;
$U_{2i} = \frac{1}{2}\left(\sqrt{L_{fr1}^2 - (L_{sti}\cos\alpha_{2i})^2}\cdot\sin\alpha_{1i} + L_{fr1}\cdot\cos\left(-\frac{\pi}{4} + \frac{\pi}{2}(i-1)\right)\right)$;
$V_{2i} = -\frac{1}{2}\left(\sqrt{(L_{fr1})^2 - (L_{sti}\cos\alpha_{2i})^2}\cdot\cos\alpha_{1i} + L_{fr1}\cdot\sin\left(-\frac{\pi}{4} + \frac{\pi}{2}(i-1)\right)\right)$. L_{sti} (i = 1–4) is the length of i-th link of the tensegrity unit 1, and L_{fr1} is the distance between

the center of mass of frame and the node A_1. α_{1i} and α_{2i} are angular parameters of the i-th R pair, and θ_i is the rotation angle of the i-th link of the tensegrity unit. It is worth noting that due to the fact that the nodes B_1, B_2,..., B_4 are always located in the plane b (Fig. 3) during the locomotion process of the robot, there is a coupling relationship between the rotation angle of each link in the tensegrity unit 1.

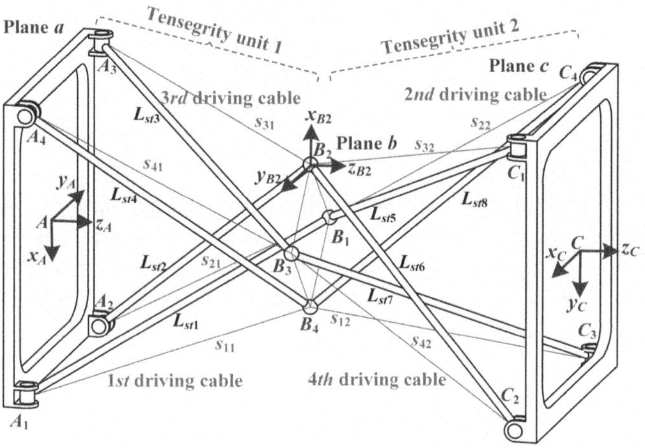

Fig. 3. Mechanism diagram of the robot

For the node B_i (i = 1–4), its position vector in the coordinate system A-$x_A y_A z_A$ can be written as

$$\begin{aligned}[\boldsymbol{B}_i]_A &= \left[u_{1i}\cos\theta_i + u_{2i} \; v_{1i}\cos\theta_i + v_{2i} \; w_{1i}\sin\theta_i \right]^T \\ &= \left[b_{i,x}^{(j)} \; b_{i,y}^{(j)} \; b_{i,z}^{(j)} \right]^T \end{aligned} \tag{3}$$

where, the expressions of u_{1i}, u_{2i}, v_{1i}, v_{2i} and w_{1i} can refer to Eq. (2). Taking the node B_1, B_2 and B_3 into account, the vector equation of the plane b composed of the three nodes in the coordinate system A-$x_A y_A z_A$ can be expressed as

$$[\boldsymbol{r}]_A \cdot [\boldsymbol{n}_b]_A = n_{b0} \tag{4}$$

where, $n_{b0} = [\boldsymbol{B}_1]_A \cdot [\boldsymbol{n}_b]_A$, $[\boldsymbol{r}]_A$ is the position vector of arbitrary point on the plane b in the coordinate system A-$x_A y_A z_A$. $[\boldsymbol{n}_b]_A$ is the normal vector of the plane b, and can be obtained by the coordinates of the node B_1, B_2 and B_3, which is expressed as

$$[\boldsymbol{n}_b]_A = [\boldsymbol{B}_1\boldsymbol{B}_2]_A \times [\boldsymbol{B}_2\boldsymbol{B}_3]_A = \left[n_{bx} \; n_{by} \; n_{bz} \right]^T \tag{5}$$

where,

$$n_{bx} = \begin{vmatrix} b_{2,y} - b_{1,y} & b_{2,z} - b_{1,z} \\ b_{3,y} - b_{2,y} & b_{3,z} - b_{2,z} \end{vmatrix}, \quad n_{by} = -\begin{vmatrix} b_{2,x} - b_{1,x} & b_{2,z} - b_{1,z} \\ b_{3,x} - b_{2,x} & b_{3,z} - b_{2,z} \end{vmatrix}, n_{bz} = \begin{vmatrix} b_{2,x} - b_{1,x} & b_{2,y} - b_{1,y} \\ b_{3,x} - b_{2,x} & b_{3,y} - b_{2,y} \end{vmatrix}$$

According to Eqs. (4)–(5), the rotation angle θ_4 of the 4-*th* link satisfy

$$A_f \cdot \cos\theta_4 + B_f \cdot \sin\theta_4 + C_f = 0 \tag{6}$$

where, $A_f = u_{14} \cdot n_x + v_{14} \cdot n_y; B_f = w_{14} \cdot n_z;\ C_f = u_{24} \cdot n_x + v_{24} \cdot n_y - n_{b0}$

On compliance with Eq. (6), the relationship between θ_4 and $\theta_1, \theta_2, \theta_3$ can be written as

$$\theta_4 = 2\arctan\left(\sqrt{\frac{1 - I_f}{1 + I_f}}\right) = f(\theta_1, \ldots, \theta_3) \tag{7}$$

where, $I_f = -\frac{\sqrt{A_f^2 + B_f^2 - C_f^2} + A_f \cdot C_f}{A_f^2 + B_f^2}$.

Insert Eq. (7) into Eq. (2), and the position of center of mass of each link in the coordinate system $A\text{-}x_A y_A z_A$ can be obtained, which is a function of θ_1, θ_2, and θ_3. Furthermore, by inserting Eq. (7) into Eq. (3), the position of the node B_1, B_2,…,B_4 in the coordinate system $A\text{-}x_A y_A z_A$ can be obtained. On this basis, the length of elastic cable of the tensegrity unit 1 can be shown as

$$L_{spi} = \begin{cases} \left\| \left[B_i B_{i-1} \right]_A \right\| = g_i(\theta_1, \ldots, \theta_3), i = 2 - 4 \\ \left\| [B_4 B_1]_A \right\| = g_1(\theta_1, \ldots, \theta_3), i = 1 \end{cases} \tag{8}$$

where, L_{spi} is the length of the *i*-th elastic cable.

The local coordinate system $B\text{-}x_B y_B z_B$ is established at the center of the plane *b*. In particular, the position of coordinate origin *B* in the coordinate system $A\text{-}x_A y_A z_A$ can be obtained as follow

$$[\boldsymbol{B}]_A = \sum_{i=1}^{4} ([\boldsymbol{G}_i]_A \cdot S_i) / \sum_{i=1}^{4} S_i \tag{9}$$

where, the plane *b* is divided into 4 triangles b_1, b_2, b_3, and b_4. $[\boldsymbol{G}_i]_A$ represents the coordinate of center of mass of each triangle in the coordinate system $A\text{-}x_A y_A z_A$, and S_i is the area of each triangle. On this basis, based on the position of the node B_i ($i =$ 1–4) and the normal vector of the plane *b*, the coordinates of the local coordinate system $B\text{-}x_B y_B z_B$ can be expressed as

$$[\boldsymbol{x}_B]_A = \frac{[\boldsymbol{BB}_4]_A}{\| [\boldsymbol{BB}_4]_A \|}, [z_B]_A = \frac{[\boldsymbol{n}_b]_A}{\| [\boldsymbol{n}_b]_A \|}, \left[y_B \right]_A = [z_B]_A \times [\boldsymbol{x}_B]_A \tag{10}$$

For the tensegrity unit 2, the coordinates of center of mass of the $[i + 4]$-th link ($i =$ 1–4) in each local coordinate system $B_i\text{-}x_{Bi} y_{Bi} z_{Bi}$ can be firstly obtained, and then the position vector of center of mass of each link in the coordinate systems $B\text{-}x_B y_B z_B$ and $A\text{-}x_A y_A z_A$ can be obtained sequentially through coordinate transformation. The specific process is as follows:

According to Fig. 3, in the local coordinate system $B_i\text{-}x_{Bi} y_{Bi} z_{Bi}$, the following relationship holds

$$\left[\boldsymbol{B}_i \boldsymbol{O}_{i+4} \right]_{B_i} \cdot \left[\boldsymbol{B}_i \boldsymbol{B}_{i-3+2p} \right]_{B_i} = \left\| \left[\boldsymbol{B}_i \boldsymbol{O}_{i+4} \right]_{B_i} \right\| \cdot \left\| \left[\boldsymbol{B}_i \boldsymbol{B}_{i-3+2p} \right]_{B_i} \right\| \cos\beta_{[i+4]p} \tag{11}$$

where, $p = 1$–2. $\beta\ [4 + i]p$ ($p = 1$–2) is the angle between $\boldsymbol{B}_i\boldsymbol{O}_{i+4}$ and $\boldsymbol{B}_i\boldsymbol{B}_{i\text{-}3+2p}$. Particularly, on the plane b, the coordinates of the node $B_{i\text{-}3+2p}$ in the coordinate system $B_i\text{-}x_{Bi}y_{Bi}z_{Bi}$ can be expressed as

$$\left[\boldsymbol{B}_{i-3+2p}\right]_{B_i} = \left[-L_{sp[i+p-1]}\cos\gamma_{ip}\ (-1)^p \cdot L_{sp[i+p-1]}\sin\gamma_{ip}\ 0\right]^T, p = 1-2 \quad (12)$$

where, $\gamma\ i1$ ($\gamma\ i2$) is the angle between $\boldsymbol{BB}_i$ and $\boldsymbol{B}_i\boldsymbol{B}_{i\text{-}1}$ ($\boldsymbol{B}_i\boldsymbol{B}_{i+1}$), which can be obtained by the coordinates of the node B_i ($i = 1$–4). $L_{sp[i+p\text{-}1]}$ is the length of each elastic cable. Insert Eq. (12) into Eq. (13), the position of center of mass of the $[i + 4]$-th link in the local coordinate system $B_i\text{-}x_{Bi}y_{Bi}z_{Bi}$ can be obtained as

$$\left[\boldsymbol{O}_{i+4}\right]_{B_i} = \left[\left[O_{i+4,x}\right]_{B_i}\ \left[O_{i+4,y}\right]_{B_i}\ \left[O_{i+4,z}\right]_{B_i}\right]^T = \begin{bmatrix} L_{st[i+4]}\cdot e_{f[i+4]} \\ L_{st[i+4]}\cdot e_{g[i+4]} \\ h_{s[i+4]} \end{bmatrix} \quad (13)$$

where, $e_{f[i+4]} = \frac{\cos\beta_{[4+i]1}\cdot\sin\gamma_{i2}-\cos\beta_{[4+i]2}\cdot\sin\gamma_{i1}}{2(\sin\gamma_{i1}\cdot\sin\gamma_{i2}-\cos\gamma_{i1}\cdot\cos\gamma_{i2})}$;

$e_{g[i+4]} = \frac{(\cos\beta_{[4+i]2}\cdot\cos\gamma_{i1}-\cos\beta_{[4+i]1}\cdot\cos\gamma_{i2})}{2(\cos\gamma_{i1}\cdot\cos\gamma_{i2}-\sin\gamma_{i1}\cdot\sin\gamma_{i2})}$;

$h_{s[i+4]} = \sqrt{L^2_{st[i+4]} - \left[O_{i+4,x}\right]^2_{B_i} - \left[O_{i+4,y}\right]^2_{B_i}}$.

Hence, the center of mass of the $[i + 4]$-th link ($i = 1$–4) in the coordinate system $A\text{-}x_Ay_Az_A$ can be expressed as

$$\left[\boldsymbol{O}_{i+4}\right]_A = {}^A_B\boldsymbol{T}\cdot{}^B_{B_i}\boldsymbol{T}\cdot\left[\boldsymbol{O}_{i+4}\right]_{B_i} \quad (14)$$

where,

$$\begin{aligned} {}^B_{B_i}\boldsymbol{T} &= Rot(z_B,\gamma_{i3})\cdot Trans(x_B, L_{sri}) \\ &= \begin{bmatrix} \cos\gamma_{i3} & \sin\gamma_{i3} & 0 & L_{sri}\cos\gamma_{i3} \\ -\sin\gamma_{i3} & \cos\gamma_{i3} & 0 & -L_{sri}\sin\gamma_{i3} \\ 0 & 0 & 1 & 0 \\ 0 & 0 & 0 & 1 \end{bmatrix}; \\ &= \begin{bmatrix} t_{11-i} & t_{12-i} & \cdots & t_{14-i} \\ t_{21-i} & t_{22-i} & \cdots & t_{24-i} \\ \vdots & \vdots & \ddots & \vdots \\ t_{41-i} & t_{42-i} & \cdots & t_{44-i} \end{bmatrix}_{4\times4} \end{aligned}$$

$$\begin{aligned} {}^A_B\boldsymbol{T} &= Trans([\boldsymbol{AB}]_A, \|[\boldsymbol{AB}]_A\|)\cdot{}^A_BRot \\ &= \begin{bmatrix} \boldsymbol{E}_{3\times3} & \{[\boldsymbol{AB}]_A\}_{3\times1} \\ \boldsymbol{0}_{1\times3} & 0 \end{bmatrix}\cdot\begin{bmatrix} \{[\boldsymbol{x}_B]_A\}_{3\times1} & \left\{\left[\boldsymbol{y}_B\right]_A\right\}_{3\times1} & \{[z_B]_A\}_{3\times1} & 0 \\ 0 & 0 & 0 & 1 \end{bmatrix} \\ &= \begin{bmatrix} t_{11} & t_{12} & \cdots & t_{14} \\ t_{21} & t_{22} & \cdots & t_{24} \\ \vdots & \vdots & \ddots & \vdots \\ t_{41} & t_{42} & \cdots & t_{44} \end{bmatrix}_{4\times4} \end{aligned}$$

where, γ_{i3} is the angle between $\boldsymbol{BB}_i$ and the positive direction of x_B, and L_{sri} is the distance between B and B_i.

Insert Eq. (14) into Eq. (13), and the position of center of mass of the $[i+4]$-th link in the coordinate system A-$x_A y_A z_A$ can be obtained as follow

$$\begin{aligned}[\boldsymbol{O}_{i+4}]_A &= \left[[O_{i+4,x}]_A \ [O_{i+4,y}]_A \ [O_{i+4,z}]_A \right]^T \\ &= \begin{bmatrix} q_{11}\cdot[O_{i+4,x}]_{B_i} + q_{12}\cdot[O_{i+4,y}]_{B_i} + q_{13}\cdot[O_{i+4,z}]_{B_i} \\ q_{21}\cdot[O_{i+4,x}]_{B_i} + q_{22}\cdot[O_{i+4,y}]_{B_i} + q_{23}\cdot[O_{i+4,z}]_{B_i} \\ q_{31}\cdot[O_{i+4,x}]_{B_i} + q_{32}\cdot[O_{i+4,y}]_{B_i} + q_{33}\cdot[O_{i+4,z}]_{B_i} \end{bmatrix}\end{aligned} \tag{15}$$

where, $q_{IJ} = \sum_{s=1}^{4} (t_{Is} t_{sJ-i})$, $I = 1-3, J = 1-3$. By referencing Eqs. (2)–(10), Eq. (25) can be expressed as a function of θ_1, θ_2, and θ_3. On this basis, the position of the node C_i $(i = 1$–$4)$ can be written as

$$[\boldsymbol{C}_i]_A = 2\cdot[\boldsymbol{O}_{i+4}]_A - [\boldsymbol{B}_i]_A \tag{16}$$

For the length of sliding cable, the following formula holds

$$s_{i\_Total} = s_{i,1} + s_{i,2} = \left\| [\boldsymbol{A}_{i+1}\boldsymbol{B}_i]_A \right\| + \left\| [\boldsymbol{B}_i\boldsymbol{C}_{i-1}]_A \right\| = f_{s,i}(\theta_1,\ldots,\theta_3) \tag{17}$$

Combining Eqs. (17) and (1), the mapping relationship between driving angle of motor and rotation angle of link can be obtained

$$a_{f,i}\cdot\cos^2\theta_i + b_{f,i}\cdot\cos\theta_i + c_{f,i} = 0,\ i = 1-3 \tag{18}$$

where, $a_{f,i} = u_{1i}^2 + v_{1i}^2 - w_{1i}^2$;
$b_{f,i} = 2u_{1i}\left(u_{2i} - L_{fr1}\cos\left(-\frac{\pi}{4} + \frac{\pi}{2}(i-1)\right)\right) + 2v_{1i}\left(v_{2i} - L_{fr1}\sin\left(-\frac{\pi}{4} + \frac{\pi}{2}(i-1)\right)\right)$;
$c_{f,i} = \left(u_{2i} - L_{fr1}\cdot\cos\left(-\frac{\pi}{4} + \frac{\pi}{2}(i-1)\right)\right)^2 + \left(v_{2i} - L_{fr1}\cdot\sin\left(-\frac{\pi}{4} + \frac{\pi}{2}(i-1)\right)\right)^2 - \left(\frac{1}{2}(s_{i\_0} + \varphi_i\cdot R_i)\right)^2$.

By solving Eq. (18), it can be concluded that

$$\theta_i = 2\arctan\left(\sqrt{\frac{1-J_{f,i}}{1+J_{f,i}}}\right) = f_{\varphi,i}(\varphi_1,\ldots,\varphi_3),\ i = 1-3 \tag{19}$$

where, $J_{f,i} = -\left(b_{f,i} - \sqrt{b_{f,i}^2 - 4a_{f,i}c_{f,i}}\right)/a_{f,i}$.

Insert Eq. (19) into Eqs. (2) and (15), and the mapping relationship between driving angle of motor and position of the robot can be obtained. Furthermore, the position and posture of each link in the coordinate system A-$x_A y_A z_A$ can be expressed as

$$\boldsymbol{q}_{O_i} = \left\{ [\boldsymbol{O}_i]_A^T \ [\boldsymbol{\alpha}_{Oi}]_A^T \right\}^T = \left\{ \boldsymbol{f}_{oi}(\varphi_1,\ldots,\varphi_3)\ \boldsymbol{f}_{\alpha i}(\varphi_1,\ldots,\varphi_3) \right\}^T \in \mathbb{R}^{6\times 1} \tag{20}$$

where, $\boldsymbol{\alpha}\ oi$ is the angle between i-th link and the plane a, which can be obtained by the coordinates of each node in the coordinate system A-$x_A y_A z_A$.

3.2 Motion Planning Based on the Kinematic Model

According to kinematic model and the locomotion mechanism, the tensegrity mobile robot proposed in this work has three basic locomotion modes, including earthworm-like, inchworm-like and turning locomotion. Since the deformation of robot is achieved by driving the sliding cables with motors, the motion planning is conducted to acquire the driving laws of each motor under different locomotion modes. Here, it is specified that in Figs. 4, 5, 6 and 7, the direction of robot movement is from left to right. The left frame of the robot is Frame 1, and the right frame is Frame 2. The sliding cables at the bottom and top of the robot are denoted as Sliding Cable 1 and Sliding Cable 3 respectively. The sliding cable on the left side of the robot's forward direction is Sliding Cable 2, while the one on the right side is Sliding Cable 4. The motor driving the Sliding cable i is denoted as Motor i, and its angle of rotation is represented by φ_i ($i = 1$–4).

The locomotion mechanism of earthworm-like movement (Fig. 4) has been described in Sect. 2 as an example. To achieve the contraction and extension of the robot while maintaining the parallelism of the two frames during movement, the four sliding cables should be contracted and extended synchronously. Therefore, the driving laws of the four motors can be formulated as

$$\varphi_1 = \varphi_2 = \varphi_3 = \varphi_4 \in [\varphi_a, \varphi_b] \tag{21}$$

where, φ_a is the rotation angle of the four motors when the robot is in its middle state of the earthworm-like locomotion, φ_b is the rotation angle of the motors when the robot is in its initial/end state. φ_a, φ_b can be solved according to kinematic model.

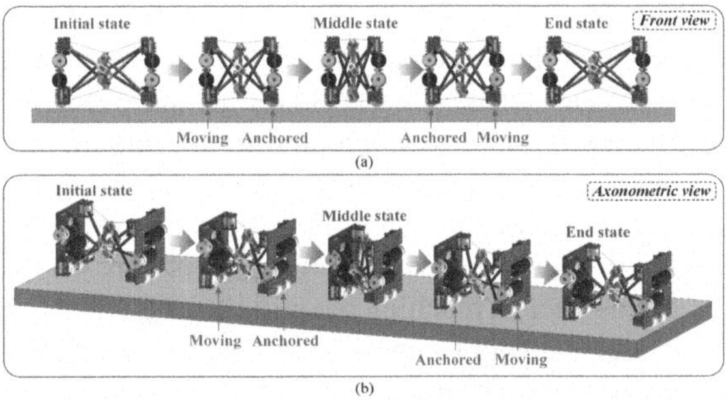

Fig. 4. Earthworm-like locomotion of the robot. (a) Front view; (b) Axonometric view.

For the inchworm-like locomotion, from its initial state to middle state, the sides of the two frames closest to the ground gradually approach each other, transitioning from a parallel state to a state with an angle between them (Fig. 5). During this process, the ratchet-based feet fixed on Frame 2 are anchored, while Frame 2 rotates clockwise around the ratchet. At the same time, the ratchet-based feet on Frame 1 moves forward as Frame 1 rotates counterclockwise around the ratchet. The situation is reversed when the robot transitions from the middle state to the end state. Such switching enables the robot to move forward under the inchworm-like locomotion (Fig. 5). To achieve this motion, the lengths of Sliding Cables 2 and 4 remain constant, while Sliding Cables 1 is first contracted and then extended. According to constraints on the lengths of the sliding cables, the length of Sliding Cable 3 can be determined by the lengths of the other three sliding cables. Therefore, the driving laws of the four motors can be formulated as

$$\varphi_2 = \varphi_4 = a,\ \varphi_1 \in [\varphi_c, \varphi_d],\ \varphi_3 = f(\varphi_1, \varphi_2, \varphi_4) \tag{22}$$

where, φ_c is the rotation angle of Motor 1 when the robot is in its middle state of the inchworm-like locomotion, φ_d is the rotation angle of Motor 1 when the robot is in its initial/end state. The rotation angle of Motor 2 and 4 is constant a. a, φ_c, φ_d can be solved according to kinematic model. In particular, the rotation angle of Motor 3 is a function of φ_1, φ_2 and φ_4.

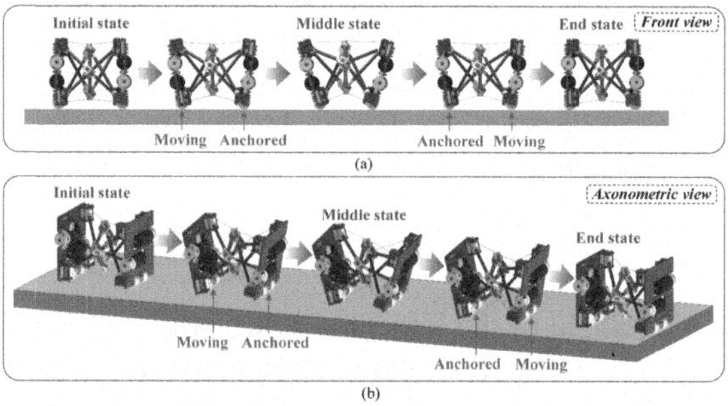

Fig. 5. Inchworm-like locomotion of the robot. (a) Front view; (b) Axonometric view.

The turning locomotion of the robot includes right turn (Fig. 6) and left turn (Fig. 7). Unlike the locomotion modes of earthworm-like and inchworm-like movements, it needs to first contract the two frames to a certain distance and then achieve the turning locomotion by a combined movement of rotation and translation of Frame 2.

For the right turn of the robot as shown in Fig. 6, in one cycle, Frame 1 is first fixed and Frame 2 is extended to rotate clockwise and move forward on the horizontal plane through extension of sliding cables, reaching the middle state. Then Frame 2 is fixed, and the sliding cables contracts, causing Frame 1 to rotate clockwise and move forward on the horizontal plane, reaching a state where both frames are parallel. During this motion, the length of Sliding Cable 2 should be equal or greater than length of Sliding Cable 4, while the length of Sliding Cable 1 and 3 are the same and between the lengths of Sliding Cable 2 and 4. Therefore, the driving laws of the four motors can be formulated as

$$\varphi_2 \le \varphi_1 = \varphi_3 \le \varphi_4,\ \begin{cases} \varphi_1 = \varphi_3 \in \left[\varphi_e^{(1)}, \varphi_f^{(1)}\right] \\ \varphi_2 \in \left[\varphi_e^{(2)}, \varphi_f^{(2)}\right] \\ \varphi_4 \in \left[\varphi_e^{(4)}, \varphi_f^{(4)}\right] \end{cases} \tag{23}$$

where,$\varphi_e^{(i)}$ is the rotation angle of Motor i when the robot is in its initial/end state of the right turn locomotion, $\varphi_f^{(i)}$ is the rotation angle of Motor i when the robot is in its middle state. $\varphi_e^{(i)}$, $\varphi_f^{(i)}$ can be solved according to kinematic model.

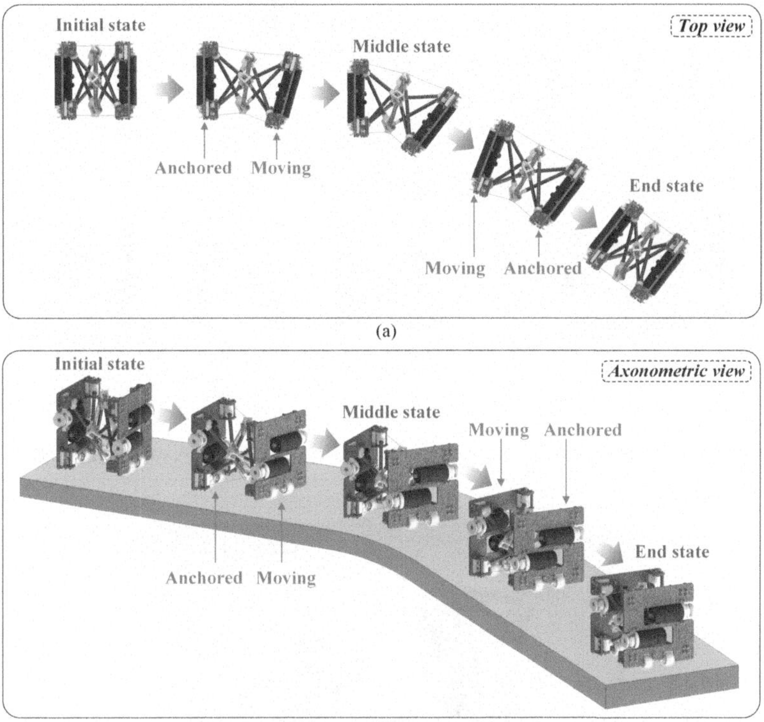

Fig. 6. Right turn locomotion of the robot. (a) Top view; (b) Axonometric view.

The principle of the robot's left turn is identical to right turn, with its frames completing counterclockwise rotation on the horizontal plane (Fig. 7). Referring to Eq. (23), by simply swapping the driving laws of Motor 2 and Motor 4, the robot's left turn motion can be achieved.

4 Experiments

4.1 Prototype of the Robot

A prototype of the spatial multi-locomotion tensegrity mobile robot, as shown in Fig. 8, is manufactured based on the 3D model described in Sect. 2. Springs are used as elastic cables, while metal wires are used as sliding cables. Two frames of the robot are made of carbon fiber, and the rods are made of aluminum alloy. Components such as ratchet-based feet and wire spools are fabricated using photosensitive resin via 3D printing.

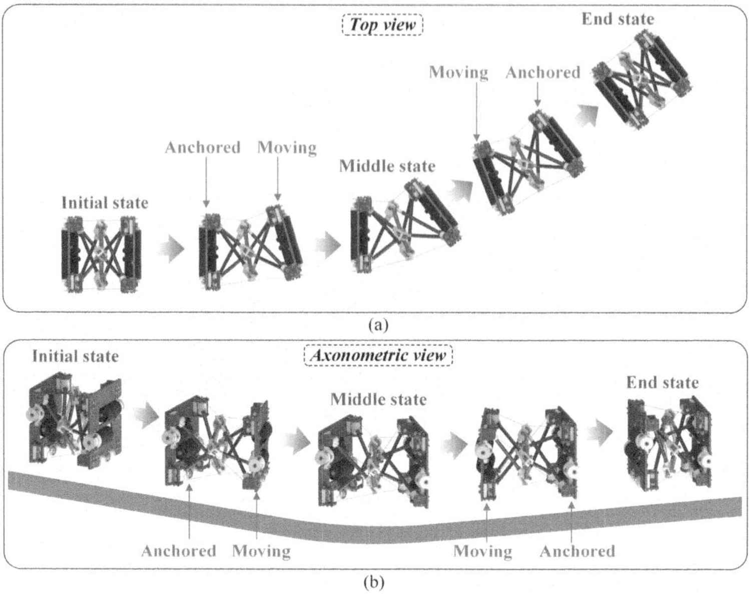

Fig. 7. Left turn locomotion of the robot. (a) Top view; (b) Axonometric view.

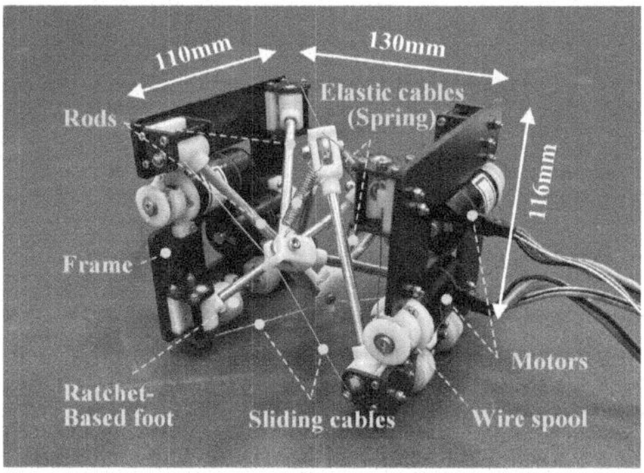

Fig. 8. Prototype of the robot

The dimensions of the robot are 130 mm × 110 mm × 116 mm, with a total weight of 680 g. The type of selected brushless DC motor is M2006 P36 with a rated torque of 1.0 Nm, controlled by an STM32 control board and powered by a 24 V lithium battery. Experiments conducted with this prototype include different locomotion modes such as earthworm-like, inchworm-like, turning, obstacle avoidance, and reverse motion.

4.2 Locomotion Test on the Robot

Earthworm-like Locomotion. The locomotion sequence and experimental data of the robot performing earthworm-like motion on a flat surface are shown in Fig. 9. The total displacement within a single earthworm-like motion cycle is 40.0 mm, with displacements of 18.5 mm during contraction and 21.5 mm during extension, taking approximately 1.0 s (as is shown in Fig. 9(a)). The relationship between displacement and velocity over time as the robot performs 25 consecutive earthworm-like motion cycles is analyzed in Fig. 9(b). It can be seen that the robot achieves a total displacement of 1004 mm over the 25 continuous motion cycles, with an average velocity of 40.16 mm/s.

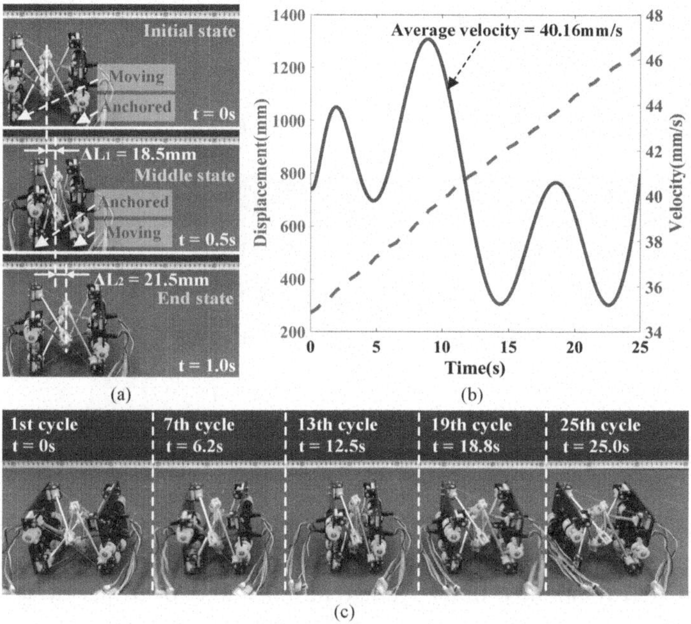

Fig. 9. Earthworm-like locomotion test. (a) Locomotion sequence of a single cycle; (b) Velocity and displacement curves; (c) Locomotion sequence of continuous motion for 25 cycles.

Inchworm-like Locomotion. Figure 10 shows the locomotion sequence and experimental data of the robot performing inchworm-like motion on a flat surface. It can be seen from Fig. 10(a) that the total displacement of the robot within a single inchworm-like motion cycle is 40.5 mm, with the maximum angle between the front and rear frames being 40°. Each motion cycle takes approximately 1.0 s. Over 25 consecutive inchworm-like motion cycles, the robot achieves a total displacement of 1013 mm, with an average velocity of 40.52 mm/s (as is shown in Fig. 10(b) and (c)).

Turning Locomotion. To verify the advantages of the robot's turning locomotion described in this study, the most basic experiments of right and left turning locomotion for the robot have been first completed. Subsequently, based on the right and left turning locomotion, obstacle avoidance and reverse motion experiments have been conducted.

Left/Right turn locomotion. The locomotion sequence diagrams for the robot's right and left turns are shown in Fig. 11(a) and Fig. 11(b) respectively. It can be seen that

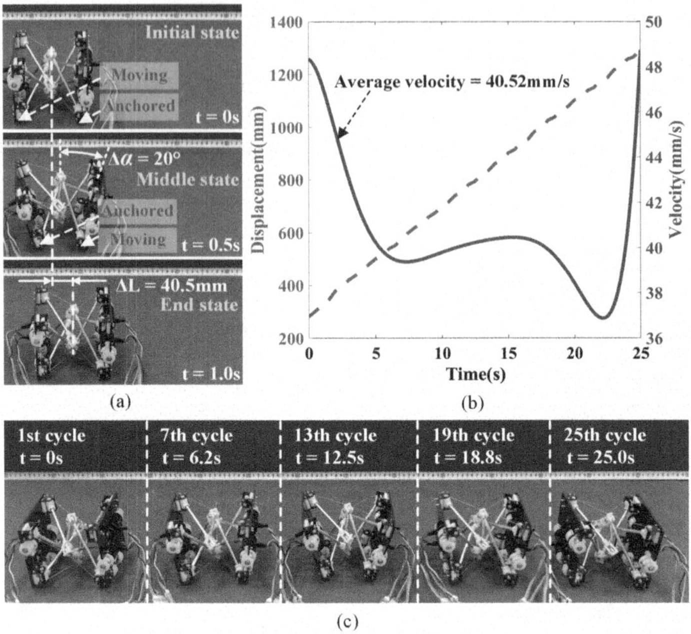

Fig. 10. Inchworm-like locomotion test. (a) Locomotion sequence of a single cycle; (b) Velocity and displacement curves; (c) Locomotion sequence of continuous motion for 25 cycles.

continuous right turns for 16 cycles result in the robot rotating 90° to the right, with an average turning angle of 5.625° per cycle. Similarly, continuous left turns for 15 cycles achieve a 90° left rotation, with an average turning angle of 6° per cycle. It is worth noting that the discrepancy in turning angles between left and right turns within a single cycle is due to assembly errors and deformation of the rods.

Obstacle avoidance motion. Two obstacles, each measuring 140mm × 100mm × 120 mm, are placed at intervals of 350 mm along the robot's forward path. The robot is driven to navigate an S-shaped route through these two obstacles to verify its turning performance. As shown in Fig. 12, when the robot approaches Obstacle 1, it begins to turn right to avoid it, then starts turning left to circumnavigate Obstacle 1. After completely circumnavigating Obstacle 1, the robot proceeds in a straight line to prepare for circumnavigating Obstacle 2, and subsequently turns right to bypass Obstacle 2, achieving obstacle avoidance movement. The experimental results indicate that the robot is capable of smooth turning locomotion through obstacles on a flat surface.

Reverse motion. Figure 13 shows the reverse motion sequence of the robot. Through 31 consecutive right turns, the robot successfully executes a U-turn, enabling it to move in the opposite direction. The experimental results demonstrate the robot's capability to perform reverse movements, significantly expanding the locomotion capabilities of the tensegrity mobile robot.

In summary, the experimental results demonstrate that the designed spatial multi-locomotion tensegrity mobile robot exhibits excellent turning capabilities, making the

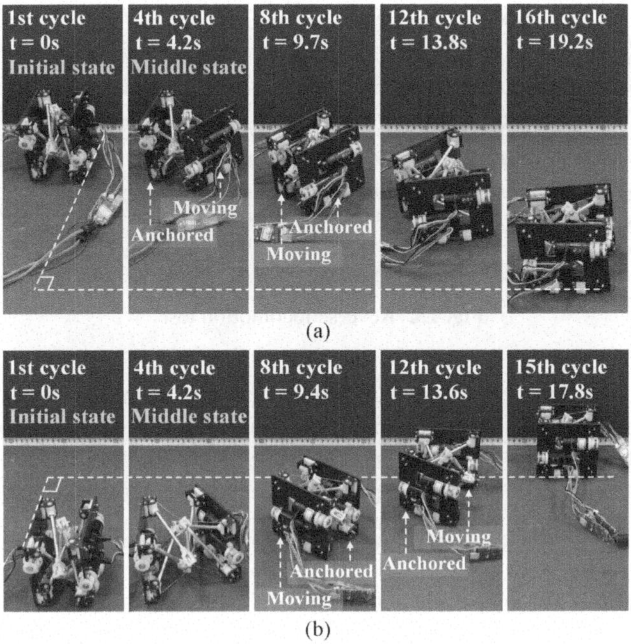

Fig. 11. Turning locomotion test. (a) Right turning locomotion sequence; (b) Left turning locomotion sequence.

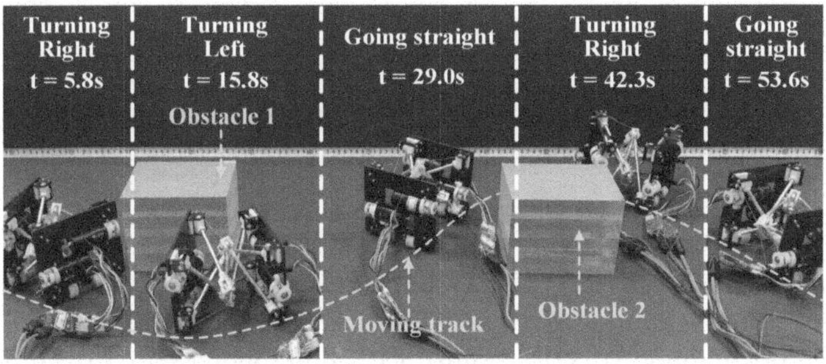

Fig. 12. Obstacle avoidance test

robot suitable for complex scenarios with obstacles, further validating the accuracy of the kinematic model and the effectiveness of the motion planning strategy.

Comparison of Our Proposed Robot and Other Related Tensegrity Robot. We have summarized tensegrity robots in the field of mobile robotics and compared their locomotion modes with ours, as shown in Table 1. It can be seen that other tensegrity mobile robots have relatively limited locomotion modes. For example, spherical tensegrity robots can only roll and jump, with turning locomotion achieved through rolling being non-smooth. Additionally, Prismatic tensegrity robots can only perform crawling and are unable to complete turning movements. Although our previous work featured

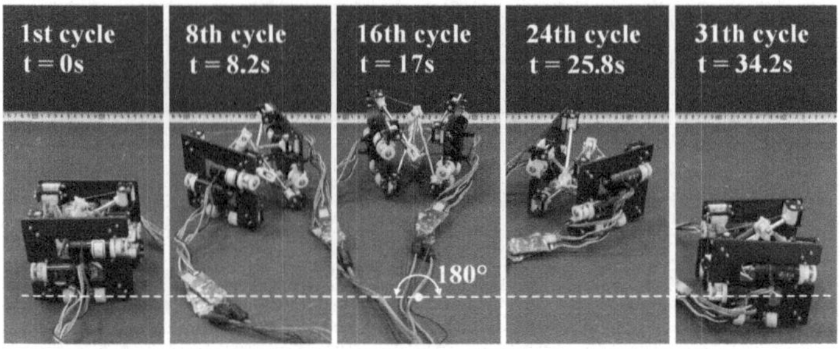

Fig. 13. Reverse locomotion test

robots with multiple motion modes [16–18], their range of motion was limited due to their planar structure, preventing them from executing turning locomotion. Therefore, the most significant highlight of the spatial multi-locomotion tensegrity mobile robot designed in this study is its ability to perform spatial turning motions, enabling it to have a larger range of motion and adapt to various motion scenarios.

Table 1. Comparison of our robot with other tensegrity robots

Related robots	Number of locomotion modes
Böhm et al.[19]	1: Worm-Like locomotion
Liu et al.[20]	1: Crawling
Kim et al.[21]	2: Hopping; rolling
Khazanov et al.[22]	1: Rolling
Our robot	3: Earthworm-like locomotion; Inchworm-like locomotion; Turning locomotion

In particular, the average speed of the robot described in this paper during earthworm-like and inchworm-like motions is 18.54 BL/min and 18.70 BL/min respectively, faster than the Three-prism robot[5] (3.0 BL/min), TT4-mini robot[13] (7.7 BL/min) and T12-R robot[15] (8.7 BL/min). It is proved that the designed robot has excellent motion performance, with a relatively high straight-line speed.

5 Conclusion

This work presents a novel spatial multi-locomotion tensegrity mobile robot. The robot can achieve multiple motion modes including earthworm-like, inchworm-like, and turning locomotion. Furthermore, the kinematic model of the robot is established, and motion planning for different motion modes is conducted based on this kinematic model. The excellent motion performance of the robot and the accuracy of its kinematic model are validated through experiments. The experimental results demonstrate that the average velocities of the robot during earthworm-like and inchworm-like locomotion reach

40.16 mm/s and 40.52 mm/s respectively. Moreover, smooth obstacle avoidance and reverse motion are achieved through consecutive left and right turns. Compared with other related robots, the spatial multi-locomotion tensegrity mobile robot proposed in this works has more motion modes and greater motion range. Because the transitions between the three motion modes is based on manual control, future work will focus on the feedback control of the robot with sensors. Miniaturizing and modularizing design of the robot will also be considered to enhance its adaptability to different terrains.

Acknowledgments. This work is funded by National Natural Science Foundation of China (grants 52275028).

References

1. Shah, D.S., et al.: Tensegrity robotics. Soft Rob. **9**(4), 639–656 (2022)
2. Liu, Y., Bi, Q., Yue, X., Wu, J., Yang, B., Li, Y.: A review on tensegrity structures-based robots. Mech. Mach. Theory **168**, 104571 (2022)
3. Luo, J., Edmunds, R., Rice, F., Agogino, A.M.: Tensegrity robot locomotion under limited sensory inputs via deep reinforcement learning. In: IEEE International Conference on Robotics and Automation 2018, ICRA, pp. 6260–6267. IEEE, Brisbane (2018)
4. Sabelhaus, A.P., et al.: System design and locomotion of SUPERball, an untethered tensegrity robot. In: IEEE International Conference on Robotics and Automation 2015, ICRA, pp. 2867–2873. IEEE, Seattle (2015)
5. Graells Rovira, A., Mirats Tur, J.M.: Control and simulation of a tensegrity-based mobile robot. Robot. Auton. Syst. **57**(5), 526–535 (2009)
6. Masic, M., Skelton, R.E., Smith, R.C.: Open-loop control of class-2 tensegrity towers. In: Smart Structures and Materials 2004, SSM, vol. 5383, pp. 298–308. IEEE, San Diego (2004)
7. Paul, C., Roberts, J.W., Lipson, H., Cuevas, F.J.V.: Gait production in a tensegrity based robot. In: 12th International Conference on Advanced Robotics 2005, ICAR, pp. 216-222. IEEE, Seattle (2005)
8. Paul, C., Valero-Cuevas, F.J., Lipson, H.: Design and control of tensegrity robots for locomotion. IEEE Trans. Rob. **22**(5), 944–957 (2006)
9. Rieffel, J., Stuk, R. J., Valero-Cuevas, F. J., Lipson, H.: Locomotion of a tensegrity robot via dynamically coupled modules (2007)
10. Kino, H., Matsutani, Y., Katakabe, S., Ochi, H.: Prototype of a tensegrity robot with nine wires for switching locomotion and calculation method of the balancing internal force. In: IEEE International Symposium on Robotics and Intelligent Sensors 2016, IRIS, vol. 105, pp. 1-6. IEEE, Tokyo (2017)
11. Zhou, D., Liu, Y., Tang, X., Sun, J., Deng, J.: A lightweight and multimotion crawling tensegrity robot driven by twisted artificial muscles. IEEE Trans. Industr. Electron. **69**(11), 11447–11457 (2022)
12. Wang, Z., Li, K., He, Q., Cai, S.: A light-powered ultralight tensegrity robot with high deformability and load capacity. Adv. Mater. **31**(7), 1806849 (2019)
13. Chen, L., et al.: Inclined surface locomotion strategies for spherical tensegrity robots. In: IEEE/RSJ International Conference on Intelligent Robots and Systems 2017, IROS, pp. 4976–4981. IEEE, Vancouver (2017)
14. Chang, J., Li, B., Liu, W., Du, W.: The path planning method of tensegrity robot based on A* Algorithm. In: Proceedings of the 8th IEEE Annual International Conference on Cyber Technology in Automation, Control, and Intelligent Systems 2018, CYBER, pp. 1502–1507. IEEE, Tianjin (2018)

15. Kim, K.: On the locomotion of spherical tensegrity robots (2016)
16. Yang, Q., Liu, X., Wang, P., Song, Y., Sun, T.: A multi-locomotion clustered tensegrity mobile robot with fewer actuators. Robot. Auton. Syst. **168**, 104504 (2023)
17. Yang, Q., Yu, Z., Liu, X., Lian, B., Sun, T.: A small-scale untethered tensegrity robot with high velocity and multi locomotion modes. IEEE Rob. Autom. Lett. **8**(11), 7503–7510 (2023)
18. Jin, Y., Yang, Q., Liu, X., Lian, B., Sun, T.: Type synthesis of worm-like planar tensegrity mobile robot. Mech. Mach. Theory **191**, 105476 (2024)
19. Böhm, V., Schorr, P., Schale, F., Kaufhold, T., Zentner, L., Zimmermann, K.: Worm-like mobile robot based on a tensegrity structure. In: IEEE 4th International Conference on Soft Robotics 2021, RoboSoft, pp. 358-363. Springer, New Haven (2021)
20. Liu, Y., Bi, Q., Dai, X., et al.: Ticbot: Development of a tensegrity-based in-pipe crawling robot. IEEE Trans. Industr. Electron. **70**(8), 8184–8193 (2022)
21. Kim, K., et al.: Hopping and rolling locomotion with spherical tensegrity robots. In: IEEE/RSJ International Conference on Intelligent Robots and Systems 2016, IROS, pp. 4369–4376. IEEE, Daejeon (2016)
22. Khazanov, M., Humphreys, B., Keat, W., Rieffel, J.: Exploiting dynamical complexity in a physical tensegrity robot to achieve locomotion. In: The Twelfth European Conference on Artificial Life 2013, ECAL, pp. 965–972. ASME, Sicily (2013)

Inverse Dynamics Model Learning for Robotic Manipulator Based on Swarm Optimization AdaBoost-LSTM

Shichao Ai[1,2], Yunhan Lin[1,2,3](✉), Wenhui Huang[3], and Huasong Min[3]

[1] School of Computer Science and Technology, Wuhan University of Science and Technology, Wuhan, China
yhlin@wust.edu.cn

[2] Hubei Province Key Laboratory of Intelligent Information Processing and Real-Time Industrial System, Wuhan, China

[3] Institute of Robotics and Intelligent Systems, Wuhan University of Science and Technology, Wuhan, China

Abstract. Inverse dynamics models of robotic manipulator can be derived using neural network training. However, in previous studies of inverse dynamics neural network model learning, there is the overfitting problem of good training effect but average estimation performance, while the configuration of hyperparameters in the model always depends on the traditional experience, which has a large room for improvement of the estimation accuracy of the model. Therefore, in this paper, we propose a method to optimize the LSTM (Long Short-Term Memory) model using AdaBoost (Adaptive Boosting) as well as Swarm Optimization Algorithm, which utilizes AdaBoost's ability to minimize the overfitting and Swarm Optimization Algorithm to optimize the model hyperparameters. In the experimental part, the method proposed in this paper is compared with previous methods using publicly available inverse dynamics datasets. Experimental results show that the method proposed in this paper has higher torque estimation accuracy and improves the performance of the inverse dynamics model.

Keywords: inverse dynamics · robotic manipulator · hyperparameter optimization · LSTM · AdaBoost

1 Introduction

Most of the task execution of the robotic manipulator that requires high control accuracy relies on the inverse dynamics model, which calculates the amount of torque required by each joint in real time to control the action of the robotic manipulator. The accuracy of the inverse dynamics model is crucial to the control effect of the robotic manipulator [1]. The methods of inverse dynamics modeling can be classified into white-box, black-box, and gray-box methods [2]. The traditional methods are based on the white-box method, which obtains more accurate inertia parameters and friction coefficients mainly through parameter identification [3]. However, this type of approach is based on an ideal physics

X. Lan et al. (Eds.): ICIRA 2024, LNAI 15201, pp. 227–240, 2025.
https://doi.org/10.1007/978-981-96-0771-6_17

model. Considering the existence of structural and non-structural uncertainties in the robot dynamics system, the errors in the parameter identification introduce structural uncertainties; the nonlinear damping of the joints, friction modeling design methods, and noise introduce non-structural uncertainties. These factors are more complex and challenging to express through physical modeling [4].

To address the difficulty of accurately modeling inverse dynamics, many black-box learning models for nonlinear modeling have been proposed. For machine learning methods, Williams et al. [5] proposed the method of Gaussian process regression (GPR); GPR is a supervised learning method, which is more widely used in regression and classification problems, this method optimizes the hyperparameters of the model by maximizing the likelihood as a way to improve the estimation accuracy and generalization, but this method has high time complexity, and is less applied on large data sets. Vijayakumar et al. [6] proposed the method of locally weighted projection regression (LWPR). The time complexity of this middle method is less, but it requires manual tuning of a large number of hyper-parameters, increasing the time cost.

The gray-box method is a hybrid modeling approach that combines the nonlinear modeling capability of the black-box method with the interpretability of the white-box method. However, at present, the gray-box method still relies on the modeling accuracy of the white-box method [7] and has not yet reached an advantageous level. Therefore, the discussion in this paper does not extend on the white-box and gray-box methods and focuses mainly on the black-box method.

Deep learning in black box method is an important branch of machine learning that has been widely used in classification and regression problems. Deep learning networks are good at extracting features from data. In Polydorus et al. [8]. And Liang et al. [9] demonstrated the high adaptability of model learning on inverse dynamics, illustrating the superiority of deep learning in the estimation performance of inverse dynamics model learning.

In recent years, recurrent neural networks have been emphasized in the field of inverse dynamics model learning based on their memory mechanism, which is capable of learning the context-dependent properties of long-term dependencies. Rueckert et al. [10] proposed a method based on the long-short-term memory network (LSTM) for inverse dynamical model learning, which has a greater improvement in estimation accuracy and time complexity compared to the traditional machine learning method with a large improvement in estimation accuracy and time complexity. Mukhopadhyay et al. [11] proposed to learn an inverse dynamics model using GRU (Gate Recurrent Unit) network, which has simpler neuron structure and less time complexity compared to LSTM network. However, both models are unidirectional networks, which are not good at extracting hidden features in the data. Liu et al. [12] proposed to learn inverse dynamics model using Bi-LSTM (Bi-directional Long Short-Term Memory) network, which takes into account the future time state of the Robotic Manipulator and is important for extracting hidden features from the data.

Although many previous studies and proposed models have improved the estimation accuracy to a certain extent, there is not much attention and research on the intrinsic problems such as model hyper-parameter optimization and model overfitting, which makes the estimation accuracy of the previous models suffer from a certain constant error.

Due to the coupling of the robotic manipulator structure, there is a correlation between the motion characteristics of the joints, where the motion of each joint of the robotic manipulator is simultaneously affected by the inertial forces caused by the motion of the other joints. This influence between joints will lead to a highly complex and unpredictable performance of the dynamics model, and therefore features that may be critical but have less weight will be discarded during model learning. AdaBoost aggregates these weak classifiers with smaller weights to form a strong classifier, recalculates the weights, and receives more attention in the next round of training, while it has the effect of solving the overfitting problem. AdaBoost is an integrated learning method that improves model performance through iterative computation. The properties and applications of this algorithm are known to have been explained and proved in many previous explained and proved in the literature [13][14]. These studies combined the AdaBoost with LSTM to obtain significant improvements in application areas such as time series estimation.

Although AdaBoost can solve the overfitting problem by constructing strong classifiers while improving the estimation accuracy, the configuration problem of hyperparameters in each weak classifier leads to low performance and some errors in the results. Therefore, the problem of hyperparameter optimization is introduced. In previous black-box methods, although the physical characteristics and various parameters of the robotic manipulator do not have to be considered, the hyperparameter settings in the model still need to be set strictly and continuously adjusted relying on experience and trial and error. Setting hyperparameter settings is a key technique for deep learning models. However, few studies and comprehensive comparative studies of different hyperparameters in these models have been reported. In the study by Liu et al.[15], the effect of hyperparameter settings on the performance of inverse dynamics models was explored, proving the importance of model hyperparameters for performance. Meanwhile, the design and training of neural networks is a challenging and unpredictable process, and automated hyperparameter optimization (HPO) has become an important research element to lower the technical threshold for common users and improving model performance [16]. In order to improve the research on hyperparameter optimization in inverse dynamics model learning, this paper proposes an architecture for hyperparameter optimization of inverse dynamics model learning networks using swarm intelligent optimization algorithms, which is of reference significance to the research on inverse dynamics model learning.

2 Method

2.1 Inverse Dynamics Analysis of Robotic Manipulator

For the n-link tandem robotic manipulator, the Euler-Lagrange method is usually used to construct the inverse dynamics model of the robotic manipulator as shown in Eq. (1).

$$M(q)\ddot{q} + C(q, \dot{q}) + G(q) + \tau_{fri} + \epsilon(t) = \tau \tag{1}$$

where $q, \dot{q}, \ddot{q} \in R^n$ denotes the joint position, velocity as well as acceleration. $M(q) \in R^{n\times n}$ denotes the inertia matrix, $C(q, \dot{q}) \in R^{n\times n}$ denotes the matrix of Coriolis and centripetal forces, $G(q) \in R^n$ denotes the gravity vector, τ_{fri} denotes the friction term, $\epsilon(t) \in R^n$ denotes the interference term influenced by the external environment, and τ denotes the joint torque. Traditional inverse dynamics models usually use linear fitting to identify the inertial parameters and calculate the friction term using the Stribeck friction model. However, all these methods are difficult to completely describe the physical properties of the robotic manipulator inverse dynamics model, making the accuracy of the model somewhat deficient. Therefore, the inverse dynamics model can be redefined when the inverse dynamics model is learned using neural networks:

$$y_i = f(q_i, \dot{q}_i, \ddot{q}_i) i = 1,2 \cdots n \tag{2}$$

In Eq. (2), y_i denotes the estimated output torque of the i-th joint, and f denotes the mapping relationship between the joint position, velocity, acceleration, and the joint torque. In this way, the inverse dynamics modeling problem of a robotic manipulator can be described as a time series estimation problem. Due to the multivariate and long time-step nature of the dynamics data, the accuracy and generalization performance of the network modeling are affected. Therefore, the model proposed in this paper is introduced.

2.2 Proposed Model

In this paper, we design a method for learning the robotic manipulator model based on AdaBoost and swarm optimization algorithm. All the joint positions, velocities, and accelerations of the robotic manipulator are taken as inputs to the model, and the torques of the joints are output. The difference between the estimated and actual torques is used as the network weights for training. Because of the large differences in physical properties between different joints of the robotic manipulator, the model in this paper trains the network separately for each joint. To distinguish the different roles of the two in the model, the model is divided into two modules, the hyperparameter optimization module and the adaptive boosting module.

Overall Modeling Framework. The overall architecture can be represented in Fig. 1. For the problem of hyperparameter optimization, the network structure of hyperparameter optimization module is designed, and the input is the inverse dynamics dataset to get the optimal hyper-parameter configuration; for the problem of generalizability as well as overfitting, the network structure of adaptive boosting is designed, and the estimations obtained from each training are used as a weak classifier, and the final set constitutes a strong classifier for further optimization to get the final model results.

In this model, there are some differences in the structure of LSTM at different locations. In the hyperparameter optimization module, the LSTM is the original structure. In the adaptive boosting module, the LSTM is the LSTM with optimal hyperparameters configuration.

The hyperparameter optimization module and the adaptive boosting module, as two independent modules, can be used as a single optimization strategy to optimize the inverse dynamics model, but considering that the hyperparameter optimization strategy can improve the performance of the network and reduce the constant error of torque estimation generated by this strategy, and considering that it can be used as a pre-input to the adaptive boosting module, it can better solve the generalization and overfitting problems. Therefore, in this paper, the result obtained by combining these two modules is used as the optimal model for inverse dynamics model learning.

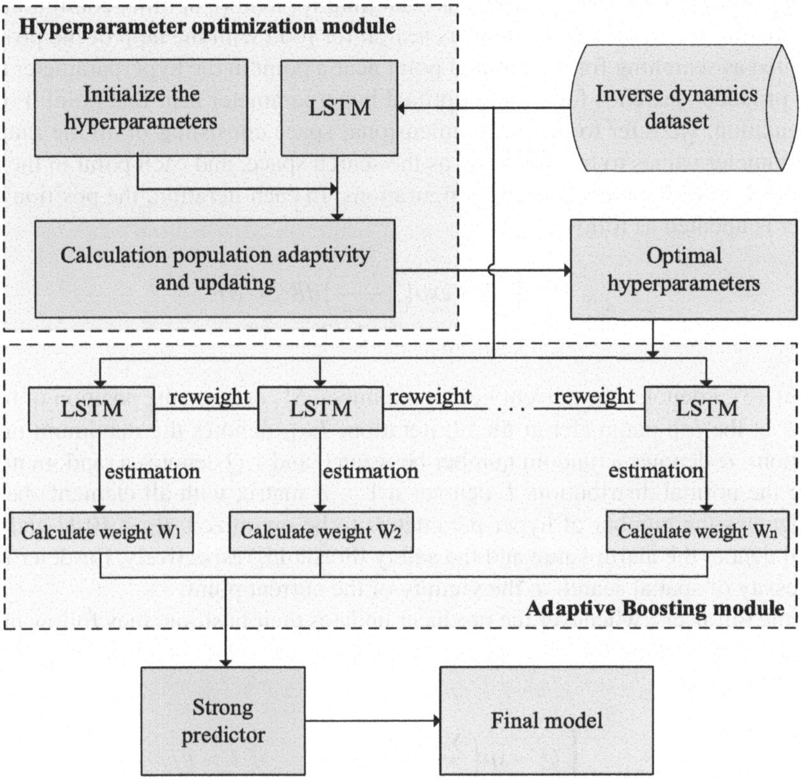

Fig. 1. Inverse dynamics model learning framework based on swarm optimization AdaBoost-LSTM

Both the hyperparameter optimization module and the adaptive boosting module revolve around the LSTM. The LSTM is better at extracting long and short-term features in a sequence. Most sequence modeling methods emphasize only the dependencies between sequence nodes and ignore other correlations. Robotic manipulator dynamics modeling due to its high complexity and spatial-temporal dependence, LSTM is more suitable for inverse dynamics model learning.

Hyperparameter Optimization Module. LSTM has many hyperparameters such as number of iterations, number of neurons, learning rate, etc., which affects the robustness and effectiveness of the model, and imperfect optimization will lead to low and unstable predictive ability [17]. To overcome this problem SSA (Sparrow Search Algorithm) [18] can be used for hyperparameter optimization problems.

SSA is a population intelligence optimization algorithm inspired by the foraging and anti-predatory behavior of sparrow populations. The algorithm can optimize multiple hyperparameters of the neural network at the same time to find the optimal result in the global search space, and at the same time has better search accuracy and convergence speed compared with the traditional PSO (Particle Swarm Optimization). There are two types of individuals in SSA, the producer has a large fitness value and is responsible for searching for food-rich areas, denoted as searching for a more optimal configuration in the hyperparameter space. The followers search for food with the help of the producer, represented as searching for the optimal point near a point in the hyperparameter space, and the producer searches for a more optimal hyperparameter near that point. For ease of presentation, we refer to the multidimensional space consisting of all the ranges of hyperparameter values to be optimized as the search space, and each point in the space represents a set of hyperparameter configurations. In each iteration, the position of the producer is updated as follows.

$$S_{i,j}^{t+1} = \begin{cases} S_{i,j}^{t} \cdot exp\left(\frac{-i}{\alpha \cdot T_{max}}\right) if R_2 < ST \\ S_{i,j}^{t} + Q \cdot L if R_2 \geq ST \end{cases} \tag{3}$$

In Eq. (3), t denotes the current iteration number, $S_{i,j}^{t}$ denotes the position of the i-th producer at the j-th parameter at the tth iteration, T_{max} denotes the maximum number of iterations. α denotes a random number between 0 and 1.Q denotes a random number obeying the normal distribution. L denotes a $1 \times d$ matrix with all elements being 1, and d denotes the number of hyper-parameters to be optimized. $R_2 \in [0,1]$ and $ST \in [0.5,1.0]$ denote the alarm value and the safety threshold, respectively, for determining the necessity of spatial search in the vicinity of the current point.

For the followers, whenever the producer updates their position, they follow up with their position, searching for better points in the space around them, and their position is updated as follows:

$$S_{i,j}^{t+1} = \begin{cases} Q \cdot exp\left(\frac{S_{worst}^{t} - S_{i,j}^{t}}{i^2}\right) & if\ i > n/2 \\ S_p^{t+1} + \left|S_{i,j}^{t} - S_p^{t+1}\right| \cdot \bar{A} \cdot L & otherwise \end{cases} \tag{4}$$

In Eq. (4), S_p denotes the optimal point where the producer is located. S_{worst} denotes the current global worst value point. Denote by A a $d \times d$ matrix consisting of -1 and 1. In this way, $\overline{A} = A^T\left(AA^T\right)^{-1}$.

If the accuracy of the estimation result at the current point exceeds the threshold, update the follower position at this point to the position of the producer with the best result. At the same time, when the estimation result accuracy equal to the threshold is encountered in the search space, their positions are updated to the nearby points with estimation results below the threshold.

$$S_{i,j}^{t+1} = \begin{cases} S_{best}^{t} + \beta \cdot \left|S_{i,j}^{t} - S_{best}^{t}\right| if f_i > f_b \\ S_{i,j}^{t} + K \cdot \left(\frac{\left|S_{i,j}^{t} - S_{worst}^{t}\right|}{(f_i - f_W) + \varepsilon}\right) if f_i = f_b \end{cases} \tag{5}$$

In Eq. (5), S_{best} denotes the optimal point of the search space. β denotes the parameter controlling the step size, which conforms to the standard normal distribution. $K \in [-1,1]$ is a random number. f_i denotes the estimation accuracy of the current point, and f_b and f_w denote the current searched optimal point and the worst point.

After the iterative optimization of the module is completed, the optimal search space, i.e., the optimal hyperparameter configuration, including the learning rate, the number of neurons, the number of iterations, etc., is derived.

Adaptive Boosting Module. The optimal hyperparameters derived from the swarm optimization algorithm will be used in the AdaBoost-LSTM model of the adaptive boosting module. LSTM and AdaBoost models have heterogeneity of independent error distributions and strong estimation ability. To further improve the estimation accuracy, the two are combined for estimation. The AdaBoost-LSTM model is adaptive in the sense that the weights of samples that have been incorrectly estimated by the previous basic classifier are increased while the weights of samples that have been correctly estimated are decreased and used to train the next basic classifier. Samples are correctly estimated will have their weights reduced and used to train the next basic classifier. Meanwhile, in each round of iterations, a new weak classifier is added until some predetermined small enough error rate is reached or a pre-specified maximum number of iterations is reached before the final strong classifier is determined. Prior to model training, the number of predictors and initialization weights D are set:

$$w_i = (w_1, w_2, \ldots w_n) = \frac{1}{n}, \frac{1}{n}, \ldots \frac{1}{n} \tag{6}$$

In Eq. (6), w_i denotes each sample in the training set and n denotes the number of samples. After initialization, the LSTM network starts iterating. In each iteration, the error of each sample from the true value is calculated. If the error of a sample exceeds a certain threshold, the sample weights are updated:

$$w_{j+1} = \begin{cases} w_i & if\ abs(error_j) < \theta \\ w_i * k & if\ abs(error_j) \geq \theta \end{cases} \tag{7}$$

In Eq. (7), $error_j$ denotes the estimation error of the j-th sample, θ denotes the error threshold, and k denotes the weight update factor. After one iteration is completed, the weak predictor weights are calculated:

$$\alpha_i = 0.5 * ln\left(\frac{1 - e_i}{e_i}\right) \tag{8}$$

In Eq. (8), α_i denotes the weight coefficient of the i-th predictor, e_i denotes the sample weight distribution of the i-th iteration. Finally, after the iteration is completed, the final strong predictor result is obtained:

$$\sum\nolimits_{i=1}^{N} W_i LSTM_i(X) \tag{9}$$

In Eq. (9), $LSTM_i(X)$ denotes the i-th training and its result N denotes the number of iterations, i.e., the number of weak predictors, and X denotes the training samples.

The result obtained is the optimal estimation obtained from the optimization of this model. This method is compared with different previous methods to verify the superiority of this method. Considering that the physical characteristics of different joints and links of the robotic manipulator are quite different, this paper trains a different model for each joint separately, which has a better estimation effect than the multi-output neural network.

3 Experiments

To verify the superiority of the model in this paper on inverse dynamics model learning, relevant experiments are designed in this section. The data are validated using publicly available datasets, selected to compute appropriate evaluation metrics, and compared with a variety of models from previous studies.

3.1 Indicators for Evaluating the Results of Experiments

The accuracy of the inverse dynamics model depends on the estimation accuracy of the torques, which in the experiments is reflected in the degree of fit of the estimated torques to the standard torques, and therefore can be evaluated in terms of the root mean square error (RMSE) and the mean absolute error (MAE).

$$RMSE = \sqrt{\frac{\sum_{i=1}^{N} \left(\tau_i - \hat{\tau}_i\right)^2}{N}} \tag{10}$$

$$MAE = \frac{1}{N} \sum\nolimits_{i=1}^{N} \left|\tau_i - \hat{\tau}_i\right| \tag{11}$$

In Eq. (10) and (11), N denotes the number of individuals in training or testing, τ_i denotes the estimated torques obtained, and $\hat{\tau}_i$ denotes the actual torques.

3.2 Data Processing

The experimental data were taken from the publicly available SARCOS manipulator inverse dynamics dataset. Its training set and test set are set as (44484, 4449) respectively. As the collected data is affected by noise which can lead to abrupt changes affecting the training results, to facilitate the feature extraction and learning convergence speed of the data, as well as to reduce the effect of noise, all the data are processed by low-pass filter and normalization. And the data of the dataset for each joint position is shown in Fig. 2. It can be seen that the SARCOS dataset exhibits disordered irregularity, and compared with the regularity of the inverse dynamics' dataset such as KUKA, the SARCOS dataset can well reflect the robustness and generalization of the model.

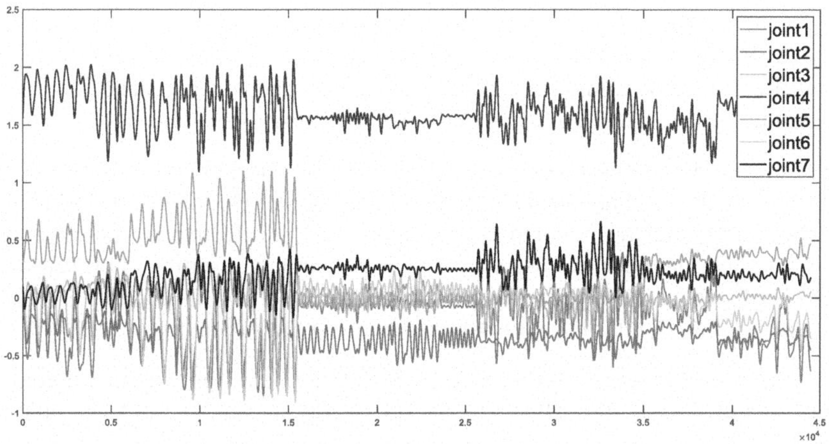

Fig. 2. Joint trajectory of the SARCOS dataset

The inputs to the model are the position, velocity and acceleration of each joint, and the outputs are the torques of the individual joints, depending on the model of the robotic manipulator used in the selected dataset, in the case of the dataset used in this paper, SARCOS, for example, which has seven joints, there are 21 inputs to the model, and seven different predictive models are output.

3.3 Experimental Setup

In the model of this paper, we select four key hyperparameters that have a large impact on the estimation results, namely, the number of neurons, the maximum number of training rounds, the learning rate, and the batch size. Since this model has two LSTM hidden layers, the number of neurons corresponds to two parameters, which are denoted as N_1, N_2, the learning rate is denoted as L, and the batch size is denoted as B. The number of neurons is denoted as N_1, N_2, the learning rate is denoted as L, and the batch size is denoted as B. In real experiments, we can optimize more hyperparameters, but the improvement obtained is limited, while it will be large in time consumption. Here we only select four hyperparameters for optimization, aiming at proving the superiority of our method and not representing the best results. It can also be adjusted as needed for different needs in practice.

In the application of SSA, its various parameter settings are decided based on experience and trial and error, while the final estimation accuracy and the cost of computation must be considered. Therefore, based on experience, and the size of the dataset, the number of searching individuals is set to 10, the proportion of producers is 20%, and the number of iterations is 5. Also, for the optimized parameters, the search ranges for these parameters are determined based on experience, N_1[5, 200], N_2[5, 200], L[0.001,0.01], and B[10,150]. Afterwards, the initial model is trained and evaluated until the optimal hyperparameter configuration is found.

The optimal hyperparameter configuration is obtained and used for the subsequent AdaBoost-LSTM model. The number of predictors is set to 10, also considering the boosting effect and time complexity. The error threshold and weight update factor among the algorithms are adjusted according to the actual estimation results.

After the training of this model is completed and the estimation results are obtained, the results are compared and analyzed using GRU model [11], LSTM model [10], Bi-LSTM model [12], and the model in this paper to verify the effectiveness of the proposed method. For these methods, we use a uniform hyperparameter setting of 60 neurons for both hidden layers, a maximum number of iterations of 100, a batch size of 128, a learning rate of 0.005 initially, and optimization using the Adam optimizer.

All codes were written to run on MATLAB R2022b on a computer configured with an Intel(R) Core (TM) i7-7700HQ CPU, 16.0 GB RAM, and an NVIDIA GeForce GTX 1050 Ti.

3.4 Experimental Results

Comparison of Estimated Indicators. Table 1 demonstrates the total estimation results of several models for different joints in the SARCOS dataset. It can be seen that the model proposed in this paper reduces the estimation error for each joint. Compared with the previous GRU, LSTM, and BI-LSTM models, The overall error of this model on the RMSE metric for torque estimation was reduced by 14.5%, 14.1%, and 8.6%, respectively, respectively. It effectively proves the superiority of the present model over the learning of inverse dynamics model for robotic manipulators.

Table 1. Estimated metrics results for different models overall on the SARCOS dataset

Methods	RMSE	MAE
GRU	0.0706	0.0535
LSTM	0.0702	0.0513
Bi-LSTM	0.0660	0.0478
Ours	**0.0603**	**0.0423**

Figure 3 demonstrates the results of the comparison of the mean square error and the mean absolute error of the torque estimation of this paper's method with different models for each joint of the SARCOS dataset, and the results are normalized. It can be seen that the estimation results of this paper's method are better than other methods in all seven joints. Due to the large differences in the physical properties of different joints and links, the indicators estimated by different joints vary overall. Among them, the errors of joints 1, 3, and 6 are relatively small.

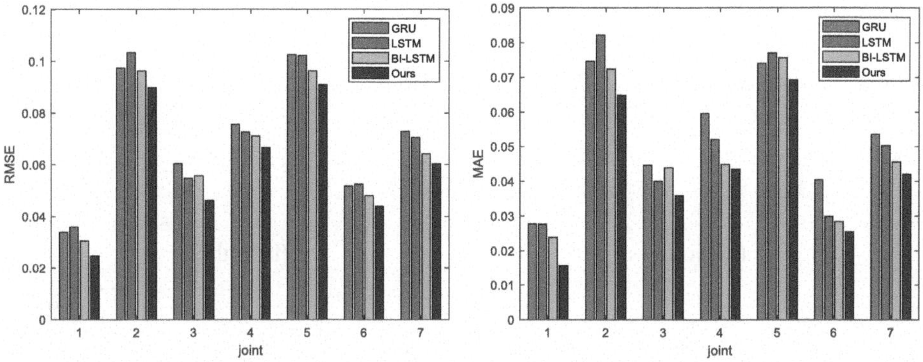

Fig. 3. Histogram of Root Mean Square Error (left) versus Mean Absolute Error (right) of Torque Estimates from Different Models on the SARCOS Dataset

Estimated Curve Comparison. The superiority of this paper's scheme can be seen in the above evaluation indexes. Meanwhile, to observe the results of the experiment more intuitively, the estimation result curves of different models and the model of this paper on seven joints are compared with the real values.

In Fig. 4, the method proposed in this paper has a better fitting degree in torque estimation, which is closer to the real value. At the same time, due to the noise and friction of the robotic manipulator itself, the estimation results of some time periods are different from the estimation results of other time periods. By analyzing the results in Fig. 4 and different evaluation indexes, the method in this paper has a significant estimation accuracy advantage in the time period when the torque fluctuation is large. The ability of the hyperparameter optimization module to improve the performance and stability of the model, as well as the ability of the adaptive boosting module to reduce the overfitting and improve the generalizability, makes the method of this paper have better results in inverse dynamics model learning.

Ablation Study. In order to further illustrate the superiority of the model proposed in this paper for inverse dynamics model learning, ablation study is conducted on this model. The hyperparameter optimization module and adaptive boosting module are treated as independent modules. The experimental results are shown in Table 2. Where the combination of the hyperparameter optimization module is denoted as SSA-LSTM and the combination of the adaptive boosting module is denoted as AdaBoost-LSTM. It can be seen that the accuracy of the torque estimation results of the two various modules in the method of this paper have been improved to some extent. Meanwhile, the overall model combining the two modules has better estimation results.

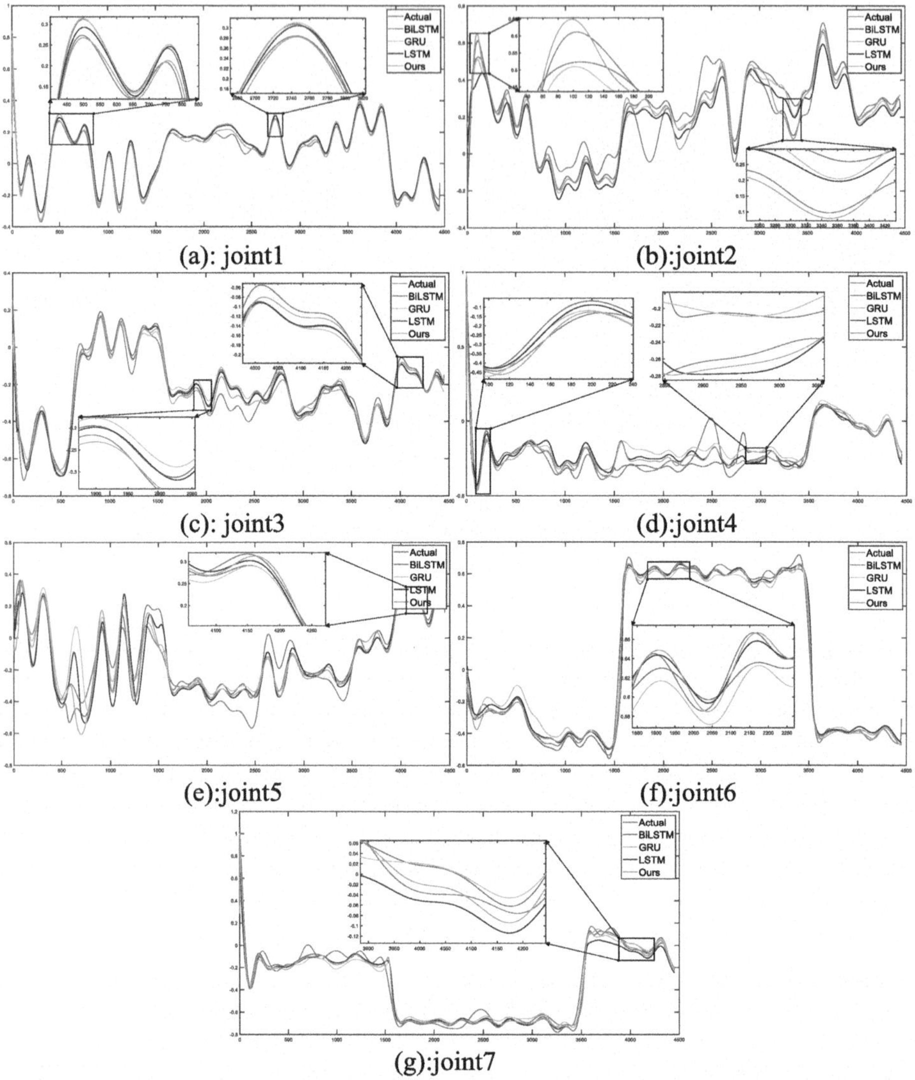

Fig. 4. Comparison of the estimation results of different models on the SARCOS dataset

Table 2. Estimated metrics results of ablation study for the different structures of the model in this paper on the SARCOS dataset overall

Methods	RMSE	MAE
LSTM	0.0702	0.0513
SSA-LSTM	0.0627	0.0454
AdaBoost-LSTM	0.0662	0.0468
Ours	**0.0603**	**0.0423**

4 Conclusion

In this paper, we propose a method to learn an inverse dynamics model using a swarm optimization algorithm combined with the AdaBoost-LSTM, which solves the problems of hyperparameter optimization and model overfitting, and improves the estimation accuracy of the torque and the model generalization ability. The method proposed in this paper provides a new theoretical basis and optimization scheme for inverse dynamics model learning and improves the accuracy of inverse dynamics model learning.

The method proposed in this paper is validated on the SARCOS dataset and compared with different previous models with better estimation results. The feasibility of the method in this paper for accurate modeling of inverse dynamics model is demonstrated. The experimental results also show that this paper's method has high estimation accuracy when the torque fluctuation is large. Therefore, the method of this paper can be applied to construct the inverse dynamics model in various situations where the motion amplitude of the robotic manipulator is large, such as the stabilization control of the end pose of the robotic manipulator, which can make the robotic manipulator have a better stability in an unknown environment. Considering the difference in physical properties between different robotic manipulator, the present model needs to be adjusted accordingly on different robotic manipulators to ensure the accuracy of estimation. For future work, on the one hand, in order to generate a robotic manipulator inverse dynamics model with higher accuracy, the various parameter settings of the model can be adjusted appropriately according to the dynamics model of the specific robotic manipulator model. On the other hand, the method of this paper will be applied and further verified in the actual operating platform.

Acknowledgement. This work is supported by the National Key R&D Program of China (grant No.: 2022YFB4700400), National Natural Science Foundation of China (grant No.: 62073249), Key R&D Program of Hubei Province (grant No.: 2023BBB011).

References

1. Nguyen-Tuong, D., Peters, J.: Model learning for robot control: a survey. Cogn. Process. **12**, 319–340 (2011)
2. Liu, Z., Peng, K., Han, L., et al.: Modeling and control of robotic manipulators based on artificial neural networks: a review. Iran. J. Sci. Technol. Trans. Mech. Eng. **47**(4), 1307–1347 (2023)
3. Wu, J., Wang, J., You, Z.: An overview of dynamic parameter identification of robots. Robot. Comput. Integr. Manuf. **26**(5), 414–419 (2010)
4. Wang, S., Shao, X., Yang, L., et al.: Deep learning aided dynamic parameter identification of 6-DOF robot manipulators. IEEE Access **8**, 138102–138116 (2020)
5. Williams, C., Rasmussen, C.: Gaussian processes for regression. Adv. Neural Inf. Process. Syst. **8** (1995)
6. Vijayakumar, S., Schaal, S.: Locally weighted projection regression: An o(n) algorithm for incremental real time learning in high dimensional space. In: Proceedings of the Seventeenth International Conference on Machine Learning (ICML 2000), vol. 1, pp. 288–293. Morgan Kaufmann (2000)
7. Çallar, T.C., Böttger, S.: Hybrid learning of time-series inverse dynamics models for locally isotropic robot motion. IEEE Rob. Autom. Lett. **8**(2), 1061–1068 (2022)
8. Polydoros, A.S., Nalpantidis, L., Krüger, V.: Real-time deep learning of robotic manipulator inverse dynamics. In: Proceedings of the 2015 IEEE/RSJ International Conference on Intelligent Robots and Systems (IROS), pp. 3442–3448. IEEE (2015)
9. Liang, B., Li, T., Chen, Z., et al.: Robot arm dynamics control based on deep learning and physical simulation. In: Proceedings of the 2018 37th Chinese Control Conference (CCC), pp. 2921–2925. IEEE (2018)
10. Rueckert, E., Nakatenus, M., Tosatto, S., et al.: Learning inverse dynamics models in O(n) time with LSTM networks. In: Proceedings of the 2017 IEEE-RAS 17th International Conference on Humanoid Robotics (Humanoids), pp. 811–816. IEEE (2017)
11. Mukhopadhyay, R., Chaki, R., Sutradhar, A., et al.: Model learning for robotic manipulators using recurrent neural networks. In: TENCON 2019–2019 IEEE Region 10 Conference (TENCON), pp. 2251–2256. IEEE (2019)
12. Liu, M., Huang, W., Min, H.: Dynamic model learning for robotic manipulators using BiLSTM networks. In: Proceedings of the 2022 IEEE International Conference on Robotics and Biomimetics (ROBIO), pp. 1270–1276. IEEE (2022)
13. Xiao, C., Chen, N., Hu, C., et al.: Short and mid-term sea surface temperature prediction using time-series satellite data and AdaBoost-LSTM combination approach. Remote Sens. Environ. **233**, 111358 (2019)
14. Bai, Y., Xie, J., Wang, D., et al.: A manufacturing quality prediction model based on AdaBoost-LSTM with rough knowledge. Comput. Ind. Eng. **155**, 107227 (2021)
15. Liu, N., Li, L., Hao, B., et al.: Modeling and simulation of robot inverse dynamics using LSTM-based deep learning algorithm for smart cities and factories. IEEE Access **7**, 173989–173998 (2019)
16. Yu, T., Zhu, H.: Hyper-parameter optimization: a review of algorithms and applications. arXiv preprint arXiv:2003.05689 (2020)
17. Khalid, R., Javaid, N.: A survey on hyperparameters optimization algorithms of forecasting models in smart grid. Sustain. Cities Soc. **61**, 102275 (2020)
18. Xue, J., Shen, B.: A novel swarm intelligence optimization approach: sparrow search algorithm. Syst. Sci. Control Eng. **8**(1), 22–34 (2020)

Design and Experiment of a Percussion Mechanism for a Self-Penetrating Drilling Robot

Zhiwei Long, Riyue Wu, Mingcong Wang, Guangfei Zhang, Haifei Zhu, Yisheng Guan, and Tao Zhang(✉)

School of Electro-mechanical Engineering, Guangdong University of Technology, Guangzhou 510006, China
tzhang@gdut.edu.cn

Abstract. In future deep planetary exploration missions, self-penetrating drilling robots (SPDRs) are expected to play a crucial role. Given the extreme environments and energy constraints of extraterrestrial planets, rotary percussion drilling emerges as the preferred drilling method for the robots. To address the drilling requirements of the SPDR on extraterrestrial planets, a design method for a highly integrated, small-sized and variable percussion frequency percussion mechanism suitable for extraterrestrial environment is proposed. On this, the dynamics model of the percussion mechanism was established and the response curves of percussion frequency and percussion work under various excitation frequencies were obtained. Subsequently, the drilling experimental system was designed and constructed. The effectiveness of the percussion mechanism was validated through comparative experiments. Results demonstrate that the percussion mechanism can enhance drilling efficiency from 16.4% to 38.3% without increasing the volume of the robot.

Keywords: Percussion mechanism · Dynamical model · Prototype testing

1 Introduction

Since the 1950 s, countries and regions such as the United States, the Soviet Union, China and the European Union have conducted numerous exploration missions on extraterrestrial objects, including the Apollo project [1], the Luna project [2] and the Chang'E project [3]. The results of the analysis of the samples obtained by these missions indicate that planetary regolith is distributed with different grain sizes and hardness classes of regolith or rocks and that the mechanical properties of the planetary regolith vary greatly among different landing sites [4]. To enhance the crushing effect of drill tools on regolith, most drilling robots are equipped with a rotary-percussion drilling unit (RPDU) [5]. Moreover, in addition to improving the drilling efficiency of the tools, the vibration induced by the percussion mechanism is favorable to chip removal and reduces the jamming of the drilling.

Supported by the National Natural Science Foundation of China (Grant No. 52275011), the Natural Science Foundation of Guangdong Province (Grant No. 2023B1515020080), and the Young Elite Scientists Sponsorship Program by CAST (Grant No. 2021 QNRC001).

X. Lan et al. (Eds.): ICIRA 2024, LNAI 15201, pp. 241–253, 2025.
https://doi.org/10.1007/978-981-96-0771-6_18

The percussion mechanism of single/multiple-pipe drilling robots (S/MPDR) is mostly integrated into the upper end of the drill tool and the percussion effect is achieved by impacting the drilling pipes. However, due to limitations in rocket thrust and energy supply on planetary surface, increasing power and mass to enhance the drilling efficiency of (S/MPDR) may not be feasible to meet the future demands of deep drilling into planetary regolith [6]. Therefore, integrating a percussion mechanism into the SPDR to achieve low reaction force and low power consumption drilling has gradually become a prominent research topic in deep planetary regolith drilling [7].

In the past decades, various percussion mechanisms for the SPDR have been designed. In 2005, a mole-style deep drilling robot called the Ground Mole Demonstrator (GMD) was developed for future planetary exploration, featuring a cam percussion design. Experimental drilling conducted at a 2 Hz percussion frequency on regolith samples with strengths of 137 MPa and 23 MPa achieved penetration speeds of 1.1 mm/h and 5.5 mm/h, respectively, generating a maximum of 0.9 J of percussion work [8]. In 2011, the Auto-Gopher system was developed, featuring a percussion based on the Ultrasonic/Sonic Driller/Corer (USDC) mechanism. This system utilizes a piezoelectric transducer to generate high-frequency vibrations at the tip of the horn, while percussion is delivered by a free mass block. The percussion mechanism can produce 60–1000 Hz high-frequency vibration [9]. During the test, the system successfully drilled 3 m into a gypsum formation with a compressive strength of 40 MPa [10]. In 2013, the Heat Flow Physical Properties Package (HP3) [11] was developed, which penetrates on the principle of mechanical percussion. This system features a percussion device housed within the submersible, released upon energy storage by a cam mechanism. The resulting kinetic energy of the mass block impacts the submersible body, thus realizing the self-penetration. The percussion mechanism has a percussion frequency of 0.25 Hz and is capable of releasing a maximum of 0.7 J of percussion work. The HP3 system successfully landed on Mars with the InSight mission. However, due to the specific regolith characteristics at the landing site, only a drilling depth of 35 cm was achieved. In 2023, the wireline self-excavating coring (WSC) robot was developed. Its percussion mechanism converts the kinetic energy of motor rotation into percussion energy through a spring-energy-storage mechanism, thus achieving a percussion frequency of 10 Hz and releasing a maximum percussion energy of 3.7 J [12].

While the aforementioned percussion mechanisms exhibit a certain degree of efficacy in percussive drilling, they encounter challenges such as high costs, excessive equipment size and fixed percussion work. In real drilling sampling, the percussion parameters directly influence the crushing efficacy of planetary regolith. The reliance on a single percussion parameter can prove inadequate for adapting to the diverse conditions encountered in the highly variable regolith of extraterrestrial planets, potentially resulting in mission failure. Thus, maximizing drilling capacity and crushing efficiency within constrained resources necessitates the design of percussion mechanisms with variable parameters, high integration, and structural stability. Furthermore, conducting kinetic modeling and analysis of these percussion mechanisms is imperative. Based on this, the paper proposes a percussion mechanism with variable percussion parameters for a SPDR.

2 Mechanism Design

The percussion mechanism is positioned in the lower section of the chip storage unit of the robot, as shown in Fig. 1(a). Together with the rotation mechanism, it constitutes the RPDU of the robot. Meanwhile, the percussion mechanism operates independently of the rotary mechanism, allowing for separate movement of each component. Considering that the percussion mechanism is applied in a SPDR that already exists in the laboratory, its dimensional parameters are constrained. Specifically, the outer diameter of the mechanism must not exceed 60 mm and its height must not exceed 200 mm.

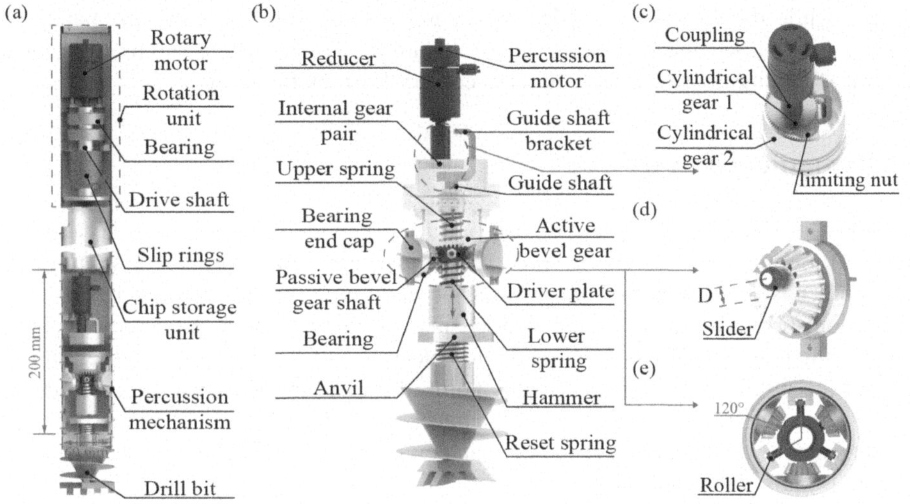

Fig. 1. Percussion mechanism design. (a) Robot configuration. (b) Percussion mechanism composition. (c) Internal gear pair. (d) Passive bevel gear shafts. (e) Horizontal diagram of the drivers.

The rotation mechanism is powered by a brushless DC gear motor (DJI, M3508 P19) whose output shaft is directly connected to the drive spindle to provide a rotary motion for the RPDU. The drive spindle is supported by a pair of deep groove ball bearings. Additionally, since the percussion mechanism is located in the rotating part of the RPDU, an overbore slip ring (MOFLON, MT2042-S12) is employed to prevent wire wrapping during powering the percussion motor and collecting data from Hall sensors.

The percussion mechanism comprises a percussion motor, an internal gear pair, an active bevel gear, a passive bevel gear shaft with an eccentric shaft, three sliders, an anvil, an upper spring, a lower spring, a reset spring, a guide shaft, a guide shaft bracket, a limiting nut, and a hammer, as shown in Fig. 1(b). The percussion mechanism is driven by a percussion motor to operate at a percussion frequency ranging from 0 to 50 Hz. When the percussion mechanism operates, the percussion motor is connected to cylindrical gear 1 via a coupling, driving cylindrical gear 2 to rotate (with an internal gear pair transmission ratio i_1 = 2:3), as shown in Fig. 1(c). As the cylindrical gear 2 is securely connected to the active bevel gear, the mechanism is further accelerated by the bevel gear (with a ratio i_2 = 2:1), transmitting power to the drive plate. At this point, the total transmission ratio can be calculated as:

$$i = i_1 \times i_2 = 1.33 \tag{1}$$

The mechanism includes three passive bevel gear shafts, each positioned 120° apart circumferentially within the drill pipe, as shown in Fig. 1(d). These shafts are supported by deep groove ball bearings and feature eccentric shafts (eccentricity D = 2.5 mm) at their front ends, as shown in Fig. 1(d), which are equipped with sliders. The sliders interact with the drive slide to facilitate the periodic vibration of the driver plate. To restrict the rotation of the driver plate, three rollers are incorporated for stabilization, as shown in Fig. 1(e). The driver plate is connected to the hammer via the upper and lower springs, while the hammer is guided by the guide shaft, forming a moving pair. This configuration allows the hammer to strike the anvil continuously as the motor rotates, thereby achieving the percussion effect necessary for rock breaking.

3 Dynamic Analysis

As shown in Fig. 2(a), the relative position of the hammer and anvil can be adjusted by modifying the stiffness coefficients of the upper and lower springs. Assuming that the hammer is in an intermediate position of static equilibrium, the upper and lower percussion springs are compressed by 30%, maintaining a bottom clearance of 2.5 mm between the hammer and the anvil and a top clearance of 5.5 mm between the limiting nut and the guide shaft bracket. At this point, the measurements can be derived: the upper spring length L_1 = 25.5 mm and the lower spring length L_2 = 22.5 mm. From the current state of force analysis, it can be seen that the elastic stiffness coefficients k_1 and k_2 need to satisfy the following equation:

$$Mg + (\frac{L_2}{0.7} - L_2)k_2 = (\frac{L_1}{0.7} - L_1)k_1 \tag{2}$$

where $k_1 > 0$ and $k_2 > 0$ represent the stiffness coefficients of the upper and lower springs respectively, M is the mass of the percussion hammer, and g is the gravitational acceleration.

Through the above conditions, it is evident that to achieve effective percussion, the hammer displacement amplitude must exceed 2.5 mm. Simultaneously, to prevent the hammer from colliding with the guiding shaft bracket within the operating frequency range of 0 to 50 Hz, the return amplitude of the hammer should be limited to 5.5 mm or less. Therefore, the maximum upward displacement of the hammer must not exceed 5.5 mm, while the minimum downward displacement must not be less than 2.5 mm. To constrain the motion of the hammer, the stiffness coefficients of the upper and lower springs need to be calculated. The percussion principle of the percussion mechanism is illustrated in Fig. 2(b), representing essentially a single-degree-of-freedom forced vibration system under basic simple harmonic excitation [13]. Considering vertical upward as the positive direction, the equation of motion for the hammer in the vibrating system can be expressed as:

$$M\ddot{X}_{(t)} + C\dot{X}_{(t)} + (k_1 + k_2)X_{(t)} = (k_1 + k_2)U_{(t)} + CU_{(t)} \tag{3}$$

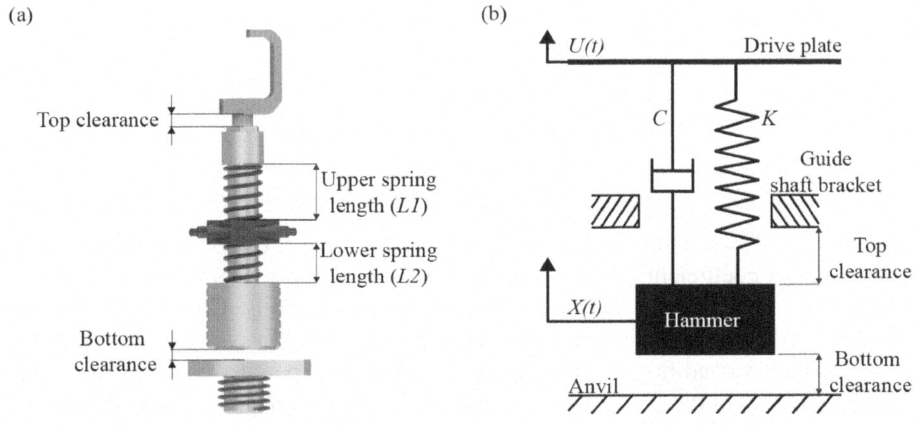

Fig. 2. Working principle of the percussion mechanism. (a) 3D model. (b) Percussion principle.

$$U_{(t)} = D\sin(2\pi ft) \tag{4}$$

where $X_{(t)}$ represents the displacement function of the hammer, $U_{(t)}$ denotes the displacement function of the driver plate, C signifies the system damping, f is the rotation frequency of the eccentric shaft that determines the excitation frequency of the system, and D is the eccentricity distance which correlates with the excitation amplitude.

The equation of motion of the vibration system is a second-order linear non-singular ordinary differential equation and the vibration response is the superposition of the generalized part and the specialized part of the second-order linear non-singular ordinary differential equation. Due to the presence of system damping, the generalized part gradually decays to zero with the increase of time and is often neglected in practical calculations. The primary focus is on the steady-state response caused by the external excitation, namely, the second-order linear non-singular ordinary differential equation of the special solution part. Therefore, the displacement function of the hammer can be expressed as:

$$X_{(t)} = D\sqrt{\frac{1+(2\,s\xi)^2}{(1-s^2)^2+(2\,s\xi)^2}}\sin(wt+\theta) \tag{5}$$

where B_d represents the steady-state vibration amplitude:

$$B_d = D\sqrt{\frac{1+(2\,s\xi)^2}{(1-s^2)^2+(2\,s\xi)^2}} \tag{6}$$

where ω_0 is the intrinsic frequency of the system itself and determined by the system parameters independent of the external excitation and initial conditions, K is the equivalent stiffness of the spring, s is the frequency ratio of the excitation frequency to the intrinsic frequency, ξ is the damping ratio of the system, and θ is the initial phase of the steady-state vibration. These vibration characteristic parameters can be expressed as:

$$\begin{cases} w_0 = \sqrt{\frac{K}{M}} \\ K = k_1 + k_2 \\ s = \frac{w}{w_0} \\ \xi = \frac{C}{2\sqrt{KM}} \\ \theta = \tan^{-1}(\frac{-2s\xi}{1-s^2}) + \tan^{-1}(\frac{Cw}{K}) \end{cases} \tag{7}$$

Substituting $X_{(t)}$ = 5.5 mm as the boundary condition into Eq. 6 and constraining the spring stiffness coefficient through Eq. 2, the spring stiffness coefficients can be calculated as k_1 = 11.8 N/mm and k_2 = 13.2 N/mm, respectively. Considering that the boundary condition has a significant influence on the vibration system, it is decided to take the boundary condition as the design parameter of the percussion mechanism. The design parameters of the percussion mechanism can be obtained, as shown in Table 1.

Table 1. Design parameters of the percussion mechanism.

Symbol	Parameter	Value	Unit
M	Hammer quality	0.138	kg
D	Eccentric distance	2.5	mm
K_1	Upper spring rigidity	11.8	N/mm
K_2	Lower spring rigidity	13.2	N/mm
Δ_1	Top clearance	5.5	mm
Δ_2	Bottom clearance	2.5	mm

Substituting the above parameters into Eq. 5, the model is analyzed using MATLAB. As shown in Fig. 3(a), the detailed process of the hammer output displacement over time and varying excitation frequencies is clearly illustrated. The hammer can contact the anvil and generate percussion within the excitation frequency range of 0 to 50 Hz. Additionally, the return amplitude of the hammer never exceeds 5.5 mm, effectively preventing collisions between components. Notably, as the excitation frequency gradually increases, the percussion frequency of the hammer synchronizes with this increase, demonstrating that the vibration system can precisely control the percussion frequency by adjusting the excitation frequency. The magnitude of the single percussion work is an important indicator of the performance of a percussion mechanism. When cylindrical springs are used as the energy storage element of the percussion system, the work generated by a single percussion can be defined as the kinetic energy of the hammer before striking the anvil. To calculate the magnitude of the percussion work, we assume that the anvil is completely rigid, the percussion does not produce deformation or displacement and collision losses are negligible. The formula for calculating the power of a single percussion can be expressed as follows:

$$W_p = \frac{1}{2}MV^2 = \frac{1}{2}M(\dot{X}_t)^2 \tag{8}$$

The velocity of the hammer, denoted as V, can be determined by differentiating the function $X_{(t)}$. Substituting the velocity of the hammer prior to generating the percussion into Eq. 8 yields the percussion work at the current excitation frequency. Figure 3(b) illustrates the detailed process of the variation in percussion work with respect to excitation frequency. It is evident that the percussion work exhibits an increasing trend as the excitation frequency rises. When the excitation frequency reaches 50 Hz, the percussion mechanism can produce a maximum of 0.16 J of percussion work. Consequently, by adjusting the excitation frequency, we can control the percussion work, allowing it to be flexibly adjusted within the range of 0 to 0.16 J.

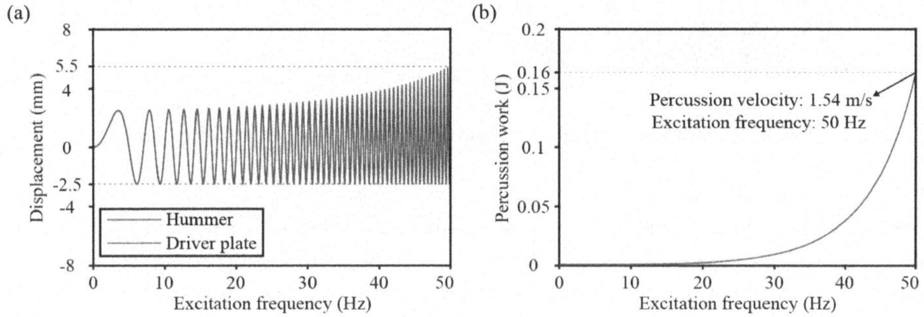

Fig. 3. Percussion parameter curves at different excitation frequencies. (a) Displacement curves at different excitation frequencies. (b) Percussion work curves at different excitation frequencies.

4 Experimental Verification

To verify the effectiveness of the proposed percussion mechanism, we constructed an experimental setup. Although the experiment was limited to a non-weightless ground environment, the results are still informative due to the general applicability of the underlying physical laws and the fact that material properties do not change with gravity. The experimental setup comprises both mechanical and control systems, as shown in Fig. 4. The mechanical system includes the auxiliary drilling equipment and the body of the RPDU, while the control system consists of a host computer and the controller.

4.1 Experimental Mechanical System

The mechanical system consists of a linear moving module, a gripper, a fixed bracket, a RPDU, and a lunar regolith container, as shown in Fig. 5(a). The fixed bracket, screwed to the table and extending 24 cm horizontally like a cantilever beam, provides support for the RPDU. The linear moving module supplies the weight on bit (WOB), pushing the RPDU downward, with both connected by a gripper. The experiment used lunar regolith simulant (LRS) contained in a lunar regolith container. To ensure consistent physical properties of the lunar regolith simulated throughout the drilling depth, we employed a layered compaction and stacking strategy: first compacting the regolith in

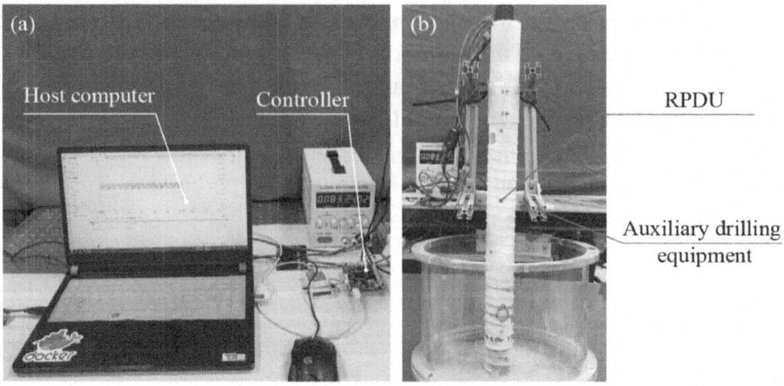

Fig. 4. Experimental setup. (a) Control system. (b) Mechanical system.

a single bucket, then fixing two buckets together, the schematic diagram of the preparation process shown in Fig. 5(b). After preparing the drilling object, the stacked lunar regolith container was placed under the RPDU. Given the outer diameter of the RPDU (62 mm) and the LRS blocks in the container (250 mm), three drilling positions can be achieved in a single preparation without affecting the boundaries of each drilling hole.

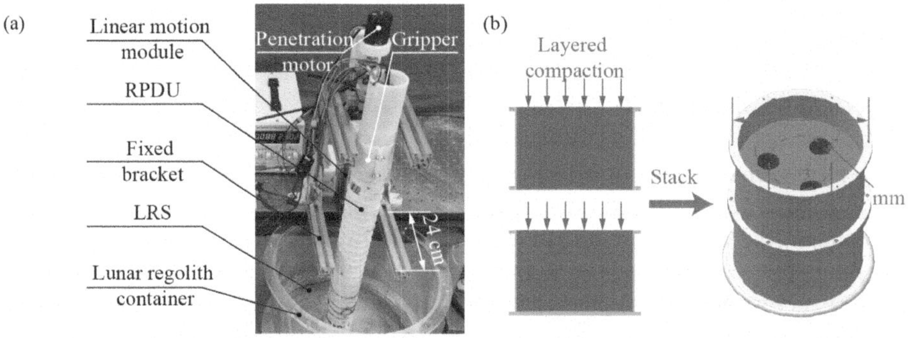

Fig. 5. Experimental mechanical system. (a) System composition. (b) Compaction stacking process to LRS.

4.2 Experimental Control System

The hardware component of the control system primarily comprises a motor speed controller (C620 Brushless DC Motor), an adjustable power, a host computer, a motor controller, and motors in each part, as shown in Fig. 4. The core of the hardware is the controller, which receives control commands from the host computer, parses these commands, and executes the necessary operations. The controller sends control signals to the speed controller via the CAN bus, enabling precise motor control. Simultaneously, the controller continuously monitors motor status parameters through Hall sensors. These data are used for the negative feedback in the closed-loop control system of the motor and are also packaged by the controller into standard frames and sent to the host computer via the serial port for subsequent analysis.

For drilling experiments, it is essential to control the WOB, rotary speed, and percussion frequency, which are correlated with the torque of the penetration motor, and the speeds of the rotation and percussion motors, respectively. Maintaining the desired output state can be challenging due to the influence of multiple factors. This difficulty may result in the loss of control over experimental variables, thereby compromising the validity of experimental data. To ensure the validity and reliability of experimental data, stable control of key parameters is achieved by implementing control algorithm [14].

The torque control of the penetration motor uses a torque Proportional-Integral-Derivative (PID) algorithm, which ensures that the penetration motor outputs a constant moment of the desired force. The PID control algorithm for the torque is:

$$u(t) = K_p e(t) + K_i \int_0^t e(\tau)\, d\tau + K_d \frac{de(t)}{dt} \tag{9}$$

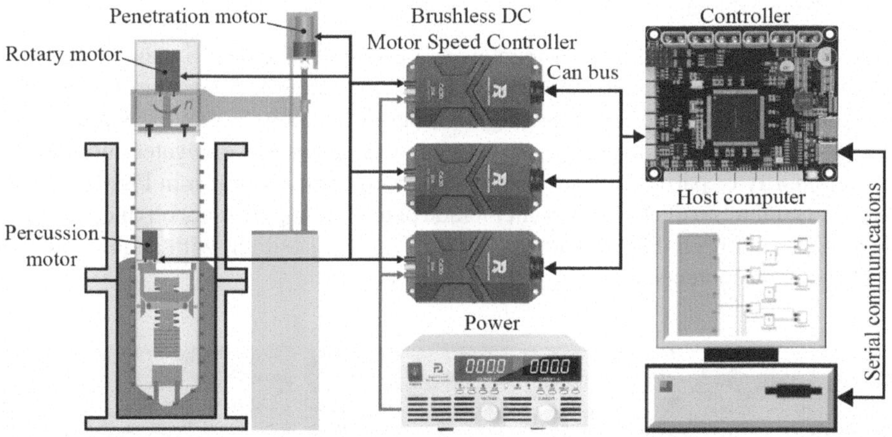

Fig. 6. Hardware components of the control system.

where $e(t)$ represents the input error of the algorithm (the difference between the desired torque and the current torque), K_p is the proportional gain used to reduce the error, K_i is the integral gain that removes the steady-state error present in the system, and K_d is the differential gain that can inhibit system jitter, and $u(t)$ is the result of the PID calculation that serving as the control quantity for the motor (Fig. 6). The speed control of the rotation motor and the percussion motor is achieved using a speed and torque double closed-loop control algorithm, as shown in Fig. 7.

The algorithm targets speed control by incorporating a speed loop as an outer loop on top of the torque loop, which serves as the inner loop. The input variable for the

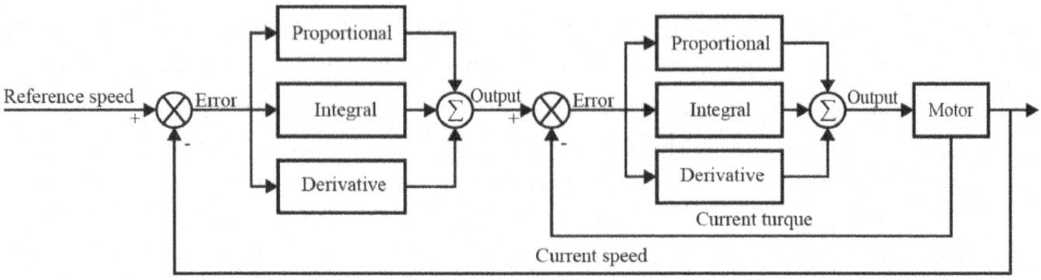

Fig. 7. Speed and torque double closed-loop control algorithm

speed and torque double closed-loop control algorithm is the difference between the desired speed and the current speed. The output of the speed PID calculation is then used as the setpoint for the torque loop, which is subsequently added to the torque PID operation. The final result of the torque PID calculation is used to control the motor. The advantage of this algorithm lies in its ability to shorten the response time of the system while accurately controlling the speed through the speed and torque double closed-loop control algorithm.

4.3 Drilling Object

The material utilized for the experimental test is the specialized LRS, fabricated specifically for ground assessments in support of China's Chang'E 5 mission. Derived predominantly from basaltic volcanic slag, the regolith exhibits a gray-brown hue, with the majority of particles displaying distinct angular shapes and elongated morphology. Only a minority of particles exhibit a more rounded form, as shown in Fig. 8(a-c). The primary crystal mineral phases present include plagioclase, pyroxene, olivine, and glass. The LRS closely resembles Apollo 14 in chemical composition, with slightly elevated Na_2O and K_2O contents and reduced CaO content [15].

Fig. 8. SEM images of simulated lunar regolith particles with different size ranges. (a) 0–50 μm. (b) 50–100 μm. (c) Particle mixture with different sizes. (Taken using Zeiss GeminiSEM 360)

4.4 Experimental Methods

The drilling experiments comprised three sets of tests at different WOB: 500, 550, and 600 N. Each set included two drilling conditions: rotary percussion and pure rotation, totaling six tests. Due to the travel limitations of the moving module, the drilling depth for each test was set to 150 mm, with the rated WOB applied by the penetration motor in each set. The rotary motor speed was maintained at a constant 120 rpm. Given the low strength of the resin material, the percussion frequency was conservatively set at 4 Hz to ensure smooth operation. During the drilling process, the control system monitored the output current and speed of the penetration motor, rotary motor, and percussion motor in real time to evaluate the percussion effect.

There are two evaluation indices for the percussion effect: the penetration speed during drilling and the time required to drill to the same depth. With the same percussion frequency and WOB, a higher penetration speed indicates greater drilling efficiency. Similarly, the shorter the time required to reach the specified depth, the more efficient the drilling process.

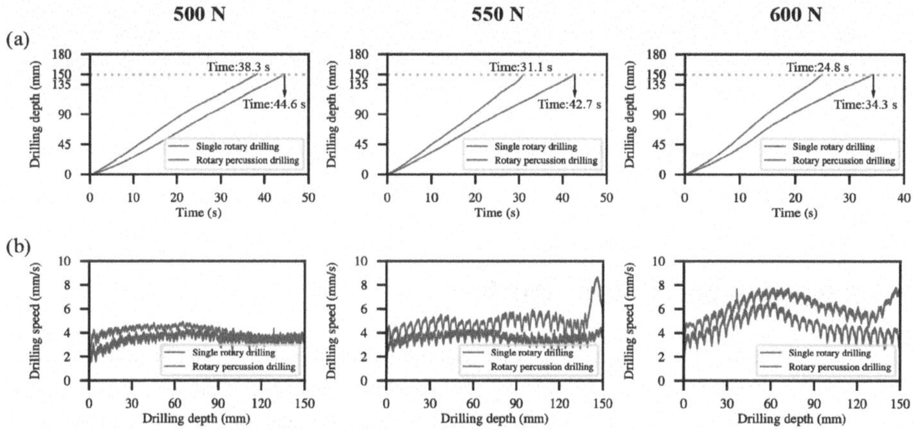

Fig. 9. Comparison of drilling under various WOB conditions. (a) Drilling depth over time. (b) Variation of drilling speed with depth.

4.5 Experimental Results

The results of the drilling experiments are presented in Fig. 9(a-b). At the WOB of 500 N, drilling to a depth of 150 mm was achieved in 38.3 s using rotary percussion drilling, compared with 44.6 s with pure rotary drilling. At the WOB of 550 N, the times required were 31.1 s and 42.7 s, respectively. When the WOB was increased to 600 N, the times were 24.8 s and 34.3 s, respectively, for the two drilling methods. Rotary percussion drilling consistently required significantly less time than single rotary drilling at all three WOBs. Rotary percussion drilling presents notable reductions in operational time compared with single rotary drilling across three distinct levels of WOB. This conclusion is further supported by the relationship between drilling speed and drilling depth. At the WOB of 500, 550, and 600 N, the average drilling speeds for rotary percussion drilling were 3.9, 4.8, and 6.0 mm/s, respectively, which are notably faster than the speeds for single rotary drilling at 3.3, 3.5, and 4.3 mm/s, respectively. These comparative experiments demonstrate that the percussion mechanism can improve drilling efficiency by 16.4–38.3% without increasing the robot size.

Figure 10(a-e) shows the process of drilling into LRS using rotary percussion at the WOB of 550 N. In the initial stage (0 s), the RPDU makes contact with the surface of the LRS. During the drilling stage (0 s–31 s), the RPDU drills downward, continuously discharging and piling up drill cuttings. The target drilling depth of 150 mm is reached in 31 s. After completing the drilling, the RPDU is retracted, as shown in Fig. 10(e).

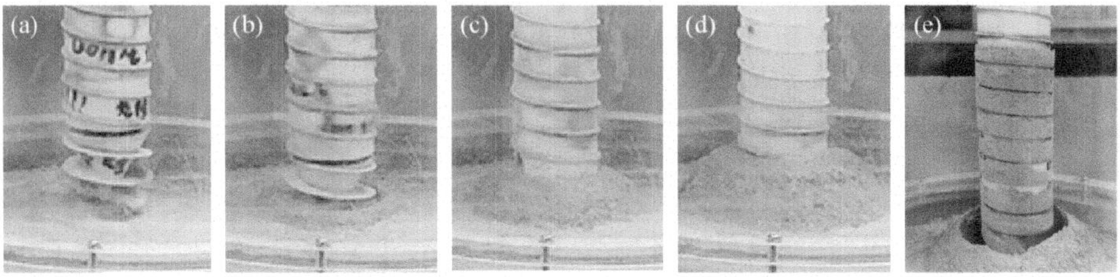

Fig. 10. Snapshots during drilling process. (a) 0 s. (b) 7 s. (c) 16 s. (d) 31 s. (e) Retraction.

5 Conclusion and Future Work

This paper presents the design of a percussion mechanism for a SPDR with variable percussion parameters, high integration, and structural stability. Subsequently, a percussion dynamics model was established, and the effectiveness of the percussion mechanism was experimentally verified. The experimental results indicate that while the inclusion of the percussion mechanism results in a modest increase in energy consumption, it effectively enhances drilling efficiency, with improvements ranging from 16.4% to 38.3%. In the subsequent phase, we will establish diversified test environments and incorporate various sensors, such as pressure sensors and vibration sensors, into the percussion mechanism. Through data acquisition and analysis, we will document the performance of the percussion mechanism under different environmental conditions. These findings will offer theoretical support for subsequent design enhancements.

References

1. Graves, C.A.: Apollo Experience Report: Mission Planning for Apollo entry. National Aeronautics and Space Administration (1972)
2. Slyuta, E.: The luna program. In: Sample Return Missions, pp. 37–78. Elsevier (2021)
3. Zhang, T., et al.: Robotic drilling for the Chinese chang'e 5 lunar sample-return mission. Int. J. Robot. Res. **42**(8), 586–613 (2023)
4. Zacny, K., Paulsen, G., Szczesiak, M.: Challenges and methods of drilling on the moon and mars. In: 2011 Aerospace Conference, pp. 1–9. IEEE (2011)

5. Li, S., Quan, Q., Tang, D.W., Jiang, S., Hou, X., Deng, Z.: Research on a rotary-percussive coring drill for lunar exploration. Appl. Mech. Mater. **233**, 297–302 (2012)
6. Zacny, K., et al.: Wireline deep drill for exploration of mars, europa, and enceladus. In: 2013 IEEE Aerospace Conference, pp. 1–14. IEEE (2013)
7. Zhang, T., et al.: Review on planetary regolith-sampling technology. Prog. Aerosp. Sci. **127**, 100760 (2021)
8. Campaci, R., et al.: Design and optimization of a terrestrial guided mole for deep subsoil exploration-boring performance experimental analyses. iSAIRAS', Munich (2005)
9. Bar-Cohen, Y., et al.: Deep drilling and sampling via compact low-mass rotary-hammer auto-gopher. In: Earth and Space 2010: Engineering, Science, Construction, and Operations in Challenging Environments, pp. 1021–1030 (2010)
10. Bar-Cohen, Y., et al.: Auto-gopher-a wireline deep sampler driven by piezoelectric percussive actuator and EM rotary motor. In: Earth and Space 2014, pp. 218–225 (2014)
11. Olaf, K., et al.: Design details of the HP3 mole onboard the insight mission. Acta Astronaut. **164**, 152–167 (2019)
12. Wen, Y., et al.: Design and dynamic analysis of the wire-line coring robot for deep lunar rocks. Appl. Sci. **13**(3), 1722 (2023)
13. Chrystal, K.: Percussion mechanism for the Mars2020 coring drill. In: Proceedings of the 45th Aerospace Mechanisms Symposium (2020)
14. Mahmud, M., Motakabber, S., Alam, A.Z., Nordin, A.N.: Control BLDC motor speed using PID controller. Int. J. Adv. Comput. Sci. Appl. **11**(3) (2020)
15. He, X., et al.: Lunar regolith simulant CUG-1A. In: 41st Annual Lunar and Planetary Science Conference, p. 1183. ASCE Library, Cambridge (2010)

Thermal-Structural Analysis of a Deployable Metamorphic Robotic Grasper with Finite Element Method

Changqing Gao[1](✉), Ruikai Fan[1], Hanlin Wang[1], Yongjie Zhao[1], Fei Liu[2], and Xuelin Du[3]

[1] Department of Mechanical Engineering, College of Engineering, Shantou University, Shantou 515063, People's Republic of China
chqgao@stu.edu.cn
[2] Industrial Training Center, Shenzhen Polytechnic University, Shenzhen 518055, People's Republic of China
[3] School of Intelligent Manufacturing and Mechanical Engineering, Hunan Institute of Technology, Hengyang 421002, People's Republic of China

Abstract. This paper takes a deployable metamorphic robotic grasper as the studied object and its thermal-structural analysis with finite element method is carried out, by which the thermal deformation of the robotic grasper can be obtained and the optimization can be performed. As a result, the mechanical performance of the robotic grasper can be greatly enhanced, which is of great significance for the on-orbit operation of space spacecraft. Firstly, the robotic grasper is sample introduced and a theoretical model of the space temperature field is established, which offers a theoretical basis for finite element simulation. In addition, by finite element analysis software, an automatic mesh partition is applied and the finite element model of the robotic grasper is then established. By loading the temperature field, the thermal deformation can be shown, which provides a clear idea for structural optimization. Finally, through a large amount of simulation data, the most thermal deformation of the robotic grasper can be optimized, and then further simulation of the optimized model is carried out, the results show that the thermal deformation effectively decreases and the theoretical model is feasible.

Keywords: metamorphic robotic grasper · thermal-structural analysis · finite element method · thermal deformation

1 Introduction

With the continuous progress of space exploration technology, more and more spacecraft are beginning to enter out space. These spacecrafts gradually lose control ability as they malfunction or end their service, and further form space debris [1]. Therefore, more and more researchers focus on the design of space robotic grasper used for grasping non-cooperative objects [2–7]. However, the out-space environment is quite complex such as temperature field, microgravity field, and electromagnetic radiation, these factors can

X. Lan et al. (Eds.): icira 2024, LNAI 15201, pp. 254–265, 2025.
https://doi.org/10.1007/978-981-96-0771-6_19

seriously affect the mechanical and control performance of the space robotic grasper, especially since the temperature field has a significant impact on the structure. Thus, thermal structural analysis is very essential for complex space tasks, and related research can be reviewed as follows.

Jin et al. investigate the influence of a modular deployable antenna support structure on the surface accuracy and stability under the space thermal alternating environment, the proposed thermal-structural analysis model could accurately estimate the behavior of thermal deformation for the modular space deployable antenna [8]. Kim et al. perform structural-thermal coupling analysis with finite element method to numerically evaluate the structural performance of the lightweight composite reflector antenna [9]. Zhang et al. analyze the thermal effect mode of the space environment on the on-orbit antenna and the differential heat conduction equation is also obtained by taking the profile as a research object [10]. Grasinger et al. investigate the thermodynamic multistability of nanoscale origami structures and the rate at which thermal fluctuations drive them is unfold-that is, its temporal stability [11]. Deravanessian et al. present a systems-level thermal analysis of a highly usable host ESPA class satellite using a combination of oscillating heat pipes and a deployable solar array-backed radiator for the primary thermal control systems architecture [12]. Guarriello et al. analyze the thermoelastic stability of a large deployable faceted reflect array and the impact of the thermoelastic deformation under a transverse thermal gradient [13]. Kuriakose et al. discuss the thermal effect on the static and dynamic behavior of deployable composite boom prototypes [14]. Li et al. propose an active surface adjustment method for a space deployable structure based on interval model updating and the kriging model to achieve high surface accuracy of the deployable structure in the presence of model parameter uncertainties caused by manufacturing and assembly errors as well as complicated space environments [15]. Cheng et al. present a numerical method to realize the thermal-mechanical coupling analysis and structural optimization of a deployable grasping manipulator, of which the hexagonal mechanism that composing the manipulator is well studied. The temperature field of the hexagonal mechanism in space is calculated by combining the thermal boundary condition analysis and the heat transfer finite element analysis [16].

From the above review, one can see that the finite element method is an important thermal-structural analysis method due to its accuracy and the main focus of thermal-structural analysis is on satellite antennas. In contrast, there are relatively few analysis cases of space robotic graspers. Based on the above, this paper will focus on a space robotic grasper as the study object and first establish the thermal conduction equation of the space temperature field, then the theoretical model for space thermal-structure analysis can be obtained. Further, the finite element model of the robotic grasper is established based on the finite element method and thermal deformation is obtained by loading different temperature fields. Finally, the position with large deformations is optimized and the comparison shows that the method is effective and feasible.

The remainder of the paper is arranged as follows: Sect. 2 briefly introduces the robotic grasper and establishes the theoretical model of thermal-structural coupling analysis; Sect. 3 conducts thermal-deformation simulation of the robotic grasper based on finite element software; Sect. 4 optimizes the structure of the robotic grasper based on simulation results; Sect. 5 do a sample conclusion for this paper.

2 Theoretical Modeling for Thermal-Structural Analysis in the Space Temperature Field

The deployable robotic grasper is shown in Fig. 1 consisting of three fingers and a palmar mechanism, the detailed mechanism design of the deployable metamorphic robotic grasper is mentioned in references [3, 4], and the dynamic performance is mentioned in references [5]. When the robotic grasper moves along a space orbit, its position and direction relative to the sun and the earth constantly change and external thermal flux and radiation exchange also constantly change, which causes the robotic grasper to undergo significant changes in high and low-temperature and thus leading to structural bending, deformation, and even vibration. For such a question, the finite element method can use a unified finite element model for thermal and structural analysis, which effectively eliminates data conversion and interface issues between thermal and structure. In this case, the computational accuracy is greatly improved. Therefore, the finite element method is particularly suitable for solving the temperature field of the robotic grasper that requires high thermal stability.

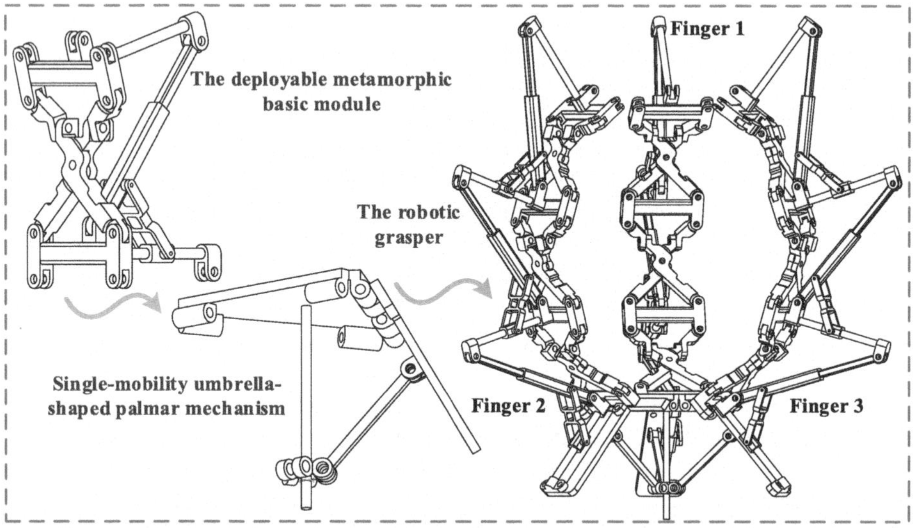

Fig. 1. The mechanism description of the robotic grasper: (a) the deployable metamorphic basic module; (b) the single-mobility umbrella-shaped palmar mechanism; (c) theoretical model of the robotic grasper with three branches structure.

The robotic grasper is mainly affected by direct sunlight and such a process can be described by establishing a thermal balance equation in the space environment. It is commonly referred to as the spatial temperature field control equation as:

$$\frac{\partial}{\partial x}\left[k_x\frac{\partial T}{\partial x}\right]+\frac{\partial}{\partial y}\left[k_y\frac{\partial T}{\partial y}\right]+\frac{\partial}{\partial z}\left[k_z\frac{\partial T}{\partial z}\right]=\rho c\frac{\partial T}{\partial t} \tag{1}$$

The boundary conditions for the radiation of the robotic grasper in the space environment can be described as:

$$k_x \frac{\partial T}{\partial x} n_x + k_y \frac{\partial T}{\partial y} n_y + k_z \frac{\partial T}{\partial z} n_z = \sigma \varepsilon (T^4 - T_\infty^4) - \alpha q \tag{2}$$

The initial conditions can be given as:

$$T(x, y, z, t = 0) = T_0 \tag{3}$$

where ρ presents material density; c presents specific thermal capacity; k_x presents the thermal conductivity coefficient of the robotic grasper in the x-direction; k_y presents the thermal conduction of the robotic grasper in the y-direction; k_z presents the thermal conduction of the robotic grasper in the *z-direction*; α presents the absorptivity; T_∞ presents the space environment temperature; σ presents the Stefan-Boltzman constant; q presents the external thermal flux; n_x presents the x-direction cosine of the outer normal; n_y presents the y-direction cosine of the outer normal; n_z presents the z-direction cosine of the outer normal.

Assuming that the interpolation form of the temperature field of each unit for the robotic grasper can be expressed as:

$$T^e(x, y, z, t) = \sum_{i=1}^{R} N_i(x, y, z) T_i(t) = N T^e \tag{4}$$

where N_i (x, y, x) presents the interpolation function; $T_i(t)$ presents the temperature of finite element unit node; R presents the number of unit nodes; N presents the interpolation function matrix; T^e presents the node temperature matrix; superscript e presents the unit.

Here, the specific form N_i (x, y, x) and T^e can be expressed as:

$$N_i(x, y, z) = \begin{bmatrix} N_1(x, y, z) \\ N_2(x, y, z) \\ \cdots \\ N_r(x, y, z) \end{bmatrix}^{\mathrm{T}} \tag{5}$$

$$T^e = [T_1(t), T_1(t), \cdots, T_R(t)]^{\mathrm{T}} \tag{6}$$

Based on the Galerkin method and the above equations including Eq. (1), Eq. (2), and Eq. (4), the weighted integration within each unit can be further deduced as:

$$J^e = C^e \frac{\partial T^e}{\partial t} + (K_c^e + K_R^e) T^e - F^e \tag{7}$$

where C^e presents the thermal capacity matrix of the unit; K_c^e presents thermal conduction matrix of the unit; K_r^e presents thermal radiation matrix of the unit; and K_r^e presents thermal load matrix of the unit.

The specific calculation methods for C^e, K_c^e, K_r^e, and F^e are as follows:

$$C^e = \int_{V^e} \rho c N^T N dV \tag{8}$$

$$K_c^e = \int_{V^e} B^T KBdV \tag{9}$$

$$K_r^e = \int_{A^e} \sigma\varepsilon(T^e)^3 N^T NdA = \int_{A^e} \sigma\varepsilon(NT^e)^3 N^T NdA \tag{10}$$

$$F^e = \int_{A^e} (\alpha q + \sigma\varepsilon T_\infty^4) N^T NdA \tag{11}$$

where B in Eq. (9) is the geometric matrix, and K is the thermal transfer coefficient matrix of the material.

By assembling the equations of each finite element in an orderly manner, the overall temperature field calculation equation can be obtained as follows:

$$\boldsymbol{C}\dot{\boldsymbol{T}} + (\boldsymbol{K}_e + \boldsymbol{K}_r)\boldsymbol{T} = \boldsymbol{F} \tag{12}$$

where $\boldsymbol{C}$ presents the overall thermal capacity matrix after assembly; K_e presents the global thermal radiation matrix after assembly; K_r presents the overall thermal load matrix after assembly; $\boldsymbol{F}$ presents the node temperature matrix after assembly.

If the thermal radiation in the stable state is considered, the above equation can be revised as follows:

$$\boldsymbol{K}_r\boldsymbol{T} = \boldsymbol{F} \tag{13}$$

Due to the complex structure of the robotic grasper, the thermal of various parts is actually uneven. Therefore, different degrees of thermal expansion may occur at different positions of the robotic grasper and the thermal stress and strain are thus formed. As a result, thermal displacement at each node of the finite element is caused. If reasonable optimization and improvement are not carried out in this case, it will ultimately lead to significant deformation of the robotic grasper and affect its space task execution. In finite element mode, the thermal stiffness equations of each finite element for the robotic grasper can be expressed as:

$$[\boldsymbol{K}^e]\{\delta^e\} = \left\{\boldsymbol{F}_Q^e\right\} \tag{14}$$

where $[\boldsymbol{K}^e]$ presents the stiffness matrix for each element of the finite element; $\{\delta^e\}$ presents the thermal potential vector at each unit node for the finite element; $\left\{\boldsymbol{F}_Q^e\right\}$ presents thermal load column vectors at each unit node of the finite element.

By assembling the equations of each finite element, the calculation equation for the overall thermal displacement of the robotic grasper can be obtained as follows:

$$[\boldsymbol{K}]\{\delta\} = \left\{\boldsymbol{F}_Q\right\} \tag{15}$$

By solving the above equation, the thermal displacement of each finite element node for the robotic grasper can be obtained. Based on the thermal displacement of each node, the thermal stress values of each finite element node can be further calculated by:

$$\{\sigma\} = [\boldsymbol{D}][\boldsymbol{B}]\{\delta^e\} - [\boldsymbol{D}]\{\varepsilon_0\} \tag{16}$$

At this point, the theoretical model of finite element analysis for the robotic grasper has been established, which lays the foundation for thermal-structural analysis.

3 Simulation with Finite Element Method for the Robotic Grasper

To further study the thermal-structural deformation of the robotic grasper, the finite element simulation model also needs to be established based on theoretical modeling. Here, finite element analysis software is applied to the calculation and the automatic meshing method with regular tetrahedra has been used. By this method, the deployable metamorphic basic module, the single-mobility umbrella-shaped palmar mechanism, and the robotic grasper in different configurations can be given as shown in Fig. 2. As the number of units increases, the accuracy of the analysis will gradually increase, but the computational workload will also increase rapidly, so which is a result of the comprehensive consideration. In practical applications, it is advisable to minimize the number of unit divisions while achieving analysis accuracy.

The working environment of the robotic grasper has a maximum temperature of nearly 150 degrees and a minimum temperature of about minus 150 degrees, which is also the temperature when the robotic grasper enters and exits the direct sunlight zone, respectively. In other on-orbit positions, the thermal load on the robotic grasper is considered within such a temperature range. Further, to complete the simulation analysis, define that the material of the robotic grasper is an aluminum alloy (Al6061). The loading process of thermal load includes two stages as follows. Firstly, the robotic grasper entering the direct sunlight zone from the non-direct sunlight zone is simulated and the temperature continuously changes from minus 150° to 150°. Secondly, the robotic grasper entering the non-direct sunlight zone from the direct sunlight zone is simulated and the temperature continuously changes from 150° to minus 150°.

In fact, temperature changes in space are influenced by multiple factors and are not linear. To simplify the computational complexity of simulation, however, one assumes that the temperature in space is linear and continuously changing. Then, thermal-structure simulation analysis with finite element analysis software is conducted for the basic module, the palmar mechanism, and the robotic grasper, and the deformation is shown in Fig. 3, from which one can see that an actual grasping configuration is selected. In addition, the maximum principal strain position is selected and further visualization of its variation process is given as shown in Fig. 4.

4 Structural Optimization and Analysis of the Robotic Grasper

Through the above finite element analysis, the position with the maximum deformation can be easily obtained, which provides a basis for further optimization. Here, the following two links are selected as the optimization objects due to their larger deformation. For the link 1 shown in Fig. 5(a), the optimization is carried out by changing the geometric parameters of the structure, the thickness of the link has increased from 5mm to 6mm. Similarly, for the link 2 shown in Fig. 5(b), the thickness of the link has increased from 2.5 mm to 3 mm. In engineering, similar structural optimization can also be achieved by changing the size of the chamfer and other material, so this is a result of comprehensive consideration that needs to be selected based on the actual situation and requirements.

After optimizing the links, thermal-structure simulation analysis with finite element analysis software is conducted again for the basic module, the palmar mechanism, and

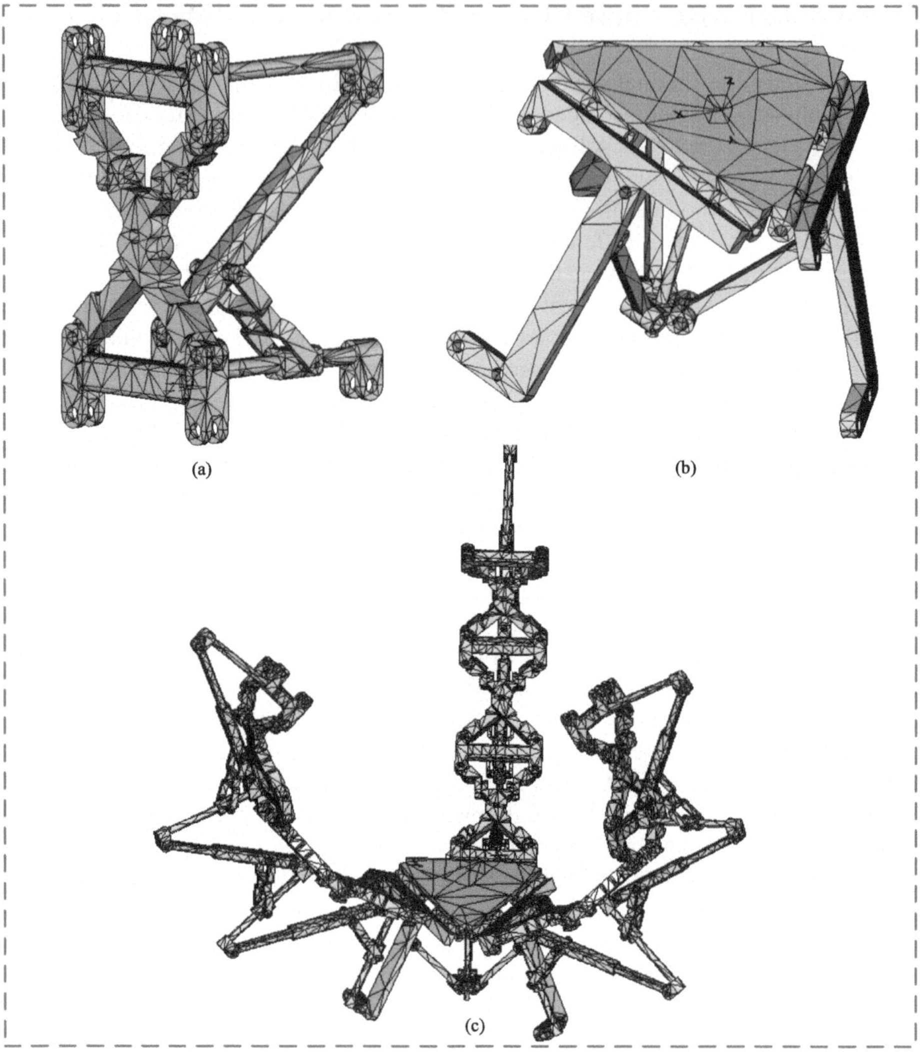

Fig. 2. The finite element simulation model: (a) the basic module; (b) the palmar mechanism; (c) the robotic grasper.

the robotic grasper, and thermal strain variation with different thermal loads is shown in Fig. 6, where the deformation is rapidly decreasing. Furthermore, a comparison for the maximum principal strain of the robotic grasper is performed in three key configurations including deployable configuration, folded configuration, and grasping configuration as shown in Table 1, by which one can see that the maximum principal strain of the robotic grasper is gradually decreasing. In practical operation, the final required accuracy of the robotic grasper can be achieved by repeatedly optimizing in this way, which is also an iterative optimization process that can effectively improve the structure of the spacecraft and thereby meeting thermodynamic requirements.

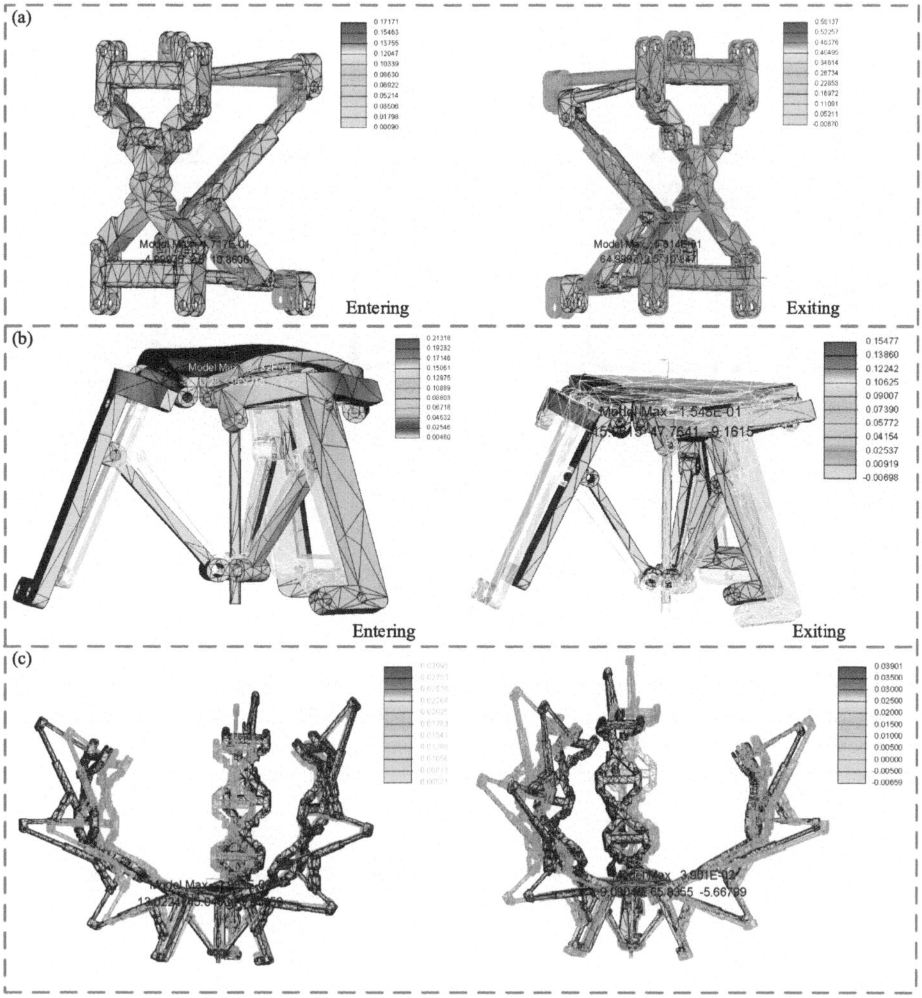

Fig. 3. Thermal-structural deformation with different thermal loads: (a) thermal-structural deformation of the basic module during the changing temperature field; (b) thermal-structural deformation of the palmar mechanism during the changing temperature field; (c) thermal-structural deformation of the robotic grasper during the changing temperature field.

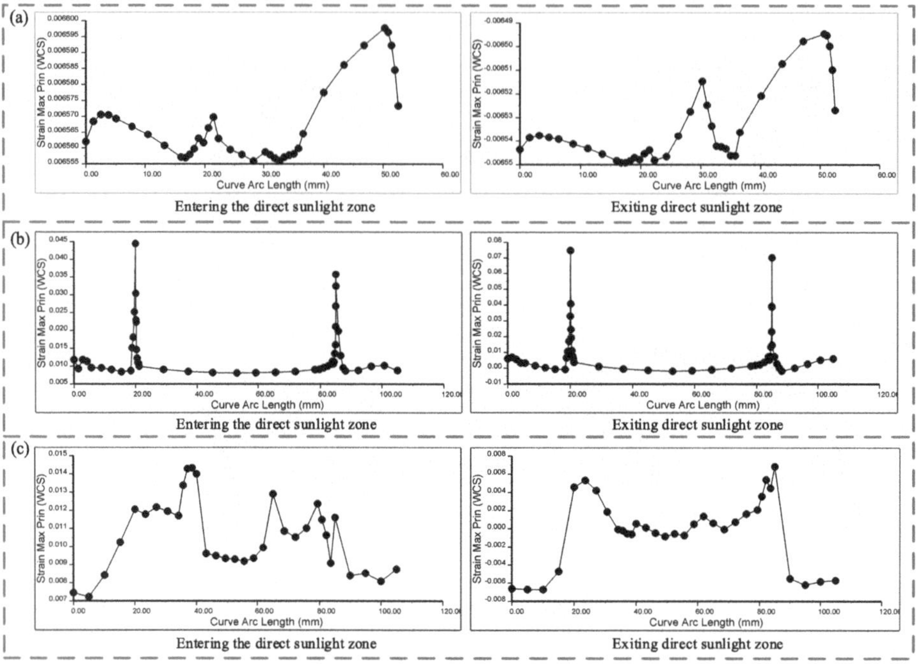

Fig. 4. Thermal strain variation with different thermal loads: (a) the maximum principal strain position of the basic module during the changing temperature field; (b) the maximum principal strain position of the palmar mechanism during the changing temperature field; (c) the maximum principal strain position of the robotic grasper during the changing temperature field.

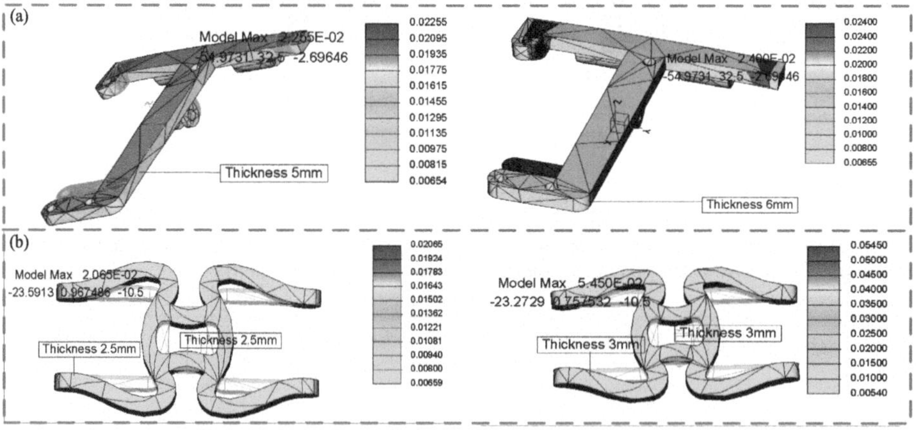

Fig. 5. Local structural optimization of the robotic grasper: (a) the key link of the basic module; (b) the key link of the palmar mechanism.

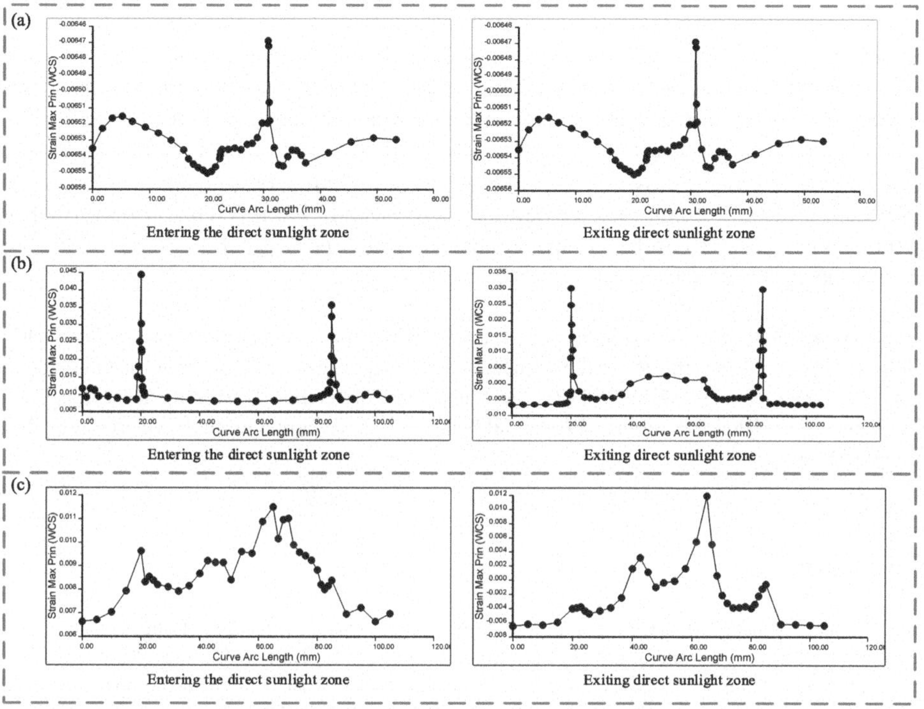

Fig. 6. Maximum thermal strain of the robotic grasper after structural optimization: (a) the maximum principal strain position of the basic module; (b) the maximum principal strain position of the palmar mechanism; (c) the maximum principal strain position of the robotic grasper.

Table 1. Numerical comparison of the maximum thermal strain before and after optimization.

Structure of the model	the maximum principal strain before optimization (mm)	the maximum principal strain after optimization (mm)
Deployable configuration	0.01100	0.00900
Folded configuration	0.00840	0.00828
Grasping configuration	0.00870	0.00820

5 Conclusion

In this paper, a truss-shaped deployable metamorphic robotic grasper is used as the studied object, and a thermal-structural analysis is performed based on the finite element method. The robotic grasper is first introduced and a theoretical model of the space temperature field is then established such as the thermal conduction equation, which provides a theoretical basis for the loading of space thermal loads. Then, the finite element simulation model of the robotic grasper is built by finite element analysis software with an automatic mesh partition. By loading different thermal loads, the key positions of thermal deformation for the robotic grasper were obtained, which require further optimization. Thus, a group of optimizations for critical structural positions is conducted. By comparing simulation results of models before and after optimization, the thermal deformation of the robotic grasper rapidly decreases and the mechanical performance of the robotic grasper can be greatly enhanced, which is of great significance for the on-orbit operation of spacecraft.

Acknowledgment. Research supported by the STU Scientific Research Initiation Grant (SRIG) (Grant No. NTF23019), the Research Projects of the Department of Education of Guangdong Province (Grant No. 2023KTSCX317), the Shenzhen Polytechnic University Research Fund (Grant No. 6023310005K), and the Provincial Natural Science Foundation of Hunan (Grant No. 2023JJ50099).

References

1. Dai, J.S., Wang, D.L., Cui, L.: Orientation and workspace analysis of the multifingered metamorphic hand—metahand. IEEE Trans. Robot. Robot. **25**(4), 942–947 (2009)
2. Gao, C.Q., Kang, X., Lei, H., et al.: Design and analysis of a novel large-span two-fold deployable mechanism. Mech. Mach. Theory **186**, 105352 (2023)
3. Gao, C.Q., Huang, H.L., Li, Y., et al.: Design and analysis of a three-fingered deployable metamorphic robotic grasper. J. Mech. Des. ASME **144**(8), 083302 (2022)
4. Gao, C.Q., Huang, H.L., Li, B., et al.: Design of a truss-shaped deployable grasping mechanism using mobility bifurcation. Mech. Mach. Theory **139**, 346–358 (2019)
5. Gao, C.Q., Zhang, Y., Kang, X., et al.: Dynamic analysis of a three-fingered deployable metamorphic robotic grasper. Mech. Mach. Theory **180**, 105140 (2022)
6. Gao, C.Q., Wang, J.H., Yang, X.J., et al.: Design and analysis of a novel truss-shaped variable-stiffness deployable robotic grasper. IEEE Access **8**, 112944–112956 (2020)
7. Gao, C.Q., Zhang, Y., Xu, P., et al.: Envelope grasping planning of a three-fingered deployable metamorphic robotic grasper. In: Proceedings of the IEEE International Conference on Cyborg and Bionic Systems, Wuhan, Hubei, China, 24–26 March 2023
8. Jin, L., Zhang, F.Y., Tian, D.K., et al.: Thermal-structural analysis of the support structure for a modular space deployable antenna. Int. J. Aerosp. Eng. **1**, 1–13 (2022)
9. Kim, H.G., Kim, D.G., Do, R.H., et al.: Development of deployable reflector antenna for the SAR-satellite: Part 1. Design and analysis of the main reflector using honeycomb sandwich composite structure. Appl. Sci. **14**(4), 1590 (2024)
10. Zhang, X., Kang, X., Huang, H.L., et al.: On-orbit thermal analysis of ring truss-type deployable antenna. In: Proceedings of IFToMM China International Conference on Mechanism and Machine Science & Engineering (CCMMS 2022), Yantai, Shandong, China, 30 July–1 August 2022
11. Grasinger, M., Sharma, P.: Thermal fluctuations (eventually) unfold nanoscale origami. J. Mech. Phys. Solids **184**(24), 105527 (2024)
12. Deravanessian, A., Anderson, K.R.: Thermal analysis of an ESPA class host satellite using oscillating heat pipes and deployable solar array backed radiator. In: Proceedings of the AIAA SciTech Forum, San Diego, USA, 3–7 January 2022

13. Guarriello, A., Loison, R., Bresciani, D., et al.: Structural and radio frequency co-design and optimization of large deployable reflect arrays for space missions. IEEE Trans. Antenn. As Propag. **71**(5), 3916–3927 (2023)
14. Kuriakose, V.M.: Thermo-structural analysis of deployable composite booms with slotted hinges for space applications. Mater. Today Proc. **56**, 3564–3570 (2022)
15. Li, T.J., Wen, J.B., Shi, Z.Y., et al.: Active adjustment method for space deployable structure considering parameter uncertainties. AIAA J. **60**(9), 1–10 (2022)
16. Cheng, W.D., Huang, H.L., Li, B., et al.: Thermal-mechanical coupling analysis and structural optimization of a deployable grasping manipulator. In: Proceedings of the 14th International Conference of Intelligent Robotics and Applications (ICIRA 2021), Yantai, Shandong, China, 22–25 October 2021

Design and Analysis of an Origami-Inspired Gripper with Passive Bistable Grasping Capability

Jieyu Wang[1,2], Weiwei Hu[1,2], Yingzhong Tian[1,2], Stéphane Caro[3], and Yinjun Zhao[4(✉)]

[1] School of Mechatronic Engineering and Automation, Shanghai University, Shanghai 200444, China
[2] Shanghai Key Laboratory of Intelligent Manufacturing and Robotics, Shanghai 200444, China
[3] Nantes Université, École Centrale Nantes, CNRS, LS2N, UMR 6004 Nantes, France
[4] School of Mechanical Engineering, University of Shanghai for Science and Technology, Shanghai 200093, China
Zhaoyinjun@usst.edu.cn

Abstract. Origami sheds light on the design of mechanisms and robots. In this paper, inspired by an origami structure, an enveloping grasping mechanism is proposed. The origami-inspired grasping mechanism (OIGM) is symmetrically designed and has only one degree-of-freedom (DOF), which can be utilized to develop a gripper that can fully enclose the objects. The kinematic characteristics of the mechanism are analyzed. In particular, we integrate a leaf-spring-based bistable mechanism with the OIGM to design a gripper with a passive bistable grasping capability. Triggered by the impact force between the gripper and the object, the gripper can passively grasp objects. To validate the passive grasping capability of the gripper, a prototype is fabricated and the grasping experiment is conducted.

Keywords: Origami-Inspired Mechanism · Bistable Structure · Passive Grasping

1 Introduction

Origami, as an ancient art of paper folding, is ubiquitous in various aspects of our lives. Origami structures can be analogized to mechanisms, with the creases and facets regarded as joints and links respectively [1]. In recent years, the exploration and utilization of origami structures in mechanical engineering have inspired researchers to innovate novel mechanisms [2–4].

Drawing inspiration from origami, several grippers have been proposed by scholars. Inspired by an origami twisted tower, Lee et al. [5] proposed an underactuated gripper driven by cables, grasping objects of different shapes, weights, sizes, and textures adaptively. A reconfigurable suction gripper, inspired by origami, was presented in [6]. Driven by a compact SMA actuator, the gripper constructed of rigid and soft components has three shape modes to pick objects with different shapes and sizes. Chen et al.

X. Lan et al. (Eds.): ICIRA 2024, LNAI 15201, pp. 266–277, 2025.
https://doi.org/10.1007/978-981-96-0771-6_20

[7] drew inspiration from an origami fortune teller and proposed a reconfigurable soft pneumatic gripper. A self-folded origami gripper was proposed in [8] and mounted on a quadcopter for object grasping by contact.

In terms of gripper design, many researchers have integrated bistable mechanisms into the gripper, resulting in the gripper with rapid response and energy efficiency due to the advantages of bistable mechanisms [9, 10]. Zhang and Tang [11] proposed a two-finger soft gripper actuated by a tendon-driven mechanism. Two types of bistable mechanisms were employed for the quick response of the gripper. Liu et al. [12] reported a soft bistable gripper with adjustable triggering conditions for dynamic object capture, leveraging the rapid occurrence of structural instability. A cable-driven mechanism was utilized to enable the gripper to return to its initial state and release the object after one grasping task. Zhang et al. [13] proposed a pneumatically actuated soft gripper in which bistable laminates were adopted to induce shape retention, which can respond at the millisecond level under low pressure. A fully passive gripper for aerial perching and grasping, operated solely by mechanical means and without any actuator, was proposed in [14]. The gripper switches from the opened state to the closed state by the impact force between the gripper and objects. The close state is maintained by external weights and the gripper will automatically open when weights are removed.

In this article, inspired by an origami structure, an enveloping grasping mechanism is developed. The kinematic characteristics of the origami-inspired grasping mechanism (OIGM) are analyzed. Structurally integrating a leaf-spring-based bistable mechanism and the OIGM, a gripper with a bistable passive grasping capability is designed. Finally, a prototype of the gripper is fabricated and a grasping experiment is conducted.

The remainder of the paper is organized as follows: Sect. 2 introduces the origami-inspired grasping mechanism and its kinematic characteristics. In Sect. 3, the gripper with passively grasping capability is designed by structurally integrating the OIGM and a bistable mechanism based on leaf springs. The prototype and experiments are described in Sect. 4. Finally, conclusions are drawn.

2 The OIGM and the Kinematic Characteristics

2.1 The Grasping Mechanism Inspired by an Origami Structure

Numerous origami artifacts in daily life exhibit distinct forms, each with unique characteristics that provide valuable insights into designing novel mechanisms and devices from the perspective of mechanical engineering [4, 7]. Figure 1(a) depicts an origami structure capable of an opening-closing motion, achieved by pulling or pushing facet A and facet B.

Inspired by the origami structure, we develop a six-link mechanism, as illustrated in Fig. 1(b)–(c). It is obtained by taking specific creases of the origami structure as revolute joints and panels as links. As shown in Fig. 1(b), the mechanism is constructed by six isosceles triangle panels P_i ($i = 1, 2, \ldots, 6$) and two of them (P_1 and P_4) are isosceles right triangle panels, connecting by seven revolute joints.

As illustrated in Figs. 1(b) and (c), the axes of joints R_1, R_2, R_3 and R_4 intersect at the point o_1 while the axes of joints R_1, R_5, R_6 and R_7 intersect at the point o_2. Plane Π_1 is formed by axes of joints R_1, R_3 and R_6 while plane Π_2 is perpendicular to the plane

Π_1 and passes through the midpoint of the line o_1o_2. It is readily to observe that the mechanism is symmetric about the planes Π_1 and Π_2, respectively. Due to the symmetric properties, the dihedral angle φ_i between panel P_i and panel P_{i+1} satisfies

$$\varphi_1 = \varphi_3 = \varphi_4 = \varphi_6, \varphi_2 = \varphi_5 \tag{1}$$

Points A, B, C, and D are points on panels P_2, P_6, P_3 and P_5 respectively, as shown in Fig. 1(b)–(c). When the mechanism is completely closed, point A coincides with point B while point C coincides with point D.

Taking the midpoint o of the line o_1o_2 as the origin of the coordinate frame, a global frame o–xyz is established and will be used for the following kinematic analysis. The z - axis of the global frame o–xyz is aligned with the axis of the joint R_1, and x - axis is coplanar with the symmetric plane Π_1. The y - axis is obtained by the right-hand rule.

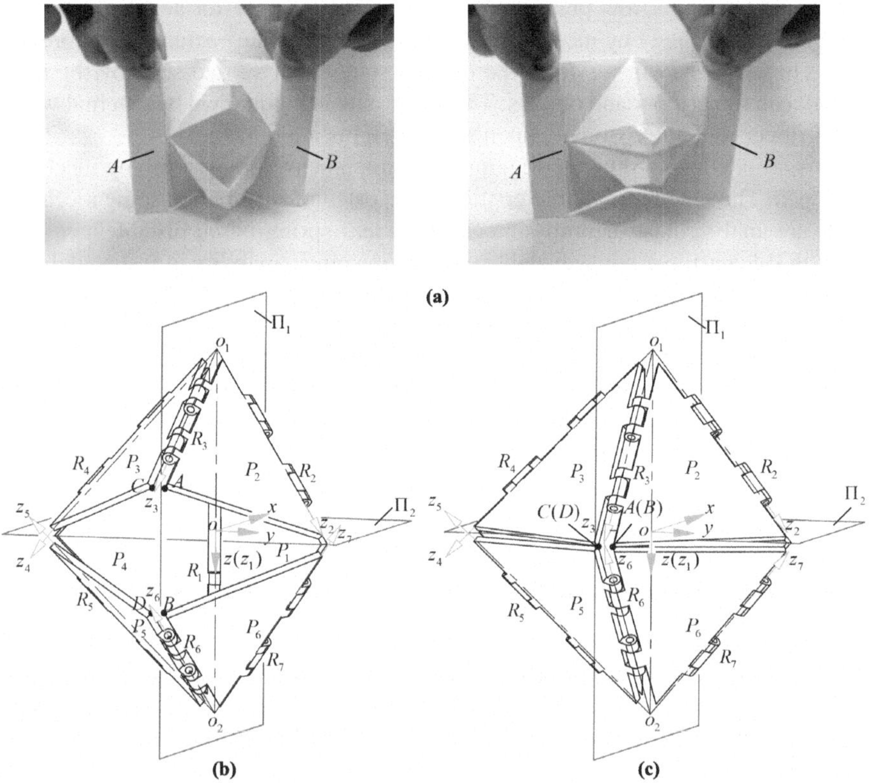

Fig. 1. An origami inspired grasping mechanism. (a) the origami structure; (b) the OIGM in opened state; (c) the OIGM in closed state.

2.2 The Kinematic Characteristics of the OIGM

To describe the kinematic characteristics of the OIGM, a Cartesian coordinate frame is attached to each link based on the modified Denavit-Hartenberg (D-H) method [15]. The coordinate frames are depicted in Fig. 1(b)–(c). The transformation matrix ${}_{i}^{i-1}T$ from the $(i-1)^{\text{th}}$ to i^{th} local coordinate is described as

$$
{}_{i}^{i-1}T = \begin{bmatrix} c\theta_i & -s\theta_i & 0 & a_{i-1} \\ s\theta_i c\alpha_{i-1} & c\theta_i c\alpha_{i-1} & -s\alpha_{i-1} & -s\alpha_{i-1}d_i \\ s\theta_i s\alpha_{i-1} & c\theta_i s\alpha_{i-1} & c\alpha_{i-1} & c\alpha_{i-1}d_i \\ 0 & 0 & 0 & 1 \end{bmatrix} \tag{2}
$$

where a_i represents the distance from z_i to z_{i+1} measured along x_i, α_i represents the angle between z_i and z_{i+1} measured about x_i, d_i represents the distance from x_{i-1} and x_i measured along z_i, θ_i represents the angle between x_{i-1} and x_i measured about z_i. s and c denote sin and cos respectively.

There are two kinematic chain loops of the OIGM in total. Panels P_1, P_2, P_3 and P_4 construct the kinematic chain loop-I while kinematic chain loop-II is formed by Panels P_1, P_4, P_5 and P_6. According to the modified D-H method, the relationship between the revolute joint angle θ_{i+1} $(i = 1,\ 2,\ \ldots,6)$ and the dihedral angle φ_i satisfies

$$
\theta_{i+1} = \pi - \varphi_i \tag{3}
$$

According to Eqs. (1) and (3), we can obtain that

$$
\theta_2 = \theta_4 = \theta_5 = \theta_7,\ \theta_3 = \theta_6 \tag{4}
$$

Therefore, the kinematic characteristics of the OIGM can be obtained just by identifying the kinematic behavior of the kinematic chain loop-I. The link parameters of the kinematic chain loop-I can be obtained as follows

$$
\begin{aligned}
&\alpha_{12} = \alpha_{23} = \alpha_{34} = \alpha_{41} = -\frac{\pi}{4} \\
&a_{12} = a_{23} = a_{34} = a_{41} = 0 \\
&d_1 = d_2 = d_3 = d_4 = 0
\end{aligned} \tag{5}
$$

The closure equation of the kinematic chain loop-I can be written as

$$
{}_{2}^{1}T{}_{3}^{2}T{}_{4}^{3}T{}_{1}^{4}T = I_4 \tag{6}
$$

or

$$
{}_{2}^{1}T{}_{3}^{2}T - {}_{1}^{4}T^{-1}{}_{4}^{3}T^{-1} = 0 \tag{7}
$$

where ${}_{i}^{i-1}T^{-1}$ is the inverse of the transformation matrix ${}_{i}^{i-1}T$. Substituting Eqs. (4) and (5) into Eq. (7), we can have

$$
\begin{bmatrix} R_{11} & R_{12} & R_{13} & 0 \\ R_{21} & R_{22} & R_{23} & 0 \\ R_{31} & R_{32} & 0 & 0 \\ 0 & 0 & 0 & 0 \end{bmatrix} = 0 \tag{8}
$$

Two equations can be obtained based on Eq. (8) as

$$\begin{aligned} R_{12} + R_{21} &= \sin(\theta_3) - \sin(\theta_1) - 2\cos(\theta_2)\sin(\theta_1) + \\ &2\cos(\theta_2)\sin(\theta_3) + \cos(\theta_2)\sin(\theta_1) - \cos(\theta_2)\sin(\theta_3) = 0 \end{aligned} \quad (9)$$

$$R_{13} = \sqrt{2}\sin(\theta_2) - \sin(\theta_1) - \sqrt{2}\cos(\theta_1)\sin(\theta_2) - \cos(\theta_2)\sin(\theta_1) = 0 \quad (10)$$

Simplifying Eq. (9), it can be derived that

$$(\sin(\theta_3) - \sin(\theta_1))(1 + \cos(\theta_2)) = 0 \quad (11)$$

Since joint 2 is always active, we can obtain that $\sin(\theta_3) - \sin(\theta_1) = 0$, which means

$$\theta_3 = \theta_1 \quad (12)$$

Solving Eq. (10), we have

$$\theta_2 = -2\arctan\left(\frac{\sqrt{2}\sin(\theta_1)}{2\cos(\theta_1) - 2}\right) \quad (13)$$

Therefore, based on Eqs. (4), (12), and (13), the kinematic relationships between the joints of the OIGM can be described as

$$\theta_1 = \theta_3 = \theta_6,\ \theta_2 = \theta_4 = \theta_5 = \theta_7 = -2\arctan\left(\frac{\sqrt{2}\sin(\theta_1)}{2\cos(\theta_1) - 2}\right) \quad (14)$$

which indicates that the OIGM is a mechanism with only one DOF.

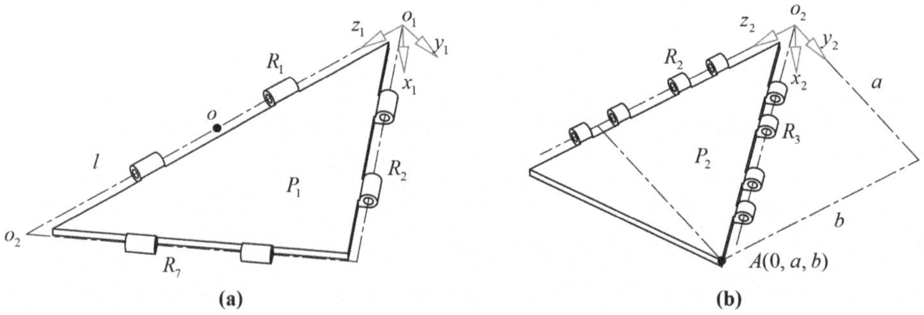

Fig. 2. Geometrical parameters and local frame denotation of the panels: (a) panel P_1; (b) panel P_2.

Figure 2 gives the names of certain geometrical parameters and local frames for panels P_1 and P_2 respectively. The coordinate frames $o_1{-}x_1y_1z_1$ and $o_2{-}x_2y_2z_2$ are attached to panel P_1, and panel P_2 respectively. As illustrated in Fig. 2(a), the length of the o_1o_2 is denoted by l. Based on the symmetric properties of the OIGM, the transformation matrix ${}^{0}_{1}T$ from the local frame $o_1{-}x_1y_1z_1$ to the global frame $o{-}xyz$ can be expressed as

$$ {}^{0}_{1}T = \begin{bmatrix} c(\theta_1/2) & -s(\theta_1/2) & 0 & 0 \\ s(\theta_1/2) & c(\theta_1/2) & 0 & 0 \\ 0 & 0 & 1 & -l/2 \\ 0 & 0 & 0 & 1 \end{bmatrix} \tag{15} $$

The coordinate of point A in $o_2{-}x_2y_2z_2$ is $A(0,\ a,\ b)$, as shown in Fig. 2(b). Therefore, the coordinate of point A in the global frame can be obtained by

$$ A_0 = {}^{0}_{1}T\,{}^{1}_{2}TA_2 \tag{16} $$

where $A_2 = [\ 0\ \ a\ \ b\ \ 1\ ]^T$.

When the OIGM is in a fully closed state, point A coincides with point B, and point C coincides with point D. Due to the symmetric properties, these points will be located on the plane Π_2, which means the z-coordinate of point A under the global frame $o{-}xyz$ is equal to zero. Based on this characteristic and Eq. (16), we have

$$ \frac{\sqrt{2}b}{2} - \frac{l}{2} - \frac{\sqrt{2}a\cos(\theta_2)}{2} = 0 \tag{17} $$

Solving Eq. (17), we can obtain

$$ \theta_2 = \arccos\left(\frac{2b - \sqrt{2}l}{2a}\right) \tag{18} $$

Based on Eqs. (14) and (18), the rotation angle of each joint can be determined when the OIGM is in the fully closed state.

3 Design of the Gripper with Passive Bistable Grasping Capability

According to the kinematic analysis of the OIGM in Sect. 2, the DOF of the OIGM is equal to one. If we designate the revolute joint R_1 of the OIGM as the actuation joint, the motion of the OIGM is suitable for designing an enveloping grasping gripper. A bistable mechanism is considered to integrate with the OIGM to design a gripper with a passive grasping capability for rapid response and energy efficiency.

A bistable mechanism is shown in Fig. 3, which has an actuation bar in the center and leaf springs on both sides. The position of the leaf spring is fixed to the base. Leaf springs will deform under an external force, leading to the energy change of the structure and making it a bistable mechanism with two stable positions. The actuation bar can undergo a linear displacement between stable position 1 (Fig. 3(a)) and stable position 2 (Fig. 3(c)), when a vertical external force is applied to it. The snap-through instability at the transition position (Fig. 3 (b)) results in the rapid linear displacement of the actuation bar between stable positions 1 and 2. In these two stable positions, there is no need for continued input of energy to make the actuation bar keep its position.

The bistable mechanism mentioned above exhibits a bistable linear displacement while the OIGM requires a rotational input to achieve the opening-closing motion for grasping. To integrate the OIGM and the bistable mechanism into designing a gripper with passive grasping capability, an additional intermediate mechanism should be employed to convert the linear displacement of the actuation bar in the bistable mechanism into the rotation motion of the joint R_1 in the OIGM.

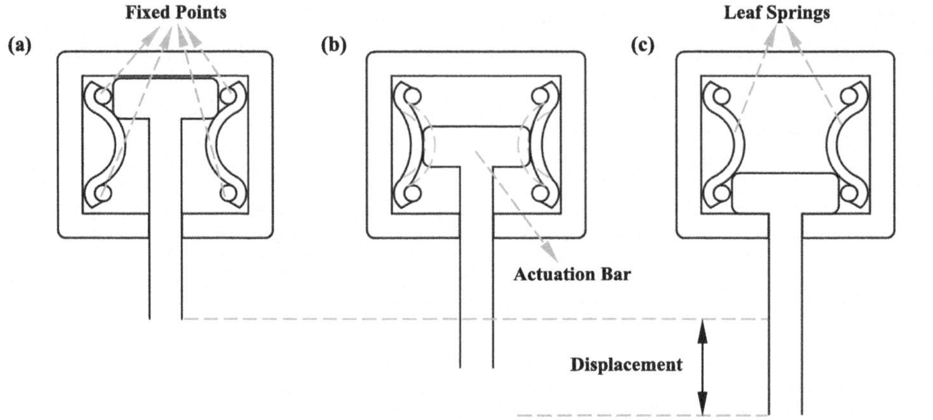

Fig. 3. Schemes of the bistable structure based on leaf springs in: (a) the stable position 1; (b) the transition position; (c) the stable position 2.

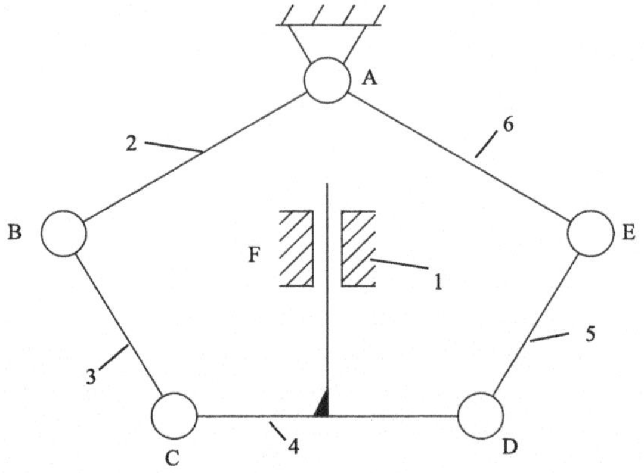

Fig. 4. The kinematic skeleton diagram of a mechanism that transforms linear displacement into rotational motion between two links.

The kinematic skeleton diagram of an intermediate mechanism capable of transforming the linear displacement of one link into rotational motion between two links is illustrated in Fig. 4. The mechanism is composed of five active links and one fixed link, with 6 revolute joints and 1 prismatic joint. The lengths of link 2 and link 6 are equal, as are the lengths of link 3 and link 5.

According to the Kutzbach-Grübler criterion [16], the DOF of the mechanism can be calculated as

$$M = 3(n - g - 1) + \sum_{i=1}^{g} f_i = 3 \times (6 - 7 - 1) + 7 = 1 \quad (19)$$

where n is the number of the total links of the mechanism, g is the number of the total kinematic joints, f_i is the DOF of the ith kinematic pair. Therefore, we can obtain that the mechanism has only one DOF, and the rotational motion between link 2 and link 6 can be achieved by linearly driving link 4.

By integrating the OIGM, the bistable mechanism, and the intermediate mechanism, a gripper with passive grasping capability is designed, which is illustrated in Fig. 5. As shown in Fig. 5(a), the gripper exhibits two symmetric planes Π_1 and Π_2, as the same as the OIGM. The joint R_1 of the OIGM is connected to the intermediate panels through a revolute joint, forming the composite hinge R_1 of the gripper. The intermediate panels are secured to the base. Figure 5(b) provides a section view of the gripper in Fig. 5(a) for a better understanding of the inner structure of the gripper. The panels of the OIGM P_1 and P_4 are connected to the trigger bar of the bistable mechanism through intermediate links by revolute joints. Therefore, the base, panels P_1 and P_4, intermediate panels, intermediate links, and the trigger bar all together, form the intermediate mechanism, enabling the linear displacement of the trigger bar to transform into the rotational motion between panel P_1 and P_4 to achieve the grasping motion of the OIGM.

The gripper is in the opened state initially, which is depicted in Fig. 5(c). Upon contacting the target object, the contact force between the target object and the gripper causes the trigger bar to move upward, exerting an external force on the leaf springs on both sides and forcing them to deform. Due to the flexibility of leaf springs, the potential energy of the gripper will change with the deformation of leaf springs. The potential energy peak appears in the transition position (Fig. 3(b)). When the contact force is sufficient to force the trigger bar to move upward and pass the transition position, the snap-through behavior of the bistable mechanism occurs, causing the gripper to rapidly transit to the closing state to grasp the target object. The closed state of the gripper is illustrated in Fig. 5(d).

The passive grasping property of the gripper is influenced by key parameters such as the thickness of the leaf springs, and the distance between the springs on both sides. Additionally, the size of objects that the gripper can passively grasp primarily depends on the geometrical parameters of the OIGM. Further exploration of these factors affecting the passive grasping performance of the gripper will be conducted in future work.

4 Prototype and Experiments

Based on the gripper design in Sect. 3, a prototype is fabricated, and a grasping experiment is conducted. Most of the components of the gripper are 3D printed using PLA, while leaf springs are 3D printed using TPU. That is because the leaf springs need to deform under an external force and recover when the external force is removed. The assembled gripper is shown in Fig. 6.

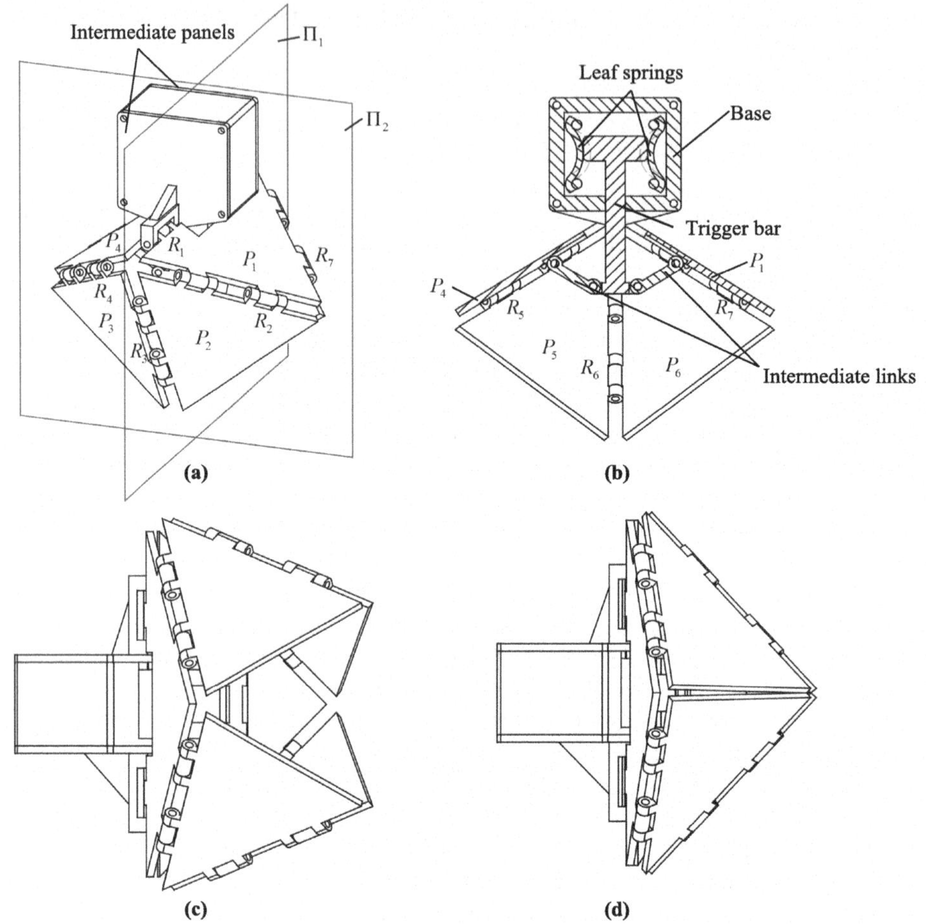

Fig. 5. The gripper with passive bistable grasping capability: (a) the structure of the gripper; (b) the section view of the gripper about plane Π_2; (c) the opened state of the gripper; (d) the closed state of the gripper.

A grasping experiment of the gripper is conducted to validate the passive grasping capability, as illustrated in Fig. 7. To passively grasp an object, the gripper in the open state approaches the object, enabling the trigger bar of the gripper to contact with the object. Grasping occurs when the contact force between the trigger bar and the object is sufficient to trigger the snap-through behavior of the bistable mechanism. Once grasped, no energy input is required to maintain the grasping state. As illustrated in Fig. 7, the gripper can passively grasp a flexible ball, a rigid ball, and a toy doll successfully, which demonstrates the feasibility of the passive grasping capability of the proposed gripper.

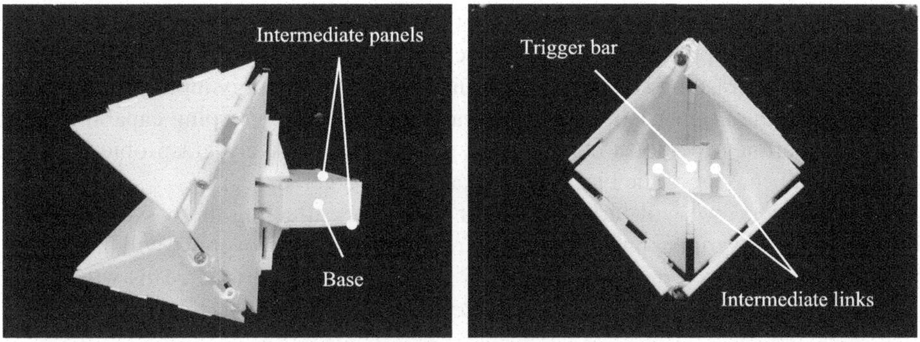

Fig. 6. The prototype of the gripper with passive grasping capability

Fig. 7. Grasping experiments of the gripper prototype.

5 Conclusion

Inspired by an origami structure, a grasping mechanism (called OIGM) is proposed in this paper. The OIGM is a six-link mechanism and is symmetric about two orthogonal planes. The kinematic characteristic analysis of the OIGM reveals that the OIGM is a mechanism with only one DOF. A gripper with a passive grasping capability is designed by integrating the OIGM with a bistable mechanism based on leaf springs and an intermediate mechanism. The bistable mechanism has a linear displacement between two stable states, and the intermediate mechanism transforms the linear displacement of the bistable mechanism into the rotation motion of the OIGM. Triggered by the impact force between the gripper and the target object, the gripper can passively grasp the object and maintain the grasping state without requiring continued energy input. Additionally, a prototype of the gripper is fabricated to validate its passive grasping capability. The grasping experiment demonstrates that the gripper can passively grasp objects if the snap-through behavior of the bistable mechanism is triggered.

In future work, we will further consider the factors affecting the passive grasping performance of the gripper and explore their relationships. Moreover, we will investigate a cable-driven actuation method for the active grasping of the gripper. This will enable the gripper to grasp objects with a wider size range, enhancing its versatility.

Acknowledgments. This study is sponsored by the National Natural Science Foundation of China (No. 52105002), and the Shanghai Pujiang Programme (No. 23PJD069).

Disclosure of Interests. The authors have no competing interests to declare that are relevant to the content of this article.

References

1. Dai, J., Rees Jones, J.: Mobility in metamorphic mechanisms of foldable/erectable kinds. J. Mech. Des. **121**(3), 375–382 (1999)
2. Barreto, R., Morlin, F., de Souza, M., et al.: Multiloop origami inspired spherical mechanisms. Mech. Mach. Theory **155**, 104063 (2021)
3. Chen, Y., Lv, W., Peng, R., et al.: Mobile assemblies of four-spherical-4r-integrated linkages and the associated four-crease-integrated rigid origami patterns. Mech. Mach. Theory **142**, 103613 (2019)
4. Wang, R., Song, Y., Dai, J.: Reconfigurability of the origami-inspired integrated 8r kinematotropic metamorphic mechanism and its evolved 6r and 4r mechanisms. Mech. Mach. Theory **161**, 104245 (2021)
5. Lee, K., Wang, Y., Zheng, C.: Twister hand: underactuated robotic gripper inspired by origami twisted tower. IEEE Trans. Robot. **36**(2), 488–500 (2020)
6. Zhakypov, Z., Heremans, F., Billard, A., et al.: An origami-inspired reconfigurable suction gripper for picking objects with variable shape and size. IEEE Robot. Autom. Lett. **3**(4), 2894–2901 (2018)
7. Chen, R., Zhang, C., Sun, Y., et al.: A paper fortune teller-inspired reconfigurable soft pneumatic gripper. Smart Mater. Struct. **30**(4), 045002 (2021)
8. Okamoto, S., Fukatsu, Y., Premachandra, C., et al.: Paper-based bistable origami gripper to make quadcopters multi-functional. IEEE Robot. Autom. Lett. **9**(5), 4511–4518 (2024)
9. Wang, Y., Gupta, U., Parulekar, N., et al.: A soft gripper of fast speed and low energy consumption. Sci. China-Technol. Sci. **62**(1), 31–38 (2018)
10. Zareei, A., Deng, B., Bertoldi, K.: Harnessing transition waves to realize deployable structures. Proc. Natl. Acad. Sci. U.S.A. **117**(8), 4015–4020 (2020)
11. Zhang, P., Tang, B.: A two-finger soft gripper based on bistable mechanism. IEEE Robot. Autom. Lett. **7**(4), 11330–11337 (2022)
12. Liu, Y., Luo, K., Wang, S., et al.: A soft and bistable gripper with adjustable energy barrier for fast capture in space. Soft Robot **10**(1), 77–87 (2023)
13. Zhang, Z., Ni, X., Wu, H., et al.: Pneumatically actuated soft gripper with bistable structures. Soft Robot **9**(1), 57–71 (2022)

14. Hsiao, H., Sun, J., Zhang, H., et al.: A mechanically intelligent and passive gripper for aerial perching and grasping. IEEE-ASME Trans. Mechatron. **27**(6), 5243–5253 (2022)
15. Granja, M., Chang, N., Granja, V. et al.: Comparison between standard and modified Denavit-Hartenberg methods in robotics modeling. In: Proceedings of the World Congress on Mechanical, Chemical, and Material Engineering (MCM 2016), pp. 1–10 (2016)
16. Zhao, J., Zhou, K., Feng, Z.: A theory of degrees of freedom for mechanisms. Mech. Mach. Theory **39**(6), 621–643 (2004)

Design of a Novel Multi-Mode Deployable Metamorphic Aerospace Mechanism

Changqing Gao[1(✉)], Hanlin Wang[1], Yongjie Zhao[1], Xuelin Du[2], and Fei Liu[1,3]

[1] Department of Mechanical Engineering, College of Engineering, Shantou University, Shantou 515063, People's Republic of China
chqgao@stu.edu.cn
[2] School of Intelligent Manufacturing and Mechanical Engineering, Hunan Institute of Technology, Hengyang 421002, People's Republic of China
[3] Industrial Training Center, Shenzhen Polytechnic University, Shenzhen 518055, People's Republic of China

Abstract. This paper develops a novel multi-mode deployable metamorphic aerospace mechanism for aerospace equipment, which is composed of a double-mode base mechanism, six metamorphic kinematic chains, and the self-locking and unlocking mechanisms. The scissor-shaped mechanism is used to afford a good deploy/fold ratio for convenient storage and transportation, the multi-loop truss-shaped structure is adopted to obtain a good stiffness property, modular and lightweight designs are applied to enhance the expandability for different aerospace tasks. Besides, a mobility bifurcation method is used to realize the transformation between the deployment motion and the bending motion. Based on the special structural design and connection method, the aerospace mechanism can be assembled and multiple motion modes can be realized, which can be used for five types of space attack-defense equipment including the space robotic grasper, the reconfigurable robot, the crawling robot, the supporting mechanism for solar array, and the supporting mechanism for large deployable antenna. The specific design and assembly methods of the aerospace mechanisms are introduced in detail, and motion analysis is then conducted. Finally, five types of key potential applications are simulated to verify their effectiveness and feasibility.

Keywords: deployable mechanism · metamorphic mechanism · self-locking and unlocking mechanism · aerospace application

1 Introduction

The deployable mechanisms are widely used in different fields and thus have become a hot study topic, especially in the aerospace industry and applications, which are also called deployable aerospace mechanisms [1–3]. However, due to the limitations of launch vehicles, the deployable aerospace mechanisms have to be fit into these vehicles during the launch process and then deployed to a predetermined form. The main applications include the space station, the communications satellite platform, the solar array, the

X. Lan et al. (Eds.): ICIRA 2024, LNAI 15201, pp. 278–291, 2025.
https://doi.org/10.1007/978-981-96-0771-6_21

space robotic grasper, and planetary exploration. Thus, a large number of researches have been performed on its design and mode synthesis [4–8]. Some related research results are reviewed as follows.

In space environments, the most common aerospace equipment includes solar arrays and deployable antennas, which are all realized by large-span deployable aerospace mechanisms. The difference is that the deployable aerospace mechanisms for solar arrays are usually planar structures and the deployable aerospace mechanisms for deployable antennas are always curved structures. In this field, Yang explored a 2-mode reconfigurable origami Nojima antenna for solar arrays [5]. Sun proposed a deployable ring mechanism using a 3-revolute-1 prismatic mechanism [9]. Han developed a scissors double-ring truss deployable mechanism, which has a good stiffness performance when the antenna has a large diameter [10]. Besides, the deployable aerospace mechanisms for space robotic grasper are also a hot study direction. More and more space debris seriously threaten the spacecraft in service and thus non-cooperative object grasping is a problem that human beings have to face. In this field, Gao developed a series of deployable robotic grasper for unknown objects in space, and the feasibility is verified by experiments [11–16]. Qiao proposed a spatial grasping mechanism based on the parallelogram mechanism with good stiffness performance [17]. Furthermore, with the increasing complexity of aerospace missions, the traditional deployable aerospace mechanisms have made it difficult to complete tasks due to their sole working mode and limited workspace. The reconfigurable mechanism for such a problem is a good selection and has been one of the emerging areas in mechanism science and robotics in the past decade, known as the metamorphic mechanism, or multiple operation modes mechanisms. Those reconfigurable mechanisms are rarely used in the design of deployable aerospace mechanisms [18] [19]. In addition to the above applications, the space station is a hot development direction, which provides the possibility for the application of space crawling robots due to various extravehicular activities. This greatly reduces the risk of human extravehicular activities and is of great research significance. The most representative in this field is the Space Station Remote Manipulator (SSRMS) [20, 21].

Compared with the gravity environment, the construction of the deployable aerospace mechanism in a low-gravity or no-gravity environment is quite difficult. More importantly, the development of deployable aerospace mechanisms can cost hundreds of millions of dollars. If it cannot be fully utilized, these large investments are already exposed to high technology and management risks. Therefore, it is necessary to construct deployable aerospace mechanisms with novel designs and a large number of mechanism modes, which can realize different aerospace functions by different working modes without influencing other performances such as deploy/fold ratio and stiffness performance. Based on the above analysis, this paper presents a multi-mode deployable aerospace mechanism, which is made up of six metamorphic kinematic chains, a double-mode base mechanism, and self-locking and unlocking mechanisms. The parallel structure is adopted by the aerospace mechanism to have higher grasping stiffness. The modular design is applied to make the deployable aerospace mechanism have good expansibility. The scissor-shaped mechanism is used to make the aerospace mechanism have a compact folded volume and large workspace. The double-mode base mechanism is designed to improve the comprehensive performance of the mechanism such as total mass and workspace. Through special structural design and assembly methods, the aerospace mechanism can form many different motion modes, which are suitable for various space missions.

The remainder of the paper is arranged as follows: Sect. 2 introduces the mechanism design, Sect. 3 demonstrates the detailed motion process of the aerospace mechanism, Sect. 4 analyzes the potential applications and completes the relevant simulation, and Sect. 5 makes a conclusion.

2 Mechanism Design of the Aerospace Mechanism

In this section, the detailed mechanical design of the aerospace mechanism is performed including the double-mode base mechanism, the self-locking and unlocking mechanism, and the metamorphic kinematic chain. Furthermore, the assembly method of the aerospace mechanism is also conducted, by which the whole aerospace mechanism can be given. The specific contents are as follows.

2.1 Design of the Metamorphic Kinematic Chain

The aerospace mechanism contains six metamorphic kinematic chains and each metamorphic kinematic chain is made up of five metamorphic basic modules, as shown in Fig. 1, where specific mechanism design, connecting method, and metamorphic motion analysis of the basic module is as mentioned in reference [12, 13], as shown in Fig. 1(a) and (b).

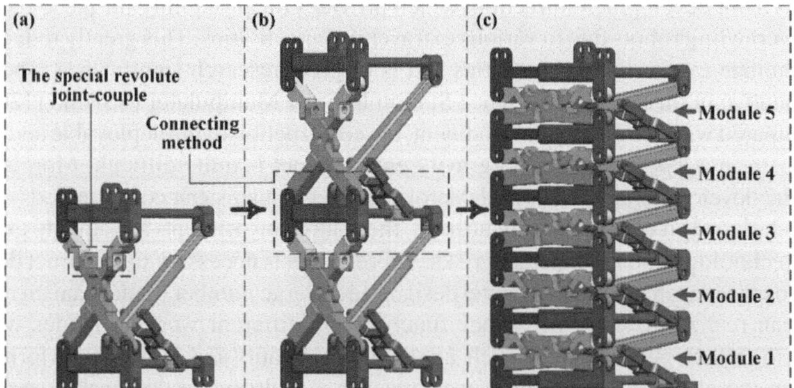

Fig. 1. Mechanism design of the metamorphic kinematic chain: (a) the metamorphic basic module; (b) the connecting method of the two basic modules; (c) the metamorphic kinematic chain with five basic modules.

Compared with the traditional serial-parallel mechanisms, the metamorphic kinematic chain has the following advantages. Firstly, a higher stiffness is ensured due to the multi-loop truss-shaped structure. Besides, the modular design is introduced to make the metamorphic kinematic chain have good expansibility, which can adjust the number of basic modules according to the task requirements. The number of basic modules can be expanded infinitely in theory, but it is a result of comprehensive consideration. Furthermore, the scissor-shaped mechanism is adapted to make the aerospace mechanism have a small folded configuration and a large deployed configuration. In addition, a special revolute joint couple is used in the scissor-shaped mechanism for mobility bifurcation, which changes its mobility from the deployment motion to the bending motion and simplifies the driving system. Finally, due to the metamorphic basic module, the metamorphic kinematic chain is a multi-metamorphic mechanism, as shown in Fig. 1(c).

2.2 Design of the Double-Mode Base Mechanism

To realize the multiple kinematic chains and the multi-mode of the aerospace mechanism, a double-mode umbrella-shaped base mechanism is designed as shown in Fig. 2. Compared with the general umbrella-shaped base mechanism, four 2R2SP (S represents the spherical joint, P represents the prismatic joint, R represents the revolute joint) limbs are added. This design makes the base mechanism have two motion modes including hexagonal mode and rectangular mode as shown in Fig. 2(d) and (e), and the movement process between the two modes is controllable. At the same time, each 2R2SP limb only introduces one degree of freedom, which is very important for the lightweight of the aerospace mechanism. Overall, it realizes the 5-DOF control of the base mechanism. Four auxiliary limbs and two main limbs together form a six-limb base mechanism with double-mode characteristics, and the folded configuration is shown in Fig. 2(b).

The specific connecting methods of links are as follows. As shown in Fig. 2(c), in two main limbs of the base mechanism, link 3 is connected with link 1 and link 7 through the revolute joints (R_3, R_2), link 8 is connected with link 7 and link 1 through the revolute joint (R_1) and prismatic joint (P_1). Revolute joints (R_1, R_2, R_3) and prismatic joint (P_1) form a planar one-degree-of-freedom 3R1P mechanism, so only one actuator is needed to control the two main limbs of the base mechanism. In four auxiliary limbs of the base mechanism, link 1 is connected with link 2 through the revolute joint (R_4), link 6 is connected with link 8 and link 5 by the spherical joint (S_1) and prismatic joint (P_2), link 4 is connected with link 5 and link 2 through the spherical joint (S_2) and revolute joint (R_5). Where the revolute joints (R_4, R_5), the spherical joints (S_1, S_2), and the prismatic joint (P_2) form a spatial 2-degree-of-freedoms 2R2SP mechanism, in which one degree of freedom is the same as the main limb used to adjust bending angle and another degree-of-freedom is used to transform the motion mode of the base mechanism. In this way, the double-mode umbrella-shaped base mechanism can be assembled, which will be an important basis for the multi-mode operation of the aerospace mechanism. The driving process of the base mechanism is shown in Fig. 2(c), the two 3R1P main limbs are driven by the prismatic joint (P_1), and the 2R2SP auxiliary limbs can be driven by the prismatic joints (P_1, P_2). Indeed, the 2R2SP auxiliary limb only adds one degree of freedom compared with the 3R1P main limb, thus, the prismatic joint (P_2), the revolute joints (R_4, R_5), and the spherical joints (S_1, S_2) can also be used as the driving joint except for the prismatic joint (P_1). However, the driving difficulty of the spherical joint is relatively high. If the revolute joint (R_4) or the revolute joint (R_5) serves as the driving joint, it is more difficult to install the actuators. In contrast, the prismatic joint (P_2) is the best choice. by the prismatic joints (P_1, P_2), the 2R2SP auxiliary limb can be effectively driven.

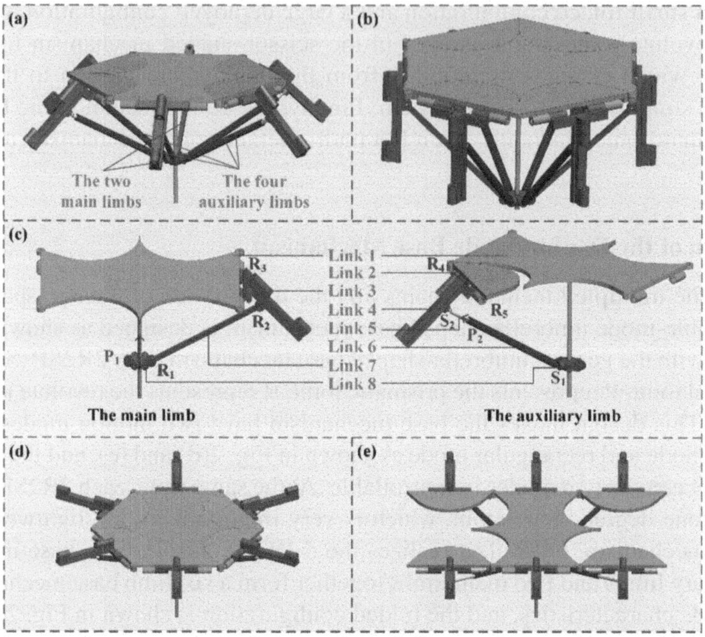

Fig. 2. Mechanism design of the double-mode base mechanism: (a) the double-mode base mechanism; (b) the folded configuration of the base mechanism; (c) the design of the moving limbs; (d) the motion mode 1 of the base mechanism; (e) the motion mode 2 of the base mechanism.

2.3 Design of the Self-locking and Unlocking Mechanism

To realize the spatial reconfiguration, a self-locking and unlocking mechanism is designed as shown in Fig. 3(a), the self-locking and unlocking mechanism is firstly assembled to the end of the metamorphic kinematic chain to realize the rapid self-locking, and then a locking and unlocking mechanism is assembled between the metamorphic kinematic chain and the base mechanism to realize the rapid unlocking. Only in this way, the control of the self-locking and unlocking process is active and cannot interfere with other movements. This design realizes the reconfiguration of the aerospace mechanism from six metamorphic kinematic chains to three metamorphic kinematic chains, it is equivalent to realizing the expansion of the workspace.

Before introducing the self-locking and unlocking process, the specific connecting method is shown in Fig. 3(b). The self-locking and unlocking mechanism is composed of two identical parts including part A and part B. In part A, link 3 is connected with link 1, link 4, and link 6 through the prismatic joints (P_3, P_4, P_5), and link 3 is connected with link 2, link 5, and link 7 through the revolute joints (R_6, R_7, R_8). The self-locking and unlocking process is shown in Fig. 3(b), when part A and part B are gradually approaching, corresponding link 2, link 5, and link 7 of part A and part B intermesh with each other, then corresponding link 1, link 4, and link 6 of part A and part B perform locking when the intermeshing reaches the maximum value, the process of which we call self-locking. When the unlocking movement needs to be performed, corresponding link 1, link 4, and link 6 of part A and part B first unlock, and then corresponding link 2, link 5, and link 7 of part A and part B are gradually far away from each other, the process of which we call unlocking. The self-locking and unlocking mechanism in this manuscript is actually a single-mobility mechanism, and thus an actuator is needed to control the motion in engineering.

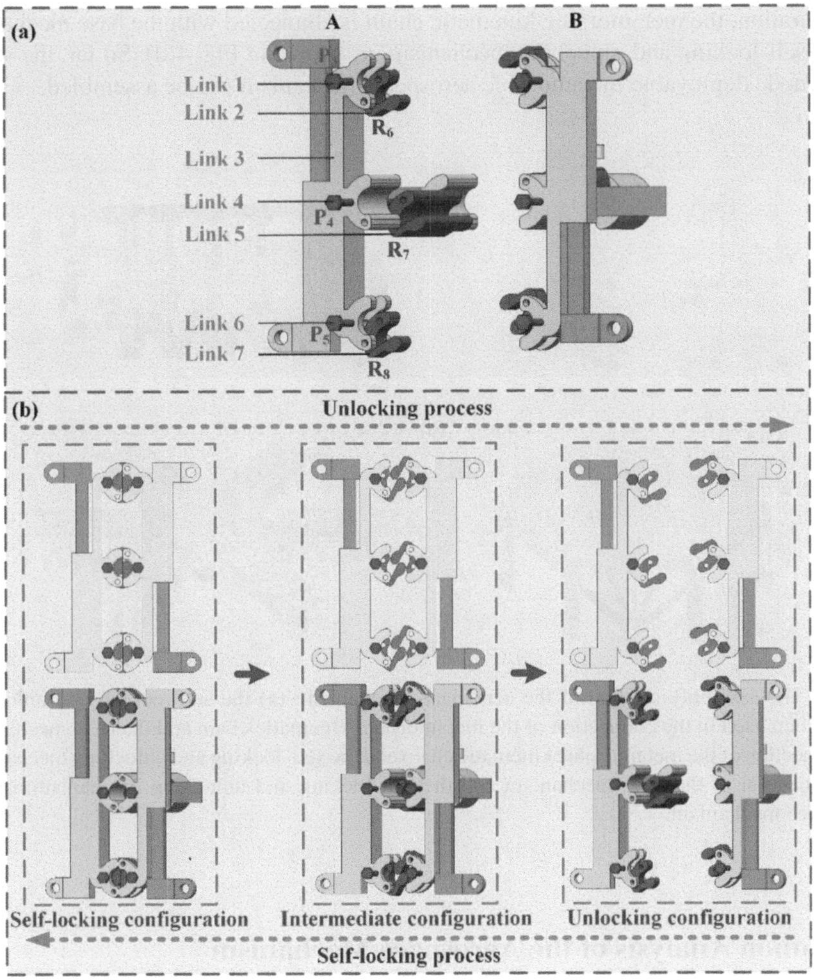

Fig. 3. Mechanism design of the self-locking and unlocking mechanism: (a) mechanism composition of the self-locking and unlocking mechanism; (b) the self-locking and unlocking process.

2.4 Assembly of the Aerospace Mechanism

To realize the crawling function, the aerospace mechanism cleverly solves this problem by designing the connection mode between the base mechanism and the self-locking and unlocking mechanism, that is, adding a revolute joint (R_{12}) between the base mechanism and the locking mechanism as shown in Fig. 4(a) and (c), which is mainly used for the forward and backward movement of each metamorphic kinematic chain, the lifting and falling of each metamorphic kinematic chain can be performed.

The connection of the metamorphic kinematic chain and the self-locking and unlocking mechanism is as shown in Fig. 4(b), where link 12 is connected with link 14 by revolute joint (R_9), link 11 is connected with link 13 by revolute joints (R_{10}, R_{11}), link 15 is rigidly connected with link 16. When the aerospace mechanism is in the folded configuration, the metamorphic kinematic chain is connected with the base mechanism by the self-locking and unlocking mechanism, as shown in Fig. 4(d). So far, the whole multi-mode deployable metamorphic aerospace mechanism can be assembled.

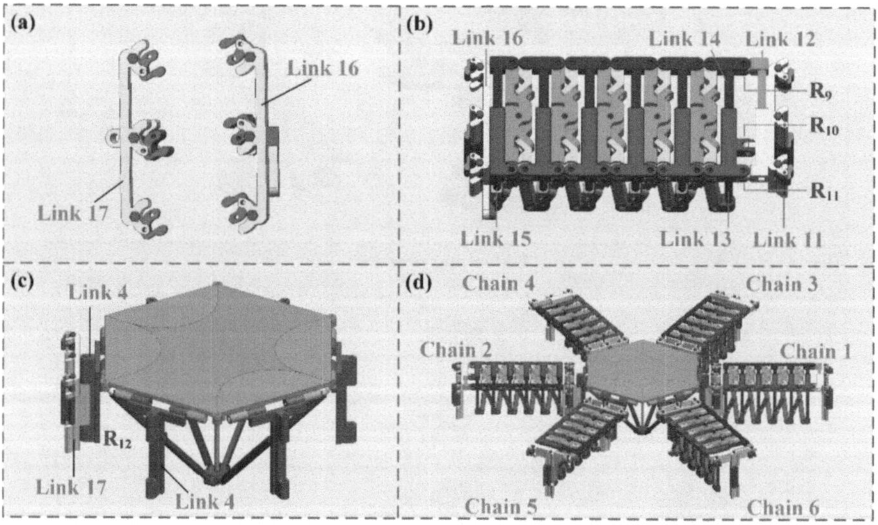

Fig. 4. The assembly method of the aerospace mechanism: (a) the self-locking and unlocking mechanism used in the connection of the metamorphic kinematic chain and the base mechanism; (b) connection of the metamorphic kinematic chain and the self-locking and unlocking mechanism; (c) connection of the base mechanism and the self-locking and unlocking mechanism; (d) the aerospace mechanism.

3 Motion Analysis of the Aerospace Mechanism

To further study the thermal-structural deformation of the robotic grasper, the finite element simulation model also needs to be established based on theoretical modeling. Here, finite element analysis software is applied to the calculation and the automatic meshing method with regular tetrahedra has been used. By this method, the deployable metamorphic basic module, the single-mobility umbrella-shaped palmar mechanism, and the robotic grasper in different configurations can be given as shown in Fig. 2. As the number of units increases, the accuracy of the analysis will gradually increase, but the computational workload will also increase rapidly, so which is a result of the comprehensive consideration. In practical applications, it is advisable to minimize the number of unit divisions while achieving analysis accuracy.

The aerospace mechanism is in folded configuration during the transportation and storage, as shown in Fig. 5(a), we call the folded configuration of the aerospace mechanism motion mode 1. In this case, the aerospace mechanism has the minimum volume, which is of great significance for aerospace equipment. The motion of the basic module is composed of the deployment motion and the bending motion as mentioned in reference [12, 13], and the deployment motion must be fully performed before the bending motion can be executed. When the aerospace mechanism enters the predetermined orbit, the six metamorphic kinematic chains conduct deployment motion while other joints remain stationary. As the six metamorphic kinematic chains are deployed to the maximum height, the whole aerospace mechanism forms a ring-shaped planar structure, which we call motion mode 2 of the aerospace mechanism, as shown in Fig. 5(b).

When the driving joint of each basic module on the six metamorphic kinematic chains drives further, the six metamorphic kinematic chains will begin to bend due to metamorphic motion. In this case, the six metamorphic kinematic chains and the base mechanism of the aerospace mechanism form a spherical surface shaped together, we call that motion mode 3 of the aerospace mechanism, as shown in Fig. 5(c). Motion mode 3 of the aerospace mechanism consists of spherical shapes with several different curvatures, which is of great significance for related applications. Besides, when the six metamorphic kinematic chains are bent to a certain extent, the base mechanism starts to move, and an enveloping grasp configuration can be formed in this case, as shown in Fig. 5(d), which we call motion mode 4 of the aerospace mechanism. From Fig. 5(d), one can see that multiple possible contact points can be formed between the aerospace and objects, which has important research value for space non-cooperative objects with different sizes and shapes. Furthermore, the base mechanism of the aerospace mechanism can transfer from mode 1 to mode 2, the aerospace mechanism in this case can form another grasping configuration, which we call motion mode 5 of the aerospace mechanism, as shown in Fig. 5(e). Motion mode 5 is suitable for grasping prism-shaped and cylinder objects. Combining the advantages of motion mode 4 and motion mode 5, one can see that the aerospace mechanism has very excellent shape adaptability, which contributes to the cost of space on-orbit maintenance. In addition, the main actuator of the base mechanism returns to the folded configuration, the six metamorphic kinematic chains and the base mechanism of the deployable mechanism, in this case, can form a cylindrical surface shaped together, we call motion mode 6 of the aerospace mechanism, as shown in Fig. 5(f). This motion mode has similar characteristics to motion mode 3, and they will also be mainly used for the same type of aerospace equipment. As the basic modules of the six metamorphic kinematic chains return deployed configuration, the aerospace mechanism can form a planar rectangular structure, which we call motion mode 7 of the aerospace mechanism, as shown in Fig. 5(g). This motion mode has similar

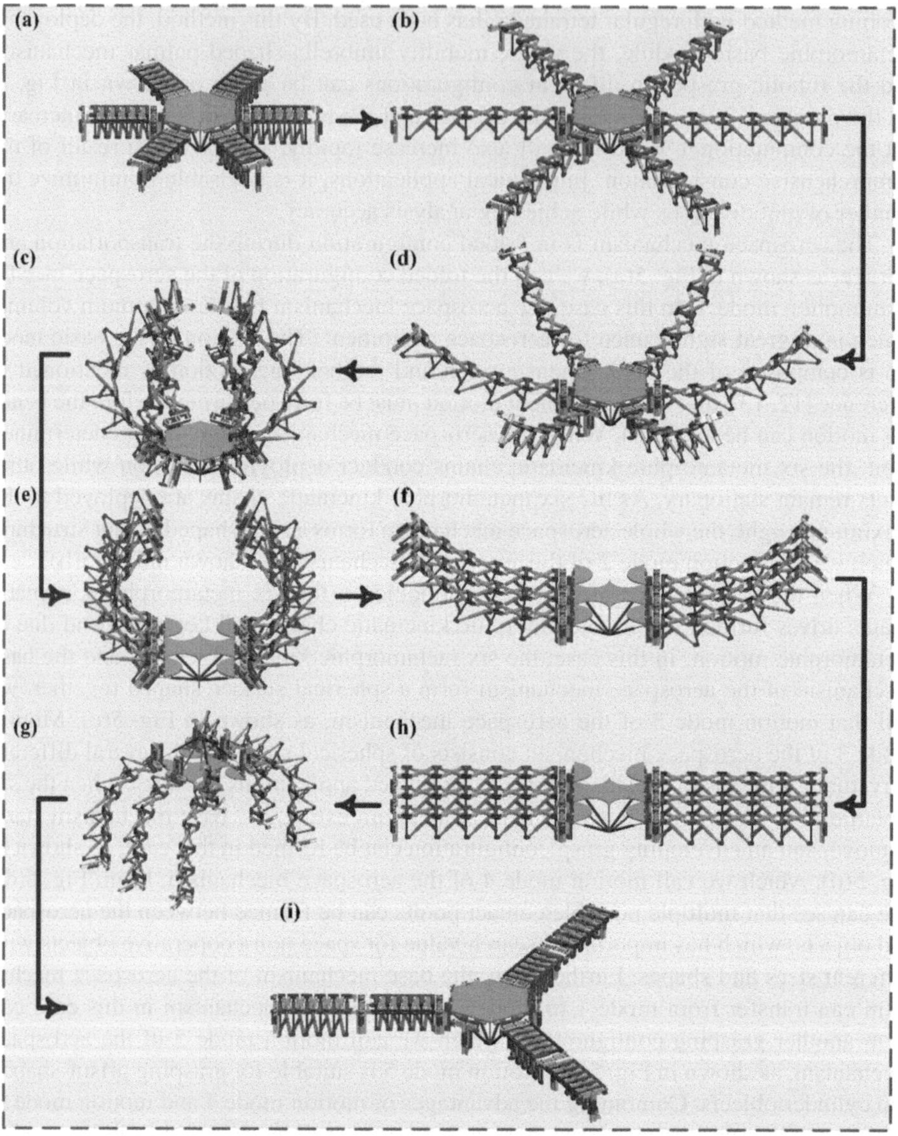

Fig. 5. Different motion modes of the aerospace mechanism: (a) motion mode 1; (b) motion mode 2; (c) motion mode 3; (d) motion mode 4; (e) motion mode 5; (f) motion mode 6; (g) motion mode 7; (h) motion mode 8; (i) motion mode 9.

characteristics to motion mode 2, they all belong to planar large-scale two-dimensional deployable structures.

To further expand the functions of the aerospace mechanism, the crawl mode is well-designed, as shown in Fig. 5(h). Where the six metamorphic kinematic chains of the aerospace mechanism are fully deployed and then bent to 90 degrees. The revolute joint (R_{12}) of each chain can be used to drive the six metamorphic kinematic chains to move. By designing the movement gait of each metamorphic kinematic chain, the aerospace mechanism can realize crawling motion. Essentially, the six metamorphic kinematic chains are equivalent to the feet of the crawling robotic and the height can be easily adjusted in this case. We call this configuration motion mode 8 of the aerospace mechanism. Finally, as the ends of fingers in relative positions are close to each other, the two metamorphic kinematic chains can be connected by the self-locking and unlocking mechanism, then the root of the metamorphic kinematic chain can be disconnected from the base mechanism by the self-locking and unlocking mechanism, such process is shown in Fig. 6. In this way, the six metamorphic kinematic chains can be reconfigured into three metamorphic kinematic chains, and thus the aerospace mechanism has a larger-scale workspace, which we call motion mode 9 of the aerospace mechanism, as shown in Fig. 5(i).

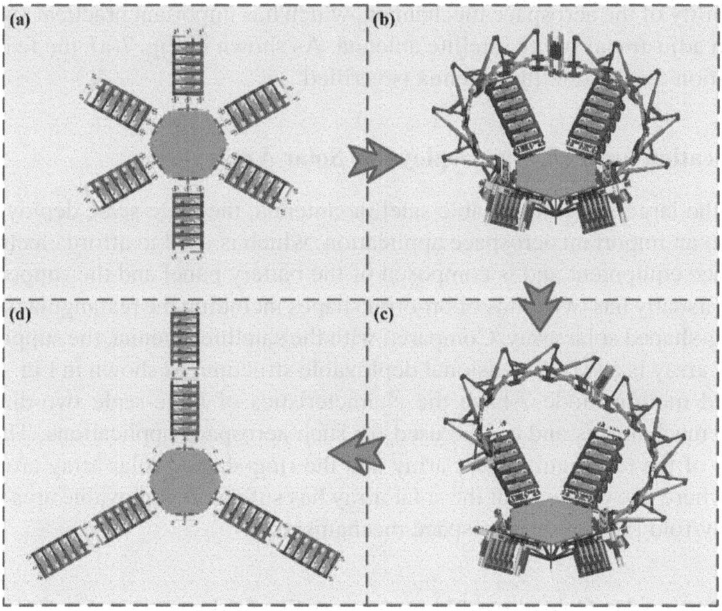

Fig. 6. Reconfigurable process of the aerospace mechanism: (a) the six metamorphic kinematic chains mode; (b) self-locking of corresponding two metamorphic kinematic chains; (c) unlocking of corresponding metamorphic kinematic chain and the base mechanism; (d) the three metamorphic kinematic chains mode.

4 Key Potential Applications and Simulation of the Aerospace Mechanism

Large-scale deployable aerospace mechanisms with multiple functions are one of the main research directions in the future, which can effectively improve economic benefits and reduce maintenance costs. This section will analyze the key potential applications based on different motion modes of the aerospace mechanism, and the corresponding simulations are conducted to verify the feasibility. The specific contents are as follows.

4.1 Application for the Large Deployable Satellite Antenna

The large-span deployable satellite antenna is usually composed of the radiator, the reflector, and the antenna support rod system. Due to the requirements of transportation and storage, the antenna support rod system is always replaced by a large-span deployable mechanism and is used to maintain the stiffness and accuracy of the reflecting surface of the satellite antenna. Up to now, there are mainly two kinds of satellite antennas, one is the spherical reflector antenna, and the other is the cylindrical reflector antenna, and thus the corresponding antenna support rod system needs to be provided. Here, as mentioned before, motion mode 3 and motion mode 6 can be suitable for such challenging aerospace applications. Furthermore, the changeable curvature radius further enhances the adaptability of the aerospace mechanism, which has important practical significance for the gain adjustment of the satellite antenna. As shown in Fig. 7(a), the feasibility of the application for the satellite antenna is verified.

4.2 Application for the Large Deployable Solar Array

Similar to the large-scale deployable satellite antenna, the large-scale deployable solar array is also an important aerospace application, which is used to afford electric energy for aerospace equipment and is composed of the battery panel and the support system. Solar array usually has two kinds of on-orbit shapes including the rectangular solar array and the ring-shaped solar array. Compared with the satellite antenna, the support system of the solar array is a two-dimensional deployable structure, as shown in Fig. 5. Motion mode 2 and motion mode 7 have the characteristics of large-scale two-dimensional deployable mechanisms and can be used for such aerospace applications. The simulation results of the rectangular solar array and the ring-shaped solar array are shown in Fig. 7(b), where one can see that the solar array has sufficient deployable area due to the good deploy/fold ratio of the aerospace mechanism.

4.3 Application for Grasping of Non-cooperative Objects

As more and more spacecraft equipment enter space, the space environment is thus becoming increasingly crowded, at the same time, a large amount of space debris is formed due to the retirement or damage of that aerospace equipment, which will undoubtedly seriously threaten the normal operation of spacecraft equipment. Therefore, on-orbit maintenance and grasp of space objects have become a hot study topic and more and more researchers have also conducted relevant research on this field. However, due to the different shapes, sizes, and qualities of these non-cooperative objects, space robotic graspers need to have excellent grasping adaptability. In this regard, motion mode 4 and motion mode 5 of the aerospace mechanism perfectly solve this problem, as shown in Fig. 7(c), which shows good shape adaptability. The grasping characteristics of the aerospace mechanism are similar to the robotic grasper in the references [14].

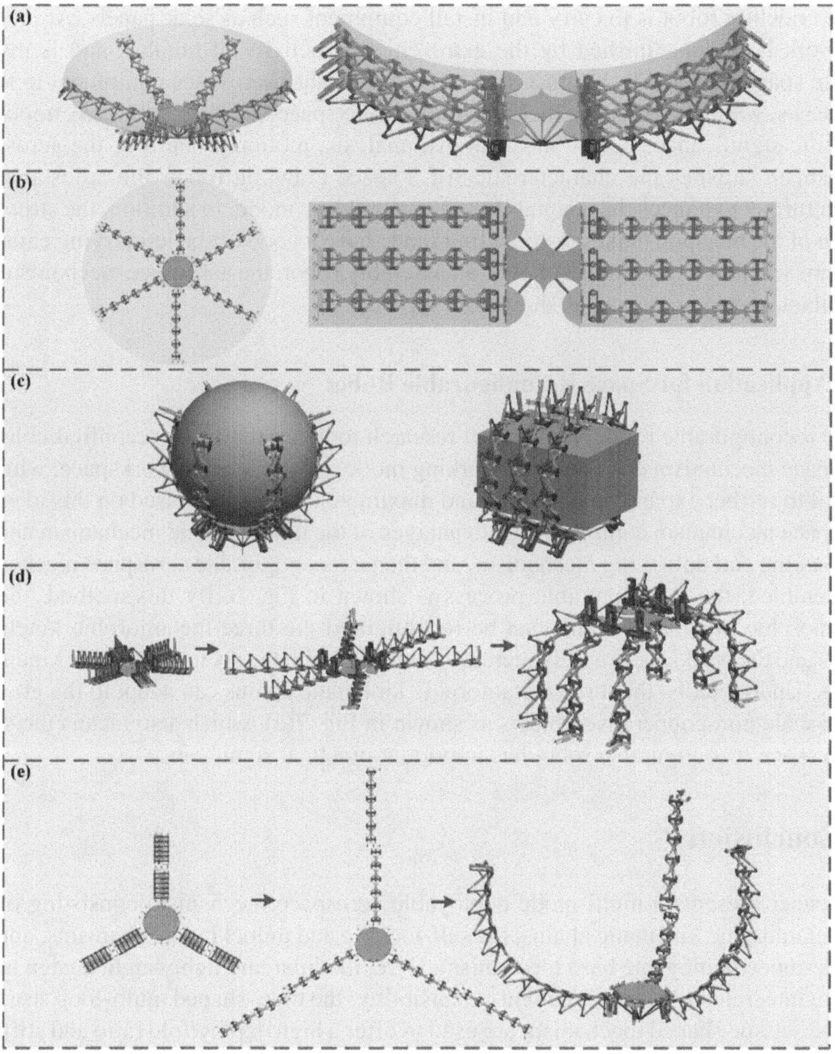

Fig. 7. Key potential applications of the aerospace mechanism: (a) supporting mechanism for the large-scale deployable satellite antenna; (b) supporting mechanism for the large-scale solar array; (c) space robotic grasper for the non-cooperative objects; (d) space crawling robot; (e) space reconfigurable robot.

4.4 Application for Space Crawling Robot

To solve the problem of energy supply for aerospace equipment, the concept of the space base station has been proposed in recent years, and the main purpose is to provide a space platform. When the space equipment with insufficient energy needs to be replenished, the space equipment will be placed on the space base station through the mechanical arm, and then maintenance will be performed by the space crawling robot. The main function of the crawling robot is to carry and install equipment such as solar panels. At present, this work is mainly finished by the extravehicular activity of humans and is mainly used in space stations. In contrast, it is difficult for other aerospace equipment to finish such tasks, which also proves that the study of the space-crawling robot has important scientific significance. Based on the above analysis, motion mode 8 of the aerospace mechanism satisfies the characteristics of a space crawling robot, the adjustable leg length further enhances the adaptability of the crawling mode. In addition, the structural design of the hexapod makes the crawling mode have a good obstacle-carrying capacity. In short, whether as a loading robot or an assembly robot, the aerospace mechanism can meet the task requirements, as shown in Fig. 7(d).

4.5 Application for Space Reconfigurable Robot

Space reconfigurable robot is also a hot research topic currently, by reconfigurable, the aerospace mechanism can adjust its working mode and change the workspace, which is helpful to further expand its functions and maximize its benefits. Based on this idea, the aerospace mechanism combines the advantages of the metamorphic mechanism and the self-locking and unlocking mechanism, and then a reconfigurable aerospace mechanism is assembled, the reconfigurable process is shown in Fig. 6. By this method, the six metamorphic kinematic chains can be reconfigured the three metamorphic kinematic chains and the workspace rapidly increase compared with the six metamorphic kinematic chains. Undoubtedly, the three metamorphic kinematic chains can adapt to the grasp of larger-scale non-cooperative objects as shown in Fig. 7(e), which also means the study of the space reconfigurable robot has important practical significance.

5 Conclusion

This paper presents a multi-mode deployable aerospace mechanism consisting of the six metamorphic kinematic chains, the self-locking and unlocking mechanisms, and the double-mode deployable base mechanism. Here, modular and lightweight design methods are integrated to obtain excellent expansibility; the truss-shaped multi-loop structure and the scissor-shaped mechanism are used to offer a high deploy/fold ratio and stiffness performance; the skillful metamorphic method further simplifies the driving system. By unique structural design and assembly methods, the aerospace mechanism can realize many different motion modes, which can be used for various space applications including space robotic grasper, solar array, deployable satellite antenna, space reconfigurable robot, and space crawling robot. Finally, simulations of each potential application are conducted and the feasibility of the aerospace mechanism is verified.

Acknowledgment. Research supported by the STU Scientific Research Initiation Grant (SRIG) (Grant No. NTF23019), the Research Projects of Department of Education of Guangdong Province (Grant No. 2023KTSCX317), the Shenzhen Polytechnic University Research Fund (Grant No. 6023310005K), and the Provincial Natural Science Foundation of Hunan (Grant No. 2023JJ50099).

References

1. Ding, X.L., Yang, Y., Dai, J.S.: Design and kinematic analysis of a novel prism deployable mechanism. Mech. Mach. Theory **63**, 35–49 (2013)
2. Puig, L., Barton, A., Rando, N.: A review on large deployable structures for astrophysics missions. Acta Astronaut. **67**, 12–26 (2010)
3. Xu, K., Li, L., Bai, S.P., et al.: Design and analysis of a metamorphic mechanism cell for multistage orderly deployable/retractable mechanism. Mech. Mach. Theory **111**, 85–98 (2017)
4. Ramadoss, V., Zlatanov, D., Ding, X.L., et al.: Design, construction, and control of curves and surfaces via deployable mechanisms. J. Mech. Des-T. ASME **11**(6), 061008 (2019)
5. Yang, Y., Peng, Y., Pu, H.Y., et al.: Deployable parallel lower-mobility manipulators with scissor-like elements. Mech. Mach. Theory **135**, 226–250 (2019)
6. Zirbel, S.A., Lang, R.J., Thomson, M.W., et al.: Accommodating thickness in origami-based deployable arrays. J. Mech. Des-T. ASME **135**(11), 111005 (2013)
7. Natori, M.C., Sakamoto, H., Katsumata, N.: Conceptual model study using origami for membrane space structures-a perspective of origami-based engineering. Mech. Eng. Rev. **2**(1), 14–00368 (2014)
8. St-Onge, D., Sharf, I., Sagnieres, L., et al.: A deployable mechanism concept for the collection of small-to-medium-size space debris. Adv. Space Res. **61**, 1286–1297 (2017)
9. Sun, Z.H., Zhang, Y.Q., Yang, D.W.: Structural design, analysis, and experimental verification of an H-style deployable mechanism for large space-borne mesh antennas. Acta Astronaut. **178**, 481–498 (2020)
10. Han, B., Xu, Y.D., Yao, J.T., et al.: Design and analysis of a scissors double-ring truss deployable mechanism for space antennas. Aerosp. Sci. Technol. **93**, 105357 (2019)
11. Gao, C.Q., Kang, X., Lei, H., et al.: Design and analysis of a novel large-span two-fold deployable mechanism. Mech. Mach. Theory **186**, 105352 (2023)
12. Gao, C.Q., Huang, H.L., Li, Y., et al.: Design and analysis of a three-fingered deployable metamorphic robotic grasper. J. Mech. Des-T. ASME **144**(8), 083302 (2022)
13. Gao, C.Q., Huang, H.L., Li, B., et al.: Design of a truss-shaped deployable grasping mechanism using mobility bifurcation. Mech. Mach. Theory **139**, 346–358 (2019)
14. Gao, C.Q., Zhang, Y., Kang, X., et al.: Dynamic analysis of a three-fingered deployable metamorphic robotic grasper. Mech. Mach. Theory **180**, 105140 (2022)
15. Gao, C.Q., Wang, J.H., Yang, X.J., et al.: Design and analysis of a novel truss-shaped variable-stiffness deployable robotic grasper. IEEE Access **8**, 112944–112956 (2020)
16. Gao, C.Q., Zhang, Y., Xu, P., et al.: Envelope grasping planning of a three-fingered deployable metamorphic robotic grasper. In: Proceedings of the IEEE International Conference on Cyborg and Bionic Systems, Wuhan, Hubei, China, 24–26 March 2023
17. Qiao, S.L., Guo, H.W., Liu, R.Q.: Self-adaptive grasp process and equilibrium configuration analysis of a 3-DOF UACT robotic finger. Mech. Mach. Theory **133**, 250–266 (2018)
18. Dai, J.S., Jones, J.R.: Mobility in metamorphic mechanisms of foldable/erectable kinds. J. Mech. Des-T. ASME. **121**(3), 375–382 (1999)
19. Liu, Y., Yao, Y.A., Kong, X.W., et al.: Type synthesis of reconfigurable single-loop mechanisms based on planar rhombus mechanisms. Mech. Mach. Theory **181**(3), 105170 (2023)
20. She, Y., Xu, W.F., Su, H.J., et al.: Fault-tolerant analysis and control of SSRMS-type manipulators with single-joint failure. Acta Astronaut. **120**, 270–286 (2015)
21. Xu, W.F., She, Y., Xu, Y.S.: Analytical and semi-analytical inverse kinematics of SSRMS - type manipulators with single-joint locked failure. Acta Astronaut. **105**, 201–217 (2014)

Modified Gear Wolfrom Reducer Joint System for the Upper-Limb of Humanoid Robot

Zhiyuan Yang[1], Weichao Guo[2], Zihang Geng[1], and Xinjun Sheng[1,2](✉)

[1] State Key Laboratory of Mechanical System and Vibration, School of Mechanical Engineering, Shanghai Jiao Tong University, Shanghai 200240, China
xjsheng@sjtu.edu.cn

[2] Meta Robotics Institute, Shanghai Jiao Tong University, Shanghai 200240, China

Abstract. It is vital to improve the joint power density for the development of humanoid robots, especially for reducing the size of the anthropomorphic upper-limb joints. This paper presents a Wolfrom reducer scheme that utilizes the gear modification principle to achieve a more compact layout with fewer components. The Wolfrom reducer configuration is characterized by a wide range of reduction ratios, capable of achieving a maximum reduction ratio of approximately 1:500 within the same dimensions through different gear matching relationships. This allows a small rotor with relatively low torque to provide a large output torque. Additionally, this paper presents a specific design of a flat reducer demonstration prototype using this modified gear Wolfrom reducer scheme, combined with a small motor, to realize a dual-degree-of-freedom joint system suitable for humanoid robotic arms. Compared to traditional robotic joint systems, this system features a more compact structure that better fits the humanoid form, along with a hollow conduit for wiring, making it suitable for practical application environments such as the shoulder joints of humanoid robots.

Keywords: Wolfrom reducer · gear modification · robotic joint

1 Introduction

The robotics industry has garnered widespread attention in recent years, and joint actuators are the most critical mechanical components of robots. From technologically mature industrial robotic arms to humanoid robots still in the developmental stage, most robots primarily use serial systems. Serial robots require joint actuators with high precision, high torque, and high power density [1]. Joint actuators typically consist of a motor, reducer, encoder, and motor controller. Among these, the design and selection of the reducer are crucial determinants for the joint precision and torque performance of robotic arms.

In the modern robotics industry, collaborative robots and industrial robots typically use harmonic reducers and 2K-H-V planetary reducer systems. In contrast, heavy-duty robotic arms with high torque requirements primarily employ RV reducers and cycloidal reducer systems. When selecting a reducer, considerations often include motor rotor inertia, transmission ratio, and friction loss, with the ultimate goal of maximizing the

X. Lan et al. (Eds.): icira 2024, LNAI 15201, pp. 292–304, 2025.
https://doi.org/10.1007/978-981-96-0771-6_22

efficiency of the joint actuator [2]. Given that motors usually operate more efficiently at high speeds, joint drive system reducers typically adopt higher reduction ratios [3]. The 3K configuration, also known as the Wolfrom configuration, is a type of planetary reducer output form. Compared to ordinary planetary gears, it offers a higher reduction ratio but relatively lower efficiency [4]. The RE series reducers from ZF Friedrichshafen AG exemplify this configuration, which are designed for applications in industrial robotics. This configuration has garnered great attention for its suitability in compact joint systems with high reduction ratios [5, 6]. However, since it eliminates backlash only by increasing gear contact stress, it has been more commonly used in early robotic arm designs [7].

Humanoid robotic arms feature a coaxial design with three joints in both the shoulder and wrist joints, which is less common in existing industrial robots and collaborative robots. If traditional serial robotic arm design approaches are applied to this configuration, it can lead to unnatural shapes at the end of shoulder joint and the front of wrist joint. However, by selecting an appropriate transmission system and motor pairing, a serial robotic arm can also achieve a smooth joint appearance and good torque performance, albeit with some loss in joint output efficiency. The 3K configuration can achieve a larger reduction ratio within limited volume and mass, with a maximum reduction ratio of nearly 1:500 [2]. López-García *et al.* have also suggested that the 3K configuration is a suitable reducer system for robots interacting with humans [8]. Therefore, this paper proposes a 3K reducer configuration that combines modified and non-modified gear systems to achieve a high reduction ratio, low backlash, and low-cost reducer system. This system allows the design of a two-degree-of-freedom joint actuator in a small space by selecting an appropriate small motor rotor.

Song T.-G. *et al.* proposed a variable reduction ratio reducer scheme that can switch between the 3K configuration and the traditional two-stage planetary reducer configuration [9]. Crispel S. *et al.* presented a compact integrated design with an ultra-high reduction ratio. Although this design lacks a hollow through-hole, it is suitable for various applications such as robotic arm ends and small high reduction ratio needs [10]. Höhn B.-R. *et al.* proposed a 3K-PGT system without a planet carrier, which features lower meshing losses and simplifies the planet carrier component [11].

2 Working Principles and Mechanical Design

This section introduces the design and principles of the modified gear reducer. This scheme adopts the 3K configuration, with its transmission system illustrated in Fig. 1. To maintain consistency with the labels in the calculation section, the parts of the reducer in the schematic diagram are defined as z_0, z_1, z_2 and z_2'. The transmission system uses the sun gear z_0 as the input driving gear, which drives the planet gear z_1 through a planetary gear set. The transmission ratio between planet gear z_1 and the second-stage internal gear z_2 is different from that of the first-stage internal gear z_2', thereby driving the second-stage internal gear z_2 to output torque as the output shaft. The planet carrier C does not directly transmit torque externally, and it is only used to stabilize the relative position of the planet gears.

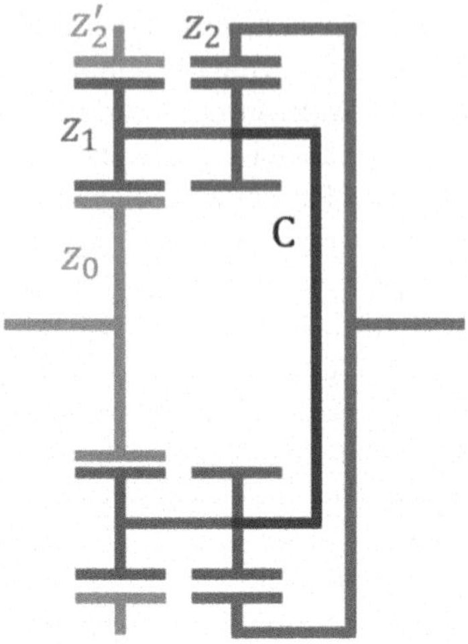

Fig. 1. Schematic diagram of the modified gear reducer.

2.1 Mechanical Design

There has been considerable research on the design methods of planetary reducers, but there is no consensus on the performance criteria for planetary reducers [12]. Additionally, the previous analysis methods typically focus only on basic performance metrics such as transmission efficiency and transmission ratio, with limited design analysis regarding to actual assembly, installation, and manufacturing. The proposed scheme primarily considers three aspects in its design approach: simplifying part complexity, reducing weight, and ensuring ease of assembly.

In the process of simplifying part complexity, it is crucial to minimize multiple clamping and positioning steps during part machining and to ensure that the working surfaces of key components, namely, the entire gear system and bearing-fixing-related parts, are machined in a single clamping whenever possible. For instance, as illustrated in Fig. 2, the working surface of the inner ring gear does not use conventional modules but is instead produced using wire EDM. The external assembly surface uses a loose fit. After the cross roller bearing in the housing and the internal gear of the output shaft are fixed, the inner ring gear is assembled along with the planetary gear and carrier. During the tightening of screws, the planetary gears are gradually rotated to minimize resistance and backlash caused by concentricity errors.

Simplifying complexity is also reflected in using gear modification instead of multistage planetary gears to achieve this configuration. In traditional 3K reducer designs, the planetary gears typically use two different modules or a scheme similar to the RE series reducers that involve tilting angles [13], employing two planetary gears as a set. This requires at least three or more parts for the planetary gears. However, using the internal gear modification scheme, the same effect can be achieved with just a single long spur gear.

Considering that this reducer is primarily intended for humanoid robots or similar mobile base robotic systems, weight reduction is essential. Aluminum is used for the

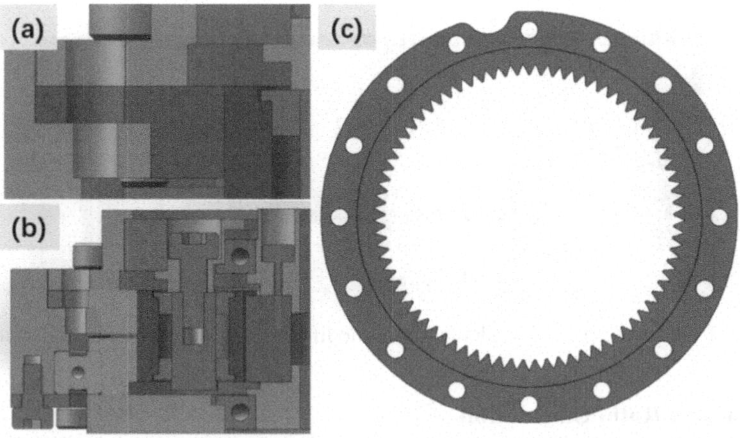

Fig. 2. Simplified part example: inner ring gear. (a) shows the installation details of the inner ring gear component assembled in the reducer base; (b) highlights the inner ring gear component and the inner ring gear portion at the output shaft end, which requires high coaxiality; (c) is the inner ring gear component.

housing and non-load-bearing parts to achieve lightweight construction, and aluminum components are also used for the low-load input shaft.

This design takes into account the need for repeated assembly and disassembly during actual testing to analyze experimental results. Therefore, most components are fixed with screws, while the cross roller bearing part uses an interference fit. Most shaft systems use an H7-h7 transition fit to allow the planetary system to float, balancing the load on each planetary gear as much as possible. These operations can improve system performance and longevity while reducing operational noise and vibration [13].

Given the significant impact of tangential errors in the positions of the planet carrier's shaft holes on the load distribution among the planetary gears, and the need for an even load distribution within the planetary gear system, a non-interference fit planet carrier is adopted [14, 15].

Overall, the design advantages of this scheme are twofold:

1) No need for multi-stage planetary gears: The processing difficulty and costs are significantly reduced. Manufacturing a set of modified internal gears is much easier than producing a dual-layer planetary gear with fixed phase angles. Especially during the laboratory testing phase, wire EDM can be used to process the internal gears, planetary gears, and sun gear.
2) Fewer required parts: The number of parts needed is reduced, and it allows for the quick substitution of similar reduction ratio schemes by replacing the modified gears. This offers high reusability and interchangeability during the early stages of joint system design. Compared to a standard 3K-PGT reducer, this scheme provides the same performance at a lower cost and offers more flexible reduction options.

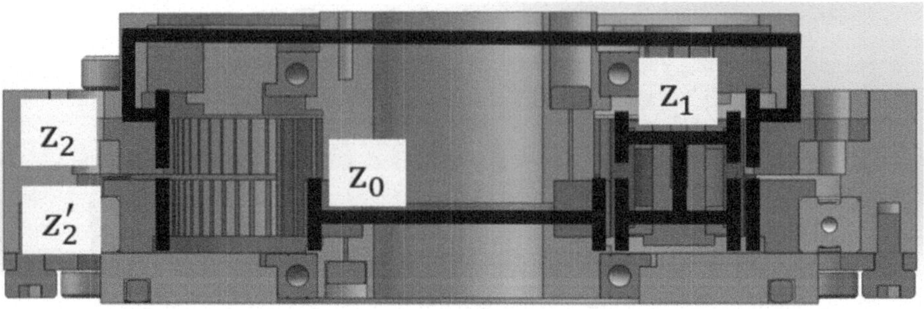

Fig. 3. Illustration for the calculation of modified gear planetary reduction ratio.

2.2 Reduction Ratio Calculation

As this scheme adopts a modified gear approach to achieve modified gear reduction, we define the non-modified internal gear and the modified internal gear by z_0 and z_2', respectively. Here, x' represents the reduction in the number of teeth after modification, which in this scheme is 3 teeth. According to mechanical design principles, internal gears typically do not have negative modification factors to ensure their strength meets requirements. This subsection will derive the mathematical relationships between the parameters and the reduction ratio of the reducer through calculations.

As shown in Fig. 3, the sun gear, planet gear, and internal gear of the reducer are respectively defined as z_0, z_1, z_2 and z_2'. It is evident that there is a relative tooth number relationship between the non-modified and modified internal gears:

$$z_2 - x' = z_2' \tag{1}$$

According to the motion relationship of the planetary gear system, we can deduce the relationship between the input speed ω_0 and the speed of the planet carrier ω_1:

$$\frac{z_0}{z_0 + z_2'} = \frac{\omega_1}{\omega_0} \tag{2}$$

On the other hand, let ω_x denote the speed of the internal gear relative to the base coordinate system on the output shaft. Then, in terms of the output shaft as the reference frame, the relationship between the input speed $\omega_{0'}$ and the speed of the planet carrier ω_1' with respect to the base coordinate system is:

$$\omega_1' + \omega_x = \omega_1 \tag{3}$$

$$\omega_0' + \omega_x = \omega_0 \tag{4}$$

Similarly, assuming the output shaft and the non-modified portion of the internal gear as the reference frame, we can deduce the relationship between the input speed ω_0' and the speed of the planet carrier ω_1':

$$\frac{z_0}{z_0 + z_2} = \frac{\omega_0'}{\omega_0'} \tag{5}$$

By rearranging the above equations, we can derive the relationship between the input and output speeds, which gives the reduction ratio of the reducer:

$$\frac{z_0 \cdot x'}{z_2(z_2' + z_0)} = \frac{\omega_x}{\omega_0} \tag{6}$$

2.3 Determination of Planetary Gear Modification Coefficient

In this scheme, it is necessary to adjust the modification coefficient of the modified gear internal gear to ensure that internal gears with concentric but different numbers of teeth can accurately mesh with the planetary gears simultaneously. On the other hand, it is also necessary to limit the tooth tip height to ensure that root cutting does not occur, as shown in Fig. 4.

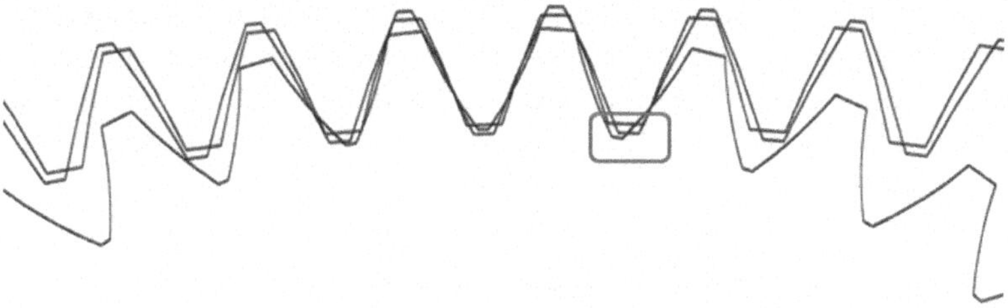

Fig. 4. Root cutting in modified gear planetary systems.

Through the calculation formula of involute spur gears, we can derive the relationship between the modification coefficient, the unmodified pressure angle a, and the modified pressure angle α':

$$x_\Sigma = (z_2' - z_1)\frac{inv(\alpha') - inv(\alpha)}{2\tan(\alpha)} = x_2 \tag{7}$$

Similarly, the center distance change coefficient also satisfies:

$$y = \frac{a' - a}{m} = \frac{z_2' - z_1}{2}\left(\frac{\cos(\alpha)}{\cos(\alpha')} - 1\right) \tag{8}$$

where the center distances before and after change are denoted as a and a' respectively:

$$a' = \frac{m}{2}(z_2' - z_1) \tag{9}$$

$$a = \frac{m}{2}(z_2 - z_1) \tag{10}$$

By rearranging the center distance relationship and considering the relationship between the number of teeth of each gear, we can determine α' as: (assuming the unmodified pressure angle is 20°)

$$\alpha' = \cos^{-1}\frac{\cos(\alpha)}{\frac{z_2' - z_2}{z_2 - z_1} + 1} \tag{11}$$

Substituting the result into Eq. (7), we can obtain the specific value of the modification coefficient x_Σ, providing a reference for the actual machining process.

3 Integration of Multi-Degree-of-Freedom Joints

Based on the mechanical design described above, we can obtain a scheme for a modified gear planetary reducer that can adjust the appropriate reduction ratio within fixed dimensions. Since it can generate relatively high reduction ratios, it allows for the use of high-power density motor rotors with smaller relative volumes and higher speeds to replace traditional joint actuators that require rotors matched to the diameter of the reducer.

Firstly, we introduce the production and implementation of the reducer. Fig. 5 shows two designs of modified gear planetary reducer systems. The first design offers a reduction ratio of 1:78, while the second design provides a reduction ratio of 1:133, suitable for different specific operating conditions. The first design is more compact in overall size, suitable for situations where there are strict requirements on joint diameter size. On the other hand, the second design emphasizes a flat design, suitable for compact multi-degree-of-freedom joint systems. In this section, we will mainly present a compact joint system integrated with two degrees of freedom.

Fig. 5. Two types of modified gear planetary reducer systems. (a) shows more compact design in overall size; (b) shows a flat design version.

In this scheme, we use M3508 rotors with a single-stage cylindrical gear transmission as the input for the modified gear planetary reducer. This setup results in a certain offset of the rotor's axis relative to the joint output shaft. On the other hand, we utilize RM08 magnetic encoders as the output shaft encoders for the joint. These encoders are characterized by their small module size and high precision. However, since these encoders are not hollow, for joints requiring hollow shafts, we employ a single-stage 1:1 transmission system as an intermediary. The specific arrangement is illustrated in Fig. 6.

Based on the mechanical design approach of this scheme, we also implemented a humanoid arm using this configuration, with the dual-degree-of-freedom joint serving as the shoulder joint, as shown in Fig. 7. This humanoid arm has basic robotic arm functions and can be remotely controlled via teleoperation equipment. It is evident that this joint system has clearly feasible application scenarios in practical use.

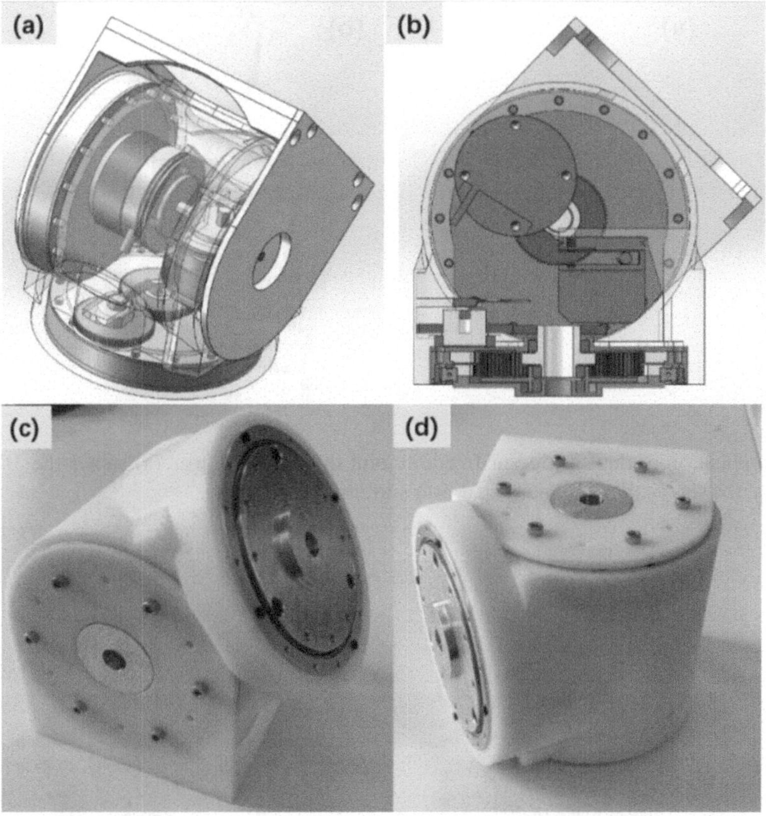

Fig. 6. Example of a dual-degree-of-freedom joint system: (a)shows the overall assembly diagram with the internal layout of the motor and encoder, (b) is a sectional view along the axis direction, (c) and (d) are actual images of the joint system.

Additionally, the modified gear Wolfrom reducer is practical for system testing and verification in joint systems with different reduction ratios. Taking the first scheme with a reduction ratio of 1:78 as an example, this reducer system has a sun gear with 40 teeth and planetary gears with 20 teeth. Depending on specific working conditions, the reduction ratio can be altered without changing the inner ring gear. For instance, in this scheme, the sun gear can be changed to 10 teeth and the planetary gears to 35 teeth. According to formula 6, the modified reduction ratio would be 1:232. This alteration involves minimal changes to the overall mechanism, making it suitable for repeated practical testing during the verification phase. The modifications before and after are shown in Fig. 8.

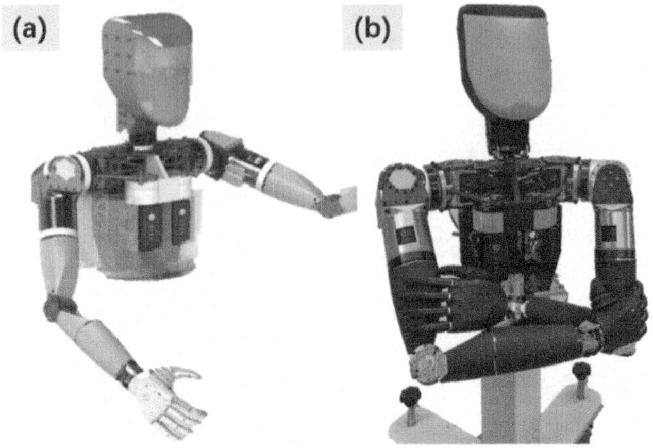

Fig. 7. Application of dual-degree-of-freedom joint in humanoid arm. (a) shows the 3D design illustration. (b) shows the humanoid dual-arm system.

Fig. 8. Comparison before and after the modification. (a) shows the reducer before modification, (b) shows the reducer after modification, (c) shows the sectional view of the axis before modification, and (d) shows the sectional view of the axis after modification.

4 Experiments and Results

For this reducer system, we utilize a traditional joint system testing platform. This platform is constructed with a hysteresis damper as a simulated load, torque sensors as data sources, and M3508 motor rotors as inputs for testing. The testing experimental platform is described in Table 1 and Fig. 9.

After actual testing, compared with the traditional Wolfrom reducer scheme [10], as shown in Table 2, it can be seen that the reducer system of this scheme has higher

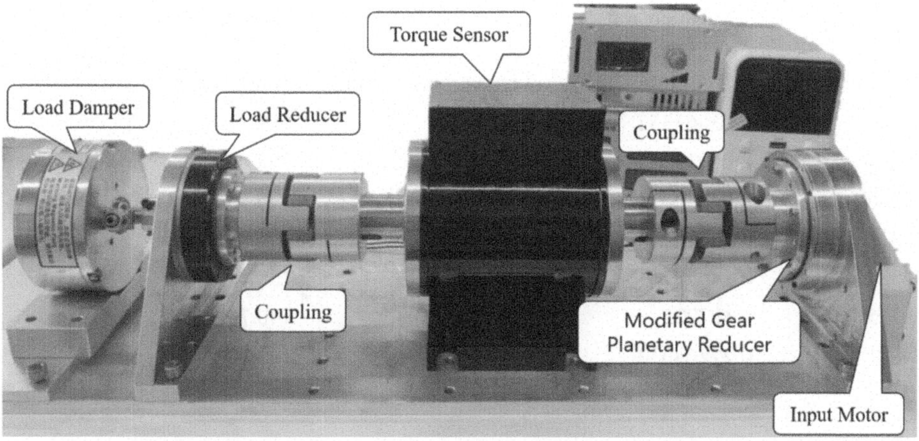

Fig. 9. Modified gear planetary reducer torque testing platform.

Table 1. Test platform selection

Parts	Type
Input Motor	M3508
Load Damper	Hysteresis Damper AHB-1M-L-A
Load Reducer	SHD17–100 Harmonic Reducer
Torque Sensor	JN-DN Dynamic Torque Sensor (0–100 Nm)

efficiency compared to the traditional Wolfrom system, and when matched with appropriate rotors, it can also provide higher torque. At the same time, its weight is limited to a relatively light range. Overall, it is a better performing scheme in the Wolfrom configuration (Table 3).

Table 2. Test result: compare with standard wolfrom reducer

Characteristic	Modified Gear Wolfrom	Standard Wolfrom [10]
Ratio	133.6	493.9
Efficiency	29.7%	25.8%
Output Torque	29.8 Nm	10.5 Nm
Input Torque	0.75 Nm	—
Weight	300 g	—

Additionally, we used the reducer torque testing platform to measure the input current and output torque. Based on the known information, we calculated the input torque

Table 3. Experimental results: relationship between efficiency and input torque

Input current	Input torque (Nm)	Output torque (Nm)	Torque ratio	Efficiency
0.141	0.03563352	9.2	259.31	0.575
0.234	0.05913648	11.4	193.02	0.428
0.296	0.07480512	14.7	196.23	0.435
0.425	0.107406	20.9	194.89	0.432
0.58	0.1465776	23.2	158.14	0.351
0.725	0.183222	25.8	140.70	0.312
0.881	0.22264632	29.8	133.85	0.297

corresponding to the input current and tested the output stall torque under different input conditions. By comparing the input-output torque ratio with the actual transmission ratio from the rotor to the output shaft, we determined the actual efficiency of the reducer. The experiments showed that the reducer had relatively high efficiency at lower input torques, and as the input torque increased, the efficiency tended to stabilize at a relatively consistent value. The results indicated that the reducer performed efficiently in low-load environments while also had a certain load-bearing capacity in high-load environments (Fig. 10).

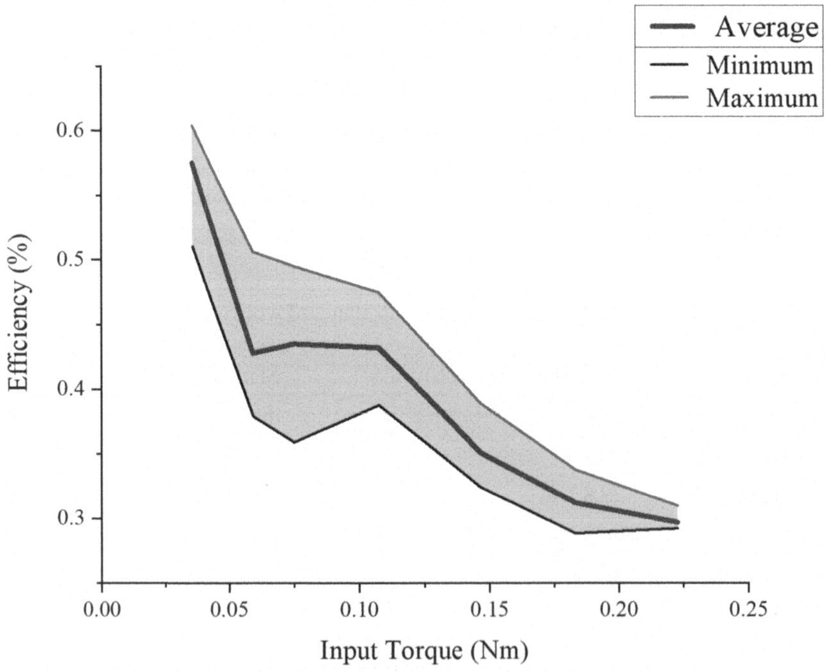

Fig. 10. The relationship between efficiency and input torque.

5 Conclusion

In this work, we introduced a novel implementation scheme for the Wolfrom reducer configuration. By utilizing the characteristic of variable tooth gears to adjust the pitch distance within a certain range, this configuration achieved higher efficiency, higher load, and lower theoretical part count compared to traditional approaches, making the structure more concise. We also confirmed geometric design issues such as tooth count and modification coefficient after confirming the reduction ratio. Furthermore, based on this design concept and configuration scheme, we specifically developed a compact two-degree-of-freedom joint system. The overall volume is controlled within a small range, providing a new approach to joint implementation in various mechanical arm devices with strict requirements on appearance and size. In practical applications, it can be used for local coupling of 2–3° of freedom such as shoulder joints and elbow joints in humanoid robotic arms, making the configuration more compact while being more operable in mechanism design and appearance design. In situations where mechanical efficiency is not high but there are strict requirements on the size of joint systems, the modified gear planetary reducer configuration presented in this article has high practical value.

Acknowledgement. This work is supported in part by the National Natural Science Foundation of China (Grant Nos. 91948302, 52175021, 52375021), in part by Natural Science Foundation of Shanghai (Grant No. 23ZR1429700).

References

1. Le, Q., et al.: Prototype Design and Efficiency Analysis of a Novel Robot Drive Based on 3K-H-V Topology. arXiv.Org, arXiv.org, 2022–10 (2022)
2. García, P.L., Crispel, S., Saerens, E., Verstraten, T., Lefeber, D.: Compact gearboxes for modern robotics: a review. Front. Robot. AI **7**, 103 (2020)
3. Rosenbauer, T.: Getriebe für Industrieroboter: Beurteilungskriterien. Kenndaten, Einsatzhinweise: Shaker (1995)
4. Crispel, S., et al.: Introducing compound planetary gears (C-PGTs): a compact way to achieve high gear ratios for wearable robots. In: International Symposium on Wearable Robotics (Pisa), pp. 485–489 (2018). https://doi.org/10.1007/978-3-030-01887-0_94
5. Kapelevich, A., AKGears, L.L.C.: High gear ratio epicyclic drives analysis. Ratio **3**, 10 (2013)
6. Arnaudov, K., Karaivanov, D.: Higher compound planetary gear trains. In: VDI International Conference on Gears, vol. 1904 (Munich: VDIBericht), pp. 327–344 (2005)
7. Schempf, H.: Comparative design, modeling, and control analysis of robotic transmissions (Ph.D. thesis). No. WHOI-90–43. Department of Mechanical Engineering, and Woods Hole Oceanographic Institute, Massachusetts Institute of Technology, Cambridge, MA, United States (1990). https://doi.org/10.1575/1912/5431
8. López-García, P., Crispel, S., Verstraten, T., Saerens, E., Vanderborght, B., Lefeber, D.: Wolfrom gearboxes for lightweight, human-centered robotics. In: Proceedings of the International Conference on Gears 2019 (Munich: VDI), pp. 753–764 (2019a)
9. Song, T.-G., Shin, Y.-H., Hong, S., Choi, H. C., Kim, J.-H., Park, H.-W.: DRPD, Dual reduction ratio planetary drive for articulated robot actuators. In: 2022 IEEE/RSJ International Conference on Intelligent Robots and Systems (IROS), pp. 443–450 (2022)

10. Crispel, S., et al.: A novel wolfrom-based gearbox for robotic actuators. IEEE/ASME Trans. Mechatron. **26**(4), 1980–1988 (2021)
11. Höhn, B.-R., Zhang, Y., Geitner, M., Otto, M.: A Wolfrom transmission without carrier. In: MATEC Web of Conferences, vol. 317, p. 1001 (2020)
12. Bodas, A., Kahraman, A.: Influence of carrier and gear manufacturingerrors on the static load sharing behavior of planetary gear sets. JSME Int. J. **47**(3), 908–915 (2004)
13. Looman, J.: Zahnradgetriebe (Gear Mechanisms). Springer-Verlag, Berlin (1996). https://doi.org/10.1007/978-3-540-89460-5
14. Singh, A.: Application of a system level model to study the planetary load sharing behavior. J. Mech. Des. **127**(3), 469–476 (2005)
15. Singh, A.: Epicyclic load sharing map development and validation. Mech. Mach. Theory **46**(5), 632–646 (2011)

Representation and Elimination of Multiple Joints Based on PF Graph

Dong Kaijie[1,2], Ren Zhouyi[1], Li Duanling[3,4](✉), Zhou Tianyu[1], and Zhang Jianhua[1]

[1] School of Mechanical Engineering, University of Science and Technology Beijing, Beijing 100083, China
[2] Innovation School, University of Science and Technology Beijing, Foshan 528300, China
[3] School of Automation, Beijing University of Posts and Telecommunications, Beijing 100086, China
liduanling_bupt@163.com
[4] College of Mechanical and Electrical Engineering, Shaanxi University of Science and Technology, Xi'an 710021, China

Abstract. The representation and elimination of kinematic chains (KCs) with multiple joints are crucial issues to be solved in mechanism research. First, the importance of mechanical innovative design and the limitations of existing methods are introduced, then the Yan's innovative design method is introduced, by comparing the shortcomings of traditional topological graphs in representing multiple joints, A modified graph—planar face graph (PF graph), is proposed. As a key concept, "face" has been put forward to represent the case that a single, specific relationship is incident with multiple incidents, and the concepts of adjacency and incidence matrices are defined, making the representation of multiple joints more accurate and easier for computer processing. Subsequently, a new method based on PF topology graphs and dendrograms is proposed to eliminate the multiple joints, which eliminates multiple joints by reducing constraints. Meanwhile, the generation of isomers in the elimination process and their naming rules are revealed. Furthermore, the generalization process of KCs containing multiple joints is discussed and the application of elimination of multiple joints in innovative mechanism design is illustrated by taking a typical SAR antenna deployable mechanism as an example. Finally, the innovativeness of the PF graph and its contribution to multiple joints elimination and mechanism generalization are summarized, the potential and value of this method in mechanical innovative design are demonstrated. It not only provides new theoretical support and practical tools for mechanical innovative design but also offers a new perspective and approach for research in related fields.

Keywords: Kinematic chains · Multiple joints · PF graph · generalization process · mechanical innovative design

1 Introductory

Mechanical innovative design methods play a pivotal role in achieving innovation in mechanical design. Currently, commonly used innovative design methods include brainstorming, analogy, bionic design, and the Theory of the Solution of Inventive Problems

X. Lan et al. (Eds.): ICIRA 2024, LNAI 15201, pp. 305–317, 2025.
https://doi.org/10.1007/978-981-96-0771-6_23

(TRIZ) [1–4]. However, most of these methods rely heavily on the rich experience and instant inspiration of designers. To address this limitation, Yan proposed an effective Yan's Creative Design Methodology based on mechanism synthesis theory [5]. This methodology starts with modifying existing mechanical devices and can systematically conceive all potential topological structures of mechanical devices. As shown in Fig. 1, the specific operation process of Yan's Creative Design Methodology is detailed.

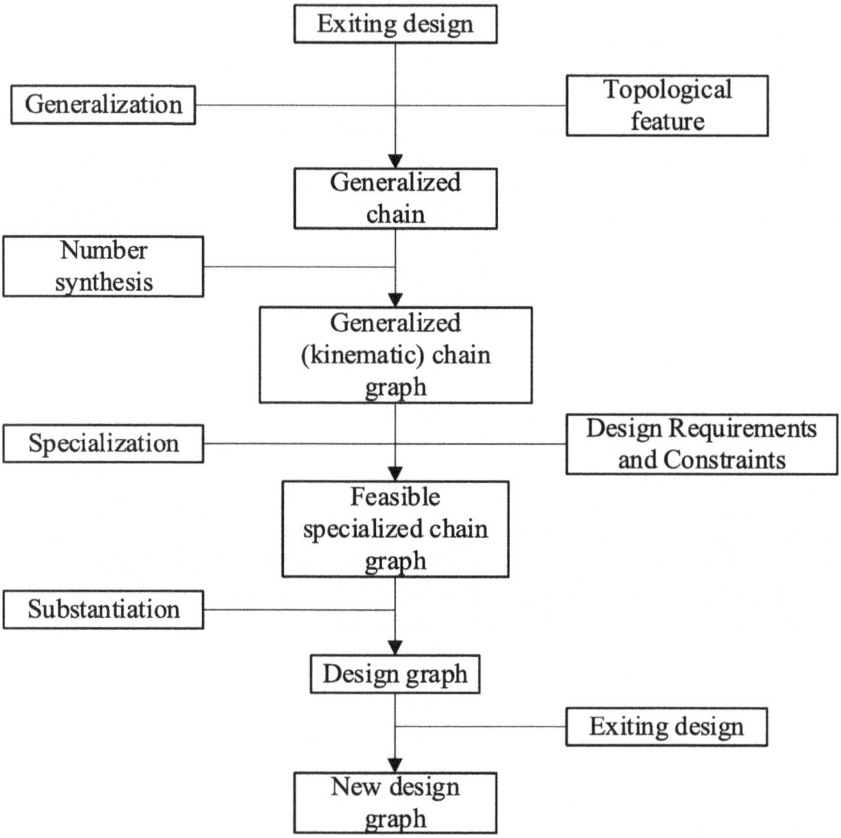

Fig. 1. Pleiades-1A satellite solar array [1]

The components of mechanical device are different, and one of the cores of Yan's Creative Design Methodology is to transform mechanical devices into generalized KCs, thereby the inherent combination mechanism of generalized mechanical devices is revealed. The generalized mechanical device is obtained by transforming the schematic diagram of a mechanical device through the application of generalization rules, while the generalized chain is obtained by removing fixed bars and eliminating multiple kinematic pairs from its corresponding generalized mechanical device. Thus, the elimination of multiple joints in the KCs is crucial for the transformation of the generalized chain.

Multiple joints are a special joint which connects two or more components simultaneously by a revolute pair at one location. Multiple joints are widely used in various complex mechanical devices to improve the maneuverability, stability, and load-bearing capacity of the devices. For generalized KCs containing only single joints, their topological representation is that transforming the KCs into a topological graph and then transforming it into a matrix for processing. However, when transforming a KC with multiple joints into a topological graph, the edges in the topological graphs can only represent the connection between two components, therefore the connection between three or more components in a multiple joint cannot be represented by a single edge, thus special processing of the multiple joints is required in the topological structure representation of the KCs. Existing methods, such as the bio-color topological graph [6, 7] or Pin component transformation method [8], either introduce one or more new elements to represent multiple joints, the topological graphs are complicated, or redefine the adjacency matrix, making it no longer a 0–1 matrix. These approaches are not conducive to complex computer calculations. Additionally, these topological models are relatively independent and lack a close connection with the topological model of single-joint KCs, which makes it inconvenient to apply mature single-joint KCs topology theories for systematic research [9].

To more effectively and conveniently represent multiple joints in KCs, a PF graph is proposed. Based on the PF graphs, the elimination of multiple joints is expounded to obtain the method of the generalized KCs. The specific structure of the paper is as follows: Sect. 2 the PF graphs and the representation of the KCs are introduced. Section 3 the method for elimination of the multiple joints is described. Section 4 the generalization of mechanisms is discussed. Finally, Sect. 5 the entire paper is summarized.

2 PF Graph and Representation of KCs

In traditional topological graphs, bars are represented by solid dot, kinematic pairs are represented by line [10]. As shown in Fig. 2 (a), it is a 3-bar KC with a multiple joint. The relationship between the bars of the 3-bar KC with a multiple joint represented by a traditional topological graph, as shown in Fig. 2 (b). As shown in Fig. 2 (c), it is adjacency matrix corresponding to the 3-bar KC with a multiple joint. Though the adjacency relationship of the bars in the KCs can be reflect accurately by adjacency matrix, the relationship between the bars and kinematic pairs of the actual mechanism is not matching with the topological graph in Fig. 2 (b): there is only one kinematic pair in the actual mechanism which are connected with three 2-joint bars, while the traditional topological graph shows three kinematic pairs are connected with three 2-joint bars in sequence; in the actual mechanism, the loop is not formed by three bars, while in the topological graph, a loop is formed by three vertices. The number of independent loops in the KCs is changed, then an inaccurate analysis is resulted.

To more accurately represent the adjacency relationship, based on the traditional topological graph and polygon representation method of multiple joints proposed by Yan [11], a concept of face is proposed to represent the adjacency relationship. As shown in Fig. 2 (d), multiple joints are represented by polygon face and the topological graph containing this face is called as PF graph, it is represented by ***G***F.

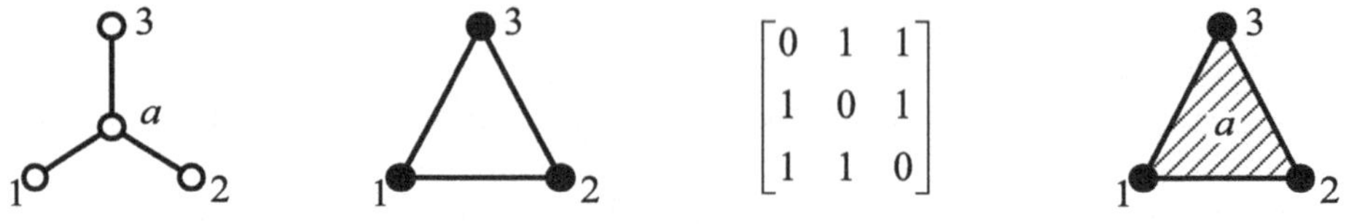

(a) 3-bar KC (b) Topological graph (c) Adjacency matrix (d) face

Fig. 2. The representation of 3-bar KC

The incidence matrix and adjacency matrix corresponding to PF graphs are:

$$\mathbf{A}(G_{\mathrm{F}}) = \left[a_{i,j} + b_{i,j}\mathrm{i}\right]_{v\times v} \tag{1}$$

$$\mathbf{M}(G_{\mathrm{F}}) = \left[m_{i,j}\right]_{v\times \varepsilon} \tag{2}$$

where, $a_{i,j}$ is the sum of the number of edges and faces connecting vertices v_i and v_j, $b_{i,j}$ is the number of faces connecting vertices v_i and v_j, i is the imaginary unit, $m_{i,j}$ is the number of associations between vertex v_i and edge e_j or face f_j, and the number of associations with faces is the number of edges of the face minus 1, ε is the total number of edges and faces in the PF graphs.

To distinguish faces of the PF graphs and complete graphs, imaginary numbers are introduced into adjacency matrix, as both of them have adjacency relationships between any two vertices. In addition, when there are no self-loops in the PF graphs, the sum of the real parts of the elements in a row (or column) of the adjacency matrix equals the degree of the corresponding vertex, and the sum of the elements in each row of the incidence matrix also equals the degree of the corresponding element, which is the same as the properties of traditional topological graphs.

As shown in Fig. 3, it is a PF graph containing a quadrilateral face. The adjacency matrix and incidence matrix corresponding to the PF graph $G_{\mathrm{F}} = (V, E, F)$ in Fig. 3 are:

$$\mathbf{A} = \begin{array}{c} \begin{matrix} v_1 & v_2 & v_3 & v_4 & v_5 & v_6 \end{matrix} \\ \begin{bmatrix} 1 & 1+\mathrm{i} & 1+\mathrm{i} & 2+\mathrm{i} & 0 & 2 \\ 1+\mathrm{i} & 0 & 1+\mathrm{i} & 1+\mathrm{i} & 1 & 0 \\ 1+\mathrm{i} & 1+\mathrm{i} & 0 & 1+\mathrm{i} & 1 & 0 \\ 2+\mathrm{i} & 1+\mathrm{i} & 1+\mathrm{i} & 0 & 0 & 1 \\ 0 & 1 & 1 & 0 & 0 & 0 \\ 2 & 0 & 0 & 1 & 0 & 0 \end{bmatrix} \end{array} \begin{matrix} v_1 \\ v_2 \\ v_3 \\ v_4 \\ v_5 \\ v_6 \end{matrix}, \quad \mathbf{M} = \begin{array}{c} \begin{matrix} e_1 & e_2 & e_3 & e_4 & e_5 & e_6 & e_7 & f \end{matrix} \\ \begin{bmatrix} 1 & 1 & 0 & 0 & 0 & 1 & 2 & 3 \\ 0 & 0 & 1 & 0 & 0 & 0 & 0 & 3 \\ 0 & 0 & 0 & 1 & 0 & 0 & 0 & 3 \\ 0 & 0 & 0 & 0 & 1 & 1 & 0 & 3 \\ 0 & 0 & 1 & 1 & 0 & 0 & 0 & 0 \\ 1 & 1 & 0 & 0 & 1 & 0 & 0 & 0 \end{bmatrix} \end{array} \begin{matrix} v_1 \\ v_2 \\ v_3 \\ v_4 \\ v_5 \\ v_6 \end{matrix} \tag{3}$$

(3)

If the self-loop e_7 is removed from Fig. 3, the sum of the real parts of the elements in the first row corresponding to vertex v_1 in the adjacency matrix is 6, which equal to its degree.

In the PF graphs, to distinguish faces and complete graphs, imaginary numbers are introduced into the adjacency matrix of the PF graphs, then the adjacency matrix is

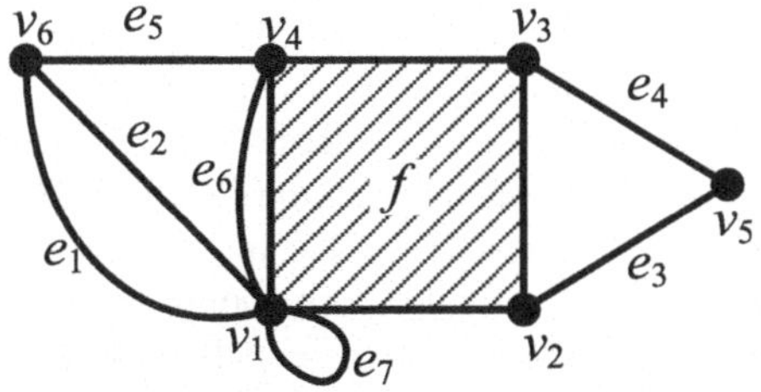

Fig. 3. A PF graph containing a quadrilateral face

no longer a 0–1 matrix or a real symmetric matrix. In fact, the KC corresponding to a complete graph does not exist in reality. A complete graph, when reflected in components and kinematic pairs, is corresponding to triangles and various complex truss structures. In kinematics, these structures are generally viewed as a multiple component. Therefore, to facilitate representation and matrix operations, the imaginary part is eliminated, forming a 0–1 real symmetric matrix.

When the relationship of the KCs is represented by PF graphs, the connection relationships of multiple joints are represented by faces. As shown in Table 1, there are several types of multiple joints and their corresponding PF graphs, as well as the adjacency and incidence matrices obtained based on Eq. (1) and (2).

Table 1. The representation of multiple joints

Multiple joints	KCs	PF graph	Adjacency matrix	Incidence matrix
3-bar multiple joints	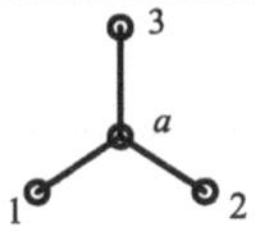	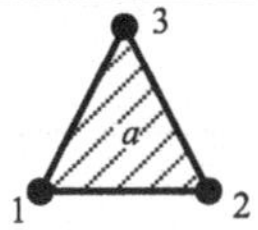	$\begin{bmatrix} 0 & 1 & 1 \\ 1 & 0 & 1 \\ 1 & 1 & 0 \end{bmatrix}$	$\begin{matrix} a \\ \begin{bmatrix} 2 \\ 2 \\ 2 \end{bmatrix} \end{matrix} \begin{matrix} 1 \\ 2 \\ 3 \end{matrix}$
4-bar multiple joints	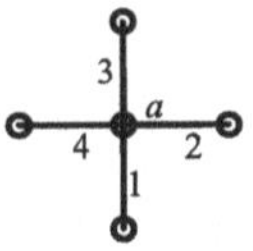	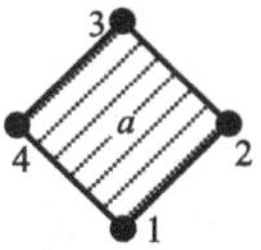	$\begin{bmatrix} 0 & 1 & 1 & 1 \\ 1 & 0 & 1 & 1 \\ 1 & 1 & 0 & 1 \\ 1 & 1 & 1 & 0 \end{bmatrix}$	$\begin{matrix} a \\ \begin{bmatrix} 3 \\ 3 \\ 3 \\ 3 \end{bmatrix} \end{matrix} \begin{matrix} 1 \\ 2 \\ 3 \\ 4 \end{matrix}$
⋮	⋮	⋮	⋮	⋮
n-bar multiple joints	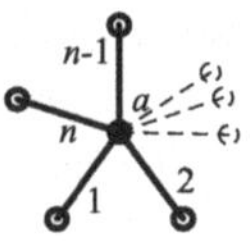	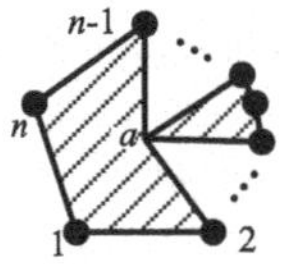	$\begin{bmatrix} 0 & 1 & \cdots & 1 & 1 \\ 1 & 0 & \cdots & 1 & 1 \\ \vdots & \vdots & \ddots & \vdots & \vdots \\ 1 & 1 & \cdots & 0 & 1 \\ 1 & 1 & \cdots & 1 & 0 \end{bmatrix}_{n \times n}$	$\begin{matrix} a \\ \begin{bmatrix} n-1 \\ n-1 \\ \vdots \\ n-1 \\ n-1 \end{bmatrix} \end{matrix} \begin{matrix} 1 \\ 2 \\ \vdots \\ n-1 \\ n \end{matrix}$

As shown in Table 2, there are two kinds of KC with multiple joints, one is an 8-bar KC with one ternary joint and the other is an 8-bar KC with one quaternary joint. It can be found that PF graph can represent the uniqueness of KCs with multiple joints and realize the one-to-one correspondence between kinematic graphs and the adjacency matrices and incident matrices. Moreover, PF graph is a further development of traditional graph, and many properties of the two graphs are concordant, which is convenient to apply some mature theories and methods of KCs with single joints to KCs with multiple joints. For example, when calculating the degree of freedom (DOF) of KCs with single joints, the DOF formula is $F = 3(n–1)–2m$, where n is bar number, m is kinematic pair number which is equal to edge number E_F of the corresponding graph. The formula is also suitable to KCs with multiple joints, where m equals to generalized edge number EF in PF graph. As we all know, when calculating DOF, a m-ary multiple joint is usually considered to have (m-1) kinematic pair.

Table 2. Representation of KC with multiple joints.

	KCs with multiple joints	PF graph	Adjacency matrix	Incidence matrix
8-bar KC with a ternar-y joint	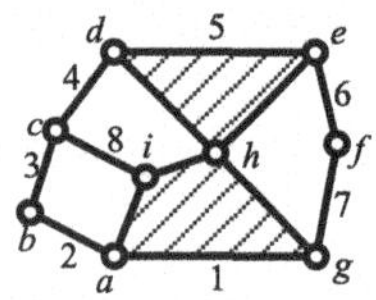	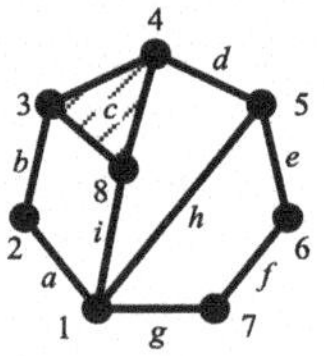	$\begin{bmatrix} 0&1&0&0&1&0&1&1 \\ 1&0&1&0&0&0&0&0 \\ 0&1&0&1&0&0&0&1 \\ 0&0&1&0&1&0&0&1 \\ 1&0&0&1&0&1&0&0 \\ 0&0&0&0&1&0&1&0 \\ 1&0&0&0&0&1&0&0 \\ 1&0&1&1&0&0&0&0 \end{bmatrix}$	$\begin{array}{ccccccccc\|c} a&b&c&d&e&f&g&h&i& \\ \hline 1&0&0&0&0&0&1&1&1&1 \\ 1&1&0&0&0&0&0&0&0&2 \\ 0&1&2&0&0&0&0&0&0&3 \\ 0&0&2&1&0&0&0&0&0&4 \\ 0&0&0&1&1&0&0&1&0&5 \\ 0&0&0&0&1&1&0&0&0&6 \\ 0&0&0&0&0&1&1&0&0&7 \\ 0&0&2&0&0&0&0&0&0&8 \end{array}$
8-bar KC with a quarte rnary joint	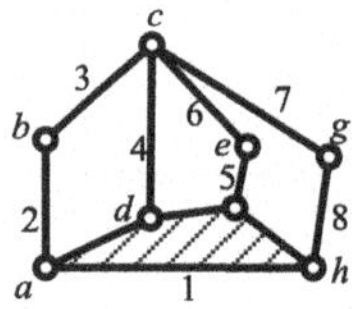	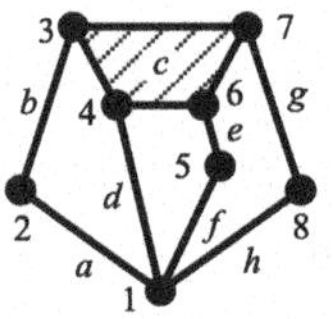	$\begin{bmatrix} 0&1&0&1&1&0&0&1 \\ 1&0&1&0&0&0&0&0 \\ 0&1&0&1&0&1&1&0 \\ 1&0&1&0&0&1&1&0 \\ 1&0&0&0&0&1&0&0 \\ 0&0&1&1&1&0&1&0 \\ 0&0&1&1&0&1&0&1 \\ 1&0&0&0&0&0&1&0 \end{bmatrix}$	$\begin{array}{cccccccc\|c} a&b&c&d&e&f&g&h& \\ \hline 1&0&0&1&0&1&0&1&1 \\ 1&1&0&0&0&0&0&0&2 \\ 0&1&3&0&0&0&0&0&3 \\ 0&0&3&1&0&0&0&0&4 \\ 0&0&0&0&1&1&0&0&5 \\ 0&0&3&0&1&0&0&0&6 \\ 0&0&3&0&0&0&1&0&7 \\ 0&0&0&0&0&0&1&1&8 \end{array}$

3 Elimination of Multiple Joint

Mechanical devices can be transformed into a generalized KC containing only single joint kinematic pairs and bars. Through generalized processing and analysis, the relationship between mechanisms can be found. Mechanisms of the same or similar generalized KCs have similarities in kinematics and dynamics characteristics. The most important thing for obtaining generalized KCs is the elimination of multiple joints [9].

The method proposed by Yan [9] to eliminate multiple joints is to sequentially add a kinematic pair to any one bar associated with the multiple joint until the original multiple joints are only associated with two bars, as shown in Fig. 4. This method of eliminating multiple joints is simple and easy to understand, however, when eliminating multiple joints in multiple bars, a large number of isomorphic configurations will appear, which requires removing them one by one, resulting in a heavy workload. Starting from the topological structure of multiple joints, this section proposes a new method for eliminating multiple joints by combining the PF graphs and tree diagrams.

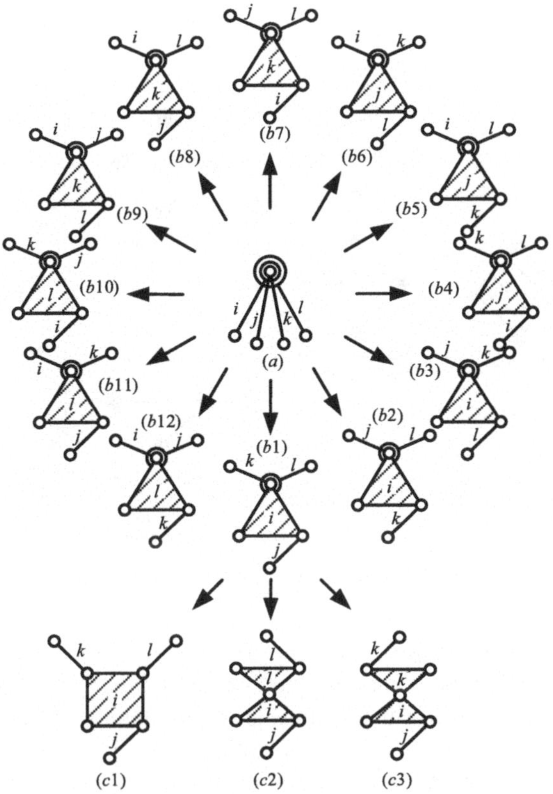

Fig. 4. The elimination of multiple joints

The elimination of multiple joints is mainly achieved by reducing constraints: In the PF graphs, when a vertex *i* in an *n*-edge polygon face *f* only reserves the adjacency relations with another vertex *j*, and removes the adjacency relations with the other (*n*-1) vertices, the *n*-edge polygon face *f* is divided into an (*n*-1)-edge polygon face *f'* and an adjacent vertex *i*. This process deletes (n-2) constraints and adds a kinematic pair $f_{i,j}$. As shown in Fig. 5, it is a process of elimination of a 4-bar multiple joint. If the adjacency relations between one vertex and its two adjacent vertices are removed, reserving only one vertex with adjacency relation, the 4-vertex face *a* is divided into a 3-vertex face *a*' and an adjacent vertex, indicating the transformation from a 4-bar multiple joint to a 3-bar multiple joint and a bar. This bar is only adjacent to one bar in the 3-bar multiple joint. This process deletes two constraints. By further eliminating a 3-bar multiple joint, it is transformed into three serially connected vertices, reducing one constraint, and thus eliminating the multiple joint in the KC.

The elimination of the 3-bar multiple joint generate two different tree configurations in the corresponding topological graph, because the positions of elimination of constraints are different. These two tree configurations, which have the same number of vertices and edges, are isomers of each other. This is similar to the isomerism phenomenon of alkanes in organic chemistry. To facilitate the distinction of isomers, alkane

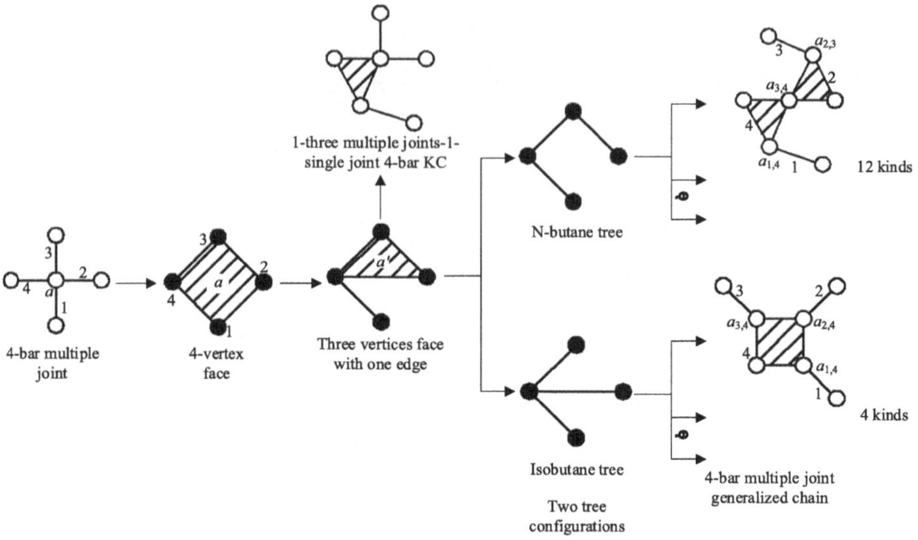

Fig. 5. The elimination of 4-bar multiple joint

naming rules are adopted to name isomeric trees. For example, the two trees generated by the elimination of the 4-bar multiple joint are n-butane tree and iso-butane tree (2-methylpropane tree). Among them, considering the number of nodes, the n-butane tree has A_4^2 kinds of permutations and combinations. However, due to the symmetry of the n-butane tree, there are $A_4^2/2 = 12$ configurations; iso-butane has $C_4^1 = 4$ kinds of configurations. As shown in Table 3, there are the tree types of generalized KCs converted from 3-bar multiple joints to 7-bar multiple joints, as well as the number of different KCs generated after the elimination of multiple joints obtained by permutation and combination. This number can also be calculated by Cayley's theorem [12] in graph theory, which indicates that there are n^{n-2} different spanning trees in K_{n}, where K_{n} represents the degree matrix, n is the order of the degree matrix, and is equal to the number of vertices. For example, the number of different KCs obtained after the elimination of the 4-bar multiple joint is $4^{4-2} = 16$, which is the same as the number obtained by permutation and combination.

4 Generalization of Mechanism

The generalization process of KCs with multiple joints is as follows: Separate the multiple joints from the KC. Based on the topological tree structure corresponding to the elimination of different multiple joints, topological graphs of the corresponding KC are obtained after numbering and arranging the bars. Then, the generalized KC corresponding to the multiple joints is obtained. By combining the obtained KC with the original partial KC, the generalized KC with multiple joints is obtained. Finally, redraw the KC graph with the largest loop in the KC as the main loop. Taking a planar 8-bar mechanism with a 3-bar multiple joint as an example, its generalization process is shown in Fig. 6. Three different generalized KCs can be obtained after generalization.

Table 3. Configurations of KCs

	Polygonal face	Tree configuration	Number of configurations	Number of KCs
3-bar multiple joints			1	3
4-bar multiple joints			2	16
5-bar multiple joints		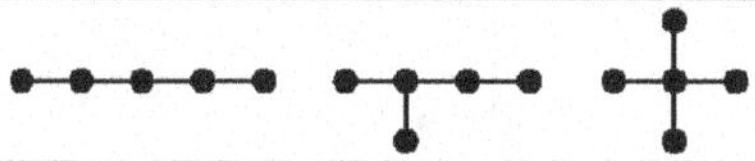	3	125
6-bar multiple joints	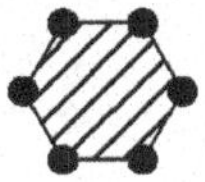	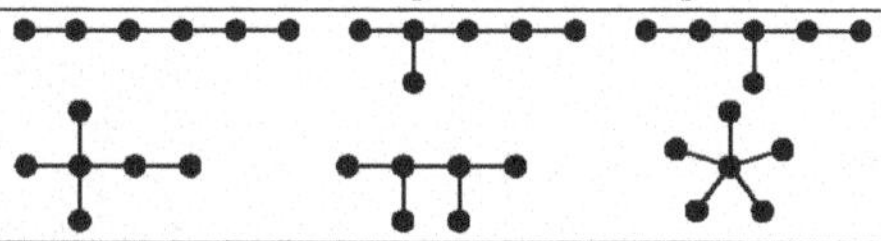	6	1296
7-bar multiple joints	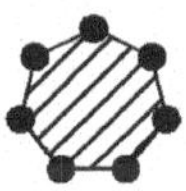	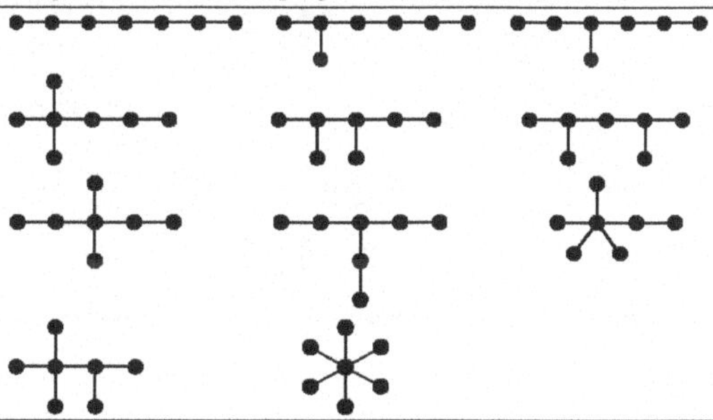	11	16807

After generalization, the number of loops of the KC with multiple joints is unchanged, thus the number of bars in partial loops through the multiple joints in the original KC is changed. In the tree structure corresponding to the KC after the elimination of the multiple joints, the bars corresponding to vertices with a degree equal to 1 are called endpoint bars, while those corresponding to vertices with a degree not equal to 1 are called intermediate bars. In the loops through the multiple joints, the number of bars in the loops containing intermediate bars is unchanged after generalization, while the number of bars in the loops that do not contain intermediate bars increases by the same number as the intermediate bars after generalization. Taking a 3-bar multiple joint as an example as shown in Fig. 6, bars 3, 4, and 8 are connected by the multiple joint *c*. After the elimination of the multiple joints, three different tree structures are obtained. In the 8-3-4 tree structure, the degree of vertices 8 and 4 are both equal to 1, representing endpoint bars, while the degree of the vertex 3 is equal to 2, not 1, representing an intermediate bar. In the original KC with multiple joints, the loops through the multiple joint *c* include 1-2-3-8, 1-8-4-5, and 1-2-3-4-5-6-7. After generalization, the number of bars in the loops 1-2-3-8 and 1-2-3-4-5-6-7, which contain intermediate bars, is unchanged, while the loop 1-8-4-5 is increased by the intermediate bar 3, the loop is transformed into 1-8-3-4-5. If the largest loop in the KC through the multiple joints contains two endpoint bars, the number of bars in the largest loop is increased after generalization, and the increase is equal to the number of intermediate bars. The characteristic of the KCs with multiple joints is beneficial to the classification of the generalized KCs based on the number of bars in loops after the generalization, to obtain the similarity relationship of generalized KCs, which facilitates further analysis and evaluation of the topological characteristics of the mechanism KCs.

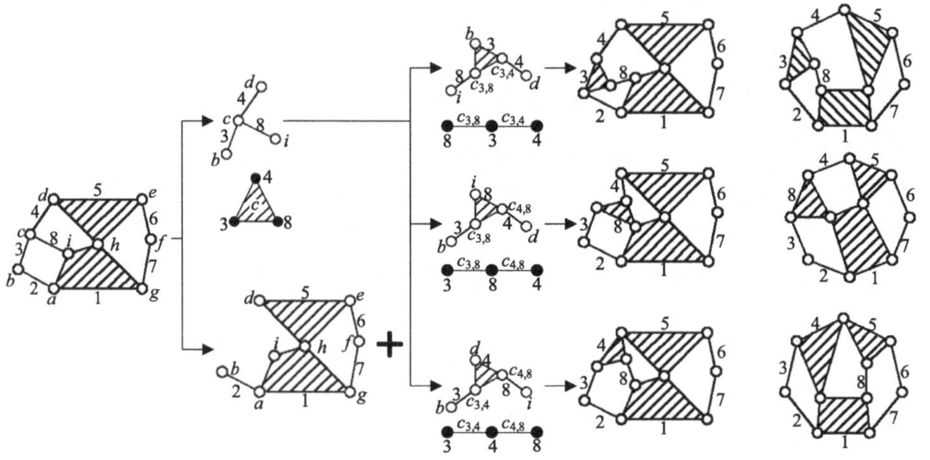

Fig. 6. The generalization process of the KCs containing multiple joints

5 Multiple Joints Elimination and Mechanism Innovation Design

Synthetic aperture radar (SAR) has important applications in military and security fields, such as border monitoring, maritime surveillance, etc. The security monitoring capabilities of country is improved through the development of high-performance planar SAR antennas, detect and respond to potential security threats in a timely manner, to maintain national security and stability [13].

The planar SAR antenna structure is composed of multiple panels. Due to the high precision and high stiffness requirements of its deployment state, most planar SAR antennas currently adopt a truss-type deployable mechanism to achieve functions such as connection unlocking, deployment control, deployment locking support, etc. After the long development, a large number of different forms of truss-type deployable mechanisms have been widely used as support mechanisms for planar SAR antennas [14, 15].

Several typical deployable mechanism configurations of SAR antennas in the world are shown in Fig. 7 [16–20]. As SAR antennas develop towards large-scale and modularization, the existing configurations are increasingly unable to meet the requirement. Currently, the largest number of antenna panels which are supported is Seasat antenna configuration, but its deployment fundamental frequency is only 0.9 Hz. The Radarsat series, which meets the fundamental frequency requirement, cannot well deploy to meet the large size requirement. Obviously, research on the configuration innovation of the deployable mechanism of the SAR antenna is still needed. The generalized KCs of the mechanism are obtained by the multiple joint elimination method, to better implement subsequent mechanism synthesis.

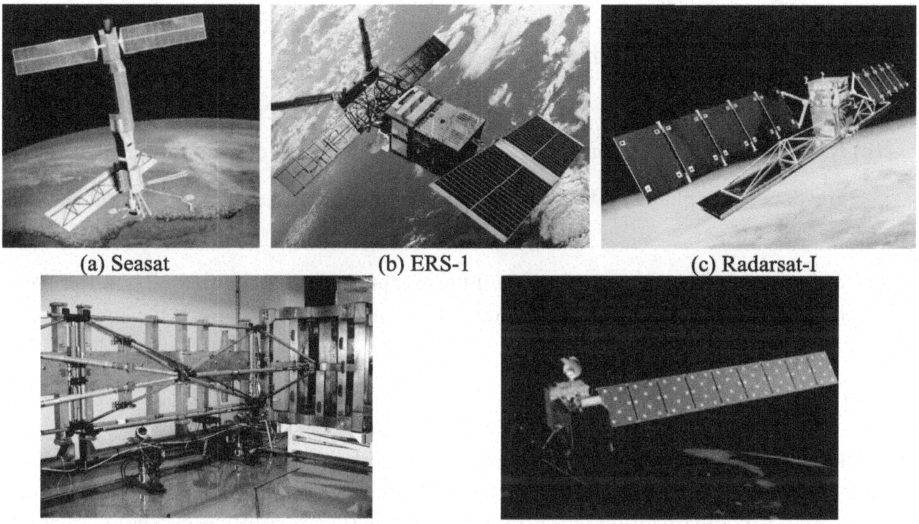

(a) Seasat (b) ERS-1 (c) Radarsat-I

(d) Radarsat-II (e) ALOS

Fig. 7. Typical planar SAR antenna

Transforming Fig. 7 (c) and (d) into planar mechanism graphs as shown in Fig. 8, the similarities between them can be obtained based on Tab. 2. The Radarsat-I configuration shown in Fig. 8 (a) and the SAR antenna configuration proposed by Liu shown in Fig. 8 (b) [21] have the same generalized chain. The Radarsat-I configuration can be transformed into the configuration shown in Fig. 8 (b) by eliminating the 4-bar multiple joints. Similarly, the Radarsat-II configuration shown in Fig. 8 (c) and the Seasat configuration shown in Fig. 8 (d) have the same generalized KCs. The same configuration as Seasat is obtained by eliminating a 3-bar multiple joint at the top from the Radarsat-II configuration. In addition, by adding a 2-bar branched chain to the Seasat configuration through the elimination and generation of the multiple joints, thesss configuration shown in Fig. 8 (b) can also be obtained.

By eliminating multiple joints, the generalized KCs of different mechanisms can be found, then the similarity between them can be judged. Mechanisms of the same generalized KC have certain similarities in topological structure, kinematic characteristics, and dynamic characteristics. Therefore, in mechanical innovation design, a mature mechanism is analyzed, the similar mechanisms with the same generalized KC can be obtained through the generation and elimination of multiple joints in the KC, and through the analysis and selection the better mechanism design scheme can be obtained

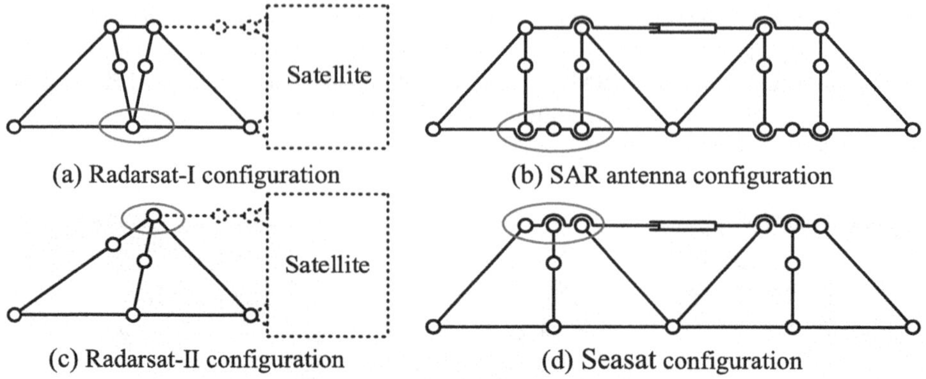

Fig. 8. Typical planar SAR antenna deployable mechanism schematic diagram

according to the working performance requirements of the mechanism. Then the work of design is more targeted and the redundant work is avoided.

6 Conclusion

(1) A PF graph is proposed in the paper that can address the limitations of traditional topological graphs in representing KCs with multiple joints. The PF graph not only accurately reflects the connection relationships between components but also effectively represents the multiple joints by introducing the concept of "face", and the concepts of adjacency and incidence matrices are defined, making the representation of multiple joints more accurate and easier for computer processing.
(2) Based on the PF graph, a new method for the elimination of multiple joints is proposed which eliminates multiple joints by reducing constraints. And the steps to obtain the generalized KC of the mechanism is provided. Meanwhile, the generation of isomers in the elimination process and their naming rules are revealed.
(3) The generalization process of KCs containing multiple joints is discussed and the fact that elimination of multiple joints is provided as a fast and simple approach for innovative mechanism design is illustrated by combining with a planar SAR antenna.

Acknowledgment. This work is funded by the Joint Funds of the National Natural Science Foundation of China (U23A20338), National Natural Science Foundation of China (No. 52175019), Beijing Natural Science Foundations (No. 3212009 and No. L222038), Guangdong Basic and Applied Basic Research Foundation (2023A1515110150) and Fundamental Research Funds for the Central Universities (FRF-TP-22-038A1).

References

1. Paulus, P.B., Kenworthy, J.B.: Effective brainstorming. Oxford Handb. Group Creativity Innov. 287–305 (2019)

2. Eppich, K.: Analogy as theory and method. SAA Archaeol. Rec. **20**(1), 31–34 (2020)
3. Ye, X., Liu, H., Chen, L., et al.: Reverse innovative design—an integrated product design methodology. Comput. Aided Des. **40**(7), 812–827 (2008)
4. Ilevbare, I.M., Probert, D., Phaal, R.: A review of TRIZ, and its benefits and challenges in practice. Technovation **33**(2–3), 30–37 (2013)
5. Yan, H., Yao, Y., et al.: Creative Design of Mechanical Devices. China Machine Press (2002). (in Chinese)
6. Chu, J., Zhang, R., Zou, Y.: Topological Structure Theory of Planar Mechanism and Its Application in Mechanism Innovative Design. Science Press, Beijing (2017). (in Chinese)
7. Chu, J., Cao, W.: Identification of isomorphism of kinematic chains through adjacent-chain table[7]. In: Proceedings of the 22nd Biennial Mechanisms
8. Liu, J., Yu, D.: Representations & isomorphism identification of planar kinematic chains with multiple joints based on the converted adjacent matrix. Chin. J. Mech. Eng. **48**, 15–21. (in Chinese)
9. Dong, K., Li, D., Kong, X.: Representation of planar kinematic chains with multiple joints based on a modified graph and isomorphism identification. Mech. Mach. Theory **172**, 104793 (2022)
10. Yang, T., Shen, H., Liu, A., et al.: Basic ideas and mathematical methods of mechanism topology theory-review of several original mechanism topology theories in a methodological perspective. Chin. J. Mech. Eng. **56**, 1–15 (2020)
11. Yan, H., Hsu, C.: Contracted graphs of kinematic chains with multiple joints. Math. Comput. Model. **10**, 681–695 (1988)
12. Suksumran, T.: The algebra of gyrogroups: cayley's theorem, lagrange's theorem, and isomorphism theorems. In: Rassias, T., Pardalos, P. (eds.) Essays in Mathematics and its Applications, pp. 369–437. Springer, Cham (2016).https://doi.org/10.1007/978-3-319-31338-2_15
13. Wang, Y., Deng, Z., Liu, R., et al.: Topology structure synthesis and analysis of spatial pyramid deployable truss structures for satellite SAR antenna. Chin. J. Mech. Eng. **27**(4), 683–692 (2014)
14. Pokuls, R., Uher, J., Pozar, D.M.: Microstrip antennas for SAR applications. IEEE Trans. Antennas Propag. **46**(9), 1289–1296 (1998)
15. Gómez-Villanueva, R., Jardón-Aguilar, H., Miranda, R.L.: State of the art methods for low SAR antenna implementation. In: Proceedings of the Fourth European Conference on Antennas and Propagation, pp. 1–4. IEEE (2010)
16. Grantham, W., Bracalente, E., Jones, W., et al.: The Seasat-A satellite scatterometer. IEEE J. Oceanic Eng. **2**(2), 200–206 (1977)
17. Rignot, E.J.M., Van Zyl, J.J.: Change detection techniques for ERS-1 SAR data. IEEE Trans. Geosci. Remote Sens. **31**(4), 896–906 (1993)
18. Haldar, D., Patnaik, C., Chakraborty, M., et al.: Identification of tall fibre crop (jute) using multi-temporal RADARSAT data in rainfed areas of eastern indogangetic plain. Asian J. Geoinformatics **11**(3) (2011)
19. Al-Bakri, J., Suleiman, A., Berg, A.: A comparison of two models to predict soil moisture from remote sensing data of RADARSAT II. Arab. J. Geosci. **7**, 4851–4860 (2014)
20. Rosenqvist, A., Shimada, M., Suzuki, S., et al.: Operational performance of the ALOS global systematic acquisition strategy and observation plans for ALOS-2 PALSAR-2. Remote Sens. Environ. **155**, 3–12 (2014)
21. Liu, R., Tian, D., Deng, Z.: Design method of truss structure with the same size module for deployable truss antenna. In: The Abstracts of the International Conference on Advanced Mechatronics: Toward Evolutionary Fusion of IT and Mechatronics: ICAM 2010.5. The Japan Society of Mechanical Engineers, pp. 480–485 (2010)

Optimum Design of a 3-SPR Parallel Manipulator with Large Parasitic Motion

Chenhao Xu[1], Fugui Xie[1,2](✉), and Xin-Jun Liu[1]

[1] State Key Laboratory of Tribology in Advanced Equipment, Department of Mechanical Engineering (DME), Tsinghua University, Beijing 100084, China
xiefg@mail.tsinghua.edu.cn

[2] Beijing Key Lab of Precision/Ultra-Precision Manufacturing Equipments and Control, Tsinghua University, Beijing 100084, China

Abstract. Parallel mechanisms with the capacity of large spatial localization are in important demand and difficult to design. In this paper, a 3-SPR parallel parameter is proposed to realize a large positioning workspace by using parasitic motion. In order to maximize the potential of the manipulator, optimum design is conducted. Firstly, kinematic analysis is carried out to investigate the characteristics of parasitic motion. Then, the motion/force transmission and constraint performance of the manipulator are evaluated, where an approach for computing the transmission and constraint indices is presented. The design indices are constructed to evaluate the size of the positioning workspace in the *xy* plane and the average level of the motion/force transmission and constraint performance. Afterwards, the parameter design space is established by the parameter-finiteness normalization method. On these bases, the region satisfying the design requirement is derived by the performance chart-based design methodology. The proportional line method is presented to determine the optimum workspace along the *Z*-axis. Finally, a group of optimum parameters is obtained, and the large spatial localization capacity of the manipulator is achieved. This work lays the foundation for the development of the 3-SPR parallel manipulator, and the methods proposed in this paper can be further applied to the design of other parallel manipulators.

Keywords: Parallel Manipulator · Optimum Design · Parasitic Motion · large positioning workspace

1 Introduction

In recent years, robotic manipulators have been well developed for industrial applications [1]. The majority of industrial manipulators commonly utilize serial mechanisms, which are known for their large workspaces and exceptional dexterity. As the counterpart of serial mechanisms, parallel mechanisms are characterized by multi-loop structures, offering benefits such as light weight, compact structure, high stiffness, and fast dynamic response [2]. However, parallel mechanisms have smaller workspaces compared to series mechanism, which may restrict the actual applications [3]. Therefore, the design of

X. Lan et al. (Eds.): ICIRA 2024, LNAI 15201, pp. 318–331, 2025.
https://doi.org/10.1007/978-981-96-0771-6_24

parallel manipulators with large workspaces has been a focus in the field. For the parallel manipulator, configuration design is a fundamental approach to realize a large workspace. Researchers have proposed diverse parallel manipulators with different configurations [4–8]. For example, some studies have used the redundant DoFs to enlarge the workspace [9].

Optimum design is the critical approach to maximize the potential of parallel mechanisms with definite configurations. The construction of design indices is a basic issue on optimum design. There are two important approaches to construct design indices for the evaluation of the workspace. For the first approach, researchers construct design indices to directly evaluate the reachable/regular/dexterous workspace based on shape (e.g. space utilization index [10], compactness index [11] and shape index [12]) and size (e.g. the volume or area of workspaces [13]). For the second approach, the workspace is determined as the region that satisfies a specific level of certain performance index, and the design index is defined by the size of the workspace. The construction of the performance index for parallel mechanisms is a challenge problem. The local conditioning index (LCI) is a typical performance index which is defined as the reciprocal of the condition number of the Jacobi matrix [14]. It has been used to evaluate the dexterity of serial manipulators. However, when the LCI is used to evaluate the performance of parallel manipulators with mixed DoFs, its value could become inconsistent as the dimensions of the elements in the Jacobi matrix are non-uniform. Inspired by the classical transmission angle theory, Liu et al. proposed a series of new performance indices to evaluate the motion/force transmission and constraint performance [15, 16]. These indices do not change with the choice of coordinate system and have a clear physical meaning. They have been well applied in the optimum design of different parallel manipulators [17, 18].

The design of optimization algorithms is also a fundamental problem for optimum design of parallel manipulators. When there are a large number of parameters to be optimized, intelligent optimization algorithms can be used for optimum design, but there may be a risk of falling into the local optimum solution [19]. When the parameter is less than four, the performance chart-based design methodology with a better level of flexibility and visualization is more suitable to obtain the ideal parameters [2].

For the lower mobility parallel mechanism, the parasitic motion is defined as the additional motion except for the motion representing the DoFs [20]. It is generally considered as a major drawback and can be eliminated by the type synthesis [21]. However, a large parasitic motion is not always a disadvantage for specific applications. For example, Exechon utilizes the parasitic motion to realize the spatial localization [22]. In this paper, we present a parallel manipulator for realizing a large positioning workspace based on the parasitic motion.

The remainder of this paper is organized as follows: In Sect. 2, the 3-SPR parallel manipulator is presented. Then, kinematic modeling and parasitic motion analysis are carried out. In Sect. 3, the motion/force transmission and constraint performance of the manipulator is evaluated, based on which the design indices are constructed. The performance chart-based design methodology and the proportional line method are adopted to obtain the optimum parameters. Section 4 concludes the paper.

2 Kinematic Analysis of the Parallel Manipulator

2.1 Configuration of the Manipulator

The configuration of the manipulator is the 3-SPR mechanism with 1T2R DoFs. The 3-SPR mechanism possesses the parasitic motion that is hopeful to be utilized for the large spatial localization. The CAD model of the mechanism is shown in Fig. 1.

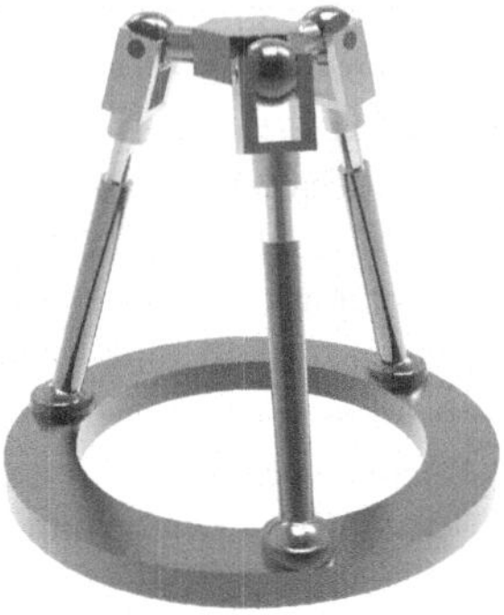

Fig. 1. CAD model of the 3-SPR mechanism.

The 3-SPR mechanism has three identical SPR limbs, where S, P, and R denote the spherical joint, prismatic joint, and revolute joint. S and R are connected to the fixed platform and moving platform, respectively. The three limbs are arranged symmetrically at the initial pose of the mechanism. The 3-SPR mechanism has a compact structure and can be actuated by ball screws with high efficiency and precision.

2.2 Kinematic Modeling and Parasitic Motion Analysis

The kinematic diagram of the 3-SPR mechanism is shown in Fig. 2. B_iP_i, $i = 1, 2, 3$, represents three SPR limbs of the mechanism. B_i, $i = 1, 2, 3$ is evenly distributed on the circle with center O and radius R_b, representing the centers of the revolute joints. P_i, $i = 1, 2, 3$ is evenly distributed on the circle with center O' and radius R_p, representing the centers of the spherical joints. The coordinate systems $O - xyz$ (denoted as $\{B\}$) and $O'-x'y'z'$ are attached to the fixed platform and the moving platform, respectively. The $\mathcal{X}$ axis is along B_3O and the Z axis is perpendicular to the fixed platform. The x' axis is along the P_3O' and the z' axis is perpendicular to the moving platform.

The position and orientation of the moving platform are represented by the vector $\boldsymbol{OO'}$ and the rotation matrix $\boldsymbol{R}(\phi, \theta, \sigma)$ as follows:

$$^{B}\boldsymbol{OO'} = \left[x\ y\ z\right]^{\mathrm{T}} \tag{1}$$

$$\boldsymbol{R}(\phi, \theta, \sigma) = \boldsymbol{R}_z(\phi)\boldsymbol{R}_y(\theta)\boldsymbol{R}_z(\sigma - \phi)$$

$$= \begin{bmatrix} c\phi c\theta c(\sigma-\phi)+s\phi s(\sigma-\phi) & -c\phi c\theta s(\sigma-\phi)+s\phi c(\sigma-\phi) & c\phi s\theta \\ s\phi c\theta c(\sigma-\phi)+c\phi s(\sigma-\phi) & -s\phi c\theta s(\sigma-\phi)+c\phi c(\sigma-\phi) & s\phi s\theta \\ s\theta c(\sigma-\phi) & s\theta s(\sigma-\phi) & c\theta \end{bmatrix} \tag{2}$$

where, ϕ, θ, and σ are the azimuth, tilt, and torsion angles.

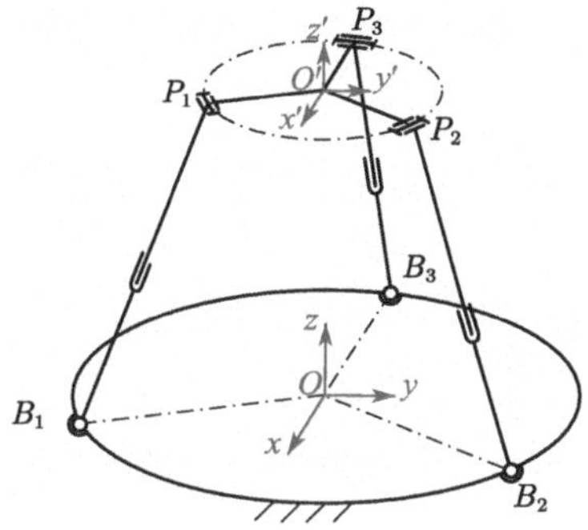

Fig. 2. Kinematic diagram of the 3-SPR mechanism.

Then, the inverse kinematics can be obtained by the closed-loop vector method:

$$^{B}\boldsymbol{B}_i\boldsymbol{P}_i = {}^{B}\boldsymbol{OO'} + \boldsymbol{R}(\phi,\theta,\sigma)\cdot{}^{P}\boldsymbol{O'P}_i - {}^{B}\boldsymbol{OB}_i \tag{3}$$

The parasitic motion is determined by the structural constraints as follows:

$$\begin{cases} ^{B}\boldsymbol{B}_1\boldsymbol{P}_1^{\mathrm{T}}\cdot\boldsymbol{R}(\phi,\theta,\sigma)\cdot{}^{P}\boldsymbol{P}_2\boldsymbol{P}_3=0 \\ ^{B}\boldsymbol{B}_2\boldsymbol{P}_2^{\mathrm{T}}\cdot\boldsymbol{R}(\phi,\theta,\sigma)\cdot{}^{P}\boldsymbol{P}_3\boldsymbol{P}_1=0 \\ ^{B}\boldsymbol{B}_3\boldsymbol{P}_3^{\mathrm{T}}\cdot\boldsymbol{R}(\phi,\theta,\sigma)\cdot{}^{P}\boldsymbol{P}_1\boldsymbol{P}_2=0 \end{cases} \tag{4}$$

Both x and y are functions of z, ϕ and θ, which can be derived from Eq. (4):

$$x = z\cos\phi\tan\theta - \frac{R_b}{4\cos\theta}\left(\cos 2\phi\sin^2\theta + 4\cos 4\phi\sin^4\frac{\theta}{2}\right) \tag{5}$$

$$y = z\sin\phi\tan\theta + \frac{R_b}{4\cos\theta}\left(\sin 2\phi\sin^2\theta - 4\sin 4\phi\sin^4\frac{\theta}{2}\right) \tag{6}$$

In addition, $\sigma = 0$ can be also obtained by Eq. (4). Therefore, the pose of the 3-SPR parallel manipulator can be described by three variables z, ϕ and θ (1T2R DoFs).

The value of parasitic motion is defined as the ratio of the distance between O' and O in the $O-xy$ plane to the radius of the fixed platform R_b, which reflects the relative magnitude of the parasitic motion:

$$\rho = \frac{\sqrt{x^2+y^2}}{R_b} \tag{7}$$

According to Eq. (5) to Eq. (7), it is clear that ρ is a periodic function of the azimuth angle with a period of 120°. The relationship between ρ and the azimuth angle when the tilt angle varies from 0° to 40° is shown in Fig. 3 (with $z = 150$ mm and $R_b = 100$ mm). Figure 3 indicates that the magnitude of the parasitic motion can exceed R_b ($\rho > 1$) when the tilt angle is large enough, which reflects the potentiality to realize large spatial localization.

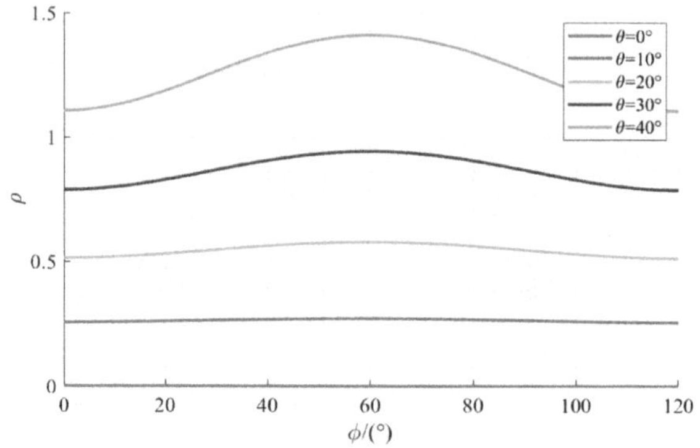

Fig. 3. The relationship between the ρ and ϕ (Z = 150 mm, R_b = 150 mm).

For the convenience of spatial localization, the pose of the manipulator should be determined by $\mathcal{X}$, y and Z. Correspondingly, the input of the inverse kinematics should change to $\begin{bmatrix} x, & y, & z \end{bmatrix}^{\mathrm{T}}$. In this case, ϕ and θ need to be represented as functions of x and y. However, the analytical expressions of $\phi(x, y)$ and $\theta(x, y)$ do not exist. Therefore, based on Eq. (5) and Eq. (6), the trust region method is used to obtain the numerical solutions of $\phi(x, y)$ and $\theta(x, y)$ with a 10^{-6} termination tolerance.

3 Performance Evaluation and Optimum Design

3.1 Motion/Force Transmission and Constraint Performance Evaluation

The goal of optimum design is to maximize the potential of the 3-SPR manipulator for the large positioning workspace. The positioning workspace of the manipulator should be defined within the region that meets the requirement of the motion/force transmission and constraint performance. In order to evaluate this type of performance, the local design index (LDI) proposed in our previous study [2] is adopted in this paper.

In order to solve the LDI, the calculation of a series of unit wrench and twist screws are necessary. The input twist screw $\$_{Ii}$, input restricted twist screw $\$_{IRi}$, transmission wrench screw $\$_{Ti}$, and constraint wrench screw $\$_{Ci}$ of the manipulator are expressed as follows:

$$\$_{Ii} = \left(0, \frac{\boldsymbol{B}_i\boldsymbol{P}_i}{|\boldsymbol{B}_i\boldsymbol{P}_i|}\right), \ i = 1, 2, 3 \tag{8}$$

$$\$_{IRi} = \left(\frac{\boldsymbol{B}_i\boldsymbol{P}_i \times \boldsymbol{P}_{i+1}\boldsymbol{P}_{i+2}}{|\boldsymbol{B}_i\boldsymbol{P}_i \times \boldsymbol{P}_{i+1}\boldsymbol{P}_{i+2}|}, \frac{\boldsymbol{OP}_i \times (\boldsymbol{B}_i\boldsymbol{P}_i \times \boldsymbol{P}_{i+1}\boldsymbol{P}_{i+2})}{|\boldsymbol{B}_i\boldsymbol{P}_i \times \boldsymbol{P}_{i+1}\boldsymbol{P}_{i+2}|} \right), \quad i = 1, 2, 3 \tag{9}$$

$$\$_{Ti} = \left(\frac{\boldsymbol{B}_i\boldsymbol{P}_i}{|\boldsymbol{B}_i\boldsymbol{P}_i|}, \frac{\boldsymbol{OB}_i \times \boldsymbol{B}_i\boldsymbol{P}_i}{|\boldsymbol{B}_i\boldsymbol{P}_i|} \right), \quad i = 1, 2, 3 \tag{10}$$

$$\$_{Ci} = \left(\frac{\boldsymbol{P}_{i+1}\boldsymbol{P}_{i+2}}{|\boldsymbol{P}_{i+1}\boldsymbol{P}_{i+2}|}, \frac{\boldsymbol{OB}_i \times \boldsymbol{P}_{i+1}\boldsymbol{P}_{i+2}}{|\boldsymbol{P}_{i+1}\boldsymbol{P}_{i+2}|} \right), \quad i = 1, 2, 3 \tag{11}$$

where, P_4 and P_5 represent P_1 and P_2 respectively.

The output twist screw $\$_{Oi}$ and output restricted twist screw $\$_{ORi}$ can be calculated by the following reciprocal relations:

$$\begin{cases} \$_{Tg}^{\circ}\$_{Oi} = 0 \quad (g = 1, 2, 3; g \neq i) \\ \$_{Ck}^{\circ}\$_{Oi} = 0 \quad (k = 1, 2, 3) \end{cases} \tag{12}$$

$$\begin{cases} \$_{Cg} \circ \$_{ORi} = 0 \ (g = 1, 2, 3; g \neq i) \\ \$_{Tk} \circ \$_{ORi} = 0 \ (k = 1, 2, 3) \end{cases} \tag{13}$$

Then, the input transmission index (ITI), the output transmission (OTI), the input constraint index (ICI), and the output constraint index (OCI) are defined as follows:

$$\gamma_I = \min_i \left\{ \frac{|\$_{Ti} \circ \$_{Ii}|}{|\$_{Ti} \circ \$_{Ii}|_{\max}} \right\}, i = 1, 2, 3 \tag{14}$$

$$\gamma_O = \min_i \left\{ \frac{|\$_{Ti} \circ \$_{Oi}|}{|\$_{Ti} \circ \$_{Oi}|_{\max}} \right\}, i = 1, 2, 3 \tag{15}$$

$$\kappa_I = \min_i \left\{ \frac{|\$_{Ci} \circ \$_{IRi}|}{|\$_{Ci} \circ \$_{IRi}|_{\max}} \right\}, i = 1, 2, 3 \tag{16}$$

$$\kappa_O = \min_i \left\{ \frac{|\$_{Ci} \circ \$_{ORi}|}{|\$_{Ci} \circ \$_{ORi}|_{\max}} \right\}, i = 1, 2, 3 \tag{17}$$

where, the maximal reciprocal product of the twist screw and the wrench screw need to be further computed.

A method to compute the above transmission and constraint indices is presented in this paper as follows:

$$\left\| \$_{wi} \circ \$_{ti} \right\|_{\max} = \sqrt{(h_{wi} + h_{ti})^2 + (d_{wi} + d_{ti})^2}, \quad i = 1, 2, 3 \tag{18}$$

where, h_{wi} and h_{ti} are the pitches of the wrench screw $\$_{wi}$ and twist screw $\$_{ti}$, respectively. d_{wi} is the distance from P_i to the axis of $\$_{wi}$, and d_{ti} is the distance from P_i to the axis of $\$_{ti}$. The physical meaning of Eq. (18) is the maximum of $\$_{wi} \circ \$_{ti}$ when the distances from the actual acting point to the axis of $\$_{wi}$ and $\$_{ti}$ remain unchanged, which reflects the potential upper limit of $\$_{wi} \circ \$_{ti}$ for a specific pose.

Finally, the LDI is obtained by calculating the minimum of ITI, OTI, ICI and OCI, which represents the overall transmission and constraint performance from both input and output parts:

$$\Lambda = \min\{\gamma_I, \gamma_O, \mathcal{K}_I, \mathcal{K}_O\} \tag{19}$$

The LDI only reflects the motion/force transmission and constraint performance for a specific pose. In order to characterize the global performance of the 3-SPR parallel manipulator with certain dimensional parameters, the construction of design indices is indispensable.

The set of position points in certain xy plane where the LDI is greater than a threshold κ is defined as the good transmission/constraint area (GTCA) of the parallel manipulator. κ is determined by the design requirement. Aiming at evaluating the localization range in the xy plane for all directions, the positioning workspace index (PWI) is defined as the minimum of the maximum parasitic motion index $\rho_{\max}(\alpha)$ that the moving platform can move along the direction (determined by the polar angle α) within the GTCA:

$$\lambda = \min_{a} \rho_{\max}(\alpha) \tag{20}$$

where, $\alpha = \mathrm{A}\tan 2(y, x)$ is the polar angle.

The planar positioning workspace is defined as the inscribed circle of the GTCA. Denoting the radius of the planar positioning workspace as R_m, the PWI can be also represented as follows:

$$\lambda = \frac{R_m}{R_b} \tag{21}$$

To evaluate the average level of the LDI in the planar positioning workspace, the global design index (GDI) is defined as follows:

$$\Gamma = \frac{\int_0^{2\pi}\left(\int_0^{R_m} \Lambda r dr\right) d\alpha}{\pi R_m^2} \tag{22}$$

As a result, two design indices (PWI and GDI) are used to optimize the dimensional parameters of the manipulator.

3.2 Optimum Design Based on Performance Charts

The critical kinematic dimensional parameters of the 3-SPR parallel manipulator are the radius of the fixed platform (R_b) and the radius of the moving platform (R_p). In addition, the distance from the center of the moving platform to the fixed platform (z) strongly influences the motion/force transmission and constraint performance of the manipulator. It is important to determine the range of the positioning workspace along the z axis. Therefore, the parameter to be optimized are R_b, R_p and z.

Without restriction, the range of the above three parameters can be $[0, +\infty]$, which makes the optimum design difficult. Owing to the two constructed design indices (PWI and GDI) are both dimensionless indices which does not change with the overall scale of the manipulator, the parameter-finiteness normalization method is adopted to normalize the parameters. The dimensionless parameters are expressed as follows:

$$r_1 = \frac{R_b}{D}, r_2 = \frac{R_p}{D}, r_3 = \frac{z}{D} \tag{23}$$

where, $D = (R_b + R_p + z)/3$ is the characteristic length of the manipulator.

In order to ensure the reasonable assembly of the manipulator, the constraint conditions of the optimum design are set as follows:

$$\begin{cases} r_1 + r_2 + r_3 = 3 \\ r_3 > r_1 > r_2 > 0 \end{cases} \tag{24}$$

The parameter design space can be constructed by the following steps: firstly, the equality constraint restricts the parameters to a plane; then, the inequality constraint determines a triangular region (shown in Fig. 4(a)); finally, the triangular region in three-dimensional space is mapped on a plane by the linear transformation (shown in Fig. 4(b)).

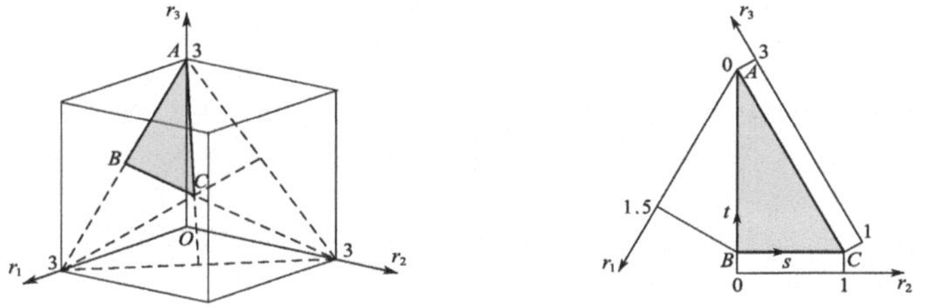

(a) (b)

Fig. 4. Parameter design space: (a) in the three-dimensional space; (b) on a mapping plane.

By means of the undetermined coefficients method, the mapping relationship between $(r_1, r_2, r_3)^{\mathrm{T}}$ and $(s, t)^{\mathrm{T}}$ can be obtained as follows:

$$\begin{cases} r_1 = \frac{3-s-\sqrt{3}t}{2} \\ r_2 = s \\ r_3 = \frac{3-s+\sqrt{3}t}{2} \end{cases} \tag{25}$$

where, s and t are the horizontal and vertical coordinates of the point in the parameter design space.

The basic elements for the optimum design of the 3-SPR parallel manipulator are shown in Table 1. The parameter design space is discretized, where discrete parameter points are selected in steps of 0.02 along s and t respectively. The PWI and the GDI (with k taken as 0.5) are calculated for each point. Then, the isopleths of the PWI and the GDI are plotted respectively in the parameter design space, forming the performance charts (shown in Fig. 5 and Fig. 6).

Table 1. Basic elements for the optimum design.

Parameters to be optimized	Parameter design space	Design index I (PWI)	Design index II (GDI)
s, t	$\begin{cases} s, t > 0 \\ \sqrt{3}s + t < \sqrt{3} \end{cases}$	$\lambda = \min\limits_{\alpha} \rho_{\max}(\alpha)$	$\Gamma = \frac{\int_0^{2\pi}\left(\int_0^{R_m} \Lambda r dr\right) d\alpha}{\pi R_m^2}$

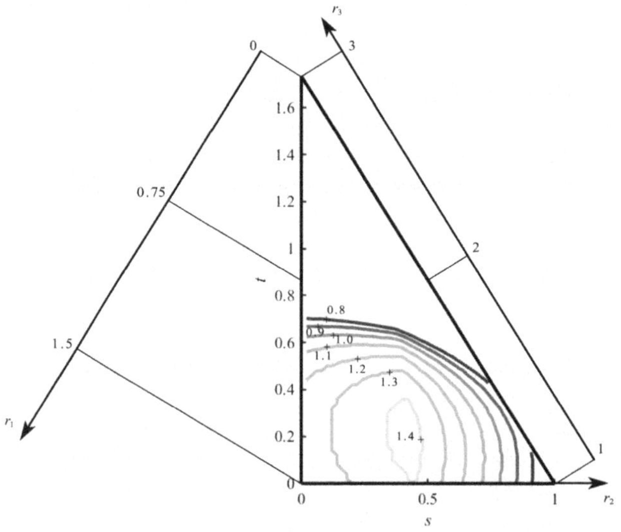

Fig. 5. Performance chart of PWI

The design requirements of the 3-SPR manipulator are $\lambda \geq 1.3$ and $\Gamma \geq 0.6$. The intersection of the regions satisfying the design requirements in the above two performance charts is defined as the qualified region (shown in Fig. 7).

In order to enlarge the workspace along the z axis, the proportional line method is presented in this paper. The ratio of r_2 to r_1 is denoted as β. Based on Eq. (25), a line equation can be derived as follows:

$$t = -\frac{\sqrt{3}}{3}\left(\frac{2}{\beta} + 1\right)s + \sqrt{3} \tag{26}$$

As shown in Fig. 8, this line pass through $(0, \sqrt{3})$ with a negative gradient. The lines with different β represent the manipulators with different R_p/R_b (equal to r_2/r_1). Different points on one line represent the corresponding manipulator at different z positions.

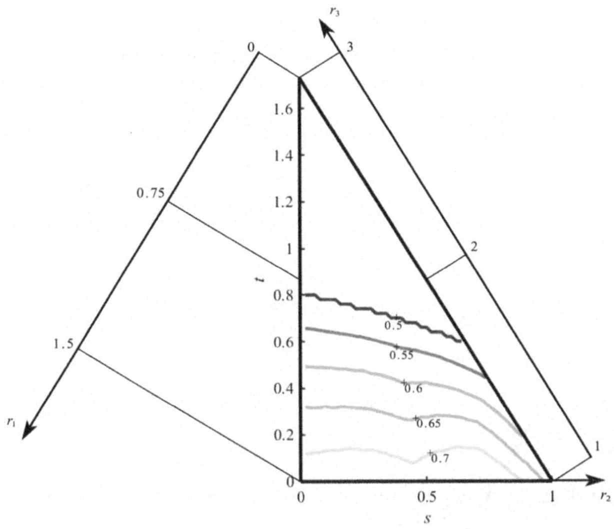

Fig. 6. Performance chart of GDI

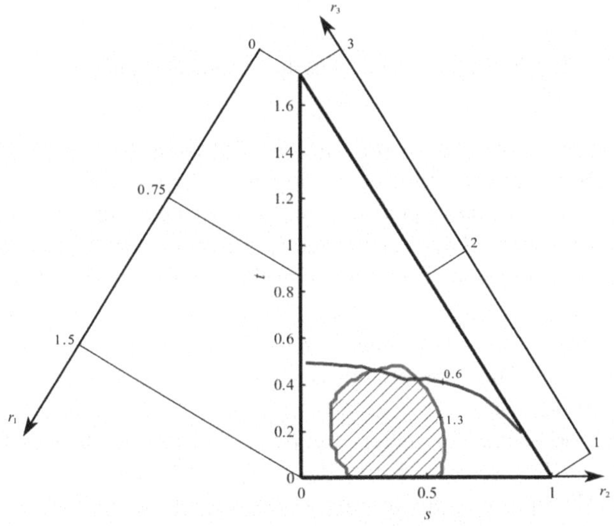

Fig. 7. Qualified region of the parallel manipulator.

The ratio of r_3 to r_1 is denoted as γ. Similarly, another line equation can be derived based on Eq. (25):

$$t = \frac{\sqrt{3}(1-\gamma)}{3(1+\gamma)}(s-3) \tag{27}$$

This line passes through (3, 0) with a negative gradient. z/R_b (equal to r_3/r_1) is positively correlated to the acute angle between the line and the S axis. The maximum range of z/R_b are determined by two lines (ℓ_1 and l_2) which are tangent to the upper and lower sides of the qualified region.

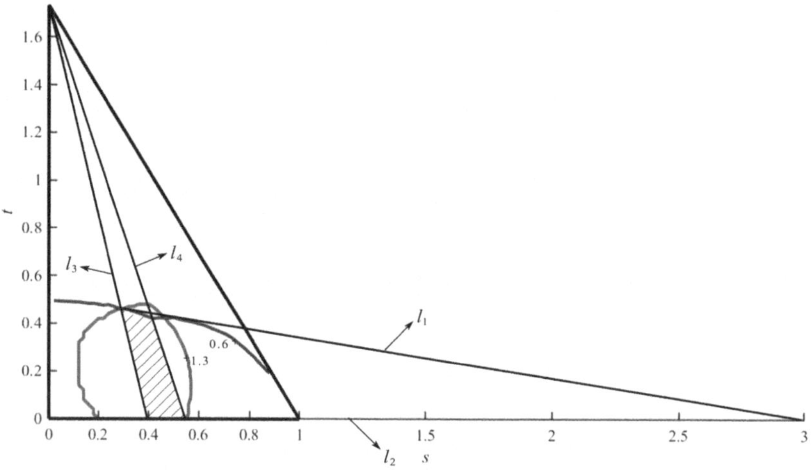

Fig. 8. Optimum region of the parallel manipulator.

The positioning workspace along the Z axis needs to be as large as possible, so the line segment obtained by intersecting the line passing through (0, $\sqrt{3}$) and the qualified region should connect ℓ_1 and l_2 as far as possible. As a result, the optimum region (the shaded region in Fig. 8) is determined by ℓ_1, l_2, l_3 and l_4. The lines passing through (0, $\sqrt{3}$) and the optimum region at the same time represent the manipulators with satisfied R_p/R_b. Finally, the line passing through (0, $\sqrt{3}$) and (0.46, 0.24) is chosen, which corresponds the manipulator with $R_p/R_b = 0.433$ and $z/R_b \in [1, 1.78]$. Based on this, the optimum positioning workspace of the manipulator is set as a cylindrical region with a radius of 1.3 R_b and a height of 0.7 R_b.

The specific dimensional parameters can be determined by the actual working conditions. In this case, R_b is set as 435 mm. Then, $R_p = 188$ mm and $z \in [435, 774]$ mm can be obtained. The optimum positioning workspace of the optimized 3-SPR parallel manipulator is the cylindrical region with a diameter of 1131 mm and a height of 339 mm. The large spatial localization capacity of the optimized 3-SPR parallel manipulator is shown in Fig. 9.

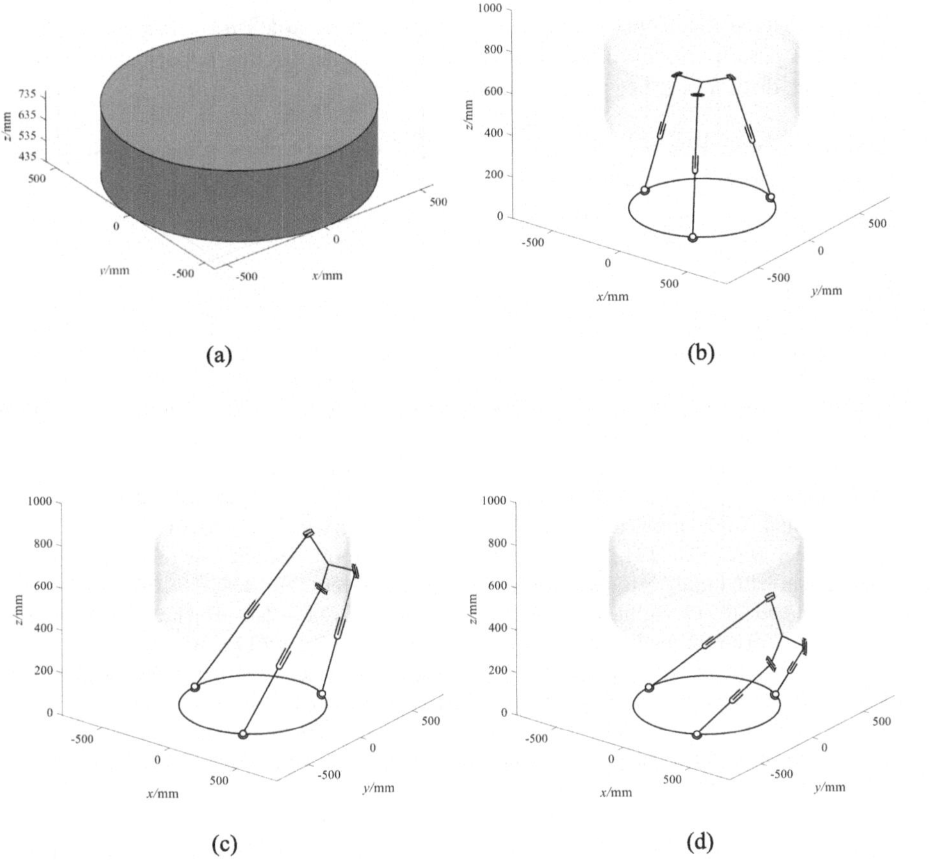

Fig. 9. Large spatial localization capacity of the 3-SPR parallel manipulator: (a) optimum positioning workspace; (b) at the middle of the positioning workspace; (c) at the upper edge of the positioning workspace; (d) at the lower edge of the positioning workspace.

4 Conclusion

In this paper, optimum design is carried out on a 3-SPR parallel manipulator with large parasitic motion. Through the kinematic analysis of the manipulator, it is proved that the parasitic motion is potential to realize a large positioning workspace. The design indices (PWI and GDI) are constructed based on the evaluation of the motion/force transmission and constraint performance. The parameter design space is established by the parameter-finiteness normalization method. The performance chart-based design methodology is adopted to illustrate the distribution of PWI and GDI. By intersecting the regions which satisfy PWI ≥ 1.3 and GDI ≥ 0.6, the qualified region is formed. In order to achieve the optimum workspace along the z axis, the proportional line method is presented, and the optimum region is partitioned from the qualified region. Finally, based on the actual working conditions, the optimum parameters ($R_b = 435$ mm, $R_p = 188$ mm and $z \in [435, 774]$ mm) are obtained, and a large cylindrical workspace (1131 mm $\times$ 339 mm) is achieved. The work in this paper lays an important foundation for the development of the 3-SPR parallel manipulator. The methods presented in this paper can be further applied to the design of other parallel mechanisms.

Acknowledgements. This work was supported by the National Natural Science Foundation of China under Grants 52375018 and 92148301.

References

1. Dzedzickis, A., Subaciute-Zemaitiene, J., Sutinys, E., et al.: Advanced applications of industrial robotics: new trends and possibilities. Appl. Sci.-Basel **12**(1), 135 (2022)
2. Liu, X.J., Xie, F.G., Wang, J.S.: Fundamentals of Parallel Robot Mechanisms. Higher Education Press, Beijing (2018)
3. Kamada, S., Laliberté, T., Gosselin, C.: Kinematic analysis of a 4-DOF parallel mechanism with large translational and orientational workspace. In: 2019 International Conference on Robotics and Automation (ICRA), pp. 1637–1643. IEEE, Montreal (2019)
4. Li, J.F., Fei, R.Y., Fan, J.H., Wu, G.Z.: Kinematic performance analysis of 3-DOF parallel mechanism with large positional workspace. Chin. J. Mech. Eng. **43**(8), 53–59 (2007)
5. Ghaedrahmati, R., Gosselin, C.: Kinematic analysis of a new 2-DOF parallel wrist with a large singularity-free rotational workspace. Mech. Mach. Theory **175**, 104942 (2022)
6. Ghaedrahmati, R., Gosselin, C.: Kinematic analysis of a new 3-dof parallel wrist-gripper assembly with a large singularity-free workspace. Actuators **12**(11), 421 (2023)
7. Khoshnoodi, H., Hanzaki, A.R., Talebi, H.A.: Kinematics, singularity study and optimization of an innovative spherical parallel manipulator with large workspace. J. Intell. Rob. Syst. **92**(2), 309–321 (2018)
8. Xu, C.H., Xie, F.G., Liu, X.J.: Optimum design and stiffness analysis of a 3-RCU parallel manipulator. In: 2023 IEEE International Conference on Robotics and Biomimetics (ROBIO), Koh Samui, Thailand, pp. 1–5 (2023)
9. Wen, K.L., Harton, D., Laliberté, T., et al.: Kinematically redundant (6+3)-DOF hybrid parallel robot with large orientational workspace and remotely operated gripper. In: 2019 International Conference on Robotics and Automation (ICRA), pp. 1672–1678. IEEE (2019)
10. Lee, J., Nam, Y., Park, M.: Kinematics and optimization of a 2-DOF parallel manipulator with a passive constraining leg and linear actuators. J. Mech. Sci. Technol. **24**(1), 1–10 (2010)
11. Hamida, B.I., Laribi, A.M., Mlika, A., et al.: Dimensional synthesis and performance evaluation of four translational parallel manipulators. Robotica **39**(1), 23–38 (2020)
12. Castelli, G., Ottaviano, E., Ceccarelli, M.: A fairly general algorithm to evaluate workspace characteristics of serial and parallel manipulators. Mech. Based Design Struct. Mach. **36**(1) (2008)
13. Saputra, V.B., Ong, S.K., Nee, A.Y.C.: A swarm optimization approach for solving workspace determination of parallel manipulators. Robotica **33**(3), 649–668 (2015)
14. Salisbsury, J.K., Craig, J.J.: Articulated hands: force control and kinematic issues. Int. J. Robot. Res. **1**(1), 4–17 (1982)
15. Liu, X.J., Chen, X., Nahon, M.: Motion/force constrainability analysis of lower-mobility parallel manipulators. J. Mech. Robot.-Trans. ASME **6**(3), 031006 (2014)

16. Wang, J.S., Wu, C., Liu, X.J.: Performance evaluation of parallel manipulators: motion/force transmissibility and its index. Mech. Mach. Theory **45**(10), 1462–1476 (2010)
17. Xie, F.G., Liu, X.J.: Design and development of a high-speed and high-rotation robot with four identical arms and a single platform. J. Mech. Robot.-Trans. ASME **7**(4), 041015 (2015)
18. Xie, F.G., Liu, X.J., Wang, J.S., et al.: Kinematic optimization of a five degrees-of-freedom spatial parallel mechanism with large orientational workspace. J. Mech. Robot.-Trans. ASME **9**(5), 051005 (2017)
19. Song, Y.M., Gao, H., Sun, T., et al.: Kinematic analysis and optimal design of a novel 1T3R parallel manipulator with an articulated travelling plate. Robot. Comput.-Integr. Manuf. **30**(5), 508–516 (2014)
20. Sun, T., Huo, X.: Type synthesis of 1T2R parallel mechanisms with parasitic motions. Mech. Mach. Theory **128**, 412–428 (2018)
21. Chen, M., Zhang, Q., Chen, W., et al.: Analysis and type synthesis of parallel mechanisms without parasitic motion based on spatial geometry. J. Mech. Eng. **57**(1), 77–85 (2021)
22. Bi, Z.M.: Kinetostatic modeling of exechon parallel kinematic machine for stiffness analysis. Int. J. Adv. Manuf. Technol. **71**(1–4), 325–335 (2014)

Pneumatic Gripper Design Concurrent Shape Topology Optimization

Nianfeng Wang(✉), Dixin Zhong, Bicheng Chen, and Xianmin Zhang

Guangdong Key Laboratory of Precision Equipment and Manufacturing Technology, School of Mechanical and Automotive Engineering, South China University of Technology, Guangzhou 510641, China
menfwang@scut.edu.cn

Abstract. The design of soft grippers is one of the most classic problems in the design and application of robots . Researchers have provided mature and complete solutions to the design problem of grippers in recent years, such as using bionics for design, mathematical modeling for simulation analysis of gripper performance. Shape and topology optimization is an effective tool for solving optimal material layout in a given field, widely used in various structural design problems, and can also be used in the structural design of flexible grippers. Compared to mature solutions with fixed force inputs, optimization tasks related to design related pressure loads remain a challenge. This article proposes a shape and topology optimization method for describing the motion pressure boundary using B-spline curves. Topological optimization is performed on the boundary shape and structure, and this method is combined to complete the design of aerodynamic compliant grippers. The design results of the clamping mechanism were post-processed and explored through pneumatic experiments to verify the feasibility of topology optimization for structural design.

Keywords: gripper design · shape and topology optimization · pressure loading problem · structural optimization · compliant mechanism

1 Introduction

With the rapid development of new materials, structural engineering, and control systems, the research scope of soft grippers is becoming more comprehensive and extensive, including in-depth research on the structure design, materials, and control of soft grippers, and the driving methods are becoming increasingly diverse. As the field gradually matures, its application scope expands to a wide range, which can be applied in various fields such as industry, agriculture, healthcare, and service industries. (Su et al. (2022); Fell C et al. (2022); Liu et al. (2020)). The existing software grippers can be divided into two forms based on their design methods: bionic design and humanoid hand design. Generally speaking, the goal of structural design is to design structures that have high economic value, high universality, and can reasonably meet different environmental usage conditions. Structural optimization design can be used in the design of

X. Lan et al. (Eds.): ICIRA 2024, LNAI 15201, pp. 332–347, 2025.
https://doi.org/10.1007/978-981-96-0771-6_25

structures, which usually includes shape optimization, size optimization, and topology optimization. Shape and topology optimization methods have been widely developed in the past decades and successfully applied in structural and multidisciplinary engineering problems (Zhu et al. (2020); Zolfagharian et al. (2019); Wang et al. (2018); Townsend et al. (2019); Sundaram et al. (2019)). A typical solution to topology optimization of structures is based on the density method (Wang et al. (2020); Wang, Hu, and Zhang (2017); Wang et al. (2019b)). Unlike fixed load inputs, this problem requires the load to vary according to the shape of the boundary, which is common in applications such as pressure loads on ships, snow loads on roof structures, and static water pressure loads on underwater machinery. The key to this problem is to deal with designable boundaries that can move and match topology evolution during the design process, in order to determine the position, size, and direction of pressure loads, and apply them to the shape of the boundary. This article studies the topology optimization of SIMP method and uses the topology optimization method to design a complete set of structures integrating gas chambers and grippers. On this basis, a shape and topology optimization method using B-spline curves to describe the motion pressure boundary is proposed. B-splines do not form boundary shapes from uncertain structural topologies, but are directly applied to the structural topology as pressure boundaries. Use the region within the equidistant curve of a B-spline with width as a solid material to form a strong boundary for pressure. Starting from this point, based on the SIMP method, a mathematical modeling method for shape optimization was explored, and the optimization of the two was linked to complete the design of the gripper and driving chamber. And manufacture and experiment the soft gripper to explore its motion mode, material deformation mode, and existing shortcomings, which can further optimize the algorithm and achieve the integrity of structural design.

2 Structural Shape and Topology Description

2.1 Pressure Loading Problem Using Prescribed Shape

In the design process of pneumatic soft grippers, the shape design of the pneumatic driving boundary is an important part. The driving part needs to bear a certain pressure and be combined with the structural part to form a complete single degree of freedom pneumatic driven gripper mechanism. To complete the design of the driving boundary, a B-spline curve with width is used to characterize the boundary.

A common task in shape and topology optimization is to plan a limited amount of material in the most favorable way. As shown in Fig. 1(a), the design domain Ω is separated into domain of void Ω_v and domain of materials Ω_m, forming the topology of the structure. $\boldsymbol{b}$ is the body forces and $\boldsymbol{\Gamma}_u$ is the fixed boundary. The additional description from the standard one is that the pressure $\boldsymbol{p}_0$ acts on the pressure boundary $\boldsymbol{\Gamma}_p$ of the material domain. The void domain inside the pressure is donated as Ω_p. The governing equation can be stated as:

$$\begin{aligned} &\boldsymbol{div\sigma}(\boldsymbol{u}) + \boldsymbol{b} = 0, && in\, \Omega_m \\ &\boldsymbol{u} = \boldsymbol{u}_0, && on\, \Gamma_u \\ &\boldsymbol{\sigma}(\boldsymbol{u})\boldsymbol{n} = \boldsymbol{p}_0, && on\, \Gamma_p \end{aligned}$$

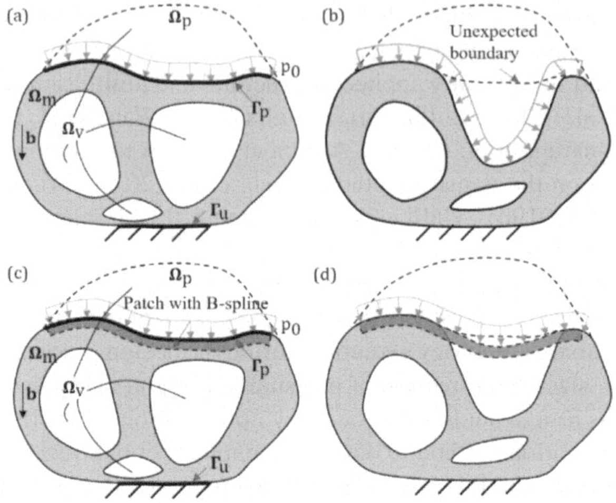

Fig. 1. Structural optimization with pressure. Ω_m is the domain of materials, Ω_v is the domain of void, and Ω_p is the domain of pressure. $\boldsymbol{b}$ is the body forces, and $\boldsymbol{p}_0$ is the pressure. $\boldsymbol{\Gamma}_u$ is the prescribed boundary, and $\boldsymbol{\Gamma}_p$ is the pressure boundary. (a) Pressure loading without constraint of boundary, and (b) unexpected boundary with rapid change. (c) Pressure loading using patch with B-spline curve, and (d) the feasible boundary for pressure.

where $\boldsymbol{div}$ is the divergent operation, $\boldsymbol{\sigma}$ is the stress, $\boldsymbol{u}$ is the displacement, $\boldsymbol{u}_0$ is the prescribed displacement, $\boldsymbol{n}$ is the normal vector of the boundary.

The pressure p_0 is expected to be applied actually in the boundary of material domain Ω_m instead of void domain Ω_p to avoid numerical difficulties, and the boundary is supposed to change slightly to avoid unsteady evolution. As the topology of structure is uncertain before convergence, and the unexpected boundary is inevitable as shown in Fig. 1 (b). The key to the problem is to constrain the topology of structure on the pressure loading boundary.

Different from previous studies that formed a boundary shape from an uncertain topology of structure, this paper directly imposes an evolutionary boundary shape into the topology of structure as the pressure boundary. As shown in Fig. 1 (c), topology of structure is patched with prescribed shape of B-spline curve on the pressure boundary $\boldsymbol{\Gamma}_p$. And the domain inside the isometric width of B-spline is designated to the material domain. On the one hand, the pressure p_0 applied can be obtained according to the shape of the B-spline. On the other hand, the isometric curve of B-spline can provide a strong pressure boundary. As shown in Fig. 1 (d), the updating of the boundary can be controlled through limiting the change of the B-spline curves so that a feasible boundary for pressure can be obtained.

2.2 B- Spline Curve with Isometric Width

B-spline curve is an extension of the Bezier curve, and the linear space formed by all spline functions within a given interval is called the B-spline basis curve. The B-spline basis function is the basis function of this linear space, and the B-spline curve can be understood as a linear combination of the basis curves. Based on the above concept, the B-spline curve can be expressed as:

$$B(t;c) = \sum_{i=1}^{n} B_{i,k}(t)P_i$$

where t is the intrinsic variable ranged from 0–1, parameter $\mathcal{C}$ is the point set of n control points of B-spline as $\boldsymbol{P}_1, \boldsymbol{P}_2, \ldots, \boldsymbol{P}_n$. $B_{i,k}$ is the i th B-spline basis function with prescribed k + 1 knots to generate a k-order curve. The B-spline basic function can be obtained by the recurrence formulation defined on the uniform knot vector $\mathbf{T} = \{t_1, t_2, \ldots, t_{n+k+1}\}$:

$$\begin{cases} B_{i,0} = \begin{cases} 1, \ if \ t_i \le t \le t_{i+1} \\ 0, \ otherwise \end{cases} \\ B_{i,k} = \frac{t-t_i}{t_{i+k}-t_i} B_{i,k-1} + \frac{t_{i+k+1}-t}{t_{i+k+1}-t_{i+1}} B_{i+1,k-1} \\ T = \{0, 0, 0, \ldots, 0, \frac{1}{m}, \frac{2}{m}, \ldots, \frac{m-1}{m}, 1, 1, 1, \ldots, 1\} \\ m = n - k \end{cases}$$

The detail information of B-spline can refer to work by Wang et al. (Wang et al. (2019a)). With the help of shared tools provided by MATLAB community (Hunyadi (2020)), the B-spline curve can be obtained directly. Figure 2 shows a 3-order B-spline curve with five control points.

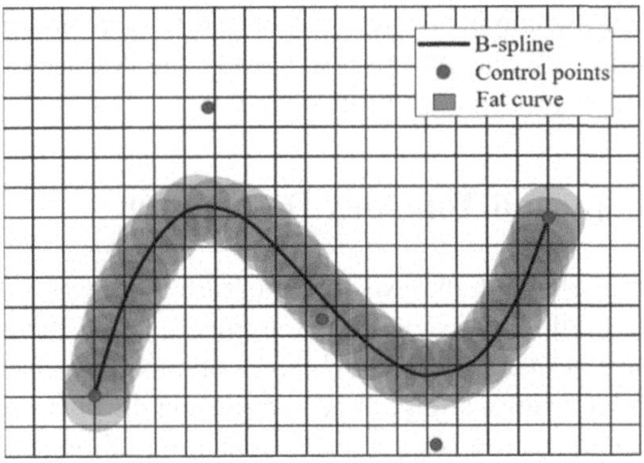

Fig. 2. B-spline curve with five control point, as k = 3, n = 5 and T = {0, 0, 0, 0, 0.5, 1, 1, 1, 1}, and a fat curve obtained by using a disk move along the curve.

B-spline curve in mathematical form is not suitable for geometry as it includes no area. A "fat curve" is obtained by using a cross-section move along a curve. The disk moves along the B-spline curve to generate the fat B-spline curve as the strong boundary as shown in Fig. 2. The fat B-spline curve can be expressed using area inside isomeric curves as:

$$\boldsymbol{B}(t;c;w) = \{\boldsymbol{X} \| \|\boldsymbol{X} - \boldsymbol{B}(t;c)\| \leq w\}$$

where w can be given by the width function of the curve $B(t;c)$ and X is the point of fat B-spline curve.

2.3 Model for Shape and Topology Optimization

Based on the description above, a shape and topology optimization model concerning a given width w0 of the B-spline curve, can be expressed as:

$$\begin{aligned}
&\min_{\rho,c} f = \boldsymbol{R}^T \boldsymbol{u} \\
&s.t.\, \boldsymbol{Ku} = \boldsymbol{F} \\
&v_1 = \sum_{e_i} (1 - \rho_i)/V_\Omega - V^p \leq 0, e_i \in \Omega_p \\
&v_2 = \sum_{e_i} \rho_i/V_\Omega - V^m \leq 0, e_i \in \Omega_m \\
&0 < \rho_{\min} \leq \rho_e = \rho_e^S + \rho_e^T \leq 1, (e = 1, 2, \ldots N)
\end{aligned}$$

where ρ is the vector of relative densities of N discretized elements as $\rho_1, \rho_2 \ldots \rho_N$. c is the control points of B-spline as **P1, P2,..., Pn**. **u** is the displacement in equilibrium state **Ku = F**, where **K** is the global stiffness matrix and F is the external load vector. f is the target function which can be obtained by a combination of displacement, and **R** is the weight vector. V_1 is the constraint of the volume of pressure area Ω_P, and V^P is the volume constraint. V_2 is the constraint of volume of material domain Ω_m, and V^m is the volume constraint. V_Ω is the total volume of the design domain. $\rho_{\min}$ is the minimum density of each element, which is taken as $\rho_{\min} = 0.001$ to avoid numerical singularity caused by zero densities. ρ_e^S and ρ_e^T are respectively the density of fat B-spline curve and basic structure discretized in each finite element.

3 Structural Shape and Topology Description

For implement of finite element analysis, the pressure loading on the shape boundary of the B-spline curve should be predetermined. Figure 3 shows the pressure imposed to the design model. The external load vector F can be obtained by assembling the element load vector F_e. Instead of using a straight line to represent the curve segment within each finite element, the load vector Fe is directly computed based on the integrated variable t as:

$$\begin{aligned}
&F = \sum_{e=1}^{N} F_e \\
&F_e = \int_L N^T \phi dL = p_0 T_0 \int_{t_s}^{t_e} N(x(t), y(t))^T \begin{Bmatrix} y'(t) \\ x'(t) \end{Bmatrix} dt
\end{aligned}$$

where N is the shape functions, L is the curve segment, Φ is the loading vector. T_0 is the element thickness, t_s and t_e are the starting point and endpoint for the curve segment. $y'(t)$ and $x'(t)$ are the components of unit load vector of Φ in x-direction and y-direction, which can be obtained by the differential of B-spline $B(t; c)$ as:

$$\begin{Bmatrix} x'(t) \\ y'(t) \end{Bmatrix} = B'(t; c) = \sum_{i=1}^{n-1} B_{i+1,k-1}(t)Q_i$$
$$Q_i = \frac{k}{t_{i+k+1} - t_{i+1}}(P_{i+1} - P_i)$$

Through variable transformation and the gauss integration, the pressure applied in the design model will be obtained as shown in Fig. 3. It shows that only the finite elements intersected by the B-spline curve will carry a part of loading.

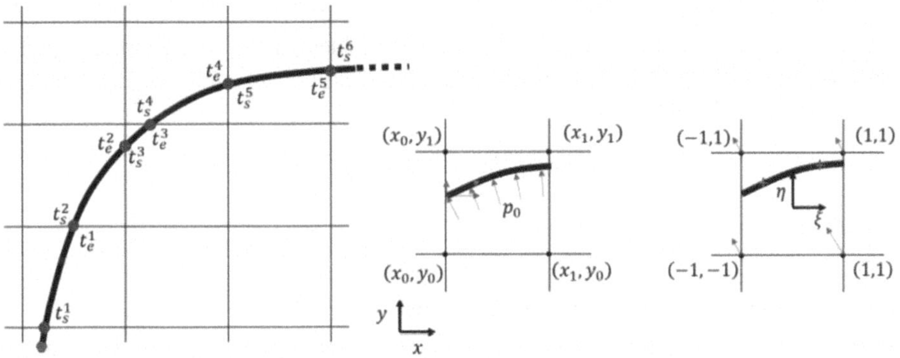

Fig. 3. Pressure loading of finite element analysis.

In order to simplify the calculation process of the above integration, the integration interval is transformed to [−1, 1], and the coordinate points are transformed, where (ξ, η) it is the coordinate of the shape function parameter. Obtain as:

$$N_1 = \tfrac{1}{4}(1-\xi)(1-\eta) \quad N_2 = \tfrac{1}{4}(1+\xi)(1-\eta)$$

$$N_3 = \tfrac{1}{4}(1+\xi)(1+\eta) \quad N_4 = \tfrac{1}{4}(1-\xi)(1+\eta)$$

$$\xi = \frac{x - x_0}{x_1 - x_0} * 2 - 1$$

$$\eta = \frac{y - y_0}{y_1 - y_0} * 2 - 1$$

$$N = \begin{Bmatrix} N_1 \; 0 \; N_2 \; 0 \; N_3 \; 0 \; N_4 \; 0 \\ 0 \; N_1 \; 0 \; N_2 \; 0 \; N_3 \; 0 \; N_4 \end{Bmatrix}$$

Using the method of two-point Gaussian integration, the pressure applied in topology optimization design will be in the finite element intersecting with the B-spline curve, and these cells will bear the applied pressure load. The finite element calculation of SIMP topology optimization and the calculation process of stiffness matrix are as follows, The global stiffness matrix K can be obtained by assembling the element stiffness K_e as:

$$K = \sum_{e=1}^{N} K_e$$
$$K_e = \int_{\Omega_e} W^T DWdV = E_e \int_{\Omega_e} W^T D^0 WdV = E_e K_e^0$$

where Ω_e is the domain of element, **W** is the matrix between strain and displacement, and K_e^0 is the stiffness matrix of solid material.

4 Design with Shape and Topology Optimization

4.1 Design Sensitivity Analysis

The adjoint variable method is utilized to evaluate the design sensitivity of the objective function. By using Lagrange multiplier method into equilibrium equation, an augmented objective function is reformed as:

$$\boldsymbol{h} = \boldsymbol{R}^T \boldsymbol{u} - \boldsymbol{I}^T (\boldsymbol{K}\boldsymbol{u} - \boldsymbol{F})$$

where $\boldsymbol{I}$ is Lagrange multiplier vector.

4.1.1 Sensitivity Analysis Topology Variables

When the topology is updated, the curves will remain constant. In this way, the pressure load on the fix boundary and the problem is the same as the typical one. Concerning the small change of topological variables, the sensitivities can be obtained as:

$$\frac{\partial h}{\partial \rho_e^T} = \frac{\partial h}{\partial \rho_e}\frac{\partial \rho_e}{\partial \rho_e} = \frac{\partial R^T}{\partial \rho_e}u + u^T(\frac{\partial R^T}{\partial u}\frac{\partial u}{\partial \rho_e})$$
$$+ R^T\frac{\partial u}{\partial \rho_e} - I^T(K\frac{\partial u}{\partial \rho_e} + \frac{\partial K}{\partial \rho_e}u)$$
$$= (u^T\frac{\partial R^T}{\partial u} + R^T - I^T K)\frac{\partial u}{\partial \rho_e}$$
$$- I^T\frac{\partial K}{\partial \rho_e}u + \frac{\partial R^T}{\partial \rho_e}u$$

Taking $I^T = (u^T \partial R^T/\partial u + R^T)K^{-1}$ to eliminate the derivative $\partial u/\partial \rho_e$ and submitting I back to the equation, it can give the sensitivities calculated at the elemental level as:

$$\frac{\partial h}{\partial \rho_e^T} = \frac{\partial h}{\partial \rho_e} = -I^T\frac{\partial K}{\partial \rho_e}u + \frac{\partial R^T}{\partial \rho_e}u$$
$$= -p\rho_e^{p-1}E^0 I_e^T K_e^0 u_e + \frac{\partial R_e^T}{\partial \rho_e}u_e$$
$$= -\frac{p}{\rho_e}I_e^T K_e u_e + \frac{\partial R_e^T}{\partial \rho_e}u_e$$

where I_e is the elemental adjoint vector and R_e is the weight vector in each element.

4.1.2 Sensitivity Analysis of Shape Variables

The change of shape will influence both the loading forces imposed and the local stiffness of the structure. Concerning the small change of shape variables, the sensitivities can be calculated as:

$$\begin{aligned}\frac{\partial h}{\partial z} &= \frac{\partial R^T}{\partial z}u + u^T\left(\frac{\partial RT}{\partial u}\frac{\partial u}{\partial z}\right) + R^T\frac{\partial u}{\partial z}\\ &- I^T\left(K\frac{\partial u}{\partial z} + \frac{\partial K}{\partial z}u + \frac{\partial F}{\partial z}\right)\\ &= \left(u^T\frac{\partial R^T}{\partial u} + R^T - I^T k\right)\frac{\partial u}{\partial z} - I^T\frac{\partial K}{\partial z}u\\ &- I^T\frac{\partial F}{\partial z} + \frac{\partial R^T}{\partial z}u\end{aligned}$$

where z denotes a shape variable of component of **c** as (x_i, y_i) for P_i. $\partial\mathbf{u}/\partial\mathbf{z}$ is the sensitivities between shape variables and displacements, and $\partial\mathbf{F}/\partial\mathbf{z}$ is the sensitivities between shape variables and loading forces. With $I^T = \left(u^T\partial R^T/\partial u + R^T\right)K^{-1}$ and the topology sensitives calculated above, the sensitivities can be simplified and calculated at the elemental level as:

$$\begin{aligned}\frac{\partial h}{\partial z} &= -I^T\frac{\partial K}{\partial z}u - I^T\frac{\partial F}{\partial z} + \frac{\partial R^T}{\partial z}u\\ &= -I^T\frac{\partial K}{\partial \rho}\frac{\partial \rho}{\partial \rho^S}\frac{\partial \rho^S}{\partial z}u - I^T\frac{\partial F}{\partial z} + \frac{\partial R^T}{\partial \rho}\frac{\partial \rho}{\partial \rho^S}\frac{\partial \rho^S}{\partial z}u\\ &= \sum_e\left(-p\rho_e^{p-1}E^0 I_e^T K_e u_e\frac{\partial \rho_e^S}{\partial z} - I_e^T\frac{\partial F_e}{\partial z} + \frac{\partial R_e^T}{\partial \rho_e}u_e\frac{\partial \rho_e^S}{\partial z}\right)\\ &= \sum_e\left(\frac{\partial h}{\partial \rho_e}\frac{\partial \rho_e^S}{\partial z} - I_e^T\frac{\partial F_e}{\partial z}\right)\end{aligned}$$

where $\partial\rho_e^s/\partial z$ and $\partial F_e/\partial z$ are approximated by their difference and the ultimate sensitivities are validated with finite element difference method. Both of them are zero for most elements except for those lying in the boundary around the fat Bezier curves.

4.2 Filtering Operation

Filtering operation is used to make solutions mesh-independent and avoid the checkerboard pattern, which can be imposed on sensitivities or the densities. Here, the density filter Sigmund (2007) is adapted and it transforms the original densities ρ_e into:

$$\overline{\rho}_e = \frac{1}{\sum_{i\in S_e} H_{ei}}\sum_{i\in S_e}(H_{ei}\rho_i)$$
$$H_{ei} = \max(0, r_{\min} - dist(e, i))$$

where *dist(e, i)* is the distance between element i and element e, H_{ei} is their weight factor, S_e is the set of element with the distance to element e smaller than the filter radius $r_{\min}$. The application of the density filter causes the original design variable ρ_e to lose its physical meaning. Instead, the filtered density $\overline{\rho_e}$ is regarded as the physical density and acted as the solution of the optimization problem . The sensitivities of the objective function f are still given by Eq. 12, provided that the variable ρ_e is changed to $\overline{\rho_e}$. And the sensitivities with respect to the design variables ρ_e are obtained by means of the chain rule as

$$\frac{\partial h}{\partial \rho_j} = \sum_{e \in S_j} \frac{\partial f}{\partial \rho_e} \frac{\partial \overline{\rho}_e}{\partial \rho_j} = \sum_{e \in S_j} \left(\frac{1}{\sum\limits_{i \in S_j} H_{ei}} H_{je} \frac{\partial f}{\partial \overline{\rho}_e} \right)$$

where S_j is the set of element with the distance to element j smaller than the filter radius.

5 Pneumatic Gripper Design

The case studies will show several examples to exam the proposed method.

This design focuses on the software gripper to achieve grasping function. For the planar design domain, a displacement degree of freedom is specified, and constraints on the design domain boundary are set. Since the symmetry of the structure can be used to simplify the optimization process, symmetric constraints are applied to the design domain. The design domain and boundary conditions are shown in the following Fig. 4:

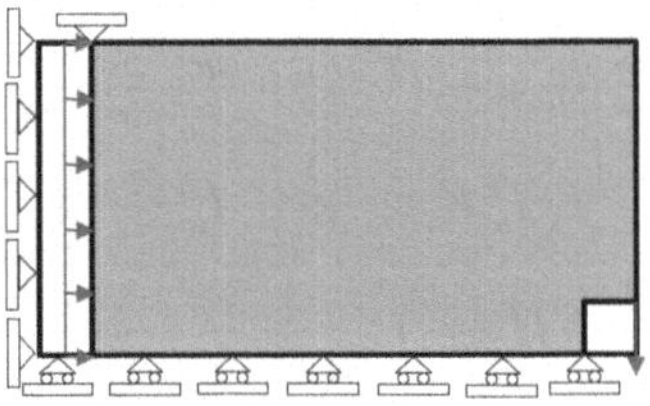

Fig. 4. Topology optimization design domain

The design domain is a gray area, and the output position hollows out a set of 10×10 units. The input is a uniformly distributed air pressure, and the output is the displacement required for the downward grasping action. The optimization result is shown in the Fig. 5:

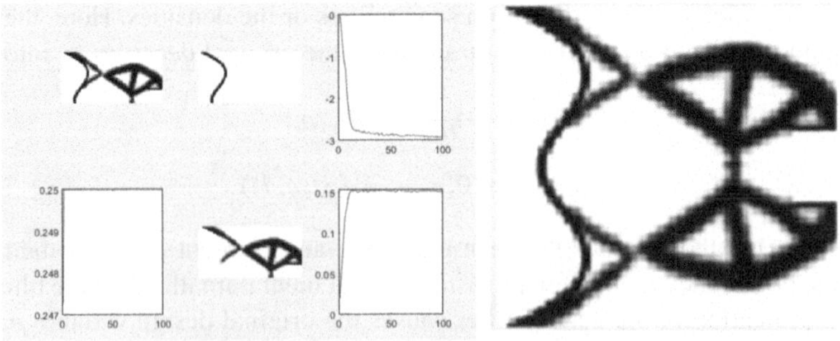

Fig. 5. Display of optimization results

From the above analysis, it can be seen that using modular thinking, the design domain can be divided into blocks, thereby designing multiple unit structures or structures with multiple degrees of freedom that are ultimately integrated. After designing a single degree of freedom structure, we will continue to study how to extend it to two or even multiple degree of freedom structure. The two degrees of freedom of grasping and pushing are also based on topology optimization design within the plane. Divide the design domain into two parts: left and right, and perform topology optimization design for pushing degrees of freedom and grasping degrees of freedom, respectively. The topology optimization design for grasping behavior is shown in the previous text, and the design for flat pushing and integrated design domain is shown in the Fig. 6:

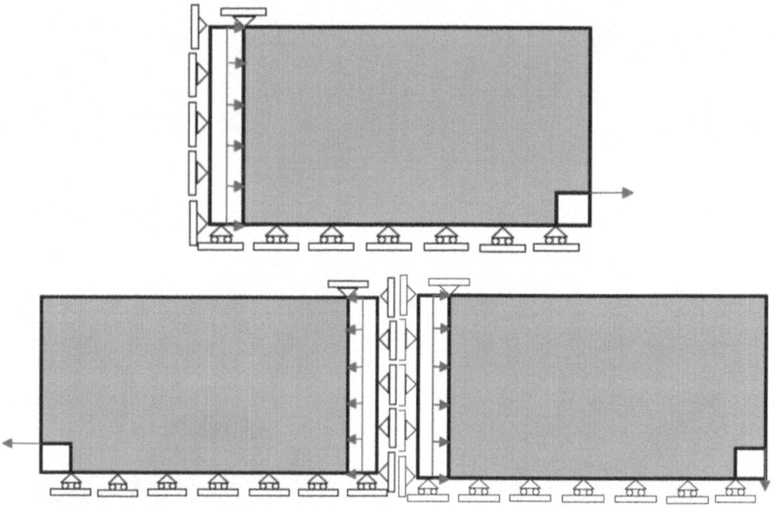

Fig. 6. Structural design domain of parallel movement degrees of freedom

The numerical calculation results of topology optimization are shown in Fig. 7:

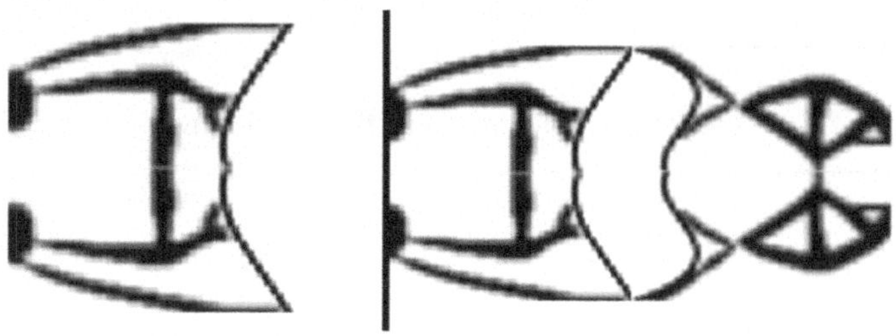

Fig. 7. Topology results and integrated structure

In order to convert the results of topology optimization into solid structures that can be used for experiments, it is necessary to convert the curves of the topology graph into closed curves with width that can be used for 3D modeling. This requires the use of contour lines to transform the design variables in topology optimization into multiple closed curves, similar to contour lines. The optimization iteration results are flattened, saved in curve form, and finally sketched for design. The contour function in MATLAB is used to draw contour maps of matrices. Import the completed design variable x into the program to obtain the contour line graph shown in the Fig. 8, after completing the contour extraction work in MATLAB, these curves are extracted and imported into SOLIDWORKS to complete the modeling process.

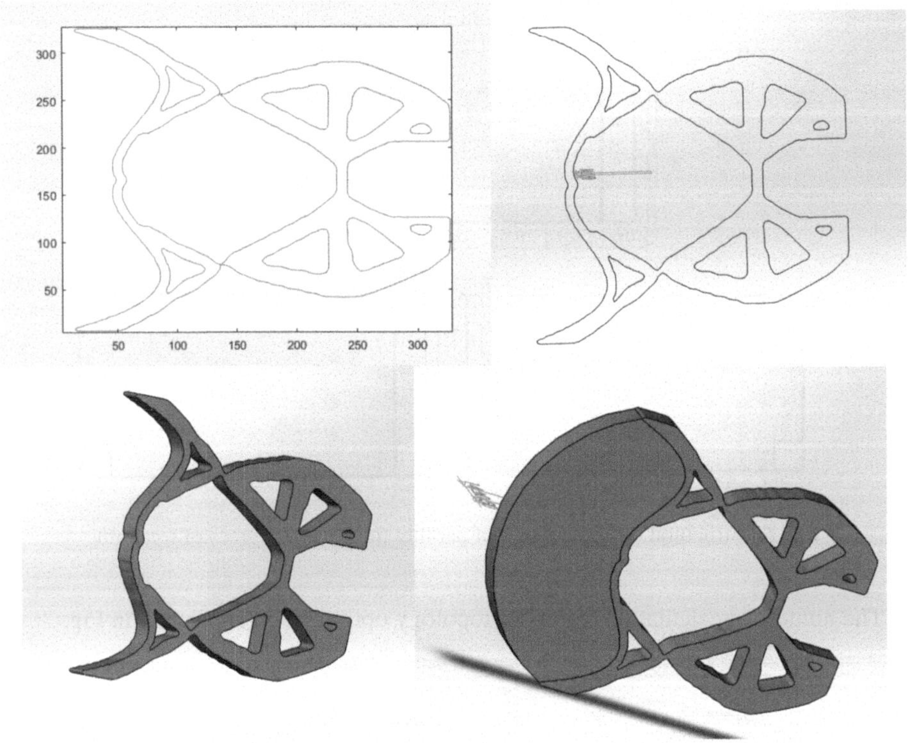

Fig. 8. The Solid Modeling Process of Claw

The structure of the air chamber is:

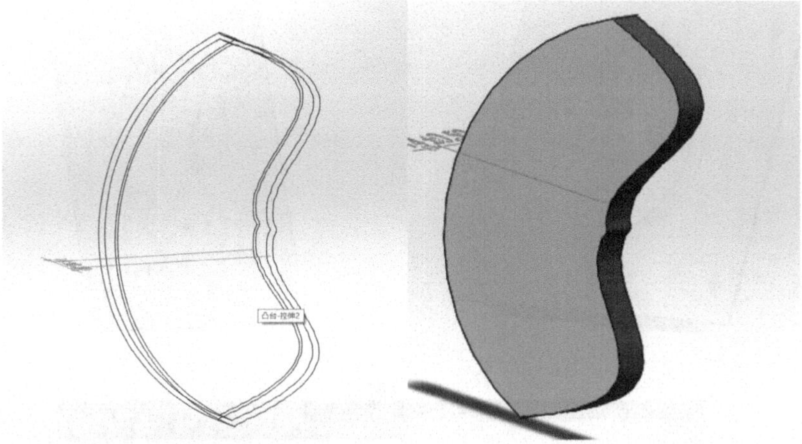

Select silicone as the material for the air chamber, mix the silicone liquid of A-30 and B-30 in a 1:1 mass ratio, and use a planetary stirrer for stirring. The parameters of the mixer are set to 1000 r/min and the rotation time is 1 min. Due to the fact that the silicone liquid is thermally cured, it is necessary to strictly control the stirring speed and stirring time to prevent the silicone from solidifying during the stirring process and affecting its fluidity, which may cause problems during the subsequent pouring process. The planetary agitator can effectively prevent the generation of bubbles. The release agent used in this article is Ease Release 200 aerosol release agent produced by Smooth-on company. Before infusion, evenly distribute the release agent.

Spray evenly on the surface of the mold. Due to the fact that the mold is also manufactured through 3D printing, heating and curing are not used. It can be completely solidified even after being left to stand for 6 to 8 h under natural air drying conditions, and demolding is very easy. This method is used for curing in this article.

The mold adopts a two half design for easy demolding. Due to the cavity structure, the edge thickness of the mold needs to be set within a reasonable range. The mold is shown in the Fig. 9(a), The blue area in the left image is the area filled with silicone, and the right image is the dustproof cover. The two are connected with screws and placed flat on a table, waiting for the silicone to solidify. After the silicone gel is completely cured, demold it, mix and stir the silicone gel as described above, pour it into a lid, and seal the air chamber, as shown in the Fig. 9(b).

After sealing, the air chamber is attached to the clamp. The clamp is obtained through 3D printing and is made of TPE flexible material. The actual product obtained is shown in Fig. 10:

Pneumatic drive is the driving method used in this article, which requires an air pump to supply air and an air valve to control the pressure. It is connected by a gas pipe and finally expands the air chamber. The pneumatic drive equipment is shown in the Fig. 11:

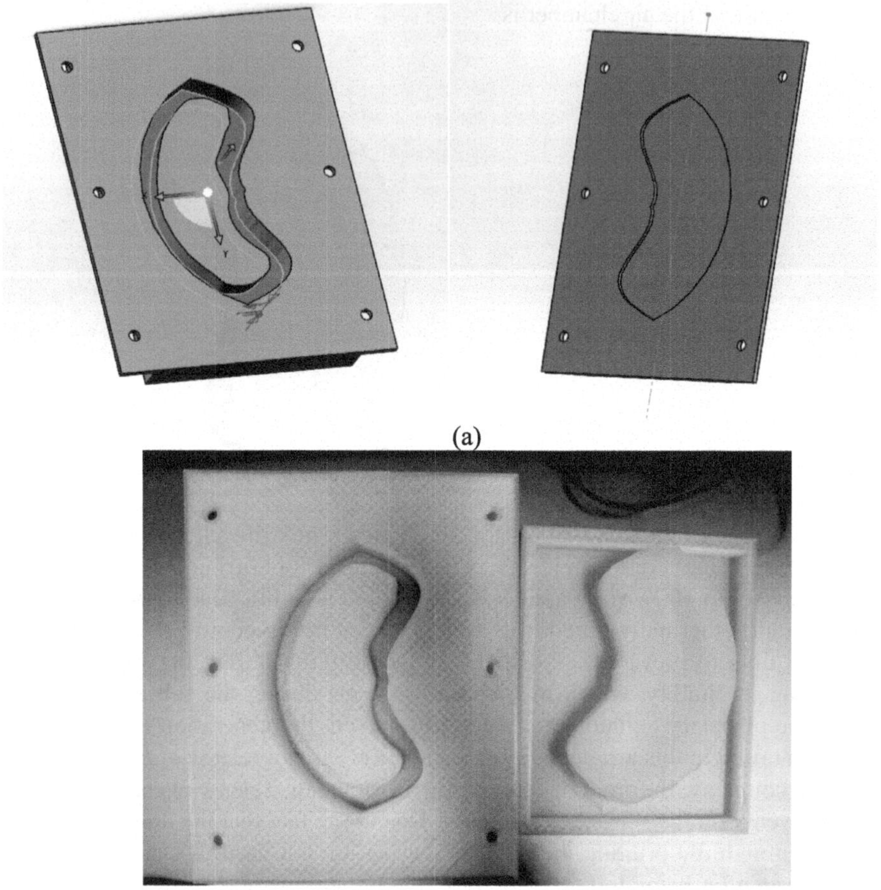

(a)

(b)

Fig. 9. Figure (a) shows the mold for manufacturing the air chamber, and Figure (b) shows the air chamber made of cured silicone material

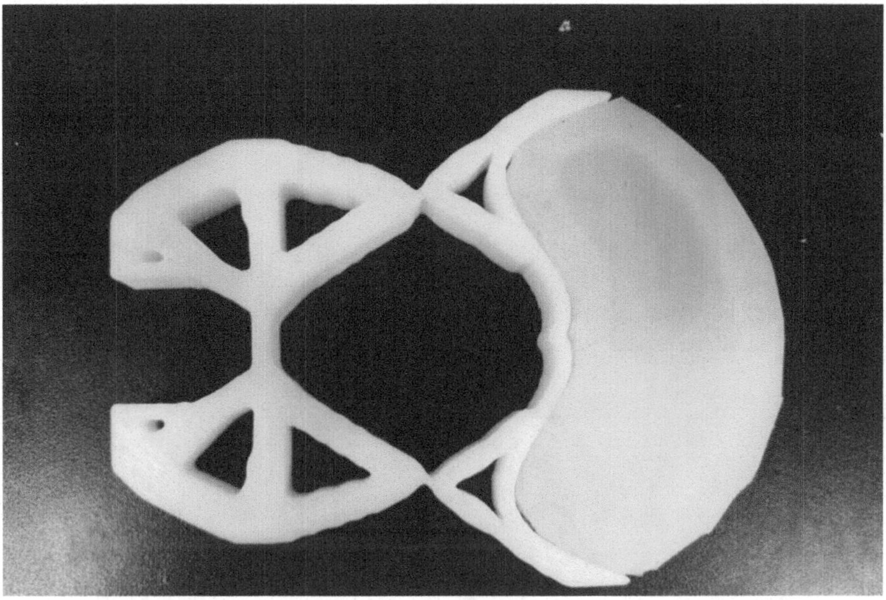

Fig. 10. Physical object of pneumatic gripper

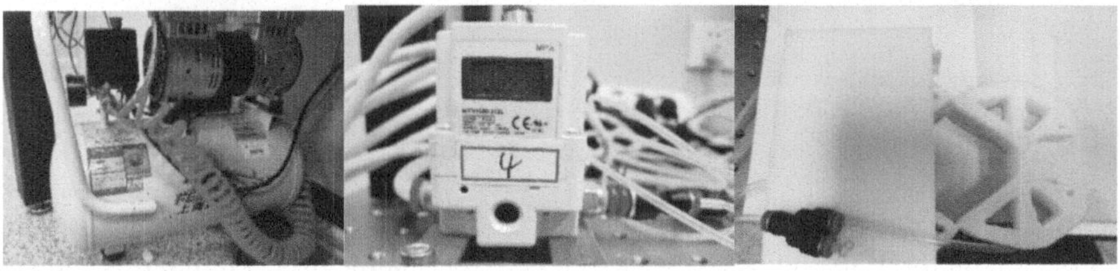

(a) (b) (c)

Fig. 11. Pneumatic drive equipment, (a) is an air pump, (b) is an air valve used to control air pressure output, (c) is a gas pipe, connecting the air valve and the air chamber

Performance demonstration of grasping objects.

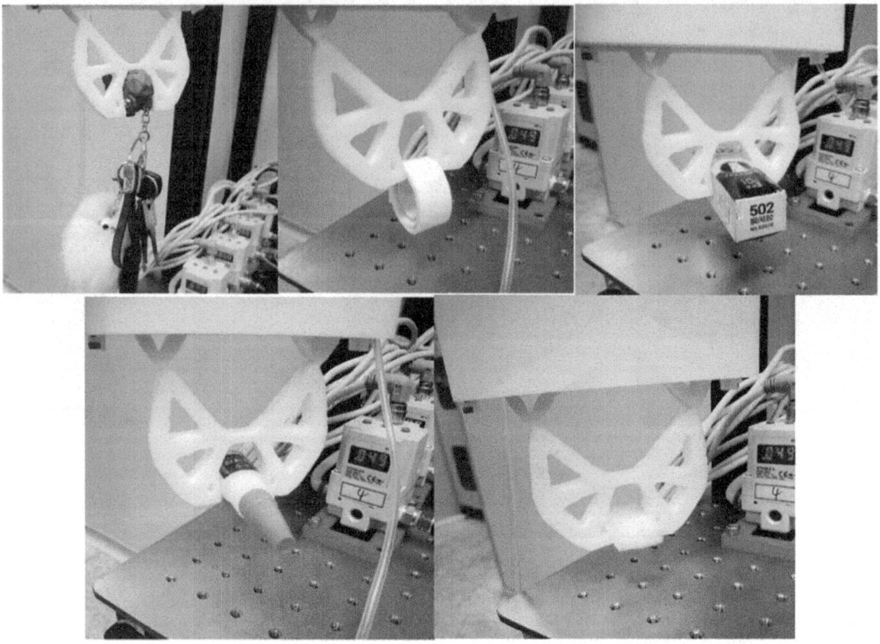

6 Conclusion

This article proposes a new design method for soft grippers. Using shape and topology optimization methods to complete the design of aerodynamic drive boundaries and gripper structures given the size of the design domain. Using B-spline curves to describe the motion pressure boundary, using the regions within the equidistant curves of B-splines with width as solid materials, to form a strong pressure boundary and stabilize its numerical operations to complete the design of the gripper boundary shape. By conducting sensitivity analysis on shape and topology design, and using gradient based optimizers to solve the design problem of grippers. This method can be extended to the research field of soft actuators involving geometric nonlinear deformation of soft materials. The numerical calculation results obtained from post-processing topology optimization were experimentally explored using pneumatic drive, verifying the practicality of topology optimization method in designing robot structures. In summary, this article proposes a structural integration design method for soft grippers based on the SIMP method.

Acknowledgements. The authors would like to gratefully acknowledge the reviewers comments. This work is supported by National Natural Science Foundation of China (Grant No. 52075180) and Guangdong Natural Science Fund (Grant No. 2024A1515011940).

References

Su, H., Hou, X., Zhang, X., et al.: Pneumatic soft robots: challenges and benefits. Actuators **11**(3), 92 (2022)

Chen, Q., Zhang, X., Zhu, B.: A 213-line topology optimization code for geometrically nonlinear structures. Struct. Multidiscip. Optim. **59**(5), 1863–1879 (2019)

Fell, C., Brooks-Richards, T.L., Woodruff, M.A., et al.: Soft pneumatic actuators for mimicking multi-axial femoropopliteal artery mechanobiology. Biofabrication **14**(3) (2022)

Xavier, M.S., Tawk, C.D., Yong, Y.K., et al.: 3D-printed omnidirectional soft pneumatic actuators: design, modeling and characterization. Sens. Actuators A **332**, 113199 (2021)

Hammer, V.B., Olhoff, N.: Topology optimization of continuum structures subjected to pressure loading. Struct. Multidiscip. Optim. **19**(2), 85–92 (2000)

Hunyadi, L.: B splines. MATLAB Central File Exchange **1**(1), 1 (2020)

Lee, E., Martins, J.R.R.A.: Structural topology optimization with design dependent pressure loads. Comput. Methods Appl. Mech. Eng. **233**, 40–48 (2012)

Liu, S., Wang, F., Liu, Z., et al.: A two-finger soft-robotic gripper with enveloping and pinching grasping modes. IEEE/ASME Trans. Mechatron. **1** (2020)

Sigmund, O.: A 99 line topology optimization code written in Matlab. Struct. Multidiscip. Optim. **21**(2), 120–127 (2001)

Sigmund, O.: Morphology-based black and white filters for topology optimization. Struct. Multidiscip. Optim. **33**(4–5), 401–424 (2007)

Sigmund, O., Clausen, P.M.: Topology optimization using a mixed formulation: an alternative way to solve pressure load problems. Comput. Methods Appl. Mech. Eng. **196**(13–16), 1874–1889 (2007)

Townsend, S., Grigg, S., Picelli, R., Featherston, C.A., Kim, H.A.: Topology optimization of vibrational piezoelectric energy harvesters for structural health monitoring applications. J. Intell. Mater. Syst. Struct. **30**, 2894–2907 (2019)

Wang, C., Zhao, M., Ge, T.: Structural topology optimization with design dependent pressure loads. Struct. Multidiscip. Optim. **53**(5), 1005–1018 (2016)

Wang, M.Y., Zong, H., Ma, Q., Tian, Y., Zhou, M.: Cellular level set in B-splines (CLIBS): a method for modeling and topology optimization of cellular structures. Comput. Methods Appl. Mech. Eng. **349**, 378–404 (2019)

Wang, N., Guo, H., Chen, B., Cui, C., Zhang, X.: Design of a rotary dielectric elastomer actuator using a topology optimization method based on pairs of curves. Smart Mater. Struct. **27**(5), 055011 (2018)

Wang, N., Guo, H., Chen, B., Cui, C., Zhang, X.: Design of dielectric elastomer actuator using topology optimization method based on genetic algorithm. Smart Mater. Struct. **28**(6), 065013 (2019)

Wang, N., Hu, K., Zhang, X.M.: Hierarchical optimization for topology design of multi-material compliant mechanisms. Eng. Optim. **49**(12), 2013–2035 (2017)

Wang, N., Zhang, X., Kuang, Y., et al.: Design of dielectric elastomer actuators using topology optimization on electrodes. Smart Mater. Struct. **29**, 075029 (2020)

Carvalho, F.S., Ruscheinsky, D., Giusti, S.M., et al.: Topological derivative-based topology optimization of plate structures under bending effects. Struct. Multidiscip. Optim. **63**(28), 1–14 (2020)

Zhang, X., Feng, Y., Hua, C., et al.: Lost wax casting and experimental analysis of pneumatic soft grippers. Forest. Mach. Woodwork. Equipment **49**(7), 46–51 (2021)

Zhu, B., et al.: Design of compliant mechanisms using continuum topology optimization: a review. Mech. Mach. Theory **143**, 103622 (2020)

Zolfagharian, A., Denk, M., Bodaghi, M., Kouzani, A.Z., Kaynak, A.: Topology optimized 4D printing of a soft actuator. Acta Mech. Solid (2019)

An Underactuated Humanoid Multi-Finger Dexterous Hand with Adaptive Synergic Grasping

Yinan Jin[1,2], Yixiao Zheng[1], Yaojie Mao[1], Zetong Li[1], Lufeng Pan[1], Bangchu Yang[1], Shibo Cai[1], Shahid Hussain[3], and Guanjun Bao[1](✉)

[1] College of Mechanical Engineering, Zhejiang University of Technology, 288 Liuhe Road, Zhejiang 310023, China
gjbao@zjut.edu.cn

[2] ZJUT Yinhu Research Institute of Innovation and Entrepreneurship, 227 Jiulong Avenue, HuangPu 311400, China

[3] School of Information Technology and Systems, University of Canberra, 11 Kirinari Street, ACT 2617, Canberra, Australia

Abstract. To address the practical requirements of daily activities, this research proposes an underactuated humanoid dexterous hand designed for multi-finger adaptive synergic grasping. This anthropomorphic hand incorporates a wheel chute actuating mechanism and an interfinger differential mechanism to enhance functionality. The compliant joints of the dexterous hand facilitate the adaptivity of grasping objects with diverse shapes. A spatial kinematic model of the robotic joints is developed based on the geometric configuration and static analysis of the dexterous hand. Additionally, the workspace and the trajectories of the fingertips are analyzed. An experimental platform has been established for conducting PID control experiments and evaluating the grasping capabilities using fingertip pressure measurements. The results reveal that the proposed underactuated humanoid dexterous hand can reliably grasp a wide range of daily necessities with a grasp weight ratio of up to 1.43, demonstrating its substantial practical utility.

Keywords: Underactuated · Humanoid Dexterous Hand · Fingertip Sensing · Adaptive Grasping

1 Introduction

The dexterous hand serves as the end effector of a humanoid robot and plays a crucial role in the robotic task execution [1]. Its application scenarios are expanding alongside the advancement of human-robot interaction requirements. Since most of daily items are designed with the consideration of human hand, a humanoid dexterous hand offers significant advantages and potential applications [2]. Moreover, anthropomorphism is an effective approach in the research of designing and controlling dexterous hands. Existing humanoid dexterous hands can be categorized into two types including fully actuated and underactuated [3]. Fully actuated hands require highly integrated designs,

X. Lan et al. (Eds.): ICIRA 2024, LNAI 15201, pp. 348–365, 2025.
https://doi.org/10.1007/978-981-96-0771-6_26

heavy cost, and pose significant control challenges [4]. In contrast, underactuated robotic hands have a simpler mechanism with less expense, and they are easier to control. They can conform to the shape of an object automatically, enveloping it without the need for precise control of each joint [5, 6]. Therefore, underactuated mechanisms are more suitable for situations with less demanding operational requirements [7, 8].

The development of underactuated dexterous hands began in the 1970s. The Soft Gripper, developed by Professor Hiroso at Tokyo University of Technology in Japan, was recognized by the industry as the first underactuated dexterous hand [9]. This hand features two fingers and ten joints, with two actuators pulling each end of a rope to control the bending and stretching of all joints. The INAIL/RTR Center in Italy advanced the conceptual design of the Soft Gripper with rope traction and developed the RTR2 Humanoid Hand [10]. This prototype applied two motors to actuate the motion of three fingers and was later transformed into underactuated Cyber Hand with five robotic fingers [11], which realized the most of human grasping operations. The SDM Hand, developed by Yale University in the United States, utilized soft material to manufacture the revolute joint instead of applying the rigid revolute shaft transmission [12]. It achieves finger resetting through the elasticity of the soft material itself, offering a novel approach to the design and manufacture of underactuated dexterous hands. The control strategy of the hand is simple and exhibits strong robustness. However, it lacks a distinct palm and does not take the human hand as a bionic model. Since the 21st century, numerous underactuated dexterous hands have emerged, achieving high integration and humanoid functionality. In 2012, a French company launched the InMoov Hand [13], noted for its highly bionic appearance and low manufacturing cost. In 2013, Japan developed the Ritsumeikan Hand [14], which placed all the actuation hardware in the palm, resulting in an overall weight of only 0.44kg. However, it lacks sensors, leading to low intelligence and limited applications. In 2014, Pisa University in Italy developed the Pisa/IIT Softhand [15], which applies just one motor to actuate 19 joints of the entire hand. It adopts concept of synergy to achieve a high degree of anthropomorphism and integration. In 2018, an upgraded version, the Pisa/IIT Softhand 2 [16], was published. It uses internal friction to achieve simple operating functions, but its grasping ability is relatively limited due to the small number of actuators. Thus, from a mechanism perspective, its grasping capability is certainly restricted. In general, most of existing underactuated dexterous hands employ either open-loop control or position sensors located on the actuators for position control, which fails to achieve accurate grasping of fragile objects. To maintain simplicity and compactness in mechanism, most of the underactuated dexterous hands either omit the force sensor or they utilize an external patch sensor for force control while performing basic grasping functions. However, this approach limits the practical application of dexterous hands.

To address above mentioned limitations, this research proposes an underactuated humanoid dexterous hand with adaptive synergies. A pressure sensor integrated within the fingertip allows for stable grasping of daily items. The Sect. 2 introduces the mechanism of the dexterous hand, covering the overall design of the fingers, palm, wrist, and forearm. The Sect. 3 discusses the motion analysis of the proposed dexterous hand, including kinematics, working space analysis, and fingertip motion trajectory analysis. The Sect. 4 presents a PID control experiment based on fingertip pressure sensing and a test of grasping ability. In Sect. 5, the overall performance of the designed dexterous hand is evaluated, and prospects for future research are outlined.

2 Mechanical Design of Underactuated Humanoid Dexterous Hand

2.1 Overall Design

The overall mechanical and transmission designs of the proposed underactuated humanoid hand are shown in Fig. 1. Its appearance and dimensions are like a human hand, with a total length of 180 mm, a total width of 82 mm, and a palm circumference of 202 mm. Using the concept of modular design approach, the robotic hand is divided into thumb, index finger, middle finger, ring finger, little finger, palm, and forearm. The modules of five robotic fingers are the primary elements for achieving dexterous manipulations. Each robotic finger has three degrees of freedom. These robotic fingers are assembled onto the robotic palm through bolt fastening connections while the robotic palm serves as the base. The robotic palm is equipped with an interfinger differential mechanism and tendon string tracks. They are used to guide the tendon strings to the actuator installed on the robotic forearm. The palm and forearm are connected by bolts and hinges to form a wrist joint with a flexural degree of freedom. The main function of the robotic forearm is to integrate the larger components of the dexterous hand, including five actuators and an actuation control board.

Figure 1(a) shows that the four robotic fingers on the dexterous hand excluding the thumb share the same mechanical structure but different in dimensions. The thumb, which plays a crucial role in grasping, is slightly larger than other robotic fingers. The little finger is slightly smaller in dimension than other fingers due to its weaker function in manipulations, which helps to avoid interference with the ring finger during the grasping process. This mechanical design aligns with the physiological characteristics of the human hand and enhances the anthropomorphic quality of the dexterous hand.

As Fig. 1(b) shows, the proposed hand has 5 actuators and 15 degrees of freedom. It utilizes tendon string transmission mechanism. The colored lines indicate the arrangement of the tendon strings in the dexterous hand. The bending of the thumb is controlled by steering gear 1, with a tendon string (blue line) passing through the DIP (Distal Interphalangeal) and MCP (Metacarpophalangeal) joints of the thumb and directly connected to the steering gear 1. The swivel motion of the thumb is independently controlled by steering gear 2, with a tendon string (purple line) passing through the CMC (Carpometacarpal) joint of the thumb and directly connected to the steering gear 2. The bending of the index finger and middle finger are controlled by steering gear 3. These fingers are connected in series by a tendon string (red line). The roots of the two fingers pass through a differential mechanism in the palm, which balances the tension of the tendon string on the two fingers to achieve their collaborative adaptive motion. The differential mechanism is connected and actuated by another tendon string (orange line) with steering gear 3. The bending of ring finger and little finger are actuated by steering gear 4. These fingers are also connected in series by a tendon string (green line), and their roots pass through another differential mechanism in the palm. This mechanism balances the tension of the tendon strings on these two fingers to enable collaborative adaptive

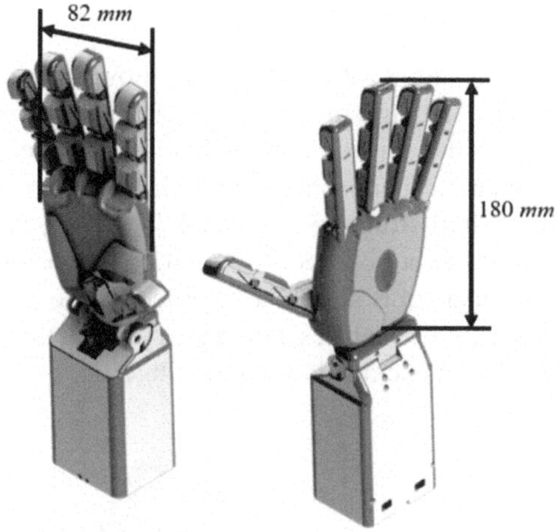

(a)

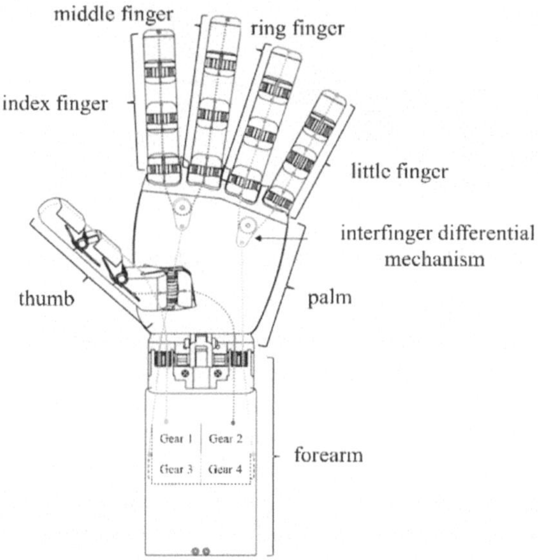

(b)

Fig. 1. Underactuated Humanoid Dexterous Hand (a) Mechanical Design, (b) Transmission Design.

motion. The differential mechanism is connected and actuated by another tendon string (cyan line) with steering gear 4.

2.2 Robotic Fingers and Palm Design

The mechanical design of a single robotic finger is shown in Fig. 2, which abandons the traditional mechanical axial structure in favor of a symmetrical hemisphere head clasp structure. By utilizing the elastic components, the robotic knuckles are fastened securely. Once the symmetrical hemisphere head clasp is fixed by the neck, a hinge mechanism with a virtual shaft structure is formed. There are two torsion springs are installed on both sides of the robotic finger to facilitate its position reset. And there is a torsion spring block mechanism is simply assembled on the robotic finger to prevent the dislodging. The robotic finger features a buckle-type structure, and a small pressure sensor (Simbatouch SBT760F) is embedded in the fingertip.

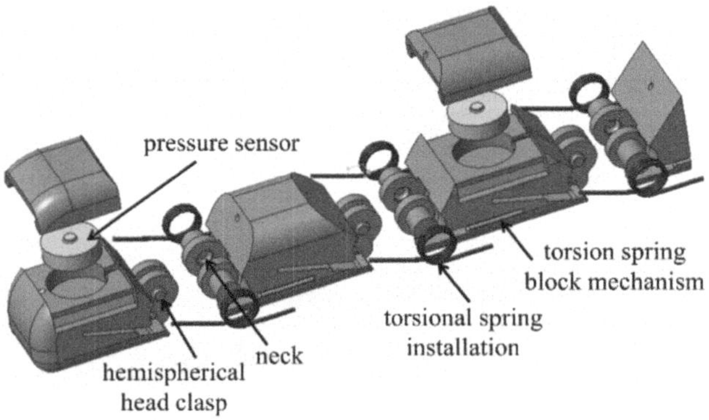

Fig. 2. Mechanical Design of a Single Robotic Finger.

Since the robotic finger joints are hollow, they are designed as a routing channel for the signal cables of the installed pressure sensor. The signal cables are routed to the finger base through this channel, preventing damage from excessive pulling and avoiding interference caused by robotic finger joints motions.

The structure of the palm is illustrated in Fig. 3, where the pulleys are used as the differential mechanism between the fingers. Figure 3(a) presents a designed pulley consists of pulley casing, bolt, pully guide rail, and a hole for tendon strings. Figure 3(b) displays the top view of the pulley after assembling. If the distance a is smaller than the diameter of the tendon string, the tendon rope will not dislodge from the pulley under stropping condition. It is also necessary to ensure that the distance b shall be greater than the diameter of the tendon string to prevent friction between the tendon string and the shell under working condition. Based on the diameter of the chosen tendon string, a shall be 0.35 mm while b is 1.1 mm. Figure 3(c) shows the trajectory of the pulley motion. A guide rail is integrated into the robotic palm design to constraint motion of pulley to ensure that the angle between the two tendon strings passing through pulley A and B remains constant. A block mechanism is designed for limiting range of robotic finger motion. The effective working distances are 44 mm and 50 mm for pulley A and pulley B, respectively.

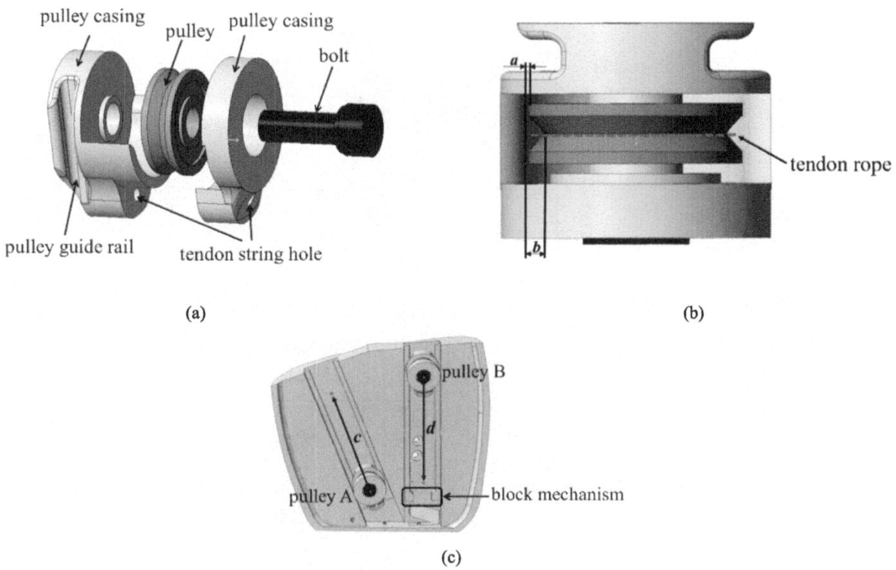

Fig. 3. Dexterous Hand Palm Design (a) Pulley, (b) Top View of the Pully, (c) Guide Rail of Pulley.

2.3 Robotic Wrist and Forearm Design

The mechanical design of the robotic wrist and forearm is presented in Fig. 4(a) and Fig. 4(b), respectively. A revolute joint is applied at the wrist, driven by a linear motor through a simple crank-rocker mechanism. The reciprocating linear motion is converted into the flexion/extension motions of the wrist. Four fixed pulleys, equipped on the robotic wrist joint, which are used to alter the motion trajectory of the four tendon strings, thereby reducing friction. Additionally, the contacting point between the tendon string and the pulley shall be aligned with the revolute center of the robotic wrist joint. When the robotic fingers and the robotic wrist move simultaneously, the moment arm of the tension applied by strings to the wrist joint is zero, therefore, the torque is zero, thus achieving the effect of motion decoupling.

The robotic forearm consists of a casing, a posteriors cap. Steering gears and linear motor are installed inside the robotic forearm. Each steering gear is secured to the forearm with four bolts to effectively prevent uncertainties caused by shaking. The robotic forearm is equipped with four threaded mounting holes used for assembling with the robotic arms.

3 Kinematic Analysis of Dexterous Hand

3.1 Joint Space Kinematics

The kinematic analysis of the joint space focuses on revealing the displacement of tendon strings and joint angle. It is a necessary condition for achieving precise motion control. Since the adduction/abduction joint of the thumb is driven by a single actuator,

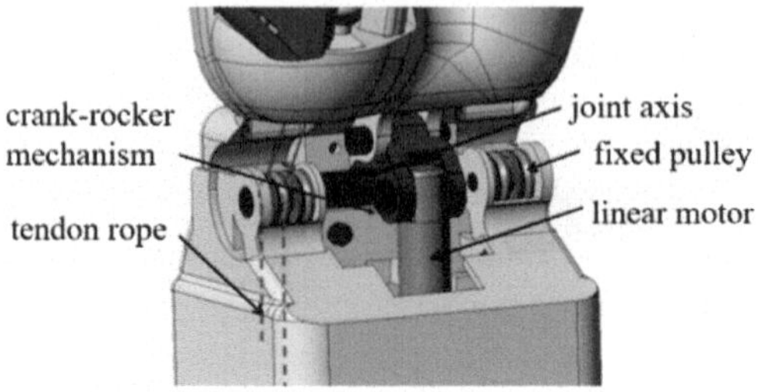

(a)

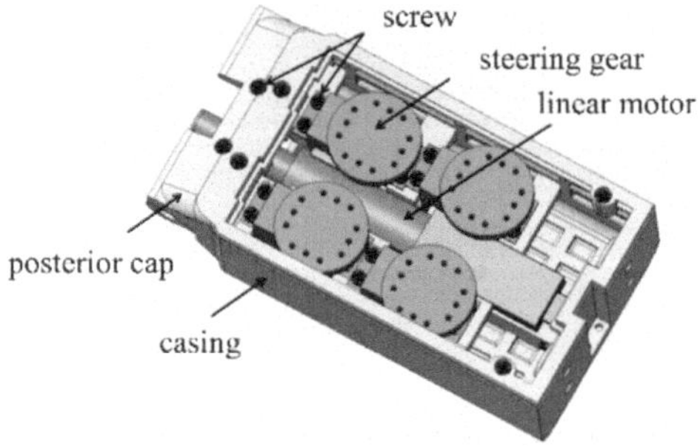

(b)

Fig. 4. Mechanical Design of (a) Robotic Wrist, (b) Forearm.

the displacement of the tendon string corresponds directly and uniquely to the motion of this joint. The remaining two joints of robotic thumb are driven simultaneously by another actuator. Unlike the thumb, robotic joints of other four fingers are actuated by a common actuator, making their kinematics more complex. Furthermore, since other four robotic fingers have the same mechanism, the index finger is analyzed as a representative example in this section.

The geometric relationship and force analysis of the robotic index finger are shown in Fig. 5, and the expression from joint angles, θ_0, θ_1 and θ_2, to tendon string displacement, Δl, can be obtained as:

$$\Delta l = (b_0 + b_1 + b_2) - 2c_0 \sin\frac{\theta_{0max} - \theta_0}{2} - 2c_1 \sin\frac{\theta_{1max} - \theta_1}{2} - 2c_2 \sin\frac{\theta_{2max} - \theta_2}{2} \tag{1}$$

where b_i represents the length of the tendon string between the two knuckles, c_i represents the distance between the revolute joint center and the contacting point of tendon string and the fingertip, and θ_{imax} denotes the maximum bending angle of the robotic joint. Based on the proposed design, the workspace of the dexterous hand shall be only determined by range of joint motion. The design objective of the prototype is to allow the fingertip to touch the palm as limiting position when it is bent. By substituting the related parameters of the dexterous hand on its limiting position into Eq. (1), the inverse

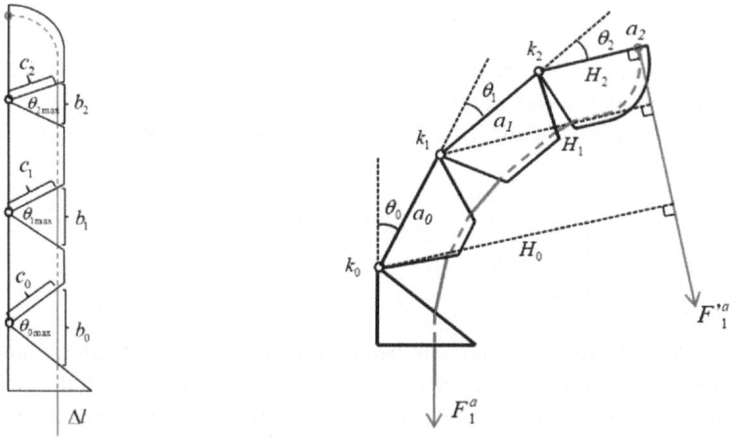

(a) (b)

Fig. 5. (a) Geometries of the Robotic Index Finger, (b) Force Analysis of the Robotic Index Finger.

kinematics expression of the index finger can be obtained by:

$$\Delta l = 43 - 20\sin\frac{90^\circ - \theta_0}{2} - 22\sin\frac{80^\circ - \theta_1}{2} - 26\sin\frac{60^\circ - \theta_2}{2} \quad (2)$$

3.2 Workspace Analysis

The geometric relationship between workspaces of those five robotic fingers can reflect the grasping ability of a dexterous hand. Whether the thumb overlaps with the other four fingers determines the ability of the dexterous hand to grasp small or flat objects by using fingertips. The Monte Carlo approach [17] was used to project the workspace of those five robotic fingers. The resulting workspace, shown in Fig. 6(a), includes a light blue area representing the thumb workspace, a red area for the index finger, deep blue region for the middle finger, yellow part for the ring finger, and green area for the little finger. Figure 6(b), 6(c), and 6(d) show the projections of the robotic fingers workspace based on the palm coordinate system on the *xoz* plane, *xoy* plane, and *yoz* plane, respectively.

The workspaces of the thumb, index finger, and middle finger significantly overlap. Within this overlapping workspace, these fingers can grasp objects with any shape theoretically. However, the workspaces of the thumb, ring finger, and little finger do not overlap. In practical applications, since smaller objects are usually lighter, using ring finger and little finger in conjunction with the thumb to grasp small volume objects is not considered. The ring finger and little finger primarily assist in grasping larger volume and massive objects. Additionally, it can be observed that when the four fingers, excluding the thumb, are bent, workspaces of their fingertips be closer to each other. This phenomenon indicates that the dexterous hand proposed in this research has the potential to achieve an interfinger clamping posture on slender objects.

3.3 Fingertips Motion Trajectory Analysis

Index finger is also chosen to be analyzed in this section. Figure 5 (b) shows the static state of the index finger during bending where H_i denote the lever of tendon tension for each joint, a_i represent the length of each knuckle. Their geometric relationship can be expressed as:

$$\begin{cases} H_0 = a_2 + a_1 \cos\theta_2 + a_0 \cos(\theta_1 + \theta_2) \\ H_1 = a_2 + a_1 \cos\theta_2 \\ H_2 = a_2 \end{cases} \tag{3}$$

The tension of the tendon string can be regarded as equal everywhere, ignoring the friction during the motion. According to the torque balance at the joint, the critical conditions for DIP, PIP (Proximal Interphalangeal) and MCP joint rotation can be obtained by:

$$k_0(20^\circ + \theta_0) = F_1^a(a_2 + a_1 + a_0) \tag{4}$$

$$k_1(20^\circ + \theta_1) = F_1^a(a_2 + a_1) \tag{5}$$

$$k_2(20^\circ + \theta_2) = F_1^a(a_2) \tag{6}$$

where k_0, k_1 and k_2 respectively demonstrate the stiffness of torsion springs located at the three joints and the initial angle of the spring is 20° in this condition.

In the process of fingertip motion, the three joints are not actuated simultaneously. According to the rule of finger motion, the kinematic relationship between the angles of finger joints θ_0, θ_1, θ_2 in different conditions can be found.

When $0 \le \theta_0 < \frac{20^\circ k_1(a_2+a_1+a_0)}{k_0(a_2+a_1)}$,

$$\begin{cases} \theta_0 = \theta_{0\max} \arcsin \frac{b_0-\Delta l}{2c_0} \\ \theta_1 = 0 \\ \theta_2 = 0 \end{cases} \tag{7}$$

When $\frac{20^\circ k_1(a_2+a_1+a_0)}{k_0(a_2+a_1)} - 20^\circ \le \theta_0 < \frac{20^\circ k_2(a_2+a_1+a_0\cos\theta_1)}{k_0 a_2} - 20^\circ$,

$$\begin{cases} \theta_0 = \frac{k_1(\theta_1+20^\circ)(a_2+a_1+a_0\cos\theta_1)}{k_0(a_2+a_1)} - 20^\circ \\ c_0 \sin\frac{\theta_{0\max}-\theta_0}{2} - c_1 \sin\frac{\theta_{1\max}-\theta_1}{2} = \frac{(b_0+b_1)-\Delta l}{2} \\ \theta_2 = 0 \end{cases} \tag{8}$$

When $\frac{20^\circ k_2(a_2+a_1+a_0\cos\theta_1)}{k_0 a_2} - 20^\circ \le \theta_0 \le 80^\circ$,

$$\begin{cases} \theta_0 = \frac{k_2(\theta_2+20^\circ)(a_2+a_1\cos\theta_2+a_0\cos\theta_1)}{k_0(a_2+a_1)} - 20^\circ \\ \theta_1 = \frac{k_2(\theta_1+20^\circ)(a_2+a_1\cos\theta_2)}{k_1 a_2} - 20^\circ \\ c_0 \sin\frac{\theta_{0\max}-\theta_0}{2} - c_1 \sin\frac{\theta_{1\max}-\theta_1}{2} - c_2 \sin\frac{\theta_{2\max}-\theta_2}{2} = \frac{(b_0+b_1+b_2)-\Delta l}{2} \end{cases} \tag{9}$$

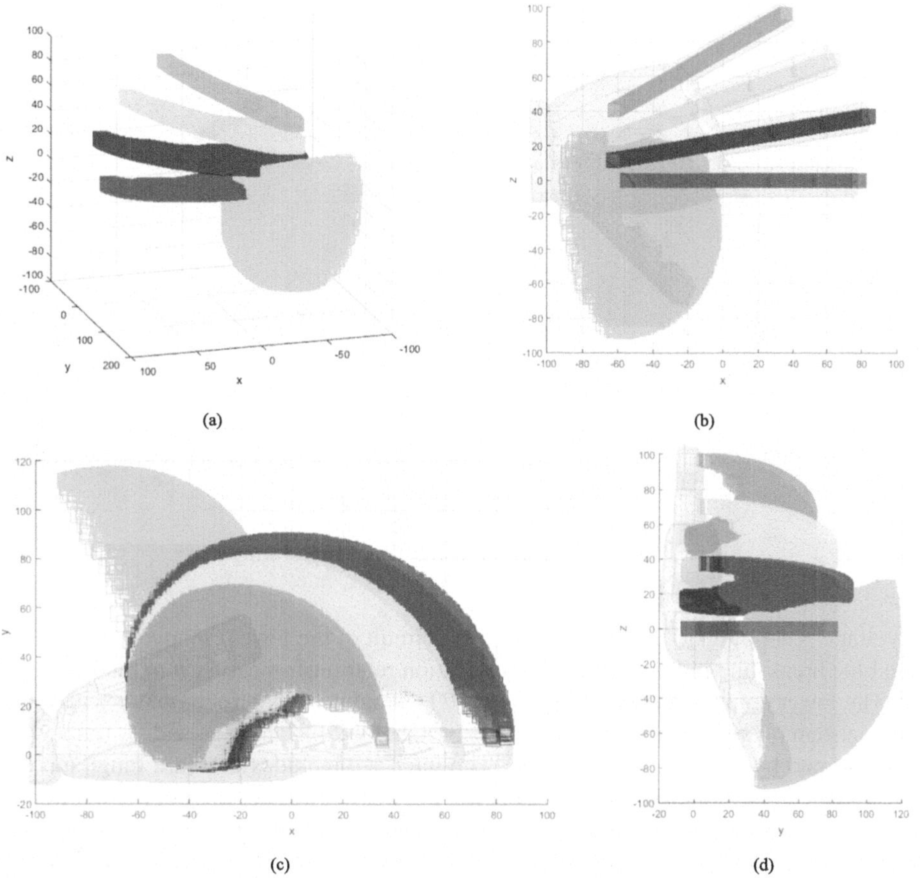

Fig. 6. Workspace (a) Stereogram, (b) Projection on *xoz* Plane, (c) Projection on *xoy* Plane, (d) Projection on *yoz* Plane.

Through forward kinematics, the motion trajectory of the fingertip of the index finger under no-load condition can be obtained. As shown in Fig. 7, the red curve is the theoretical trajectory, while the blue curve is the actual measured trajectory. The deviation between the two curves is mainly caused by the frictional resistance of the tendon string during the motion, which leads to the unstable motion relationship between the three joints, and the maximum trajectory uncertainty is about 3mm. It is 12.5% of the finger width, in other words, it can be ignored.

4 Experimental Results and Discussion

4.1 Control System

The control system for the experimental setup is shown in Fig. 8 where black line represents the power supply relationship. 24 V switching power supply is used to supply power, 8.3 V voltage is output to the steering gear through the step-down module, and 5

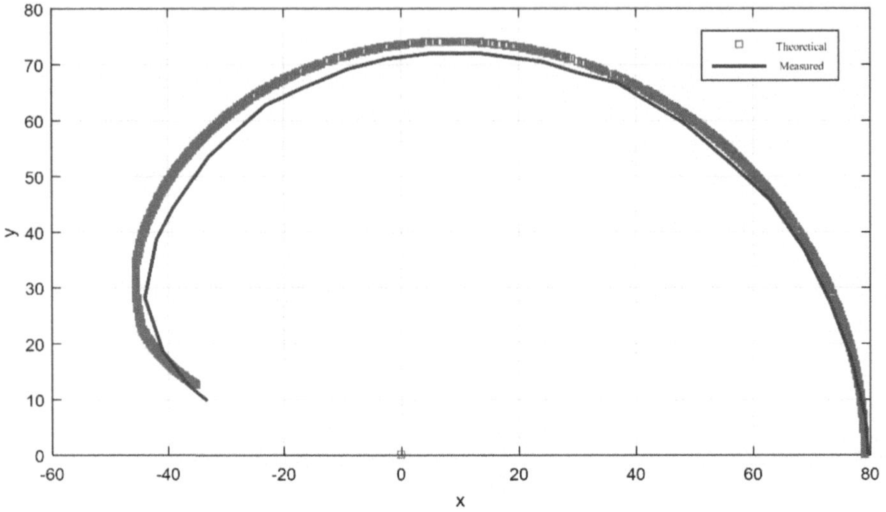

Fig. 7. Theoretical and Measured Trajectory of Fingertip.

V voltage is supplied to the signal processing circuit of the lower computer and sensor. The blue break-line indicates the communication relationship between modules.

The lower computer uses STM32F103C8T6 single chip microcomputer with minimum system board. The upper computer is written by C++ language and Qt framework and operated by Linux Ubantu system. The interface includes pressure range module and kinematics estimation module. Considering that the actual operating condition of dexterous hand will be affected by the electromagnetic influence of the actuator, leading the uncertainty in data transmission. Thus, the communication protocol designed in this research can not only carry out multidimensional verification of the communication content, but also directly read the source data of serial communication, so that the user can verify and solve the error.

4.2 PID Control Experiment Based on Fingertip Pressure Sensing

In this research, the holding operation of the underactuated humanoid dexterous hand is segmentally controlled, which is divided into two stages including position open loop control based on inverse kinematics and PID force feedback control based on pressure sensing. The control strategy flow chart is shown in Fig. 9.

The reasonableness and validity of the designed finger mechanism shall be verified by pinching experiments of thumb, index finger and middle finger. Raw eggs with moderate volume, quality and fragileness are chosen as the grasping target. Firstly, the open loop control, based on forward and inverse kinematics, shall be applied to actuate the index finger and middle finger of the proposed dexterous hand to touch and rest on the surface of the targeted egg. Then, the robotic thumb shall be controlled to touch the surface of the chosen egg. The sensors on the fingertips can accurately measure the contacting force and the control system shall apply an error compensation if the force is less than the setting threshold, τ, which is equal to 0.05 N. Once the contacting force reaches the setting threshold, a PID closed-loop control is applied to pinch eggs. In PID closed-loop control, the expected contacting force is set to be 0.4 N based on the mass and delicacy of the targeted egg. And the classical PID control outputs a PWM wave to control the servo angle until the output forces of fingertips matches the expected contacting force. In this experiment, the maximum response frequency of the pressure sensor is 90 Hz, and the maximum response frequency of the steering gear is 50 Hz. In PID force feedback closed-loop control strategy, k_p=27, T_i=1, and T_d=0.8.

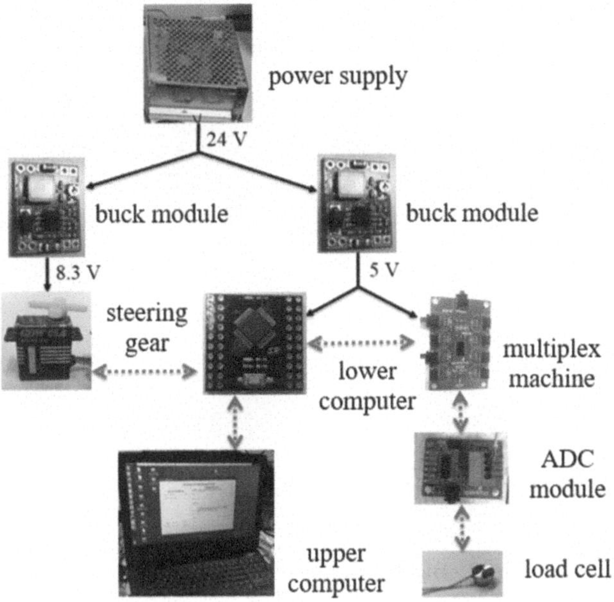

Fig. 8. Instrumentation for Experimental Setup.

The change of the output signal of the thumb fingertip pressure sensor over time is shown in Fig. 10. The output signal of using open loop control and PID control can both reach 0.4 N approximately. The experimental results show that the finger mechanism designed in this research can address the requirement of pinching manipulation. Compared with open-loop control, PID closed-loop control can ensure that the thumb tip pressure quickly reaches the expected pressure value. At the same time, because there is no feedback in the open-loop control, the error will continue to accumulate, resulting in further increasing in uncertainties. This phenomenon has been better handled in the PID closed-loop control, which can control the thumb motion to make the fingertip output stable pressure.

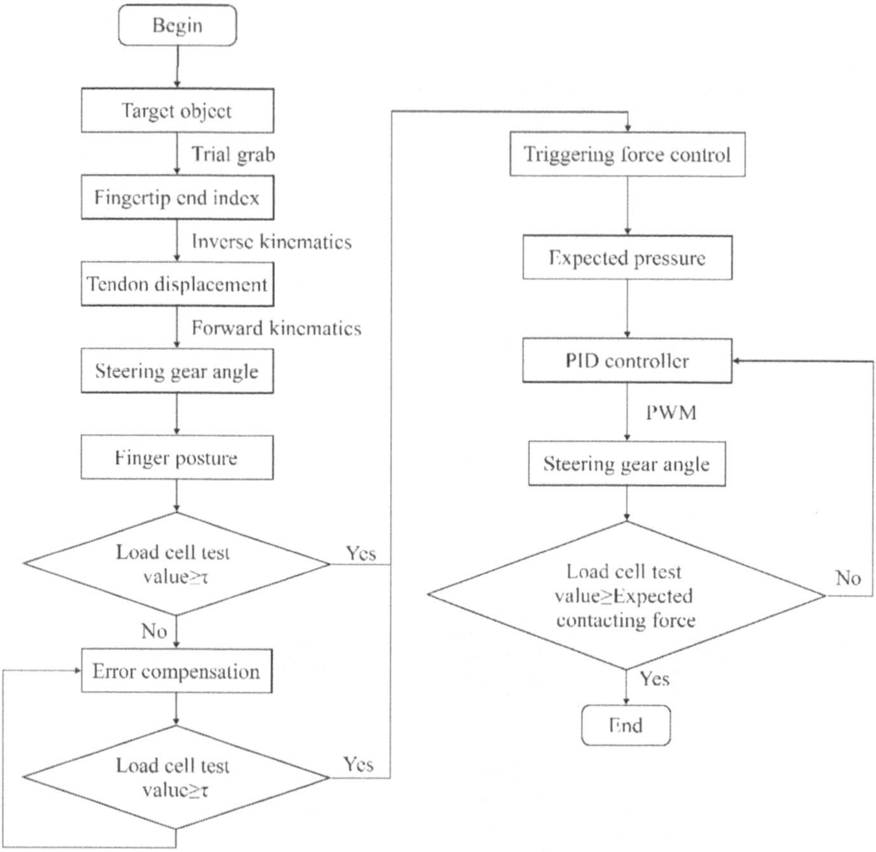

Fig. 9. Block Diagram of Control Strategy.

4.3 Tests of Grasping Ability

In this section, the performance of the underactuated dexterous hand is verified by the grasping performance tests, which include the repetition experiment of the grasping posture, the grasping strength test, and the grasping weight ratio test.

4.3.1 Tests of Grasping Posture

To better identify specific bionic targets for designing dexterous hands, several researchers have already classified and analyzed various grasping operations based on their characteristics [18, 19]. The grasping test applied in this research is used to verify one by one the 33 kinds of grasping postures in the GRASP classification [20]. The dexterous hand is fixed vertically, the target object is artificially moved to the appropriate position, and the dexterous hand is driven to grasp the target object with the corresponding grasping posture. The grasping posture is regarded as successful when it is held steadily for 10 s. In this experiment, common objects with equivalent shape were selected as the target objects.

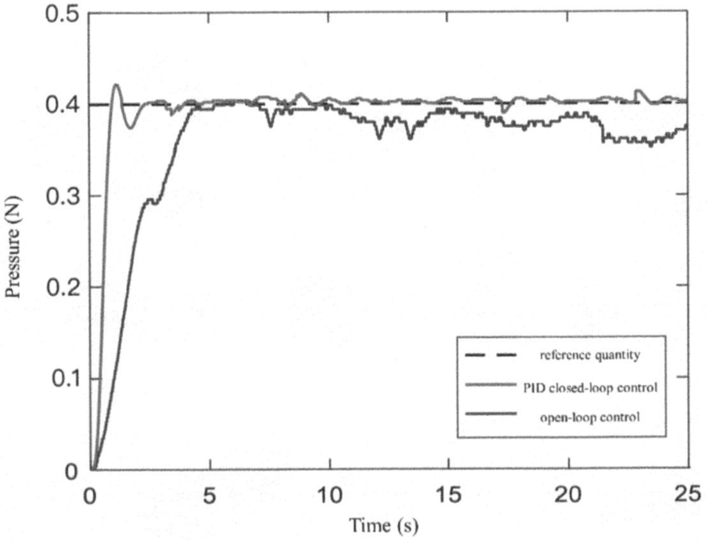

Fig. 10. Experimental Results Verified by Static Model.

Figure 11 shows the grasping posture of the dexterous hand prototype on objects of different shapes and sizes. The objects in the figure are respectively orange, egg, pen, potato chip cylinder, plastic bottle, glasses case, medicine bottle, double-sided tape, pen, ruler, and student card. Total of 20 grasping postures in the GRASP classification can be achieved with a total frequency of 66%, including power grasping with five fingers on large objects ((a), (d), (e), (f)), using the tips of the thumb, index and middle fingers for precise pinching of small objects ((b), (g), (i), (j)), using the index and middle fingers to pick up slender objects ((c)), and pinching the sheet object ((k)) with the tip of the thumb and the side of the index finger. Total of 13 grasping cases are failed, 10 of them were because of the linkage problem between the index finger and the middle finger, two were caused by the linkage between the four-finger MCP joints and the PIP joints, and one was due to the insufficient friction on the finger surface leading to the object falling. However, the underactuated humanoid dexterous hand proposed in this research has enough flexibility to adaptive grasp most of daily necessities in general.

4.3.2 Tests of Grasping Strength

As shown in Fig. 12, the test platform for grasping strength was built. The dexterous hand was fixed on one end of aluminum rods and the digital tension measurer was placed on the other end. The tension measurer is connected to the pull rod by fishing line. The pull rod naturally falls on the four fingers under the action of gravity, slowly drags the PWM control bar on the upper computer, and the four fingers gradually bend and adaptively hook the pull rod under the action of the differential mechanism to apply force along the direction of the palm. Dexterous hand adjusted the position of the slider to make the dynamometer move back, repeating the experiment until the slider moves back to the point where the finger cannot hold the pull bar, drag the control bar to the ultimate

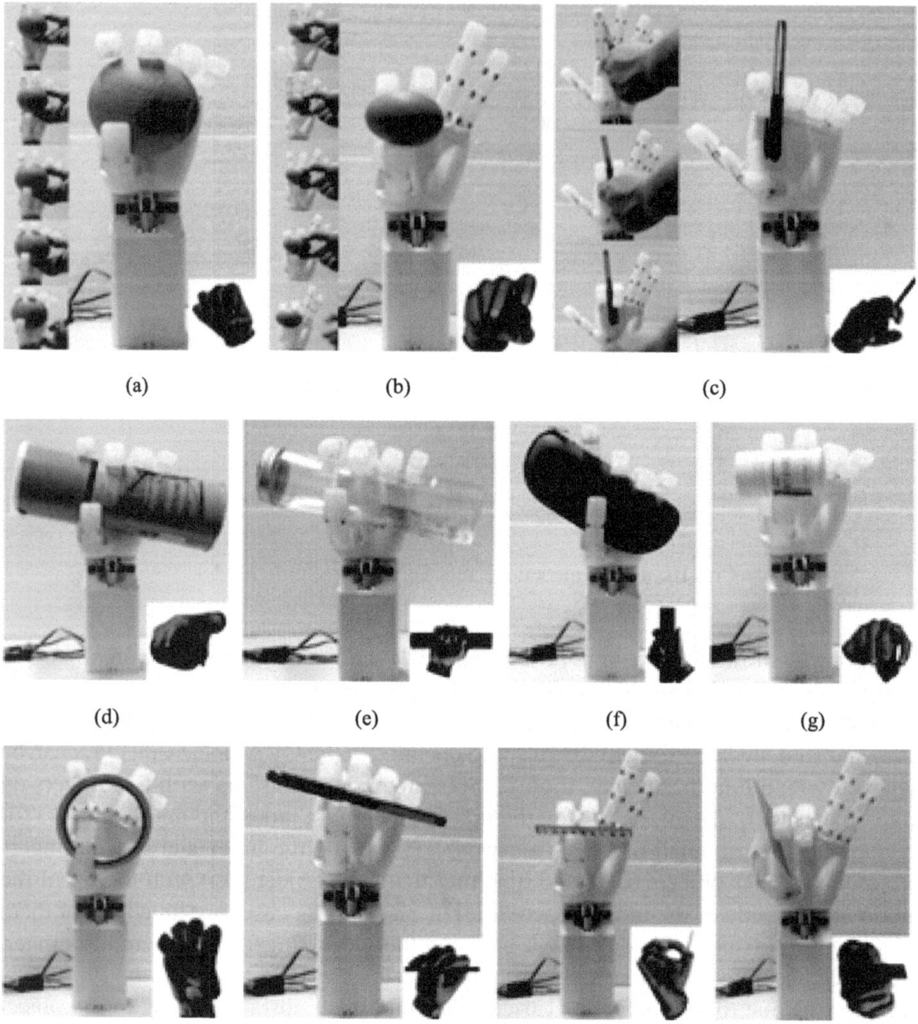

(a) (b) (c)

(d) (e) (f) (g)

(h) (i) (j) (k)

Fig. 11. Grasping Posture of the Dexterous Hand on Different Objects.

position, and the maximum active grasping force can be measured as 4.8N. Due to the limited length of the robotic fingers, it can be verified that the dexterous hand can provide a maximum active grip strength of 4.8N under this experimental platform. Because the test of ultimate grasping force may destroy the motor. The loading test is not performed when the proposed dexterous hand achieves the design requirements.

4.3.3 Tests of Grasping Weight Ratio

Different from the grasping strength test, the grasping weight ratio test not only requires the finger to provide enough pressure, but also requires the finger joint to resist the

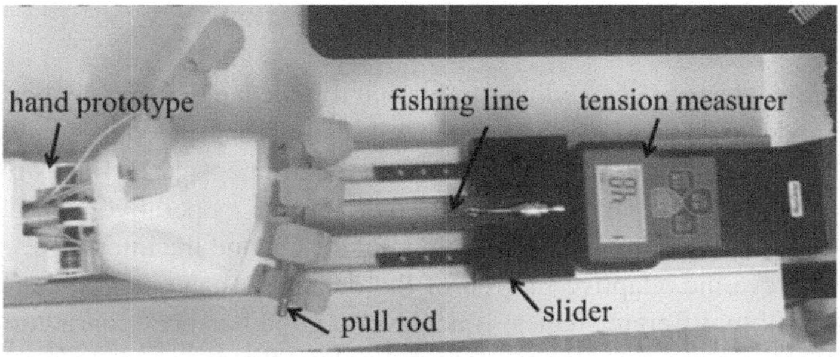

Fig. 12. Grasping Strength Test Platform.

tangential torque generated by friction, which is an important index to measure the grasping ability and structural robustness of the dexterous hand [21]. According to the design objectives, the 500 g weight was chosen in this experiment. The weight was placed in a large cylindrical plastic bottle as a grasping target, and the dexterous hand was worn with protective gloves to increase the friction on the robotic finger surface.

The voltage of the steering gear is given as 8.3V. When driving each steering gear to the ultimate position using the open-loop control, the dexterous hand can firmly grasp the plastic bottle and artificially lift the dexterous hand holding the bottle vertically away from the table for 10 s, without relative displacement between the bottle and the dexterous hand, as shown in Fig. 13. The test is repeated by choosing different positions of the bottle body as grasping points. All grasping tests are successful without relative displacement. The experiment reveals that the grasping weight ratio of the proposed dexterous hand is around 1.43.

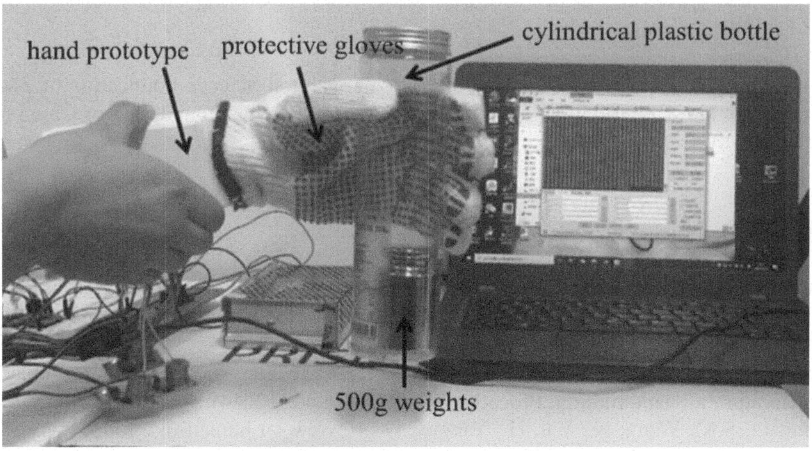

Fig. 13. Grasping Weight Ratio Test Platform.

5 Conclusion

Due to the limited degrees of freedom, traditional robotic hands typically perform a single function and can be adapted for a wide variety of tasks. They are often designed to fulfill specific functions based on the application requirements [22]. In this research, an underactuated humanoid dexterous hand with multi-finger cooperative adaptive grasping is proposed for daily operation. The flexible joint design and the interfinger differential mechanism achieve the adaptive motion of the dexterous hand, which can adaptively grasp objects within different shapes. It achieves a good balance of structural simplicity and functional diversity. Experimental results show that the proposed underactuated humanoid dexterous hand can grasp common objects including power gripping, fingertip pinching, finger side pinching and interfinger pinching. It can lift and pick up 0.5 kg objects with a grasping weight ratio of 1.43, which has great practical value. As a multifunctional intelligent system, the proposed dexterous robotic hand shall be applicable across a broader range of working conditions. It may have numerous potential applications because of its sufficient designed degrees of freedom and robust capabilities of sensing feedback.

In near future, the mechanical design of the dexterous hand will be further optimized, such as the optimization of the stiffness ratio of the torsion spring on a single finger, and the motion trajectory of the finger under no-load condition will be optimized by adjusting the stiffness ratio of the torsion spring. On the one hand, the driven strings and electrical components shall be fully integrated inside the hand, and new sensors shall be applied to establish a hybrid force/bit control system, thereby improving the grasping performance of the dexterous hand. On the other hand, in view of the underactuated motion characteristics of dexterous hand, the multi-dimensional, high-speed, and modular information transmission mechanism shall be extended, and an offline simulation platform for the realization of dexterous hand is established to achieve a good human-robot interaction control system.

Acknowledgments. This research is supported by the Natural Science Foundation of Zhejiang Province (Grant No. LZ23E050005), the National Natural Science Foundation of China (Grant No. U23A20338).

References

1. Akin, D.L., Carignan, C.R., Foster, A.W.: Development of a four-fingered dexterous robot end effector for Space operations. In: IEEE International Conference on Robotics and Automation 2002, vol. 3, pp. 2302–2308. Washington, USA (2002)
2. Virgala, I., Kelemen, M., Varga, M., Kurylo, P.: Analyzing, modeling and simulation of humanoid robot hand motion. Procedia Eng. **96**, 489–499 (2014)
3. Sampath, S.K., Wang, N., Wu, H., Yang, C.G.: Review on human-like robot manipulation using dexterous hands. Cogn. Comput. Syst. **5**(1), 14–29 (2023)
4. Birglen, L., Laliberté, T., Gosselin, C.: Underactuated Robotic Hands. 1st edition. Springer Tracts in Advanced Robotics, vol. 40 (2008)
5. Odhner, L.U., Dollar, A.M.: Dexterous manipulation with underactuated elastic hands. In: IEEE International Conference on Robotics and Automation 2011, pp. 5254–5260. Shanghai, China (2011)

6. Dong, Y.K., Zhang, W.Z.: Multi-mode compound grasping robot finger driven by linkage. Appl. Sci. **13**(9), 5550 (2023)
7. He, B., Wang, S., and Liu, Y. J.: Underactuated robotics: a review. Int. J. Adv. Robot. Syst. **16**(4) (2019)
8. Bottin, M., Rosati, G.: Comparison of under-actuated and fully actuated serial robotic arms: a case study. J. Mech. Robot. **14**(3) (2021)
9. Hirose, S., Umetani, Y.: The development of soft gripper for the versatile robot hand. Mech. Mach. Theory **13**(3), 351–359 (1978)
10. Massa, B., Roccella, S., Carrozza, M.C., Dario, P.: Design and development of an underactuated prosthetic hand. In: IEEE International Conference on Robotics and Automation 2002, vol. 4, pp. 3374–3379. Washington, USA (2002)
11. Carrozza, M.C., Cappiello, G., Micera, S., Edin, B.B., Beccai, L., Cipriani, C.: Design of a cybernetic hand for perception and action. Biol. Cybern. **95**(6), 629–644 (2006)
12. Dollar, A.M., Howe, R.D.: A robust compliant grasper via shape deposition manufacturing. IEEE/ASME Trans. Mechatron. **11**(2), 154–161 (2006)
13. Lenzi, T., Lipsey, J., Sensinger, J.W.: The RIC arm—a small anthropomorphic transhumeral prosthesis. IEEE/ASME Trans. Mechatron. **21**(6), 2660–2671 (2016)
14. Mitsui, K., Ozawa, R., Kou, T.: An under-actuated robotic hand for multiple grasps. In: IEEE/RSJ International Conference on Intelligent Robots and Systems 2013, pp. 5475–5480. Tokyo, Japan (2013)
15. Catalano, M.G., Grioli, G., Farnioli, E., Serio, A., Piazza, C., Bicchi, A.: Adaptive synergies for the design and control of the Pisa/IIT SoftHand. Int. J. Robot. Res. **33**(5), 768–782 (2014)
16. Santina, C.D., Piazza, C., Grioli, G., Catalano, M., Bicchi, A.: Toward dexterous manipulation with augmented adaptive synergies: the Pisa/IIT SoftHand 2. IEEE Trans. Rob. **34**(5), 1141–1156 (2018)
17. Rubinstein, R.Y., Kroese, D.P.: Simulation and the Monte Carlo Method. 1st edition. John Wiley & Sons (2017)
18. Feix, T., Pawlik, R.: A Comprehensive Grasp Taxonomy (2009)
19. Taylor, C.L., Schwarz, R.J.: The anatomy and mechanics of the human hand. Artif. Limbs **2**(2), 22–35 (1955)
20. Feix, T., Romero, J., Schmiedmayer, H.-B., Dollar, A.M., Kragic, D.: The GRASP taxonomy of human grasp types. IEEE Trans. Hum.-Mach. Syst. **46**(1), 66–77 (2016)
21. Li, H.L., Yao, J.T., Wei, C.J., Zhou, P., Xu, Y.D., Zhao, Y.S.: An untethered soft robotic gripper with high payload-to-weight ratio. Mech. Mach. Theory **158** (2021)
22. Melchiorri, C., Kaneko, M.: Robot Hands. 1st edition. Springer (2008)

Kinematic Analysis and Optimal Design of 2SPS-RR Parallel Wrist in Humanoid Robot

Siyuan Peng, Yaming Li, Peng Xu(✉), and Bing Li

School of Mechanical Engineering and Automation, Harbin Institute of Technology (Shenzhen), Shenzhen 518055, China
xupeng919@hit.edu.cn

Abstract. Humanoid robots are a hot research topic in robotics nowadays and show broad application prospects. Among the various components of humanoid robots, the wrist is essential as it enables the completion of complex motions. Compared to the serial configuration, the wrists with parallel configurations show the advantage of compactness and high stiffness. In this paper, the kinematic and optimal design of a robotic wrist with a 2SPS-RR parallel mechanism are performed. Firstly, the position, velocity, and singularity are analyzed and the workspace is presented. Secondly, an optimization model that considers multiple performance indexes is proposed. The function is simple to calculate, which takes into account the effects of the area of the workspace, the expected boundary and the singular trajectory. Then, a global optimization of the mechanism is conducted based on the design parameters, and a set of optimal parameter values is obtained. The results indicate that the desired workspace of the mechanism is distant from the singular trajectory with the optimized parameters, and the coverage of the workspace relative to the desired workspace is considerable. Furthermore, the sensitivity and condition number of the design parameters are analyzed. Finally, the driving force and driving speed of the mechanism are analyzed in conjunction with the optimal parameters, which provides a theoretical reference for the design of the humanoid robot wrist.

Keywords: Humanoid robot · Parallel configurations · Global optimization

1 Introduction

The field of *humanoid robotics* is currently experiencing a surge in interest. The goal of humanoid robot design is to achieve a high degree of resemblance to humans [1]. For humanoid robots, the joints play a pivotal role in determining the robot's overall flexibility, mobility, and load-bearing capacity. The development of lightweight and dexterous joints represents a significant area of research within the field of humanoid robotics. As a key component of the upper limb, the wrist joint plays a pivotal role in determining the motion performance of the robot's upper limb. One of the most crucial metrics of whether a robot is deemed *humanoid* is the ability of its wrist to perform complex movements that are comparable to those of humans.

X. Lan et al. (Eds.): ICIRA 2024, LNAI 15201, pp. 366–380, 2025.
https://doi.org/10.1007/978-981-96-0771-6_27

The main configurations for the wrist joint of humanoid robots are serial and parallel structures. Schwartz et al. [2] designed a humanoid robot called TOCABI, which used a wrist design scheme by connecting three active 1-degree-of-freedom (DoF) rotating units in series, with the rotation axes of the three rotating units arranged orthogonally. Sun et al. [3] developed a bionic tensegrity wrist, which drove the universal joint component through the contraction and tension of the spring in the tension body component to achieve wrist movement. In recent years, the use of parallel mechanisms as the wrist joints in humanoid robots has increased, demonstrating enhanced potential and flexibility. The Robonaut 2 humanoid robot [4] developed by General Motors in collaboration with NASA used a U-2PSU 2-DoF parallel mechanism for the wrist. The U-joints connected the hand to the robot's forearm, and the PSU linkage was actuated through the P-joints to achieve wrist motion. This enabled the robot to perform a similar motion as a human wrist. Kim et al. [5] designed a RoboRay humanoid robot with a U-2PUR 2-DoF parallel mechanism for the wrist to achieve wrist motion. In the aforementioned studies of humanoid robot wrists, the use of serial structures may result in a less compact design, rendering the wrist unsuitable for specific applications [6, 7]. This is because the serial mechanism consists of multiple joints successively connected to form an open chain of motion. This structure makes it difficult to greatly reduce the length and volume of the serial mechanism, which leads to the reduction of design compactness. In contrast, the parallel mechanism is a closed-loop mechanism, which allows for a certain degree of design compactness. Concurrently, it is important to optimize the design of parallel mechanisms.

To achieve the optimal design of a parallel mechanism, it is necessary to consider two main aspects: configuration optimization and structural parameter optimization. For a given configuration, the optimization of its structural parameters is particularly important, because the parameters directly affect the performance of the mechanism. Huang et al. [8] took the workspace, stiffness, and dexterity as performance indexes and implemented a multi-objective optimization using genetic algorithms to enhance the mechanism's performance. However, the defined stiffness and dexterity were challenging to quantify. Srivastava et al. [9] proposed a 3-DoF wrist joint mechanism and performed finite element analysis of the mechanism with the aid of ANSYS and performed multi-objective optimization of the dimensional parameters of the mechanism using deformation and equivalent stress as performance indexes, but did not consider the workspace, which was an important performance index. Mustafa et al. [10] selected the matching metric between the workspace of the mechanism and the workspace of the human wrist and the global stiffness as the optimization metrics for workspace optimization. Li et al. [11] proposed a new workspace metric that excludes the singularities within the workspace. This metric was then used to analyze the workspace of a 3-RPR parallel mechanism. Babu et al. [12] proposed a multi-objective optimization approach based on a linear combination of global stiffness, workspace volume and global number of conditions of the 3-PRS mechanism. This approach was implemented using Genetic Algorithms to improve the stiffness performance of the mechanism while reducing the workspace volume.

On the whole, the optimization design of the wrist joint of a humanoid robot plays a pivotal role in determining the robot's overall performance and motion dexterity.

The application of diverse structural parameter optimization methodologies enables the enhancement of performance indexes, including workspace, stiffness and dexterity, thereby facilitating the precision and flexibility of robot wrist movements. In addition, the selection of different configurations and the optimization of structural parameters directly impact the practical application of humanoid robots. During the design process, it is essential to consider a range of performance indexes to ensure that the goal of optimization can be achieved. Consequently, in consideration of the advantages of the parallel configuration over the serial configuration, this paper presents a kinematic analysis and optimal design of the wrist of a robot with the parallel structure of 2SPS-RR. The results are expected to provide a reference for the development of humanoid robot wrists.

In Sect. 2, the kinematic analysis of the parallel wrist is conducted, and the design parameters are selected. In Sect. 3, workspace optimization and evaluation are conducted. In Sect. 4, a static optimization analysis is conducted to propose an optimization objective function that considers the workspace, singularity and mechanical properties. This objective function is used to identify a structural parameter with a large workspace, good mechanical properties and singularity avoidance.

2 Kinematic Analysis

Kinematic analysis serves as the foundation for optimization work. This paper presents a derivation of the Jacobi matrix of a parallel wrist mechanism and the selection of optimized design parameters. Subsequently, the singular trajectories of the mechanism under the specified structural parameters are solved based on the supplementary equations and numerical methods. Additionally, typical singularities are analyzed in conjunction with inverse kinematics.

2.1 Position and Velocity

The parallel wrist configuration presented in this paper is based on the 2SPS-RR configuration, and the geometry is modeled according to Fig. 1(a). The mechanism has three sets of supporting chains. Among them, two sets of SPS chains and one set of RR chain connect the manipulator connection platform. The actuator chains consist of spherical joints and prismatic joints. The prismatic joints connect the base and the manipulator connection platform via the spherical joints. The support chain is comprised of two revolute joints. The manipulator connection platform is equipped with two rotational degrees of freedom. The mechanism is depicted in Fig. 1(b), wherein the origin of the coordinate system of the fixed plane is fixed at $\{O_1\}$ and the origin of the coordinate system of the movement plane is fixed at $\{O_2\}$. A_1 and A_2 represent the two spherical joint center points at the proximal end of the fixed plane. Similarly, B_1 and B_2 represent the two spherical joint center points at the proximal end of the movement plane. l_1 and l_2 represent the lengths of the lines connecting the spherical joint center points at the two ends of the movement plane. The lengths of the rods are also included. $\boldsymbol{n}_1$ and $\boldsymbol{n}_2$ are the unit vectors along the direction of the movement plane. H_1 is the perpendicular height from the origin of the fixed plane coordinate system, O_1, to the first revolute joint axis.

H_2 is the vertical height between two revolute joint axes. e_1 denotes the negative bias of O_1 with respect to O_2 along the y-axis of the coordinate system of the fixed plane, and takes a positive value. e_2 represents the negative bias of B_1B_2 along the z-axis in the coordinate system of the movement plane, and takes a positive value. $\boldsymbol{P}$ represents the origin of $\{O_2\}$ in $\{O_1\}$. Figure 2 depicts the assembly of a manipulator with a parallel wrist and a robotic arm. The manipulator is connected to the connection platform, which is connected to the manipulator, and the manipulator is connected to the wrist.

The orientation matrix of $\{O_2\}$ with respect to $\{O_1\}$ can be expressed as.

$$\boldsymbol{R} = \mathrm{Rot}(Y, \beta)\mathrm{Rot}(X, \alpha) \quad (1)$$

where α and β are the two angles of the mechanism.

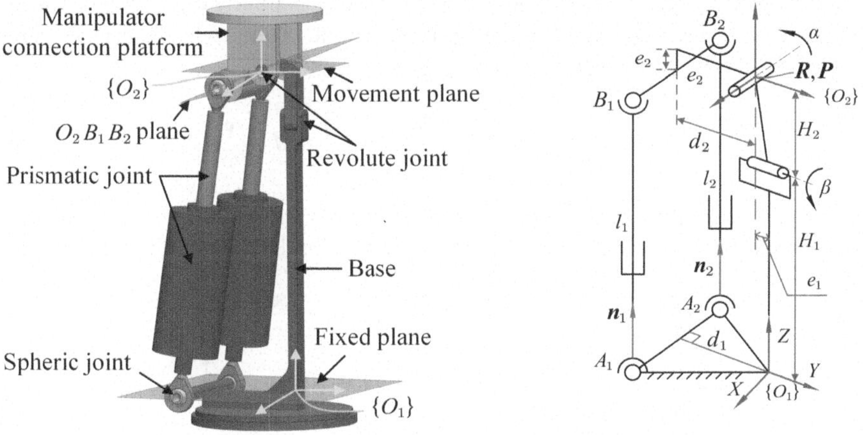

(a) Assembly model of parallel wrist (b) Topology diagram of parallel wrist

Fig. 1. Assembly model of the parallel wrist and topology of the 2SPS-RR configuration

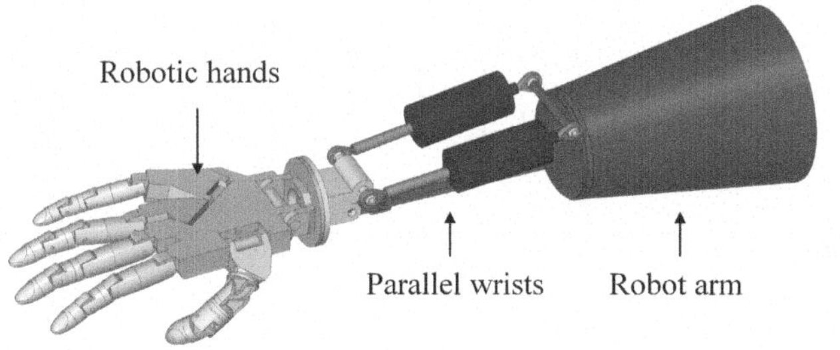

Fig. 2. Schematic of the assembly model of the robot hand and parallel wrist and arm

According to the closed-loop vector method, it can be deduced that.

$$l_i\boldsymbol{n}_i = \boldsymbol{B}_i - \boldsymbol{A}_i \quad (i = 1, 2) \quad (2)$$

where $\boldsymbol{B}_i$ is the vector representation of the center point B_i of the spherical joints in $\{O_1\}$ and $\boldsymbol{A}_i$ is the vector representation of the center point A_i of the spherical joints in $\{O_1\}$. The elongation of the moving prismatic joints and the direction vector of the line where the prismatic joints are located can be solved by using Eq. (2) and the initial rod length.

The Jacobi matrix represents the mapping relationship between the velocity of the moving platform and the velocities of the two actuators, which serves as the foundation for singular and static analyses. The motion of the moving platform can be described by the twists of the origin and the Euler angles. The derivative of $\boldsymbol{B}_i$ with respect to time is.

$$\dot{\boldsymbol{B}}_i = \boldsymbol{v} + \boldsymbol{\omega} \times (\boldsymbol{B}_i - \boldsymbol{P}) \tag{3}$$

where $\boldsymbol{v}$ and $\boldsymbol{\omega}$ are the velocity and angular velocity of O_2 with respect to $\{O_1\}$.

The velocity of the moving joints can be obtained by projecting the velocity at point B_i along the direction of the moving joints. This velocity is finally organized as Eq. (4), which responds to the mapping relationship between the origin twist of the movement plane and the velocity of the actuator.

$$\begin{bmatrix} i_1 \\ i_2 \end{bmatrix} = \begin{bmatrix} \boldsymbol{n}_1^{\mathrm{T}} & (\boldsymbol{B}_1 - \boldsymbol{P}) \times \boldsymbol{n}_1^{\mathrm{T}} \\ \boldsymbol{n}_2^{\mathrm{T}} & (\boldsymbol{B}_2 - \boldsymbol{P}) \times \boldsymbol{n}_2^{\mathrm{T}} \end{bmatrix} \begin{bmatrix} \boldsymbol{v} \\ \boldsymbol{\omega} \end{bmatrix} = \boldsymbol{J}_1 \begin{bmatrix} \boldsymbol{v} \\ \boldsymbol{\omega} \end{bmatrix} \tag{4}$$

The angular velocity can be represented by Euler angles, and the twist at the origin of the movement plane can be mapped from the first-order derivative of the Euler angle.

$$\begin{bmatrix} v \\ \omega \end{bmatrix} = \begin{bmatrix} 0 & H_2 \cos\beta \\ 0 & 0 \\ 0 & -H_2 \sin\beta \\ \cos\beta & 0 \\ 0 & 1 \\ -\sin\beta & 0 \end{bmatrix} \begin{bmatrix} \dot{\alpha} \\ \dot{\beta} \end{bmatrix} = \boldsymbol{J}_2 \begin{bmatrix} \dot{\alpha} \\ \dot{\beta} \end{bmatrix} \tag{5}$$

A mapping of the derivative of the Euler angle to the velocity of the actuator can be derived.

$$\begin{bmatrix} \dot{i}_1 \\ \dot{i}_2 \end{bmatrix} = \boldsymbol{J}_1 \boldsymbol{J}_2 \begin{bmatrix} \dot{\alpha} \\ \dot{\beta} \end{bmatrix} \tag{6}$$

2.2 Singularity

The singularity judgment condition is.

$$\det(J) = 0 \tag{7}$$

As $\boldsymbol{J}_1$ is not a square matrix and the primary focus of analysis is the angular velocity of rotation of the movement plane, an equivalent transformation can be performed so that the equivalent Jacobi matrix is square.

To facilitate the calculation of the singular discriminant, supplementary Eq. (8) is added.

$$[\sin\beta \quad 0 \quad \cos\beta]^T \boldsymbol{\omega}_{o_2} = \mathbf{m}\cdot\boldsymbol{\omega}_{o_2} = 0 \tag{8}$$

The mapping relationship between the origin velocity and the angular velocity of the moving plane is.

$$\boldsymbol{v} = \begin{bmatrix} 0 & H_2\cos\beta & 0 \\ 0 & 0 & 0 \\ 0 & -H_2\sin\beta & 0 \end{bmatrix} \omega = G\omega_{o_2} \tag{9}$$

Simultaneous Eqs. (4), (8) and (9) can be derived.

$$\begin{bmatrix} 1 & 0 \\ 0 & 1 \\ 0 & 0 \end{bmatrix}\begin{bmatrix} \dot{i}_1 \\ \dot{i}_2 \end{bmatrix} = \boldsymbol{H}\begin{bmatrix} \dot{i}_1 \\ \dot{i}_2 \end{bmatrix} = \begin{bmatrix} \boldsymbol{J}_1 & \\ \boldsymbol{0}_{3\times3} & \boldsymbol{m} \end{bmatrix}\begin{bmatrix} \boldsymbol{G} \\ \boldsymbol{I}_{3\times3} \end{bmatrix} = \boldsymbol{J}'\boldsymbol{\omega} \tag{10}$$

The equivalent Jacobi matrix is.

$$J' = \begin{bmatrix} \boldsymbol{k}_1 \\ \boldsymbol{k}_2 \\ \boldsymbol{k}_3 \end{bmatrix} = \begin{bmatrix} \boldsymbol{n}_1{}^T\boldsymbol{G} + \left({}_{o_1}\boldsymbol{P}_{\boldsymbol{B}_1} \times \boldsymbol{n}_1\right)^T \\ \boldsymbol{n}_2{}^T\boldsymbol{G} + \left({}_{o_1}\boldsymbol{P}_{\boldsymbol{B}_1} \times \boldsymbol{n}_2\right)^T \\ \sin_\beta \quad 0 \qquad \cos_\beta \end{bmatrix} \tag{11}$$

From the mixed product formula, it can be deduced that.

$$|J'| = (\boldsymbol{k}_1 \times \boldsymbol{k}_2)\cdot \boldsymbol{k}_3 \tag{12}$$

From a geometric point of view, the singularity condition is satisfied when the normal vector of the plane formed by vectors $\boldsymbol{k}_1$ and $\boldsymbol{k}_2$ is perpendicular to vector $\boldsymbol{k}_3$, at which point the pose is at the singularity point. From the equivalent Eq. (10), $\boldsymbol{H}$ is a constant value matrix and is a unit matrix after removing the last row. Therefore, there is no inverse solution singularity. While $\boldsymbol{J}$' contains structural parameter variables and may have positive solution singularity.

According to Eq. (11), the singular trajectory can be plotted in Fig. 3(a). At this point the line $\beta = 0$ and the singular trajectory exists at the intersection points C_1 and C_2. Draw the side view of the topological map of the wrist, as Fig. 3(b). The geometrical significance of C_1 and C_2 at this point is the intersection of the line where A_1O_2 is located with the circle centered at O_2 with radius O_2B_1. At point C_1, the rod lengths are at the shortest point. At this time, the elongation of the prismatic joints is increased, and the α-rotational motion of the movement plane becomes uncertain. At point C_2, the length is at the longest point at the same time. At this time, to shorten the elongation of the mobile joints, the α-rotational movement of the moving plane is uncertain. These two points are the typical singularity points of the parallel wrist.

Taking the typical singular points as the benchmark, with the increase of β angle, the prismatic joints move close to the limit state, which leads to the uncertainty of the rotational motion at the spherical joints of the unilateral movement plane. The collection of these points together constitutes the singular trajectory of the parallel wrist. Meanwhile, since the force arm of the driving force with respect to O_2 tends to 0 when approaching the singular trajectory, the joint driving force will tend to infinity at this point. Therefore, in the subsequent optimization process, it is necessary to stay as far as possible from the singular trajectory to ensure the certainty of the motion as well as the reasonableness of the magnitude of the driving force.

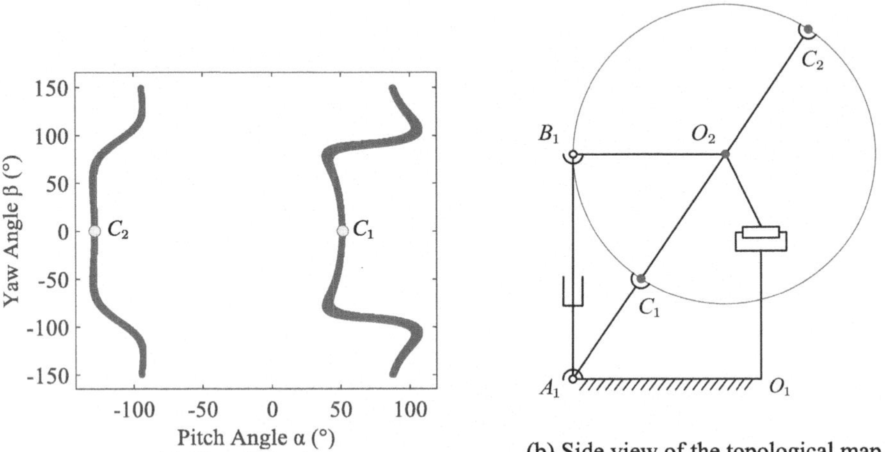

(a) Singular trajectory

(b) Side view of the topological map of the wrist

Fig. 3. Analytical plots of singular trajectories

2.3 Workspace

In this paper, the sequence of Euler angles (α, β) is employed to describe the position of the movement plane that can be reached by the attitude, which is traversed via the grid search method. This entails determining the rod length and spherical joints angle at each search point, given the search interval and search step of α and β. The sequence of the position is finally generated.

It is necessary to provide the limit of the rotational angle of the spherical joints. Given the limited practical applications of spherical joints, equivalent spherical joints are typically employed in their stead. This involves combining revolute joints and universal joints to achieve a configuration analogous to that of spherical joints. In this configuration, the axes of revolute joints at the hinge point pass through the center of universal joints, thereby maintaining three degrees of freedom at the hinge point. The topology and kinematic relationships are identical to those of the previous configuration, although the restriction on the rotation of the spherical joints is no longer in effect.

The limitation of the equivalent spherical joints at the proximal end of the fixed plane to the workspace can be determined by (13), where $\boldsymbol{\theta}_A$ is the rotational cone angle of the equivalent spherical joints, $\boldsymbol{e}_3$ is the z-axis vector of the fixed plane, $\boldsymbol{n}_i$ is the unit direction vector along the two rods, and $\boldsymbol{\theta}_{A\text{-max}}$ is the limiting value of the rotational cone angle. For the equivalent spherical joints at the proximal end of the movement plane, the rotational cone angle, $\boldsymbol{\theta}_B$, can be determined by (14), where $\boldsymbol{e}_3$' is the z-axis vector of the movement plane, $\boldsymbol{\theta}_{B\text{-max}}$ is the limit value of the rotational cone angle, and $\boldsymbol{\theta}_B$ is the rotational cone angle of the equivalent spherical joints. In light of the possibility of interference between the actuator and the movement plane in practical applications, it can be determined by (15), where $\boldsymbol{\theta}_{\min}$ is the minimum value of $\angle A_2B_2B_1$ and $\angle A_1B_1B_2$ in the non-interference state.

$$\theta_A = \arccos(\boldsymbol{e}_3 \cdot \boldsymbol{n}_i) \le \theta_{A-\max} \tag{13}$$

$$\theta_{\mathrm{B}} = \arccos(\boldsymbol{e}_{3'} \cdot \boldsymbol{n}_{\mathrm{i}}) \le \theta_{\mathrm{B\ -\ max}} \tag{14}$$

$$\angle A_2B_2B_1 > \theta_{min},\ \angle A_1B_1B_2 > \theta_{min} \tag{15}$$

3 Workspace Optimization and Evaluation

From the perspective of demand, the rotation range of the parallel wrist should be as close as possible to that of the human wrist. Therefore, it is necessary to evaluate the size of its workspace reasonably and analyze the variables affecting the workspace simultaneously. In this paper, the seven proposed design parameters are globally optimized by a genetic algorithm, and the effects of the seven design parameters on the workspace are analyzed. The results of the optimization are evaluated.

3.1 Design Parameters

The parallel wrist has two revolute joints and two platforms. The variables related to the characteristics mentioned above are designated as the design parameters. The design parameters selected in this paper are presented in Table 1. The constraint Eqs. (16) are introduced concerning the length of the human forearm, so that the overall dimensions of the parallel wrist can be harmonized with the real dimensions of the human body.

$$H_1 + H_2 = 200\text{mm} \tag{16}$$

In this paper, the upper and lower bounds of seven design parameters are presented, considering the overall size and structural rationality. These bounds are presented in Table 2.

3.2 Objective Function

In order to perform global optimization, it is necessary to define the evaluation function for the optimization objective. Furthermore, the total number of reachable location points after the grid search provides an indication of the size of the workspace, although the range of the search must be specified. In this paper, the size of the workspace is

Table 1. Design parameters

Parameter	Meaning
a	Length between points A_1 and A_2
b	Length between points B_1 and B_2
d_1	The vertical distance from O_1 to line A_1 A_2
d_2	The vertical distance from O_2 to line B_1 B_2
e_1	The offset of O_1
e_2	The offset of B_1 B_2
H_1	Vertical height from fixed plane to revolute joints

Table 2. Upper and lower bounds for design parameters

Variable	Lower bound (mm)	Upper bound (mm)	Variable	Lower bound (mm)	Upper bound (mm)
a	55	55	e_1	8	30
b	55	55	e_2	0	15
d_1	10	10	H_1	140	190
d_2	55	55			

evaluated by the area of the reachable area in the boundary of the desired workspace. This is achieved by generating m_1 equally spaced points within the boundary of the desired workspace using α, and similarly generating m_2 equally spaced points within the boundary of the desired workspace using β. The number of reachable locations n is recorded after the grid search, which can be used to compute the coverage of the reachable area relative to the desired workspace. By specifying the area of the desired workspace, the area of the reachable region can be calculated.

For the desired workspace, this paper refers to human motor anatomy. The flexion motion of the palm can reach 80° ~ 90°, the extension motion can reach 70°–80°, the radial deviation can reach 15° ~ 30°, and the ulnar deviation can reach 30°–40°, as shown in Fig. 4. Combining with the range of motion of the human wrist, and taking into account the smaller range of motion of the parallel mechanism, this paper defines the boundaries of the desired workspace of the parallel wrist as a rectangular region, i.e., the rotation range of α-direction is from −80° to 50°, and the rotation range of β-direction is from −30° to 30°.

The search range of the workspace is the rectangular area of the desired workspace, i.e., $\alpha_{min} = -80°$, $\alpha_{max} = 50°$, $\beta_{min} = -30°$, $\beta_{max} = 30°$. In theory, the smaller the l_{min}, the larger the l_{max}, the larger the working space. But in practice, l_{min} and l_{max} are determined by the drive itself, this paper refers to H_1 and H_2, so that l_{min} and l_{max} are coordinated with the length of the mechanism. At the same time, consider the actual travel of the electric push rod on the market. Taking $l_{min} = 170$ mm, $l_{max} = 220$ mm.

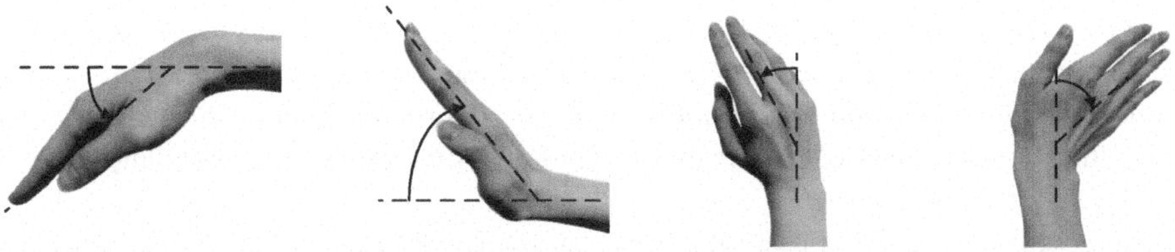

Fig. 4. Schematic of human wrist movement

The purpose of this is, on the one hand, to make the analysis results closer to the actual design situation. On the other hand, the given limit of rod length reduces the difficulty of subsequent optimization.

In order to achieve the desired boundary coverage and to avoid singular trajectories, the objective function is selected as in Eq. (17), where k_1, k_2 and k_3 are the weight values. The value of γ is the α forward singular angle of the mechanism, which corresponds to the C_1 point in Fig. 3(b). Similarly, $\alpha_{\min}$ represents the minimum value of α in the sequence of reachable poses, which can be obtained by traversing the numerical method. Finally, $\alpha_{\exp}$ represents the desired minimum value of α, which is set to -80° in this paper. The coefficient of $k_2\gamma$ is 100, which serves to make the three components in Q of approximately the same order of magnitude. Given that the driving of the mechanism tends towards infinity when approaching the singular trajectory, the forward singular angle value is the focus of avoidance in this paper, and finally $k_1 = 0.3, k_2 = 0.4, k_3 = 0.3$

$$Q = -k_1 \frac{Sn}{m_1 m_2} - 100k_2\gamma - k_3 \left(\frac{1}{(a_{\min} - a_{\exp})^2} \right) \tag{17}$$

where S is the area of the desired workspace.

3.3 Optimization Result

Table 3 shows the optimization results. Figure 5 shows the resultant plots calculated by the objective function.

Table 3. Optimization results using the objective function

Variable	Values (mm)	Variable	Values (mm)
a	60	e_1	8
b	55	e_2	3
d_1	13	H_1	140
d_2	20		

Figure 5(a) shows the superposition of the workspace with the singular trajectory corresponding to the parameter values of the best individual, at which point the coverage is 78.31%. The green area in the figure is the workspace of the mechanism, and the red trajectory is the singular trajectory. The boundary of the desired workspace of the parallel wrist is the blue rectangular region in Fig. 5(a), i.e., the rotation range of α is from $-80°$ to $50°$, the rotation range of β is from $-30°$ to $30°$, and the desired boundary is away from the singular trajectory.

The magnitude of the condition number of the Jacobi matrix reflects the degree to which the pose of the mechanism is close to the singularity, and the ratio of the maximum singular value and the minimum singular value of the matrix $\boldsymbol{J}_1\boldsymbol{J}_2$ in Eq. (6) is used to define the condition number of the Jacobi matrix as in Eq. (18).

$$\mathrm{cond}(\boldsymbol{J}_1\boldsymbol{J}_2) = \frac{\sigma_{\max}}{\sigma_{\min}} \tag{18}$$

Figure 5(b) shows the distribution of the optimized condition numbers, and it can be seen that the values of the condition numbers on the right side of the distribution are relatively large, but the absolute values are all less than 20, indicating that the boundary of the desired workspace is far away from the singular trajectory at this point.

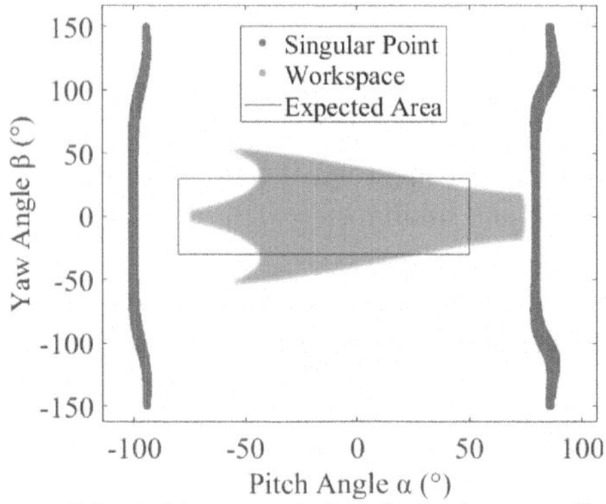

(a) workspace and singular trajectory after the optimization

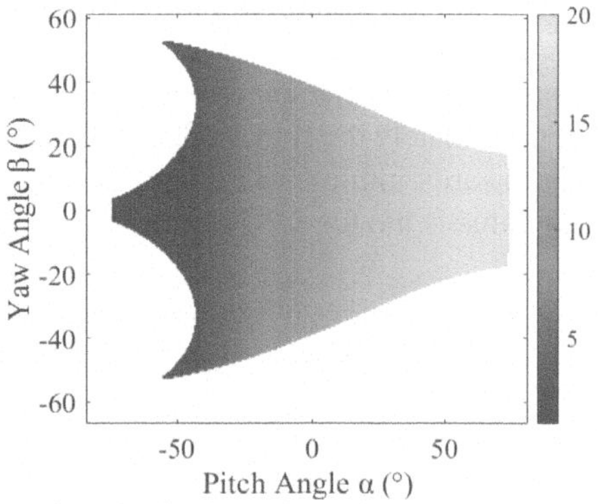

(b) Distribution of condition numbers

Fig. 5. Plot of the workspace distribution corresponding to the optimal individual parameters; Plot of the distribution of condition numbers. For the number of conditions, the closer to 1 the better

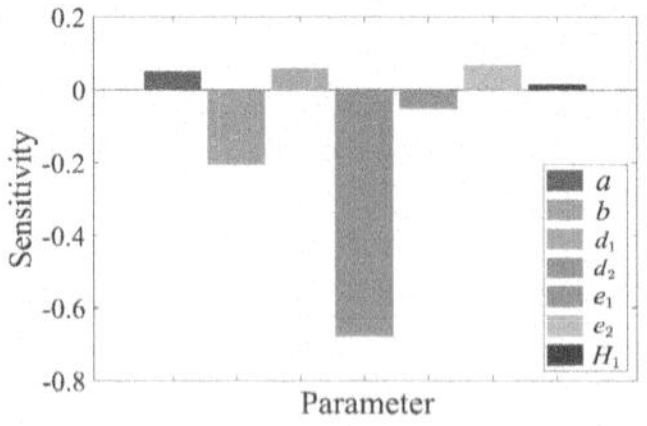

Fig. 6. Results of sensitivity analysis

Figure 6 illustrates the sensitivity values for the seven design parameters. It can be observed that d_2, b, and e_1 are negatively correlated with the size of the workspace.

Among the aforementioned parameters, d_2 exerts the most significant influence on the workspace. Furthermore, an increase in b will result in a more substantial reduction in the extent of the workspace. The remaining four parameters exhibit positive sensitivity values due to the random nature of the mutation of the genetic algorithm and the limited density of the grid search. Consequently, the final optimization result may be a very small value near the true extreme value. However, the sensitivity values of these parameters are relatively low, indicating that the result obtained by the genetic algorithm is an acceptable approximation of the desired optimization result in this paper.

4 Driving Force and Driving Speed of Joints

Indicators of the mechanics of the parallel wrist influence the choice of cylinder or electric actuator model, and this paper analyzes the joint driving forces and drive speed of the mechanism after optimization of the workspace. Equation (19) can be derived from the Principle of Virtual Work and Eq. (6).

$$\tau = \boldsymbol{J}_2(\boldsymbol{J}_1\boldsymbol{J}_2)^{-1}\boldsymbol{F} \tag{19}$$

where $\boldsymbol{\tau}$ is a two-dimensional joint driving force vector, and $\boldsymbol{F}$ is a six-dimensional load external force vector on the movement plane.

In this paper, the load is equivalent to a 4 kg particle with a distance of 100 mm along the z-axis of the movement plane, and the direction of the force is along the y-axis of the fixed plane. Hence, the load $\boldsymbol{F}$ is.

$$\boldsymbol{F} = \begin{bmatrix} \boldsymbol{f}_{\text{load}} \\ \boldsymbol{m}_{\text{load}} \end{bmatrix} = \begin{bmatrix} 0\ 4g\ 0 \end{bmatrix}^{\text{T}} \begin{bmatrix} \boldsymbol{p}_{\text{load}} \times \boldsymbol{f}_{\text{load}} \end{bmatrix} \tag{20}$$

where $\boldsymbol{p}_{\text{load}} = \begin{bmatrix} 0\ 0\ 0.1 \end{bmatrix}^{\text{T}}$, $g = 9.8\ \text{m/s}^2$.

Figure 7 is the joint driving forces distribution calculated using the optimization objective function, and the maximum driving force is 354.4N. There is no sharp increase in the joint driving forces at this time, which indicates that the boundary of the desired workspace at this time has no intersection with the singular trajectory, which agrees with the results of condition number analysis.

The linear actuator speed of the prismatic joints is an important selection evaluation index, under the condition of the same rotation speed of the movement plane, the absolute value of the linear actuator speed should be as small as possible. The reason is that this not only reduces the inertia force of the actuator movement, but also reduces the wear and tear of the mechanism, resulting in a relatively longer life of the mechanism.

The parallel wrist has two rotational degrees of freedom, given the sequence of movement plane attitude, keep the rotational speed of one of the axes corresponding to the Euler angle as 0, and specify the rotational speed of the other Euler angle, the linear actuator speed law can be obtained under the rated rotational speed of a single axis. In this paper, the numerical method is adopted, the calculation range of α is from $-80°$ to $45°$, the calculation range of β is from $-45°$ to $45°$. Through the mapping relationship of Eq. (6), the velocity distribution can be plotted. Figure 8(a) is the linear actuator velocity plot when keeping the rotational speed of β-angle as 0 and the rotational speed of the

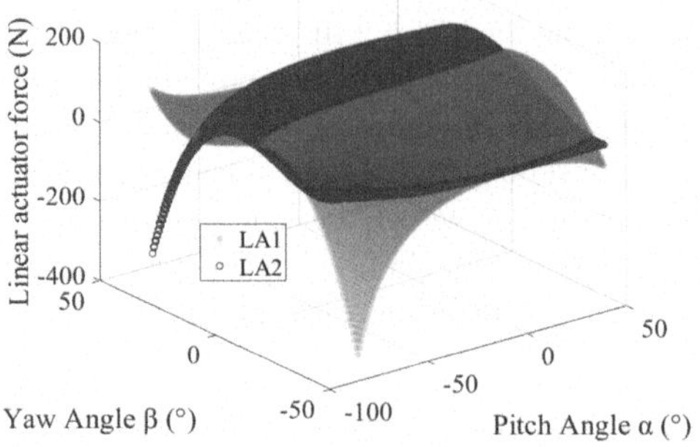

Fig. 7. Joint driving forces after the optimization

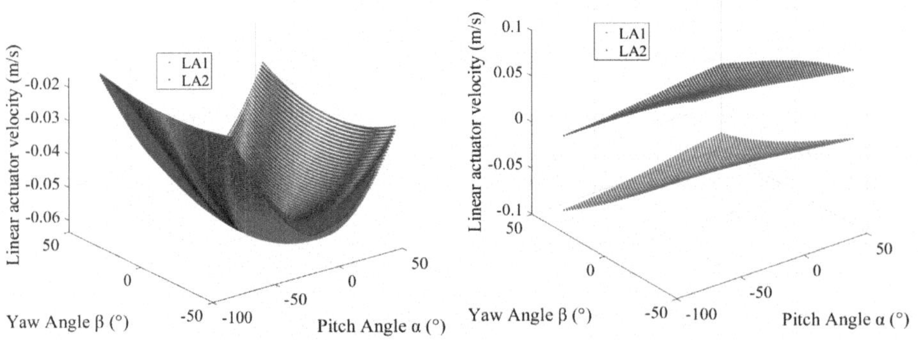

(a) linear actuator speed (α) (b) linear actuator speed (β)

Fig. 8. The distribution of linear actuator velocity

α-angle as π rad/s, Fig. 8(b) is the linear actuator speed plot when the rotational speed of α angle is kept as 0 and the rotational speed of β angle is π rad/s. The absolute values of the maximum actuator speed in the two states are 0.063 m/s and 0.098 m/s. The absolute values of the actuator speed at this time are less than 0.1 m/s, which are in the acceptable range.

5 Conclusion

In this paper, seven design parameters were proposed for the structural design of the 2SPS-RR parallel wrist. Based on the design parameters, the position, velocity and typical singular position of the mechanism were analyzed and the workspace was solved. An optimization function considering multiple performance indexes was proposed, and based on this, a global optimization was carried out, and the optimized workspace achieved a coverage of 78.31% in the desired workspace. A workspace sensitivity analysis was performed, and it was found that the vertical distance from O_2 to line B_1 B_2

had the greatest impact on the area of the workspace based on the optimization results in this paper. The optimization results were evaluated by condition number, which showed that the desired workspace is far away from the singular trajectory when the value was taken as the optimal parameter. Finally, this paper analyzed the driving force and speed of the wrist, and obtained the distribution map about the values of these two indexes. The results showed that the driving force did not have the condition of a sharp increase in value when the value was taken as the optimal parameter, which was consistent with the analysis results of the condition number. This paper provided a basis for theoretical analysis of the subsequent design and optimization of the humanoid robot wrist. In the future, other performance indexes, such as the stiffness of the mechanism, can be considered to be introduced into the optimization function and based on which the dynamic performance can be optimized.

Acknowledgement. This work was supported by the National Natural Science Foundation of China under Grant 52305016, Guangdong Basic and Applied Basic Research Foundation under Grants 2022B1515120078 and 2023A1515240062, and Shenzhen Science and Technology Program under Grants JSGGZD20220822095401004, GXWD20220811151912002 and JCYJ20230807094311023.

References

1. Saeedvand, S., Jafari, M., Aghdasi, H.S., Baltes, J.: A comprehensive survey on humanoid robot development. Knowl. Eng. Rev. **34**, e20 (2019)
2. Schwartz, M., Sim, J., Ahn, J., Hwang, S., Lee, Y., Park, J.: Design of the Humanoid Robot TOCABI. In: 2022 IEEE-RAS 21st International Conference on Humanoid Robots (Humanoids), pp. 28–30 (2022)
3. Sun, J., Cao, X., Song, G.: Design method for a bionic wrist based on tensegrity structures. Biosurface and Biotribology **6**(2), 31–36 (2020)
4. Bridgwater, L.B., Ihrke, C.A., Diftler, M.A., Abdallah, M.E., Linn, D.M.: The Robonaut 2 hand - designed to do work with tools. In: Proceedings - IEEE International Conference on Robotics and Automation, pp. 3425–30 (2012)
5. Kim, Y.J., Lee, Y., Kim, J., Lee, J.W., Choi, J.Y.: RoboRay hand: A highly backdrivable robotic hand with sensorless contact force measurements. IEEE (2014)
6. Bajaj, N.M., Spiers, A.J., Dollar, A.M.: State of the art in prosthetic wrists: Commercial and research devices. In: IEEE International Conference on Rehabilitation Robotics (2015)
7. Bajaj, N.M., Spiers, A.J., Dollar, A.M.: State of the art in artificial wrists: a review of prosthetic and robotic wrist design. IEEE Trans. Rob. **35**(1), 261–277 (2019)
8. Huang, G., Guo, S., Zhang, D., et al.: Kinematic analysis and multi-objective optimization of a new reconfigurable parallel mechanism with high stiffness. Robotica: Int. J. Inform., Educ. Res. Robot. Artif. Intell. **36**(2), 187–203 (2018)
9. Srivastava, S., Salunkhe, S., Pande, S., Naranje, V.: Design of Prosthetic Finger Using Topology Optimization. In: 2021 International Conference on Computational Intelligence and Knowledge Economy (ICCIKE) (2021)
10. Mustafa, S.K., Yang, G., Yeo, S.H., Lin, W., Pham, C.B.: Development of a Bio-Inspired Wrist Prosthesis. IEEE (2006)

11. Li, H., Gosselin, C.M., Richard, M.J.: Determination of maximal singularity-free zones in the workspace of planar three-degree-of-freedom parallel mechanisms. Mech. Mach. Theory **41**(10), 1157–1167 (2006)
12. Ramana Babu, S., Ramachandra Raju, V., Ramji, K.: Design optimization of 3PRS parallel manipulator using global performance indices. J. Mech. Sci. Technol. **30**(9), 4325–4335 (2016)

An Innovative Hierarchical Approach to Multi-rigid Body Modeling and Control Using Constraint-Following Method

Xiao Su[1], Yutong Yuan[1], Longjie Fan[1], Duanling Li[1](✉), and Jin Huang[2](✉)

[1] School of Automation, Beijing University of Posts and Telecommunications, Beijing 100876, China
duanlingli@bupt.edu.cn

[2] School of Vehicle and Mobility, Tsinghua University, Beijing 100084, China
huangjin@tsinghua.edu.cn

Abstract. The modeling and control of complex multi-rigid-body systems remain challenging due to the systems' pronounced coupling and nonlinearity. In this paper, we propose a novel extended hierarchical modeling method for complex multi-rigid body systems, obtain an analytical model of system dynamics, and introduce a constraint-following control method to address the challenges of system modeling and control. In this approach, constraints are categorized into two levels: structural constraints constitute the first level, and motion constraints form the second level. Within the second level constraints, arbitrary initial conditions can lead to trajectory divergence. Consequently, we propose the asymptotic convergence criterion to address this issue. Subsequently, the analytical dynamic equation and trajectory tracking control force for the mobile robot are derived simultaneously. Numerical simulations of the mobile robots are performed to demonstrate the efficacy and accuracy of this methodology.

Keywords: Multi-Rigid Body · Hierarchical Modeling · Constraint-Following

1 Introduction

The dynamic model underpins the control theory of multi-rigid body systems. Previously, several dominant approaches to multibody modeling have been established.

In the Newton-Euler method [1–3], motion equations for each rigid body are separately established using Newton-Euler equations, subsequently enabling the assembly of the system's dynamic model via forward and backward recursion to ascertain coupling conditions. This approach is notably intuitive and straightforward to implement. However, as the count of rigid bodies within the system

X. Lan et al. (Eds.): ICIRA 2024, LNAI 15201, pp. 381–395, 2025.
https://doi.org/10.1007/978-981-96-0771-6_28

escalates, the complexity of coupling and constraints amongst these bodies intensifies considerably. Given that the forces on each rigid body require individual consideration, the system's unknown variables proliferate substantially, thereby augmenting the modeling workload.

The Lagrange multiplier method [4–6] develops the dynamic model of multi-rigid bodies from an energy perspective under unconstrained conditions before employing the Lagrange multiplier to incorporate constraints, thus deriving the system's dynamic model under such constraints. This method ensures compliance with constraints by embedding a constraint equation into the system via the Lagrange multiplier. Nonetheless, the approach is not intrinsically unique owing to the presence of arbitrary vectors within the Lagrange multipliers and yields a unique solution exclusively under specific conditions.

In the Gibbs-Appell method [7–9], the Gibbs function is formulated using the auxiliary variables of pseudo velocity and pseudo acceleration; subsequently, the dynamic model of the rigid body system is resolved using the Appell equation. While this method is cumbersome in holonomic constraint systems compared to the Lagrange multiplier method, it offers significant advantages in nonholonomic constraint systems.

In the Kane method [10,11], the generalized inertial force equation is formulated through generalized pseudo-velocity, which then facilitates the establishment of the dynamic model of the rigid body system using Kane's equations. Generally, the Kane method bears similarity to the Gibbs-Appell method, representing essentially an alternate form articulated through different auxiliary variables.

Although traditional multi-rigid-body modeling methods are widely utilized in the engineering field, they present several shortcomings. For example, establishing a dynamic analytical model for complex multi-rigid-body systems proves challenging. The modeling process under non-holonomic constraints becomes cumbersome. Additionally, when faced with non-ideal constraints [12], it is problematic to model mechanical systems, such as in cases where an analytical model of the system's friction force is unattainable.

This paper introduces a novel hierarchical modeling method, grounded in the Udwadia-Kalaba method [13–15], to address the shortcomings of existing modeling approaches. In this approach, a multibody system is segmented into a class of subsystems that are connected kinematically. Suppose the equations of motion of the unconstrained subsystems can be obtained. The constraint forces, which are induced by the constraints, can be calculated without using any auxiliary variables. As a result, the analytic expressions of the equations of motion of the constrained subsystems can be obtained.

2 Udwadia-Kalaba Theory and Extended Hierarchical Modeling Methods

2.1 Udwadia-Kalaba Theory

The Udwadia-Kalaba theory, which provides the equations of motion for multibody systems under constraints, has been a significant development in the Lagrangian community over the past 30 years.

Assuming the system is composed of s particles and a rigid body, with the generalized coordinates $q \in R^n$ being an n-dimensional generalized coordinate vector, $\dot{q} \in R^n$ being a generalized velocity vector, and $\ddot{q} \in R^n$ being a generalized acceleration vector, the equation of motion for the system under unconstrained conditions is:

$$M\left(q(t), t\right)\ddot{q}(t) = Q\left(q(t), \dot{q}(t), t\right), \tag{1}$$

where $t \in R$ is the independent variable time. In addition, $M \in R^{n\times n}$ is the inertia matrix, $Q \in R^n$ is the impressed (or applied) force plus all Coriolis/centrifugal and gravitational terms. The functions $M(\cdot)$ and $Q(\cdot)$ are posited to be continuous.

A set of constraints is imposed on the unconstrained system. It is supposed that $m\,(m \leq n)$ consistent constraints of the following form are applied:

$$\sigma_i\left(q, \dot{q}, t\right) = 0, i = 1, 2, \cdots, m, \tag{2}$$

where $\sigma(\cdot) : R^n \times R^n \times R \to R$, $\sigma_i(\cdot)$ is sufficiently smooth (up to the level that is required for differentiation).

The class of constraints comprises common types of holonomic and nonholonomic constraints. Moreover, all these constraints are presumed to possess sufficient smoothness, ensuring their differentiability with respect to time t allows for transformation into second-order form:

$$A\left(q, \dot{q}, t\right)\ddot{q} = b\left(q, \dot{q}, t\right), \tag{3}$$

where $A \in R^{m\times n}$ denotes the constraint matrix, and $b \in R^{m\times 1}$ represents an m-dimensional vector.

Due to the presence of constraints, additional 'generalized forces of constraints' should be imposed on the system. Thus, the explicit equation of motion for the constrained system can be expressed as:

$$M\left(q(t), t\right)\ddot{q}(t) = Q\left(q(t), \dot{q}(t), t\right) + Q^e\left(q(t), \dot{q}(t), t\right), \tag{4}$$

where $Q^e \in R^n$, arising due to the holonomic and nonholonomic constraints, the additional term of forces is imposed on the system. Our task is to determine the constraint force Q^e. Based on Gauss's principle of least constraint, Udwadia and Kalaba [16] proposed that the constraint force vector is explicitly given by:

$$Q^e = M^{\frac{1}{2}}\left(AM^{-\frac{1}{2}}\right)^+\left(b - AM^{-1}Q\right), \tag{5}$$

where the superscript '+' denotes the Moore-Penrose generalized inverse.

The Moore-Penrose generalized inverse of the constraint matrix A plays a substantial role in describing constrained motion. It is not required to know the rank of the matrix A to obtain the explicit equation of motion governing the constrained dynamical system, which allows deeper insights into the nature of constrained motion. The Moore-Penrose generalized inverse A^+ uniquely satisfies the following four conditions:

$$AA^+A = A \tag{6}$$

$$A^+AA^+ = A \tag{7}$$

$$AA^+ = \left(AA^+\right)^T \tag{8}$$

$$A^+A = \left(A^+A\right)^T. \tag{9}$$

The explicit equation of motion that governs the evolution of the constrained system is:

$$M\ddot{q} = Q + M^{\frac{1}{2}}\left(AM^{-\frac{1}{2}}\right)^+(b - Aa), \tag{10}$$

$$\ddot{q} = a + M^{-\frac{1}{2}}\left(AM^{-\frac{1}{2}}\right)^+(b - Aa), \tag{11}$$

where $a = M^{-1}Q$.

Equation 10 is renowned as the "fundamental equation of constrained motion". It boasts mathematical conciseness and equips us with an efficacious tool for handling constraints.

2.2 Extended Hierarchical Modeling Methods

According to the hierarchical properties of the Udwadia-Kalaba equation [17], a particle, rigid body system, or other multibody system can be decomposed into several subsystems, and a multibody system model can be established based on the constraint relationships among each subsystem.

Based on Eq. 5, the constraint force Q^e is determined by Q. This formulation enables the equation of motion to be expressed in a cascading manner as additional constraints are imposed on the system. Suppose the unconstrained system:

$$M(q,t)\ddot{q} = Q_0(q,\dot{q},t), \tag{12}$$

is subject to the constraint $A_1(q,t)\ddot{q} = b_1(q,\dot{q},t)$, then one can formulate the equation of motion as

$$M(q,t)\ddot{q} = Q_1(q,\dot{q},t), \tag{13}$$

where

$$Q_1 = Q_0 + Q_1^e, \tag{14}$$

$$Q_1^e = M^{\frac{1}{2}}\left(A_1M^{-\frac{1}{2}}\right)^+\left(b_1 - A_1M^{-1}Q_0\right). \tag{15}$$

One can interpret Eq. 13 to be in the same form as Eq. 12, an unconstrained mechanical system. Next, suppose there is an additional constraint $A_2(q,t)\ddot{q} = b_2(q,\dot{q},t)$, added to the system motion. Then, one can formulate the equation of motion as:

$$M(q,t)\ddot{q} = Q_2(q,\dot{q},t), \tag{16}$$

where

$$Q_2 = Q_1 + Q_2^e, \tag{17}$$

$$Q_2^e = M^{\frac{1}{2}}\left(A_2 M^{-\frac{1}{2}}\right)^+ \left(b_2 - A_2 M^{-1} Q_1\right). \tag{18}$$

This iterative process can be implemented with additional constraints. Now, letting the constraints be $A_i(q,t)\ddot{q} = b_i(q,\dot{q},t)$, where $(i = 1, 2, \ldots, l)$, the equation of motion for the constrained system is given by:

$$M(q,t)\ddot{q} = Q_i(q,\dot{q},t), \tag{19}$$

where

$$Q_i = Q_{i-1} + Q_i^e, \tag{20}$$

$$Q_i^e = M^{\frac{1}{2}}\left(A_i M^{-\frac{1}{2}}\right)^+ \left(b_i - A_i M^{-1} Q_{i-1}\right). \tag{21}$$

3 Analytical Modeling of Hierarchical Dynamics

A dynamic modeling method based on nested constraint design, utilizing the Udwadia-Kalaba equation, is proposed. The multi-rigid body intelligent system is envisaged as a composite of multiple module subsystems that correspond to each other. Starting from the unconstrained dynamic model of these modular units, corresponding constrained kinematic models are embedded to develop a constrained dynamic model. Building on this, a new constrained kinematic model is integrated with other modules to establish a dynamic model for the reassembly module. This iterative process facilitates the nested modeling of multi-agent transportation system dynamics. By modeling each module independently and leveraging nested constraint relationships, the overall model is enhanced with the capability for modules to be freely added, removed, or replaced without impacting other parts, thus significantly enhancing the adaptability of the overall system.

Assuming a multibody system is composed of k_0 basic units, these units can be combined into k_1 first-level subsystems based on their kinematic or constraint relationships. The constraint relationships are unique and non-overlapping, indicating that a basic unit can only contribute to one first-level subsystem and cannot simultaneously participate in multiple first-level subsystems. In a similar fashion, k_1 first-level subsystems can form k_2 second-level subsystems; likewise, $k_n - 1$ subsystems at the $n-1$ level can develop into k_n subsystems at the n level; ultimately, these k_n subsystems at the n-level constitute the entire multibody system.

The specific process of the dynamic modeling method, based on hierarchical constraint design, proceeds as follows: First, establish the dynamic models for each basic unit, the motion equations of these units can be expressed as:

$$M_{j0}\left(q_{j0}, t\right) \ddot{q}_{j0} = Q_{j0}\left(q_{j0}, \dot{q}_{j0}, t\right), \tag{22}$$

where $j = 1, 2, \ldots k_0$, M_{j0} is the mass matrix of $n_{j0} \times n_{j0}$, q_{j0} is n_{j0}-dimensional state vector, Q_{j0} is n_{j0}-dimensional generalized force applied to the system.

The constraints imposed on the system are expressed in the form of matrix equations as follows:

$$A_{j0}\left(q_{j0}, \dot{q}_{j0}, t\right) \ddot{q}_{j0} = b_{j0}\left(q_{j0}, \dot{q}_{j0}, t\right), \tag{23}$$

where A_{j0} expresses the constraint matrix of $m_{j0} \times n_{j0}$, b_{j0} is n_{j0}-dimensional vector.

The motion equation of a constrained system can be described as:

$$\begin{aligned} M_{j0}\left(q_{j0}, t\right) \ddot{q}_{j0} &= Q_{j0}\left(q_{j0}, \dot{q}_{j0}, t\right) + Q_{j0}^{e}\left(q_{j0}, \dot{q}_{j0}, t\right) \\ &=: \hat{Q}_{j0}\left(q_{j0}, \dot{q}_{j0}, t\right), \end{aligned} \tag{24}$$

where Q_{j0}^{e} is n_{j0}-dimensional constraint torque matrix, the display expression is:

$$Q_{j0}^{e} = M_{j0}^{\frac{1}{2}}\left(A_{j0} M_{j0}^{-\frac{1}{2}}\right)^{+}\left(b_{j0} - A_{j0} M_{j0}^{-1} Q_{j0}\right). \tag{25}$$

Secondly, following the development of dynamic models for each basic unit, unique and non-overlapping constraint relationships are employed to create k_1 primary level subsystems. These constraints are expressed as matrix equations:

$$A_{j1}\left(q_{j1}, \dot{q}_{j1}, t\right) \ddot{q}_{j1} = b_{j1}\left(q_{j1}, \dot{q}_{j1}, t\right), \tag{26}$$

where $j = 1, 2, \ldots k_1$, A_{j1} expresses the constraint matrix of $m_{j1} \times n_{j1}$, b_{j1} is m_{j1}-dimensional vector, q_{j1} is n_{j1}-dimensional state vector, composed of state variables aggregated from various basic units within its first-level subsystem.

The motion equation of the first-level subsystem, derived from the constraint relationships in Eq. 26, is described as follows:

$$\begin{aligned} M_{j1}\left(q_{j1}, t\right) \ddot{q}_{j1} &= Q_{j1}\left(q_{j1}, \dot{q}_{j1}, t\right) + Q_{j1}^{e}\left(q_{j1}, \dot{q}_{j1}, t\right) \\ &= Q_{j1}\left(q_{j1}, \dot{q}_{j1}, t\right) + M_{j1}^{\frac{1}{2}}\left(A_{j1} M_{j1}^{-\frac{1}{2}}\right)^{+}\left(b_{j1} - A_{j1} M_{j1}^{-1} Q_{j1}\right) \\ &=: \hat{Q}_{j1}\left(q_{j1}, \dot{q}_{j1}, t\right), \end{aligned} \tag{27}$$

where $M_{j1} \in n_{j1} \times n_{j1}$, $M_{j1} = diag[M_{j0}]$, composed of related basic unit quality matrix of M_{j0}, $Q_{j1} \in n_{j1} \times 1$, composed of related basic units Q_{j0} stacked together, Q_{j1}^{e} is n_{j1}-dimensional constraint torque matrix.

Next, based on establishing the dynamic models of each first level subsystem, k_2 second level subsystems will be formed by the constraint relationships between each subsystem, which can be expressed as:

$$A_{j2}\left(q_{j2}, \dot{q}_{j2}, t\right) \ddot{q}_{j2} = b_{j2}\left(q_{j2}, \dot{q}_{j2}, t\right), \tag{28}$$

where $j = 1, 2, \ldots k_1$, A_{j2} expresses the constraint matrix of $m_{j2} \times n_{j2}$, b_{j2} is m_{j2}-dimensional vector, q_{j2} is n_{j2}-dimensional state vector, formed by the aggregation of state variables from each first-level nested subsystem within its second-level nested subsystems.

The motion equation of the second-level subsystem, derived from the constraint relationships in Eq. 28, is described as follows:

$$\begin{aligned} M_{j2}(q_{j2}, t)\, \ddot{q}_{j2} &= Q_{j2}(q_{j2}, \dot{q}_{j2}, t) + Q_{j2}^{e}(q_{j2}, \dot{q}_{j2}, t) \\ &= Q_{j2}(q_{j2}, \dot{q}_{j2}, t) + M_{j2}^{\frac{1}{2}} \left(A_{j2} M_{j2}^{-\frac{1}{2}} \right)^{+} \left(b_{j2} - A_{j2} M_{j2}^{-1} Q_{j2} \right) \\ &=: \hat{Q}_{j2}(q_{j2}, \dot{q}_{j2}, t), \end{aligned} \tag{29}$$

where $M_{j2} \in n_{j2} \times n_{j2}$, $M_{j2} = diag[M_{j1}]$, composed of related basic unit quality matrix of M_{j1}, $Q_{j2} \in n_{j2} \times 1$, composed of related basic units Q_{j1} stacked together, Q_{j2}^{e} is n_{j2}-dimensional constraint torque matrix.

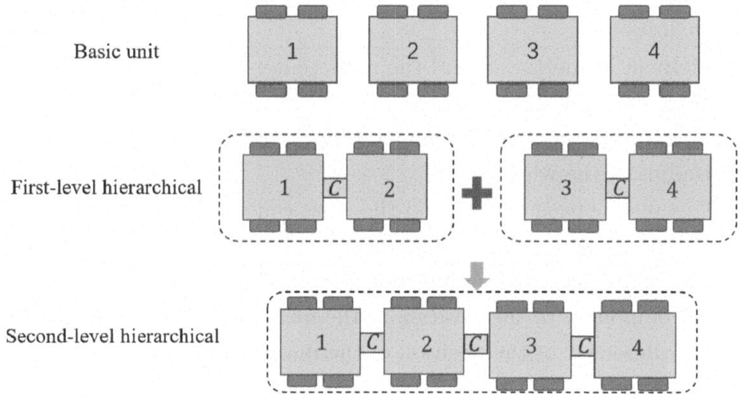

Fig. 1. Schematic diagram of hierarchical modeling.

Similarly, if additional constraint relationships exist, the process can persist until the final tier of k_s s-level nested subsystems. Eventually, as shown in Fig. 1, through the constraint relationships among the subsystems, the ultimate multi-body dynamics model is obtained.

4 Hierarchical Dynamic Model of the Mobile Robots

This section applies the dynamic modeling method based on hierarchical constraint design mentioned above, and uses a fleet of four mobile robots as an example to demonstrate the above method. As shown in Fig. 2, require the entire fleet to travel along a circle with a radius of $R = 10$ meters, and set the centroid distance between each mobile robot to $L = 1$ meter. The entire system consists of four basic units (mobile robots), with each two basic units forming a first level hierarchical model. Finally, two first level hierarchical models form a second level hierarchical model.

Firstly, establish the dynamic models of each basic unit, using the four-wheel mobile robot dynamic model established by Sun et al. [18], and organize it into the following matrix form (Table 1):

$$M\left(q,t\right)\ddot{q}=Q\left(q,\dot{q},t\right), \tag{30}$$

where

$$M=\begin{bmatrix} m & 0 & 0 \\ 0 & m & 0 \\ 0 & 0 & I/l \end{bmatrix} \ddot{q}=\begin{bmatrix} \ddot{x} \\ \ddot{y} \\ \ddot{\theta} \end{bmatrix} Q=\begin{bmatrix} -m\dot{y}\dot{\theta}+\frac{\cos\theta}{r}u_r+\frac{\cos\theta}{r}u_l \\ m\dot{x}\dot{\theta}+\frac{\sin\theta}{r}u_r+\frac{\sin\theta}{r}u_l \\ \frac{1}{r}u_r-\frac{1}{r}u_l \end{bmatrix}. \tag{31}$$

Table 1. The symbol definition of the mobile robot variables and parameters.

Parameter	Definition
I	Moment of inertia around the mass center of the mobile robot
m	Mass of the mobile robot
θ	Orientation angle of the mobile robot
r	Radius of the wheels
l	Distance between wheel and the mass center of the mobile robot
u_l	Driving torque of the left motor
u_r	Driving torque of the right motor
x	X component of the position of the mass center of the mobile robot
y	Y component of the position of the mass center of the mobile robot
$\dot{x}$	X component of the velocity of the mass center of the mobile robot
$\dot{y}$	Y component of the velocity of the mass center of the mobile robot
$\ddot{x}$	X component of the acceleration of the mass center of the mobile robot
$\ddot{y}$	Y component of the acceleration of the mass center of the mobile robot

Establish dynamic models for each primitive module based on Eqs. 22 and 30, where $j=1,2,3,4$. Due to the mobile robot traveling in a circle with a radius of 10 m, it is subject to the following kinematic constraints:

$$x_i^2+y_i^2=R^2. \tag{32}$$

Take the derivative of the constraint equation over time from Eq. 32 and organize it into the form shown in Eq. 23:

$$A_{j0}\left(q_{j0},\dot{q}_{j0},t\right)\ddot{q}_{j0}=b_{j0}\left(q_{j0},\dot{q}_{j0},t\right), \tag{33}$$

where $A_{j0}=\left[x_j\ y_j\ 0\right]$, $b_{j0}=\left[-\dot{x}_j^2-\dot{y}_j^2\right]$, $\dot{q}_{j0}=\ddot{q}$, $j=1,2,3,4$.

Secondly, based on the establishment of dynamic models for each basic unit, a first-level subsystem is formed by the constraint relationships between each unit. Due to the centroid distance of 1 m between each mobile robot, there are the following constraint relationships for the first-level subsystem:

$$(x_1 - x_2)^2 + (y_1 - y_2)^2 = L^2. \tag{34}$$

According to Eqs. 24 and 25, the motion equation of the constrained mobile robot j can be described as follows:

$$\begin{aligned} M_{j0}(q_{j0}, t)\, \ddot{q}_{j0} &= Q_{j0}(q_{j0}, \dot{q}_{j0}, t) + Q^e_{j0}(q_{j0}, \dot{q}_{j0}, t) \\ &=: \hat{Q}_{j0}(q_{j0}, \dot{q}_{j0}, t). \end{aligned} \tag{35}$$

Extract constraints from time twice and organize them into a constraint matrix form:

$$A_{11}(q_{11}, t)\, \ddot{q}_{11} = b_{11}(q_{11}, \dot{q}_{11}, t), \tag{36}$$

where

$$A_{11} = \left[(x_1 - x_2)\ (y_1 - y_2)\ 0\ (x_2 - x_1)\ (y_2 - y_1)\ 0 \right], \tag{37}$$

$$b_{11} = \left[-(\dot{x}_1 - \dot{x}_2)^2 - (\dot{y}_1 - \dot{y}_2)^2 \right], \tag{38}$$

$$q_{11} = \begin{bmatrix} q_{10} \\ q_{20} \end{bmatrix}, \dot{q}_{11} = \begin{bmatrix} \dot{q}_{10} \\ \dot{q}_{20} \end{bmatrix}, \ddot{q}_{11} = \begin{bmatrix} \ddot{q}_{10} \\ \ddot{q}_{20} \end{bmatrix}. \tag{39}$$

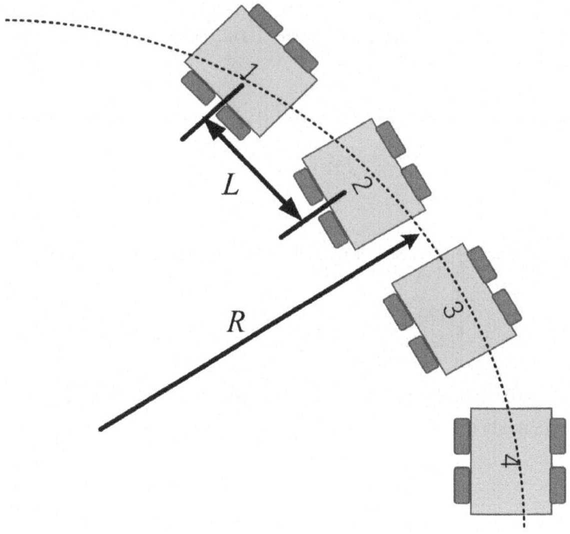

Fig. 2. Schematic diagram of trajectory tracking.

Similarly, based on the establishment of dynamic models for each basic unit, a first level subsystem is formed by the constraint relationships between each unit.

$$(x_3 - x_4)^2 + (y_3 - y_4)^2 = L^2. \tag{40}$$

Extract constraints from time twice and organize them into a constraint matrix form.

$$A_{21}(q_{21}, t)\,\ddot{q}_{21} = b_{21}(q_{21}, \dot{q}_{21}, t), \tag{41}$$

where

$$A_{21} = \left[(x_3 - x_4)\ (y_3 - y_4)\ 0\ (x_4 - x_3)\ (y_4 - y_3)\ 0\right], \tag{42}$$

$$b_{21} = \left[-(\dot{x}_3 - \dot{x}_4)^2 - (\dot{y}_3 - \dot{y}_4)^2\right], \tag{43}$$

$$q_{21} = \begin{bmatrix} q_{30} \\ q_{40} \end{bmatrix}, \dot{q}_{21} = \begin{bmatrix} \dot{q}_{30} \\ \dot{q}_{40} \end{bmatrix}, \ddot{q}_{21} = \begin{bmatrix} \ddot{q}_{30} \\ \ddot{q}_{40} \end{bmatrix}. \tag{44}$$

The motion equation of the first-level subsystem 1 can be described as:

$$\begin{aligned} M_{11}(q_{11}, t)\,\ddot{q}_{11} &= Q_{11}(q_{11}, \dot{q}_{11}, t) + Q_{11}^{e}(q_{11}, \dot{q}_{11}, t) \\ &=: \hat{Q}_{11}(q_{11}, \dot{q}_{11}, t), \end{aligned} \tag{45}$$

where

$$Q_{11}^{e} = M_{11}^{\frac{1}{2}}\left(A_{11}M_{11}^{-\frac{1}{2}}\right)^{+}\left(b_{11} - A_{11}M_{11}^{-1}Q_{11}\right), \tag{46}$$

$$M_{11} = \begin{bmatrix} M_{10} & 0 \\ 0 & M_{20} \end{bmatrix} \ddot{q}_{11} = \begin{bmatrix} \ddot{q}_{10} \\ \ddot{q}_{20} \end{bmatrix} Q_{11} = \begin{bmatrix} Q_{10} \\ Q_{20} \end{bmatrix}. \tag{47}$$

Similarly, the motion equation of the first level nested subsystem 2 can be described as:

$$\begin{aligned} M_{21}(q_{21}, t)\,\ddot{q}_{21} &= Q_{21}(q_{21}, \dot{q}_{21}, t) + Q_{21}^{e}(q_{21}, \dot{q}_{21}, t) \\ &=: \hat{Q}_{21}(q_{21}, \dot{q}_{21}, t), \end{aligned} \tag{48}$$

where

$$Q_{21}^{e} = M_{21}^{\frac{1}{2}}\left(A_{21}M_{21}^{-\frac{1}{2}}\right)^{+}\left(b_{21} - A_{21}M_{21}^{-1}Q_{21}\right), \tag{49}$$

$$M_{21} = \begin{bmatrix} M_{30} & 0 \\ 0 & M_{40} \end{bmatrix} \ddot{q}_{21} = \begin{bmatrix} \ddot{q}_{30} \\ \ddot{q}_{40} \end{bmatrix} Q_{21} = \begin{bmatrix} Q_{30} \\ Q_{40} \end{bmatrix}. \tag{50}$$

Based on the establishment of dynamic models for the first level nested subsystem, establish constraint relationships between them.

$$(x_1 - x_2)^2 + (y_1 - y_2)^2 = L^2, \tag{51}$$

$$(x_2 - x_3)^2 + (y_2 - y_3)^2 = L^2, \tag{52}$$

$$(x_3 - x_4)^2 + (y_3 - y_4)^2 = L^2. \tag{53}$$

Extract constraints from time twice and organize them into a constraint matrix form.

$$A_{32}\left(q_{32},t\right)\ddot{q}_{32}=b_{32}\left(q_{32},\dot{q}_{32},t\right), \tag{54}$$

where

$$A_{32}=\begin{bmatrix}A_{11}\\A_{21}\\A_{31}\end{bmatrix},b_{32}=\begin{bmatrix}b_{11}\\b_{21}\\b_{31}\end{bmatrix}, \tag{55}$$

$$q_{32}=\begin{bmatrix}q_{11}\\q_{21}\end{bmatrix},\dot{q}_{32}=\begin{bmatrix}\dot{q}_{11}\\\dot{q}_{21}\end{bmatrix},\ddot{q}_{32}=\begin{bmatrix}\ddot{q}_{11}\\\ddot{q}_{21}\end{bmatrix}, \tag{56}$$

where

$$A_{31}=\left[0\;0\;(x_2-x_3)\;(y_2-y_3)\;(x_3-x_2)\;(y_3-y_2)\;0\;0\right], \tag{57}$$

$$b_{31}=\left[-\left(\dot{x}_2-\dot{x}_3\right)^2-\left(\dot{y}_2-\dot{y}_3\right)^2\right]. \tag{58}$$

The motion equation of the second-level subsystem (a fleet of four mobile robots) can be described as:

$$M_{32}\left(q_{32},t\right)\ddot{q}_{32}=Q_{32}\left(q_{32},\dot{q}_{32},t\right)+Q_{32}^{e}\left(q_{32},\dot{q}_{32},t\right), \tag{59}$$

where $M_{32}=\begin{bmatrix}M_{11}&0\\0&M_{21}\end{bmatrix}$, $Q_{32}=\begin{bmatrix}Q_{11}\\Q_{21}\end{bmatrix}$, $Q_{32}^{e}=M_{32}^{\frac{1}{2}}\left(A_{32}M_{32}^{-\frac{1}{2}}\right)^{+}\left(b_{32}-A_{32}M_{32}^{-1}Q_{32}\right)$.

5 Numerical Example

In this section, the analytical results detailed in Sects. 3 and 4 are corroborated through numerical simulations. We strive to determine the necessary control torques that allow the mobile robot to follow a specified trajectory illustrated in an example.

Using the Udwadia-Kalaba theory [19–21], we calculate the control torque required by each mobile robot. To mitigate errors originating from initial conditions, the following controller is employed:

$$\tau=p_1\left(q,\dot{q},t\right)+p_2\left(q,\dot{q},t\right), \tag{60}$$

$$p_1\left(q,\dot{q},t\right)=M^{\frac{1}{2}}\left(AM^{-\frac{1}{2}}\right)^{+}\left(b-AM^{-1}Q\right), \tag{61}$$

$$p_2\left(q,\dot{q},t\right)=-\kappa MA^{T}\left(AA^{T}\right)^{-1}\left(A\dot{q}-c\right), \tag{62}$$

where τ represents the control input, $\kappa>0$ is a constant, $A\dot{q}-c$ can be derived by formulating the constraint equation in its first-order form.

In addition, by replacing the constraint forces Q^e with τ at each level, we obtain the revised dynamic model of the mobile robot fleet system. Using Udwadia-Kalaba theory, the control torque for each mobile robot is derived:

$$\tau = hu, \tag{63}$$

$$u = h^+ \left[p_{321}(q_{32}, \dot{q}_{32}, t) + p_{322}(q_{32}, \dot{q}_{32}, t)\right], \tag{64}$$

where $h = \begin{bmatrix} h_1 & 0 & 0 & 0 \\ 0 & h_2 & 0 & 0 \\ 0 & 0 & h_3 & 0 \\ 0 & 0 & 0 & h_4 \end{bmatrix}$, $h_g = \begin{bmatrix} \frac{\cos\theta_g}{r} & \frac{\cos\theta_g}{r} \\ \frac{\sin\theta_g}{r} & \frac{\sin\theta_g}{r} \\ \frac{1}{r} & -\frac{1}{r} \end{bmatrix}$, $g = 1, 2, 3, 4$, $u = \left[u_1\ u_2\ u_3\ u_4\right]^T$, $u_g = \left[u_{gr}\ u_{gl}\right]$, $g = 1, 2, 3, 4$.

$$p_{321}(q_{32}, \dot{q}_{32}, t) = M_{32}^{\frac{1}{2}}\left(A_{32}M_{32}^{-\frac{1}{2}}\right)^+ \left(b_{32} - A_{32}M_{32}^{-1}Q_{32}\right), \tag{65}$$

$$p_{322}(q_{32}, \dot{q}_{32}, t) = -\kappa M_{32}A_{32}^T\left(A_{32}A_{32}^T\right)^{-1}\left(A_{32}\dot{q}_{32} - c_{32}\right). \tag{66}$$

The simulation results are presented in Fig. 3, while the initial conditions are detailed in Table 2.

Table 2. Initial condition.

Parameter	Value	Parameter	Value	Parameter	Value	Parameter	Value
x_1	10.50 m	x_2	10.45 m	x_3	10.30 m	x_4	10.05 m
y_1	−0.50 m	y_2	−1.50 m	y_3	−2.49 m	y_4	−3.46 m
θ_1	1.5708 rad	θ_2	1.4708 rad	θ_3	1.3707 rad	θ_4	1.2707 rad
$\dot{x}_1$	0 m/s	$\dot{x}_2$	0.9987 m/s	$\dot{x}_3$	1.9875 m/s	$\dot{x}_4$	2.9564 m/s
$\dot{y}_1$	10 m/s	$\dot{y}_2$	9.9500 m/s	$\dot{y}_3$	9.8005 m/s	$\dot{y}_4$	9.5530 m/s
$\dot{\theta}_1$	1 rad/s	$\dot{\theta}_2$	1 rad/s	$\dot{\theta}_3$	1 rad/s	$\dot{\theta}_4$	1 rad/s

Figure 3 displays both the actual and ideal trajectories of the mobile robots, illustrating that despite each robot starting with a specific initial error, the actual trajectories eventually align with the ideal trajectories over time.

Figure 4 depicts the trajectory errors between the actual and ideal trajectories of the mobile robot, demonstrating that the final errors gradually converge to zero.

Figures 5 and 6 illustrate the drive torques of the right front wheel and left front wheel of mobile robots, respectively. Initially, the torque curves rise and then fall within the first two seconds as the mobile robot corrects its initial error with a higher torque. Once the actual trajectory aligns with the ideal trajectory, which is a perfect circle, the torques stabilize due to this alignment.

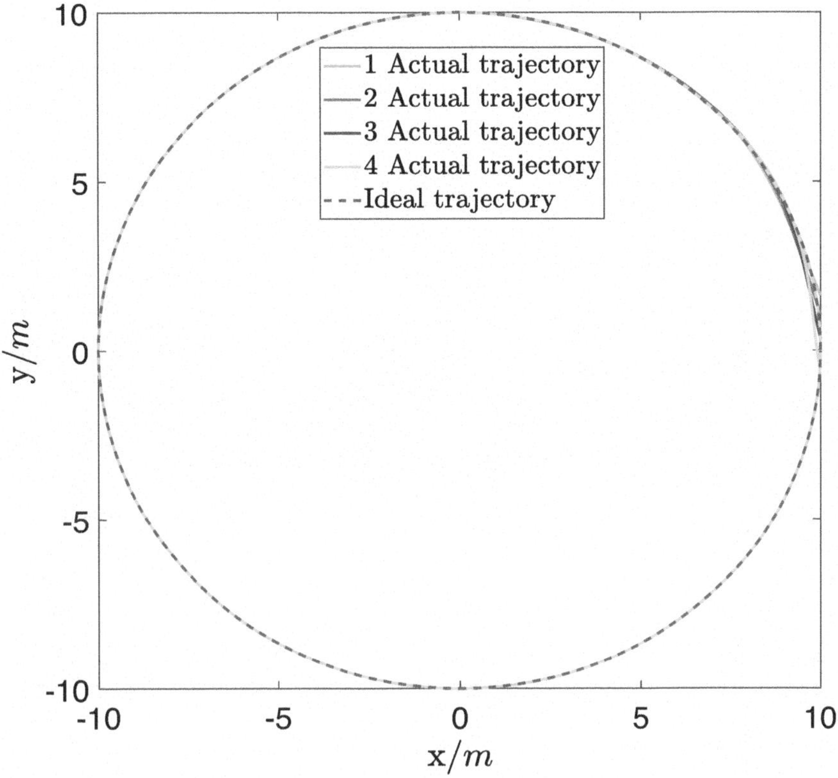

Fig. 3. The trajectory of mobile robot 1,2,3,4.

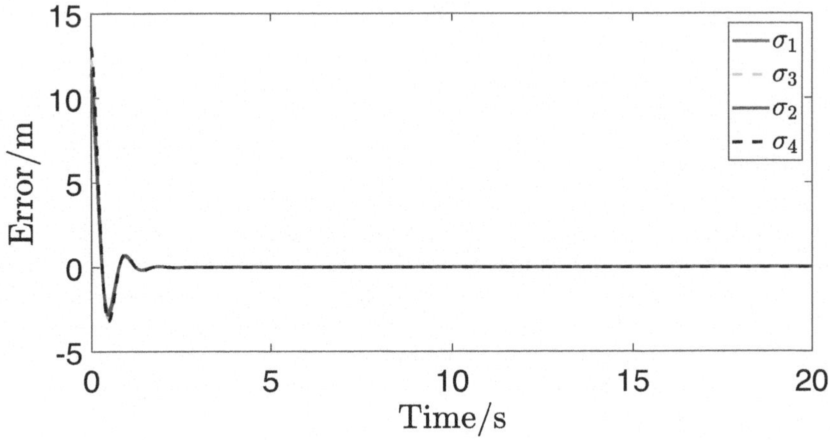

Fig. 4. The error of trajectory of mobile robot 1,2,3,4.

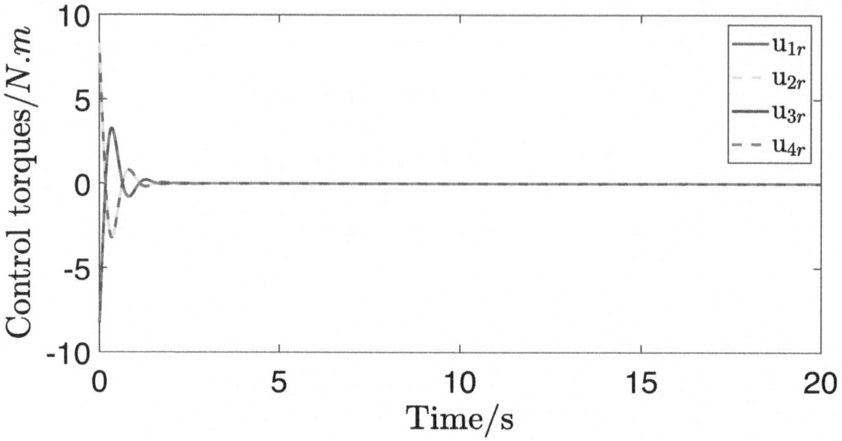

Fig. 5. The control torques of right motors.

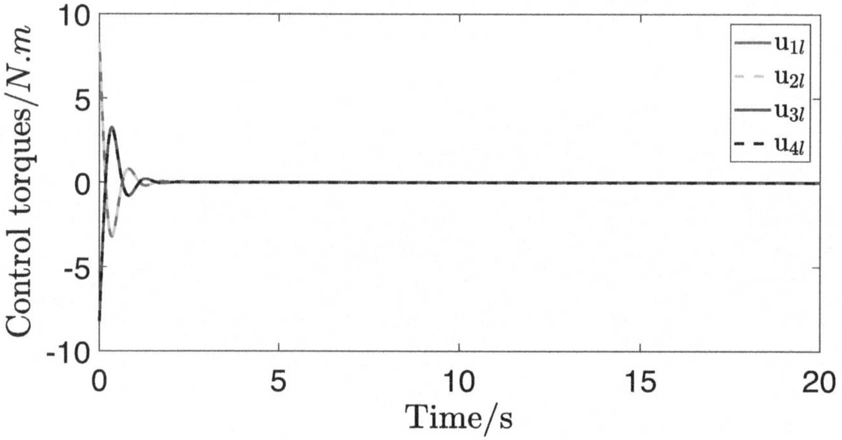

Fig. 6. The control torques of left motors.

6 Conclusion

This article applies the Udwadia-Kalaba theory to propose a hierarchical analytical modeling method for multi-body mechanical system dynamics, particularly suitable for complex systems. This approach models the system as multi-level nested subsystems that collectively form the desired multi-body configuration. Notable advantages of this method include its high adaptability-it allows for modifications such as additions, deletions, and replacements without impacting other system components.

Acknowledgment. This research was sponsored in part by the NSFC Program (No.52175019, No. 61872217, No. U20A20285, No. 52122217, No. U1801263, No.

52102438) and Beijing Natural Science Foundations(No. 3212009, No. L222038). The research is also sponsored in part by the key R&D projects of the ministry of science and technology (No. 2020YFB1710901).

References

1. Rosenberg, R.M., Schmitendorf, W.: Analytical dynamics of discrete systems. J. Appl. Mech. **45**(1), 233 (1978)
2. Ginsberg, J.: Engineering Dynamics, vol. 10. Cambridge University Press (2008)
3. Luh, J.Y., Walker, M.W., Paul, R.P.: On-line computational scheme for mechanical manipulators. J. Dyn. Sys., Meas. Control. **102**, 69–76 (1980)
4. Lagrange, J.L.: Mécanique Analytique, vol. 1. Mallet-Bachelier (1853)
5. Hollerbach, J.M.: A recursive lagrangian formulation of maniputator dynamics and a comparative study of dynamics formulation complexity. IEEE Trans. Syst. Man Cybern. **10**(11), 730–736 (1980)
6. Featherstone, R.: Rigid Body Dynamics Algorithms. Springer (2014)
7. Gibbs, J.W.: On the fundamental formulae of dynamics. Am. J. Math. **2**(1), 49–64 (1879)
8. Appell, P.: Sur une forme générale des équations de la dynamique. Gauthier-Villars et cie (1925)
9. Papastavridis, J., Yagasaki, K.: Analytical mechanics: a comprehensive treatise on the dynamics of constrained systems; for engineers, physicists, and mathematicians. Appl. Mech. Rev. **56**(2), B22 (2002)
10. Kane, T.R., Levinson, D.A.: Dynamics, Theory and Applications. McGraw Hill (1985)
11. Murray, R.M., Li, Z., Sastry, S.S.: A Mathematical Introduction to Robotic Manipulation. CRC Press (2017)
12. Udwadia, F.E., Kalaba, R.E.: Nonideal constraints and lagrangian dynamics. J. Aerosp. Eng. **13**(1), 17–22 (2000)
13. Udwadia, F.E., Kalaba, R.E.: A new perspective on constrained motion. Proc. Roy. Soc. London Ser. A Math. Phys. Sci. **439**(1906), 407–410 (1992)
14. Udwadia, F.E., Kalaba, R.E.: On the foundations of analytical dynamics. Int. J. Non-Linear Mech. **37**(6), 1079–1090 (2002)
15. Udwadia, F.E., Kalaba, R.E.: Equations of motion for mechanical systems. J. Aerosp. Eng. **9**(3), 64–69 (1996)
16. Kalaba, R., Udwadia, F.: Equations of motion for nonholonomic, constrained dynamical systems via gauss's principle. J. Appl. Mech. **60**(3), 662–668 (1993)
17. Huang, J., Chen, Y., Guo, K.: Novel approach to multibody system modeling: cascading and clustering. J. Aerosp. Eng. **27**(2), 279–290 (2014)
18. Sun, H., et al.: Application of the udwadia-kalaba approach to tracking control of mobile robots. Nonlinear Dyn. **83**, 08 (2015)
19. Chen, Y.-H.: Constraint-following servo control design for mechanical systems. J. Vib. Control **15**(3), 369–389 (2009)
20. Chen, Y.-H., Zhang, X.: Adaptive robust approximate constraint-following control for mechanical systems. J. Franklin Inst. **347**(1), 69–86 (2010)
21. Zhang, B., Chen, Y.-H., Jia, Y., Huang, J., Yang, D., Zhong, Z.: Accuracy and safety: tracking control of heavy-duty cooperative transportation systems using constraint-following method. IEEE Trans. Intell. Transp. Syst. **25**(5), 3628–3641 (2024)

Design and Analysis of Deployment Mechanism Based on Sliding Disc for Solid Surface Deployable Antenna

Hao Li(✉), Xiaofei Ma, Dayu Zhang, Guanlong Su, Huanxiao Li, and Zexing Yu

Xi'an Institute of Space Radio Technology, Xi'an 710100, Shaanxi, China
lh651628333@stu.xjtu.edu.cn

Abstract. This paper designs a deployment mechanism based on sliding disc for solid surface deployable antenna. Firstly, a method for determining the folded petal posture based on particle swarm optimization algorithm is proposed, combined with the equivalent axis angle theorem to achieve the 1DOF deployment requirement. The deployment mechanism of solid surface deployable antenna is abstracted as a single closed-loop parallel platform. Based on the calculation of spatial mechanism degrees of freedom, the configuration synthesis of this type of antenna is established, and 136 feasible configurations are topologically identified. A detailed design analysis is conducted using the PUSR mechanism as an example. A kinematic model of the PUSR mechanism is constructed based on the closed vector method. The analysis results showed that the deployment process is stable and reliable, verifying the feasibility of the design scheme. Meanwhile, the analysis methods and conclusions can provide technical references for the design of solid surface deployable antennas.

Keywords: Solid Surface Deployable Antenna · Configuration Synthesis · Kinematic Analysis

1 Introduction

With the exploration of the space mysteries by human beings, traditional satellites can no longer meet the requirements of space observation. The development of ultra large and high-precision satellites and space stations is becoming increasingly urgent [1–3]. As the equipment for receiving signals, the antenna plays a crucial role in the satellite field such as wireless communication, space exploration, remote sensing, and radio astronomy [4–6].

Due to the limitation of the rocket envelope, large aperture antennas are usually designed as deployable structures [7–9], which exhibit a folded state during transportation and a deployed state after reaching the predetermined orbit. Compared to antennas that use metal mesh [10–12] or thin films as reflector surfaces [13–15], solid surface antennas can provide higher operating frequency bands and gains [16–20] due to their excellent surface accuracy. Therefore, the solid surface antenna receives increasing attention by researchers.

X. Lan et al. (Eds.): icira 2024, LNAI 15201, pp. 396–411, 2025.
https://doi.org/10.1007/978-981-96-0771-6_29

The typical solid surface deployable antenna consists of a central petal and several petals, which together form the reflector surface. The earliest solid surface deployable antenna is Sunflower developed by TRW company [21], which consists of six main petals hinged on the central part and six sub petals between adjacent main petals. However, the folded volume of this form antenna is large, so its application is limited. Currently, the most widely used form is the petal shaped solid surface antenna proposed by the European Space Agency (ESA) [22]. Its deployment process usually consists of two parts, that is, petals first deploy radially around the radial axis, and then deploy circumferentially around the axis. Chae [23] designs a solid surface deployable antenna with carbon fiber reinforced plastic, using a layout of 30 petals. Each petal can independently complete the radial and circumferential deploying processes. To improve the synchronization, Bujakas [24] designs a solid surface antenna that deploy along two axes. The difference is that a micro linear driver is set between the petals to improve the deployment synchronization. Huang [25] proposed a solid surface deployable antenna that uses a torsion spring to drive petals to rotate and deploy along two orthogonal axes. The advantage of this arrangement is that it can independently adjust the posture of each petal, but at the same time, due to the large number of motion pairs and driving sources, the synchronization and reliability of the system are poor.

To solve the problem caused by the deployment of petals along two axes, Xu [26] and Huang [27] propose a design scheme of deployment along a single axis. Tan [28] proposes a single degree of freedom(DOF) design scheme using the Bennett mechanism in the solid surface deployable antenna. However, this over constrained mechanism is prone to jamming in practical engineering, making it difficult to complete the predetermined deployment.

In response to the above problems, this paper proposes a method for determining the folded petal posture based on particle swarm optimization algorithm, combined with the equivalent axis angle theorem to achieve the one degree of freedom deploying requirement. By abstracting the mechanism of this type of antenna as a single closed-loop parallel platform, and using the spatial degree of freedom calculation method to synthesize the configuration of this type of antenna, 136 feasible configurations are identified. Taking a 10 m aperture solid surface deployable antenna as an example, a detailed design and simulation analysis are carried out using a PUSR mechanism. The kinematic analysis results show that the deployment process of the antenna designed in this paper is stable and reliable, verifying the feasibility of the design scheme.

2 Antenna Structure

Figure 1 shows a typical petal shaped solid surface deployable antenna, which mainly consists of four parts: feed source system, reflector panel, drive and transmission components, supporting and connection components. The antenna is installed on the satellite with supporting and connecting components, and stored in the rocket envelope. After the satellite is launched into the predetermined orbit, the reflector petals deploy to the service attitude through the driving and transmission components, and works with the feed system to achieve the predetermined function.

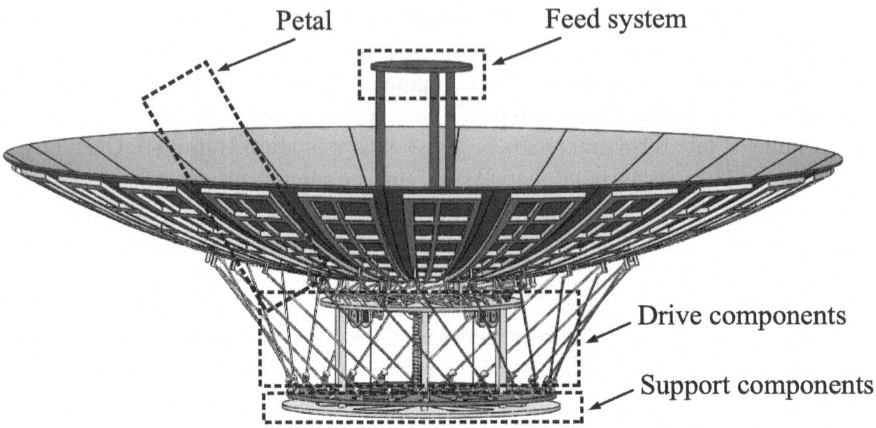

Fig. 1. Schematic diagram of the solid surface deployable antenna structure

3 Deployment Mechanism Design

3.1 Axis Calculation

The deploying process of traditional solid surface deployable antennas can be divided into two stages: radial and circumferential deployment, as shown in Fig. 2. This process requires the petals to rotate around two orthogonal axes. Due to its simple and controllable advantages, it has been widely used in research literature.

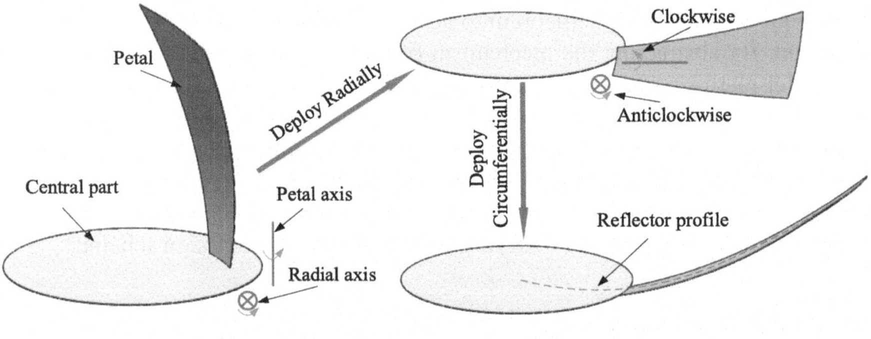

Fig. 2. Schematic diagram of 2DOF deployment

However, compared to the traditional 2DOF process, simplifying the antenna deployment into 1DOF process can further simplify the structural design and improve system reliability, which is the research objective of this article.

The petals of a solid surface antenna can be considered as rigid motion during the deployment, so the position of the petals can be defined using any three points that are not in the same plane. To clearly describe this process, a schematic diagram of the

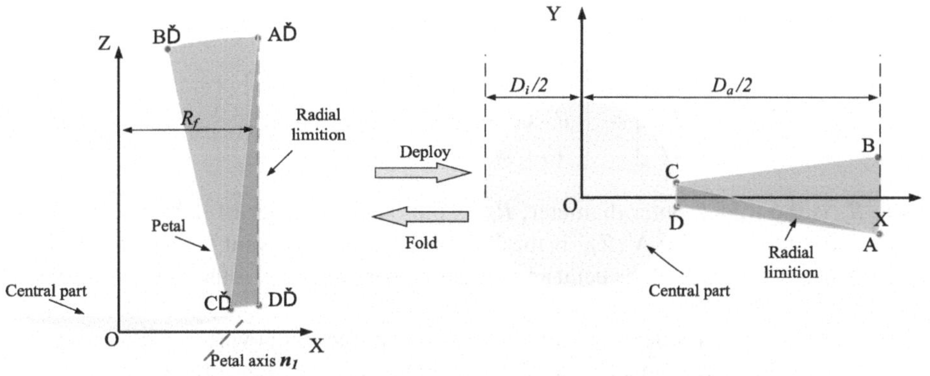

Fig. 3. Schematic diagram of rigid motion [28]

deployment process is established as shown in Fig. 3. The deployed state is defined by A, C, D, while the folded state is defined by A′, C′, and D′.

Based on the principle of coordinate transformation, the rigid motion problem can be summarized as the solution of three parameters: (1) the rotation axis vector $\boldsymbol{n_r}$; (2) anchor point $\boldsymbol{P}$; (3) Rotation angle θ.

According to the task requirements and antenna surface division, the spatial coordinates of the petal (A, C, D) are known. Due to the requirement of the envelope, it is usually possible to set the folded position of the antenna, which means A′C′ and D′ coordinates are given.

Therefore, at the beginning of designing the 1DOF deployment mechanism, it is necessary to clarify whether there is a unique axis that can make the petal rotates from A′, C′, and D′ to A, C, and D.

Taking a 10 m aperture solid surface deployable antenna as an example, the outer diameter of the antenna is $D_a = 10000$ mm, the center panel diameter is $D_i = 2400$ mm, the focal length is $f = 4350$ mm, the number of petals is 24, and the radial storage limit of the envelope is $R_f = 1600$ mm. Based on this, we can obtain the coordinates of points A, C and D as Eq. (1):

$$\begin{bmatrix} \boldsymbol{A} \\ \boldsymbol{C} \\ \boldsymbol{D} \end{bmatrix} = \begin{bmatrix} \frac{D_a}{2}\cos\frac{\pi}{24} & -\frac{D_a}{2}\sin\frac{\pi}{24} & \frac{D_a^2}{16f} \\ \frac{D_i}{2}\cos\frac{\pi}{24} & \frac{D_i}{2}\sin\frac{\pi}{24} & \frac{D_i^2}{16f} \\ \frac{D_i}{2}\cos\frac{\pi}{24} & -\frac{D_i}{2}\sin\frac{\pi}{24} & \frac{D_i^2}{16f} \end{bmatrix} \tag{1}$$

To avoid interference between the petals during deployment and facilitate the binding of the folded state, the requirements for the spatial position of the petals in the folded state are: (1) Points A′, and D′ are on the same radial line; (2) The lowest point of the petal is higher than the outer edge of the center part; (3) The line connecting points A′ and D′ is parallel to the Z-axis. Compared to the literature, the constraint conditions proposed in this paper can make the outer edge of the petal coincide with the envelope generatrix, making it easier to store.

It can be assumed that the spatial position of the petal in the folded state is:

$$\begin{bmatrix} \boldsymbol{A}' \\ \boldsymbol{C}' \\ \boldsymbol{D}' \end{bmatrix} = \begin{bmatrix} R_f \cos 0 & R_f \sin 0 & z_{A'} \\ R_{c'} \cos\theta_c & R_{c'} \sin\theta_c & h + \mathrm{C}(z) \\ R_f \cos 0 & R_f \sin 0 & z_{D'} \end{bmatrix} \tag{2}$$

where R_f is the folded outer diameter; $R_{c'}$ is the outer diameter of point C′, $Z_{A'}$ is the Z-axis coordinate of point A′, $Z_{D'}$ is the Z-axis coordinate of point D′, h is the distance between the lowest point of the petal and the center part, and C(z) is the Z-axis coordinate of point C.

It can be seen that when the value of h is given, the unknowns in Eq. (2) are $Z_{c'}$, $Z_{A'}$ and $Z_{D'}$. Considering that the petal is a rigid body, the distance between each node remains unchanged, that is:

$$\begin{cases} L_{AC} = L_{A'C'} \\ L_{AD} = L_{A'D'} \\ L_{CD} = L_{C'D'} \end{cases} \tag{3}$$

Substitute Eq. (1) and (2) into (3) to obtain the spatial position of the folded petal: **A**′ [1600; 0; 4216.78], **C'** [1302.18; 89.19; 144.24], **D**′ [1600; 0; 182.76].

Considering that the petals deploy around a certain axis in space, the rotation axis vector should always be perpendicular to the plane composed of $\boldsymbol{AA'}$ and $\boldsymbol{CC'}$, $\boldsymbol{AA'}$ and $\boldsymbol{DD'}$, $\boldsymbol{CC'}$ and $\boldsymbol{DD'}$. Based on this assumption, it can be obtained:

$$\begin{cases} \boldsymbol{n}_1 = \dfrac{\boldsymbol{AA'} \times \boldsymbol{CC'}}{\left|\boldsymbol{AA'} \times \boldsymbol{CC'}\right|} = (0.3877, 0.8842, 0.2606) \\ \boldsymbol{n}_2 = \dfrac{\boldsymbol{AA'} \times \boldsymbol{DD'}}{\left|\boldsymbol{AA'} \times \boldsymbol{DD'}\right|} = (-0.2157, 0.8601, -0.4624) \\ \boldsymbol{n}_3 = \dfrac{\boldsymbol{CC'} \times \boldsymbol{DD'}}{\left|\boldsymbol{CC'} \times \boldsymbol{DD'}\right|} = (-0.3266, 0.2788, 0.9031) \end{cases} \tag{4}$$

Due to the non-collinearity of $\boldsymbol{n}_1$, $\boldsymbol{n}_2$, and $\boldsymbol{n}_3$, it indicates that there is no rotation axis at the given coordinates that can cause the petal to rotate from the folded state to the deployed state.

To achieve the requirement of 1DOF deployment, this paper proposes the pose transformation shown in Fig. 4, which achieves a configuration that can be deployed through 1DOF rotation:

$$\begin{bmatrix} \boldsymbol{A}'' \\ \boldsymbol{C}'' \\ \boldsymbol{D}'' \\ 1 \end{bmatrix} = \begin{bmatrix} \cos\Delta\theta_z & -\sin\Delta\theta_z & 0 & 0 \\ \sin\Delta\theta_z & \cos\Delta\theta_z & 0 & 0 \\ 0 & 0 & 1 & 0 \\ 0 & 0 & 0 & 1 \end{bmatrix} \begin{bmatrix} 1 & 0 & 0 & \Delta x \\ 0 & 1 & 0 & 0 \\ 0 & 0 & 1 & \Delta z \\ 0 & 0 & 0 & 1 \end{bmatrix} \begin{bmatrix} \boldsymbol{A}' \\ \boldsymbol{C}' \\ \boldsymbol{D}' \\ 1 \end{bmatrix} \tag{5}$$

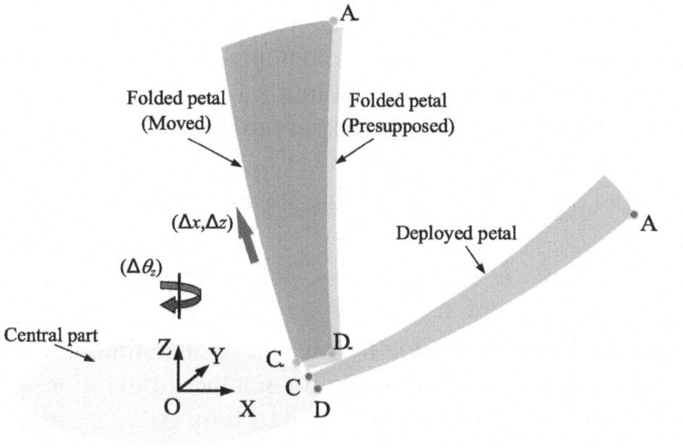

Fig. 4. Schematic diagram of petal pose transformation

Using the newly obtained coordinates of A″, C″, and D″ to update the axis vector described in Eq. (4):

$$\begin{cases} \boldsymbol{n}_1 = \dfrac{\boldsymbol{AA''} \times \boldsymbol{CC''}}{|\boldsymbol{AA''} \times \boldsymbol{CC''}|} \\ \boldsymbol{n}_2 = \dfrac{\boldsymbol{AA''} \times \boldsymbol{DD''}}{|\boldsymbol{AA''} \times \boldsymbol{DD''}|} \\ \boldsymbol{n}_3 = \dfrac{\boldsymbol{CC''} \times \boldsymbol{DD''}}{|\boldsymbol{CC''} \times \boldsymbol{DD''}|} \end{cases} \tag{6}$$

Due to the petal deploys with a single axis, vectors $\boldsymbol{n}_1$, $\boldsymbol{n}_2$, and $\boldsymbol{n}_3$ should be collinear:

$$|\boldsymbol{n}_1 \cdot \boldsymbol{n}_2| = |\boldsymbol{n}_1 \cdot \boldsymbol{n}_3| = |\boldsymbol{n}_2 \cdot \boldsymbol{n}_3| = 1 \tag{7}$$

The problem of the petal deployment is simplified as a multi parameter optimization problem, that is, by adjusting the parameters Δx Δy $\Delta\theta_z$ in Eq. (5) to make the newly obtained A″, C″, and D″ satisfy Eq. (7). To solve this problem, this paper adopts particle swarm optimization algorithm for multi parameter optimization, and constructs the objective function G as shown Eq. (8):

$$G(\Delta x, \Delta z, \Delta\theta_z) = \left|\sum \left|\boldsymbol{n}_i \cdot \boldsymbol{n}_j\right| - 1\right| \tag{8}$$

When the objective function G is small enough, it can be considered that the newly obtained petal position meets the requirements of uniaxial rotation. To ensure that the process of moving petals does not significantly affect the storage of the antenna and does not interfere with the central panel, the displacement is limited to a specified range:

$$\Delta x \in [-200, 200];\ \Delta z \in [-200, 200];\ \Delta\theta_z \in \left[-10^\circ, 10^\circ\right] \tag{9}$$

In the optimization process, the $k+1$st action of particle i is defined as $s_i(k+1)$, which inherits the parameter $s_i(k)$ from the previous action:

$$s_i(k+1) = ws_i(k) + c_1r_1(p_{Best} - s_i(k)) + c_2r_2(g_{Best} - s_i(k)) \tag{10}$$

where k is the number of iterations; w is the inertia coefficient; c_1 and c_2 are defined acceleration coefficients; r_1 and r_2 are random numbers; p_{Best} is the optimal solution of the population; g_{Best} is the global optimal solution.

During the calculation process, it is necessary to dynamically adjust the inertia coefficient w in order to balance the relationship between global search and local search, in order to achieve rapid detection in the starting stage and fine search in the later stage.

$$w = w_{\max} - \frac{(w_{\max} - w_{\min})k}{N} \tag{11}$$

where w_{max} is the maximum inertia coefficient; w_{min} is the minimum inertia coefficient; k is the number of iterations; N is the maximum number of iterations.

Based on the optimization results $\Delta x = -110$ mm, $\Delta z = 24$ mm, $\Delta\theta_z = 7.5°$ are obtained.

$$\begin{bmatrix} A'' \\ C'' \\ D'' \end{bmatrix} = \begin{bmatrix} 1477.25 & 194.48 & 4240.78 \\ 1170.34 & 244.04 & 168.24 \\ 1477.25 & 194.48 & 206.75 \end{bmatrix} \tag{12}$$

At this point, the process of the deployment is simplified as solving the spatial transformation problem from [A, C, D] T to $\left[A'', C'', D'\right]$ T. According to the equivalent axis angle theorem, this process can be described as:

$$\begin{bmatrix} \boldsymbol{A} \\ \boldsymbol{C} \\ \boldsymbol{D} \end{bmatrix} = \begin{bmatrix} \boldsymbol{R}_\omega(\theta) & (\boldsymbol{I} - \boldsymbol{R}_\omega(\theta))\boldsymbol{C_P} \\ \boldsymbol{0} & 1 \end{bmatrix} \begin{bmatrix} \boldsymbol{A}'' \\ \boldsymbol{C}'' \\ \boldsymbol{D}'' \end{bmatrix} \tag{13}$$

where $\boldsymbol{R}_\omega(\theta)$ is the rotation matrix; $\boldsymbol{C_P}$ is the coordinate of the anchor point; $\boldsymbol{I}$ is the identity matrix.

By solving the above nonlinear equation system, the deployment parameters can be obtained:

$$\begin{cases} \boldsymbol{n}_r = \left[-0.4167\ 0.5866\ -0.6944\right]^T \\ \boldsymbol{C_P} = \left[946.33\ 452.64\ -185.52\right]^T \\ \theta = 1.8577 \end{cases} \tag{14}$$

3.2 Configuration Synthesis

This type of antenna is symmetrical about the center of the parabolic focal axis and has a spatial rotation axis $\boldsymbol{n_r}$. Therefore, the deployment form of this type of antenna is a typical staggered axis transmission process shown in Fig. 5.

Compared to transmission methods such as belts and gears, linkage mechanisms have higher transmission efficiency. Therefore, this paper takes the central sliding plate linkage mechanism as an example to design the configuration of the deployment mechanism.

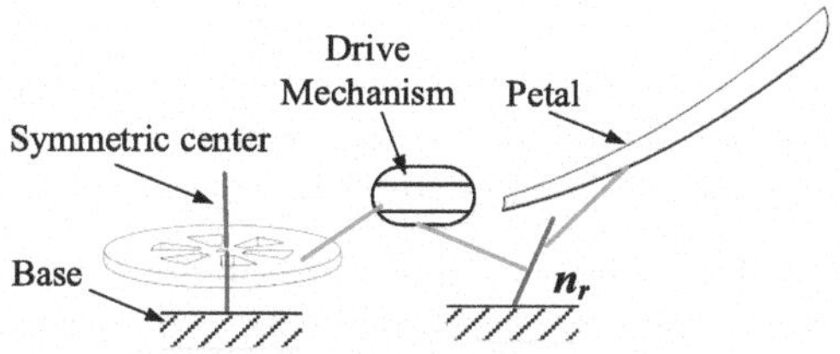

Fig. 5. Schematic diagram of antenna deployment form

To meet the 1DOF deployment requirement of the antenna, degree of freedom analysis should be performed firstly. Equation (15) is the formula for calculating the DOF of spatial closed chain mechanisms:

$$F = d(n - p - 1) + \sum_{i=1}^{p} f_i + \upsilon - \lambda \tag{15}$$

where d is the order of the mechanism, n is the number of components, p is the number of motion pairs, f_i is the i-th degree of freedom of the motion pair, υ is the virtual constraint, and λ is the local degree of freedom.

Due to the possibility of functional failure in over constrained mechanisms, only non over constrained design forms are considered in this paper, that is the order of the mechanism $d = 6$. Meanwhile, to simplify the design, virtual constraints and local degrees of freedom are not taken into account. At this point, the formula for the degree of freedom of the deployment mechanism evolves into:

$$F = d(n - p - 1) + \sum_{i=1}^{p} f_i = 1 \tag{16}$$

According to the design requirements, the antenna requires at least three components: a base, a sliding disc, and a petal, that is, $n \geq 3, p \geq 3, f_1 = 1, f_2 = 1$. The following analysis and design will be conducted:

(1) $n = 3, p = 3$; According to Eq. (16), at this point $F = -4$, it does not meet the design requirements;
(2) $n = 4, p = 4$; According to Eq. (16), $f_3 = 5$, it is not possible to use a lower pair;
(3) $n = 5, p = 5$; According to Eq. (16), the sum $f_3 + f_4 = 5$, where f_3 and f_4 are II and III pairs respectively, can meet the design requirements. Combined with the existing moving and rotating pairs, a total of four configurations can be generated. The comprehensive configuration is shown in Table 1;
(4) $n = 6, p = 6$; According to Eq. (16), the sum of $f_3 + f_4 + f_5 = 5$. The combination forms of f_3, f_4, and f_5 can be (I, I, and III) and (I, II, and II). Combined with the existing moving and rotating pairs, a total of 36 configurations can be generated. The comprehensive configurations are shown in Table 2;
(5) $n = 7, p = 7$; According to Eq. (16), if $f_3 + f_4 + f_5 + f_6 = 5$, the combination form of f_3, f_4, f_5, and f_6 should be I, I, I, and II pairs. Combined with existing moving and rotating pairs, a total of 64 configurations can be generated;

(6) $n = 8, p = 8$; According to Eq. (16), if $f_3 + f_4 + f_5 + f_6 + f_7 = 5$, the combination form of f_3, f_4, f_5, f_6, and f_7 should be I, I, I, I, and I pairs. Combined with existing moving and rotating pairs, a total of 32 configurations can be generated;
(7) $n > 8, p > 8$; Without local degrees of freedom, Eq. (16) cannot be solved.

Therefore, under the aforementioned constraints in this paper, the total number of configurations of the deployment mechanisms for the solid surface antenna driven by sliding pairs is 136.

Table 1. Configuration synthesis at $n = 5$ and $p = 5$

Number	configuration	quantity	diagram
1	P(US)R	2	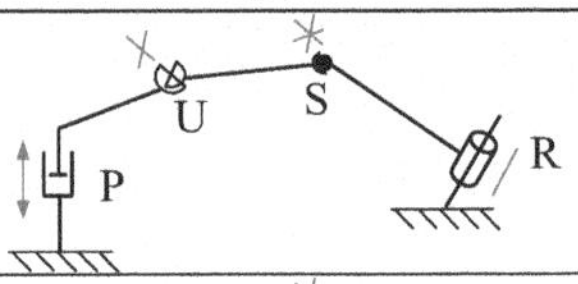
2	P(CS)R	2	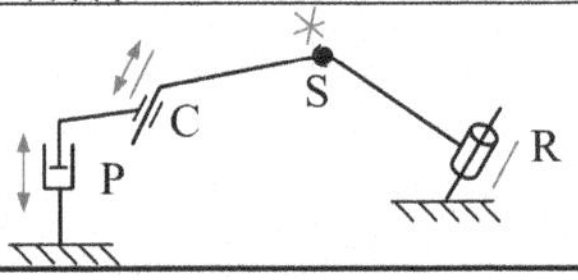

This paper selects the PUSR mechanism as the basic deployment unit, and its structure is shown in Fig. 6. During the deployment process, the sliding disc slides downwards driven by the spring, and the petals are deployed to the working position by the Hooke joint, transmission link, and ball joint. The speed control motor and rope group control the deployment speed of the sliding disc to reduce the impact of motion.

The 1DOF mechanism only needs to lock any motion pair to lock the entire motion chain. Therefore, the Maxwell connector shown in Fig. 7 can be adopted. This mechanism consists of three rigid spheres distributed on equilateral triangles and corresponding V-shaped grooves. The constraint line diagram consists of three intersecting constraint lines. According to the Grassman geometry theory, the mechanism can generate six constraints after constraint combination, that is, lose all degrees of freedom.

4 Kinematic Modeling and Simulation

4.1 Closed Vector Model

For the sliding disc deployment mechanism, the kinematic model of the PUSR mechanism can be abstracted as the schematic diagram shown in Fig. 8. The vector of sliding pair collinear with the parabolic focal axis. The origin of the global coordinate system is established at the vertex of the paraboloid (O_0); The common perpendicular between the focal axis and the deployment axis determines the positions of O_1 and O_2; The center of the ball joint is the origin of the coordinate system O_3; The midpoint of the Hooke hinge is defined as O_4 and O_5; The position of O_6 is determined by the common perpendicular between the sliding pair and the Hooke hinge.

Table 2. Configuration synthesis at $n = 6$ and $p = 6$

Number	configuration	quantity	diagram
1	P(RRS)R	3	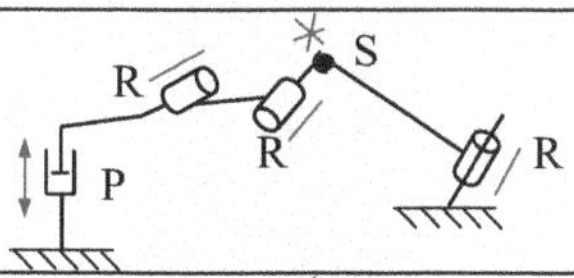
2	P(PPS)R	3	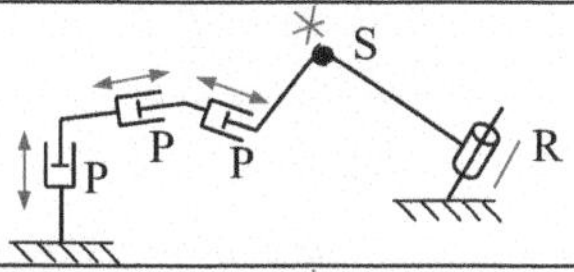
3	P(RPS)R	6	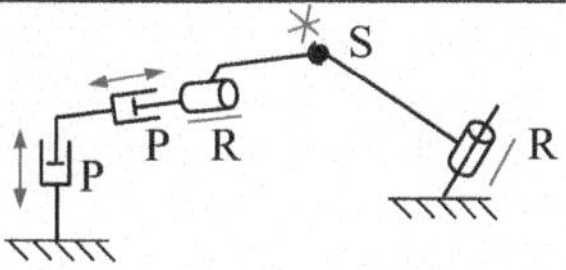
4	P(RUC)R	6	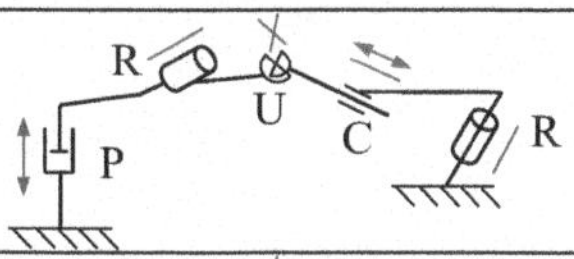
5	P(PUC)R	6	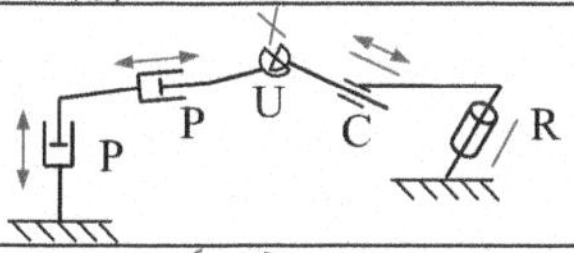
6	P(RCC)R	3	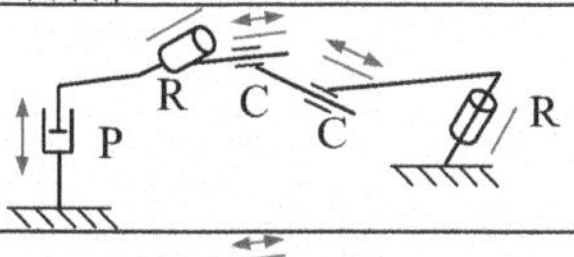
7	P(PCC)R	3	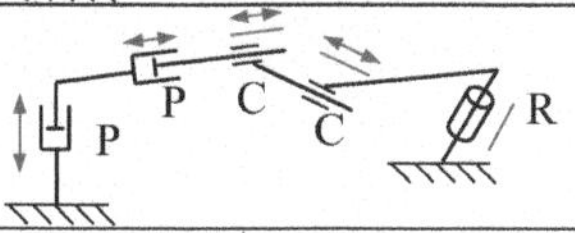
8	P(RUU)R	3	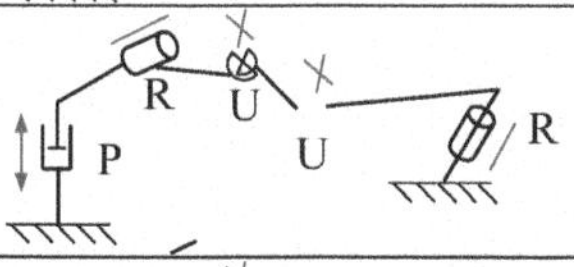
9	P(PUU)R	3	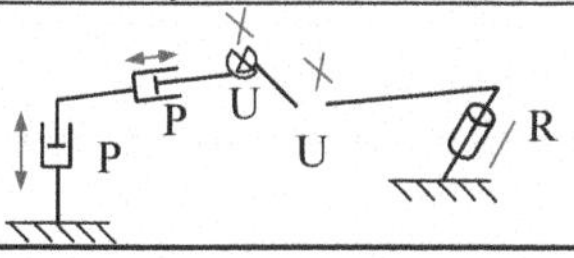

After obtaining the local coordinate system origin O_i of each motion pair, the local coordinate system can be established by the right-hand Cartesian coordinate rule. It can be seen that due to the assumption of a rigid rod, the distances between O_0 and O_1, O_1

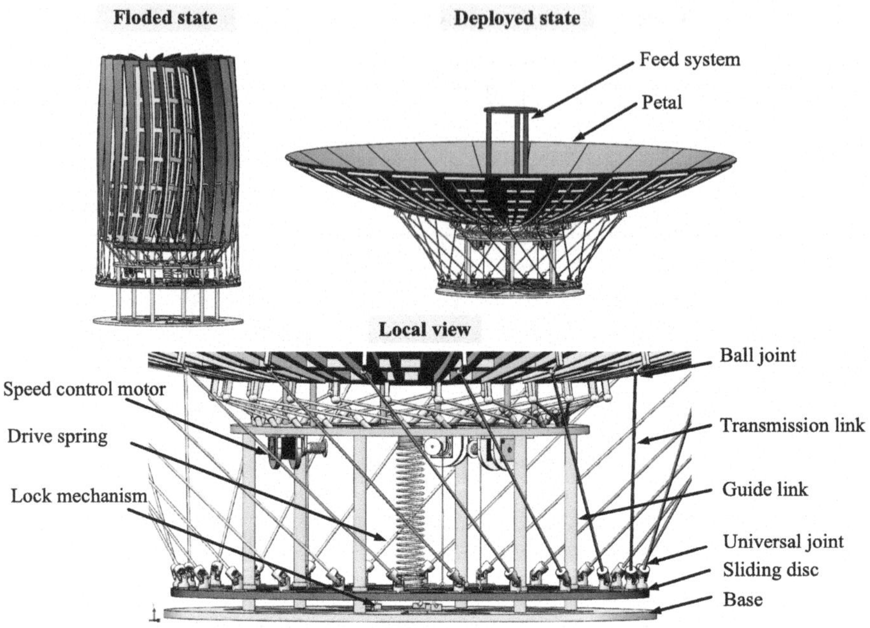

Fig. 6. Deployment scheme based on PUSR mechanism

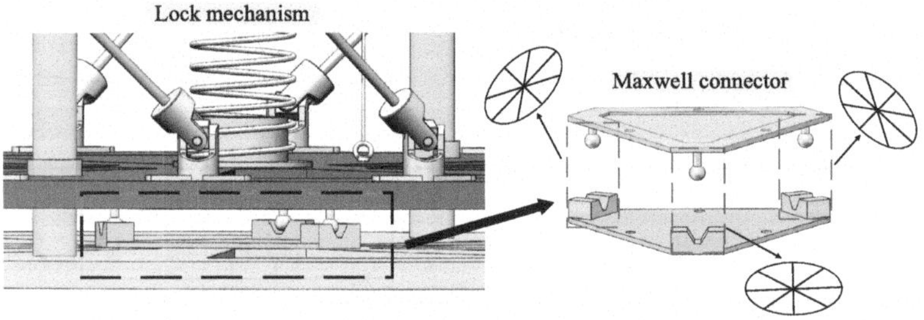

Fig. 7. Lock mechanism of antenna

and O_2, O_3 and O_3, O_3 and $O_4(O_5)$, and $O_4(O_5)$ and O_6 remain constant throughout the entire motion.

Based on the constructed local coordinate systems of each motion pair, the kinematic analysis of the deployment mechanism is carried out using the front D-H coordinate method. The kinematic parameter table shown in Table 3 is obtained through geometric relationships, where ‘const’ represents that the parameter remains constant during the deployment process, ‘var’ indicates that the parameter will change during the deployment process.

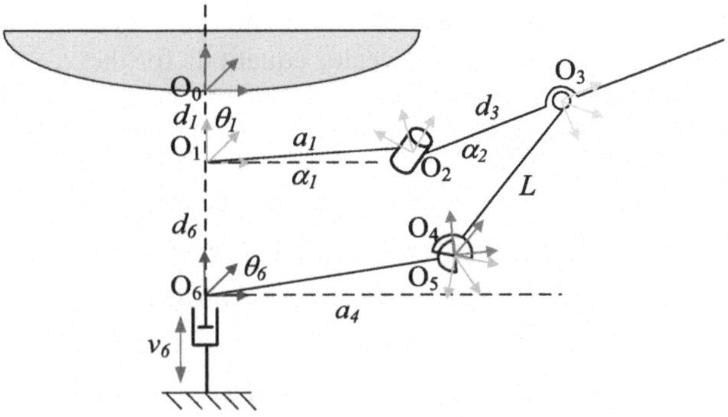

Fig. 8. Kinematic model of the PUSR mechanism

Table 3. D-H Parameters of deployment Mechanism

i	α_{i-1}	a_{i-1}	d_i	θ_i
1	0	0	$d_1 = \text{const}$	$\theta_1 = \text{const}$
2	$\alpha_1 = \text{const}$	$a_1 = \text{const}$	0	$\theta_1 = \text{var}$
3	$\alpha_2 = \text{const}$	0	$d_3 = \text{const}$	0
6	0	0	$d_6 = \text{var}$	$\theta_6 = \text{const}$
5	$\pi/2$	$a_6 = \text{const}$	0	$\theta_5 = \text{var}$
4	$\pi/2$	0	0	$\theta_4 = \text{var}$

It can be seen that the variables are θ_1, θ_4, θ_5 d_6. Considering that the basic unit is a spatial closed chain mechanism, the spatial closed vector method can be used for description. Based on the local coordinate system origin of each motion pair, a closed vector schematic diagram is constructed as shown in Fig. 9, and the vector expression can be obtained:

$$\overrightarrow{O_0O_1} + \overrightarrow{O_1O_2} + \overrightarrow{O_2O_3} = \overrightarrow{O_0O_6} + \overrightarrow{O_6O_5} + \overrightarrow{O_5O_4} \tag{17}$$

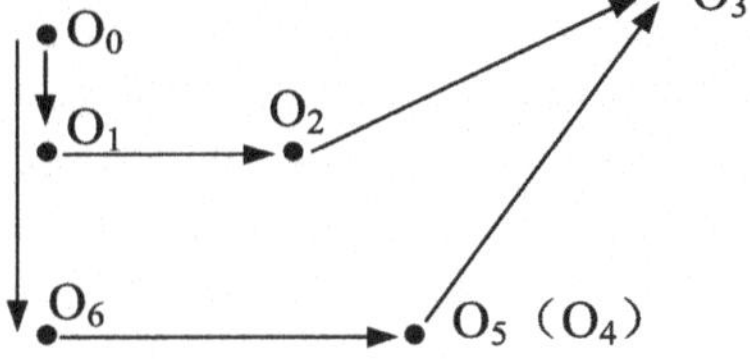

Fig. 9. Schematic diagram of closed vector model

By projecting Eq. (16) onto the spatial coordinate system and combining with the parameters shown in Table 3, the closed vector equations for the *x*, *y*, and *z* directions can be obtained as follows:

$$\begin{aligned} & d_1\cos(z_1, x_0) + a_1\cos(x_1, x_0) + d_3\cos(z_3, x_0) = \\ & d_6\cos(z_6, x_0) + a_4\cos(x_6, x_0) + L\cos(x_4, x_0) \\ & d_1\cos(z_1, y_0) + a_1\cos(x_1, y_0) + d_3\cos(z_3, y_0) = \\ & d_6\cos(z_6, y_0) + a_4\cos(x_6, y_0) + L\cos(x_4, y_0) \\ & d_1\cos(z_1, z_0) + a_1\cos(x_1, z_0) + d_3\cos(z_3, z_0) = \\ & d_6\cos(z_6, z_0) + a_4\cos(x_6, z_0) + L\cos(x_4, z_0) \end{aligned} \tag{18}$$

where $\cos(i, j)$ is the cosine value between the *i*-axis and the *j*-axis.

It can be seen that there are four variables in Table 3, and Eq. (18) can be supplemented with three constraint equations. Therefore, when any of the parameters θ_1, θ_4, θ_5 or d_6 are determined, the petal posture can be uniquely determined. Combining with the driving form, d6 is established as the independent variable and the other parameters as the dependent variables, the kinematic analysis of the basic deployable unit can be completed.

4.2 Kinematic Analysis

According to the task requirements of our laboratory, parameters shown in Table 4 are used in this paper.

Table 4. Structural parameters of solid surface deployable antenna

Structural parameters	Value
Aperture	10 m
Focal diameter ratio	0.435
Center part diameter	2.4 m
Number of petals	24
Storage ratio	0.3130
DOF of deployment	1

It can be concluded that the displacement of the sliding disc d_6 is 682.73 mm during the deployment action. In the calculation process, the displacement driving function is Eq. (19), and the antenna deployment is completed within 500 s. The calculated curves of the rotation angles of each motion pair are shown in Fig. 10.

$$d_{in}(t) = \frac{3}{t_f^2} d_f t^2 - \frac{2}{t_f^3} d_f t^3 \tag{19}$$

where d_f represents the total displacement; t_f is the total duration; t is the exercise time.

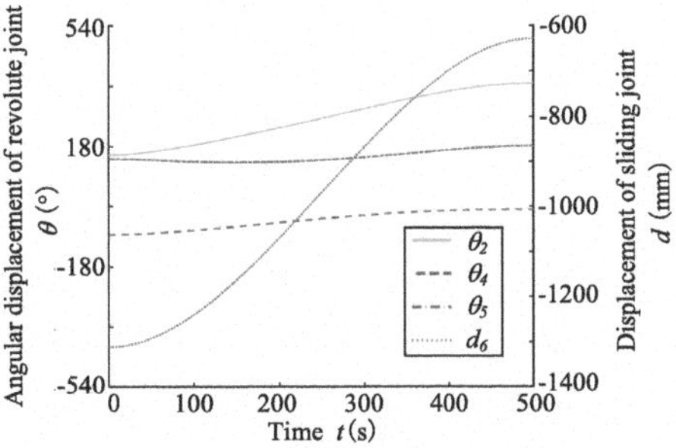

Fig. 10. Variation curves of displacement for each motion pair

By solving for the first and second derivatives of the angular displacements of each motion pair obtained from Eq. (19), the velocity and acceleration within the time range shown in Fig. 11 can be obtained.

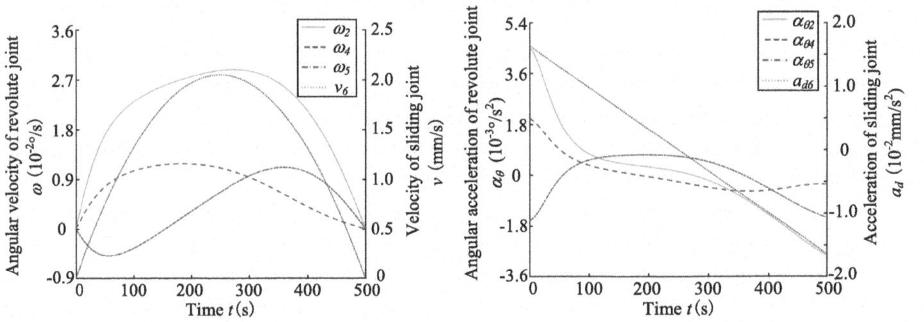

(a) Velocity (b) Acceleration

Fig. 11. Variation curves of velocity and acceleration for each motion pair

As shown in Fig. 10 and 11, the displacement, velocity and acceleration of each motion pair are stable, indicating that there is no severe impact vibration during the deployment process.

The positions of each motion pair in the global coordinate system are shown in Fig. 12. it can be seen that when using the PUSR mechanism as the basic folding unit of the antenna, the O_3 corresponding to the ball joint, the $O_4(O_5)$ corresponding to the Hooke joint, and the O_6 corresponding to the sliding joint undergo significant displacement in space. The displacement of O_3 is spatial displacement, specifically manifested as rotation around O_2. The displacement of $O_4(O_5)$ and O_6 is in the XZ plane.

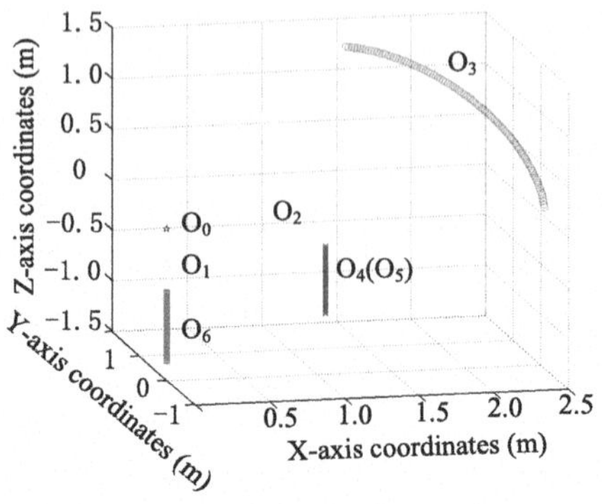

Fig. 12. The positions of each motion pair

5 Conclusion

This paper designs a 1DOF deployment mechanism of the solid surface deployable antenna and conducts the kinematics analysis, the main conclusions are as follows:

(1) A petal posture determination method based on particle swarm optimization algorithm was proposed, and a technical solution for 1DOF deployment design was provided by combining the equivalent axis angle theorem;
(2) A comprehensive analysis of the configuration was conducted, and a detailed design based on PUSR mechanism was established;
(3) A D-H kinematic model was constructed, and the closed vector projection method was used for kinematic analysis of the antenna deployment process. The variation of displacement, velocity, and acceleration of the PUSR mechanism were obtained. The results showed that the motion curve was continuous and smooth, indicating that the design scheme was reliable.

References

1. Li, C.S., Yu, Z., Chen, J.: Overview of techniques for improving high resolution spaceborne SAR imaging and image quality. J. Radars **8**(6), 717–731 (2019)
2. Teng, F., Wan, J.X., Liu, J.: Review of terahertz antenna technology for science missions in space. IEEE Aerospace Electron. Syst. **38**(2), 16–32 (2023)
3. Davarian, F., Babuscia, A., Baker, J., et al.: Improving small satellite communications in deep space a review of the existing systems and technologies with recommendations for improvement. IEEE Aerosp. Electron. Syst. Mag. **35**(7), 8–25 (2020)
4. Duan, B.Y.: Spaceborne deployable antennas (LSDAs) a comprehensive summary. Chin. J. Electron. **29**(1), 1–15 (2020)
5. Chen, C.Z., Dong, J.B., Chen, J.B., et al.: Large spaceborne parabolic antenna: research progress. Acta Aeronautica et Astronautica Sin. **42**(01), 133–153 (2021)
6. Buend, G.G., Liberto, S., Goussetis, G., et al.: Review of antenna technologies for very high frequency data exchange systems. Int. J. Satell. Commun. Netw. **41**(2), 122–133 (2021)
7. Liu, R.Q., Shi, C., Guo, H.W., et al.: Review of space deployable antenna mechanisms. J. Mech. Eng. **56**(05), 1–12 (2020)

8. Ma, X.F., Li, Y., Xiao, Y., et al.: Development and tendency of large space deployable antenna reflector. Space Electron. Technol. **15**(02), 16–26 (2018)
9. Chandra, M., Kumar, S., Chattopadhyaya, S., et al.: A review on developments of deployable membrane-based reflector antennas. Adv. Space Res. **68**(9), 3749–3764 (2021)
10. Liu, L.K., Zhou, Z.C., Zheng, G.T., et al.: Advance of dynamics and control of the satellite with large mesh deployable antenna. Chin. Space Sci. Technol. **34**(2), 1–12 (2014)
11. Zheng, S.K., Ji, Y.Z., Cui, Z.Y., et al.: Design and analysis of HJ-1-C satellite SAR antenna. J. Radars **3**(3), 266–273 (2014)
12. Tang, Q.Y., Li, T.J., Chen, C.C.: Design and analysis of a new hoop tensegrity structure for space deploable antenna. J. Xidian Univ. **49**(04), 193–200 (2022)
13. Thomas, M.: Inflatable space structures. IEEE Potentials **11**(4), 29–32 (1992)
14. Zhou, X.T., Ma, X.F., Li, H.X.: Review of flexible tensioned thin-film deployable antennas. Chin. Space Sci. Technol. **42**(04), 77–91 (2022)
15. Wei, J.Z., Miao, C.Q., Du, X.W.: Simulation analysis of deployment process of inflatable planar antenna structure. J. Harbin Inst. Technol. **39**(9), 1398–1401 (2007)
16. Escrig, F.: Expandable space structures. Int. J. Space Struct. **1**(2), 79–91 (1985)
17. Luo, A.N., Liu, H.P., Zhang, T.M., et al.: Structural analysis of flowerlike deployable antenna. China Mech. Eng. **23**(14), 1656–1658 (2012)
18. Liu, R.Q., Tian, D.K., Deng, Z.Q.: Research status and prospects of spaceborne deployable antenna structure. Mech. Des. **27**(9), 1–10 (2010)
19. Shi, C., Liu, M.L., Guo, H.W., et al.: Mechanism design and dynamic analysis of large-scale two-dimensional deployable planar antenna. Opt. Precis. Eng. **29**(12), 2868–2876 (2021)
20. Tian, D.K., Fan, X.D., Jin, L., et al.: Surface accuracy analysis for hexagonal prism modular deployable antenna. Opt. Precis. Eng. **29**(12), 2855–2867 (2021)
21. Nakano, H., Yamauchi, J., Hashimoto, S.: Sunflower spiral antenna. Trans. Inst. Electron. Commun. Eng. Jpn. Sect. E **64**(12), 763–769 (1981)
22. Guest, S.D., Pelegrino, S.: A new concept for solid surface deployable antennas. Acta Astronaut. **38**(2), 103–113 (1996)
23. Chae, S., Oh, Y., Lee, S.: Deployment behaviors of CFRP reflector under zero gravity environment. Int. J. Aerosp. Syst. Eng. **7**(1), 1–6 (2020)
24. Bujakas, V.I., Kamensky, A.A.: Self-setting locks for petal type deployable space reflector. Microactuators Micromechanisms **45**, 177–187 (2017)
25. Huang, H., Cheng, Q., Zheng, L., et al.: Development for petal-type deployable solid-surface reflector by uniaxial rotation mechanism. Acta Astronaut. **178**(2), 511–521 (2021)
26. Xu, Y., Cheng, Q., Huang, H., et al.: Study of deploying process of solid-surface deployable antenna rotating along a single axis. Chin. J. Eng. Des. **27**(3), 301–306 (2020)
27. Huang, H., Guan, F.L., Xu, Y., et al.: Design and deploying study of a new petal-type deployable solid surface antenna. Acta Astronaut. **148**, 99–116 (2018)
28. Tan, G.D., Duan, X.C., Niu, D.C., et al.: Visual synthesis of uniaxial synchronous deployment mechanisms for solid-surface deployable antennas. Mech. Mach. Theory **178**, 105073 (2022)

Design of High Obstacle-Crossing Robot Based on Flexible Spine Structure

Bing Li[1], Linsen Xu[1,2,3](✉), Zhihuan Wang[1], and Lisheng Wang[1]

[1] School of Mechanical and Electrical Engineering, Hohai University, Changzhou 213000, China
lsxu@hhu.edu.cn

[2] Changzhou Key Laboratory of Intelligent Manufacturing Technology and Equipment, Changzhou 213000, China

[3] Suzhou Research Institute, Hohai University, Suzhou 215000, China

Abstract. Facing complex non-structural environments, such as post-disaster rescue, pipeline inspection, industrial maintenance, and scientific investigation, etc., higher requirements are placed on the robot's ability to pass through, but the existing robots are not well adapted to complex environments. In this paper, based on the flexible spinal structure of animals, we combine the characteristics of tracked robots and reconfigurable robots to design mobile robots with both high obstacle-crossing and flexibility. The maximum height of the robot and its constraints are analyzed from the kinematic point of view, and the dynamics model of the robot's obstacle-crossing process is established by using the Newton-Euler method, and the driving torque is derived according to the maximum height of the obstacle-crossing and its constraints. According to the maximum obstacle-crossing height derived from the theoretical calculation, a robot simulation platform was established to simulate the obstacle-crossing process of the robot and verify the correctness of the theoretical calculation.

Keywords: Vertebral replica · Reconfigurable · Crawler robot · Kinematics · Dynamics

1 Introduction

A mobile robot is a robotic system with a mobile function that consists of mechanisms such as sensors, remote operators, and automatic controllers. They can replace people in hazardous or hostile environments and have greater mobility and flexibility than typical robots. According to the mobile mechanism robots can be categorized as wheeled, tracked, footed, etc. Among them, tracked robots can be used for tasks such as surveillance of suspicious areas or buildings, inspection of hazardous objects, search for survivors of collapsed rubble, coal mine gas detection, disaster relief, combat operations, planetary exploration, etc. [1, 2].

Due to the advantages of reconfigurable tracked robots such as obstacle-crossing ability and environmental adaptability, many scholars have conducted extensive research.

X. Lan et al. (Eds.): ICIRA 2024, LNAI 15201, pp. 412–424, 2025.
https://doi.org/10.1007/978-981-96-0771-6_30

Zong et al. developed a variable-angle tracked robot, and the team developed an adaptive passive device that allows the track to maintain the necessary tension during obstacle crossings [3]. The self-reconfiguring tracked mobile robot (RLMA) developed by Liu et al. can climb stairs stably [4]. Luo et al. proposed a reconfigurable wheel-track hybrid mobile robot (RHMBot) that can realize three modes of motion: wheeled, tracked, and tilted [5]. Takayama et al. developed an actively attached crawler robot (Souryu-I) with only three degrees of freedom, capable of passing through a variety of complex terrain [6]. Kamegawa et al. developed a snake-shaped rescue robot (KOHGA) that can both cross obstacles and adapt to complex terrain [7]. Wang et al. developed a rescue robot for mining research, which was equipped with two pairs of swing arms at the front and back to improve its obstacle-crossing performance [8]. Luo et al. proposed a reconfigurable tracked mobile robot (RTMB) based on a four-link mechanism, which can be structurally adapted to different terrains to cross obstacles, gullies, and other [9]. Zhou et al. developed a reconfigurable robot with multimodal locomotion, which can be interchanged between wheeled, legged, and tracked and their intermediate modes by changing the shape of the reconfigurable wheels [10]. A reconfigurable robot with an integrated two-degree-of-freedom active docking mechanism was proposed by Sohal et al. The team developed an active docking mechanism that allows multiple robots to be coupled or decoupled from each other [11]. Huang et al. developed a parent-child robot, in which the parent robot is a wheel-legged quadruped hybrid robot; the child robot is a number of modular reconfigurable tracked microrobots, which can either act alone or be reconfigured by several modules to form a chain or ring robot, and both the chain and ring robots can improve the obstacle-crossing ability of the child robot [12]. However, all of the above studies have been conducted to improve the robot's obstacle-crossing performance, ignoring the environment's requirement for high robot dexterity.

In this paper, a reconfigurable tracked robot with both high obstacle-crossing and high dexterity is designed by mimicking the structure of the animal spine and combining the advantages of tracked robots with the advantages of reconfigurable robotic locomotion. In this paper, the maximum height of the robot and its constraints are analyzed from the kinematics point of view, and the dynamics model of the robot in the process of motion is established by using the Newton-Euler method, and the driving torque of the robot is derived according to the maximum height of the robot and its constraints. The correctness of the theoretical analysis results is verified by simulation.

2 Design of Mechanical Systems

In order to solve the shortcomings of mobile robots with poor barrier-crossing and flexibility, this paper proposes a mobile robot that combines the features of crawler robots and reconfigurable robots, as shown in Fig. 1. The robot includes a track module, a drive module, a support module, and a follower module. The support module is used to connect the active module and the drive module, and to support the track module. The robot can achieve various lifting angles to adapt to different heights when crossing obstacles, and the overall flexibility of the robot also increases the flexibility of the robot during the movement process.

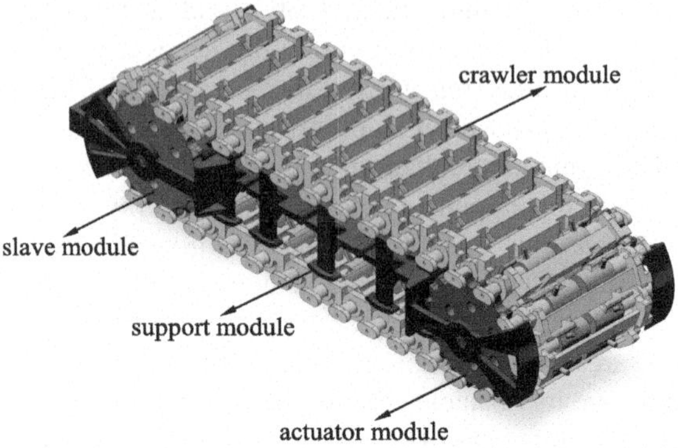

Fig. 1. General view of the robot.

2.1 Crawler Module Design

The track module consists of a number of track chains, and a single track chain consists of a track plate, a 0-degree locking pin, and a 16-degree locking pin, as shown in Fig. 2. The 0-degree locking pin and the 16-degree locking pin can make a helical movement around the track plate, and when the 0-degree/16-degree locking pin makes a helical movement around the track plate to the end, it can make the neighboring track plate lock to 0°/16°, as shown in Fig. 3.

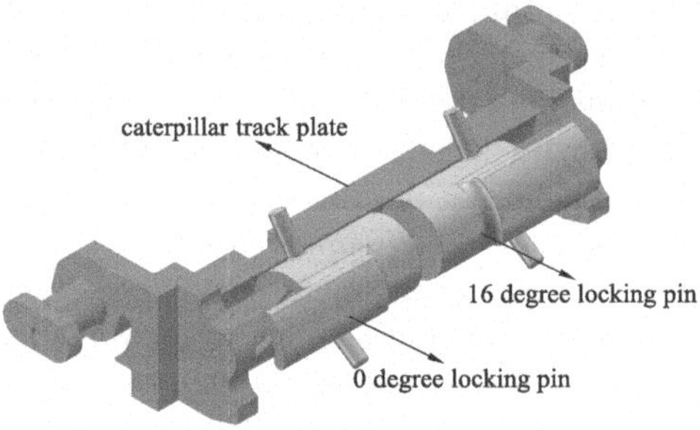

Fig. 2. Crawler Chain

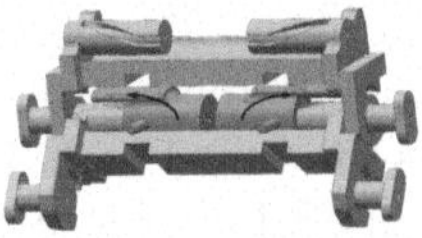

Fig. 3. Track chain locking 0 degree/16 degree.

2.2 Driver Module Design

The drive module includes a drive mechanism and a locking mechanism, as shown in Fig. 4. The locking mechanism consists of a locking motor, a locking gear and a locking plate, which drives the locking plate to move left or right through the forward or reverse rotation of the locking gear to make the locking plate contact with the 0-degree/16-degree locking pins, so as to make the two neighbouring crawler plates in a locking state, and the locking process is shown in Fig. 5.

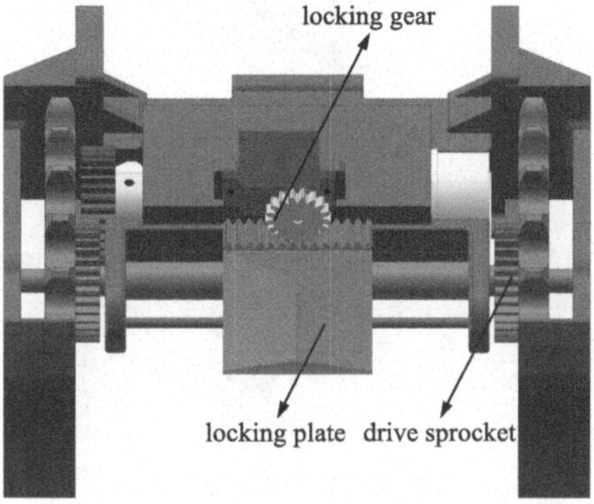

Fig. 4. Driver module.

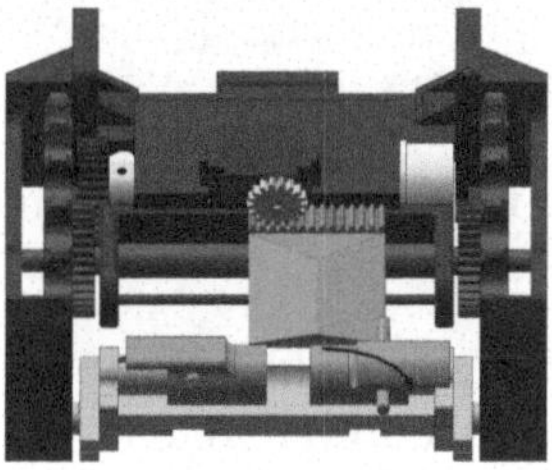

Fig. 5. Locking pin locking process.

2.3 Slave Module Design

The follower module includes the follower sprocket and the unlocking plate, as shown in Fig. 6. When the 0°/16° locking pin in the locked state moves to the unlocking plate, as the track chain continues to move, the locking pin contacts the unlocking plate so that the locking pin resumes the unlocking state, and the unlocking process is shown in Fig. 7.

3 Kinematics and Dynamics Analysis

The motion process of the robot climbing up the step is shown in Fig. 1, which is divided into three stages according to the robot crossing state. Among them, (a)→(b) is the lifting stage, in which the front end of the robot lifts up and contacts the step;

Fig. 6. Slave module.

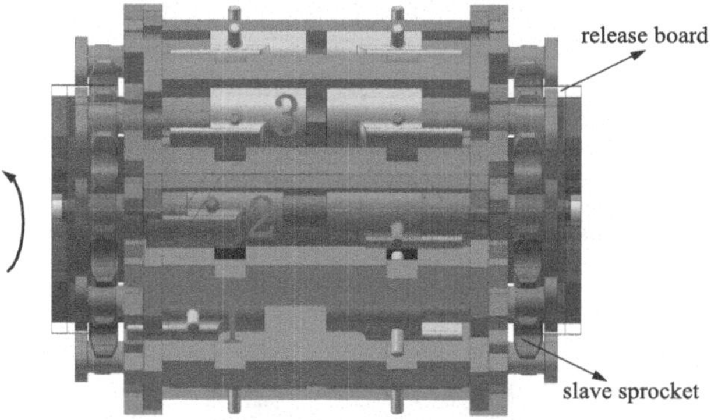

Fig. 7. Locking pin unlocking process.

(b)→(c)→(d) is the supporting stage, in which the robot's head climbs up to the upper edge of the step, and the tail is at the lower edge of the step; (d)→(e) is the crossing stage, in which the robot's tail climbs up to the upper edge of the step. From the robot crossing process, it can be seen that states (b) and (d) are the key states for the robot to climb up the step, so only states (b) and (d) are analyzed kinematically and dynamically in the following. The following assumptions need to be made before performing the robot kinematic characterization (Fig. 8):

(1) The floor is rigid;
(2) Neglecting friction between parts during robot operation;
(3) No sliding between the track and the ground.

3.1 Lift Phase State (B) Robot Kinematic Analysis

As shown in Fig. 9, the robot is divided into two segments to be analysed separately. In the robot coordinate system *xoy*, the centre of mass coordinates of segment 1 and

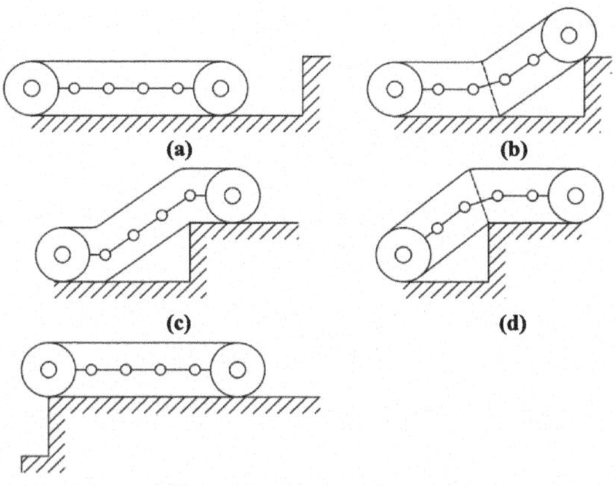

Fig. 8. Analysis of robot gait over obstacles.

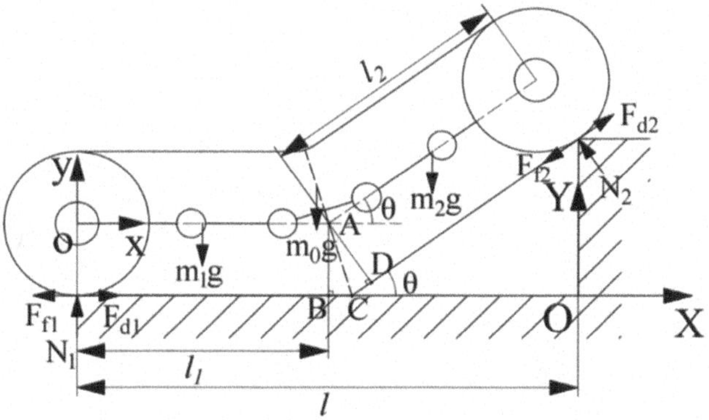

Fig. 9. Robot lifting phase state (b) force analysis.

segment 2 are respectively

$$\begin{cases} x_1 = \frac{l_1}{2}, y_1 = 0 \\ x_2 = l_1 + \frac{l_2}{2}\cos\theta, y_2 = \frac{l_2}{2}\sin\theta \end{cases} \tag{1}$$

where l_1 and l_2 are the lengths of segment 1 and segment 2, respectively, and θ is the angle between segment 2 and the ground.

Then its centre of mass coordinates of segment 1 and segment 2 in the world coordinate system XOY are respectively

$$\begin{cases} x_{G1} = \frac{l_1}{2} - l, y_{G1} = r \\ x_{G2} = l_1 + \frac{l_2}{2}\cos\theta - l, y_{G2} = \frac{l_2}{2}\sin\theta + r \end{cases} \tag{2}$$

where l is the distance between the robot coordinate system xoy and the world coordinate system XOY in the X-axis direction. By the RHS theorem, it can be deduced that

$$l = l_1 + l_2 \cos\theta + r \tan\frac{\theta}{2}(1 + \cos\theta) \tag{3}$$

In summary, in the world coordinate system XOY, the coordinates of the centre of mass of segment 1 and segment 2 are respectively

$$\begin{cases} x_{G1} = -\frac{1}{2}l_1 - l_2\cos\theta - r\tan\frac{\theta}{2}(1+\cos\theta),\ y_{G1} = r \\ x_{G2} = -\frac{1}{2}l_2\cos\theta - r\tan\frac{\theta}{2}(1+\cos\theta),\ y_{G2} = \frac{1}{2}l_2\sin\theta r \end{cases} \tag{4}$$

In the world coordinate system, the robot's overall centre of mass coordinates are

$$\begin{cases} x_{G0} = \frac{m_1x_1+m_2x_2}{m_1+m_2} - l \\ y_{G0} = \frac{m_1y_1+m_2y_2}{m_1+m_2} + r \end{cases} \tag{5}$$

where m_1 and m_2 are the masses of segment 1 and segment 2 respectively, and $m_0 = m_1 + m_2$, m_0 is the total weight of the robot.

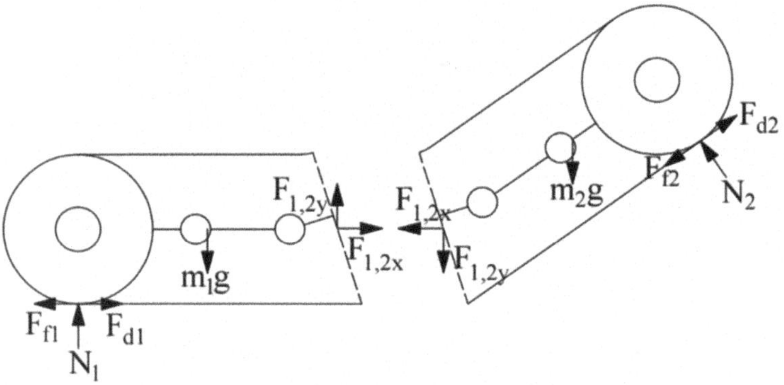

Fig. 10. Robot lifting stage state (b) Force analysis of each module.

The velocity and acceleration of segment 1 and segment 2 are obtained by first and second order derivatives of the centre of mass coordinates of segment 1 and segment 2 respectively.

$$\begin{cases} \dot{x}_{G1} = -\frac{1}{2}\dot{l}_1 - \dot{l}_2\cos\theta + \dot{\theta}\sin\theta\left(l_2 + r\tan\frac{\theta}{2}\right) - r\dot{\theta} \\ \dot{y}_{G1} = 0 \\ \dot{x}_{G2} = -\frac{1}{2}\dot{l}2\cos\theta + \dot{\theta}\sin\theta\left(\frac{1}{2}l2 + r\tan\frac{\theta}{2}\right) - r\dot{\theta} \\ \dot{y}_{G2} = \frac{1}{2}\left(\dot{l}_2\sin\theta + l_2\dot{\theta}\cos\theta\right) \end{cases} \tag{6}$$

$$\begin{cases} \ddot{x}_{G1} = -\frac{1}{2}\ddot{l}_1 - \ddot{l}_2\cos\theta + \dot{l}_2(1+\dot{\theta})\sin\theta + \left(l_2 + r\tan\frac{\theta}{2}\right)\left(\dot{\theta}^2\cos\theta + \ddot{\theta}\sin\theta\right) + \frac{r\dot{\theta}^2\sin\theta}{1+\cos\theta} - r\ddot{\theta} \\ \ddot{y}_{G1} = 0 \\ \ddot{x}_{G2} = -\frac{1}{2}\ddot{l}_2\cos\theta + \dot{l}_2\dot{\theta}\sin\theta + \left(\frac{1}{2}l_2 + r\tan\frac{\theta}{2}\right)\left(\dot{\theta}^2\cos\theta + \ddot{\theta}\sin\theta\right) + \frac{r\dot{\theta}^2\sin\theta}{1+\cos\theta} - r\ddot{\theta} \\ \ddot{y}_{G2} = \frac{1}{2}l_2\left(\ddot{\theta}\cos\theta - \dot{\theta}^2\sin\theta\right) + \dot{l}_2\dot{\theta}\cos\theta + \frac{1}{2}\ddot{l}_2\sin\theta \end{cases} \tag{7}$$

3.2 Lift Phase State (B) Robot Dynamics Analysis

As shown in Fig. 10, the dynamics of segment 1 and segment 2 are modelled according to the Newton-Euler equation respectively

$$\begin{cases} F_{d1} - F_{f1} + F_{1,2x} = m_1 \ddot{x}_{G1} \\ N_1 - m_1 g + F_{1,2y} = m_1 \ddot{y}_{G1} \\ (F_{d1} - F_{f1})r - N_1 l_1 + m_1 g \frac{l_1}{2} = J_1 \ddot{\beta}_1 \end{cases} \tag{8}$$

$$\begin{cases} \left(F_{d2} - F_{f2}\right)\cos\theta - N_2 \sin\theta - F_{1,2x} = m_2 \ddot{x}_{G2} \\ \left(F_{d2} - F_{f2}\right)\sin\theta + N_2 \cos\theta - m_2 g - F_{1,2y} = m_2 \ddot{y}_{G2} \\ (F_{d2} - F_{f2})r + N_2 l_2 - m_2 g \frac{l_2}{2}\cos\theta = J_2 \ddot{\beta}_2 \end{cases} \tag{9}$$

where m_1 and m_2 are the masses of segment 1 and 2 respectively, J_1 and J_2 are the rotational inertia of segment 1 and 2 respectively, $F_{1,2x}$ and $F_{1,2y}$ are the forces of interaction between segment 1 and 2 in the x-direction and y-direction, F_{d1} and F_{d2} are the driving force on segment 1 and 2 respectively, F_{f1} and F_{f2} are the resistance on segment 1 and 2 respectively, N_1 and N_2 are the support force on the ground for segment 1 and 2 respectively.

The drive force of a tracked robot is generated by the shear between the tracks and the ground, and since the robot travels on a hard surface, then its maximum drive force $F_{d\max}$ can be expressed as [13]

$$F_{d\max} = N \tan\varphi \tag{10}$$

where φ is the internal shear resistance angle of the ground, which is taken as 35° in this paper.

The resistance to travel experienced by tracked robots during movement consists of internal and external resistance. Internal resistance is the resistance of the robot due to mutual friction of parts, vibration and other reasons during travelling; external resistance is the resistance to movement due to the compaction of the track on the ground. Since the robot travels on a hard surface, its resistance F_{fi} can be expressed as [14]

$$F_{fi} = \mu N_i \tag{11}$$

where μ is the rolling resistance coefficient, which is taken as 0.026 in this paper [15].

When the projection of the robot's overall centre of mass onto the X-axis of the world coordinate system is at point C, the robot can climb to a maximum height $H_{1\max}$

$$x_{G0} = \frac{m_1 x_1 + m_2 x_2}{m_1 + m_2} - l = l_1 + r\tan\frac{\theta}{2} - l \tag{12}$$

3.3 Cross Phase State (D) Robot Kinematic Analysis

(Fig. 11).

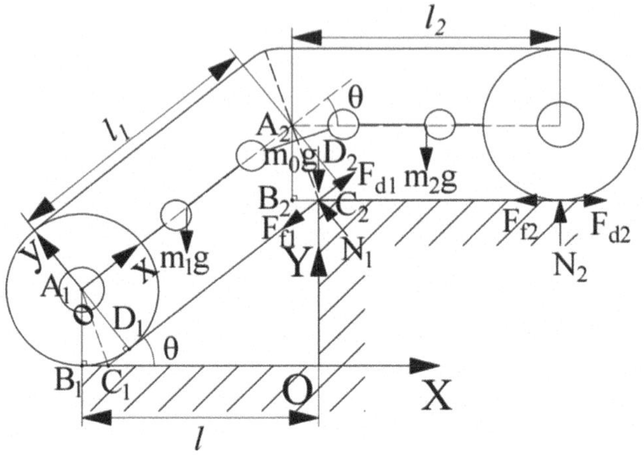

Fig. 11. Robot crossing phase state (d) force analysis.

As shown in Fig. 4, in the robot coordinate system *xoy*, the coordinates of segment 1 and segment 2 are

$$\boldsymbol{c}_1 = \begin{pmatrix} \frac{l_1}{2} \\ 0 \\ 0 \end{pmatrix}, \boldsymbol{c}_2 = \begin{pmatrix} l_1 + \frac{l_2}{2}\sin\theta \\ -\frac{l_2}{2}\cos\theta \\ 0 \end{pmatrix} \tag{13}$$

The transformation matrix of the robot coordinate system *xoy* with respect to the world coordinate system *XOY* in this state is

$${}_R^G\boldsymbol{T} = \begin{pmatrix} \cos\theta & -\sin\theta & 0 & -l \\ \sin\theta & \cos\theta & 0 & r \\ 0 & 0 & 1 & 0 \\ 0 & 0 & 0 & 1 \end{pmatrix} \tag{14}$$

Then its centre of mass coordinates of segment 1 and segment 2 in the world coordinate system *XOY* are respectively

$$\boldsymbol{c}_{G1} = \begin{pmatrix} \frac{l_1}{2}\cos\theta - l \\ \frac{l_1}{2}\sin\theta + r \\ 0 \end{pmatrix}, \boldsymbol{c}_{G2} = \begin{pmatrix} l_1\cos\theta + \frac{l_2}{2} - l \\ l_1\sin\theta + r \\ 0 \end{pmatrix} \tag{15}$$

By the *RHS* theorem, it can be deduced that

$$l = l_1\cos\theta + r\tan\frac{\theta}{2} \tag{16}$$

In summary, in the world coordinate system XOY, the centre of mass coordinates of robot segments 1 and 2 are respectively

$$\boldsymbol{c}_{G1} = \begin{pmatrix} -\frac{l_1}{2}\cos\theta - r\tan\frac{\theta}{2} \\ \frac{l_1}{2}\sin\theta + r \\ 0 \end{pmatrix}, \boldsymbol{c}_{G2} = \begin{pmatrix} \frac{l_2}{2} - r\tan\frac{\theta}{2} \\ l_1\sin\theta + r \\ 0 \end{pmatrix} \tag{17}$$

In the world coordinate system XOY, the robot's overall centre of mass coordinates are

$$\begin{pmatrix} \boldsymbol{c}_{G0} \\ 1 \end{pmatrix} = {}^{G}_{R}\boldsymbol{T}\frac{m_1\boldsymbol{c}_1 + m_2\boldsymbol{c}_2}{m_1 + m_2} \tag{18}$$

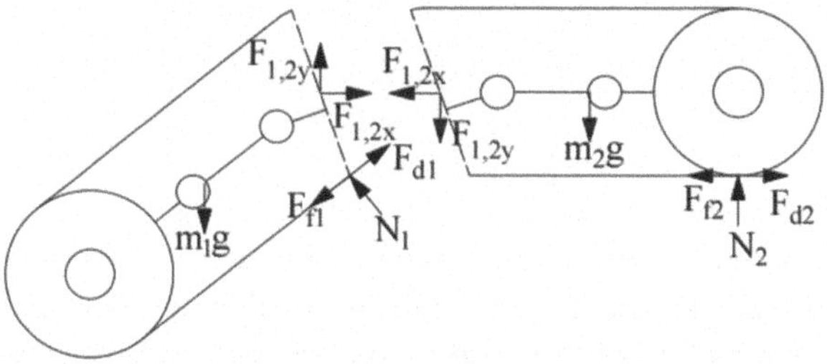

Fig. 12. Robot crossing stage state (d) force analysis of each module.

First-order and second-order derivatives of the centre-of-mass coordinates of segment 1 and 2 are used to obtain the velocity and acceleration of segment 1 and 2, respectively

$$\dot{\boldsymbol{c}}_{G1} = \begin{pmatrix} -\frac{\dot{l}_1}{2}\cos\theta \\ \frac{\dot{l}_1}{2}\sin\theta \\ 0 \end{pmatrix}, \dot{\boldsymbol{c}}_{G2} = \begin{pmatrix} \frac{\dot{l}_2}{2} \\ \dot{l}_1\sin\theta \\ 0 \end{pmatrix} \tag{19}$$

$$\ddot{\boldsymbol{c}}_{G1} = \begin{pmatrix} -\frac{\ddot{l}_1}{2}\cos\theta \\ \frac{\ddot{l}_1}{2}\sin\theta \\ 0 \end{pmatrix}, \ddot{\boldsymbol{c}}_{G2} = \begin{pmatrix} \frac{\ddot{l}_2}{2} \\ \ddot{l}_1\sin\theta \\ 0 \end{pmatrix} \tag{20}$$

3.4 Cross Phase State (D) Robot Dynamics Analysis

As shown in Fig. 12, the dynamics of segment 1 and segment 2 are modelled according to the Newton-Euler formulation respectively

$$\begin{cases} \left(F_{d1} - F_{f1}\right)\cos\theta - N_1\sin\theta + F_{1,2x} = m_1\ddot{x}_{G1} \\ \left(F_{d1} - F_{f1}\right)\sin\theta + N_1\cos\theta - m_1g + F_{1,2y} = m_1\ddot{y}_{G1} \\ \left(F_{d1} - F_{f1}\right)r + m_1g\frac{l_1}{2}\cos\theta - N_1 r\tan\frac{\theta}{2} = J_1\ddot{\beta}_1 \end{cases} \tag{21}$$

$$\begin{cases} F_{d2} - F_{f2} - F_{1,2x} = m_2\ddot{x}_{G2} \\ N_2 - m_2 g - F_{1,2y} = m_2\ddot{y}_{G2} \\ \left(F_{d2} - F_{f2}\right)r + N_2 l_2 - m_2 g \frac{l_2}{2} = J_2\ddot{\beta}_2 \end{cases} \tag{22}$$

When the tail of the robot is just off the ground and the projection of the robot's centre of mass onto the X-axis of the world coordinate system is at a point, the robot can climb to a maximum height $H_{2\,\max}$

$$x_{G0} = \frac{m_1\left(-\frac{l_1}{2}\cos\theta - r\tan\frac{\theta}{2}\right) + m_2\left(\frac{l_2}{2} - r\tan\frac{\theta}{2}\right)}{m_0} = 0 \tag{23}$$

The maximum height that the robot can climb the steps is calculated to satisfy Eq. (24)

$$H_{\max} = \min\{H_{1\,\max}, H_{2\,\max}\} = 55mm \tag{24}$$

4 Simulation

In order to further verify the obstacle-crossing ability of the robot, a robot model was established in Adams. An obstacle model was established based on the maximum obstacle-crossing height derived from theoretical calculations, and the dynamics simulation of the robot crossing the obstacle was carried out, and its obstacle-crossing process is shown in Fig. 13, and the driving torque versus centre-of-mass change curves required for the robot to cross the obstacle were obtained, as shown in Fig. 14 and Fig. 15.

Figure 14 shows the change of driving torque of the robot in the process of crossing the obstacle, and its maximum torque is $1.8N \cdot m$, which is smaller than the blocking torque of the selected motor and meets the performance requirements. Figure 15 shows the change of centre of mass of the robot crossing the obstacle, its initial height is 7.03

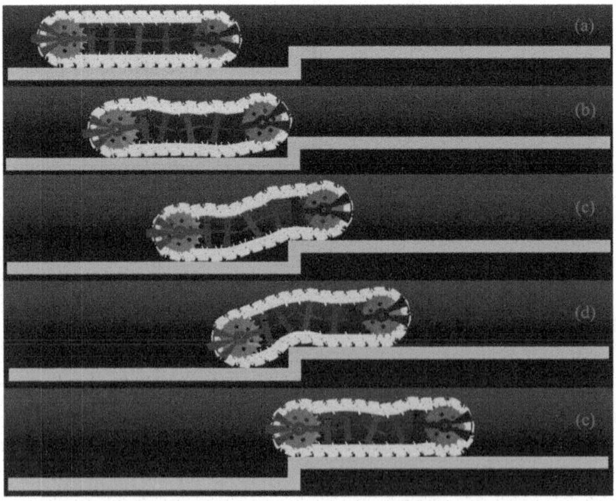

Fig. 13. Robot overpassing process.

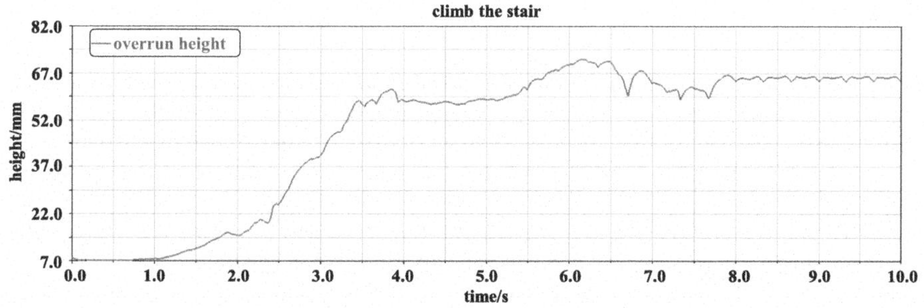

Fig. 14. Driving torque for robot obstacle crossing.

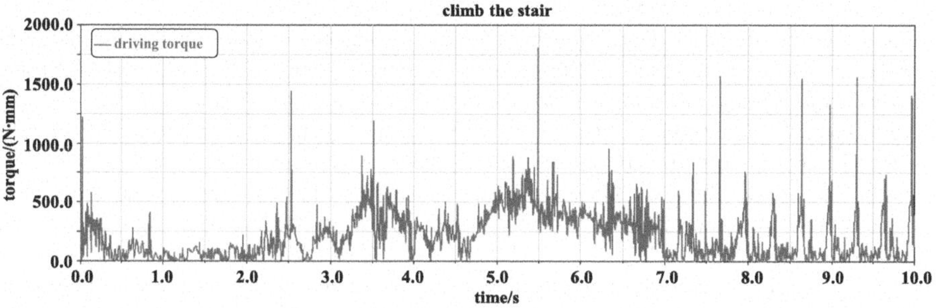

Fig. 15. Centre-of-mass changes for robotic obstacle crossing.

mm, and the final height is 64.48 mm, so the height of crossing the obstacle is greater than the theoretically calculated value 55 mm, which proves the correctness of the theoretical calculation.

5 Conclusion

A reconfigurable tracked robot with both high obstacle-crossing and flexibility is designed by combining the advantages of tracked robots and reconfigurable robot locomotion, modelled on the spinal structure of animals. In this paper, the maximum height of the robot and its constraints are analysed from the kinematics point of view, and the Newton-Euler method is used to establish the dynamic model of the robot in the process of movement and derive the driving torque of the robot according to the maximum height of the robot and its constraints, so as to ensure that the drive motors are correctly selected, and then the robot's obstacle-crossing performance is verified. Based on the theoretically calculated maximum height, a simulation platform was established to simulate the robot crossing the obstacles, which further verified the robot's obstacle-crossing performance.

References

1. Zong, C., Ji, Z., Chen, Z.: A joint double-tracked robot with passive track adjusting device. In: 2018 Chinese Control and Decision Conference (CCDC), pp. 4148–4153 (2018)
2. Wu J, Liu Z.: The control strategy of swarm tracked robots for intelligent transportation based on parallel formation. In: 2012 Third Global Congress on Intelligent Systems, pp. 348–351 (2012)
3. Zong, C., Ji, Z., Yu, J., et al.: An angle-changeable tracked robot with human-robot interaction in unstructured environments. Assem. Autom. **40**(4), 565–575 (2020)
4. Liu Y, Liu G.: Track--stair interaction analysis and online tipover prediction for a self-reconfigurable tracked mobile robot climbing stairs. IEEE/ASME Trans. Mechatron. **14**(5), 528–538(2009)
5. Luo, Z., Shang, J., Wei, G., et al.: A reconfigurable hybrid wheel-track mobile robot based on Watt II six-bar linkage. Mech. Mach Theory, pp.16–32 (2018)
6. Takayama, T., Hirose, S.: Development of Souryu-I connected crawler vehicle for inspection of narrow and winding space. In: 26th Annual Conference of the IEEE Industrial Electronics Society, pp.143–148 (2000)
7. Kamegawa, T., Yarnasaki, T., Igarashi, H., et al.: Development of the snake-like rescue robot kohga. In: IEEE International Conference on Robotics and Automation, pp. 5081–5086 (2004)
8. Wang, W., Du, Z., Sun, L.: Obstacle performance analysis of mine research robot based on terramechanics. In: 2007 International Conference on Mechatronics and Automation, pp. 1382–1387 (2007)
9. Zhou, F., Xu, X., Xu, H., et al.: Implementation of a reconfigurable robot to achieve multimodal locomotion based on three rules of configuration. Robotica **38**(8), 1478–1494 (2020)
10. Sohal, S.S., Sebastian, B., Ben-Tzvi, P.: Autonomous docking of hybrid-wheeled modular robots with an integrated active genderless docking mechanism. J. Mech. Robot. **14**(1), 011010 (2022)
11. Huang B, Li M, Sun L.: The research of a parent-children type robot system. In: 2006 IEEE International Conference on Robotics and Biomimetics, pp. 977–981 (2006)
12. Wong, J.Y.: Theory of Ground Vehicles. John Wiley & Sons (2022)
13. Kitano, M., Kuma, M.: An analysis of horizontal plane motion of tracked vehicles. J. Terrramech. **14**(4), 211–225 (1977)
14. Liu, Y., Liu, G.: Interaction analysis and online tip-over avoidance for a reconfigurable tracked mobile modular manipulator negotiating slopes. IEEE/ASME Trans. Mechatron. **15**(4), 623–635 (2009)

Research on Folding Method of High Storage Ratio Parabolic Cylindrical Antenna Based on Six-Fold Origami Structures

Yuqing Feng[1,2], Jialong Zhu[1,2], Xiaofei Ma[1(✉)], Rongqiang Liu[2], Fei Hu[1], and Huan Wang[1]

[1] China Academy of Space Technology (Xi'an), Xi'an 710100, China
maxf041600@sina.com

[2] State Key Laboratory of Robotics and System, Harbin Institute of Technology, Harbin 150001, China

Abstract. Aiming at the problem of folding methods for deployable parabolic cylindrical antennas with high storage ratio, a reverse parameterized model from known 3D parabolic cylindrical surface to unknown 2D plane fold is established based on the classical six-fold origami structures. In order to meet the large-angle rotation requirements of the parabolic cylindrical antenna in cylindrical direction, a method is proposed to achieve the folding of the cylindrical width to a large angle by adding large folding elements. Finally, according to the folding method proposed in this paper, an experimental verification was carried out using polyimide film, a commonly used material in aerospace. The results show that the sample storage capacity is increased by 5.27 times compared with the ordinary parabolic antenna after the folding unit enlarged, which confirms the correctness of the method proposed in this paper. The crease reverse parameterization design method can provide a reference for the folding mode of parabolic antenna, and can be extended to multiple configuration structures with strong adaptability.

Keywords: Parabolic Cylinder Antenna · High Storage Ratio · Six-Fold Origami · Reverse Design · Folding Method

1 Introduction

Space deployable antennas are used as the "eyes and ears" of spacecraft to receive and transmit electromagnetic waves. Due to the limited volume of the rocket fairing, the deployable antennas are stowed on the ground and in transportation, and deployed when launched into space [1]. At present, the reflectors of deployable antennas are mostly in the form of paraboloids, such as ring antennas, umbrella antennas and frame antennas [2]. The aperture of such antennas is difficult to exceed tens of meters because of the folding mode and the size of the folded state. In view of the future requirements of extremely large aperture deployable antennas, it is necessary to explore the folding method of parabolic cylindrical antennas based on the modular splicing idea [3].

X. Lan et al. (Eds.): ICIRA 2024, LNAI 15201, pp. 425–436, 2025.
https://doi.org/10.1007/978-981-96-0771-6_31

As a traditional art form in China, origami can fold 2D planes into the desired 3D structural form through established peak valley creases [4]. It has advantages such as high storage ratio and flexible folding and unfolding, and is widely used in aerospace, medical equipment and other fields [5, 6]. With the rapid development of computer technology, scholars have further conducted related research on classic origami methods such as Miura origami. Lu Chenhao [7] constructed a reverse design method for a four-fold conical origami structure based on deep neural networks, achieving reverse design from 3D structure to 2D crease diagram. Cai Jianguo [8] designed a segmented cylindrical flexible structure unfolding sequence based on origami theory. Zhang [9] constructed a Miura thick plate origami with five vertices based on a spherical 4R mechanism and a Bennett mechanism, and used hinge removal technology to form a parabolic cylindrical antenna. Xiao Hong [10] developed a folding scheme design for axially repeatable retractable protective covers based on the Miura origami principle. Footdale [11] studied the folding method of planar thin films in optical systems based on the Flash model. Liu [12] designed a thick plate origami structure that can be quickly reconstructed between specified configurations based on a zero thickness four fold tubular configuration.

It can be seen that there are currently many research methods based on the classic four fold and six fold folding methods. However, no scholar has studied the folding method of parabolic cylindrical antennas with large folding ratios, based on the engineering requirements of high storage ratio of space deployable antennas. So, this paper establishes a reverse parameterized design model from a known 3D parabolic cylinder to an unknown 2D plane fold based on six-fold origami, from analytical geometric perspective. To meet the motion requirements of parabolic cylindrical antenna's with a large rotation in the cylindrical direction, a method is proposed to achieve a wide angle folding of the cylindrical width by adding crease elements. Experiments were conducted for the proposed methods using polyimide films, which commonly used in aerospace, to demonstrate the correctness of proposed methods. The research content can provide folding reference for the design of large parabolic cylindrical antennas.

2 Based on Six-Fold Reverse Origami Design of High Storage Ratio Cylindrical Antenna

2.1 Establishment of Six-Fold Origami Model for Ordinary Parabolic Cylindrical Surface

The classic origami model can be divided into four-fold origami and six-fold origami based on the number of node creases. For parabolic cylindrical structures, six-fold model are commonly used for analysis. The basic unit of six-fold origami and its partially unfolded state are shown in the Fig. 1, where the red solid line represents peak line and the blue dashed line represents valley line. The peak line represents crease pointing upwards, while the valley line represents crease pointing downwards. The angle between the valley line and peak line β is defined as the top corner of a six-fold origami unit.

The parabolic cylinder is formed by the motion of the parabola along the line, so it can be applied to the parabolic cylinder by designing its creases based on the parabola. When accurately designing the β of six-fold unit, it can be ensured that the line connecting the

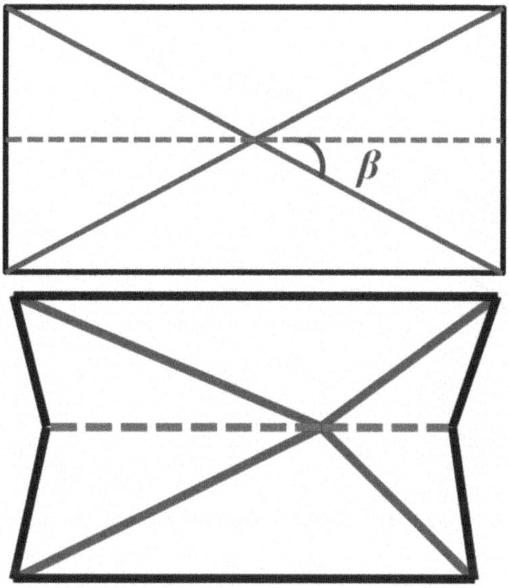

Fig. 1. Schematic diagram of six-fold units

outermost node is in a parabolic shape. It can be seen that as the number of six-fold origami units increases (including four units in the Fig. 2), the simulation accuracy of the parabola is higher (Fig. 3).

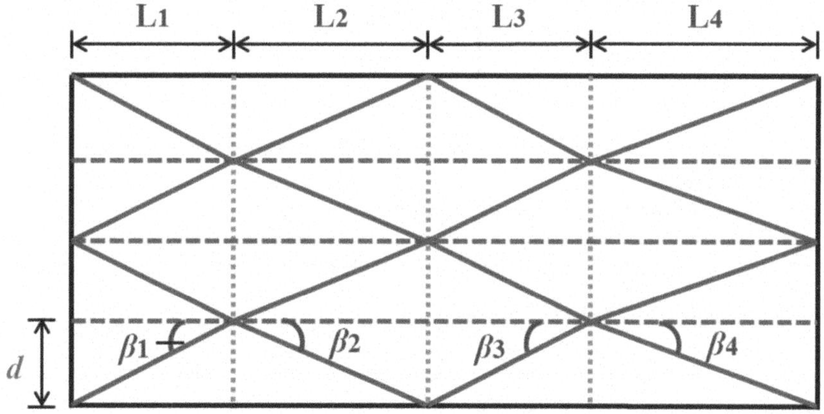

Fig. 2. Schematic diagram of cylindrical shell structure based on irregular elements

Set the parabolic equation as:

$$x = ay^2 \tag{1}$$

where, $a = \frac{1}{4f}$, f is the parabolic focal length.

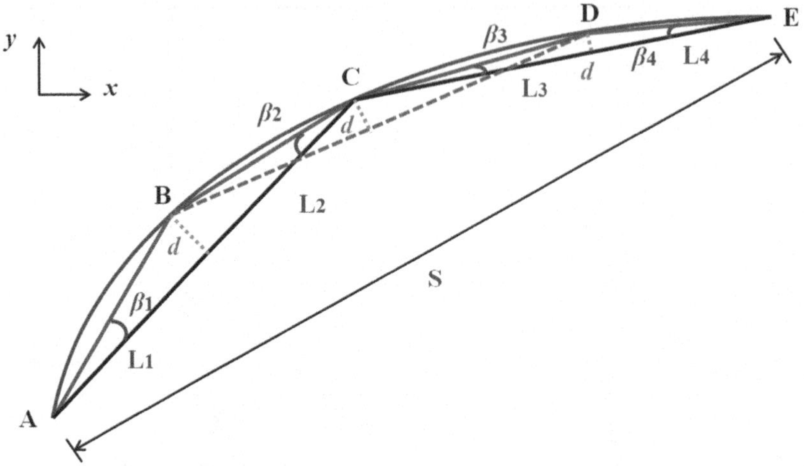

Fig. 3. Schematic diagram of six-fold simulated parabola

Assuming four six-fold elements are used to simulate a parabola, based on the principle of equal curvature fitting, all fold vertices are arranged on the paraboloid. The simulated parabolic equation and endpoints are known, so it is possible to uniquely confirm the coordinates of points A and E, which are (x_A, y_A) and (x_E, y_E), respectively. Therefore, the unknown variables are the coordinates of point B (x_B, y_B), point C (x_C, y_C), and point D (x_D, y_D).

Since points B, C, and D are all on the parabola, so:

$$\begin{cases} x_B = ay_B^2 \\ x_C = ay_C^2 \\ x_D = ay_D^2 \end{cases} \tag{2}$$

According to analytic geometry, the width d of the origami corresponding to different six-fold units is equal.

The equation of the line passing through points A and C is:

$$(y_A - y_C)x + (x_C - x_A)y + x_A y_C - x_C y_A = 0 \tag{3}$$

The distance d from point B to line AC is:

$$d = \frac{|(y_A - y_C)x_B + (x_C - x_A)y_B + x_A y_C - x_C y_A|}{\sqrt{(y_A - y_C)^2 + (x_C - x_A)^2}} \tag{4}$$

Similarly, the equation of the line passing through points B and D is:

$$(y_B - y_D)x + (x_D - x_B)y + x_B y_D - x_D y_B = 0 \tag{5}$$

The distance d from point C to line BD is:

$$d = \frac{|(y_B - y_D)x_C + (x_D - x_B)y_C + x_B y_D - x_D y_B|}{\sqrt{(y_B - y_D)^2 + (x_D - x_B)^2}} \tag{6}$$

The equation for the line passing through points C and E is:

$$(y_C - y_E)x + (x_E - x_C)y + x_C y_E - x_E y_C = 0 \tag{7}$$

The distance d from point D to line CE is:

$$d = \frac{|(y_C - y_E)x_D + (x_E - x_C)y_D + x_C y_E - x_E y_C|}{\sqrt{(y_C - y_E)^2 + (x_E - x_C)^2}} \tag{8}$$

According to the principle that the width d of any six-fold unit is equal, and by combining the above equations, it can be obtained:

$$\begin{cases} \frac{|(y_A - y_C)x_B + (x_C - x_A)y_B + x_A y_C - x_C y_A|}{\sqrt{(y_A - y_C)^2 + (x_C - x_A)^2}} = \frac{|(y_B - y_D)x_C + (x_D - x_B)y_C + x_B y_D - x_D y_B|}{\sqrt{(y_B - y_D)^2 + (x_D - x_B)^2}} \\ \frac{|(y_A - y_C)x_B + (x_C - x_A)y_B + x_A y_C - x_C y_A|}{\sqrt{(y_A - y_C)^2 + (x_C - x_A)^2}} = \frac{|(y_C - y_E)x_D + (x_E - x_C)y_D + x_C y_E - x_E y_C|}{\sqrt{(y_C - y_E)^2 + (x_E - x_C)^2}} \end{cases} \tag{9}$$

It can be seen that the system of equations contains 6 unknown variable x_B, y_B, x_C, y_C, x_D, y_D, and 5 known equations. Therefore, the system of equations is an indefinite equation with infinite solutions. In other words, when the parabolic span S is determined (i.e. points A and E are determined), the width d of the six-fold element does not have a unique solution, but when d is confirmed, the overall fold is uniquely determined.

2.2 Establishment of Six-Fold Origami Model for High Storage Ratio Parabolic Cylindrical Antenna

To reduce the volume of the parabolic cylindrical antenna after folding, combined with the requirements of antenna mechanism 180° large-angle folding, a method is proposed to achieve the folding of the cylindrical width to a large angle by adding crease units. According to the parabolic reverse crease design proposed in the previous section, two crease units are added based on the 3-unit six-fold structure to form a 5-unit six-fold structure (Fig. 4).

The dimensions L_1, L_2, and width d can be determined in advance. Based on the geometric relationship, the unit vertex angles β_1 and β_2 can be determined as:

$$\begin{cases} \beta_1 = \arctan(d/L_1) \\ \beta_2 = \arctan(d/L_2) \end{cases} \tag{10}$$

The 5-unit model in the folding and unfolding state are shown in the Fig. 5.

To achieve 180° large angle folding of the antenna deployable mechanism, so AB and DE are parallel to each other when folded. According to analytical geometry, it is necessary to meet the following requirements:

$$\begin{cases} 2 * (\frac{\pi}{2} - \beta_4) + (\frac{\pi}{2} - \beta_1) = \pi \\ 2 * (\frac{\pi}{2} - \beta_5) + (\frac{\pi}{2} - \beta_2) = \pi \end{cases} \tag{11}$$

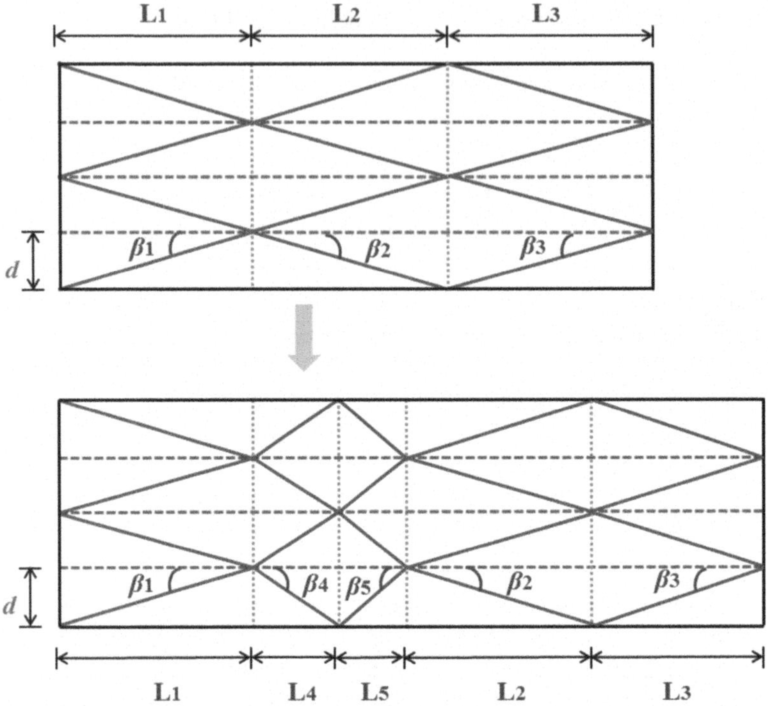

Fig. 4. Schematic diagram of six-fold transformation

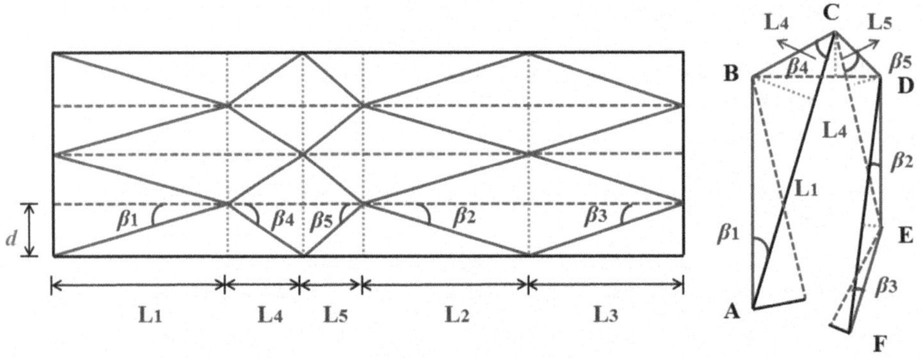

Fig. 5. 5-unit six-fold origami model in the folding and unfolding state

Based on the known vertex angle β_1 and β_2. It can be uniquely determined β_4 and β_5, then the length of L_4 and L_5 are:

$$\begin{cases} L_4 = \dfrac{d}{\tan(\beta_4)} \\ L_5 = \dfrac{d}{\tan(\beta_5)} \end{cases} \tag{12}$$

Since the parabola can be folded in half after folding, the cylindrical width storage ratio is greatly improved compared to the original storage state.

3 Sample Test

Polyimide film has the characteristic of high modulus and is commonly used in aerospace. So we made samples using this material to verify the correctness of the proposed method.

The parabolic sample is folded through 3-unit six-fold origami. Assuming that the focal length of the forward fed parabolic cylindrical antenna is 310 mm and the aperture is 750 mm, the parabolic equation is (Fig. 6):

$$y^2 = 1240x \tag{13}$$

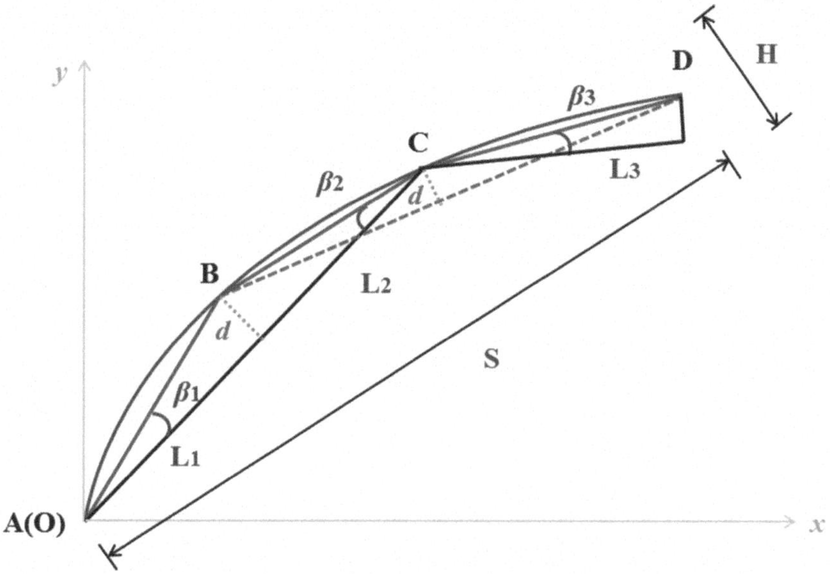

Fig. 6. Schematic diagram of a simulated parabola with 3-unit six-fold origami

According to the parabolic equation, it is easy to obtain the coordinates of points A and D:

$$\begin{cases} x_A = 0, y_A = 0 \\ x_D = 750\,\text{mm},\ y_D = 453.63\,\text{mm} \end{cases} \tag{14}$$

The folded arch length *S* and arch height *H* of the structure are:

$$\begin{cases} S = 876.52\,\text{mm} \\ H = 97.04\,\text{mm} \end{cases} \tag{15}$$

According to the inference in Sect. 2.1, when $d = 48$ mm, the lengths of the 3-unit creases can be obtained as follows:

$$\begin{cases} L_1 = 186.28\,\text{mm} \\ L_2 = 390.89\,\text{mm} \\ L_3 = 311.69\,\text{mm} \end{cases} \tag{16}$$

The coordinates of points B and C are:

$$\begin{cases} x_B = 29.16\,\text{mm},\ y_B = 190.14\,\text{mm} \\ x_C = 227.07\,\text{mm},\ y_C = 530.63\,\text{mm} \end{cases} \tag{17}$$

To meet the demand for a large folding ratio, two crease units were added between the longest units L2 and L3, so that the creases are parallel after the structure was completely folded (Fig. 7).

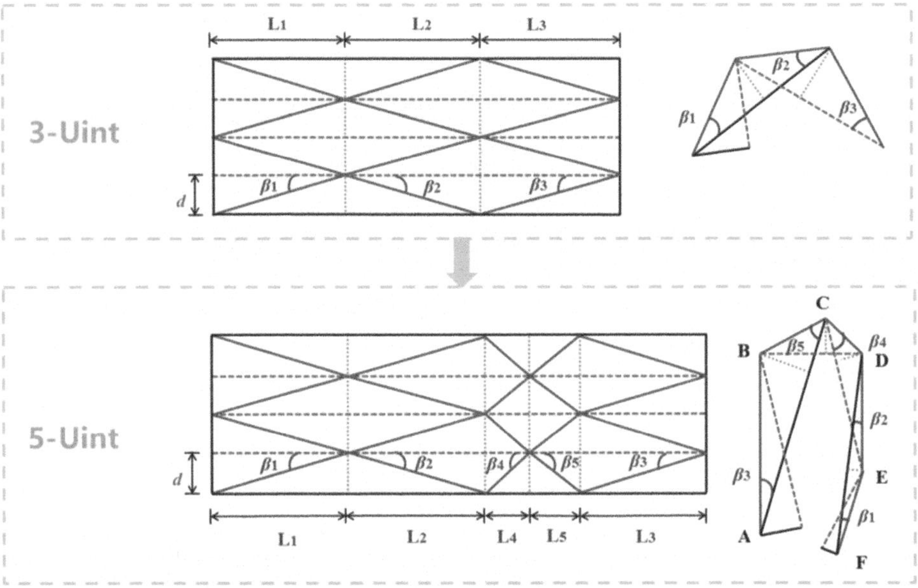

Fig. 7. Example of Six-fold Model Transformation

Calculate the top angle β_1, β_2 and β_3 are:

$$\begin{cases} \beta_1 = \arctan(\frac{48}{186.28}) = 14.45^\circ \\ \beta_2 = \arctan(\frac{48}{390.89}) = 7^\circ \\ \beta_3 = \arctan(\frac{48}{311.69}) = 8.75^\circ \end{cases} \tag{18}$$

Therefore, the top corner β_4 and β_5 are:

$$\begin{cases} \beta_4 = 41.5^\circ \\ \beta_5 = 40.63^\circ \end{cases} \quad (19)$$

The length of the middle two creases added to the 5-unit six-fold origami are:

$$\begin{cases} L_4 = \dfrac{48}{\tan(41.5^\circ)} = 54.24\,\text{mm} \\ L_5 = \dfrac{48}{\tan(40.63^\circ)} = 55.94\,\text{mm} \end{cases} \quad (20)$$

Therefore, in order to achieve large angle folding for parabolic cylindrical antenna, the 5-unit six-fold model size parameters are (Fig. 8):

$$\begin{cases} L_1 = 165.74\,\text{mm} \\ L_2 = 347.78\,\text{mm} \\ L_3 = 277.32\,\text{mm} \\ L_4 = 48.25\,\text{mm} \\ L_5 = 49.77\,\text{mm} \\ d = 42.71\,\text{mm} \end{cases} \quad (21)$$

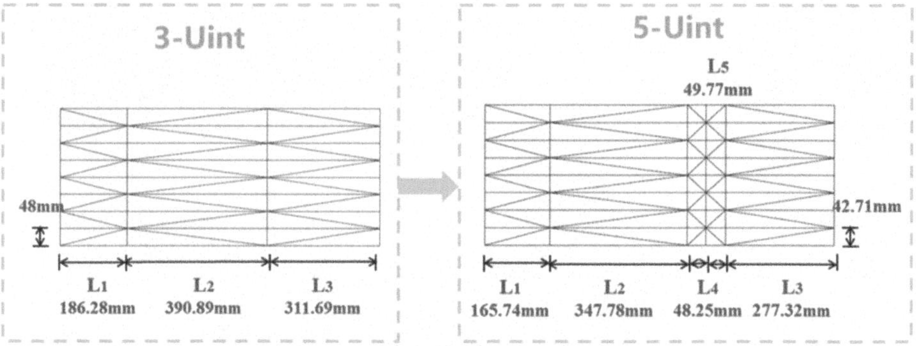

Fig. 8. Dimensions of Six-fold Origami

According to the results, ordinary parabolic cylindrical and high storage ratio parabolic cylindrical antenna samples were made using polyimide film materials. The folded, and unfolded state are shown in the following Fig. 9 (Fig. 10) (Table 1).

After the test, it was found that the width storage ratio of the ordinary parabolic cylindrical sample with 3-unit six-fold was relatively small, about 1.01. However, in the condition of the same width in cylindrical direction, the width storage ratio of 5-unit six-fold sample can reach 5.325, which is 5.27 times higher than the initial sample, verifying correctness of the method proposed in this paper.

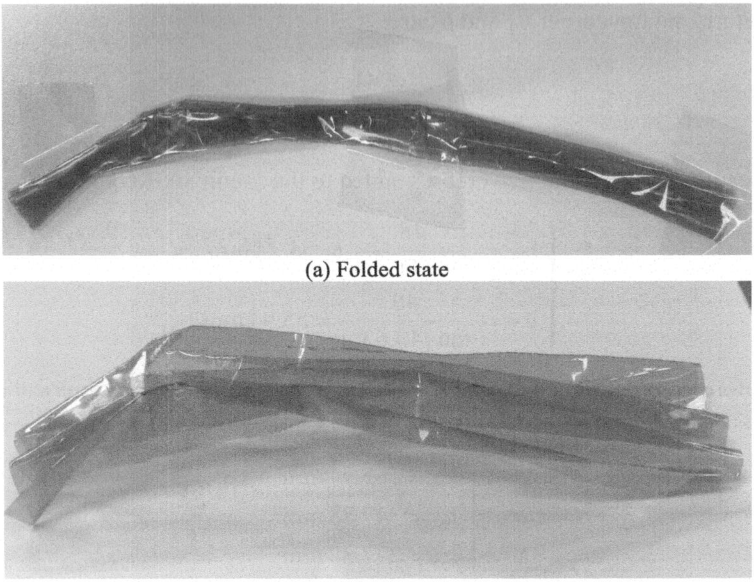

(a) Folded state

(b) Unfolded state

Fig. 9. Ordinary six-fold parabolic cylindrical folding sample

(a) Folded state (b) Unfolded state

Fig. 10. High storage ratio six-fold parabolic cylindrical folding sample

Table 1. Test results of saples

No	Folding method		Width of cylinder	
			Folded	Unfolded
1	Ordinary parabolic cylindrical 3-unit six-fold sample	Size/mm	210	213
		Storage ratio	1.01	
2	5-unit six-fold sample with high storage ratio	Size/mm	40	213
		Storage ratio	5.325	

4 Conclusion

Meeting the demand for deployable parabolic cylindrical antennas with high storage ratio, this article conducts research on the folding method based on the classic six-fold origami, and obtains the following conclusions:

(1) Based on analytical geometry, a reverse crease design model was established from known 3D parabolic cylinder to unknown 2D plane, and the correctness of the model was verified through physical experiments.
(2) Meeting large angle rotation demand, a method was proposed to expand the width of the cylindrical surface by adding crease units, and a sample was produced. The results showed that the storage capacity of the antenna was 5.27 times larger than that ordinary parabolic cylindrical antenna, verifying the correctness of the method.
(3) The proposed reverse parameterization design method for parabolic cylindrical antennas can be extended to various structural forms and has strong adaptability.

References

1. Ma, X., Li, T., Ma, J., et al.: Recent advances in space-deployable structures in China. Engineering **17**(10), 207–219 (2022)
2. Ma, X., Li, Y., Xiao, Y., et al.: Development and tendency of large space deployable antenna reflector. Space Electron. Technol. **15**(02), 16–26 (2018)
3. Liu, R., Shi, C., Guo, H., et al.: Review of space deployable antenna mechanisms. J. Mech. Eng. **56**(5), 1–12 (2020)
4. Bern, M., Hayes, B.: The complexity of flat origami. In: Proceedings of the 7th Annual ACM-SIAM Symposium on Discrete Algorithms, pp. 175–183. ACM, Atlanta (1996)
5. Lin, Q., Zhang, Q., Jia, W., et al.: Deployable configuration design and analysis of large space membrane sunshield structures. J. Mech. Eng. **56**(05), 13–20 (2020)
6. Boatti, E., Vasios, N., Bertoldi, K.: Origami metamaterials for tunable thermal expansion. Adv. Mater. **29**(26), 1700360 (2017)
7. Lu, C., Chen, Y., He, R., et al.: Developing four-fold conical origami structures using deep neural network. J. Mech. Eng. **59**(21), 167–176 (2023)
8. Cai, J., Zhong, Y., Wang, L., et al.: Deployment scheme of deployable cylindrical flexible structure with large storage ratio. J. Mech. Eng. **58**(01), 19–28 (2022)
9. Zhang, Y., Li, M., Chen, Y., et al.: Thick-panel origami-based parabolic cylindrical antenna. Mech. Mach. Theory 182, **105233** (2023)

10. Xiao, H., Wang, H., Guo, H., et al.: Design and analysis of the repeatable development and collapse mechanism film protective cover of space camera. Opt. Precis. Eng. **29**(12), 2877–2890 (2021)
11. Footdale, J.N., Murphey, T.W., Peterson, M.E.: Design and testing of self-deploying membrane optic support structure using rollable composite tape springs. In: 54th AIAA/ASME/ASCE/AHS/ASC Structures, Structural Dynamics, and Materials Conference, April 8–11, Boston, USA (2013)
12. Liu, W., Song, Y., Chen, Y., et al.: Reconfigurable thick-panel structures based on a stacked origami tube. J. Mech. Robot. **16**(12), 121005 (2024)

Adaptive Neural Network Sliding Mode Controller for Welding Robot with Uncertain Model in Nuclear Power Plant

Jiale Huan[1,2], Qingxin Shi[1,2], Pu Chen[1,2], and Xingguang Duan[1,2](✉)

[1] The School of Mechatronical Engineering, Beijing Institute of Technology, Beijing 100081, China
[2] The Key Laboratory of Biomimetic Robots and Systems Beijing Institute of Technology, Ministry of Education, Beijing 100081, China
duanstar@bit.edu.cn

Abstract. The welding robot in nuclear power plant is used for repairing tasks of control rod guide tubes, thermocouple guide tubes, and baffle screws to prevent loosening welds. It can effectively replace manual operations in high radiation underwater environments. Due to the model uncertainty of the robot system itself and external disturbances, it is difficult for the robot to accurately track operational trajectories. This paper proposes an Adaptive Neural Network Sliding Mode Controller (ANNSMC) applied to welding robots in nuclear power plants, which includes three parts: sliding mode controller (SMC), neural network (NN)controller, and barrier Lyapunov function (BLF) output-constrained controller. The controller uses NN to improve adaptability to uncertain parts of the system and utilizes BLF to ensure tracking capability of trajectories when subjected to external disturbances. A simulation was conducted on a 2-link robot to evaluate the performance of this controller. The steady-state position error at the end of the robot is better than 0.01 rad.

Keywords: Sliding mode control · Neural network control · Output-constrained control

1 Introduction

The welding robot of the nuclear power plant is used for the reinforcement of the thermocouple catheter in the component pool. The storage environment of the reactor components is shown in Fig. 1 (a). The anti-loosening weld structure of the thermocouple column catheter in the pool is shown in Fig. 1(b), and the weld width is only 3mm, which requires the robot system to achieve accurate end positioning and accurate trajectory tracking control [1].

This work was supported by National Key Research and Development Program, the Ministry of Science and Technology (MOST) of China (No. 2022YFB4701100).

X. Lan et al. (Eds.): ICIRA 2024, LNAI 15201, pp. 437–448, 2025.
https://doi.org/10.1007/978-981-96-0771-6_32

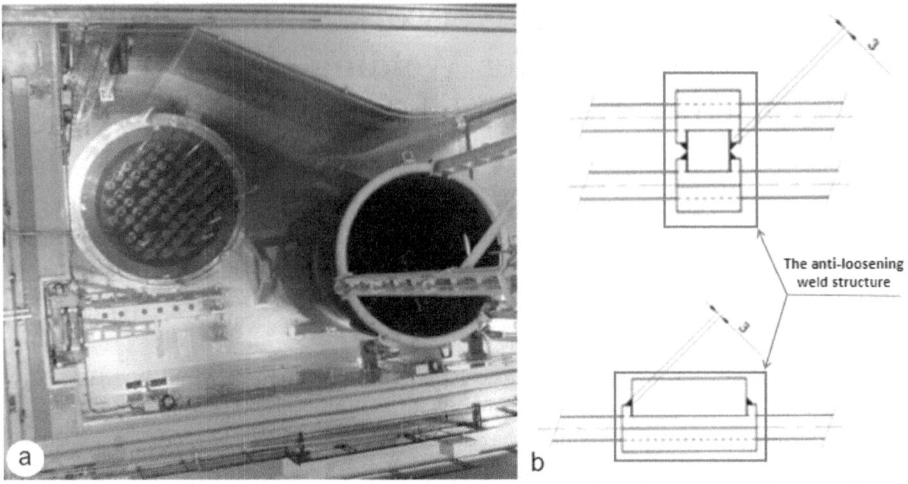

Fig. 1. (a) Storage environment of reactor components; (b) The anti-loosening weld structure.

Sliding mode control is a kind of typical variable structure controller. The principle of sliding mode control is to design the switching hyperplane of the system according to the desired dynamic characteristics of the system. Once the system reaches the switching hyperplane, the control action will ensure that the system reaches the origin along the switching hyperplane. This process of sliding along the switching hyperplane towards the origin is called sliding mode control [2,3]. The limitation of sliding mode control is that it is sensitive to external interference, easy to aggravate its own buffeting phenomenon, and has limited adaptability to system uncertainties [4]. The fitting ability of the neural network to the unknown part of the system combined with the sliding mode control is applied to the control of nonlinear systems, which can effectively reduce the switching gain of the sliding mode control and improve the robustness of the system to the unknown term [5,7]. Radial basis function (RBF) neural network has good generalization ability. It is a common control method to design an output limited controller with the help of the barrier Lyapunov equation [8,10]. The output limited controller can limit the system error and ensure the tracking effect of the system when it is subjected to large external interference [11,13].

The purpose of this paper is to ensure that the welding robot can maintain robustness and reduce steady-state tracking error when its own model is uncertain and it receives large external interference. Therefore, the main work of this paper can be summarized as follows: (1) An output constrained adaptive neural network sliding mode controller ANNSMC is proposed, which includes sliding mode controller, neural network controller and output constrained control. On the basis of traditional sliding mode control, radial basis function neural network is used to fit the uncertainty of the system. The barrier Lyapunov function is used to control the output limit, which guarantees the trajectory tracking performance of the system under the condition of large external force. (2) The performance of ANNSMC is evaluated through comprehensive simulation, and the results confirm that ANNSMC can improve the robustness of the system while maintaining good tracking accuracy. The rest of this paper is organized as follows: The second section introduces the welding robot system; The third section introduces ANNSMC in detail and analyses the system stability. The fourth section gives the simulation results. Finally, the fifth section summarizes the thesis.

2 Welding Robot System

The welding robot used to strengthen the anti-loosening weld in the pool of a nuclear power plant is shown in Fig. 2. Its structure consists of a three-stage sleeve in the Z direction, a 6-DOF mechanical arm, an environmental camera, an end depth camera and a end welding workpiece. The robot base is installed on the moving platform above the pool, and the translation in the X/Y direction is realized through the guide rail of the moving platform, and the movement in the Z direction is realized by the three-stage sleeve. The six-degree-of-freedom robot arm makes the welding operation more flexible and allows visual servo control through the guidance of the ambient camera and the end depth camera. The robot arm used in the system is independently designed and manufactured, which can control the position, speed and current. The dynamic model error is large, and an adaptive controller is required.

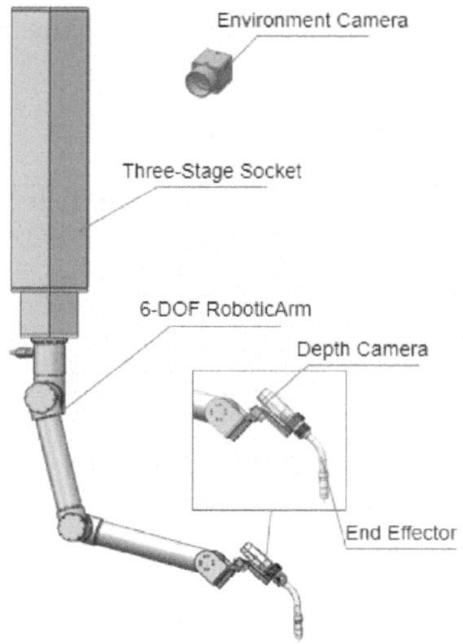

Fig. 2. Welding robot system composition.

3 Controller Design

3.1 Robot Dynamic Model

The dynamics of an n-link rigid robotic system are described by [14]

$$M(q)\ddot{q} + C(q,\dot{q})\dot{q} + G(q) = \tau(t) + f(t) \tag{1}$$

where $q, \dot{q}, \ddot{q} \in \mathbf{R}^n$ are the position, velocity, and acceleration vectors, respectively, $\tau \in \mathbf{R}^n$ is the input torque, $M(q) \in \mathbf{R}^{n\times n}$ represents a symmetric positive definite inertia matrix, $C(q,\dot{q}) \in \mathbf{R}^n$ denotes the centripetal and Coriolis torques, and $G(q) \in \mathbf{R}^n$ is the gravitational force. In the actual robot model, $C(q,\dot{q}), G(q)$ is the uncertain part, $f(t)$ is the external disturbance caused by human or contact with the environment, and $f(t) = 0$ when there is no external contact.

Assumption 1: We assume that the constrained force $f(t)$ is uniformly bounded, i.e., there exists a constant $\bar{f} \in \mathbf{R}^+$, such that $| f(t) | \leq \bar{f}, \forall t \in [0,\infty)$.

Since the position and speed of the robot are known, the acceleration can be calculated. Then we set $x_1 = q, \quad x_2 = \dot{q}$, and then we can write the robot model as follows:

$$\begin{aligned} \dot{x}_1 &= x_2 \\ \dot{x}_2 &= M^{-1}(\tau(t) - Cx_2 - G) \end{aligned} \tag{2}$$

The tracking trajectory of the robot is the ideal position trajectory $\mathrm{q_d} = [\mathrm{q_{d1}}, \mathrm{q_{d2}}, ..., \mathrm{q_{dn}}(\mathrm{t})]^{\mathrm{T}}$ and the ideal speed trajectory $\dot{\mathbf{q}}_{\mathrm{d}} = [\dot{\mathbf{q}}_{\mathrm{dl}}, \dot{\mathbf{q}}_{\mathrm{d2}}, ..., \dot{\mathbf{q}}_{\mathrm{dn}}(\mathrm{t})]^{\mathrm{T}}$ in the world coordinate system, while ensuring that the points passed by all the trajectories do not exceed the limit range.

3.2 Model-Based Controller Design

Assuming the model $M(q), C(q,\dot{q}), G(q)$ is known, define the error function $e = [e_1, e_2, ..., e_n] = x_1 - qd$ and $\dot{e} = [\dot{e}_1, \dot{e}_2, ..., \dot{e}_n] = x_2 - \dot{qd}$, then we choose the following BLF:

$$V_{BLF} = \frac{1}{2}\sum_{i=1}^{n} \ln \frac{\rho_i^2}{\rho_i^2 - e_i^2} \tag{3}$$

where $\rho = [\rho_1, \rho_2, ..., \rho_n]$ is the BLF parameter, used to adjust the position error boundary. Taking the derivative of V_{BLF} yields:

$$\dot{V}_{BLF} = \sum_{i=1}^{n} \frac{e_i \dot{e}_i}{\rho_i^2 - e_i^2} \tag{4}$$

Combined with sliding mode control for controller design, the following sliding mode surface is selected:

$$S = [s_1, s_2, ..., s_n]^T = \dot{e} + \Lambda e \tag{5}$$

where $\mathbf{\Lambda}$ is the positive diagonal matrix, derivation of which:

$$\dot{S} = [\dot{s}_1, \dot{s}_2, ..., \dot{s}_n] = \dot{x}_2 - \ddot{q}_d + \Lambda \dot{e} \tag{6}$$

On the basis of (3)–(6), the following Lyapunov equation is further designed:

$$V_1 = \frac{1}{2}\sum_{i=1}^{n} \ln \frac{\rho_i^2}{\rho_i^2 - e_i^2} + \frac{1}{2}\sum_{i=1}^{n} s^T s| \tag{7}$$

Then take the derivative of V_1 to get:

$$\begin{aligned} \dot{V}_1 &= \sum_{i=1}^{n} \frac{e_i \dot{e}_i}{{\rho_i}^2 - {e_i}^2} + \sum_{i=1}^{n} s\dot{s} \\ &= \sum_{i=1}^{n} [\frac{e_i \dot{e}_i}{{\rho_i}^2 - {e_i}^2} + (c_i e_i + \dot{e}_i)(c_i \dot{e}_i + M^{-1}(\tau - Cx_2 - G) - \ddot{q}_d)] \end{aligned} \tag{8}$$

where $c_i, i = 1, 2, ..., n$ is an element of the positive diagonal matrix $\mathbf{\Lambda}$ in Eq. (5). On the basis of $\dot{V}_1$, we design the following controller:

$$\tau = M(-\Lambda \dot{e} - vec(\frac{e_i}{{\rho_i}^2 - {e_i}^2}) + \ddot{q}_d) + Cx_2 + G \tag{9}$$

By substituting Eqs. (9) into (8), we get:

$$\dot{V}_1 = -\sum_{i=1}^{n} \frac{c_i e_i^2}{\rho_i^2 - e_i^2} \leq 0 \tag{10}$$

The above formula shows that $\dot{\nu}_1$ is negative semi-definite, thus ensuring the stability of the control system.

3.3 Adaptive Neural Network Sliding Mode Control

According to the universal approximation theory of neural networks, the RBF neural network can effectively simulate an unknown function $f = W^{*T}h(x) + \varepsilon$, where W^* represents the ideal weight value of the RBF network, x represents the input of the network, $\boldsymbol{\varepsilon}$ represents the approximation error of the network, and satisfies $\| \varepsilon \| \leq \bar{\varepsilon}$, $\bar{\varepsilon}$ represents a positive number, $\mathbf{h} = [h_j]^T$ represents the output of the Gaussian function of the network, and the j th element can be written as:

$$h_j = \exp(\frac{\| x - c_j \|^2}{2b_j^2}), j = 1, 2, ..., l \tag{11}$$

In Eq. (11), c_j represents the j th column of c, c and b respectively represent the center of the receptive field and the width of the Gaussian kernel function. Since $C(q, \dot{q}), G(q)$ in Eq. (9) are unknown, let f be a completely uncertain vector, and the RBF network is responsible for fitting f. The theoretically ideal fitting expression is:

$$f = W^{*T}h(x) + \varepsilon \tag{12}$$

However, the actual fitting effect is:

$$\hat{f} = \hat{W}^T h(x) \tag{13}$$

where $\hat{f}$ is the actual fitting result for f, and $\hat{W}$ represents the estimated result for W^*. The weight error $\widetilde{W}^T$ is defined as:

$$\widetilde{W}^T = \hat{W} - W^* \tag{14}$$

Then, we select the following Lyapunov equation:

$$V_2 = V_1 + \frac{1}{2\gamma}\widetilde{W}^T\widetilde{W} \tag{15}$$

Taking the derivative of V_2, we obtain:

$$\begin{aligned}
\dot{V}_2 &= \sum_{i=1}^{n} \frac{e_i \dot{e}_i}{\rho_i^2 - e_i^2} + \sum_{i=1}^{n} s\dot{s} + \frac{1}{\gamma}\widetilde{W}^T\dot{\hat{W}} \\
&= \sum_{i=1}^{n} \frac{e_i \dot{e}_i}{{\rho_i}^2 - {e_i}^2} + \sum_{i=1}^{n} s(c_i\dot{e}_i + M^{-1}(\tau + f) - \ddot{q}_o) + \frac{1}{\gamma}\widetilde{W}^T\dot{\hat{W}} \\
&= \sum_{i=1}^{n} [\frac{e_i \dot{e}_i}{\rho_i^2 - e_i^2} + (c_i e_i + \dot{e}_i)(c_i\dot{e}_i + M^{-1}(\tau + f) - \ddot{q}_d)] + \frac{1}{\gamma}\widetilde{W}^T\dot{\hat{W}}
\end{aligned} \tag{16}$$

Combine RBF to design the controller:

$$\tau = M(-\Lambda\dot{e}_i - vec(\frac{e_i}{{\rho_i}^2 - {e_i}^2}) + \ddot{q}_d - K\text{sgn}(s)) - \hat{f} \tag{17}$$

Substituting Eqs. (17) into (16), we obtain:

$$\begin{aligned}
\dot{V}_2 &= \sum_{i=1}^{n} [\frac{e_i \dot{e}_i}{{\rho_i}^2 - {e_i}^2} + (c, e_i + \dot{e}_i)(M^{-1}(f - \hat{f}) - \frac{e_i}{{\rho_i}^2 - {e_i}^2} - K\text{sgn}(s))] + \frac{1}{\gamma}\widetilde{W}^T\dot{\hat{W}} \\
&= -\sum_{i=1}^{n} \frac{c_i {e_i}^2}{\rho_i^2 - e_i^2} + s(-M^{-1}\widetilde{W}^T h(x) + \varepsilon - K\text{sgn}(s)) + \frac{1}{\gamma}\widetilde{W}^T\dot{\hat{W}} s \\
&= -\sum_{i=1}^{n} \frac{c_i {e_i}^2}{\rho_i^2 - e_i^2} + \varepsilon s - K \mid s \mid + \widetilde{W}^T(\frac{1}{\gamma}\dot{\hat{W}} - sM^{-1}h(x))
\end{aligned} \tag{18}$$

Let $K > \bar{\varepsilon}$, design the adaptive law as follows:

$$\dot{\hat{W}} = \gamma s M^{-1} h(x) \tag{19}$$

Substituting Eqs. (19) into (18), we obtain:

$$\dot{V}_2 = -\sum_{i=1}^{n} \frac{c_i e_i^2}{\rho_i^2 - e_i^2} + \varepsilon s - K \mid s \mid \leq 0 \tag{20}$$

This indicates that $\dot{V}_2$ is negative semi-definite at $s \neq 0$, ensuring the asymptotic stability of ANNSMC.

4 Simulation Results

4.1 Simulation Model

To test the effectiveness of ANNSMC, we conducted a simulation experiment on a 2-link robot system. Its dynamic equations can be expressed as:

$$\begin{bmatrix} M_{11}, M_{12} \\ M_{21}, M_{22} \end{bmatrix} \begin{bmatrix} \ddot{q}_1 \\ \ddot{q}_2 \end{bmatrix} + \begin{bmatrix} C_{11}, C_{12} \\ C_{21}, C_{22} \end{bmatrix} \begin{bmatrix} \dot{q}_1 \\ \dot{q}_2 \end{bmatrix} + \begin{bmatrix} G_1 \\ G_2 \end{bmatrix} = \begin{bmatrix} \tau_1 \\ \tau_2 \end{bmatrix} + \begin{bmatrix} F_1 \\ F_2 \end{bmatrix} \tag{21}$$

where:

$$\begin{aligned} M_{11} &= p_1 + p_2 + 2p_3 \cos q_2, M_{22} = p_2 \\ M_{12} &= M_{21} = p_2 + p_3 \cos q_2 \\ C_{11} &= -p_3 \dot{q}_2 \sin q_2 \\ C_{12} &= -p_3(\dot{q}_1 + \dot{q}_2) \sin q_2 \\ C_{21} &= p_3 \dot{q}_1 \sin q_2, C_{22} = 0 \\ G_1 &= p_4 g \cos q_1 + p_5 g \cos(q_1 + q_2) \\ G_2 &= p_5 g \cos(q_1 + q_2) \end{aligned} \tag{22}$$

where $\mathbf{p} = [2.9, 0.76, 0.87, 3.04, 0.87]$, F_1, F_2 are external disturbance terms, which are zero when there is no external contact.

4.2 Simulation Experiment Design

The ANNSMC proposed in this paper is compared with the sliding mode controller and the adaptive neural network sliding mode controller. The initial state of the system is $x_0 = [0, 0, 0, 0]$, and the inputs for the two joint angles are $q_{d1} = q_{d2} = 0.1 \sin(t)$. The control parameter $K = diag\{20, 20\}$, $\Lambda = diag\{5, 5\}$, and the parameters in BLF are chosen as $\rho_1 = \rho_2 = 0.2$. The control system design was carried out using Matlab, and a total of three simulation experiments were conducted.

First, the robustness of the SMC was verified under the premise of model uncertainty. Subsequently, the adaptability and robustness of the adaptive neural network sliding mode controller were tested in both presence and absence of external disturbances. Finally, the feasibility and steady-state performance of ANNSMC were tested under conditions of model uncertainty and external disturbances.

4.3 Simulation Results and Analysis

Using SMC for simulation experiments, it was found that under model uncertainty, SMC is unable to correct the unknown parts of the model and cannot achieve trajectory tracking. The results are shown in Fig. 3. In the figure, the red line represents the ideal trajectory, and the blue line represents the actual output trajectory. The results indicate that the actual trajectory is unable to converge. The control outputs for the two joints are depicted in Fig. 4.

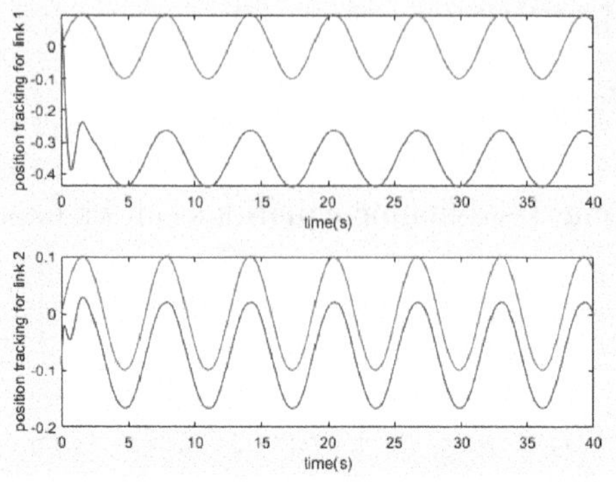

Fig. 3. SMC trajectory tracking effect.

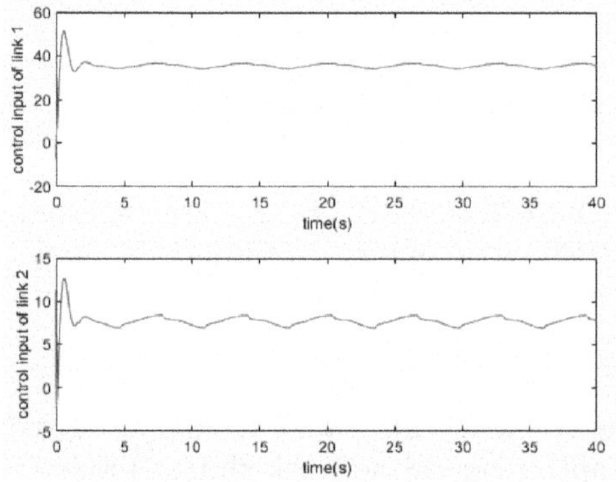

Fig. 4. SMC joint output.

Using the adaptive neural network sliding mode controller for simulation experiments under the same conditions and parameters, the simulation results show that it has good tracking performance and a better fitting effect on the uncertain parts of the model, as shown in Fig. 5. In Fig. 5, the red line represents the ideal trajectory, and the blue line represents the actual trajectory. The system is able to converge even in the presence of initial errors.

Figure 6 demonstrates the fitting effect of RBF network on uncertain terms in the model. The red line in the figure represents the fitted values of the neural network, while the blue line represents the actual values of the model. The results indicate that the neural network can effectively estimate the model. Adding an external disturbance term $F_2 = 10\sin(t)$ for simulation experiments based on this, due to its limited adjustment capability, the controller cannot effectively track trajectories, as shown in Fig. 7. In the figure, the red line represents the ideal trajectory, while the blue line represents the actual trajectory.

Under the condition of external disturbances, simulation experiments were conducted using ANNSMC, and the results are shown in Fig. 8. In the figure,

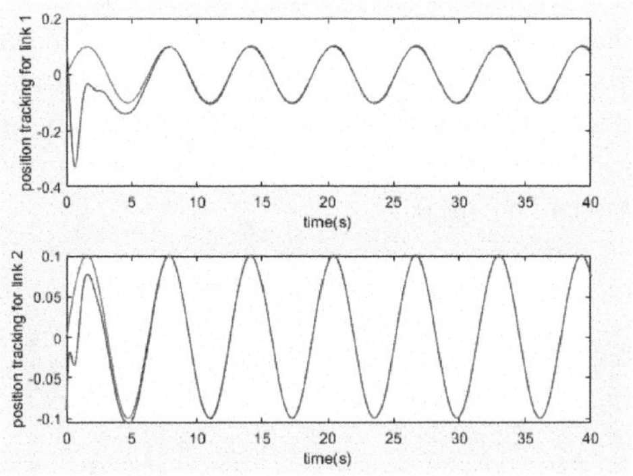

Fig. 5. Trajectory tracking effect of the adaptive neural network sliding mode controller.

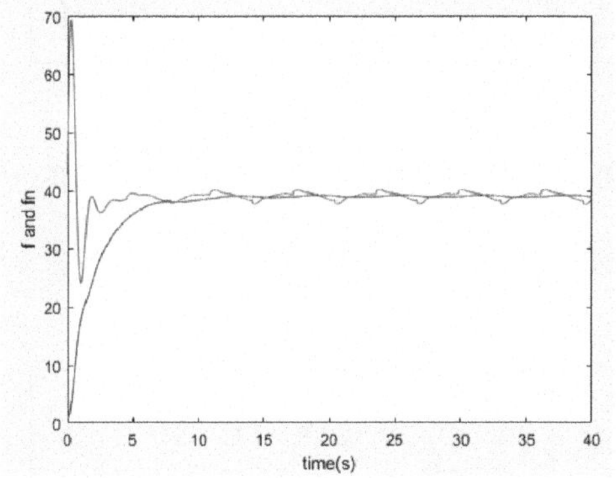

Fig. 6. The fitting effect of the RBF network.

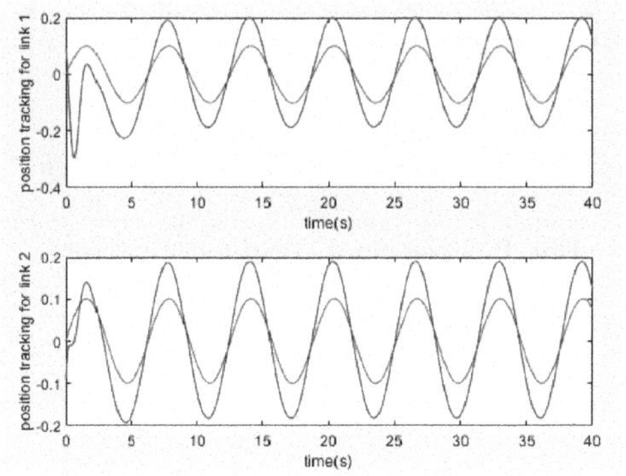

Fig. 7. Trajectory tracking effect under external disturbances.

the red line represents the ideal trajectory, while the blue line represents the actual trajectory. The results indicate that the controller has good adaptability to uncertain model parts and external disturbances. Through BLF correction of external disturbances, it achieved joint angle position and velocity tracking while maintaining good steady-state performance, with a positional steady-state error better than 0.009 rad (Fig. 9).

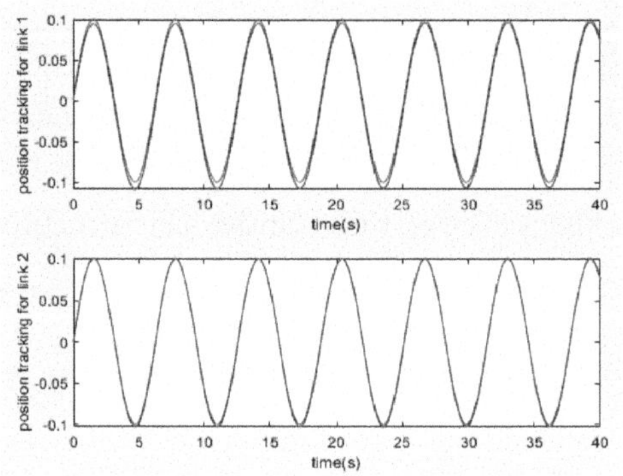

Fig. 8. ANNSMC trajectory tracking effect.

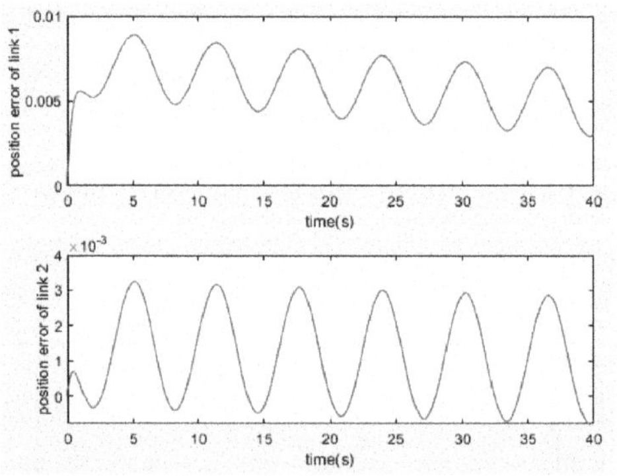

Fig. 9. Positional steady-state error.

5 Conclusion

In this paper, an ANNSMC controller for model uncertain welding robot in nuclear power plant is designed. NN is used to approximate the uncertain part of the model to improve the adaptability of the system. In order to deal with the external disturbance in robot operation, BLF is used to design the position output limited control. The simulation results show that ANNSMC can effectively approximate the uncertain part of the model, and can effectively track the trajectory in the presence of large external interference, while maintaining good steady-state characteristics.

Acknowledgments. This work was supported by National Key Research and Development Program, the Ministry of Science and Technology (MOST) of China (No. 2022YFB4701100).

References

1. Luo, Y., Tao, J., Sun, Q., Deng, L., Deng, Z.: A new underwater robot for crack welding in nuclear power plants. In: 2018 IEEE International Conference on Robotics and Biomimetics (ROBIO), Kuala Lumpur, Malaysia, pp. 77–82 (2018)
2. Azeem, M.F., Kareem, A.: A fuzzy logic based super-twisting sliding mode control scheme for electronic throttle control. In: 2016 IEEE International Conference on Fuzzy Systems (FUZZ-IEEE), Vancouver, BC, Canada, pp. 485–492 (2016)
3. Heidarpoor, S., Tabatabaei, M., Khodadadi, H.: Speed control of a DC motor using a fractional order sliding mode controller. In: 2017 IEEE International Conference on Environment and Electrical Engineering and 2017 IEEE Industrial and Commercial Power Systems Europe (EEEIC/I&CPS Europe), Milan, Italy, pp. 1–4 (2017)
4. Kamal, S., Chalanga, A., Ramesh, K.P., Bandyopadhyay, B.: Multivariable continuous integral sliding mode control. In: 2015 International Workshop on Recent Advances in Sliding Modes (RASM), Istanbul, Turkey, pp. 1–5 (2015)
5. Si, Y., Pu, J., Lu, B., Sun, L.: An improved adaptive neural network sliding mode method for tracking control. In: 2018 Chinese Automation Congress (CAC), Xi'an, China, pp. 3967–3972 (2018)
6. Chen, Y., Fei, J., Chen, F.: Adaptive terminal sliding mode control of single-phase active power filter using novel recurrent neural network. In: 2020 Chinese Control And Decision Conference (CCDC), Hefei, China, pp. 256–260 (2020)
7. Tian, H., Liang, Y.: Research on adaptive sliding mode robust control algorithm of manipulator based on RBF neural network. In: 2020 Chinese Automation Congress (CAC), Shanghai, China, pp. 4625–4629 (2020)
8. Zhang, Y., Kong, L., Zhang, S., Yu, X., Liu, Y.: Improved sliding mode control for a robotic manipulator with input deadzone and deferred constraint. IEEE Trans. Syst. Man Cybern. Syst. **53**(12), 7814–7826 (2023)
9. Guo, X.-G., Xu, W.-D., Wang, J.-L., Park, J.H., Yan, H.: BLF-Based neuroadaptive fault-tolerant control for nonlinear vehicular platoon with time-varying fault directions and distance restrictions. IEEE Trans. Intell. Transp. Syst. **23**(8), 12388–12398 (2022)
10. Zhang, X.-Y., Xie, X., Park, J.H., Liu, Y., Sun, J.: Integral BLF-based adaptive dynamic event-triggered boundary control for a flexible riser system. IEEE Trans. Cybern. **54**, 5555–5564 (2024)
11. Liu, L., Cui, Y., Liu, Y.-J., Tong, S.: Adaptive event-triggered output feedback control for nonlinear switched systems based on full state constraints. IEEE Trans. Circuits Syst. II Express Briefs **69**(9), 3779–3783 (2022)

12. Xu, Z., Deng, W., Shen, H., Yao, J.: Extended-state-observer-based adaptive prescribed performance control for hydraulic systems with full-state constraints. IEEE/ASME Trans. Mechatron. **27**(6), 5615–5625 (2022)
13. Hu, Z., Chen, Q., Hu, Y., Chen, C.: Barrier lyapunov function based finite-time backstepping control of quadrotor with full state constraints. In: 2018 37th Chinese Control Conference (CCC), Wuhan, China, pp. 9877–9882 (2018)
14. He, W., Chen, Y., Yin, Z.: Adaptive neural network control of an uncertain robot with full-state constraints. IEEE Trans. Cybern. **46**(3), 620–629 (2015)

Design of Optimal Control System for AGV Power Converter

Yuming Meng(✉), Ziyu Wang, Song Wang, and Duanling Li

Beijing University of Posts and Telecommunications, Beijing 100876, China
mengyuming@bupt.edu.cn

Abstract. There are the current issues of unification, inefficiency, and low precision in the control strategies of unmanned vehicles across various scenarios. The optimal control system for AGVs is the critical research. Firstly, the kinematic characteristics of AGVs is analyzed. A three-dimensional model of a dual-drive differential speed unmanned vehicle is built with CoppeliaSim. Then a trajectory tracking algorithm is designed based on the concept of the PID algorithm to enhance the precision of AGV control. Simulation is conducted through communication between MATLAB and CoppeliaSim, Additionally, the various speed planning models are analysis. An AGV speed planning decision model is provided. The indicators for evaluating the optimal control system is established. Four types of speed planning models are solved by MATLAB. Precise controlling of unmanned vehicles is achieved in multiple scenarios.

Keywords: AGV Motion · Digital Twin · Trajectory Tracking · Optimal Control

1 Introduction

Automated Guided Vehicle (AGV) is a type of load-carrying mobile robot that can transport production materials to the target location and features autonomous obstacle avoidance and navigation capabilities [1]. This paper aims to conduct an in-depth study of the AGV system to more precisely control AGVs and their control strategies for different scenarios.

Motion control strategy plays a crucial role in AGV research, as it directly influences the working performance of the AGVs. The differential drive AGV system, characterized as a typical multi-input multi-output, strongly coupled, underactuated nonlinear system, makes trajectory tracking control a critical area of study [2]. Various researchers have contributed to this field: Kang and colleagues have focused on the kinematic model of the AGV, proposing a segmented tracking-based speed control strategy to achieve precise trajectory tracking [3]. Similarly, Ai and others have introduced a kinematic sliding mode control method that enhances the control output by adjusting the approaching rate, though it does not address the control of the system's power output [4]. Additionally, Gao J and his team have developed an adaptive sliding mode control strategy that modifies the system dynamics control inputs to stabilize the system by estimating the sideslip angle [5]. While these studies have advanced AGV motion trajectory tracking, they exhibit

X. Lan et al. (Eds.): icira 2024, LNAI 15201, pp. 449–460, 2025.
https://doi.org/10.1007/978-981-96-0771-6_33

limitations, such as neglecting the effects of parameter coupling, which impedes the achievement of precise control model accuracy.

A digital twin system is introduced in this paper to simulate and emulate various real-world scenarios, thereby aiding in the development of optimal control strategies for AGVs. The digital twin system collects, processes, and analyzes data from the real world to create a corresponding virtual environment. This virtual environment not only mirrors the properties and characteristics of the real world but also reflects real-time changes occurring within it [6]. Consequently, the digital twin system allows for the conducting of simulation experiments and predictive analyses of AGV motion control in a virtual setting, thereby optimizing and enhancing its application in actual scenarios.

Firstly, the stability of AGV motion is analyzed by establishing the AGV coordinate system and modeling the AGV kinematic equations. On this basis, this paper develops a trajectory tracking algorithm, constructs a dual-drive differential speed motion model of the AGV, and conducts motion simulations. The results of these simulations are then analyzed, leading to the design of a trajectory tracking control algorithm for precise AGV control. Secondly, using numerical analysis methods, multi-objective evaluation metrics are established based on the efficiency, energy consumption, and stability requirements of logistics delivery. By analyzing the outputs of various speed planning models, optimal control strategies for each scenario are produced, concluding that the polynomial speed planning model is optimal in terms of stability and efficiency. Finally, the paper summarizes the main research work, discusses the shortcomings of the study, and looks forward to the work that needs to be improved in the future.

2 AGV Motion Stability Analysis

The optimal motion control strategies are designed for AGVs in various scenarios. Thus, necessitating a deeper understanding of the underlying logic of AGV vehicle motion through motion modeling. The kinematic model of the AGV vehicle is established, which includes the relationships among the linear velocity, angular velocity of the center of mass of the AGV, and the angular velocities of the left and right drive wheels. The relationships between the displacement state variables of the AGV and the angular velocities of the drive motors are deter-mined through integration.

2.1 AGV Kinematic Modeling

An AGV equipped with a differential drive system featuring two wheels is explored in this paper. Characterized by its simple architecture and direct control mechanisms, the differential drive method allows the vehicle to perform in-place turns [7].

Establishment of AGV Coordinate System. A mathematical model for the kinematics of the AGV is outlined in this paper, with emphasis on the importance of establishing a coordinate system to facilitate the analysis of variable relationships. The world coordinate system, denoted as XOY in Fig. 1, is adopted as the universal framework to determine the AGV's positioning. Within this system, the centroid M of the AGV acts as the origin, forming a local coordinate system, termed the AGV coordinate system, which remains stationary relative to the AGV itself. Illustrated in the figure, point P serves as a reference point located in both the XOY system and the AGV coordinate system. The transformation relationship between these two coordinate systems is then detailed:

$$\begin{cases} X_P = X_M + X_{PM} cos\theta + Y_{PM} sin\theta \\ Y_P = Y_M - X_{PM} sin\theta + Y_{PM} cos\theta \end{cases} \tag{1}$$

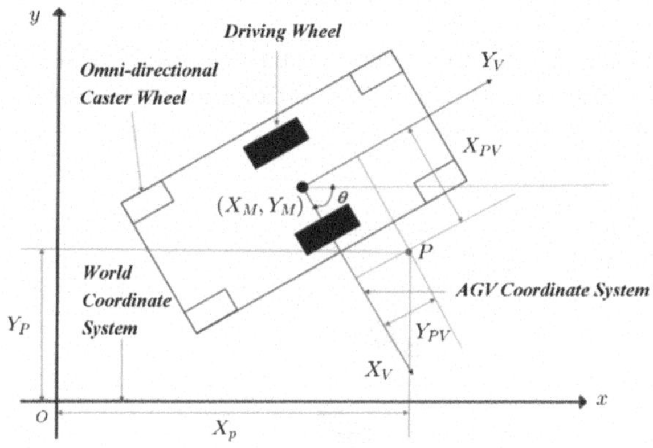

Fig. 1. Establishment of AGV Coordinate System

AGV Kinematic Modeling and Analysis. To simplify the development and analysis of the kinematic model for the AGV, the subsequent assumptions are posited regarding the AGV's motion platform [8]: The AGV is considered a rigid body in motion, operating exclusively on a horizontal plane; the drive wheels of the AGV are identical in size, subjected to uniform forces, and exhibit no relative sliding with the motion plane; the effects of the AGV's mass, frictional resistance, and load on its velocity are disregarded.

Figure 2 illustrates the motion model of the AGV, which includes the motor speeds of the drive wheels, labeled as ω_L and ω_R, the angular velocity of the AGV itself represented as ω, and the forward speed denoted as V. Given that the radius of the drive wheels is r and the distance between the drive wheels is d, the following relationship is established:

$$\begin{bmatrix} \dot{x_M} \\ \dot{y_M} \\ \dot{\theta} \end{bmatrix} = \begin{bmatrix} \frac{r\cos\theta}{2} & \frac{r\cos\theta}{2} \\ \frac{r\sin\theta}{2} & \frac{r\sin\theta}{2} \\ -\frac{r}{2} & \frac{r}{2} \end{bmatrix} \begin{bmatrix} \omega_L \\ \omega_R \end{bmatrix} \tag{2}$$

From the equation presented, it is determined that at time t, the coordinates of the AGV in the global frame are expressed as follows:

$$\begin{cases} x_{i+1} = \frac{rcos\theta_i \int_{t_i}^{t_{i+!}} (\omega_L(t)+\omega_R(t))dt}{2} \\ y_{i+1} = \frac{rsin\theta_i \int_{t_i}^{t_{i+!}} (\omega_L(t)+\omega_R(t))dt}{2} \\ \theta_{i+1} = \frac{r \int_{t_i}^{t_{i+!}} (\omega_L(t)-\omega_R(t))dt}{2} \end{cases} \tag{3}$$

By discretizing Eq. (3), the state equation of the AGV is derived and expressed as follows:

$$\begin{bmatrix} x(n+1) \\ y(n+1) \\ \theta(n+1) \end{bmatrix} = \begin{bmatrix} x(n) + \frac{Trcos\theta(\omega_{Li}+\omega_{Ri})}{2} \\ y(n) + \frac{Trsin\theta(\omega_{Li}+\omega_{Ri})}{2} \\ \theta(n) + \frac{Tr(\omega_{Li}-\omega_{Ri})}{2} \end{bmatrix} \tag{4}$$

As indicated by Eq. (4), the difference in rotational speed between the drive wheels governs the directional angle of the AGV. This differential in rotational speed is regulated by the voltage applied to the drive motors.

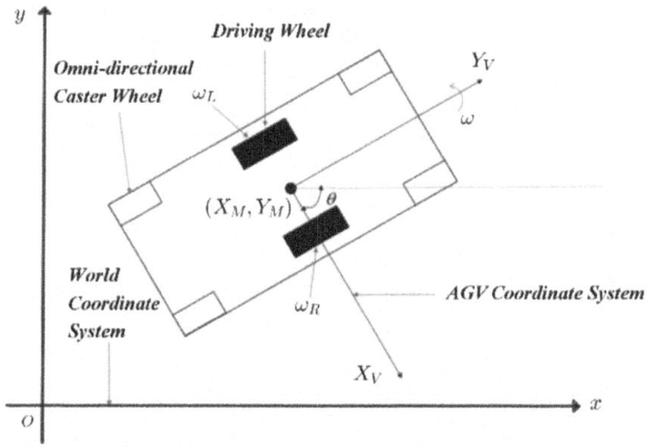

Fig. 2. Schematic Diagram of the AGV Motion Model

From Eq. (2), the inverse kinematic model of the AGV can be derived and is presented as follows:

$$\begin{bmatrix} \omega_R \\ \omega_L \end{bmatrix} = \begin{bmatrix} V + \frac{d}{4}\omega \\ V - \frac{d}{4}\omega \end{bmatrix} = \begin{bmatrix} 1 & \frac{d}{4} \\ 1 & -\frac{d}{4} \end{bmatrix} \begin{bmatrix} V \\ \omega \end{bmatrix} \tag{5}$$

2.2 AGV Trajectory Tracking Control

In the inertial coordinate system, the variables x and y correspond to the horizontal and vertical positions of the AGV, while a represents the AGV's angular acceleration. The desired positions and velocities -x_r, y_r and ω_r for horizontal, vertical, and angular velocities, respectively - along with the system-defined forward velocity V^d and rotational velocity ω^d, set the operational parameters. Consequently, the error $e(t)$ within the AGV's coordinate system is articulated as follows:

$$e(t) = \begin{bmatrix} e_x(t) \\ e_y(t) \\ e_\omega(t) \end{bmatrix} = \begin{bmatrix} cos\theta & sin\theta & 0 \\ -sin\theta & cos\theta & 0 \\ 0 & 0 & 1 \end{bmatrix} \begin{bmatrix} x_r(t) - x(t) \\ y_r(t) - y(t) \\ \omega_r(t) - \omega(t) \end{bmatrix} \tag{6}$$

Therefore, to adjust the error and ensure precise movement of the AGV along the designated trajectory, the following control system has been established [9]:

$$v(t) = k_1 e_x(t) + V^d cos e_\omega(t) \tag{7}$$

$$\omega(t) = \omega^d(t) + k_2 V^d \frac{sin e_\theta(t)}{e_\omega(t)} e_y(t) + k_3 e_\omega(t) \tag{8}$$

Utilizing the Lyapunov equation, the gain of the error in the AGV trajectory is adjusted and determined, followed by a straightforward linearization fitting. Ultimately, the constants k_1, k_2, k_3 are established as:

$$k_1 = k_3 = 2\zeta\sqrt{(\omega^d)^2 + g(V^d)^2} \tag{9}$$

$$k_2 = g \tag{10}$$

2.3 AGV Motion Control Simulation and Analysis

Construction of the Three-Dimensional AGV Model. CoppeliaSim_Edu_V4_1_0, running on Windows 11 64-bit Professional Edition, is utilized as the simulation development software in this paper. Python is employed to control the AGV within the simulation environment and output results through the Carla API. CoppeliaSim, an advanced robotic simulator, supports six programming approaches: embedded scripts, plugins, add-ons, ROS nodes, remote client APIs, and a robust kinematic solver for both inverse and forward kinematics. The software also supports data recording and visualization with time-distance graphs, X/Y plots, or three-dimensional curves, and offers an integrated graphic editing mode [10].

CoppeliaSim includes a built-in model of Mecanum wheels. However, the AGV model discussed in this paper is a dual-drive differential speed smart vehicle that uses only two of these wheels, controlled primarily by two joints located at the central axes of the AGV's left and right drive wheels, thereby managing the vehicle's overall motion. The AGV's exterior is designed in SolidWorks to create a three-dimensional model, which is subsequently imported into CoppeliaSim. Drive wheels and joints are then integrated into the model by drag-and-drop under the designed shell, effectively assembling the dual-drive differential speed AGV model.

As illustrated in Fig. 3, this study employs Python and CoppeliaSim for remote communication to simulate and control the AGV using a method similar to G-code. This involves transmitting commands between the Python environment and the V-REP side in the format of strings like "G80 G0 L* R** \r", where 'L' and 'R' represent the speeds of the left and right wheels, respectively. On the CoppeliaSim side, commands are parsed using Lua script to execute control, stop, and continue commands.

Simulation Results Analysis. The overall setup for the AGV motion simulation in Simulink is depicted in Fig. 4:

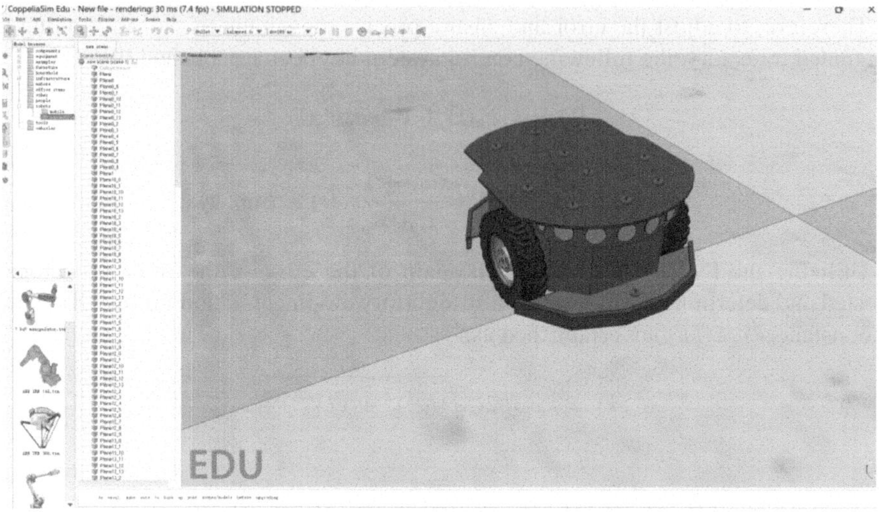

Fig. 3. Dual-Drive Differential Speed AGV Model in CoppeliaSim

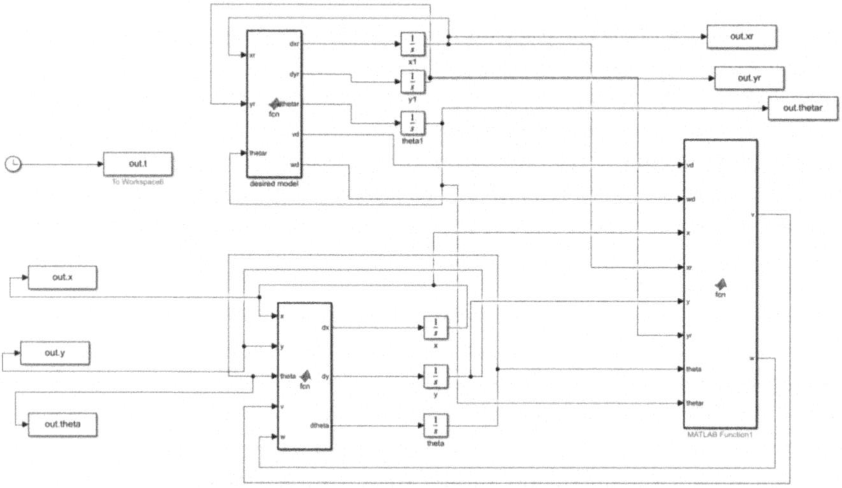

Fig. 4. AGV Motion Simulation Simulink Model

Following the construction of the AGV motion Simulink model, the controller's feasibility is verified by conducting a circular motion test with the AGV. Initially, the rotational speed of the AGV is set to 0 radians per second, with a target testing speed of 0.1 radians per second. The results obtained from this test are presented below (Figs. 5 and 6):

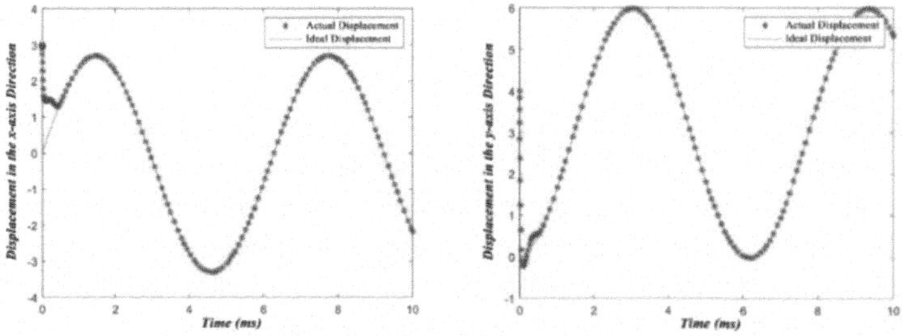

Fig. 5. Comparison of Actual vs. Ideal AGV Horizontal and Vertical Movements in Simulation

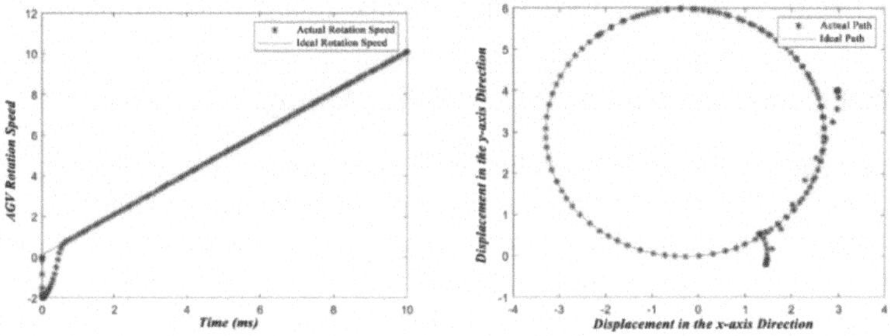

Fig. 6. Comparison of Actual vs. Ideal AGV Rotational Speeds and Movement Trajectories in Simulation

The simulation results confirm that the controller's design allows the AGV to navigate precisely along the designated trajectory within a short time frame, thereby meeting the design objectives for accuracy and swift responsiveness.

3 Optimal Control Strategy Design for AGVs in Diverse Scenarios

Unmanned delivery vehicles require effective trajectory planning to expedite logistic distribution tasks, utilizing optimal control outputs. Specific algorithms in trajectory planning generate a safe and efficient path from the starting point to the destination, incorporating both path and speed planning. The key optimization objectives for AGV trajectory planning and control design in logistic distribution are:

1. Safety: To ensure avoidance of collisions with both static and dynamic obstacles, with additional strategies to reduce risks from the unpredictable movements of dynamic obstacles.
2. Stability: To address the significant inertia and limited flexibility of the vehicle, ensuring both the physical feasibility of the trajectory and the stability of the control system.
3. Driving Efficiency: To enable faster vehicle speeds that shorten transit times without compromising safety and stability.

Trajectory planning must consider various physical constraints that affect the vehicle's performance, such as:

1. Acceleration and Deceleration Constraints: Governed by the limits of the vehicle's propulsion and braking systems, and by the safety considerations for the goods.
2. Nonholonomic Constraints: Arising because the vehicle has three degrees of motion freedom but only two degrees of control, defining the trajectory's physical feasibility.
3. Dynamic Constraints: Restrictions on the curvature and yaw rate during the driving process, based on the vehicle's dynamics and stability [11].

Developing suitable AGV trajectory planning and control strategies for different scenarios is crucial to enhance delivery efficiency and stability, necessitating a tailored approach to meet specific operational requirements.

3.1 Optimal Control Metrics for AGVs Across Multiple Scenarios

The AGV, as an autonomous mobile robot, utilizes a camera (vision sensor) to determine its position and gather surrounding information for movement planning. Section 2.3 presents an analysis of the local trajectory planning model for the dual-drive differential speed AGV, achieving high-precision trajectory tracking. Additionally, the development of a complete AGV motion planning system requires the selection of effective speed planning strategies to enhance efficiency and conserve energy.

The initial goal involves identifying the shortest path to the destination, thereby generating the most efficient route while accommodating the requirements for goods delivery and timing. This challenge resembles the Traveling Salesman Problem with Time Windows, typically addressed through heuristic algorithms such as simulated annealing, ant colony optimization, and genetic algorithms, which are beyond the detailed scope of this paper.

Scenarios in which the route environment from starting point A to endpoint B is known are the focus of this paper. The AGV's journey from A to B is facilitated using an optimal motor control strategy, given the known distance of 1 between these points.

Assuming a short travel distance s_f, or the AGV and a total travel time T_f, as indicated in Eq. (11), penalty functions are established to enhance movement accuracy according to predefined speed and trajectory parameters, as detailed in Eqs. (12) and (13):

$$T_f = \int_0^{s_f} \frac{1}{v(s)} ds \tag{11}$$

$$\int_0^{s_f} \|x(s) - x_{ref}(s)\| ds \tag{12}$$

$$\int_0^{s_f} \|v(s) - v_{ref}(s)\| ds \tag{13}$$

In this context, $x(s)$ describes the function mapping the actual output trajectory of the AGV to the movement distance s, while $x_{ref}(s)$ relates to the ideal motion trajectory over the same distance. Similarly, $v(s)$ and $v_{ref}(s)$ represent the functions correlating the actual and ideal motion speeds of the AGV to the movement distance s, respectively.

Additionally, considering the delivery of fragile items, it is crucial to ensure the stability of the AGV's movement. Stability is indicated by the smoothness of the trajectory, denoted as $sm(s)$, as outlined in Eq. (14):

$$sm(s) = \int_0^{s_f} \| \dddot{x} \|^2 ds \tag{14}$$

The analysis must also account for the AGV's speed constraints, which are captured by $P(s)$, representing the sum of velocity curvatures, and $k(s)$, which describes the relationship between the trajectory's slope and the movement distance s, as detailed in Eq. (15):

$$P(s) = \int_0^{s_f} \|k(s)\|^2 ds \tag{15}$$

In the optimal control model under consideration for the AGV, the objective function is represented by Z:

$$minZ = m_1 T_f + m_2 sm + m_3 P \tag{16}$$

In the model, m_1, m_2 and m_3 are weight coefficients for each objective, ranging between 0 and 1, with the sum of $m_1 + m_2 + m_3$ equaling 1. The values of these weight coefficients, which users can adjust, define the system's requirements.

3.2 Mathematical Model for Optimal Speed Planning of AGVs

Currently, research on speed planning for dual-drive differential speed mobile robots mostly uses the following four speed planning models: trapezoidal speed planning, cosine speed planning, polynomial speed planning and seven-phase S-curve speed planning. Generally, the input parameters are: travel distance: S, initial speed: v_s, final speed: v_e, maximum speed: v_c, acceleration: acc ($acc \leq 250m/min$), secondary acceleration: $jerk$. For the problem discussed in this article, since the AGV needs to deliver goods from point A to point B, both the initial and final speeds are zero, i.e., $v_s = v_e = 0$. After conducting a simulation analysis of four types of speed planning models based on specified metrics, the polynomial speed planning model emerged as the most stable and efficient. Consequently, this paper concentrates on detailing the mathematical model associated with polynomial speed planning.

Polynomial speed planning models the AGV velocity distribution as $v = \sum_{i=0}^{5} a_i t^i$, where a_i are arbitrary real numbers. Similar to the trapezoidal speed planning approach, this method can also be categorized into three types depending on whether the maximum speed is reached before the destination is achieved. The characteristics of this model include smooth transitions in position and velocity, continuous acceleration, and secondary acceleration that is not smooth, with a discontinuity in tertiary acceleration. While velocity, acceleration, and secondary acceleration are controllable, higher-order dynamics remain uncontrollable (Figs. 7, 8 and 9).

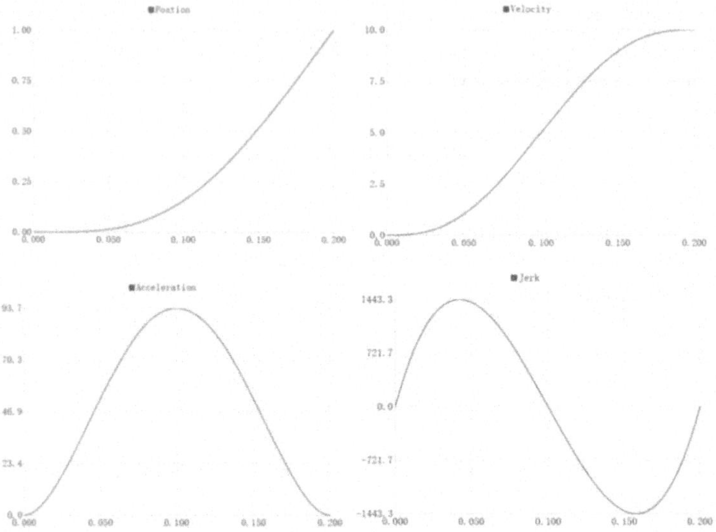

Fig. 7. Dynamics of Position, Speed, and Multiple Accelerations Over Time in Single-Phase Polynomial Speed Planning

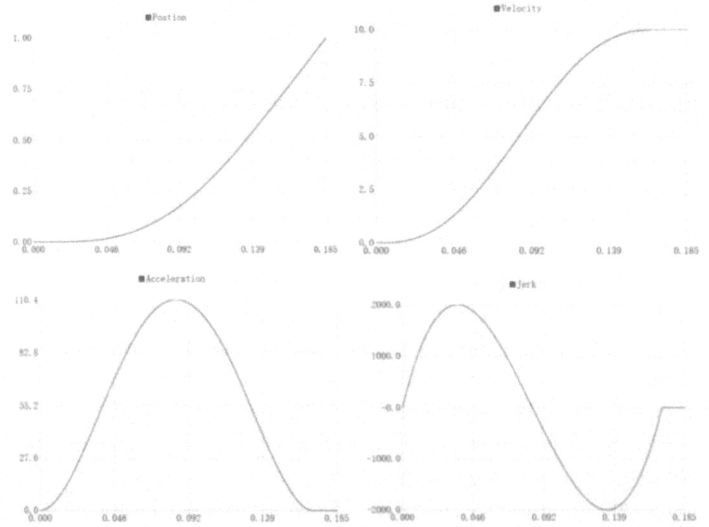

Fig. 8. Dynamics of Position, Speed, and Multiple Accelerations Over Time in Two-Phase Polynomial Speed Planning

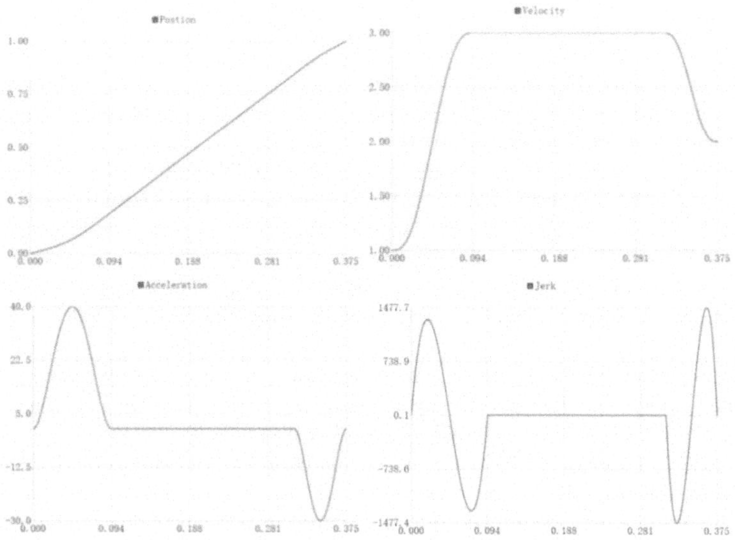

Fig. 9. Dynamics of Position, Speed, and Multiple Accelerations Over Time in Three-Phase Polynomial Speed Planning

4 Conclusion and Discussion

A detailed analysis of the kinematic characteristics of AGVs is performed in this paper, resulting in the construction of a three-dimensional model and the implementation of trajectory tracking control. These developments significantly enhance the precision of AGV trajectory planning. Additionally, a mathematical model for AGV control strategies is established, complete with a comprehensive set of evaluation metrics that demonstrate the superiority of these strategies. Moreover, after analyzing four types of speed planning models, the polynomial speed planning model is identified as the most stable and efficient.

An innovative integration of multiple indicators - efficiency, stability, and energy consumption - is introduced in this paper for selecting models for AGV control strategy metrics, accompanied by the construction of a mathematical model. Although the current model does not yet consider potential collisions with obstacles, this foundational work enables future research to explore AGV control strategies more deeply and address the associated decision-making and selection challenges.

Acknowledgement. This study was co-supported by the National Natural Science Foundation of China. (Grant No. 62206027), Xiaomi Foundation/Xiaomi Young Talents Program, the Fundamental Research Funds for the Central Universities (Project No. 2024ZCJH06).

References

1. Archila, J.F., Becker, M.: Mathematical models and design of an AGV (Automated Guided Vehicle). In: IEEE 8th Conference on Industrial Electronics and Applications, pp. 1857–1862. IEEE, Melbourne, VIC, Australia (2013)
2. Nguyen, H.T., Ly, T.T.K.: Trajectory tracking control for differential-drive mobile robot by a variable parameter PID controller. Int. J. Mech. Eng. Robot. Res. **11**(8), 614–621 (2022)
3. Kang, Z.Q., Liu, Y., Xu, J.B., et al.: AGV path tracking based on preview point control method. Manufac. Autom. **42**(10), 125–128+136 (2020)
4. Ai, Q.L., Wang, G.D., Xu, Q.N.: Tracking control for a flexible steel structure inspection robot based on improved approaching law sliding mode. High Technol. Lett. **30**(12), 1264–1273 (2020)
5. Gao, J., Wang, H., Quan, W., et al.: Adaptive sliding mode trajectory tracking control of automated guided vehicles with sideslip angle. In: 2021 IEEE 10th Data Driven Control and Learning Systems Conference (DDCLS), pp. 1339–1344. IEEE (2021)
6. Nguyen, H.X., Trestian, R., To, D., et al.: Digital twin for 5G and beyond. IEEE Commun. Mag. **59**(2), 10–15 (2021)
7. Myint, C., Win, N.N.: Position and velocity control for two-wheel differential drive mobile robot. Int. J. Sci. Eng. Technol. Res. **5**(9), 2849–2855 (2016)
8. Deshmukh, R.A., Hasamnis, M.A.: An improvement to the conventional PD scheme for the speed control of a two-wheeled differential steering mobile robot. Int. J. Inf. Technol. **15**(6), 3093–3101 (2023)
9. Oriolo, G., De Luca, A., Vendittelli, M.: WMR control via dynamic feedback linearization: design, implementation, and experimental validation. IEEE Trans. Control Syst. Technol. **10**(6), 835–852 (2002)
10. Girbes-Juan, V., Schettino, V., Demiris, Y., Tornero, J.: Haptic and visual feedback assistance for dual-arm robot teleoperation in surface conditioning tasks. IEEE Trans. Haptics **14**(1), 44–56 (2020)
11. Geisslinger, M., Poszler, F., Lienkamp, M.: An ethical trajectory planning algorithm for autonomous vehicles. Nat. Mach. Intell. **5**(2), 137–144 (2023)

Analysis and Prospects of the Current Research Status of Robotics for In-Situ Inspection in Confined Spaces

Ruichao Ma[1], Zhonghai Zhang[1,2](✉), Xinmeng Ma[1,2], and Linbin Zhao[1,2,3]

[1] School of Mechanical Engineering, Hebei University of Technology, Tianjin 300401, China
zhzhonghai@sina.com

[2] Key Laboratory of Advanced Intelligent Protective Equipment Technology, Ministry of Education, Tianjin 300401, China

[3] Key Laboratory of Hebei Province On Scale-Span Intelligent Equipment Technology, Hebei University of Technology, Tianjin 300401, China

Abstract. With the development of robotics technology, the application fields of robots are becoming more and more extensive. High-end equipment, facilities, and equipment are also more and more complex, and the structure is more precise, and miniaturized. When corrosion, wear, and cracks occur inside the equipment, it is very difficult to detect without damaging the equipment. With the development of micro-small robotic technology, in-situ detection of robots in a narrow space can solve the internal detection problems of complex high-end equipment and facilities. The types of in-situ detection robots in narrow spaces are described. The technical characteristics of miniaturization, intelligence, versatility, and remote operation of in-situ detection robots in narrow spaces are analyzed. The challenges and future development directions of perception, positioning, and autonomous control of in-situ detection robots in narrow spaces are prospected.

Keywords: Confined space · In situ inspection · Robotics · Miniaturization · Intelligence

1 Introduction

With the development of science and technology and the increase in the demand for high-end equipment, the current high-end equipment and facilities have a complex internal structure, diverse functions, and a high degree of integration, and internal space gradually tends to be miniaturized [1]. For example, the iterative upgrading of aviation warplanes, and the design of aviation engines is more complex and sophisticated, coupled with the rapid development of the petroleum, chemical, nuclear, natural gas, and other industries, pipeline transportation devices in the industry have been in an increasingly critical position. However, due to the long-term working conditions, corrosion, abrasion, cracks, and other defects will occur within the product structure, reducing the working performance of the product [2]. Therefore, regular inspection and maintenance of the product is very important.

X. Lan et al. (Eds.): ICIRA 2024, LNAI 15201, pp. 461–475, 2025.
https://doi.org/10.1007/978-981-96-0771-6_34

In-situ inspection tasks in tight spaces have always been a challenging problem in fields such as industry and aerospace. The aero-engine consists of more than 30,000 components that constitute a precise and complex system [3]. Traditional aero-engine maintenance and inspection relies on manual labor, firstly removing the engine from the aircraft, and then using ultrasonic inspection aids to perform the inspection, the whole process requires high capital and time costs. Therefore, it is necessary to eliminate the process of removing aero-engines to reduce costs and perform in-situ inspection and maintenance. In addition, the overall structure of industrial pipelines is lengthy, and pipeline inspection is generally performed by manpower, which is a heavy workload and low efficiency. Some pipelines transport harmful chemical substances or have complex and narrow internal structures, resulting in the inability of staff to carry out detection, and may even affect health, the application of pipeline inspection robots is crucial [4]. Therefore, when carrying out maintenance and inspection in narrow spaces, avoid disassembly, carry out inspection in the original position, and use mobile robots instead of manual labor to carry out inspection. So the rapid development of in-situ inspection robots in narrow spaces with the advantages of flexible maneuvering, fast movement, high efficiency, low cost, etc., has become a hot spot for domestic and foreign scholars to study at present.

In-situ inspection refers to the inspection and testing of machine parts, equipment, and systems in their original installation position without disassembly [5]. In-situ inspection generally consists of defect detection [6], fault diagnosis [7], performance parameter determination [8], and condition detection and monitoring [9]. Depending on the concept both destructive and non-destructive methods can be used, but it is optimal not to damage the test object.

In this paper, we will review the current research status of the narrow space in-situ inspection robot, describe the current application of the narrow space in-situ inspection robot type, summarize the current narrow space in-situ inspection robot has the technical characteristics of the outlook of the narrow space in-situ inspection robot challenges as well as the direction of future development.

2 Types of Robots for In-Situ Inspection in Confined Spaces

A confined space in-situ inspection robot is an autonomous mobile robot that performs in-situ inspection tasks in confined, complex, or hazardous environments, and this class of robots has a wide range of application prospects in the fields of industry, medical care, injury detection, and disaster rescue.

2.1 Pipeline Robot

A pipeline robot is a robot specifically designed to inspect, maintain, and repair pipeline systems. Pipeline robots typically have a small, flexible design that allows them to move through narrow, complex pipeline environments and perform a variety of tasks [10]. Pipeline robots are usually equipped with a variety of sensors, cameras, and tools that allow them to complete their work without the need for manual access to hazardous environments, and the use of pipeline robots improves efficiency, reduces labor costs, and decreases risks to worker health and safety. Currently, pipeline robots are a research hotspot in the field of mobile robotics.

Pipeline robots are categorized into wheeled [11–13], tracked [14–16], inchworm [17–19], pressure-wall [20–22], and screw [23–25] according to the different ways of moving as shown in Fig. 1, and pipeline robots with different ways of moving have their advantages and limitations.

Wheeled pipeline robots rely on motor-driven wheels to travel, similar to a small car. Due to the characteristics of simple structure, fast movement speed, smooth traveling, and low cost, wheeled pipeline robots are widely used in the power drive of actual pipeline inspection robots. As shown in Fig. 2, the number of wheels of common wheeled pipeline inspection robots mainly have four or six wheels, and along with the increase in the number of wheels, the contact area between the robot and the pipeline increases, and the stability of the movement in the pipeline is improved [26]. According to the size and internal environment of the pipeline and the requirements of the inspection quality, the pipeline robot with the appropriate number of wheels can be selected for inspection. However, wheeled pipeline inspection robots have poor obstacle-crossing ability and are usually suitable for more spacious and flat pipeline environments, and it is more difficult to use wheeled pipeline robots for pipeline scenarios with complex terrain and more obstacles.

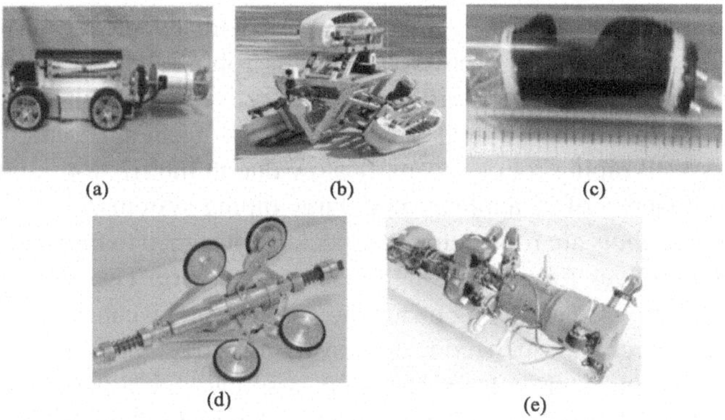

Fig. 1. Pipeline robots with different types of movement: (a) wheeled (b) tracked (c) inchworm (d) pressure-wall (e) screw-type

Crawler pipeline robots walk on motor-driven tracks, which have the advantages of large traction force, good stability and balance, and strong obstacle-crossing ability, and are mainly used in uneven, rugged, and obstructed pipeline environments, and are capable of performing complex and challenging pipeline inspection tasks. Due to its complex structure and large size, it is relatively difficult and consumes more power to generate turning maneuvers in pipelines, and the overall drive and control are relatively complex.

The inchworm pipeline robot utilizes the robot's gripping force to travel in a peristaltic manner, which can be applied to a wide range of pipeline types and sizes and is

Fig. 2. Wheeled pipeline robot

mainly used in twisted, curved, and narrow pipeline environments. However, the inchworm pipeline robot moves slowly, the detection time is longer, the overall structural load-bearing capacity is poor, the function is limited, and it is difficult to complete more complex tasks.

Pressure-wall pipeline robots are special robots designed to move inside pipelines, utilizing the friction of the pipeline walls to propel themselves forward. Pressure-wall pipeline robots can also be adapted to various types and sizes of pipes. Compared to some other pipeline robots, pressure-wall robots do not require additional devices or mounts for stability and can move more easily inside pipelines with less disruption to the pipeline system. Since the movement of a press-wall piping robot relies on the friction of the inner wall of the pipeline, it may be difficult or ineffective to move the robot if the inner wall of the pipeline is uneven or the surface material is unsuitable, and the movement speed of a press-wall piping robot is usually slow due to the friction limitation, which may affect the efficiency of its application in large piping systems.

Screw pipeline robots are robots that are specially designed to move inside pipelines by propelling themselves forward through a screw structure. The screw-type pipeline robot has high stability when moving inside the pipeline, and it can advance in a straight line along the axis direction, which reduces the swaying and oscillation during the moving process. Due to its linear propulsion structure, a screw-type pipeline robot typically has a high mobility efficiency and can move inside a pipeline quickly and stably. The movement of the screw-type pipeline robot is limited by the internal structure of the pipeline, such as the curvature of the pipeline and the obstacles inside the pipeline, which may affect the movement efficiency and stability of the robot, and in addition, the screw-type pipeline robot has a complex screw structure and a control device, and the screw-type pipeline robot has a high cost of manufacturing, which may increase the investment and maintenance costs.

In practice, with the use of pipeline systems for a long time, there will be obstacles and sediment accumulation inside the pipeline to reduce the operating space, resulting in pipeline systems of different sizes, which requires pipeline robots to have a certain degree of adjustability to adapt to changes in the internal environment of the pipeline, which not only improves the detection flexibility of pipeline robots but also increases the application of pipeline robots. Currently, most of the mobile and tracked pipeline robots are only suitable for pipeline inspection of the same diameter size, while inchworm, pressure-wall, and screw pipeline robots can adapt to complex pipelines of different diameter sizes by changing the overall volume size through their structural changes.

Therefore, most scholars have researched more on inchworm, pressure wall, and screw-type pipe robots. Yonsei University in South Korea developed a tracked pipeline robot with a diameter range of 400–700 mm [27], which is adjusted by a ball screw-nut sub-system so that the left nut is close to the screw and the right nut is far away from the screw when the screw is rotated either clockwise or counterclockwise, which drives the linkage underneath to rotate, and thus realizes the change of the pipeline robot's inner diameter. Yu [28] et al. designed a flexible pipeline robot that is simple and easy to fabricate by mimicking the principle of geometrid movement, which is the same as the geometrid. The robot consists of a front and rear deformation part and a middle expansion part, the deformation part is used for bending positioning and fixing, and the expansion is used for compression and length, so the flexible pipe robot can move in pipes of different diameters and sizes. Liu[29] and others also designed a flexible pipe robot, which mainly consists of an elongated pneumatic actuator, radial expansion pneumatic actuator, and space bending pneumatic actuator. Actuator and space-bending pneumatic actuator, by using the soft radial expansion actuator to produce a large deformation, so that it can adapt to the pipe of different diameter sizes.

Although the flexible pipeline robot has the characteristics of softness and high flexibility and can adapt to the pipeline environment of different pipe diameters, its moving speed is slow, the carrying capacity is poor, and the overall inspection efficiency is low, which limits the practical application of many scenarios. To improve the moving speed, Zheng et al. [30] designed a pressure-wall pipeline robot, the overall structure of the robot is divided into the head, waist, and tail, and the two ends of the waist are installed with servomotor active articulated joints to connect the head and tail, and the use of tracks as the robot's walking unit, respectively, in the head and the tail to install two tracks. This not only ensures that the pipeline robot can adapt to the complex pipeline environment but also improves the robot's moving speed. Ma et al. [31] designed an active variable-diameter pipeline robot, which consists of three branched-chain structures, each branched chain end connected to two pulleys close to the inner wall of the pipeline, through the collaborative control of the three branched chains, the mechanical structure of the pipeline inspection robot can be reconfigured, to adapt to the pipeline of different diameters and through the existence of obstacles in the pipeline function can be realized. For the detection of sub-centimeter pipelines, the Laboratory of Modern Mechanisms and Robotics at Tsinghua University has developed a sub-centimeter pipeline inspection robot [32], which adopts a high power density, long-life dielectric elastomer actuator as an artificial muscle, an intelligent composite microstructure-based high-efficiency anchoring unit as a transmission device, and uses an adjustable number of magnetic units to quickly assemble the robot to adapt to sub-centimeter diameter and variable curvature pipes.

Current pipeline robots must be adaptive to ensure smooth passage through complex pipeline environments and to complete the inspection of the assigned tasks, Table 1 summarizes the parameters of pipeline robots and the range of pipe diameters adapted to the pipelines proposed in this section.

Table 1. Pipe robot parameters and pipe diameter range

Reference	Author	Type of movement	Robot Dimensions	Pipe diameter range
[27]	Park et al	Tracked	Length: 390 mm Weight: 7.8 kg	400–700 mm
[28]	Yu et al	Inchworm	Length: 55–60 mm diameter: 6–10 mm	20–42.4 mm
[29]	Liu et al	Inchworm	Length: 25 mm	50–65 mm
[30]	Zheng et al	Pressure-wall	Length: 108 mm	100–180 mm
[31]	Ma et al	Pressure-wall	Length: 212–240 mm diameter: 230–300 mm	290–325 mm
[32]	Tang et al	Inchworm	Length: 47 mm diameter: <10 mm Weight: 2.2g	$\geq$9.8 mm

2.2 Bionic Robot

Bionic robots are robotic systems that are inspired by living organisms in nature and prepare robotic systems with both biological structural and functional characteristics by mimicking the external structure or function of these organisms [33]. For smaller crawling organisms such as snakes [34] and spiders [35], researchers have developed corresponding bionic robots. For in-situ inspection in confined spaces, these bionic robots can replace manual access to the interior of the structure to complete the inspection.

Continuum robots are robots modeled after the shape of a snake, with a "spineless" flexible structure that does not have any discrete joints or rigid connecting rods [36]. Compared with traditional rigid robots, continuum robots have higher flexibility and deformability. Thus continuum robots have the potential to perform tasks in narrow, deep, and confined spaces [37]. As shown in Fig. 3, continuum robots have been widely used in confined spaces such as aerospace maintenance [38], nuclear power plant overhaul [39], aero-engine inspection [40], and automobile charging [41].

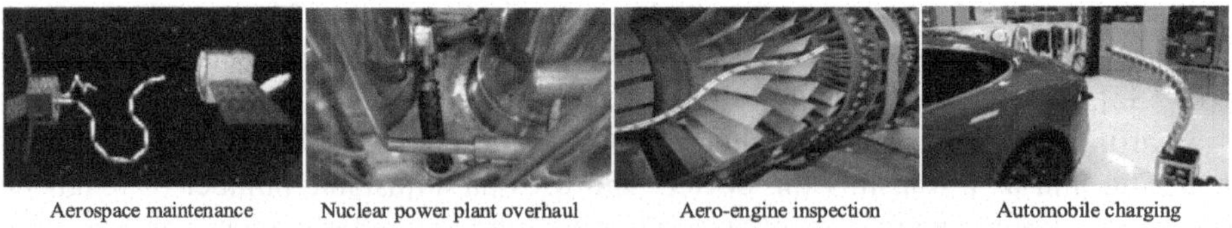

Fig. 3. Continuum robots in confined spaces [38–41]

For the application of continuum robots for in-situ inspection in confined spaces, many companies, as well as scholars, have developed continuum robots for practical testing NASA designed a robot called Tendril robot for inspecting the depths of cracks in aerospace equipment [42], which has an aspect ratio of the diameter of the carcass to the length of the carcass 1:100, and its arm length can be as long as 2,500 m. The robot is a highly flexible and slender continuum robot for inspecting aerospace engines. Dong, Alatorre, et al. [43, 44] designed a highly flexible slender continuum robot for the inspection of aero-engines. The robot has 25 degrees of freedom, an arm length of 1200 mm, a carapace diameter of 15 mm, and the ability to unfold from a drum to provide the forward motion needed to enter crowded environments, and the end-effector is equipped with a camera that enables photographing the interior of the engine and inspecting the engine blades. Also, Dong [45] et al. designed a continuum robot with a dual pivot flexible joint structure that minimizes twisting around the axes and is suitable for a wide range of structures. Jorge et al. [46] investigated a slender, small-diameter, and ultra-redundant continuum robot for the inspection of an aero-engine, which has an arm length of only 175 mm and is only applied in some environments with small depths. Zhou et al. [47] designed a wire-driven continuum robot capable of multi-degree-of-freedom wide-range detection of targets in a confined space with a radius of 99.33 mm. In the medical field, Bamoriya et al. [48] designed a continuum robot consisting of multiple tendon-driven segments, which can highly dexterously pass through complex body environments to reach a designated position for surgical treatment, and has been applied in minimally invasive surgeries. Zhang et al. [49] designed a biomimetic composite continuum robot based on the ordinary concentric tube continuum robot combined with a notched continuum robot. Continuum robot, this composite continuum robot combines the advantages of the two continuum robots and increases flexibility and workspace size. At present, continuum robots are widely used in a variety of application scenarios, but with their simple composition structure, poor load-bearing capacity, and the number of actuators installed at the end of a small number of single functions, it is difficult to complete the complex inspection tasks.

Spider-proof robots are designed by utilizing bionics, combining spider physiology and robotics [50]. The anti-spider robot is structurally different from other types of bionic robots, with a multi-legged structure, so that it walks in poor road conditions, can adapt to a variety of harsh environments, can move on uneven ground, complete obstacle avoidance, and can replace the human to complete the work of sampling and detection in a small environment.

The structure of the spider-like robot is the carrier of flexible movement, which determines the advantages and disadvantages of the robot's performance. Expressed as a multi-legged form is mainly composed of two components: torso and legs, most of which are six-legged robots, and there are also eight-legged robots. Sun et al. [51] designed a six-legged bionic spider robot, each leg adopts a tandem mechanism consisting of the hip, femur, and tibia, with three degrees of freedom, and uniformly distributed around the circular torso. Zhao et al. [52] designed a bionic hexapod robot based on pneumatic multidirectional bending flexible joints, which can realize the functions of advancing, translating, and turning through the deformation of the flexible joints of the legs under pneumatic pressure as a drive, and the maximum speed of movement of this robot is 100 mm/s, and the loading capacity is only 0.5 kg. From the mechanistic point of view, it is difficult for the octopedal spider imitation robots to be completely bionic according to their physiological characteristics Festo has introduced a spider-like robot named "Bionic Wheel Bot" [53], as shown in Fig. 4, which has eight legs, six of which are used for walking, and the other two legs are folded on the abdomen of the robot as push legs. In walking mode, the six legs adopt a tripod gait, and each time it moves, three legs land on the ground and the other three legs lift to move forward, and so on, to complete the forward movement. In roll mode, the six legs are folded to form a wheel, and the two push legs are spread out to contact the ground to push, realizing the rolling action. The inertial sensors inside the Bionic Wheel Bot robot can instantly know its position and roll continuously, and the rolling speed is much faster than the traveling speed, and can also climb up to 5° off the slope.

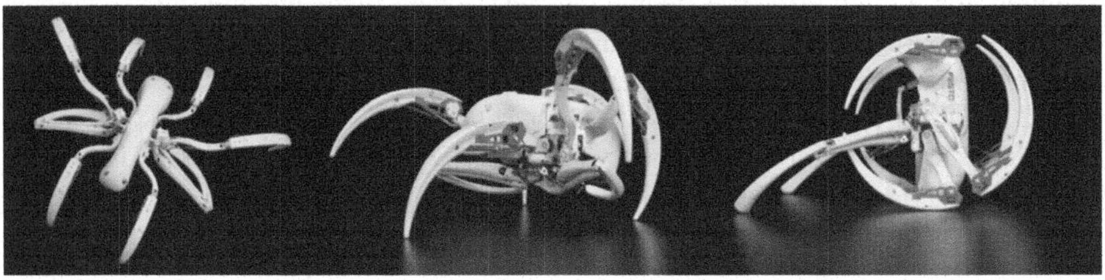

Fig. 4. Bionic Wheel Bot Spider-like Robot [53]

3 Technical Analysis

Narrow space in-situ inspection robots perform tasks in complex environments with miniaturization, intelligence, versatility, and remote operability features, which can support robots to complete a series of narrow space inspection tasks.

3.1 Miniaturization

A miniaturized mechanical structure is the key to achieving miniaturization of in-situ inspection robots for confined spaces. The robot adopts a lightweight, compact design to minimize volume and weight, enabling the robot to carry out a series of operations in a confined space. The use of high-strength, lightweight materials for the robot, such as carbon fiber composites, titanium alloys, and aluminum alloys, reduces the robot's deadweight while ensuring structural strength, helping to achieve a miniaturized robot design. In addition, when the robot meets the miniaturized mechanical structure, it needs to be equipped with a miniaturized power system to provide sufficient power and driving force. The use of high-efficiency micro-motors, gearboxes, and drives, as well as high-energy-density batteries or wire charging, effectively reduces the size and weight of the power system.

When operating in a confined space, robots need to have a certain degree of flexibility and deformability to adapt to different working environments and task requirements. Therefore, the use of flexible materials, deformable mechanisms, or deployable designs provides robots with greater adaptability and flexibility, as well as the use of flexible connectors, joints, or soft transmissions to enable robots to move flexibly in tight spaces and adapt to complex environments with different shapes and curvatures.

3.2 Intelligence

Intelligent in-situ inspection robots in confined spaces are characterized by research in various aspects of perception, decision-making, planning, and control. When performing tasks in confined spaces, robots need to have the ability to perceive and acquire the necessary information about the surrounding environment. This includes the ability to perceive objects, obstacles, environmental structures, etc., as well as changes in external conditions. The robot realizes the perception of different types of information through cameras, LIDAR, ultrasonic sensors, etc. mounted on the body to provide data support for subsequent decision-making and planning. When the robot perceives the information of the surrounding environment, the robot needs to have the intelligent decision-making ability to make reasonable decisions. Using intelligent technologies such as machine learning and deep learning, it analyses and processes the sensed data to achieve understanding and judgment of the environment and make corresponding countermeasures.

The robot autonomously performs tasks and completes various operations based on sensory information and decision-making results. This includes control of motion control, attitude adjustment, and end-work platform operation. Feedback control algorithms and motion planning algorithms are used to achieve stability and precise operability of the robot in complex environments and to confirm the successful completion of inspection tasks. Intelligent optimization techniques such as augmented learning and genetic algorithms are also used to improve the robot's ability to learn and optimize, continuously improving its performance and behavioral strategies through feedback information and experience, and improving adaptability and intelligence.

3.3 Versatility

In small and complex environments, completing the specified detection tasks requires the robot to be able to carry various types of detection sensors, as shown in Fig. 5, including cameras, lidar, infrared thermography, ultrasonic sensors, gas sensors, and so on. These sensors can provide different types of information such as image, distance, temperature, gas concentration, etc. for performing different detection tasks. Robots can be designed with expandable functional modules, which can be added or replaced as needed to achieve different detection tasks or to cope with different working environments. These function modules can provide different functions and services for hardware devices, software algorithms, or control strategies. The robot can perform multiple inspection tasks simultaneously by carrying multiple sensors and functional modules, for example, pipe inspection, environment inspection, and object recognition at the same time, to improve work efficiency and resource utilization.

3.4 Remote Operability

A confined space in-situ inspection robot that supports remote operation and real-time monitoring requires that the robot meets the following conditions: 1) It is equipped with a remote control interface, which typically communicates with an external control device via a network connection (e.g., Wi-Fi, Bluetooth, 4G/5G, etc.). These interfaces can be standard network communication interfaces or specially designed communication interfaces for connecting to specific teleoperation devices.2) Equipped with a teleoperation interface, which is realized through a software application or a web interface. This interface provides robot status information, sensor data, operation control buttons, and other functions, enabling inspectors to monitor the robot's status in real-time and operate it remotely.

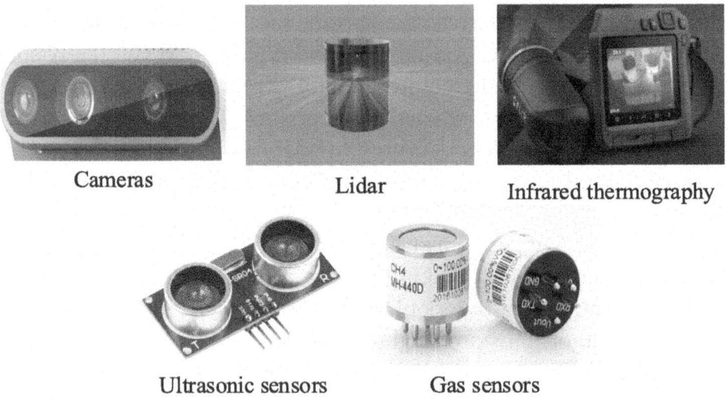

Fig. 5. Robots can be equipped with a variety of detection sensors

The robot is remotely controlled to enable real-time video transmission of the video images seen by the robot to the inspector's terminal device in real-time. This real-time video transmission can be achieved using a camera or other visual sensor to provide real-time visual feedback to the inspector. The inspector remotely controls the direction, speed, and tool use of the robot using a remote control or an operating handle. In addition, the robot's teleoperating system includes a remote troubleshooting function that monitors the robot's operating status in real-time and reports abnormalities promptly. The inspector can obtain fault information through the remote troubleshooting system, and carry out fault analysis and troubleshooting, to ensure the normal operation of the robot.

4 Prospects for Future Development

Although the narrow space in-situ inspection robot in the aero-engine blade inspection, high-end equipment and industrial pipeline internal in-situ inspection, as well as earthquakes, fires, and other scenarios in the search and rescue and survey and other areas of application, but also faces a lot of challenges, the future in the further miniaturization and micro-miniaturization, manipulation of the integration of the development of a set of sensing and localization, autonomy and control of the integration of the intellectualization of the main future development direction. Future development will be the main development direction.

4.1 Perception and Localization

Currently, accurately sensing and localizing robot positions in complex environments is still a difficult task. Environments in confined spaces are usually complex, including various obstacles, pipes, equipment, etc., making the robot perception task more difficult. These complexities require that the robot's sensing system be able to overcome various disturbances and accurately perceive the surrounding environment. Complex environments limit the layout and installation of robotic sensors, while there may be problems such as occlusion and interference that affect the sensing effect of the sensors. In a confined space, the robot's localization accuracy is required to be very high, usually at the sub-centimeter or even millimeter level. Robots need to have a fast response capability to sense environmental changes in real-time and make corresponding control actions. However, the processing and transmission of sensor sensing data may be delayed, affecting the real-time performance of the robot.

In this regard, the future direction of development is to utilize multiple sensor technologies for fusion, including vision, LiDAR, ultrasonic, inertial sensors, etc. Through the fusion of multimodal sensing data, the robot's ability to perceive and adapt to the environment in a narrow space is improved; intelligent environment modeling methods are studied, and automatic modeling and recognition of the environment are achieved through machine learning, deep learning, and other technologies. Use intelligent environment modeling technology to improve the robot's ability to understand and analyze the environment within a narrow space; research new positioning technologies, such as visual positioning, inertial navigation, wireless positioning, etc. Adopt advanced positioning technology to improve the positioning accuracy and stability of the robot in a narrow space; optimize the real-time sensing and control system, reduce the delay of sensor sensing data processing and transmission, and improve the real-time response ability of the robot. Optimize the real-time sensing and control system to improve the operation efficiency and safety of the robot in a narrow space.

4.2 Autonomous Control

Environments in confined spaces are often complex and variable, with many obstacles and constraints. Robots need to plan their paths efficiently, taking into account obstacles, spatial constraints, and dynamics. In addition, the robot needs to perform precise motion control to ensure that it can accurately reach the target location and perform the desired operation. However, spatial constraints and environmental complexity may have an impact on motion control, increasing the difficulty of control. Robots need to be able to make autonomous decisions in complex environments and have the adaptability to adjust their decisions and behaviors in real-time in response to changes in the environment and mission requirements. This requires the robot to have strong intelligence and learning ability. In addition, the autonomous control of robots needs to take into account safety and risk management. Robots need to be able to recognize and avoid potential safety risks promptly when performing tasks to safeguard the safety of personnel and equipment.

Therefore, the future direction of development is to study intelligent path-planning algorithms, which utilize machine learning, deep learning, and other technologies to realize the automatic planning of optimal paths in complex environments. This intelligent path-planning algorithm can take into account the dynamic changes in the environment and the robot's characteristics to improve the efficiency and accuracy of path planning. Research on precise motion control technology, real-time feedback control algorithms based on vision, laser, inertia, and other sensors, and high-precision actuator design. This precise motion control technology ensures that the robot can accurately perform a variety of complex tasks in a small space. Further enhance the autonomous decision-making and learning ability of the robot, through augmented learning, deep reinforcement learning, and other technologies to achieve autonomous decision-making and intelligent behavior of the robot in complex environments, this autonomous decision-making and learning ability enhancement can make the robot more adaptable to different task requirements and environmental changes. Research on safety risk identification and management systems, through the integration of sensing, decision-making, and control functions, to realize the timely identification and effective management of potential safety risks in the environment, through the safety risk identification and management system can ensure the safe operation and task execution of the robot in a small space.

5 Conclusion

This paper reviews and analyzes the current research status of in-situ inspection robots in confined space, describes the application of pipeline robots and bionic robots in in-situ inspection robots in confined space, analyzes the in-situ inspection robots in confined space with miniaturization, intelligence, versatility, and remote operability technical characteristics, and looks ahead to the challenges of the in-situ inspection robots in confined space in terms of perception and localization and autonomous control and the future development direction of the robot. The challenges and future development direction of in-situ inspection robots in sensing and localization and autonomous control in narrow space. With the continuous innovation and progress of science and technology, the importance of narrow-space in-situ inspection robots in industry, high-end equipment aerospace, and other fields will continue to increase. In the future, narrow-space in-situ inspection robots will take on more tasks, including maintenance, overhaul, and inspection, thus improving productivity and reducing costs, and are expected to explore a wider range of application areas.

Acknowledgements. This work was supported by the Chinese National Natural Science Fund (Grant No.:12072005 U23A2067), the Hebei Natural Science Foundation (Grant No.:F2024202052), the Project of Introducing High-Level Talents in Hebei Province (2021HBQZYCSB009), and the Science and Technology Innovation Project of Hebei Province (SJMYF2022X20).

References

1. Masato, D., Lucchetta, G.: Editorial for the special issue on advances in micro and nano manufacturing: process modeling and applications. Micromachines **12**(8), 3 (2021)
2. Chen, Y.J., Ding, Y.Y., Zhao, F., et al.: Surface defect detection methods for industrial products: a review. Appl. Sci.-Basel **11**(16), 25 (2021)
3. Huang, S.L., Peng, L.S., Sun, H.Y., et al.: Review of non-destructive testing and online monitoring technology for aero-engine blade defects. Measure. Control Technol. **42**, 1–11 (2023)
4. Song, K., Wu, W., Ma, Z.Y., et al.: Comprehensive evaluation method of industrial pipeline safety barrier in natural gas purification plant. J. Northwest Univ. Nat. Sci. Edn. **51**(4), 621–631 (2021)
5. Zhang, L.: In-situ ultrasonic detection of high-pressure disc cracks based on longitudinal wave reflection method. Dalian University of Technology, Dalian (2020)
6. Ding, M., Wu, B., Xu, J., et al.: Visual inspection of aircraft skin: automated pixel-level defect detection by instance segmentation. Chin. J. Aeronaut. **35**(10), 254–264 (2022)
7. Li, Y.S., Li, C.S., Kong, F.S., et al.: Analysis of common fault diagnosis methods for aero-engine. In: Prognostics and Health Management Conference. IEEE Computer Society, Paris, France (2023)
8. Liao, W.H., Guo, J.X., Liu, X.Y., et al.: Uncertainty analysis in scramjet performance parameters measurements. J. Aerospace Power **35**(11), 2421–2428 (2020)
9. Chai, H., Wu, M.M., Wang, H.B., et al.: Research status and development prospect of ship pipeline detection technology. Ordnan. Mater. Sci. Eng. **46**(2), 145–150 (2023)
10. Wang, Y., Shao, L.: Overview of the latest development of pipeline inspection robots. Petrol. Pipes Instrum. **2**(04), 6–10 (2016)
11. Sawabe, H., Nakajima, M., Tanaka, M., et al.: Control of an articulated wheeled mobile robot in pipes. Adv. Robot. **33**(20), 1072–1086 (2019)
12. Park, J., Luong, T., Moon, H.: Development of a wheel-type in-pipe robot using continuously variable transmission mechanisms for pipeline inspection. Biomimetics **9**(2), 113 (2024)
13. Min, J.H., Setiawan, Y.D., Pratama, P.S., et al.: Development and controller design of wheeled-type pipe inspection robot. In: 3rd International Conference on Advances in Computing, Communications and Informatics. New Delhi, India (2014)
14. Zhao, W.T., Zhang, L., Kim, J.W.: Design and analysis of independently adjustable large in-pipe robot for long-distance pipeline. Appl. Sci. **10**(10), 3637 (2020)
15. Bogdan, P.A., Wheadon, J., Klein, F.B., et al.: Magnetic tracked robot for internal pipe inspection. In: 10th European Conference on Mobile Robots (ECMR). University Bonn, Electrical Network (2021)
16. Kumar, V., Agarwal, S., Vadapalli, R., et al.: Design and analysis of modular pipe climber-III with a multi-output differential mechanism. In: IEEE/ASME International Conference on Advanced Intelligent Mechatronics, Electrical Network (2021)
17. Kusunose, K., Akagi, T., Dohta, S., et al.: Development of inchworm type pipe inspection robot using extension type flexible pneumatic actuators. Int. J. Automot. Mech. Eng. **17**(2), 8019–8028 (2020)
18. Nakagawa, K., Dohta, S., Akagi, T., et al.: Improvement of pipe holding mechanism for pipe inspection robot using flexible pneumatic cylinder. In: International Conference on Robotics and Automation Sciences. Hong Kong (2017)
19. Kamata, M., Tachibana, K., Tanise, Y., et al.: Proposal of one-inch pipe inspection robot "PI-RO I". In: 7th IEEE International Conference on Biomedical Robotics and Biomechatronics. Enschede, Netherlands (2018)

20. Rusu, C., Tatar, M.O.: Adapting mechanisms for in-pipe inspection robots: a review. Appl. Sci. **12**(12), 6191 (2022)
21. Feng, G.H., Li, W.H., Li, Z.G., et al.: Development of a wheeled and wall-pressing type in-pipe robot for water pipelines cleaning and its traveling capability. Mechanika **26**(2), 134–145 (2020)
22. Elankavi, R.S., Dinakaran, D., Chetty, R.M.K., et al.: Mobility of modular in-pipe inspection robot inside curved and l-branch pipes. In: 3rd IEEE Conference on Norbert Wiener in the 21st Century - Being Human in a Global Village. Anna University, College Engineering Guindy Campus, Chennai, India (2021)
23. Ren, T., Zhang, Y., Li, Y.J., et al.: Driving mechanisms, motion, and mechanics of screw drive in-pipe robots: a review. Appl. Sci. **9**(12), 2514 (2019)
24. Zhang, Z., Hu, L.H., Li, X.H., et al.: Motion analysis of screw drive in-pipe cleaning robot. Proc. Inst. Mechan. Eng. Part C-J. Mech. Eng. Sci. **236**(10), 5605–5617 (2022)
25. Deng, J.M., Shen, H.P., Xue, C.Y., et al.: Design and development of screw-drive in-pipe robot. In: 6th China-Japan International Conference on Mechatronics. Jiangsu University, Zheng Jiang, Peoples r China (2010)
26. Elankavi, R.S., Dinakaran, D., Chetty, R.M.K., et al.: A review on wheeled type in-pipe inspection robot. Int. J. Mechan. Eng. Robot. Res. **11**(10), 745–754 (2022)
27. Park, J., Kim, T., Yang, H.: Development of an actively adaptable in-pipe robot. In: IEEE International Conference on Mechatronics (2009)
28. Zhang, Y., Huang, P.Y., Bo, Y., et al.: Design and motion simulation of a soft robot for crawling in pipes. Appl. Bion. Biomechan. **2023**, 1–8 (2023)
29. Liu, X.M., Song, M.Z., Fang, Y.H., et al.: Worm-inspired soft robots enable adaptable pipeline and tunnel inspection. Adv. Intell. Syst. **4**(1) (2021)
30. Zheng, T., Wang, X., Li, H., et al.: Design of a robot for inspecting the multishape pipeline systems. Trans. Mechatron. (2022)
31. Ma, W.Z., Zhang, D., Liu, J., et al.: Design and prototype verification of an active variable diameter pipe inspection robot. J. Fudan (Natl. Sci. Edn.) **62**, 627–636 (2023)
32. Tang, C., Du, B.Y., Jiang, S.W., et al.: A pipeline inspection robot for navigating tubular environments in the sub-centimeter scale. Sci. Robot. **7**(66), 13 (2022)
33. Men, B., Fan, X.K., Chen, Y.X.: Research on the development status and trend of bionic robots. Robot. Technol. Appl. **27**(05), 15–19 (2019)
34. Yang, X.L., Zheng, L., Lu, D., et al.: The snake-inspired robots: a review. Assem. Autom. **42**(4), 567–583 (2022)
35. Islas, G.E., Ceccarelli, M., Tapia, H.R., et al.: Pipeline inspection tests using a biomimetic robot. Biomimetics **6**(1), 16 (2021)
36. Sun, L.N., Hu, H.Y., Li, M.T.: A review of research on continuous robots. Robotics **32**(05), 688–694 (2010)
37. Robinson, G, Davies, J.B.C.: Continuum robots - a state of the art. In: International Conference on Robotics Kc Automation. IEEE (1999)
38. Wooten, M., Frazelle, C., Walker, I.D., et al.: Exploration and inspection with vine-inspired continuum robots. Robot. Autom. (2018)
39. Mohammad, A., Russo M., Fang Y., et al.: An efficient follow the leader strategy for continuum robot navigation and coiling. Robot. Autom. Let. (2021)
40. Russo, M., Raimondi, L., Dong, X., et al.: Task-oriented optimal dimensional synthesis of robotic manipulators with limited mobility. Robot. Comput.-Integrat. Manufac. **69**, 102096 (2021)
41. Lou, Y.N.: Design and plug-in study of rope-driven robot for automatic charging of new energy vehicles. Harbin Institute of Technology, Harbin (2022)
42. Mehling, J.S., Diftler, M.A., Chu, M., et al.: A minimally invasive tendril robot for in-space inspection. Biomed. Robot. Biomechatron. (2006)

43. Dong, X., Axinte, D., Palmer, D., et al.: Development of a slender continuum robotic system for on-wing inspection/repair of gas turbine engines. Robot. Comput.-Integrat. Manufac. **44**, 218–229 (2017)
44. Alatorre, D., Nasser, B., Rabani, A., et al.: Teleoperated, in situ repair of an aeroengine: overcoming the internet latency hurdle. IEEE Robot. Autom. Mag. **26**(1), 10–20 (2019)
45. Dong X., Raffles M., Cobos, G.S., et al.: A novel continuum robot using twin-pivot compliant joints: design, modeling, and validation. J. Mechan. Robot. **8**(2) (2016)
46. Barrientos, D.J., Dong, X., Axinte, D., et al.: Real-time kinematics of continuum robots: modelling and validation. Robot. Comput.-Integrat. Manufac. **67** (2021)
47. Zhou, Z.D., Jia, J.S., Wei, S.S., et al.: Structure design and kinematics analysis of continuum detection robot through narrow cavity. J. Southeast Univ. Natl. Sci. Edn. **50**(6), 1030–1037 (2020)
48. Bamoriya, S., Kumar, C.S.: Kinematics of three segment continuum robot for surgical application. In: 4th International and 19th National Biennial Conferences on Machines and Mechanisms. Springer-Verlag Singapore Pte Ltd, Indian Institute of Technology Mandi, Suran, India (2019)
49. Zhang, G., Du, F.X., Xue, S.W., et al. Design and modeling of a bio-inspired compound continuum robot for minimally invasive surgery. Machines **10**(6) (2022)
50. Sun, C., Yuan, M.H., Li, F., et al.: Design and simulation analysis of hexapod bionic spider robot. In: International Conference on Computer Information Science and Application Technology. IOP Publishing Ltd, NE Petroleum University, Daqing, Peoples r China (2018)
51. Sun, C., Yuan, M.H., Li, F., et al.: Design and simulation analysis of hexapod bionic spider robot. J. Phys: Conf. Ser. **1168**(2), 022094 (2019)
52. Zhao, Y.W., Geng, D.X., Liu X M, et al.: Gait planning and motion performance of a pneumatic flexible joint bionic hexapod robot. J. Agric. Machin. **49**, 385–394+418 (2018)
53. Festo, Bionic Wheel Bot. https://www.festo.com.cn

Author Index

X. Lan et al. (Eds.): ICIRA 2024, LNAI 15201, pp. 477–479, 2025.
https://doi.org/10.1007/978-981-96-0771-6

The manufacturer's authorised representative in the EU is Springer Nature Customer Service Centre GmbH, Europaplatz 3, 69115 Heidelberg, Germany. If you have any concerns regarding our products, please contact ProductSafety@springernature.com

Printed and bound by CPI Group (UK) Ltd, Croydon, CR0 4YY
01/10/2026
02225933-0003